THE FREE PORT OF LIVORNO AND THE TRANSFORMATION OF THE MEDITERRANEAN WORLD, 1574–1790

The Free Port of Livorno and the Transformation of the Mediterranean World, 1574–1790

COREY TAZZARA

OXFORD
UNIVERSITY PRESS

OXFORD
UNIVERSITY PRESS

Great Clarendon Street, Oxford, OX2 6DP,
United Kingdom

Oxford University Press is a department of the University of Oxford.
It furthers the University's objective of excellence in research, scholarship,
and education by publishing worldwide. Oxford is a registered trade mark of
Oxford University Press in the UK and in certain other countries

First Edition published in 2017

Published in the United States of America by Oxford University Press
198 Madison Avenue, New York, NY 10016, United States of America

British Library Cataloguing in Publication Data
Data available

ISBN 978–0–19–879158–4

Acknowledgments

The monograph is the most obedient of all genres to Montaigne's injunction in *On Cannibals*. The French philosopher condemned those travelers who, "having seen Palestine, want the privilege of telling us news about the rest of the world." To share their petty scraps of knowledge, such authors "undertake to write all of natural philosophy," producing those tedious tomes that are such a pleasure for modern antiquarians. In Montaigne's view, travelers must content themselves with their own adventures. "A person may have some special knowledge or experience of the nature of a river or a spring, who in other matters knows only what everybody knows." Hence the humble monograph.

Like all historians, I am a bit like Montaigne's traveler, having spent the past decade devoted to the Tuscan port of Livorno. This city—Leghorn to the English merchants who used it as an entrepôt—is almost as obscure today as the American indigenes were to Montaigne's readers: although continental historians have documented important aspects of its history, it remains little known to Anglophone scholarship. And yet, in its own day, Livorno presented a rich tableau of officials, merchants, mariners, and slaves, buffeted about by the currents of Mediterranean life. Nobody could have predicted in 1600 that their activities would contribute a chapter in the history of free trade. The story of Livorno shows the seeds of liberalism emerging, not from the studies of philosophers, quill in hand, but out of the nexus between commerce, politics, and identity in the early modern Mediterranean.

For every historian of early modern Europe, the Republic of Letters is more than a fusty prelude to the Enlightenment: it is a living reality. Countless scholars have contributed toward making this a better book. At Stanford University: Avner Greif, Philippe Buc, Aron Rodrigue, Laura Stokes, David Como, Lydia Barnett, Elizabeth Thornberry, Suzanne Sutherland, Nick Valvo, Hannah Marcus, Catherine Chou, and Brad Bouley. In Tuscany: Lucia Frattarelli Fischer, Andrea Addobbati, Richard Goldthwaite, Renata Ago, Marcella Aglietti, Renato Ghezzi, Edward Goldberg, Elizabeth Mellyn, Patrizia Urbani, Guillaume Calafat, Lisa Lille, Francisco Javier Zamora, Kathryn Jasper, and Stephanie Nadalo. At the University of Chicago: Fredrik Albritton Jonsson, John Padgett, Paul Cheney, Rachel Fulton Brown, Constantin Fasolt, Julius Kirshner, Cornell Fleischer, Carlos Grenier, Nicole Beckmann, David Lyons, Lisa Scott, Jennifer Timmons, and Joseph Franklin. At the Claremont Colleges: George Gorse, Lori Anne Ferrell, Andre Wakefield, Andrew Aisenberg, Rita Roberts, Julie Liss, Dion Scott-Kakures, Thomas Koenigs, Tessie Prakas, and Rosemary Kepple. In Los Angeles: Jacob Soll, Jessica Goldberg, Jean-Laurent Rosenthal, Tracy Dennison, Keith Pluymers, Jessica Marglin, Rebecca Emigh, and Farley Ziegler. And on the conference circuit: William Bulman, Nicholas Popper, Robert Fredona, Edward Muir, William Caferro, Thomas Allison Kirk, Cynthia Houng, Daniel Hershenzon, Naor Ben-Yehoyada, and Koen Stapelbroek. My anonymous readers also provided friendly and constructive criticism.

Five people must be singled out for their exceptional assistance. My dissertation advisor, Paula Findlen, guided me through graduate school with consummate patience and critical acumen. Noah Millstone and Jeffrey Miner read every chapter, sometimes more than once, and provided careful field-specific criticism. Sophus Reinert likewise read the entire manuscript and offered a wealth of erudite commentary. And lastly, very special thanks go to Francesca Trivellato for her intellectual mentorship throughout the process of researching and writing. Many of the bright ideas of this book originated in conversations with these five scholars; any errors of fact or emphasis are mine alone.

Finally, I would like to express my gratitude to my friends and family. They have followed my peregrinations with curiosity and enthusiasm; and they have forced me to articulate the significance of my research in clearer terms than is my custom. I have also found that it was salutary to escape academic life from time to time: I therefore extend heartfelt thanks to John Gahbauer, Kyle Liston, and Will McPherson for our excursions these past few years (and Will for his advice on the manuscript as well). And I would like to thank Abby Lynn for her support throughout the process of seeing the book into print.

I dedicate this work to my parents.

Contents

List of Figures

List of Tables

List of Abbreviations

AF	Antica finanza
AS	Archivio segreto
ASF	Archivio di Stato di Firenze
ASG	Archivio di Stato di Genova
ASL	Archivio di Stato di Livorno
ASP	Archivio di Stato di Pisa
ASV	Archivio di Stato di Venezia
BL	British Library
BNF	Biblioteca Nazionale di Firenze
CGA	Capitano poi Governatore poi Auditore vicario
CO	Colonial Office
CSG	Cancellieri di San Giorgio
DBI	Dizionario biografico degli italiani
DG	Depositeria generale
GCM	Governo civile e militare
LCF	Libri di commercio e famiglia
LCL	Lettere dei consoli di Livorno
MM	Miscellanea medicea
MP	Mediceo del principato
NA	National Archives
ODNB	Oxford Dictionary of National Biography
PS	Pratica segreta
SP	State Papers

Terminology and Units of Measurement

TERMINOLOGY AND TRANSLATION

I have generally employed an English translation for Italian institutional terms. While these terms are glossed when they first appear in the text, the principal translations are: the Customs Office (Dogana); the Construction Office (Ufficio della Fabbrica): the Health Board (Ufficio di Sanità); the liberal/perpetual gift (beneficio libero/perpetuo); the Privy Council (Pratica Segreta); and the Venetian Trade Board (Cinque Savi alla Mercanzia). The Office of Plenty (Abbondanza) was responsible for purchasing cereals, whereas the Victual Office (Grascia) was responsible for distributing flour and other viands. I have retained the term *auditore* (a legal counselor) in the original Italian, to avoid the misleading translation of *auditor*. I use the term "free port" (porto franco or porto libero) without quotation marks throughout the book, although its meaning crystallized only gradually throughout the seventeenth century.

I have provided transcriptions only for quotations from unpublished archival material. I have not modernized spelling in the primary sources, but I have modified punctuation to facilitate readability. All translations and transcriptions are mine, except where noted.

MONETARY UNITS

The primary currency of international commerce in Livorno was the silver piece of eight (*pezza da otto reali*), also known as the Spanish real. By accounting convention, one piece of eight equaled six lire *moneta lunga* or five lire and fifteen soldi *moneta corta*. Fiscal reckoning in Tuscany was conducted in scudi, lire, soldi, and denari: one scudo was worth seven lire; one lira was worth twenty soldi; and one soldo was worth twelve denari. In summarizing data, I have generally rounded to the nearest lira for the sake of simplicity.

The long seventeenth century was a period of monetary stability in Tuscany. The Florentine lira contained 4.5 grams of silver between 1555–6 and 1710–11; 4.29 grams of silver between 1711–12 and 1730–1; 4.19 grams of silver between 1731–2 and 1740–1; and 3.9 grams of silver between 1741–2 and 1780–1; see Malanima, "Wheat Prices in Tuscany, 1260–1860." Exchange rates fluctuated widely, however. For typical exchange rates between local and international currencies, see Trivellato, *The Familiarity of Strangers*, xi–xii; and Stumpo, "La circolazione monetaria sulla piazza di Livorno."

WEIGHTS AND MEASURES

The Tuscan pound weighed about 340 grams. Most goods were imported into Livorno by bale (*balla* or *collo*), although the bale's weight varied by commodity, ranging from 370 Tuscan pounds (for pepper) to 1500 Tuscan pounds (for flax). Many other units of measure were also employed, such as the *sacco*, *cantaro*, and *barile*. I have presented data in the unit most commonly found in the literature—thus, cotton appears in quintals, grain in hectoliters, and wool in Tuscan pounds. See the appendix for the complete list of equivalencies used in compiling data.

CALENDAR

Dates in the main text are presented according to the modern Gregorian calendar. Most Tuscan documents until 1751 employed the Florentine calendar, however, in which the new year began on March 25 (the Feast of the Annunciation). I have retained the original dating in the footnotes. For clarity, I have placed "ab inc." (for *ab incarnatione*) or AD (for *anno Domini*) next to dates between January 1 and March 24.

Introduction

In 1656, the government of Tuscany minted a rare gold coin, with a man's portrait on one side and the image of a city on the other. The man was Ferdinando II de' Medici (r. 1620–70), grand duke of Tuscany, scion of the fabled Medici family: international bankers and patrons of the arts who became the hereditary rulers of Florence, producing two popes and two queens of France. Affable and intelligent, sensitive to politics and aesthetics alike, Ferdinando presided over a state whose political stability astonished his contemporaries, in which wise rule and good fortune had spared his subjects "the rapine, the burnings, and the sacrileges" associated with the Thirty Years' War.[1] Tuscany was renowned for its luxury crafts and had one of the most vibrant scientific communities in Europe. No lesser a personage than Galileo Galilei—somewhat prematurely, given the grand duke's failure to protect him from the Roman Inquisition—declared that under Ferdinando's "happy dominion there is no one who is troubled by any of the hardships that afflict the [rest of the world] these days" (see Fig. 0.1).

The city was Livorno, the Medici state's greatest prize and the most innovative port in Italy. The coin bore a maritime view of the town, with its lighthouse, fortifications, and ship-filled harbor. A hundred years earlier, there would have been little to see but a swampy fortress. Almost everything had been constructed by Ferdinando's forebears over the previous century. "Livorno is entirely a new city," noted a French traveler. "It is situated on a flat terrain and surrounded by beautiful fortifications fronted with brick. Its roads are quite large, all arranged in straight parallel lines. Its buildings are generally equal in height and almost all painted on the outside."[2] In stark contrast to the convoluted medieval cityscapes of Europe, Livorno's simple, uniform, and elegant design was more akin to that of a colonial town, planned and executed from scratch by an absolutist state. Livorno was one of Europe's internal frontiers.

A Latin legend curled around the image of the town: *diversis gentibus una*, "out of many peoples, one." This motto recalls the foundation myth of Livorno as a cosmopolitan paradise, open not only to commerce, but to any person who wanted to settle in the port. The city came to house communities of Jews, English, Dutch, French, Armenians, and Greeks. These different *gentes* did not melt seamlessly into one people, contrary to the propaganda of the coin: the Medici regime policed religious boundaries in Livorno almost as thoroughly as elsewhere in Tuscany. But

[1] The quotes are from Cochrane, *Florence in the Forgotten Centuries*, 191–4.
[2] Misson, *Nouveau voyage d'Italie*, 5th ed., vol. 2, 320.

Fig. 0.1. The 1656 gold *tollero*. This coin weighed 3.48 grams and was made of 23.5 carat gold. Its motto, *diversis gentibus una*, celebrates the cosmopolitan identity of Livorno. Merchants preferred silver, however, so the coin was discontinued after just two emissions. The grand duke's silver coins had more success in the Ottoman Empire, where they competed with Spanish reales, but they bore a different motto.
Credit: Kunsthistorisches Museum, Vienna.

the effort to attract foreigners did lay the basis for the city's prosperity, enmeshing it in mercantile networks that stretched across the Old World. In a continent riven by religious antagonism, Livorno came to exemplify the virtues of commercial toleration. The resemblance of the coin's slogan to that of the United States, *e pluribus unum*, is not a coincidence: both mottoes emerged out of a common discourse that treated foreign hospitality as a means of economic development.

Ferdinando's coin—full of symbolism though it was—had a practical purpose: it was destined for export to the Ottoman Empire. In its earliest days, Livorno was a local port, serving the needs of Tuscany alone. By 1600, Medici activism had turned it into a major market for the sale of pirated goods. Livorno was second only to Malta as a center of Christian corsairing, which sought to combat Muslim shipping by seizing their goods and enslaving their crews. But the city invented a more significant if less exotic role over the course of the seventeenth century. Thanks to incentives for the storage and transit of merchandise, Livorno became the principal entrepôt of long-distance commerce connecting northwestern Europe, Italy, and the Levant. Silver and gold were essential commodities for doing business in the Ottoman Empire, where European goods were never in as much demand as precious metals. The coin was thus a tangible artifact of Livorno's role in commercial mediation. One Englishman remarked, somewhat unfairly, "here are no considerable libraries, nor any academy of wits; and indeed the town is unfit for any letters, but those of exchange and traffick."[3] No other port in the central Mediterranean was more

[3] Nugent, *The Grand Tour*, 374.

connected to the rise of the Atlantic world than Livorno—although more as partner than subordinate, thanks to the wealth of the Italian hinterland.[4]

History, of course, is littered with such cities, their fortunes rising and falling according to the shifting contours of empires, entrepôts, and trade routes. But far from being simply the latest Mediterranean boomtown, Livorno represented the emergence of something radically new—and something which, in time, came to be one of the most contested aspects of the modern world. Namely, Livorno was the earliest and most successful instance of a free port in Europe. Free ports were places where wares could be imported, exchanged, or exported without paying customs duties; or where merchants of any nation or religion could trade on equal terms. They are the lineal ancestors of the modern special economic zone, although their commercial function was rather different in the seventeenth and eighteenth centuries. For contemporaries, moreover, Livorno provided evidence of the link between liberty on the one hand and "trade, navigation, and riches" on the other.[5] Its model was imitated and debated. In pairing the grand duke's portrait with the first free port in Europe, Ferdinando's coin marked a set of transitions in early modern Europe that are still imperfectly understood: the passage from feudalism to capitalism, and from an international marketplace strictly controlled by public authorities to one given a wide margin of autonomy. A neglected chapter in the history of liberalism, Livorno upends the received notion of free trade as the brainchild of philosophers. Free trade emerged from the dusty floorboards of the customs house a century before it was theorized during the Enlightenment.

It has long been common to treat Livorno as a curiosity that bears little relationship to the larger historical experience of Italy. In a sense, Livorno certainly did have a "very special nature," distinct from that of Tuscany: "because although it is ruled by the same laws as the grand duchy, there are many cases in which regard for its commerce and foreign communities requires not insisting on their scrupulous observation."[6] In addition to the compromises involved in managing trade, Livorno also benefited from peculiar institutional arrangements. The city had no guilds, no nobility, and a weak ecclesiastical and municipal establishment. Theoretically, the monarch enjoyed a large amount of control untroubled by the vested interests that elsewhere frustrated princely activism. For this reason, Montesquieu supposedly admired Livorno as "the policy masterpiece of the Medici," punning on the family's fame as patrons of the arts.[7]

Yet this unusual city was intimately related to the Italian hinterland in two ways. First, Livorno served as a port of entry for food provisions and industrial raw materials for much of north-central Italy. It also became a hub for the export of Italian

[4] On this coin, see Balbi de Caro, "La monetazione granducale per Livorno," 151; Frattarelli Fischer and Villani, "'People of Every Mixture,'" 104.

[5] Bethel, *French Usurpation upon the Trade of England*, 22–3.

[6] Quoted by Aglietti, *I governatori di Livorno*, 140; see also 10 and 28. For the exceptionalist case in general, see Mangio, "Livorno nel Granducato."

[7] Quoted by Braudel and Romano, *Navires et marchandises*, 28. I have not been able to trace the original citation, which may be spurious. The phrase gained currency through Repetti's geographic dictionary, which uses the phrase "capo d'opera della dinastia Medicea." Repetti, *Dizionario geografico*, vol. 2, 741.

manufactured goods, though not to the degree envisioned by Medici ambition. Its distinctive institutions never produced an economic divorce from the hinterland.[8] In addition, Livorno provided the chief model for nearby port cities as they crafted their own policies. In that crucible of rivalry that was the Italian peninsula, the Tuscan port stood at the epicenter of the reorganization of maritime trade. Indeed, if the notion of Italian unity has any meaning for this period—the peninsula was divided among several independent states—it is as a field of emulation rather than as a single economy or polity. By the mid-eighteenth century, all major ports in Italy were effectively free ports of some kind. Livorno's policies of hospitality were exceptional more in degree than in kind, and they are conspicuous above all for their success.[9]

FREE PORTS IN THE CENTRAL MEDITERRANEAN

Livorno has not figured prominently in our picture of commercial change. In a telling remark in his history of capitalism, Fernand Braudel cited Livorno as an example of a marginal place that demonstrated the coherence of the European economy.[10] In Braudel's interpretation, followed by scholars influenced by world systems theory, Livorno and other free ports served as outposts whereby the "sharp-toothed young capitalism" of northwestern Europe launched its economic penetration of the Mediterranean. As vehicles for extracting surplus capital and precursors of colonial domination, free ports were mere extensions of the more dynamic economies of northwestern Europe—where lay the real story of modern economic growth. Insofar as the Mediterranean has entered into this history, it has done so in the guise of economic decline and eventual dependency.[11]

In framing Livorno as a vehicle for northern domination, these narratives have overlooked the ways in which the region's economy remained surprisingly autonomous. Livorno did indeed become a crucial broker mediating trade between the Levant, Italy, and northwestern Europe; its meteoric rise was connected to that of the Atlantic economies. But the European economy was not as coherent as Braudel and his followers believed, and not as ripe for the mechanisms of commercial domination that began to appear by the late eighteenth century. Despite the glamor of its long-distance trade, Livorno's development remained linked to local and regional dynamics. The spread of free ports was an adaptive response to changing

[8] Contrary to a long tradition of scholarship: Sonnino, *Saggio sulle industrie, marina e commercio*, 28–32; Baruchello, *Livorno e il suo porto*, 245, 264, 301; Mori, "Linee e momenti," 7, 11, 14; Filippini, *Il porto di Livorno*, vol. 1, 48–9 and vol. 2, 125–9. For contemporary views, see the quotations in Pagano de Divitiis, "Il porto di Livorno," 62–3; and Pagano de Divitiis, *English Merchants*, 121.

[9] In addition to the works already cited, essential bibliography includes Frattarelli Fischer, "Livorno città nuova"; Frattarelli Fischer, "Livorno 1676"; Frattarelli Fischer, *Vivere fuori dal ghetto*; Engels, *Merchants*; Ghezzi, *Livorno e il mondo islamico*; Ghezzi, *Livorno e l'Atlantico*; and Addobbati, *Commercio, rischio, guerra*.

[10] Braudel, *Civilization and Capitalism*, vol. 3, 75–6.

[11] Wallerstein, *The Modern World-System*, 50, 146, 175–6, 196–8; Arrighi, *The Long Twentieth Century*, 130–62; Tabak, *The Waning of the Mediterranean*, *passim*. The quote is from Braudel, *The Mediterranean*, 640. For this approach applied to Italian free ports, see Caracciolo, *Le port franc d'Ancône*, 163–4, 179–80; and M. Costantini, *Porto, navi e traffici*, 21–4.

patterns of long-distance trade and commercial competition among the small states of north-central Italy.

The famous Italian ports of the Renaissance had an active commerce. They hosted native merchant marines and centralized exchange around their own markets. Venice for instance used its maritime power to capture lucrative economic rents.[12] Livorno, by contrast, became famous for its passive trade, for its reliance on foreign shipping and its inability to control exchange. It was open to foreign merchants, goods, and shipping; much of its long-distance commerce was en route to other destinations. "The trade of Livorno is no more than the commerce of transit, or of an entrepôt, that merchants of other cities conduct by commission," confessed the grand duke in the late eighteenth century. "Considering it in any other way is an illusion."[13] The grand duke's tone of frustration is misleading, however. Livorno became a crossroads of trade under such circumstances because the pursuit of commercial monopoly in the Mediterranean was no longer possible by the mid-sixteenth century. Amidst the prevailing conditions, a program of hospitality toward goods and merchants was a more viable strategy for participating in global commerce (Fig. 0.2).

To interpret the difference between Venice and Livorno, between the ages of active and passive trade, it is essential to distinguish between commercial power and economic output. Commercial power is the capacity to structure economic exchange, whether by force or diplomacy. It is influenced by economic factors—by the aggregate output of a society's productive forces—but it also depends on political and military organization. Commercial power is a zero-sum game in which antagonists seek to control the behavior of one another.[14] These considerations suggest that the oft-made distinction between relative and absolute *economic* decline is not in fact helpful for understanding the rise of free ports like Livorno.[15] From an economic standpoint, aggregate output in Italy remained roughly stable across the early modern period; what changed was Italy's position in the hierarchy of European economies.[16] Yet the relative performance of the Italian economy does not explain patterns of change in the region. More important was the absolute decline in Italy's commercial power, which made it impossible to pursue monopolistic strategies of capital accumulation. In a nutshell: before the sixteenth century, Italian polities were capable of exercising commercial power; thereafter, this capacity waned until they were marginal players on the European scene. That decline

[12] Lane, "Economic Consequences of Organized Violence"; Lane, *Venice*, 30–43, 56–85, 124–34, 144–6, 166–70, 172–201, 224–49, 284–307; Greif, "On the Political Foundations of the Late Medieval Commercial Revolution"; S. A. Epstein, *Genoa and the Genoese*, 133–5, 205–8; Miner, "Lest We Break Faith with Our Creditors," 103–33. On passive and active trade, see Salvemini and Visceglia, "Pour une histoire des rapports économiques," 352–65.

[13] Pietro Leopoldo d'Asburgo Lorena, *Relazioni*, 60–1.

[14] There were multiple paths to power in the early modern period; today, a large national state and a diversified industrial economy are essential. Tilly, *Coercion, Capital, and European States*, *passim*, esp. 47–66.

[15] Rapp, *Industry and Economic Decline*, 1–6; Pagano de Divitiis, *English Merchants*, 9–10; Engels, *Merchants*, 34; Lanaro, ed., *At the Centre of the Old World*, 38–9.

[16] Sella, *Crisis and Continuity*; Aymard, "La fragilità di un'economia avanzata"; and especially Malanima, *La fine del primato*.

Fig. 0.2. Map of Italy, 1559. This map represents the chief political boundaries at the end of the Italian Wars. Most of the port cities shown would be free ports by the early eighteenth century.

in power—not any decline in wealth, absolute or relative—set the stage for the spread of free ports.

True, Italy was poorly situated for the direct exploitation of the Indies. The Tyrrhenian and Adriatic were "mere ponds" compared to the Atlantic Ocean.[17] Yet

[17] Botero, *On the Causes of the Greatness of Cities*, 63.

more important than geography was the political condition of Italy, some of whose small states were subordinate to the Spanish crown. Had Machiavelli's dream of unity been realized, Italy might have pursued overseas empire with as much gusto as other European powers. Political fragmentation was the primary reason why Italian states did not sponsor armed trading ventures in the Indies. All of Italy's long-distance trade with the Americas, and much of its trade with Asia, was destined to be mediated by the Atlantic powers. Venice forfeited its lucrative pepper trade, "like the loss of milk to a new-born babe," while certain cash-crops such as sugar migrated across the ocean.[18] But this position also constituted an opportunity. Unlike in the national states, which tended to privilege one port over another, no single port in Italy could engross all commerce with the Atlantic world. Instead, Italian ports competed with one another for as much traffic as the market would bear. And again unlike the Atlantic powers, which relied on trading companies or conquest, controlled liberalization was the principal weapon in the arsenal of ports like Livorno.

Exclusion from the Atlantic sphere was due in part to Italy's loss of hegemony in its traditional Mediterranean markets. The mercantile networks headed by the Genoese, Florentines, and Venetians contracted in the decades after 1600. Ships from northwestern Europe took over routes once plied by Italian ships. Urban wool industries saw their markets in the Levant shrink before cheaper competitors. "Let us face it," said one Enlightenment economist, "Our economy rested on a monopoly. We waxed rich thanks to the barbarous ignorance and indolence of others. Now the other nations... have dispensed with our services as they can make themselves the things which they formerly allowed us to make for them."[19] This analyst was not quite correct: the northern nations never fully dispensed with Italian services. Many luxury industries remained vibrant after 1600—silk most notably, but also glass, paper, and artistic objects. More importantly for our purposes, northerners continued to rely on Italian ports for commercial mediation with the Near East. They tended to use their own shipping, but they relied on Italian harbor and warehousing facilities. This arrangement generated fiscal benefits for governments, market access for merchants, and economic opportunities for local inhabitants. If Italy did not establish direct ties with the Indies, neither did northwestern Europe establish direct ties with the Levant. Italy remained the intermediary, albeit without the monopoly rents of yesteryear.

While some historians have been tempted to view free ports as pockets of liberalism and hence as avatars of modernity, most have reacted sharply against this view. For these scholars, free ports were instruments of the mercantilist state, opportunistic if not disingenuous tools of *raison d'état*.[20] States jealously protected

[18] Braudel, *The Mediterranean*, vol. 1, 543.

[19] Paolini, *Della legittima libertà del commercio*, vol. 1, 231, as quoted by Sella, *Crisis and Continuity*, 104.

[20] Masson, *Ports francs*, 21; Minoletti, *I porti franchi*, 67; Caracciolo, *Le port franc d'Ancône*, 50; Dermigny, "Escales, échelles et ports francs," 522; Kirk, *Genoa and the Sea*, 176–85. Among scholars who emphasize their relative liberalism, see Giacchero, *Origini e sviluppo*, 10–13; and more ambivalently, Hovy, *Het voorstel van 1751*, 161–81.

their legal prerogatives and projected their jurisdiction over maritime space, even as they crafted controlled marketplaces on the land.[21] Despite the illiberal intentions of state officials, however, free ports did relax ethno-religious restrictions and lower customs barriers in Italy. Free ports consolidated the role of Italian intermediation between the Levant and northwestern Europe until the advent of the steamship in the nineteenth century; and they helped Italian economies participate in the expansion of European commerce while facilitating the import of raw materials and provisions on the best possible terms. As competitive trading institutions, moreover, they constituted a breach in the ambitions of other European powers. Interloping merchants relied on Italian ports to elude French and English efforts to construct commercial monopolies in the Mediterranean. Far from being a vehicle for colonialism, Livorno fostered a competitive trading zone that frustrated monopolistic projects.

Nobody could control international trade in the central Mediterranean—not so much because of state weakness, but because competition itself imposed severe constraints on the exercise of commercial power. Italy's moment of free trade was not directed by the homogenizing hand of empire, imposed by stronger states upon weaker ones, or prompted by the dictates of ideology. It was the product of an environment in which states sought to preserve their traffic while drawing rival commerce to their own ports. Venetian officials observed that Italian states had all created free ports "at opportune moments," leaving Venice little choice but to temper the "exorbitance" of its customs regime.[22] The Italian case illustrates how an international free trade regime may emerge because of the pressures of a competitive system.

The spread of free ports was by no means automatic. Although Livorno set the gold standard for free trade throughout the period, Italian regimes did not create carbon copies of the Tuscan port. They debated the merits of policies, tinkered with their customs rules, and anxiously tracked the flow of commerce. Every free port entailed compromises with the larger fiscal system. The "profit of the prince" remained a paramount consideration for elites who were not actuated by the principles of liberal ideology.[23] Free ports therefore varied widely in institutional structure and in the degree of hospitality extended to goods and foreigners. In conceptualizing the nature of the maritime free trade zone, we should not imagine an abstract market produced by identical institutional structures. Marketplace freedoms differed greatly from place to place.

PEOPLE AND COMMODITIES IN EARLY MODERN TRADE

The development of Livorno and its rival free ports amounted to the appearance of a new kind of marketplace. As the Brothers Savary suggested in their commercial

[21] Calafat, "Une mer jalousée," 352–4.
[22] From a 1735 Trade Board report published by Caracciolo, *Le port franc d'Ancône*, 130.
[23] *Lettera di un mercante*, in ibid., 125–6.

dictionary, free ports had peculiar procedures for treating merchants and goods. They were "free to any merchant, of whatever nation, to import and export their merchandise" without paying dues, so long as wares did not change ownership. The term also described the "total franchise and exemption" that merchants enjoyed from duties when importing or exporting goods into a port.[24] This double definition draws our attention to the role of commercial privileges in promoting two principal functions of the free port, either as an emporium for merchants or an entrepôt for merchandise.[25] This distinction between emporium (open to people) and entrepôt (open to goods) is best seen as complementary rather than oppositional, since there was an essential connection between commodities and merchants in early modern trade. The key achievement of the free port of Livorno lay in modifying the terms of this connection. It changed the social foundations of the marketplace by redefining who was allowed into the market and by altering the rules of exchange.

Commodity markets are places for trading physical goods such as grain or pepper. Some scholars treat such markets as natural, almost ahistorical in the way they brought together buyers and sellers. Given basic political and judicial protections, markets will develop as a result of "a certain propensity in human nature... to truck, barter, and exchange one thing for another."[26] Others emphasize that commodity markets, while relatively mature by the seventeenth century, were nonetheless subject to mercantilist distortions or capitalist manipulation.[27] This ambivalence does not merely reflect differing methodological commitments between economists and historians; how to conceptualize historically specific markets is an open question.[28]

Even Karl Polanyi took commodity markets for granted. He analyzed the formation of markets in land and labor—what he called "fictitious commodities"—but said little about commodities proper, thereby obscuring the social underpinnings of regular markets.[29] Yet in my view, Polanyi's concept of social embeddedness offers a promising avenue for understanding early modern commodity markets. In this economy, access to the market was conditioned by one's status of belonging, including citizenship, religion, and guild membership. Groups enjoyed certain economic privileges—sometimes preferential, such as the right to pay fewer taxes, and sometimes monopolistic, such as the right to the exclusive production or sale

[24] J. Savary des Bruslons and P.-L. Savary, *Dictionnaire universel*, vol. 3, 962. This definition was cited by Azuni, *Dizionario universale*, vol. 3, 306; and it was repeated by Livorno's own legal experts in 1762 in ASL, Governo, 1025, ins. 13: on which, see "The System of Livorno" in chapter 7.

[25] Kirk, *Genoa and the Sea*, 155.

[26] Smith, *Wealth of Nations*, bk 2.I.ii (p. 24). The most influential modern economic history adopting this perspective is North and Thomas, *The Rise of the Western World*, esp. 54, 92–4, 134–8.

[27] Braudel, *Civilization and Capitalism*, vol. 2, 27–9, 51, 93–7, 194, 412, 416–23; and vol. 3, 236–9.

[28] See Ogilvie, *Institutions and European Trade*, 51–71, for the longstanding restrictions on the free flow of goods and people; and 34–5, 70, 410–11, on the gradual liberalization after *c.*1500 in a few of the most advanced markets of the day. See also Pomeranz's account in *The Great Divergence*, esp. 12–15, 166–9, 199–201.

[29] Polanyi, *The Great Transformation*, 75–8, 138. Braudel criticized Polanyi's inattention to market development in *Civilization and Capitalism*, vol. 2, 225–9.

of a good. Prices, when they emerged in the marketplace, were the result of social practices far removed from the market itself. They were determined not only by factor costs, but also by the formal and informal terms with which groups participated in the market. The history of collective privilege in early modern commerce is also the history of commodity markets.[30]

Commerce is about the exchange of goods. In theory, even over long distances, buyers and sellers need never meet in person. As long as information flows are dense enough or the judicial system reliable enough, traders could conduct all negotiations from the comfort of home; goods need only be handled by transport personnel. In practice, commerce in the premodern world was conditioned by slow information, thin markets, and difficulties of contract enforcement. This situation prompted some merchants to travel in person to a locality to conduct spot transactions; it also engendered various forms of agency relations, in which principals relied upon others to conduct their business. In both cases, agents and merchants were often foreign guests of a larger host society. The movement of goods and the movement of people were two aspects of the same problem.

Long-distance commerce in the late Middle Ages depended on particularistic political arrangements. For instance, cartels or other merchant guilds such as the Hanseatic League pursued commercial privileges for members while excluding outsiders from their activities.[31] Sometimes, access to the marketplace was predicated on citizenship status or ethno-religious identity. The Venetian commercial empire, for example, employed diplomatic and military power to establish an archipelago of privilege for Venetian citizens. Arrangements for conducting cross-cultural trade between the Islamic and Christian ecumenes likewise depended on an ensemble of privileges. Some more inclusive trading institutions did develop. The fairs erected by enterprising rulers made it possible for merchants from across Europe to conduct trade and settle accounts. But these fairs were temporary (if regular) and politically fragile establishments. More often, privileges to participate in long-distance commerce entailed efforts to exclude those who did not belong to one's city, religious group, or cartel.

Free markets were not the rule in early modern Europe: many of the exclusionary policies of the medieval city were adopted by the national states. The rise of monopolistic trading companies further restricted market access. In spite of this, intensified commercial competition, and the negotiating power of certain mercantile interests, did have the effect of liberalizing some commodity markets. The most celebrated exemplar of free trade was Amsterdam, which enjoyed low tariffs and an absence of restrictions on the flow of people and commodities through its port. The republican publicist Pieter de la Court (1618–85) praised the city's religious

[30] Just as technologies of transport, sorting, and storage inform the history of nineteenth-century commodity markets: see Cronon, *Nature's Metropolis*, pt II.

[31] The Hanseatic towns—"free" (i.e. privileged or franchised) cities—have sometimes been mistakenly called free ports, as for instance in Minoletti, *I porti franchi*, 8. They are better understood as cartels that regulated membership and applied violent sanctions to preserve their privileges against non-members. See Dollinger, *The German Hansa*, 47–51, 65–78, 85–90, 108–12, 189–90, 199–203, 300–2, 371–2; and more generally Mauro, "Merchant Communities."

liberty, the "taxes equally charging all, whether inhabitants or strangers," and the freedom to engage in retail or wholesale trade without regard to citizenship status.[32] Of course, the Dutch entrepôt benefited from organized violence in the colonial sphere and was ultimately buttressed by a social alliance between Dutch political leaders, the Calvinist establishment, and elite merchants.[33] The free market's foundations lay in the peculiar soil of Dutch social history. That substratum explains why de la Court's maxims of policy were honored as much in the breach as by the observance.

There was another, southern European path to the commodity market. Beginning in the 1590s, Livorno coped with chaos in the international trading sphere by opening its doors to foreign merchants of all nations: commerce remained tied to personal status, except that everybody enjoyed equal privileges, "even our enemies the Turks."[34] The evacuation of group privilege from the marketplace was a central innovation of the seventeenth century, occurring at approximately the same time in Livorno and in Amsterdam. But as the double definition of the free port reminds us, liberalizing the treatment of goods was also crucial for creating more competitive commodity markets. Here, too, Livorno was important in experimenting with new methods for treating goods. The early free port benefited from a complex set of incentives around the warehousing and transiting of merchandise. A reform act in 1676 eliminated customs duties and applied a universal stallage tariff, assessed upon the arrival of goods with no further inquiry into their provenance, destination, or transactional destiny. By the early eighteenth century, most ports in the central Mediterranean modeled their customs regime after Livorno—they were open to foreign traders and had simplified rules for the import, storage, and export of goods. This situation was less the result of a social alliance, as in the Netherlands, than of the competitive environment outlined above.

The spread of free ports had implications for commercial organization around the central Mediterranean. This region was distinguished from others by the absence of armed trading companies and the vibrancy of cross-cultural trading networks. Explanations have focused on the capacity of such networks to transmit information and police agency relations as effectively as bureaucratic organizations such as trading companies.[35] But institutional context was also crucial in shaping commercial organization. We must explain not only why agency relations were possible across cultural and political frontiers, but also why spot transactions between merchants of different ethno-religious groups became easier in the early modern Mediterranean.

[32] De la Court, *The True Interests and Political Maxims of the Republick of Holland*, 52–3. De la Court was not an ideological liberal but rather a pragmatic mercantilist. See E. S. Reinert, "Emulating Success," 28–31, 36.

[33] Padgett, "Country as Global Market."

[34] ASF, MP, 2160, f. 132, 02/16/1645 [AD], Pandolfo Attavanti to Domenico Pandolfini.

[35] See Trivellato, *The Familiarity of Strangers*, chs 6 and 7; Grafe and Gelderblom, "The Rise and Fall of Merchant Guilds"; Aslanian, *From the Indian Ocean to the Mediterranean*, 99–102, 119; Fusaro, *Political Economies of Empire*, 182–8.

The internalization of protection and transaction costs are two rationales for armed trading companies.[36] By lowering such costs—by lowering customs and transaction costs for all merchants—free ports promoted informal commercial networks over armed organizations. The other rationale for trading companies is the pursuit of monopoly, which is often hard to differentiate from internalizing protection costs (both involved violence). And yet the prospects of armed monopoly certainly declined in the central Mediterranean, even as it proved profitable in East Asia and the Americas.[37] As noted, long-distance trade in the Middle Ages often depended on negotiated privileges exacted by the use or threat of force. In the era of free trade, however, organized violence was generally unnecessary for commerce and would have been resisted; Italian states were small but not weak by the standards of the day, and they were also shielded by the international diplomatic situation. In short, the expenses of internalizing protection costs were high, as were the expenses of pursuing violent monopolies; and the rewards diminished as Italian port cities liberalized their treatment of goods and people. The rents accruing to group privilege fell markedly as Italian regimes extended privileges to everybody.

Countless harbor views from the seventeenth and eighteenth centuries show a colorful array of peoples from distant lands. This was not a romantic genre offering a timeless portrait of Mediterranean trade. Consciously or not, painters were depicting the avant-garde of commercial life in the middle sea. Cross-cultural trading networks grew in importance after the sixteenth century, with the decline of Italian maritime power and the consolidation of the Ottoman Empire. The absence of armed trading companies is not a sign of the region's backwardness, where there were no rich trades worth monopolizing.[38] It was a function of competitive commercial institutions and strong states. Informal networks proved more competitive than armed companies because the high costs of bureaucratic organization were not recompensed with efficiency gains or economic rents.

One official identified Livorno as "a continuous fair of foreigners."[39] The free port exemplified the political protection of goods and people typical of fairs, but extended to encompass all the peoples of the world and rendered into a permanent infrastructure of commerce. This transition had implications beyond the exchange of merchandise. Imagine what would have happened had the carnivalesque inversions of the fair become the ordinary state of affairs in early modern Europe. That revolution is precisely what, from an economic perspective, the creation of continuous commodity markets meant. It helped produce a set of shared social

[36] The case for trading companies as bureaucratic institutions capable of reducing transaction costs and internalizing protection costs is made most notably by K. N. Chaudhuri, who also underscores their use of violence: *The Trading World of Asia*, chs 2 and 6; and *Trade and Civilisation*, 82, 88; see too Carlos, "Principal-Agent Problems."

[37] Jones and Ville, "Efficient Transactors or Rent-Seeking Monopolists?"; Ogilvie, *Institutions and European Trade*, 321–30.

[38] Cf. Tabak, *The Waning of the Mediterranean*, ch. 2.

[39] ASF, MP, 2160, from an undated memorandum appended to 01/16/1645 [AD], Pandolfo Attavanti to Domenico Pandolfini. Amsterdam too was often likened to a permanent fair: see Braudel, *Civilization and Capitalism*, vol. 3, 236.

and cultural practices across merchant communities divided by faith or ethnicity.[40] It also contributed to a general program of religious toleration. "Take a view of the Royal Exchange in London," wrote Voltaire during the high-noon of the Enlightenment: "There the Jew, the Muslim, and the Christian transact together as though they all professed the same religion, and give the name of Infidel to none but bankrupts."[41] Although commercial toleration never translated directly into the acceptance of religious minorities—least of all in Livorno itself—the permanent commodity market made it easier for thinkers like Voltaire to imagine a more tolerant world.[42]

FROM REASON OF STATE TO A SCIENCE OF COMMERCE

I have been using terms such as "free port," "rent," or "monopoly" as unproblematic categories of analysis. These words do have a genealogical relationship to those used in early modern Europe, but today they are embedded in an economic framework alien to their original contexts. That does not mean that we should jettison their use: doing so would make it impossible to study economic history for a culture yet to produce a distinct notion of economics. But while I believe that modern categories are essential for interpreting the past, it is important to examine the potential anachronisms in projecting our own sciences upon historical actors. Livorno presents a compelling glimpse into this problem, since the city was crucial in generating the very notion of a free port. It offers a case study in how the economic history of Europe is itself bound up with the origins of a science of economics.

The rise of political economy is one of the paradigmatic events of early modern Europe, a close concomitant of state development and the commercialization of society. Although it is impossible to identify a single canon of texts with these processes, works that treated the economy as a distinct sphere for government action began appearing in print in the late sixteenth century with Giovanni Botero's discourse on reason of state (1589). Many of the early writers on economic matters were merchants and projectors, men such as Thomas Mun, Josiah Child, John Cary, and Johan Joachim Becher. Another strand of reflection was represented by jurists expanding on the scholastic inheritance, such as Spanish thinkers of the Salamanca school or natural law theorists like Hugo Grotius or Samuel Pufendorf.[43]

[40] Trivellato, *The Familiarity of Strangers*, chs 6 and 7.

[41] Voltaire, *Letters Concerning the English Nation*, 44, adapted from the quote by Grell and Porter (eds), *Toleration in Enlightenment Europe*, 4. As Grell and Porter point out on p. 20 n. 12, Sir William Temple made a similar point in his *Observations upon the United Provinces of the Netherlands*. See also the slightly earlier comment on the Amsterdam bourse by the Dutch poet Jérémias de Decker in Donatella Calabi, *The Market and the City*, 183.

[42] The success of Livorno's model of toleration probably hindered social integration, at least among Jews: Bregoli, *Mediterranean Enlightenment*, 15–19, 208–18.

[43] Heckscher, *Mercantilism*; Schumpeter, *History of Economic Analysis*; Coleman, ed., *Revisions in Mercantilism*; Fox-Genovese, *The Origins of Physiocracy*; Grice-Hutchinson, *Early Economic Thought*; de Maddalena, "Il mercantilismo"; P. Smith, *The Business of Alchemy*; Magnusson, *Mercantilism*.

The challenge lies in tracing the transformation of a disparate set of writings into an organized body of knowledge that was called the science of commerce by the mid-eighteenth century. The crystallization of political economy was attended by the appearance of new academies and university positions devoted to economic issues, the quickening of a public sphere, and a program of translation and publication. More-or-less public intellectuals were responsible for articulating the new science. Their key concerns included debating free trade versus protectionism, promoting practical knowledge, and making private interests serve the public good. A revolution in moral philosophy, drawing on Epicurean and Augustinian principles, helped make this human science possible.[44]

The weakness of recent historiography is that it examines the science of commerce strictly as a problem of intellectual history. One of the most distinguished scholars of the Enlightenment, John Robertson, states that the success of political economy owed to the "methodological and philosophical convictions" it carried; and that the project of Enlightenment "stood or fell on its intellectual merits."[45] Accordingly, given his focus on philosophical underpinnings, Robertson denies that the literature on reason of state is even part of his subject's lineage because it was preoccupied with questions of princely resources rather than "the analysis of economic activity in its own right, and for its own sake."[46] In fact, political economy's longtime entanglement with the apparatus of governance was a motivating force behind Enlightenment economic thought. The move to free the analysis of wealth from the policy process was political in the most direct sense of the word: it was meant to limit the interference of the ministers, projectors, and merchants who for two centuries had directed economic life in Europe.

A reluctance to look beyond high intellectual life has been especially detrimental to the study of free ports. When contemporaries first described Livorno as a free port, the phrase meant "a port with privileges." It referred primarily to the city's openness to foreigners regardless of religion, ethnicity, indebtedness, and criminal history; and secondarily to various derogations from the normal customs regime. Many refinements to this definition occurred via negotiations between officials, merchants, and the central government in Florence. Eventually, the phrase came to indicate a fiscal regime in which goods were lightly or simply taxed; or, more formally, where taxes were solely intended to cover infrastructural expenses, not to raise revenue. The definition provided by the Brothers Savary thus had a long history behind it. In fact, their gloss did not even encompass one of the principal meanings of the term, ill-favored by regimes intent on exercising regulatory mastery: "a general notion of unrestrained liberty" for merchants to trade without bureaucratic interference.[47] The free port was the most notable invention of seventeenth-century Italian political economy, but one would never know that by

[44] Rothschild, *Economic Sentiments*; Wahnbaeck, *Luxury and Public Happiness*; Hont, *Jealousy of Trade*; Robertson, *The Case for the Enlightenment*, esp. 9, 29–30; S. Reinert, *Translating Empire.*

[45] Robertson, *The Case for the Enlightenment*, 375–6; see also Venturi, whose approach to the Enlightenment strongly influenced Robertson: e.g. *Utopia and Reform*, 15–16.

[46] Robertson, *The Case for the Enlightenment*, 154.

[47] Cf. ASL, Governo, 1025, ins. 13.

reading treatises or pamphlets. The free port requires us to encompass a range of texts sometimes neglected in studies of economic thought: principally memoranda or other ephemera written for ad hoc purposes. Recovering and contextualizing these texts requires a further move, however, one corrosive to a purely discursive approach to the history of political economy.

Accounting for changes in terminology requires attention to the strategic field in which contemporaries wrote. Scholars of discourse influenced by the Cambridge School have been too willing to accept native analytic categories at face value. Their histories allow discourse to unfold according to its own logic of language and ideas within a static context.[48] By contrast, historians of political practice identify actor strategies as an important factor in discursive production.[49] What individuals meant by terms such as "free port"—and hence how meanings changed over time—was conditioned by their underlying enterprises. People deployed the free port to suit their own concerns, sometimes respecting inherited meanings, at other times acting creatively or disingenuously. Actors' goals must be identified as best as possible. Since discussions about the free ports were often intended to influence policies, actors' position in the policy process and what they hoped to get from it were critical determinants of how they wrote.[50]

Questions of authority and consensus were central to the production of knowledge in the natural sciences.[51] The same was true in matters of political economy. There as in the natural sciences, authoritative knowledge hinged upon social position, proximate context, and appropriate argumentative procedures. For centuries before the Enlightenment, the legitimate purveying of economic advice was tied to the policy process. That is, an individual's capacity to make economic arguments depended on his relationship to the regime and his mastery of the genre conventions associated with bureaucratic memoranda. Much of this discursive production occurred within state-sponsored institutions for administering taxes, guilds, or trade; even those addressed directly to the prince required following courtly norms. Institutions conditioned how individuals wrote about economic matters by making some argumentative strategies sensible and others feckless. Arguments needed not only to be true or plausible, but above all, they needed to have political efficacy in the eyes of the administrators to whom they were addressed. The entanglement of expert knowledge in the policy process was one of the great problems that

[48] For introductions, see Pocock, *Politics, Language, and Time*; and Tully, ed., *Meaning and Context*. Foundational works are Pocock, *The Machiavellian Moment*; Skinner, *The Foundations of Modern Political Thought*. For criticism of the Cambridge School's approach to political economy in theory and practice, see Pincus, "Neither Machiavellian Moment nor Possessive Individualism"; Cheney, *Revolutionary Commerce*, 10–12.

[49] See especially Millstone, *Manuscript Circulation*, 12–17, and the bibliography cited therein.

[50] Although Foucauldian approaches to the origins of political economy have not been very common, at least among historians, my criticism of the Cambridge School extends to any methodology that relies primarily on discourse analysis. For an example, see Germano, *From Oikonomia to Political Economy*.

[51] Shapin and Schaffer, *Leviathan and the Air-Pump*; Latour and Woolgar, *Laboratory Life*; Dear, *The Literary Structure of Scientific Argument*; Dear, *Discipline and Experience*; Shapin, *A Social History of Truth*; Ash, *Power, Knowledge, and Expertise*; Ash, "Introduction"; Ashworth, "Quality and the Roots of Manufacturing 'Expertise.'"

exercised political economists during the Enlightenment. The search for disinterested knowledge—the regulation of who was entitled to produce such knowledge—was a major impetus for the elaboration of the new science of commerce. But Enlightened political economy also developed its own norms, practices, and institutions, often centered around cultural elites. It was no purer than its predecessor, although its practitioners were committed to obscuring some of its sociological preconditions.

My perspective on the science of commerce raises a potential problem: institutional analysis requires the detailed examination of local experience, but all of Western Europe participated in the rise of political economy. Certainly we should not minimize the impact of shared transformations in the Republic of Letters, which stretched across the continent. Equally important, however, was a process of institutional emulation that preceded and accompanied changes in moral philosophy. This process proceeded from the humble capillary organizations that regulated economic life or from the new bodies erected to oversee them (such as boards of trade or chambers of commerce). These institutions were at once highly localized and cosmopolitan. Localized, because how they functioned depended on how they were embedded in the political and fiscal landscape. But such institutions were also cosmopolitan, because they were often the products of direct emulation, and because their users were often merchants with international connections. People and policies were mobile. Even before the Enlightenment, economic knowledge produced in different local contexts bore a family resemblance.

The proliferation of new commercial institutions such as free ports was cause and consequence of European economic expansion. These institutions shaped economic debate in ways that their architects found hard to control. The "general notion of unrestrained liberty" was certainly not something that any regime was eager to contemplate, let alone propagate. Likewise, institutions structured economic activity itself in unanticipated ways, in part because they were embedded in larger networks of power, in part because they fostered patterns of interaction that were strategic in nature.[52] When one pamphleteer declared that all free ports required a clear and definite "constitution" like that of Livorno, he was indulging in the same advocacy as modern-day experts who seek to transfer policies from one context to another.[53] Although such direct transference was rarely possible, the effort to reproduce models nonetheless brought about a more integrated institutional environment. These were not the lofty political bodies such as parliaments that bargained over tax rates and property rights; the extent to which these mattered for early modern economic growth remains under dispute.[54] Rather, they were ground-level institutions such as customs houses whose actions and inactions

[52] I follow many of Greif's methodological insights while jettisoning his ahistorical (and triumphalist) accounts of historical change. See Greif, *Institutions and the Path to the Modern Economy*, pts 2 and 4.

[53] Sheeres, *A Discourse Touching Tanger*, 46.

[54] Cf. North and Weingast, "Constitutions and Commitment." Historians have subjected neo-institutional accounts of early modern growth to substantial criticism: see n. 6 in chapter 2 and n. 11 in chapter 4.

regulated the flow of commerce. They were the basic infrastructure of the unity of Europe. Institutional emulation and commercial competition were two sides of the same coin.

PLAN OF THE BOOK

This book is structured chronologically to provide a coherent account of the development of the free port. The narrative arc moves from Medici projects of merchant hospitality to liberalizing the treatment of goods. The last three chapters focus on Livorno's influence in reordering commerce in the central Mediterranean and on Enlightenment debates about the nature of the free port. Each chapter also has an analytic focus, aligned with the chief problems raised by the chronology. The following précis is intended to help readers with particular concerns locate the chapters of greatest interest.

The first two chapters examine Medici efforts to promote industry, foster a merchant marine, and tap into foreign markets. Hospitality was central to all three goals. Chapter 1 examines the theoretical tools and institutional framework that the grand dukes had at their disposal when planning Livorno. Although contemporary theories of reason of state authorized a range of interventions in economic life, the regime lacked organizations for analyzing, evaluating, and implementing economic policy. Policy was a function of ambitions formulated at the center and unforeseen institutional dynamics at the periphery. Chapter 2 argues that endemic insecurity in the Mediterranean and the instability of religious boundaries conditioned the expansion of Livorno. The process of settling merchants in Livorno raised issues of contract enforcement comparable to that of commerce itself. Medici legislation did not offer sufficient protections against expulsions of settlers and expropriations of property. Regime agents worked tirelessly to provide adequate assurances that Livorno's privileges would be enforced. These negotiations channeled the city's growth in unexpected directions. Rather than provide Tuscan merchants with a means of breaking directly into distant markets, Livorno came to serve foreign merchants as a center of deposit and transit for goods traversing the shores of the Mediterranean.

The following three chapters examine the consolidation of the free port during the seventeenth century. The legislative framework erected by the Medici was full of lacunae and uncertainties. Chapter 3 shows how a system of supplications was responsible for elaborating the theory and practice of the free port in the first half of the century. Although the central government played a formal role in resolving requests, in practice local officials made decisions in particular cases. Supplications functioned according to a bureaucratic logic that tended to serve the interests of the growing merchant community in Livorno. Chapter 4 argues that the Customs Office played a unique role in structuring economic life in the port. It shows that the procedures associated with the early free port complicated rather than simplified efforts to administer trade. The office cultivated ties with merchants to facilitate revenue collection, coordinate policy decisions, and grease the wheels of commerce—often illicitly. Chapter 5 examines the creation of the classic free port, which taxed only for commercial services. Amidst intensified commercial competition throughout the central Mediterranean, the Medici regime launched a panel of interventions aimed at improving the grand duchy's economic position. For Livorno, this program culminated in the reform of 1676, which eliminated import/export duties and simplified collection procedures. This reform constituted an important moment in the development of commodity markets and secured Livorno's role in brokering trade between northwestern Europe, Italy, and the Levant.

The final three chapters explore the wider implications of the free port. Chapter 6 offers a quantitative examination of the commercial development of Livorno, showing how it plugged local and regional exchange networks into the currents of global commerce. Despite dense connections between north-central Italy and the free port, however, international commerce did not substantially affect productive relations in the hinterland. North-central Italy remained an autonomous region; rather than a colonial outpost subservient to northern capitalism, Livorno was a large marketplace connecting otherwise distinct economies. The Tuscan city's success in organizing trade eventually provoked a competitive response by neighboring ports. Chapter 7 shows how commercial crisis in Livorno, combined with debates over its distinctive institutions, helped introduce scientific political economy to Tuscany. The status of foreigners in Livorno and the city's inability to promote Tuscan industry convinced elites of the need for an economic strategy focused on domestic agriculture and industry. Chapter 8 situates Livorno amidst a larger picture of competition in the central Mediterranean. It analyzes the spread of free ports by considering the two axes along which Italian ports liberalized during the early modern period: hospitality toward merchants and openness toward goods. Despite much institutional variation, a maritime free trade zone was in existence by the mid-eighteenth century. The intellectual legacy of free ports such as Livorno was nonetheless ambivalent. Though some Enlightenment thinkers used free ports to formulate general theories of free trade, others believed they promoted "the servitude of commerce": the subjection of state policy to foreign merchants.[55]

The conclusion draws on the book's key themes to revisit models of the policy process in early modern Europe, particularly that of rent-seeking as understood by public choice economists. It shows that the fight against monopoly was co-constituted with the origins of a science of commerce during the Enlightenment. If the mercantilist state of the Ancien Régime was an outgrowth of a rent-seeking society, it was because the rent-seekers themselves enjoyed a monopoly on economic expertise until the eighteenth century. The new science of economics did not expel local merchants from regime counsels as much as reformers might have desired, however. It gave merchants a powerful rhetorical arsenal concerning economic liberty that helped secure localities from unwanted interference by the central government.

And finally, it is necessary to offer a few comments about the fragmentary condition of the sources. The peculiar customs of the free port meant that certain

[55] Montesquieu, *De l'esprit des loix*, bk 20, ch. 11. See chapter 8, nn. 89 and 90.

kinds of records were never produced. Although quarantine officials documented long-distance imports, other kinds of trade—regional imports, and all export and transit flows—usually escaped bureaucratic notice. To make matters worse, the destruction of the Customs Office archive in 1877 eliminated the most important repository for commercial information about Livorno. I relied extensively on the archives in Florence for telling the history of the free port: the letters, memoranda, shipping reports, and fiscal information that officials in Livorno transmitted to their superiors in the capital city. This procedure could not pretend to be a complete reconstruction of the city's commercial history, but it did have the merit of making every document into a problem of the relationship between center and periphery. And that in turn revealed new vistas into discursive production about the free port that more straightforward documentation might have concealed. Even economic history can be brushed against the grain.[56]

[56] The phrase of course is from Benjamin, *Illuminations*, 257.

1

Livorno and Political Economy in the Late Renaissance

In 1591 the grand duke of Tuscany issued an invitation for merchants to settle in the city of Pisa or the nearby port of Livorno. The preamble reads like a roll call of Mediterranean peoples: it was addressed to "Easterners, Westerners, Spanish, Portuguese, Greeks, Germans, Italians, Jews, Turks, Moors, Armenians, Persians, and [merchants] of other states."[1] The grand duke encouraged these foreigners to conduct their business in Tuscany, "hoping thereby to benefit all of Italy, our subjects, and especially the poor." The remainder of the text outlined the pledges of security and exemptions that merchants would enjoy. The privilege was reissued in modified form in 1593, and in time the pair became known as the Livornina and served as a foundational text of the free port. Although the document is coy about what "worthy considerations" prompted the grand duke to make such extensive provisions for foreigners, the Livornina was the culmination of several decades of investment in the backwards port of Livorno—a project embedded in new forms of state intervention in economic life and incipient theories of economic growth.

Although Cosimo I (r. 1537–74) turned his attention to maritime commerce in the early 1560s, Livorno remained little more than a castle with a few docks at the time of his death. It was Francesco I (r. 1574–87) who developed a strategy in which Livorno would play a key role in attracting Ottoman merchandise and selling Tuscan textiles. He commissioned his finest architect to begin constructing a fortified port that could accommodate some ten thousand inhabitants. Francesco's plans faltered upon his preference for state-directed development. Ferdinando I (r. 1587–1609) adapted his brother's strategy to the evolving conditions of Mediterranean trade. His legislation aimed at populating the new port with merchants, Jews, artisans, and mariners. It also created the basis for subsequent policy development in Livorno.

The Medici regime has been hailed as one of the first in Europe to pursue a coherent economic policy. The grand dukes planted mulberry trees throughout their realm to support an indigenous silk industry, adopted measures for ensuring access to raw materials, reorganized customs houses, and sought (less successfully) to strengthen direct trading ties with the Ottoman Empire. Above all, they

[1] Guarnieri, *Livorno medicea*, doc. 5.

persuaded foreign artisans and merchants to settle in Tuscany.[2] But though Cosimo and his sons have won the lion's share of historiographical attention, governments elsewhere in Italy adopted similar policies. Italian princes had been wooing foreign merchants since the 1530s, especially Jews. Many also took measures to promote the silk industry, and by the late sixteenth century north-central Italy had come to be a magnet for manufacturing and commercial projects of all kinds. The Medici were just one of many contributors to the invention of political economy.

Renaissance Italy produced a rich discourse about the state's role in promoting commerce and industry. This new body of economic thought emerged out of the tradition of *ragione di stato* (reason of state). At the hands of its originators such as Niccolò Machiavelli, reason of state treated political problems such as how to manage conquered peoples or whether Christian morality was compatible with the requirements of rulership.[3] But with the consolidation of territorial states during the sixteenth century, some writers began to consider the factors that made states wealthy. The new economic theories are sometimes described as "mercantilist," owing to their unabashed concern with the state rather than the producer or consumer, as well as for their focus on export-oriented sectors rather than the entire economy.[4] While Renaissance economic thought certainly had a statist bias, however, the mercantilist label does a disservice in other respects. Commercial rivalry, and with it a sense of trade as a zero-sum game, was a subordinate consideration in Italian texts of the late Renaissance. Italy was internationally weak and politically fragmented. Thinkers devoted their energies to exploring what domestic actions princes could take to sustain economic development. In doing so they examined the conditions for population growth, the dynamics of cross-cultural trade, and the logic of customs regimes.

For some scholars, Renaissance economic thought is a subject manqué. One even declares that a gap in the historiography reflects a real absence of sources: "I mean of printed sources that document a capacity for observing and shaping the social world; of naming, understanding, and evaluating economic processes in ways that do not depend directly on theological or ecclesiastical premises."[5] Leaving aside the unjustifiable focus on printed sources, this definition privileges the exploration of first principles rather than the spread, reception, and transformation of economic ideas. These issues are central to the history of every discipline. In addition, it divorces intellectual discussion from other spheres of life. By contrast, I will argue that the transmission of old ideas into new political and social contexts

[2] Brown, "Concepts of Political Economy," 278–93; Diaz, *Il Granducato di Toscana*, 257–66; Frattarelli Fischer, "Livorno città nuova," 875–6.

[3] Gilbert, *Machiavelli and Guicciardini*; Pocock, *The Machiavellian Moment*; Skinner, *The Foundations of Modern Political Thought*; Pagden, ed., *The Languages of Political Theory*; Viroli, *From Politics to Reason of State*; Burke, "On Tacitus," 479–98; Soll, *Publishing the Prince*.

[4] See n. 43 in the introduction.

[5] Pesante, "Un pensiero economico laico?," 72; see also Pesante, "Il commercio nella repubblica"; and Goldthwaite, *The Economy of Renaissance Florence*, 484–516, 590–4. Other scholars have rightly emphasized the novelty of economic thought in this period: Jurdjevic, "Virtue, Commerce, and the Enduring Republican Moment"; S. Reinert, introduction to *A "Short Treatise."*

made late Renaissance economic thought possible. The project of Livorno was inconceivable a century earlier.

THE QUICKENING OF MEDICI POLITICAL ECONOMY

The history of Livorno begins with a question of military defense. The Republic of Genoa was strapped for cash and pressed hard by the forces of the duke of Milan. In June, 1421, the Genoese sold Livorno along with the adjacent Porto Pisano to the Republic of Florence for 100,000 gold florins.[6] The Florentines did not receive much for their money—only a small fortress and two docks in Livorno, and a modest haven in Porto Pisano. The lands were swampy and sparsely populated, and the port was scarcely touched by the currents of Mediterranean trade. The air was notoriously unhealthy, and at least six Florentine naval officers were cut down by the fearsome *febbre livornina* or Livorno fever.[7] One sixteenth-century official composed a poem likening the place to Dante's Inferno and complained of being posted in that "bed of fevers, that nest of pestilence."[8] But the Florentine Republic had conquered Pisa in 1406 and sought to strengthen its authority by eliminating Genoese interlopers. When the duke of Milan objected to the sale of Livorno, the Florentines claimed that "they would not return Livorno for all the money in the world."[9]

The Florentine Republic did little to develop commercial infrastructure in Livorno. Instead, the Republic bolstered the town's fortifications while devoting its energies to Pisa, which remained the chief port of Tuscany until the mid-sixteenth century. From 1422 to 1480, the Republic's galleys departed from Porto Pisano, sometimes in numbers comparable to the Venetian convoys that fetched spices from the East. These ships brought raw wool from England and carried finished cloth to the Levant. The Republic abandoned the galley system, however, after merchants discovered that it was cheaper to rely on third-party shipping facilities.[10] Meanwhile, Pisa itself was in decline. Its population had plummeted from forty thousand people at the height of its glory in the thirteenth century to less than ten thousand by the mid-fifteenth century.[11] The Florentines delivered the coup de grace in the War of Pisa (1494–1509), during which a rebellious Pisa fought unsuccessfully to establish its independence. Its commerce and industry lay in shambles by the conflict's end, and the irrigation network of the surrounding countryside was shattered. By then, the silting of its harbor had rendered it unfit for heavy maritime traffic. The grand dukes eventually succeeded in revivifying the

[6] Guarnieri, *Da Porto Pisano*, 139; and in general, Baruchello, *Livorno e il suo porto*, pt 1. Pisa and its countryside, a larger and more developed piece of land, only cost 200,000 florins less than two decades earlier.

[7] Mallet, *The Florentine Galleys*, 14.

[8] Pietro Orsilago: his poem is reproduced in G. Vivoli, *Annali*, vol. 3, 10–14.

[9] Quoted by Guarnieri, *Da Porto Pisano*, 141.

[10] Mallet, *The Florentine Galleys*, 40, 108–13.

[11] Della Pina, "Andamento e distribuzione della popolazione," 25.

city, but they could do little for its harbor. Livorno now offered the best prospects for access to the sea.

Circumstances were changing both in Tuscany and in Italy by the time the Medici principate was established in 1532.[12] The Medici, conscious of the prestige of their dynasty and the interests of their entire state, had clearer incentives to invest in a seaport than the merchant oligarchs who had run the Republic but whose wealth had never depended on a native merchant marine. In addition, Italian governments by the mid-sixteenth century were more likely than ever before to make large-scale interventions in economic life. This concern for the economy owed to the spread of a culture of projecting and the birth of what would soon be called political economy. Both developments were implicated in the consolidation of the territorial state. Italian political and economic life had focused on cities since the High Middle Ages. During the first stage of territorialization, from the twelfth century to the Peace of Lodi in 1454, city-states constructed their domains by conquering rival towns and relegating them to subordinate positions via a series of submission agreements. This situation began to change in the sixteenth century as rulers like Cosimo I created a nobility for all of Tuscany, or as Venetian patricians bought land and invested in enterprises on the Venetian mainland. Regimes increasingly pursued state-wide projects as they extended their administrative apparatus into subject lands. It would be a mistake to exaggerate the modernity of these polities. Capital cities continued to claim special economic and political status; for instance, Genoa blocked the development of rival ports in Liguria. But the new developments had an important effect on economic thought and policy.

When Cosimo I unexpectedly came to the throne in 1537, he set about controlling his new territory with a determination and subtlety reminiscent of Machiavelli's prince. He laid the foundation for the Medici state through the conquest of Siena (1555), suppression of republican allegiances, reorganization of the Tuscan bureaucracy, and cooptation of traditional elites. Though he did not alter the system of special jurisdictions that had characterized the republican regime, Cosimo and his successors controlled the old system with new supervisory bodies and personnel. These agents of central authority ensured that the grand dukes ruled and not merely reigned in Tuscany. In many ways, his policies were a continuation of those that developed under the Republic. What changed was the introduction of a Medici court apparatus and the bureaucraticization of governance in the form of a larger administration staffed by permanent officials.[13] Cosimo capped his success

[12] The Medici family governed Florence informally after 1434 by maintaining republican political forms while directing the city's affairs through their control of balloting and patronage networks. The family's expulsion in 1494 ushered in an era of political instability for Florence, in which Medici, oligarchic, and popular factions vied for control of the government. Instability came to an end when the Medici Pope Clement VII had the Emperor Charles V install his illegitimate son Alessandro de' Medici as the first hereditary duke of Florence in 1532. When Alessandro was killed by a cousin only five years later, the title passed to Cosimo I. Diaz, *Il Granducato di Toscana*, 1–72; Najemy, *A History of Florence*, chs 9, 10, and 12.

[13] Fasano Guarini, *Lo stato mediceo di Cosimo I*; Fasano Guarini, "Center and Periphery"; Fasano Guarini, *L'Italia moderna e la Toscana dei principi*; Litchfield, *Emergence of a Bureaucracy*; Waquet, *Le Grand-Duché de Toscane*; Mannori, *Il sovrano tutore*; Connell and Zorzi, eds, *Florentine Tuscany*. For

by winning recognition from Pope Pius V in 1569 as *Grand Duke of Tuscany*. This title, unique in the Italian context, encapsulated the status of Tuscany vis-à-vis other powers—stronger and more independent than Milan, Naples, and Genoa, but not as autonomous as Venice or the Papal States.

Security was of paramount importance to Cosimo during the first half of his reign. Following the murder of Alessandro de' Medici in 1537, the Spaniards had occupied Livorno and several other Tuscan fortresses along the coast. Cosimo obtained restitution of Livorno in 1543 and built an array of fortresses in Tuscany's major towns as well as along the periphery of his state. In the years before Lepanto, moreover, the Ottoman fleet remained a threat to the coast of Tuscany, exacerbating the need for maritime defense.[14] Cosimo did take a few steps toward promoting Livorno's commerce by replacing the customs "shed" with a new building in 1546 and issuing privileges in the mid-1540s for attracting mariners. The new customs house would in turn be replaced with a larger building in 1605, however, suggesting that he had not yet developed a vision for the long-term growth of the port when he started the structure in 1546. In general, Cosimo's initial efforts in Livorno were geared toward strengthening the port's defenses.[15]

The onset of the *Pax hispanica* in 1559 allowed Italian princes to cultivate more peaceful pursuits, and in his later years Cosimo felt safe enough to focus on his commercial ambitions.[16] He began by constructing new port facilities. The infrastructure of the town was woefully unprepared for large-scale commerce. The new customs house possessed an unknown number of warehouses, probably not many; the grand duke himself owned only twelve storehouses. Slowly other edifices appeared, such as a stockpile for the galleys, a few underground grain silos, and a small arsenal for shipbuilding and repairs. In 1563 he began a channel (the *Canale dei navicelli*) to connect Livorno to the Arno River. The waterway, completed in late 1574, made it easier to transport merchandise to Pisa and beyond. Cosimo also built a dike to join the mainland to its lighthouse as well as a pier that jutted off from the lighthouse to run parallel with the city. This infrastructure increased the number of ships that could be harbored in Livorno. The canal and the pier were the first major projects oriented toward commerce rather than defense.

other Italian states, see esp. Chittolini, *La formazione dello stato regionale*; Chittolini, "The 'Private,' the 'Public,' the State"; for France, see Beik, *Absolutism and Society*; for England, Braddick, *State Formation in Early Modern England*; and in general, Elliott, "A Europe of Composite Monarchies."

14 Galluzzi, *Storia del granducato di Toscana*, vol. 4, 10; Baruchello, *Livorno e il suo porto*, 107–9, 166; Matteoni, *Livorno*, 13.

15 Cosimo's abolition of the *provveditore* over maritime traffic in 1551 likewise indicates a lack of certainty about the port's future. Baruchello, *Livorno e il suo porto*, 115; Nudi, *Storia urbanistica di Livorno*, 90; G. Vivoli, *Annali*, vol. 3, 26–8, 53.

16 The Treaty of Câteau Cambrésis (1559) ended the war between France and Spain over control of the Italian Peninsula. For the following century and a half, Spain ruled directly over Naples, Sicily, Sardinia, and the Duchy of Milan while exerting informal control over Genoa, Rome, Tuscany, and a host of minor states. Although Spanish domination rested in the last instance on a network of naval bases and garrisons flung across the western Mediterranean, webs of patronage, marriage alliances, and business or military ties reconciled Italian elites to Spanish rule. Dandelet and Marino, *Spain in Italy*; Spagnoletti, *Principi italiani*; Hanlon, *The Twilight of a Military Tradition*; Musi, ed., *Nel sistema imperiale*.

In 1573 Cosimo spoke of expanding Livorno's fortifications and harbor, but it was his son Francesco who put his intentions into practice three years later.[17]

Cosimo had inherited a chaotic customs regime that frustrated Tuscan maritime goals or even the collection of duties. Abuses were rife in the Customs Office of Pisa, and Livorno did not even have an autonomous customs house—it was a mere appendage of Pisa. Regulations concerning both cities were scattered, disorganized, and poorly known to officials. New laws in 1556 and 1561 eliminated disorders in Pisa. Livorno's turn came in 1566, when Cosimo instituted a new customs regime that endured for over a century. The 1566 law created a hierarchy of officials and granted the Customs Office of Livorno its own director. Although the law was a consolidation of prior arrangements, a traditional reform rather than a novel departure, this legislation came to constitute a cornerstone of the free port.[18]

Livorno began its experimentation with free trade less by manipulating tariff levels (a hallmark of modern policy) than by erecting a system of storage, transit, and commercial exemptions that left import/export duties intact. These measures eventually made Livorno into a center of the deposit and transit trade, but their immediate aim was to integrate a backwards port into the networks of Mediterranean commerce. Privileges included a tax exemption for shipboard victuals, the permission to salt fish in transit without paying duties, and provisions in favor of merchandise from Lucca or Milan. Other clauses were intended to help state industries, as the exemption on alum tariffs imported for the Wool Guild of Florence or on raw materials for soap production. But the most significant concession was the "liberal gift" (*beneficio libero*), which allowed merchants to store wares for up to a year in Livorno duty-free before transshipping them to another place. Goods that changed ownership only paid export taxes. The chief caveat was that wares had to come or go by sea and from beyond one hundred miles, excluding rivals such as Genoa. Even goods that arrived from nearby states, whether by sea or by land, received a discount of two-thirds off tariff dues (the "two-thirds gift"). The same tax reduction applied to foreign grain shipped through Livorno.

One scholar has detected in the liberal gift a "will to sacrifice fiscal logic to the economic development of the port."[19] In fact, the logic of the reform was rather ambivalent. Levying export taxes on goods that changed hands was at odds with creating a port of deposit, and it later occasioned systemic abuses in the administration of trade. Commercial competition had already kept transit taxes low for a long time in Tuscany, moreover, suggesting that it is a mistake to ascribe a perspicacious new vision to an essentially conservative reform. In addition, Cosimo I was keen to assert his dominion over the sea: the one hundred mile rule

[17] ASF, MP, 797, f. 43, 04/02/1588, Bartolomeo Ammannati to Ferdinando I.

[18] G. Vivoli, *Annali*, vol. 3, 40–1, 66–70; Baruchello, *Livorno e il suo porto*, 119–36; Mannini, "La riforma." The Customs Office of Livorno remained subordinate for the time being to the Consoli del Mare (Sea Consuls) in Pisa, but gradually it asserted its de facto independence. See "Paperwork and Checkpoints" in chapter 4.

[19] Mannini, "La riforma," 69.

may have had a jurisdictional rather than economic aim.[20] The transit exemptions were probably not intended to create a true staple, then, but to entice incidental shipping to call in Livorno while en route to other destinations. Above all, they were meant to encourage Florentine commercial houses to settle in Livorno. The law gave Tuscan manufacturers an interest in shipping their wares via a local port rather than through Venice, Ancona, or Genoa.

The reform of 1566 sought to channel Florentine capital toward the sea, but the Medici developed the port of Livorno without altering the basic political economy of their state. The Tuscan economy was organized according to the old agreements between Florence and its hinterland that defined the status of subject communities, so that while Florence was truly the *dominante* (dominant city), it ruled less like a modern state and more like a feudal lord. The fiscal regime reflected divisions among the cities, their *contado* (immediate countryside), and their *distretto* (district). Cosimo formally respected these arrangements. He exercised control over the economy through supervisory officials, the creation of new institutions, and the codification of fragmentary rules. He did not modify the fiscal system itself. Even more than the 1566 legislation in Livorno, reforms in Pisa (1561), Prato (1563), and Florence (1577) consolidated rather than swept away prior dispositions. Medici absolutism was above all a scrupulous regard for entrenched interests.[21] The grand dukes had a free hand in Livorno owing to the town's small size, the absence of a native elite, and institutional underdevelopment relative to other communities. But the port's ability to reshape the Tuscan economy remained limited by the framework inherited from the Republic.

The city of Livorno was planned and its first stones were laid under Francesco's watch. In 1576 he decided "to enlarge Livorno with an abundance of inhabitants."[22] Livorno was to be a big port capable of accommodating a great number of people, ships, and merchandise. He entrusted the design of the city to Bernardo Buontalenti (1536–1608), one of Tuscany's preeminent architects and a loyal companion to Francesco. Buontalenti was influenced by the Platonic tradition that took man as microcosm and the urban space as macrocosm. He was also indebted to the two "ideal cities" constructed during the reign of Cosimo I, Cosmopolis (Portoferraio) and Terra del Sole. These cities wedded the aesthetic ideals of the Renaissance to Medici propaganda and the particular functions of the cities.[23] Buontalenti's

[20] The liberal gift of 1566 was a lineal descendent of a Florentine concession in 1419 to recently conquered Pisa and appears as chapter forty in the text of the reform; it was first extended to Livorno with the 1451 "beneficio della ritratta," which permitted the partial suspension of dues on goods re-exported by the same firm within a certain time period. Mori, "Linee e momenti," 4; Mannini, "La riforma," 69–70; S. R. Epstein, "Market Structures," 97–9; Addobbati, *Commercio, rischio, guerra*, 66; Calafat, "Une mer jalousée," 440–5. See "Revenue Collection as Collaboration" in chapter 4.

[21] See Teicher, "Politics and Finance in the Age of Cosimo I," 343–62; Menning, *Charity and State in Late Renaissance Italy*; Parigino, *Il tesoro del Principe*; and in general, Mirri, "Formazione di una regione economica"; S. R. Epstein, "Cities, Regions and the Late Medieval Crisis."

[22] ASF, MP, 686, ff. 377–378, 06/06/1576, Luigi Dovara to Francesco I, quoted by Matteoni, *Livorno*, 14; for what follows see also Nudi, "Il progetto di Bernardo Buontalenti per la città nuova."

[23] In 1548 Cosimo began to construct Cosmopolis (Portoferraio), named after himself but with humanist echoes of the kosmos, the ideal of order. In 1564 he founded a fortress-town in the frontier region of the Romagna called Terra del Sole. Cosmopolis and Terra del Sole were significant not only

pentagonal diagram encompassed the existing fortress and town while laying out a grid that could accommodate some ten thousand souls (see Fig. 1.1). The single large piazza at the center signified that commerce would be intimately bound to the religious and civic life of Livorno. Medici economic policy was inscribed in the urban fabric of the city.

When Francesco commissioned Buontalenti to design a new city, Livorno was still a malaria-infested town of five hundred people. Over the following years some progress was made in making the place habitable. In 1576 an Uffizio della Fabbrica

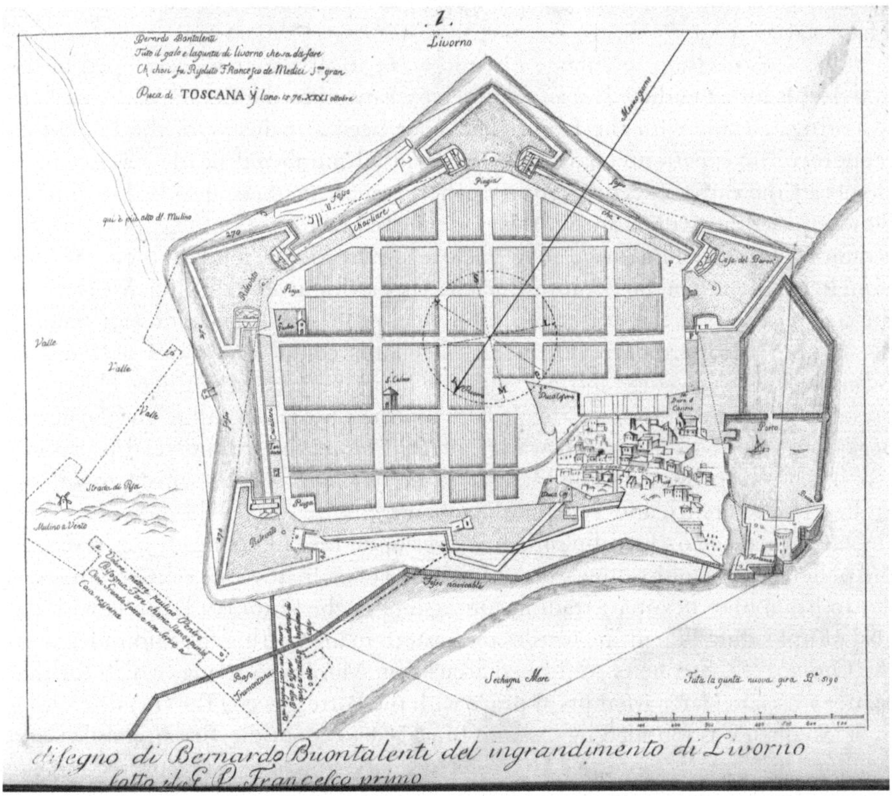

Fig. 1.1. Bernardo Buontalenti, "Plan for Livorno." Buontalenti sought to delineate the fortifications and was less interested in the city's internal space. His ideal city underwent many modifications both large and small: note, for instance, the absence of the huge Piazza d'Armi, which today dominates the urban landscape. The jumble of buildings in the bottom-right represents the old medieval village. © Victoria and Albert Museum, London.

as formal models, but also for the political precedents they set. In each town, a bureaucracy was set up to plan and manage construction. Architects sent almost daily reports to the grand duke, who intervened regularly in planning decisions. Battaglini, *Cosmopolis*; Donatini, *La città ideale*; in general, see Garin, "The Ideal City"; Fortunati, "Progetti utopici ed architettonici."

(Construction Office) was instituted to manage building projects. The Construction Office administered land expropriations, pressured pious foundations to develop residential and commercial property, and oversaw building sites. In 1577, the stone for the first bulwark was put into place with an elaborate ceremony blending astrology with theology.[24] Francesco intended to fund the fortifications through public means while leaving real estate development to private merchants and religious organizations. Both groups proved skittish about investing before seeing something more than savagely unimproved lands.[25] A slowdown in the Tuscan economy during the 1580s further deterred investors from sinking money into a risky venture, and Francesco's building program turned out to be something of a false start.

Francesco's decision to enlarge Livorno was part of a strategy developed in the mid-1570s for extending Tuscan commerce eastward to the Levant and westward to Portugal. Trade with the Levant had once been a mainstay of the Florentine economy. The expatriate community in Istanbul numbered nearly seventy merchants in the early sixteenth century, when eastern markets absorbed a third of Florentine cloth production. Yet this trade proved fragile for both geopolitical and economic reasons. Florentine manufacturers increasingly sourced their raw silk from Italy rather than the Levant, which had to pay for its cloth in gold. Meanwhile, the consolidation of the Ottoman Empire had profound implications for trade in the Eastern Mediterranean. Ottoman merchants could now travel overland to Adriatic cities like Venice and Ancona, obviating the need for a direct Florentine presence in the Levant. The struggle between the Ottoman Empire and Spain for hegemony over Mediterranean waters affected Florentine commercial prospects, too. It is not surprising that the Medici regime, as clients of the Spanish crown, lost ground before French and Venetian merchants.[26]

One of Francesco's first diplomatic moves upon his father's death was reversing the policy of antagonism toward the Sublime Porte. In 1574 he sent an ambassador to Istanbul to negotiate trading concessions in the Ottoman Empire, with the goal of unloading Florentine textiles on Eastern markets. This effort foundered on the Order of St. Stephen's continued attacks on Muslim shipping, which for that matter frustrated later attempts at peace with the Porte as well. The chivalric Order of St. Stephen was founded by Cosimo I in 1561 to coopt the Tuscan nobility and promote his dynasty's prestige. Its chief military functions were protecting the Tuscan coastlines and assaulting Muslim shipping. During negotiations with the Ottomans, Tuscan diplomats sought without avail to distance the grand duke from the allegedly "independent" Order. While Medici devotion to the *corso* has usually been chalked up to domestic political concerns, the failure to establish reciprocal diplomatic ties was typical of an era when states had few incentives to commit to maritime peace. It was an age of corsairs.[27]

[24] Nudi, *Storia urbanistica*, 100–3.

[25] ASF, MP, 1181, f. 113, 11/24/1578, Luigi Dovara to Antonio Serguidi.

[26] Goldthwaite, *The Economy of Renaissance Florence*, 182–93.

[27] Guarnieri, *I cavalieri di Santo Stefano*; Angiolini, *I cavalieri e il principe*. See "An Expanding Port in a Time of Crisis" in chapter 2.

Meanwhile, Francesco sent Antonio Vecchietti in 1575 to negotiate for the Portuguese pepper monopoly. King Sebastião I had decided to farm out the royal spice outfit to raise money for his ill-starred Africa expedition. A consortium of merchants won the contract even before the Tuscan ambassador arrived in Lisbon.[28] Vecchietti, though ill, proceeded to Lisbon anyway in the hopes of persuading the new pepper contractors to steer their ships to Livorno (a task that met with more success).[29] In brief, the Tuscans aspired to compete with the major commercial powers of Europe for the Levantine trade and also to insert themselves in the global networks directed by the Portuguese crown. Livorno was supposed to serve as the departure point for Florentine cloth and as the center for redistributing Portuguese colonial goods.

The scale of Francesco's ambitions signals a new moment in the history of political economy. Rulers throughout Italy embarked on projects for expanding industry, trade, and agriculture. Increasing cloth production was a central plank in the grand duke's platform. Since Florentine industry had long been dependent on foreign raw silk, in 1576 Francesco obligated landowners to plant mulberry trees and cultivate silkworms on their property.[30] He also took a passionate interest in industrial and alchemical processes. Under his direction the Medici Foundry (*Fonderia*) was established in various locations throughout Florence to produce wrought gold, glassware, porcelain, and other luxury goods.[31] Above all, Francesco lent an attentive ear to men with new proposals or inventions. These "projectors" were closely associated with state development and court culture in the late sixteenth century.[32]

In the last ten years of Cosimo's reign (1564–73), only nine commercial or industrial patents were granted, and most of these were handled through Francesco's chancery rather than Cosimo's.[33] But when Francesco assumed the reins of government in his own right, the number of patents multiplied: in the following decade (1574–83) he issued twenty-six, and in the remaining four years of his reign he granted another nineteen (Fig. 1.2).[34] Francesco even contemplated granting himself a patent for a new method of producing loaves of bread, which "came out so white and flavorful that we ate them at my dinner table"; he died before he had a

[28] Boyajian, *Portuguese Trade in Asia under the Habsburgs*, 18.

[29] Baruchello, *Livorno e il suo porto*, 143–56; Diaz, *I Medici*, 257–9; Frattarelli Fischer, "Livorno città nuova," 875–6.

[30] Malanima, *Decadenza*, 107–19; Battistini, *Gelsi, bozzoli e caldaie*, 39–42, 45–59, 101–8. Ferdinando issued similar laws in 1590, 1595, and 1597. By the mid-seventeenth century, domestic silk met about two-thirds of the industry's needs.

[31] Berti, *Il principe dello studiolo*, 75–97. The earliest Foundry was in the Palazzo Vecchio, but later it moved to the Boboli Gardens, the Uffizi, and the Casino di San Marco.

[32] Thirsk, *Economic Policy and Projects*; Ash, *Power, Knowledge, and Expertise*; Ravid, "A Tale of Three Cities"; Smith, *The Business of Alchemy*; Biagioli, *Galileo, Courtier*; Biagioli, "From Print to Patents," 149.

[33] Cosimo went into semi-retirement in 1564, when his son Francesco took over as regent. Francesco managed day-to-day affairs such as the handling of supplications, but Cosimo retained real power. It is customary to date the start of Francesco's reign upon the death of his father in 1574.

[34] Francesco issued 3.5 patents per year during his reign, which bears comparison to his brother Ferdinando's activities (5 per year).

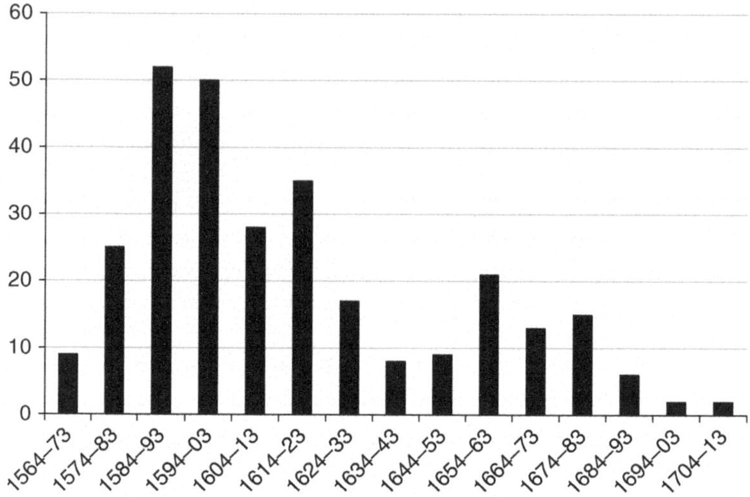

Fig. 1.2. Industrial and commercial patents by decade, 1564–1720.

Note: I have excluded printing presses because they were regulated according to a political rather than economic logic. I have also excluded renewals, common in the reign of Cosimo III. They signaled a different approach to patent granting.

Source: ASF, PS, 188–96.

chance to issue the privilege.[35] There is little doubt that the projecting that characterized his reign owed in part to his personal interests and the kind of court he created.[36] But he was far from the only prince from whom inventors could expect a reward, so long as their ideas were not "absurd and vain."[37]

Francesco's program failed to account for some of the epochal changes underway in Mediterranean commerce. These included the appearance of lightweight textiles that outcompeted Florentine woolens and the rise of Anglo-Dutch shipping, which eventually suppressed hopes for a native merchant marine. The twin trades that the regime expected to animate Livorno—textiles and spices—likewise required reconsideration. Failure to establish ties with the Sublime Porte meant that Florentines remained unable to sell cloth or buy goods directly in the Levant. Similarly, Portugal's loss of independence in 1580 made the spice trade less accessible to Tuscan capital. The sluggish pace of construction in Livorno owed

[35] ASF, MP, 269, f. 127, 08/26/1586, Francesco to Cesare Carafa.

[36] The Medici court grew rapidly from the late sixteenth century on. In 1564, it consisted of a mere 168 people. This was less than half the average among Italian princes. But under Francesco I the court grew to 233 members and continued to develop at an even faster clip under Ferdinando I to reach, at the death of Cosimo II (1621), 457 people. By the end of the seventeenth century, there were about eight hundred court dependents. Fantoni, "La formazione del sistema curiale mediceo," 165–78; Fantoni, ed., *La corte del Granduca*.

[37] ASF, MP, 269, f. 79, 06/20/1586, Belisario Vinta to Iseppo Paganini and Luigi Portelli. The patent institution developed in Venice in the late fifteenth century to encourage foreigners to bring their skills to the Republic and gradually spread throughout Western Europe. See Berveglieri, *Inventori stranieri a Venezia*; Molà, "Artigiani e brevetti," 57–79; Molà, "Il mercato delle innovazioni."

not only to an ailing economy, therefore, but also to changes in the geopolitical outlook. But where the alchemist prince failed to make the town into a bustling port, his *politique* brother Ferdinando succeeded. Ferdinando approached Livorno with a strategy more attuned to Mediterranean conditions. Before turning to his legislation it is worth examining economic thought in the late Renaissance to better contextualize the intellectual resources available to the Medici regime. Francesco in his failure and Ferdinando in his success both founded their plans upon a new body of economic thought that instructed rulers in the art of making their states rich.

LATE RENAISSANCE ECONOMIC THOUGHT

Economic thought in the High Renaissance was concerned with the practical activities of merchants, morality in the marketplace, and the effects of wealth on civic life. Although most contemporaries believed that industry and maritime power made cities richer than agriculture, they did not devote much time to investigating the underlying causes of national wealth.[38] The late Renaissance witnessed an outpouring of texts that theorized at length about what made states rich and what steps princes could take to harness economic life. These treatises were yet another concomitant of the territorial state.

Reflecting on the link between power and wealth first emerged as common practice in Italian diplomatic circles, where Venetian ambassadorial reports began to frame state power in terms of economic resources. It was only a small step to apply this analysis to the burgeoning reason of state literature, hitherto preoccupied with problems of political stability, defense, and conquest. Intensified commercial competition probably contributed to this move as well. The Venetians worried about the effect of Portuguese navigation on their spice monopoly when news of Vasco da Gama's success reached the Serenissima, and the Genoese were concerned as early as 1568 about the transit incentives in Livorno. By the 1570s, Daniel Rodriguez identified the implications of competitive tariff reductions in Italy, where key ports (Genoa, Livorno, Naples, Ancona, Venice) lay in the hands of different princes. By the late sixteenth century, all the ingredients of the new discourse were in place: techniques for managing political life, the question of the state's resources, and relentless commercial rivalry.[39]

[38] Some Quattrocento writers did address, albeit briefly, what policies conduced to the wealth of the city. These authors include Matteo Palmieri (*Vita civile*) and Diomede Carafa (*Memoriali*). Although they did not influence writers in the late Renaissance directly, they often figure in general histories of Italian economic thought.

[39] Braudel, *Civilization and Capitalism*, vol. 3, 120–1; Preto, *I servizi segreti di Venezia*, 217–18; Kirk, "Genoa and Livorno," 5; Contini, "L'informazione politica sugli stati italiani non spagnoli nelle relazioni veneziani," 30; Ravid, *Economics and Toleration*, 61; Ravid, "An Autobiographical Memorandum by Daniel Rodriga." On late medieval precedents, see Wilson, "Trade, Society, and the State," 496–8.

The most original thinker was Antonio Serra, whose 1613 treatise analyzed the difference between industrial and agricultural economies. But Serra was just one of several Italians who applied analytic reason to the sources of state wealth. For our purposes the most important authors were Filippo Sassetti and Giovanni Botero. Sassetti's *Treatise on Commerce* (1577) offers pivotal insights into Medici policy in Livorno. Botero's *Reason of State* (1589), although it exerted no direct influence on the grand dukes, illuminates the populationist policies which the regime employed to foster settlement in its new port. For both writers, the key to tapping into larger currents of trade was an open-door policy towards immigrants and merchants.

Like other Florentine elites, Filippo Sassetti (1540–88) spent time in his teens working in business. Even after he enrolled at the University of Pisa in 1568, he continued to act as a dealer in Ancona, although he abandoned commerce in favor of literary pursuits a few years later.[40] His treatise outlining Tuscan commerce prospects was composed in 1577. Sassetti claimed in the epistle dedicatory that he merely contributed "the words," while the ideas themselves belonged to the grand duke. That is undoubtedly a half-truth: while the strategic vision probably did come from Francesco and his ministers, the technical argumentation must have been Sassetti's own. The treatise was not printed until the late nineteenth century and did not circulate widely; it was a courtly document intended to martial patrician support for peace with the Ottoman Empire as Francesco prepared a second (failed) overture to Istanbul.[41] In the absence of a richer paper trail, it provides the best entrée into Livorno's privileges for toleration and trade.

The *Treatise* presented an analysis of the Mediterranean luxury trades stretching from the Levant to Antwerp. In it, Sassetti argued that Florentines could replace the mediating role then played by Venice while developing new markets for their textiles. Ottoman subjects would continue to use overland routes to the Adriatic for high-value wares such as silk, but bulk goods such as leather, slaves, or wax could travel by sea to Livorno.[42] The presence of Ottoman subjects would also draw French and Dutch merchants to Livorno: Levantine goods were in great demand, after all. In exchange, Ottoman subjects would buy Florentine silk and wool cloth, possibly even cheaper imitations of Venetian fabric. Sassetti framed the development of Tuscan trade in terms of state power:

> It is true that, in the end, we could live without Levantine products: spices come in equally great quantities via Portugal, and flax may be grown in our country. But the amount of traffic in goods produced here, either by agriculture or by industry, is very

[40] Sassetti, *Lettere da vari paesi*; Milanesi, *Filippo Sassetti*; Karl, "Galanterie di cose rare. . . ."; cf. Scrosoppi, "Attività commerciale del porto di Livorno." On the commercial apprenticeships of Florentine youth, see Litchfield, *Emergence of a Bureaucracy*, 168–70.

[41] The dedicatee of the treatise was Bongianni Gianfigliazzi (1549–1616). A Knight of Malta and a notable figure in the court of Francesco I, Gianfigliazzi was one of the chief proponents of peace with the Ottomans. He had been captured in the Battle of Lepanto (1571) and spent several years in Constantinople. Gianfigliazzi was sent back to Istanbul in 1578 to negotiate a commercial treaty. As in 1574, this mission foundered on the Order of St. Stephen's ongoing assault on Muslim shipping and the opposition of Venetian merchants resident in Istanbul. Arrighi and Klein, "Da mercante avventuriero a confidente dello stato"; Diaz, *I Medici*, 258–9; and Galluzzi, *Storia del granducato*, vol. 4, 66–7.

[42] Sassetti, "Ragionamento sul commercio," 175.

> important to the power of a country. Multiplying manufacturing increases wealth, and therein lies population growth.[43]

Trade would spur innovation and output; the wealth thereby accumulated would support a larger population and a stronger state.

Unlike later plans for increasing Tuscan commerce, Sassetti's proposals were not a plea of desperation. His advice was intended to safeguard the prosperity of a wool industry that had reached new heights over recent decades.[44] Florentine cloth had been making inroads into the markets of southern Europe and were again competing with Venetian products in the East. In addition, Sassetti imagined Livorno as the nexus for spices coming through Portugal (the sea route) and the Levant (the land route). Antwerp had served as the Portuguese spice entrepôt since 1501, but this role met with increased difficulties after the start of the Dutch Revolt in 1568; the city was sacked in 1576. In view of the troubles in Antwerp, the sale of the royal pepper monopoly in 1575, and the frailties in the Venetian stranglehold over the Levant, the spice trade seemed to be up for grabs.

The task was to make Livorno a profitable destination for people from different cultures, particularly Ottoman subjects. In general, people only want to trade in places where they have "experience and knowledge" and where they themselves are already known. A new port must therefore offer an unusual degree of utility, security, and convenience if it is to attract trade.[45] Sassetti recalled the commodious fonduks of Antwerp as an example. These dual storage/housing facilities had many well-appointed rooms and could lend out clothing or other necessities to new arrivals. The customs regime in Ancona likewise loomed large in Sassetti's mind. Earlier in the century Ancona had attracted the international trade in bulk commodities through low duties and hospitality towards foreigners. Sassetti approved of these incentives, but he thought that it would be better to assess duties by the amount of a product rather than its estimated value.[46] This rate would provide more predictability for merchants and eliminate arbitrary decisions by officials. Due to the greater distance, it was costlier to ship from the Levant to Livorno than to Ancona or Venice. Low duties were the best way to make this extra distance profitable, "since there is no surer or better profit than money never spent."[47]

[43] Ibid., 183. On these themes, see Viner, "Power versus Plenty as Objectives of Foreign Policy"; and my discussion of Botero below.

[44] Some scholars have read the treatise through the lens of the subsequent decline of the wool industry; e.g. Frattarelli Fischer, "Livorno città nuova," 878–80. But Paolo Malanima cannot locate a more precise date for the start of the decline than "*c.*1575." In the following five years, the number of apprentices in the industry began to decline, as did the investments of the Riccardi family (though the latter soon rose again). There is no evidence of alarmism in the sources, and it is likely that these first troubles were viewed as normal business fluctuations rather than the start of a terminal crisis. Malanima, *Decadenza*, 293–305; Sella, "L'industria della lana," 545. See "Livorno and its Hinterlands" and "The Limits of Market Development" in chapter 6.

[45] His terms are "pratiche e conoscenze," and "utilità, sicurtà e comodità." Sassetti, "Ragionamento sul commercio," 171–2.

[46] Ibid., 174, 176, 183. See Earle, "The Commercial Development of Ancona"; Delumeau, "Un ponte fra oriente e occidente"; Kafadar, "A Death in Venice," 195–8. Some Florentine merchants were skeptical that a local port was necessary; they found doing business in Ancona and relying on third-party shipping quite profitable.

[47] Sassetti, "Ragionamento sul commercio," 176.

Sassetti perceived a close connection between exemptions, port facilities, and cross-cultural trade. Commerce between Tuscany and the Ottoman Empire could be profitable for both parties despite stark cultural differences. The Turks offered special difficulties in this regard:

> Concerning the Turks' stay here among us, it is necessary to think long and hard about whether the customs of the Christians are similar to theirs. For they are allowed in their own lands to commit many injuries without being punished. For instance, if fury so prompts them, they take it upon themselves to deprive us of whatever is aggravating them. This proceeds not so much from their barbarous manners, as from the pride which their large empire gives them, and the excessive power with which [the Turks] dominate everyone else. For these reasons they despise all other nations and consider them vile, chalking up to their generosity everything which they do not simply take from others.[48]

Sassetti's concern was that Ottoman merchants were unaccustomed to fair business dealings because of their excessive power vis-à-vis other nations: they could simply plunder when negotiation was a hassle. What is interesting is less the truth of Sassetti's claims than his perception that trade with members of another religion and political allegiance was possible.[49] He suggested that the grand duke could mollify Turkish pride by offering prompt and fair justice in disputes, "convenience" in unloading ships and paying customs, lodging in their own buildings, and "utility" in trading. The conviction that religious differences could be sidelined by commerce lay at the heart of political culture in Livorno as it emerged in the seventeenth century, although it was rarely theorized as explicitly as by Sassetti.

For all his attention to accommodating Ottoman subjects in Livorno, Sassetti eyed greater profits in the Levant itself. Tuscans (he said) paid twice as much for Levantine goods as they cost in the East, for the simple reason that Florentines no longer had any merchant communities in the Levant capable of long-term negotiations. Florentines who did trade there in person were forced by the brevity of their stay to accept lower prices for their textiles and higher prices for Ottoman goods. As a result, Florentines found it more profitable to trade via Ancona or Venice. "And this is the origin of the proverb, *double your profit without going to the Levant.* But this is just a saying.... The tales they now tell about our ancestors and the great riches they made there are thought to be fables today, contrary to experience."[50] If Tuscan merchants had capitulation agreements with the Ottoman sultan, they could establish themselves in Constantinople and Aleppo, compete with Venetian factors, and earn greater profits. For Sassetti, port facilities and tax incentives in Livorno needed to be paired with reciprocal arrangements in the East.

[48] Ibid., 173. The insecurity of property in the Ottoman Empire was a common stereotype, often repeated in Venetian ambassadorial reports; see e.g. the 1585 report of Gianfrancesco Morosini in Albèri, *Le relazioni degli ambasciatori veneti*, 272–3. The "anti-commercial" nature of the Ottomans is simply a myth: Kafadar, "A Death in Venice," 209–12.

[49] On contemporary concern with cross-cultural trade, see Trivellato, *The Familiarity of Strangers*, 15–16; cf. the judgment of Stumpo, "Livorno in età granducale," 106.

[50] Sassetti, "Ragionamento sul commercio," 182.

Although Sassetti's treatise was meant to explicate the regime's investments in Livorno, there was a wide gulf between his ideas and outcomes in the port city. His approach to the problem of cross-cultural trade harked back to traditional, medieval antecedents. He dealt with reciprocal relations with Turks rather than with Jews, who were the primary recipients of the privileges granted in 1591 and 1593. The emphasis on Turks made good sense given the grand duke's initiative to establish trading relations with the Sublime Porte and reflects the assumption that business relations would be organized as in the Levant. The Ottoman subjects whom Sassetti imagined flocking to Livorno would remain under the political authority of the sultan, and their commerce would have been regulated by treaty. Accordingly, Sassetti advocated fonduks in which merchant-nations would temporarily live and work in their own palaces. As it turned out, the privileges of Livorno allowed foreigners to own their own property and encouraged the indiscriminate settlement of ethno-religious groups on a permanent basis.[51] Officials avoided defining the status of foreign merchants sojourning in Tuscany and, when they could not finesse the issue, insisted on maintaining absolute jurisdiction. Nor did Sassetti's prophecies about Tuscan economic prospects come true. His treatise was primarily about replacing Venice as an intermediary. He dwelt upon the export of local textiles and the import of Eastern luxuries. He said little about grain or transshipment, key functions of Livorno from the 1590s onward, while the Dutch and the English received only cursory mention.

Sassetti assumed that diplomacy was capable of regularizing international trade. The chaotic entry of new players onto the maritime scene soon rendered this notion obsolete. Yet his emphasis on port infrastructure, customs incentives, and cross-cultural trade continued to actuate Medici policy over the ensuing decades. To it was joined a conviction that Tuscany could not rely on negotiated treaties with foreign rulers but had to go it alone. The Livornina and other ducal legislation of the early 1590s sought to attract merchants, artisans, and laborers to Livorno without any presumption of reciprocal arrangements for Tuscan subjects. Giovanni Botero's influential *Reason of State* (1589) is a good guide to the rationale of this legislation. As a secretary to the prominent Borromeo family of Milan, Botero had first-hand knowledge of the machinations that drove European politics—and the importance of a buoyant fisc in weathering them.[52] Although his writings were known in Florence shortly after their publication, his work was not a direct inspiration of Medici policy so much as an elaboration of its implicit assumptions.

Botero argued that a large population was the foundation of state power, both through the men that could serve as soldiers and through the wealth it brought the treasury: rich princes were powerful princes. Population (and hence wealth) was a function of commerce, industry, and agriculture: "Italy and France have no mines of gold or silver, yet they possess more of both these metals than any other country

[51] Informal fonduks did develop, just as ethnic and religious groups tended to cluster in certain areas. For example, the Casa dei Corsi on the Via di S. Giovanni served as a meeting place for Corsican merchants and a storehouse for their wares. Lami, "I Corsi a Livorno," 74.

[52] Baldini, ed., *Botero e la "Ragion di Stato"*; Descendre, *L'état du monde*, 133–212.

in Europe, for no other reason than their inestimable number of inhabitants, who draw in money from the ends of the earth by way of trade and commerce."[53] Botero offered a battery of advice concerning economic development, ranging from customs duties and industry, to infrastructure and public works. Princes themselves could engage in trade if an enterprise lay beyond the means of subjects, as did colonial expeditions; to prevent subjects from growing excessively wealthy; or to serve the public good, such as purchasing grain in times of famine. All Botero's counsel aimed at creating a powerful state and a flourishing population.

Immigration was the most obvious way to expand the population. Botero encouraged the settlement of impecunious foreigners to develop the human potential of one's territory, but artisans and merchants were the most valuable additions to national wealth. No wonder he saw the expulsion of Jews from Spain (1494) and Portugal (1497) as an appalling episode of political stupidity. In his estimation, some 800,000 Jews were driven from the Iberian peninsula (the real figure was closer to 200,000). "This caused Bayezid King of the Turks, considering such a huge affair, to say that he marveled at King Ferdinand's prudence in depriving himself of what made most kingdoms great and rich, namely, of so many people": the sultan gladly settled the expelled Jews in his own domains.[54] This example was especially eloquent because Jews were considered a rich and industrious people.[55] Botero's populationist attitude was common among commercial writers of the late Renaissance—although curiously, this position is not always ascribed to Botero himself.[56]

Botero cited fairs to illustrate the attractive power of tariff exemptions: this is an early instance in which the free city was conceptualized as a permanent extension of the commercial fair. "People are taxed so heavily by their rulers, who are driven partly by greed and partly by necessity, that they eagerly go wherever they discover the slightest hope of fiscal immunity or franchise."[57] Although he did not mention Livorno in this connection, the congruence between his prescriptions and Medici action is unmistakable. Ferdinando I implemented a program of demographic growth, with commercial and industrial expansion playing notable if subordinate roles. Everybody was welcome to settle in Livorno regardless of ethno-religious

[53] Botero, *Della ragion di stato*, VII, 193. [54] Ibid., 195.

[55] Sir Thomas Shirley maintained as much in his 1607 proposal to resettle the Jews in England, and the Venetian Board of Trade repeatedly argued that Venice depended on Jews. Even some commercial writers in Spain, where persecution was most intense, thought the state should harness Jewish economic might. Samuel, "'Sir Thomas Shirley's Project for Jewes,'" 195–7; Ravid, *Economics and Toleration*, 36–7; Israel, *European Jewry*, 55–7.

[56] Jean Bodin and Antoine Montchretien espoused similar views for different reasons. See Cole, *French Mercantilist Doctrines*, 51–6, 196–200; Vidal, *La pensée démographique*, 23–30; Descendre, *L'état du monde*, 154–5; and on the Italian context, Fasano Guarini, "La politica demografica." Nevertheless, Joseph Schumpeter (*History of Economic Analysis*, 254–5) ascribes proto-Malthusian ideas to Botero because of the latter's recognition of theoretical limits to population growth, and his reputation as an "anti-populationist" has been repeated elsewhere: see e.g. Statt, *Foreigners and Englishmen*, 107.

[57] Botero, *Delle cause della grandezza e magnificenza delle città*, in *Della ragion di stato*, II, 321 and III, 333–5; translation by Symcox, *On the Causes of the Greatness of Cities*, 46. Botero did not relate the issue of exemptions for cities to the fiscal requirements of the state, suggesting that he did not fully realize his ideas on the relationship between territorial and urban space.

identity, from merchants to laborers. Yet there was an important difference between Botero's pronouncements and the Tuscan port. Botero did not advocate eliminating customs tariffs for foreign merchants: in his view, it was perfectly reasonable to tax aliens more than subjects.[58] What he wanted was foreign settlement, the transformation of an alien into a subject. The right of merchants to trade in Livorno on equal terms irrespective of citizenship status became one of the hallmarks of the free port. This liberty was not envisioned by Renaissance theorists and implied a bending of the populationist principle to accommodate the needs of commerce.

Botero and Sassetti are often designated mercantilists. By positing a subterranean intellectual architecture throughout the long seventeenth century, mercantilism ignores the existence of distinct discursive traditions of economic thought.[59] Zero-sum international competition is often taken as a bedrock concern for mercantilist writers, for instance. But although commercial rivalry had certainly exercised Italians for some time, it played a marginal role in the work of Botero and Sassetti. It is true that Sassetti was concerned with capturing Venetian cloth markets, but the gravity of his piece lay in analyzing the benefits of hospitality toward foreign merchants and efficient customs incentives. Botero's disinterest in rivalry perhaps owed to his project of softening the aggressive overtones of Machiavelli and rehabilitating a notion of Christian rulership.[60] Both writers focused on internal development, appropriate for small states with little scope for military adventures. In doing so they drew on examples from contemporary and ancient history to understand which policies worked and which were ruinous. In that sense, "emulation" remained central even when issues of competition were marginal.[61]

THE PRIVILEGES OF LIVORNO

"I have no desire to describe the land of Livorno," declared the Florentine patrician Giovanni Rondinelli in 1591, before heaping praise upon the town's fortifications, fortress, walls, fountains, and the "innumerable quantity of treasure that these princes have spent here."[62] The subject of his letter was the sovereign care that Grand Duke Ferdinando I paid to the port. The grand duke had transformed Livorno from a swamp into a "clean, healthy, and comfortable place." Some fourteen or fifteen hundred people, including Christian peasants and Muslim slaves, were impressed

58 Botero, *Della ragion di stato*, VII, 186. This too was a common position: e.g. Juan de Mariana, *De monetae mutatione*, in *Tractatus VII*, 201, 220; and Christoph Besold, *De aerario publico*, 46. Besold's debt to Botero is evident throughout his work: see e.g. the discussion of foreign artisans and merchants on p. 69.

59 For these reasons, Magnusson (*Mercantilism*, 8–15, 174–6) confines the word "mercantilism" to a specific group of English writers in the mid- and late seventeenth century. Despite a tendency among historians of economic thought to use the term cautiously or avoid it altogether, it remains a staple in historical writing.

60 E. Reinert discusses Botero as a non-zero-sum economist in "Emulating Success," 23–4.

61 On international competition, imitation, and analytic borrowing, see S. Reinert, *Translating Empire*.

62 Letter from Rondinelli to the Cardinal of Lorraine. Reproduced in Guarnieri, *Livorno medicea*, 253–7.

into a frenzy of draining water and clearing dirt. Ferdinando himself was involved: "The grand duke continuously went about, surveying everything, commanding regally, ordering justly, and looking after things patiently" (Fig. 1.3).

Historians have generally seconded Rondinelli's praise, according Ferdinando the seat of honor in the history of Livorno.[63] A cardinal since the age of fourteen, Ferdinando was schooled in the labyrinthine games of papal politics. He had long been wary of Francesco's philo-Spanish policies.[64] Whether he was responsible for his brother's untimely death in late 1587 remains uncertain, but there is no doubt that Ferdinando assumed the helm of Tuscany with gusto. Under Ferdinando's tenure, the grand duchy reached the height of its international prestige and power. He married his daughter Marie de Médicis to Henri IV and was a steadfast supporter of the embattled French king. His galleys cruised the Mediterranean and sacked the North African city of Bône in 1607. At home, he put an end to the banditry that plagued parts of his state and cultivated a reputation for justice. He pursued the economic goals of his predecessor with greater prudence, persistence, and, above all, flexibility.

Fig. 1.3. Jacques Callot, "Ferdinando I orders the fortifications of Livorno." This image depicts Ferdinando overseeing the building of the port. The regime glorified his personal involvement in Livorno, and historians have followed suit. Note the coerced labor in the background.
Credit: The Newberry Library, Chicago.

[63] Aglietti, *I governatori di Livorno*, 33–4.

[64] Fasano Guarini, "'Roma officina di tutte le pratiche del mondo'"; see too Berner, "Florentine Society."

In the early sixteenth century, the city-state was still the essential site for reflecting on political relations and crafting policy. The absolute dominance of the capital city is clear from any analysis of Machiavelli's oeuvre. But the rise of the territorial state changed the political calculus of rulers like Cosimo I. The grand duke came to treat his cities as part of a network of military relations, for instance, by founding Cosmopolis and Terra del Sole to control the periphery of his territory.[65] Ferdinando's central innovation was to transpose this optic of differentiated urban spaces onto the economic sphere. The centerpiece of his strategy was a division of Livorno as port, Pisa as market, and Florence as manufacturer. The three cities were supposed to serve complementary but distinct functions. Realities in the Mediterranean quickly transformed much of this strategy, as we shall see. But Ferdinando's short-lived strategy had long-term consequences through his investments and legislation.

The pace of construction in Livorno reached a frenetic pitch under Ferdinando, because, as the Venetian agent in Florence noted, "when he resolves to undertake something he cannot wait to see it completed."[66] He delegated general oversight to Don Giovanni de' Medici, the bastard son of Cosimo, who had a mastery of architectural theory and was a faithful executor of his brother's will. Along with Buontalenti, Don Giovanni presided over a team of engineers who reshaped the urban landscape and established building traditions in the city. Thanks to a variety of fiscal incentives and loans, the problem of finding investors vanished, leaving in its wake a housing frenzy administered by the Construction Office. Not without pressure from Ferdinando, the Ceppi di Prato (a charitable organization) purchased entire blocks on the central axes of the city, starting in 1592 with their first thirty-two houses for 15,000 scudi.[67] These often contained a shop on the ground level and were commonly frescoed on the outside. Livorno become yet another theater of self-celebration for the Medici as city dwellers saw the festivals of Florence, the life of the port, and the battles of the Order of St. Stephen depicted on their homes.[68]

Buontalenti's spare design had been more concerned with fortifications than the city itself. Ferdinando's regime thought seriously about how urban space could channel trade and settlement. The enormous, porticoed Piazza d'Armi (or Piazza Grande) was constructed as the commercial heart of Livorno, flanked by the civic and governmental bodies that regulated the city's life. To accommodate the burgeoning numbers of mariners kept in quarantine, a new lazaretto, complete with

[65] Likewise, the dukes of Savoy remade Turin in a deliberate attempt to create a capital city for an absolutist ruler. Symcox, "Turin *ca* 1560–1750." See too n. 23 on the ideal cities.

[66] ASV, *Dispacci di ambasciatori al Senato: Firenze*, V–IX (1590–94), f. 222. Quoted by Frattarelli Fischer, "Livorno città nuova," 884.

[67] The three biggest landowners in the city were the Ceppi di Prato, the Order of St. Stephen (forced to invest in 1616 and again in 1625), and the Customs Office itself. The Construction Office erected houses, but once built they were entrusted to the Customs Office, which both sold houses and administered leases. The leases owned by charitable organizations were deposited in the Monte di Pietà of Florence with an interest rate of five percent. Frattarelli Fischer, "Livorno città nuova," 888; Frattarelli Fischer, "La costruzione," 93.

[68] Matteoni, *Livorno*, 29–30, 37; Fasano Guarini and Matteoni, "L'Ufficio della Fabbrica."

chapel and warehouses, was built by 1597; a decade later a Health Board (Sanità) was commissioned for Livorno. An enlarged arsenal for the construction and repair of ships was also set up, as were new storehouses for the flush of commodities that began to arrive after 1591 and a "little port" or Porticciolo for loading wares onto transport barks. The Porticciolo was paid for by a temporary anchorage tax abolished in 1609.[69]

The city was structured to minimize mixing between free and unfree, Christian and non-Christian. The synagogue acted as a magnet for concentrating Jewish settlement in the absence of a ghetto, although Jews were hypothetically free to live where they wished. Likewise, the new churches that were springing up throughout the city promoted orthodoxy by focalizing the religious energies of immigrant communities. Foreign Catholics began constructing altars in the Chiesa della Madonna (completed in 1608–9), for instance, and the Uniate Greek Church of the Santissima Annunziata helped suppress schismatic practices among the Greek population.[70] To house the unfree populations amounting to some two thousand people, a *bagno* modeled after that of Algiers or Malta was made in the cramped space between the old city, its fortifications, and the more open new city. This fortress in the center of Livorno was meant to control slaves' movements, but it did not keep prisoners from trucking and dealing throughout the city.[71]

The labor regime underscored the distinct, and distinctly absolutist, character of Livorno. The Medici had long treated Livorno as a kind of container for the disorderly elements of Tuscan society. The grand dukes frequently relegated prisoners, madmen, and bandits to a spell of confinement in Livorno, often with labor.[72] Botero cited this policy as a potential way to increase a town's inhabitants, but he disapproved of "force and necessity" as a strategy for urban development: "because people who are constrained to stay in one place are like seeds cast upon the sand, where they never put down roots."[73] Bad for the character of the city, perhaps, but good for its infrastructure. The Order of St. Stephen's corsair activities moreover kept the *bagno* stocked with galley slaves whose winter season could be devoted to public works.[74] When forced labor and slaves were not enough, there was always the peasantry: the regime paid derisory wages to local peasants, whose services were not exactly voluntary. The Construction Office's pharaonic activities depended on a large pool of unfree or cheap labor.

Ferdinando issued a body of legislation that came to serve as the fundamental laws of the port. His first privileges sought skilled workmen to build infrastructure in Livorno. Like the later and more famous decrees, the orientation of this legislation was demographic: it was intended to populate the city. On October 8, 1590,

[69] Baruchello, *Livorno e il suo porto*, 180. [70] Matteoni, *Livorno*, 44.

[71] On the *bagno* and urban space more generally, see Nadalo, "Constructing Pluralism," ch. 5.

[72] For examples see Mellyn, *Mad Tuscans*, 76–80; and Goldberg, *Jews and Magic*, 41, 88, 117, 167. Goldberg also examines a controversy over establishing a Sephardic prayer house in Florence for those Sephardim in Livorno or Pisa who traveled to the capital city. The strategy of containing disorder to Livorno inevitably involved unforeseen compromises: ibid., 59, 62–4, 115–16, 236–7.

[73] Botero, *Delle cause della grandezza e magnificenza delle città*, in *Della ragion di stato*, II, 321.

[74] Salvadorini, "Traffici con i paesi islamici," 206–55; cf. Davis, *Christian Slaves*, 13–15, 23.

he published a notice that foreign "makers of mast shrouds, caulkers, wood-choppers, carpenters of all kinds, masons, woodworkers, stone workers, fishermen, mariners, smiths, and all other manual trades except for farm hands and laborers" were to be welcomed in Livorno along with their families and possessions. They would be employed in building fortifications, serving in galleys, and constructing the facilities that Rondinelli praised.[75] In fact, immigrants had in theory to become investors in the new port: to settle in the city, every head of household had to deposit fifty scudi in the Monte di Pietà of Pisa at five percent annual interest, or had to employ such a sum in buying real estate in Livorno.[76] Other legislation pursued similar aims. In January 1590 Ferdinando issued a decree exempting Greek mariners and shipwrights from various duties.[77] In March 1591 he invited artisans to Livorno, freeing them from the payment of taxes on their personal property and shop tools.[78]

The first Livornina was issued on July 1, 1591, and the second on June 10, 1593.[79] Both were directed explicitly at merchants of every nation, that is, toward people with money and connections. Still, most such individuals were promised nothing aside from the privileges and exemptions issued in previous years: safe conduct against debts contracted before their settlement in Livorno, freedom from prosecution for crimes committed outside of Tuscany (except heresy, counterfeiting, assassination, and lèse-majesté), and housing loans. There were personal tax exemptions as well, including the right to exercise a trade without paying guild fees. For non-Jewish immigrants this legislation did not offer anything new.[80] The long-term significance of the Livornina lay in its codification of earlier privileges guaranteeing visitors safety and security, their scriptural pronouncements on the nature of the port, and the gradual extension of their principles to unforeseen issues. But in the short run the Livornina mattered chiefly as a means to entice Jews to settle in Livorno and Pisa. Of the letter's forty-four provisions, forty-one dealt with the Jewish community to be established in Livorno and Pisa.[81] The Livornina contained many guarantees of life, limb, and property, freedom to practice Judaism, tax exemptions, communal autonomy, and assurances of fair judicial treatment.

75 Document 3 in Guarnieri, *Livorno medicea*, 257–9. For the drafting of this privilege, see ASF, MP, 1829, f. 223.

76 Housing contracts only required a one-third down payment; the remaining two-thirds could be paid over the next three or even seven years. These investment requirements did not survive the 1590s, however: by the early seventeenth century, virtually any visitor in Livorno enjoyed the city's exemptions. See the introduction to chapter 3.

77 Frattarelli Fischer, "La costruzione," 89. Not by chance was the first governor of Livorno a Greek. Bonifacio, "Il primo governatore di Livorno"; Aglietti, *I governatori di Livorno*, 34–46.

78 Dated 03/30/1591 and published in Castignoli and Frattarelli Fischer, eds, *Bandi per il popolamento di Livorno*, 473, n. 8.

79 Frattarelli Fischer, *Vivere fuori dal ghetto*, 36–51.

80 In February 1592, seven months after the first Livornina, Ferdinando issued another open letter inviting people to settle in Livorno that resembled the more famous document. This draft entitled captains and scriveners to bear arms. Later, in 1595, Ferdinando directed an invitation to the Jews of Lombardy, mostly of Italian or German rather than Iberian origin. This last call did not prove very effective. See Guarnieri, *Livorno medicea*, doc. 4, 259–60; Frattarelli Fischer, *Vivere fuori dal ghetto*, 58–62.

81 This tally is taken from the 1593 version.

Some unusual provisions were made, such as the right of Jews to attend the University of Pisa, for Jewish doctors to care for Christians, and for Christian wet nurses to suckle Jewish infants.[82]

The chief difference between the first and second Livornina concerned the internal regulation of the Jewish community. The first Livornina owed to the activity of a remarkable Jew from Padua named Maggino di Gabriello. Maggino began his career by marketing a method for producing two silk harvests per season.[83] He won privileges from the Duke of Savoy, Pope Sixtus V, and Tuscan Grand Duke Francesco I. When the atmosphere for Jews in Rome grew tense following the death of Sixtus V in 1590, Maggino found a welcome reception in the Grand Duchy of Tuscany.[84] With his assistance, Ferdinando's legal experts drafted the provisions of the first Livornina.[85] This charter made Maggino the head of a *universitas* on the model of the consular system in the Levant, "with all the authority and honors and graces that Christian consuls in the Levant enjoy."[86] It also entrusted him with 100,000 scudi to encourage Jewish settlement in the city, presumably to cover the costs of relocation or provide initial capital to newly arrived Jews. Over the following two years Maggino worked tirelessly to promote immigration, sending copies of the privileges to his contacts in other cities and assuring cautious Jews that Ferdinando would not renege on his promises. Ultimately, he was a victim of his own success. Several "people of quality" were interested in Livorno but disliked being subordinate to Maggino. The second Livornina (1593) ousted him as consul and instituted an oligarchic self-government for Jews.[87] The resulting arrangement resembled the Ottoman *millet* system for Jews, although other ethnic or religious groups in the port did not enjoy similar privileges of autonomy.

The Livornina was the most far-reaching of several earlier efforts to attract rich Jews to Italian states. Amidst ghettoization and expulsions throughout the sixteenth century, including the confinement of Tuscan Jews in Florence and Siena in 1570, some Italian princes had been wooing mercantile Jews since the 1530s.[88] In 1547

[82] Though see chapter 2, n. 53.

[83] Frattarelli Fischer, *Vivere fuori dal ghetto*, 39–44, 56–67, 86–91, 97–101; Molà, *The Silk Industry*, 204–14.

[84] Grand Duke Ferdinando I granted Maggino a silk privilege, a glass-making privilege, a linseed oil privilege, and huge loans for selling Florentine cloth in the Levant. By contrast, Francesco I had refused Maggino both the silk privilege and the loan in 1587. ASF, MP, 270, f. 115, 05/12/1587, and ibid., f. 119, 06/18/1587; ASF, PS, 189, ff. 48–49, 05/30/1587, ibid., ff. 64–65, 06/18/1588, and ibid., f. 206, 12/29/1593.

[85] Maggino even had to remind a secretary to publish the new privileges some two weeks after the grand duke had approved them. ASF, Riformagioni, 18, ins. 111.5, f. 661.5, 07/14/1591.

[86] Article 8 of the 1591 version.

[87] The governing body was known as the *senhores do Ma'amad* (*Massari* in Italian). Maggino's ambitions were unchecked, however. He traveled to Lorraine, Aachen, and Württemberg to establish a network of Jewish merchants whose center of gravity would lay in Tuscany. These later projects appear to have failed, and we lose track of Maggino after 1598. ASF, MP, 844, f. 130; ASF, Riformagioni, 19, ins. 100; Frattarelli Fischer, *Vivere fuori dal ghetto*, 44.

[88] Jonathan Israel argues that European states sought to expel or control their Jewish populations from about 1470 to 1570. The anti-Jewish campaign reached a fevered pitch with the papal bull *Cum nimis absurdum*, issued by Paul IV in 1555 to ghettoize the Jews of the Papal States. *Cum nimis*

Pope Paul III granted a charter for Jews to settle in Ancona. The Duchies of Urbino (1548), Tuscany (1549), and Ferrara (1550) issued privileges that mimicked the language as well as intent of Ancona's privileges. Like the Livornina, such laws often offered toleration for *marranos* (Judaizing Christians) and commercial incentives.[89] The Tuscan legislation was distinctive because it permitted Jews to own property, live an unghettoized life, and dress without distinguishing marks.[90] Above all, Livorno's privileges were special because the grand dukes stuck by and even extended key provisions to the Jewish community.[91] One observer noted in 1607 that the "*politique* Duke of Florence will not leave his Jews for all other merchants whatsoever."[92]

Ferdinando abandoned the capitulatory approach pursued by his brother. Settlement in Livorno would not be based on bilateral agreements between sovereigns, but rather upon a set of privileges granted unilaterally by the regime and geared toward artisans, laborers, mariners, merchants, and Jews. This was a sensible move for rulers influenced by contemporary thought, which located power and wealth in a state's population. The regime's legal advisors were steeped in reason of state.[93] Ferdinando justified the settlement of Jews in Livorno on the same grounds. When critiqued for having signed a trade agreement with Protestant England, Ferdinando replied with an affirmation of his own independence: "I said to the pope that I am a free prince by the grace of god and should not be deprived of that reason with which states are governed."[94] He then noted that the pope himself hosted Jews in Ancona and Rome. In making such claims Ferdinando was participating in the gradual process whereby Catholic rulers asserted their sovereign autonomy from the papacy and the emperor. Ferdinando was less committed to a specific economic vision for Livorno than his brother had been. He did not pin his hopes on breaking into the spice trade or distributing textiles in the Levant. Instead his priority was populating the city. He protected *conversos* who returned to

absurdum was overturned with *Christiana pietas* (1586), a generous charter that Grand Duke Ferdinando may have been familiar with as cardinal. These liberal provisions were overruled a few years later with *Caeca et obdurata hebraeorum perfidia* (1593), although the papal government continued to make compromises with Jews for commercial reasons. The tide was clearly changing. In the 1530s Duke Ercole II welcomed Sephardic Jews and *marranos* in Antwerp into his city. More important as a precedent, however, was the 1547 invitation for Ancona mentioned in the text. Israel, *European Jewry*, 1–69; Stow, *Catholic Thought and Papal Jewry Policy*; Segre, "La Controriforma"; Siegmund, *The Medici State and the Ghetto of Florence*; di Leone Leoni, *The Hebrew Portuguese Nations in Antwerp and London*, ch. 9.

89 Even the language of the Livornina resembles that of many of these charters. Ravid, "Venice, Rome, and the Reversion of New Christians to Judaism," 151–93, esp. 153–5, 166.

90 Jews tended to live near their synagogue, however. The grand duke steadfastly squashed periodic attempts by some Catholics to ghettoize the Jews. Frattarelli Fischer, "Proprietà e insediamento ebraici a Livorno"; Frattarelli Fischer, "Tipologia abitativa degli ebrei a Livorno."

91 Unlike (for instance) Emanuele Filiberto's abortive charters for Savoy, granted in 1572 but revoked in 1574 under papal pressure. Israel, *European Jewry*, 46–7.

92 Samuel, "'Sir Thomas Shirley's Project for Jewes,'" 196.

93 Pietro Cavallo and Carlo Dal Pozzo were Ferdinando's chief legal advisors. Fasano Guarini, "I giuristi," 235–403.

94 ASV, *Dispacci al Senato: Firenze*, VI, c. 43v–44, 05/15/1591. Quoted by Frattarelli Fischer, "Livorno città nuova," 886.

Judaism and even tolerated the presence of Protestant merchants for whom the Livornina made no special provisions. Welcoming Jews was but one component in a program of attracting productive people to Tuscany.

Ferdinando's legislation aimed at settlement in Pisa as well as Livorno. In the 1590s, the regime envisioned Livorno primarily as a port city. Commerce was supposed to take place in Pisa, whose growth in absolute numbers outstripped Livorno's in the early seventeenth century. Pisa doubled in size between 1552 and 1613, from about eight thousand inhabitants to sixteen thousand.[95] Although the majority of immigrants came from the Tuscan countryside, the most conspicuous new arrivals were foreign merchants and industrialists. For instance, the Ximenes, an illustrious mercantile family from Portugal, were given a Medici palace in Pisa and admitted into the Order of St. Stephen. The Genoese Paolo di Battista Borzone became a large coral merchant-producer in Pisa, eventually branching out into the usual panoply of commodities traded on the Mediterranean scene. The grand duke conceded privileges to foreigners in export industries such as soap, glass, and textiles.[96] Medici ambitions for Pisa are best symbolized by the construction of the Merchants' Gallery (the *Loggia dei Mercanti*) by Buontalenti between 1603 and 1605 as a structure for merchants to display their wares and conduct business.

Remaking Pisa's emporium was not the only dimension of the city's urban renewal. The grand dukes made Pisa the home of a major university whose faculty attracted students from all over Catholic Europe. They also made it the seat of the Order of St. Stephen, assuring the city a political and social role in the state. Giorgio Vasari created the Piazza dei Cavalieri, redesigned the communal palace into the knights' headquarters, and constructed the Chiesa dei Cavalieri where Turkish standards still hang as a testament to the Order's naval victories.[97] Most importantly, the Medici established their arsenal in Pisa in 1548. This structure took some forty years to complete. By the end of the century it comprised five thousand square meters and regularly employed about one hundred people between shipwrights, carpenters, and functionaries. Gradually, however, merchants came to prefer doing business in Livorno itself and began to establish their residence in the port. The process of transferring mercantile operations from Pisa to Livorno reached a tipping point around 1615; by 1640 the movement was complete.[98] For political and cultural reasons, Pisa remained the second city of Medici Tuscany. But Livorno was its undisputed commercial center.

[95] Della Pina, "Andamento e distribuzione della popolazione," 25–6; and Della Pina, "La formazione di un nuovo polo demografico."

[96] On the Ximenes, see Frattarelli Fischer, *Vivere fuori dal ghetto*, 78–85; on Borzone, see Mazzei, *Pisa medicea*, 33–4; on various manufacturing endeavors, see ibid., 63–97.

[97] G. Vivoli, *Annali*, vol. 3, 246–7; Spini, "Introduzione"; Codini, *Piazza dei Cavalieri*.

[98] Pisa's population growth fell off in about 1615. Livorno's population exceeded Pisa's after about 1640 and expanded throughout the Ancien Régime. Baruchello, *Livorno e il suo porto*, 231–5, 380; Della Pina, "Andamento e distribuzione della popolazione," 28. See "An Expanding Port in a Time of Crisis" in chapter 2.

CONCLUSION

Italian city-states had long undertaken economic projects or fought one another over access to markets. But they had pursued these activities in the absence of a theoretical interest in the sources of economic growth or the relationship between wealth and power. Writers began to supply this theory in the late Renaissance. The early incarnation of conscious economic thought was closely tied to the consolidation of the territorial state. The regularization of relations between capital and subject cities, and the bureaucratic or courtly institutions established to supervise them, raised problems about the territorial economy ignored by the city-centered political analysis of an earlier age. The challenges posed by the consolidation of the Ottoman Empire and the genesis of an Atlantic sphere also directed attention to new modes of economic analysis. While these issues began to exercise observers throughout Europe, the political fragmentation and (after 1559) military pacification of the Italian peninsula helps account for the accent upon internal development characteristic of economic thought in Italy. The grandest project of the age was not a trading company or a colonial venture, but the construction of a port city for receiving foreign merchants.

The new theories are best identified not with mercantilism but with reason of state. In my view, the persistence of mercantilism as a term nonetheless reflects a need to categorize thinkers during this period as part of a common genus. Rather than a set of ideas or policies, seventeenth-century writers all shared a pre-scientific institutional position. They wrote in an era when norms of scientific credibility in economic matters were still being established. There were no organizations such as professorships, academies, or government bodies to confer special authority on one's economic ideas. Still less were there core texts that served as touchstones for later developments and established standards of argumentation and methodology. "Mercantilist" writers could and did exploit other sources of authority, such as shared political norms, the prestige of antiquity, and (in the case of Antonio Serra) scholastic methodology. But they had no set of authorized economic knowledge upon which to found their arguments.

It is true that some scholars attribute scientific stature to the English mercantilist writers of the late seventeenth century, celebrating their systematic theorizing or their Baconian empiricism.[99] My position is that neither theory nor method is sufficient for producing a science in the absence of a social framework that authorizes such knowledge. While that framework may have been in place in late-seventeenth century England, it did not exist in Renaissance Italy. To the epistemological revolution that separated reason of state from Enlightenment political economy we must acknowledge an institutional transformation, too. Of course, figures like Sassetti did write within a social matrix, chiefly the court and the literary academy. But the kind of knowledge fostered by such institutions militated against the genesis

[99] Appleby, *Economic Thought and Ideology*, 49–51, 80–1, 93; and Magnusson, *Mercantilism*, 10–12, 76–8. See "From Reason of State to a Science of Commerce" in the introduction.

of a new epistemology proper to studying economic phenomena. Reason of state is best seen as a variant of humanist political theory rather than a distinct discipline.

The interest of the sovereign is one of the red threads of reason of state, a bedrock certitude that buttressed the rest of the analysis.[100] But even if a prince's interests could be specified, his freedom of action was a trickier matter. When treating of economic affairs, authors like Botero and Sassetti placed tremendous—and unwarranted—confidence in his capacity to control outcomes. Perhaps this conviction stemmed from their status as courtiers disinclined to explore the limits of sovereign action. For whatever reason, they did not apply the rich Italian tradition of institutional analysis to the problems of generating wealth.[101] They did not analyze regulatory bodies such as customs houses or guilds. They left unexplored the problems of exploiting information about economic trends, managing projects, and controlling interest groups. They took for granted the sovereign's control over his territories: a "stylized fact" that was highly misleading in the conditions of the day. It was possible to construct a new city and strategize about its role in economic development, then, but other relevant institutions remained uninspected. Italians in the twilight of the Renaissance were intent on recapturing the commercial hegemony of their forefathers, of proving that "the tales they now tell about our ancestors" were not mere fables.[102] They had absorbed the insights of late Renaissance economic thought, but they worked through traditional institutions to achieve their goals.

Livorno offers special insight into how contemporaries conceived of the management of commerce. Inspired by populationist principles, the Medici unilaterally extended the privileges of the city to would-be settlers. The terms on which Protestants and schismatic Greeks would live in Livorno remained unclear, as did the status of temporary visitors to the port. But despite such ambivalence in the settlement privileges, Medici legislation began the process of generalizing access to the marketplace. Sassetti's discourse on commerce indicates how trade privileges could be a means of lowering the costs of doing business in Livorno for a specific group: Ottoman subjects. The decision to offer unilateral privileges made it possible to decouple citizenship status from the right to trade. In theory, ethno-religious identity could have continued to define market access even under the unilateral privileges. The Medici could have welcomed Jews while excluding (for instance) Orthodox Greeks. But the populationist principles that actuated Medici policy helped avert this possibility. Trade costs would be lower for everybody.

100 Hirschman, *The Passions and the Interests*, 31–40.

101 Serra also failed to detail the institutional mechanisms for regulating and manipulating economic life. Unlike most of his contemporaries, however, he did not have great faith in the ability of the prince or republic to create economic growth (*A "Short Treatise,"* 127–33). Thinkers elsewhere were more interested in institutions even if they did not examine institutional practice. Laffemas, for instance, was keen on establishing fairs, guilds, a bureau of manufactures, and a chamber of commerce. Such enthusiasm was not found in Italy, perhaps because the Middle Ages had already bequeathed a host of regulatory institutions. Cole, *French Mercantilist Doctrines*, 64, 72–5; and 227 on the "childlike" belief in the omnipotence of princes common among commercial writers.

102 Sassetti, "Ragionamento sul commercio," 182.

The regime governing the treatment of goods remained poorly conceived in comparison to foreign hospitality. Sassetti and Botero treated the question of taxing trade as one connected essentially with the identity of the merchant, above all whether he was a subject or a foreigner. Apart from tariff rates, the fiscal and economic implications of commercial regulation escaped their interest. Medici legislation likewise remained ambivalent—or, to be more precise, traditional. The grand dukes envisioned several ethno-religious trading networks converging upon Livorno in the service of specifically Florentine needs. The reform of 1566 insisted on taxing exchange within the port and instituted complex procedures for monitoring the flow of goods. There was no idea that the networks might become entangled with one another in a more expansive marketplace, or that third-party merchants might use Livorno as a warehouse for their own commerce. These limitations did not spring from any obtuseness on the part of the grand dukes, who had good reasons for linking the port to Tuscan commerce. It is simply that the notion that a free port was supposed to serve for the deposit and transit of wares did not yet exist.

Ferdinando remarked in 1603 that Livorno was the "key of my states."[103] But a key for what? The regime's choice to preserve existing institutions throughout Tuscany rather than create new bodies meant that Livorno would be nestled into an existing structure; it would not be part of a general refashioning of the territory. Secondly, reason of state did not provide detailed guidance to economic policy. Instead, it carved out a sphere of legitimate princely action by linking the economic wellbeing of a territory—its population, trade, industry, and agriculture—to the integrity of the state. This outlook enabled the strategic policy planning exemplified by Sassetti's discourse and Ferdinando's legislation. It justified lavish expenditures on new infrastructure and other economic projects. But it did not instruct the regime on how a free port was supposed to function. The fundamental laws of Livorno remained laden with lacunae, uncertainties, and unresolved complexities. Among the institutions most capable of taking control of policy were the new ones set up in Livorno itself, principally the Customs Office and the Governor's Office. Over the course of several decades, local officials acting in conjunction with merchants, seamen, and artisans elaborated and modified the regime created by Medici legislation. These considerations turn our attention away from state-level choices about policy and toward the new city that the regime had called into being.

[103] ASF, MP, 67, f. 299, 04/11/1603. Quoted by Frattarelli Fischer, "Livorno città nuova," 892.

2

Insecurity and Opportunity in the Middle Sea

From an undistinguished trading post on the shores of the Tyrrhenian Sea, Livorno quickly became "one of the most famous places for trade in all Christendom."[1] Explaining the port's success requires moving beyond Medici legislation to examine the process of negotiation between the grand duke and prospective merchants or settlers. Consider an episode involving a ship captain named Honoré De Cuges, his fellow citizens in Marseille, and the Medici regime. De Cuges began to use Livorno as his base of operations in 1599 and urged his countrymen to direct their ships there as well. However, the merchants of Marseille were afraid that mariners would exploit the exemptions of Livorno to defraud them of their merchandise. What recourse would merchants enjoy if their agents absconded with their property? Grand Duke Ferdinando I promised De Cuges that officials would carefully investigate every new arrival before granting the exemptions of Livorno. In practice, seamen and merchants continued to accede to the free port's liberties almost without question. The grand duke had lied.[2]

The anxieties of the Marseillais merchants and the grand duke's facile promise to De Cuges were typical of the age. Two forms of insecurity plagued Mediterranean commerce during the seventeenth century: risk of predation on the seas, and risk of arbitrary government on the shore. Few ships were immune to danger, whether belligerent or neutral, Christian or Muslim. Several factors account for these maritime perils: the retreat of the Spanish and Ottoman imperial fleets after the Battle of Lepanto (1571); the disruptive entry of Dutch and English navigation; and the rise of privateering in the conflicts associated with the Dutch Revolt. At the same time, merchants faced a volatile atmosphere for trade. Religious reformation and the spread of Machiavellian rationality encouraged princes to renege on their agreements with alarming frequency—such, at least, was their unsavory reputation. These two forms of insecurity, though distinct, were often linked: controversies over property rights frequently emerged out of incidents at sea. While some states were victims of this unsettled environment, others tried to profit from it, occasionally by indulging in their own misbehavior. This situation led to a vicious

[1] Mun, *England's Treasure*, 24–5.

[2] ASL, CGA, 2602, vol. 1, f. 170, 02/25/1605. On De Cuges, see Engels, *Merchants*, 142, 177, 199, 202. Over a decade later, in 1618, another Marseille merchant had a similar complaint: ASL, GCM, 2602, vol. 2, f. 137. See the episode of the *Royal Exchange* in "Negotiating Trade and Settlement"; and the introduction to chapter 3.

cycle of insecurity until the stabilization of religious and political boundaries after the Peace of Westphalia (1648) and the introduction of naval convoys by the principal European fleets around 1650.[3]

Religious affiliation grew in importance during the late sixteenth century, as states lost the capacity or willingness to regulate commerce according to norms of citizenship. Malta, for instance, defined legitimate trade along religious lines, whereas Venice privileged citizenship. Other regimes oscillated opportunistically between favoring citizenship and religious status. As a result, the legitimacy of a merchant's contracts or the security of his property varied from place to place, sometimes depending on his state affiliation, sometimes on his religion.[4] The free port of Livorno pioneered a novel solution to the problem of insecurity by divorcing identity from commercial activity. Anyone could trade in Livorno regardless of ethnic, state, or religious affiliation. Religion and citizenship remained important in structuring actual trading networks, but they did not affect an individual's right to do business in the free port.

Insecurity in the Mediterranean bequeathed a massive commitment problem to the grand dukes. As Honoré De Cuges's difficulties in convincing the merchants of Marseille to trade with Livorno indicate, the novelty of the port's privileges raised issues of trust for contemporaries that were comparable to the trust problem between principals and agents.[5] In both cases, information flows were crucial in creating formal and informal sanctions for good behavior. But settlers or merchants negotiated with princes (i.e. their representatives) rather than with individual traders. Since princes presided over coercive power, they could and sometimes did default on their contracts with relative ease. In the late Middle Ages, merchant guilds, consulates, and collective retaliation helped rulers commit to protecting foreign commercial interests by imposing unacceptable costs in cases of violated trust.[6] Although these medieval institutions were in decline by the Renaissance, the state remained unable to promise foreign merchants impartial justice or security against expropriation. If anything, princes were even less to be trusted in the seventeenth century than in an earlier age.

This predicament raises a special problem for scholars of Livorno. Historians have tended to assume the bona fides of the Medici grand dukes, privy as they are to the regime's internal deliberations. Contemporaries lacked scholarly hindsight. We must explain why the regime remained committed to the port's liberties as well as how it convinced skeptics.[7] Not by chance was this the golden age of the "agent,"

[3] See n. 31 in chapter 6.

[4] Greene, "Beyond the Northern Invasion"; Greene, *Catholic Pirates and Greek Merchants*, 9–10, 194–200, 226–31; Rothman, *Brokering Empire*, *passim*, esp. 11–15. An earlier view posited well-defined English and Dutch nations rapidly gaining commercial hegemony over the Mediterranean: see Rapp, "The Unmaking."

[5] Trivellato, *Familiarity of Strangers*, intro., chs 6 and 7; and Aslanian, *From the Indian Ocean to the Mediterranean*, ch. 7.

[6] Greif, *Institutions and the Path to the Modern Economy*, chs 4 and 10; and the more historical approach in Grafe and Gelderblom, "The Rise and Fall of Merchant Guilds."

[7] Most scholarship on Livorno treats immigration in terms of Tuscan domestic considerations, the exigencies of the Jewish diaspora, or the particularistic interests of national communities (the English,

an informal representative of a prince. Tuscan agents abroad furnished individualized assurances that merchants or mariners would find a hospitable reception in Livorno and served as channels of communication between foreigners and the grand duke. Local officials likewise negotiated with immigrants to ensure that the regime stood by its promises of security and impartiality. Until the free port became a well-defined institution, these personal negotiations were an essential "infrastructure" for supporting trade and immigration.

AN EXPANDING PORT IN A TIME OF CRISIS

Medici officials knew by early August that the harvest of 1590 was going to be bad. Ferdinando commissioned Neri Giraldi and Riccardo Riccardi to buy Baltic grain to fight the specter of famine. Riccardi was one of the grand duke's richest subjects, while the young Girarldi had spent several years as a factor in Cracow. Traveling in secrecy to Nuremberg—they did not want to alert speculators of their intentions—the pair met up with another Florentine and proceeded to Danzig. There they purchased immense quantities of grain and arranged for English, Hanseatic, and Dutch ships to carry victuals to Livorno. Their mission was a huge success. Between December and April of the following year about thirty grain ships landed in the Tuscan port. From an average of 19,000 hectoliters of grain per year in the period between 1580–3, Livorno unloaded an average of 170,000 hectoliters per annum in 1590/1–1592/3.[8]

The arrival of grain heralded the beginning of Livorno's fortunes as a port. Previously, Livorno had participated in the cabotage (short-distance tramping) that characterized Mediterranean ports, with a smattering of connections further afield. In the decades after 1590 it became a center for redistributing grain to a region in regular need of foodstuffs. Eventually Livorno served as an entrepôt connecting Italian economies to the outside world while brokering trade between the Levant and northwestern Europe. On its way from grain port to entrepôt, Livorno passed through a period in which predation was an important industry. Indeed, the few cameos that Livorno makes in general histories are often in its guise as corsair haven, which gives a misleading impression of the port's economic and cultural significance.[9] Nevertheless, corsairing was critical for attracting Dutch and especially English personnel to Livorno.

The grand dukes were vigorous participants in the corsair wars that flourished during the first half of the seventeenth century. In May 1605 the Order of

the Dutch, etc.). Examining the systemic condition of insecurity reveals the commonalities that shaped all their experiences in settling or trading in Livorno. See e.g. Baruchello, *Livorno e il suo porto*, 149–50, 171–2; Engels, *Merchants*; Frattarelli Fischer and Villani, "'People of Every Mixture'"; Frattarelli Fischer, *Vivere fuori dal ghetto*, 78–108.

[8] Braudel and Romano, *Navires et marchandises*, 22, 117; Engels, *Merchants*, 89; Mazzei, *Itinera mercatorum*, 348–63. Braudel and Romano's figures for the number of Hanseatic ships are too high and those for the Dutch are too low, since many "Hanseatic" ships were owned and captained by Dutchmen.

[9] E.g. Greene, *Catholic Pirates and Greek Merchants*, 81–95; Kaplan, *Divided by Faith*, 308–9.

St. Stephen assaulted Prevesa, in August 1607 they raided Bône, and in October 1608 they engaged the Turks in a sea battle near Rhodes.[10] The grand dukes also commissioned corsairs, who were obliged to sell their prizes in Livorno and give ten percent of their booty to the fisc. Over a dozen corsairs were based in the free port during these years, and they found investors among the mercantile elite as well as the regime.[11] Like their counterparts elsewhere, they participated in both peaceful and predatory commerce, but their richest haul was undoubtedly in human beings. Their activities gave rise to a permanent market for slave redemptions between Livorno and Algiers.[12] Medici naval glory remains inscribed in the fabric of Livorno by the monument of the *Quattro Mori*. In this piece, a tall Ferdinando towers over four shackled slaves. The slaves' bodies writhe in pain or, perhaps, anger. The "free port" was not free for everybody (Fig. 2.1).

Predation played a visible role in Livorno's economy. Saharan products such as gold and ivory arrived from North Africa, as did the wax, wool, grain, leather, and cloth that normally plied Mediterranean routes. Some of these goods had been plundered on the high seas and brought to market in Tunis or Algiers. The Venetian dragoman Giovanni Battista Salvago wrote about the ties between Livorno and North Africa in 1625. According to Salvago, European merchants "buy all the stolen goods and send them to the extremely free port of Livorno, from where they are distributed to all of Italy."[13] The preference for Livorno owed to low taxes and provisions for duty-free warehousing. "Every ship that is lost to other ports when it is seized by corsairs winds up in Livorno." Salvago lamented that corsairs could only prey on commerce because the Tuscan port offered an attractive market for stolen goods. This kind of promiscuity occasioned periodic reprisals against Livorno's trade.[14]

Braudel called Livorno a second Algiers because of its role in the corsair economy, but it was also a second Izmir. Like the Anatolian city, Livorno benefited from the appearance of Dutch and English shipping in the Mediterranean. The early period, from about 1590 to 1640, was one of fluid boundaries befitting a city that supported corsair ventures and enjoyed extensive relations with North Africa. Among foreign nations, the Dutch were preeminent in the volume and value of the goods they carried, but all the seafaring nations were present. The 1630s witnessed

[10] R. C. Davis, *Christian Slaves*, 30–1, 59–60; Boni, *Corsari nel Mediterraneo*.

[11] Surviving supplications from the Governor's Office contain five requests for patents in the period 1595–1629. They are Luigi Marchegiano, 1603 (vol. 1, f. 94); Luigi Marsilione, 1614 (vol. 1, f. 610); Alessandro Sauli, 1628 (vol. 2, ff. 385–387); Antonio Manfredini, 1628 (vol. 2, f. 517); Andrea Langetto, 1629 (vol. 2, f. 484). All are in ASL, CGA, 2602. Other corsairs include Jan Davids Rutz, Niels Van der Steen, Ercole Rusca, Robert and Giles Thornton, Robert Gifford, William Ingram, Jacob Duppart, and Antonio Buleggio. See *ad vocem* in Engels, *Merchants*; and Pagano de Divitiis, *English Merchants*.

[12] For example, the merchants Jacob Beaulieu and Theodoor Reiniers invested in Jan David Rutz's piracy missions; the mother of the grand duke (and her grocer!) invested in yet another corsair ship. In the 1640s many members of the Italian *nazione* invested in Arrigo Antelmi's ventures. ASF, LCF, 134–46; Engels, *Merchants*, 78, 146; Salvadorini, "Traffici e schiavi fra Livorno e Algeria." Cf. R. C. Davis, *Christian Slaves*, 49.

[13] Masi, "Relazioni fra Livorno e Algeri," 183–4.

[14] Baruchello, *Livorno e il suo porto*, 328–31, 342.

Fig. 2.1. Pietro Tacca, "The Monument of the Four Moors." A statue of Ferdinando I by Giovanni Bandini (1599, not shown) rests atop the pedestal. The four slaves testify to Medici corsairing rather than the commercial toleration for which Livorno became famous.
Credit: photo by author.

a crisis in trade compounded by plague. Thereafter, the English consolidated their position in Livorno and used the port to organize their commerce in the Mediterranean. Growing rivalry among the maritime powers after 1650 reinforced the neutrality of Livorno and thereby its role as a secure depot where merchants could trade despite national enmities. By then, Livorno had come to serve as a center for redistribution for Italy as well as the principal node for commerce between the eastern and western Mediterranean.

The population of the city grew apace with its commerce. In 1590, Livorno was a mere village with some five hundred inhabitants. By 1642, it had about twelve thousand people, and it had over forty thousand by the end of the Ancien Régime.[15] Livorno's population explosion figures among the most remarkable in early modern Europe. Within Italy, only that of Turin and Trieste is comparable, and most other fast-growing cities were capitals of centralizing states.[16] During the period

[15] See Trivellato, *The Familiarity of Strangers*, 54.

[16] De Vries, *European Urbanization*, 141. The only Christian ports in the Mediterranean that grew in the seventeenth century were Malaga and Cadiz.

between 1591 and 1609 the majority of immigrants came from Tuscany itself (seventy-two percent), attracted by opportunities for work on the city's infrastructure and pushed by the dismal prospects afforded by the sharecropping system. Many of the remaining immigrants (sixteen percent) came from Liguria, Provence, Naples, Rome, and Corsica.[17] From a demographic standpoint, the development of Livorno was primarily a Tuscan and secondarily a Tyrrhenian phenomenon. But still, many people came from further afield as the seventeenth century wore on. These included large numbers of "Iberian" Jews, but also Greeks, French, English, Dutch, and Armenians. These groups possessed a significance beyond their size due to their connections to international trading networks. In addition, a population of Muslim slaves comprised about five percent of Livorno's population, and there were large numbers of transient mariners present as well.[18]

The streets of Livorno were "a veritable masquerade, and the language that of the Tower of Babel."[19] A Babel, but not a melting pot. Commercial toleration in Livorno was of a distinctly Catholic Reformation cast. Social groups remained closed and suspicious of outsiders; political authorities policed religious boundaries with care. Conversions from Catholicism to Protestantism were forbidden as a matter of course; even conversions from Judaism to Catholicism fell under intense state scrutiny. Social mixing occurred in the marketplace rather than the more private spheres of life. For instance, although one Jew was notorious for frequenting Christian prostitutes (and for paying the hefty fine attached to this crime), most johns preferred to patronize women of their own ethno-religious affiliation. Coffeehouses might have become a venue for general sociability, but here too groups preferred to attend distinct establishments, "to play common games, or to talk and spend time," as the governor put it in the mid-eighteenth century.[20] Life in the free port scarcely resembled the cosmopolitan ideals of Enlightenment thinkers or their intellectual heirs. But the experience of Livorno testifies to the effectiveness—purely instrumental, from the state's point of view—of commercial toleration in the Ancien Régime.[21]

Several factors conspired to transform Livorno into the "warehouse of Italy and the Mediterranean."[22] The late-Renaissance crisis in Italian shipping created an

[17] Pardi, "Disegno della storia demografica di Livorno"; Fasano Guarini, "Esenzioni e immigrazioni"; Fasano Guarini, "La popolazione." The figures for Tuscany include the independent republic of Lucca. The Tyrrhenian region comprises Genoa (i.e. Liguria), Lunigiana, Rome, Naples, Piombino, and Cagliari. On the relationship between Livorno and the sharecropping regime, see Addobbati, *Commercio, rischio, guerra*, 60–1; and "The Limits of Market Development" in chapter 6.

[18] Although a free Islamic trading community never developed in Livorno, Muslim merchants did visit the city. At least between 1720 and 1740, they were also able to use Melkite translators to make recourse to the Tuscan courts. Calafat, "Ramadam Fatet," esp. 427.

[19] De Brosses, *Lettres familières écrites d'Italie*, 125.

[20] The quote is from Bregoli, *Mediterranean Enlightenment*, 166. For conversions and sexuality, see Frattarelli Fischer, *Vivere fuori dal ghetto*, 240–306; Villani, "Donne inglesi a Livorno"; and Donati, *Tra inquisizione e granducato*.

[21] Tazzara, "Maintaining Religious Boundaries"; Trivellato, *The Familiarity of Strangers*, ch. 3; and in general, Kaplan, *Divided by Faith*, *passim*. Cf. Schlereth, *The Cosmopolitan Ideal*, esp. 100–3; and Jacob, *Strangers Nowhere in the World*, ch. 3.

[22] Quoted by Frattarelli Fischer, "Merci e mercanti," 65.

opportunity for other seafaring nations such as the Dutch, English, and (eventually) French. Second, the growth of English and Dutch trade with the Indies and the development of the Atlantic economy put northerners in a position to satisfy the demand in Mediterranean lands for colonial products. And finally, Italian textiles faced stiff competition from the inexpensive cloth manufactured in the Netherlands and England. As market opportunities in the Ottoman Empire grew for the northern nations, so too did the need for a port from which to distribute their products. Situated halfway between the Strait of Gibraltar and the Levant, Livorno was an excellent place for northerners to organize their commerce. The Tuscans had a weak maritime tradition, but they had a strong mercantile background and plenty of investment capital. In addition, Tuscany was relatively independent from both the papacy and from Spain, making Livorno well placed to serve as a neutral zone for commerce during moments of political tension or war.

The core decades of the seventeenth century were a period of crisis, stagnation, and economic restructuring. This "general crisis" struck earlier in the Mediterranean than in northern Europe, in the early 1620s, and was marked by declines in prices, populations, and agricultural production (though Livorno itself was spared until the 1630s). Italian manufacturing and banking suffered, tied as they were to demand elsewhere in Europe. In the short run, the crisis exacerbated maritime insecurity by diminishing the incentives of fair dealing. In the long run, it led to a permanent shift in the center of growth of the European economy, away from the Mediterranean and toward northwestern Europe. These developments did not convert the Mediterranean into a backward periphery, but they did affect the region's ability to participate in the Atlantic economy and the industrious revolution.[23]

Livorno was one of the few Mediterranean cities that benefitted from the general crisis. At first blush, the reasons are obvious: it had close ties with the English and Dutch, the "winners." It was the most successful among several ports that offered harbor and warehouse facilities to these maritime newcomers. But there is a problem of chronology. The Medici regime was most active in cultivating ties with the northern nations (and Jewish merchants) during the period from 1591 to 1621, when Cosimo II died and which in retrospect turned out to be an important inflection point in the Mediterranean economy. It took a long time for contemporaries to appreciate these changes, however; the foundations for trade between Livorno and the northern nations were laid decades before the northern ascendancy became clear after 1650. We must lay aside the general crisis as an explanation for Livorno's expansion and focus instead on the regime's efforts to populate their port during a period of maritime insecurity and surprising opportunities. The free port in the early seventeenth century was less an institution than a social reality created by Medici zeal in promoting settlement and trade in their new city.

[23] See Parker and Smith, eds, *The General Crisis of the Seventeenth Century*, especially the essay by Romano, "Between the Sixteenth and Seventeenth Centuries"; and de Vries, "The Economic Crisis of the Seventeenth Century."

PAPER PROMISES

In the summer of 1609, the ship *Catelana* arrived from Lisbon carrying thirty-nine Portuguese passengers interested in settling in Tuscany. They were reputed to be rich New Christians bent on escaping persecution in Portugal. In deference to their wealth and connections, the grand duke had instructed Customs Director Ludovico Niccolini to prepare a lavish welcome. Niccolini arranged for six women "of their nation" to greet the newcomers at the mouth of the harbor and provide them with carriages or canal-boats.[24] Niccolini promised to find housing for these New Christians quietly, without alarming anybody; perhaps he did not want to rouse the attention of the Inquisition or raise the hackles of the Jews in Pisa, since he thought it likely that families would increasingly choose to live in Livorno rather than the older city. But the welcome party never went off. At first Niccolini wrote to Florence to explain that the new arrivals were not the ones expected. The next day he sent a further clarification. Their relatives, already established in Livorno, confessed that the *Catelana*'s passengers were in fact the right ones—they had just not been dressed properly for such an elaborate reception. This appeared to be an excuse to Niccolini. "I believe that they were ashamed that we paid them so much honor. I went to the lazaretto to visit them, and judging by appearances, they do not seem to be people of much quality or wealth. Nevertheless, I could be wrong, and for this reason I will be as courteous as possible with them."[25] Appearances could be deceiving.

Niccolini's solicitude for the new arrivals provides a rare glimpse into the process of shepherding immigrants to Livorno. Reliable information about migrants was hard to obtain. By itself, Ferdinando's legislation drew only the most desperate—criminals, debtors, and manual laborers. A Livorno populated by such people would be no different from the "reign of fraud and avarice" the poet-administrator Pietro Orsilago had found there in the early sixteenth century: a place where "one cannot find a sign of faith or pity" among the inhabitants.[26] More desirable immigrants such as merchants and artisans needed to be courted.

Initially, publicity was a central aim of the Livornina (1591/93), which served as an open statement of the grand duke's desire to build a community of merchants in Livorno. Nevertheless, it is easy to overstate the importance of the Livornina to the city's development. Although copies of the privilege made their way to the chief cities of Europe in the early 1590s, the Livornina served primarily as a framework for the internal regulation of the Jewish communities in Livorno and Pisa. The Livornina was generally called the "privileges of the Jews." Only in the 1640s

[24] ASF, MP, 2140, f. 778, 07/19/1609, Ludovico Niccolini to Marcello Accolti.

[25] "[E] per dirla in una parola mi credo che si vergognassero, di tanto onore se li faceva. Io sono stato a lazzaretto a visitarli, e per quello che posso giudicare così esteriormente, non mi paiono gente, né di molta qualità, né anco di troppa facoltà; tuttavia posso ingannarmi, né resterò per questo di fare loro ogni sorte di cortesia." ASF, MP, 2140, f. 722, 07/29/1609, Ludovico Niccolini to Marcello Accolti.

[26] G. Vivoli, *Annali*, vol. 3, 10–14. The regime began scaling back protections from criminal prosecution in 1603: Baruchello, *Livorno e il suo porto*, 366–7.

did the documents, now known as the "privileges granted to the merchants of all nations," get identified as the foundation of the free port.[27] In the meantime, Ferdinando I tried to deflect attention away from the Livornina for fear of alarming the Holy See and the Spanish king. The external reaction to the privileges is captured by the words of Antonio Fernández de Cordóva, the Spanish ambassador in Rome. In his dispatches he detailed how the grand duke welcomed the English, Dutch, and "those Jews who come from Portugal and the other kingdoms of Spain. Knowing full well that they are baptized, he receives them in Pisa with little respect for God and Your Majesty and lets them publicly practice Judaism."[28] Ferdinando, deft dissimulator that he was, repeatedly assured the Holy See that he had no knowledge of such practices. Rather than annul the Livornina, in 1603 the grand duke forbade his chancellery from producing copies of the text and even from letting people see it without his permission. In less than a decade, the Livornina went from being a bold declaration to a secret privilege.[29]

Many merchants sought individual assurances known as safe-conducts *ad personam* when they arrived at Livorno. These documents protected people from prosecution for debts contracted outside of Tuscany and recapitulated the guarantees afforded by the port's general exemptions. For example, when a merchant of Genoa learned that disaster befell a ship on which he had 20,000 scudi worth of goods, his creditors swooped in like vultures to demand repayment. The Genoese merchant asked for a safe-conduct to live and trade in Livorno; free from prosecution, he could compose his debts and claim his insurance money in peace.[30] There was a spate of requests *ad personam* during the 1590s and the first decade of the seventeenth century, but officials came to consider them superfluous as their understanding of the free port evolved.[31] One official apologized for troubling a privy secretary with a captain's request for a safe-conduct, "which His Highness gives to everybody who asks for it. Because he is afraid that he'll get slammed [with a lawsuit], he begged me to send the present courier at his own expense."[32] Officials were prompt in providing extra assurances to skittish individuals.[33]

The grand duke issued dozens of industrial patents to encourage foreign entrepreneurs to settle in Livorno. These were a special kind of privilege *ad personam*,

[27] Frattarelli Fischer, *Vivere fuori dal ghetto*, 54; see "The Free Port as a Work in Progress" in chapter 3.

[28] Quoted by ibid., 53; see too Aglietti, *I governatori di Livorno*, 38, 44–5.

[29] Fischer, *Vivere fuori dal ghetto*, 42–3.

[30] ASF, Riformagioni, 21, ins. 59, f. 202 (1596). The merchant was named Domenico Ansaldo.

[31] E.g. ASF, Riformagioni, 18, ins. 50, f. 205 (1590); ASF, Riformagioni, 18, ins. 60, f. 275 (1590); ASF, Riformagioni, 21, ins. 32, f. 141 (1595); ASF, Riformagioni, 21, ins. 47, ff. 216–223 (1595); ASL, CGA, 2602, vol. 1, f. 85 (1604); ASF, MP, 2139, f. 305 (1606); ASL, CGA, 2602, vol. 1, f. 294 (1608); ASL, CGA, 2602, vol. 1, f. 323 (1608); ASL, CGA, 2602, vol. 1, ff. 319, 320 (1608); ASL, CGA, 2602, vol. 1, f. 341 (1609); ASL, CGA, 2602, vol. 1, 02/17/1614; ASL, CGA, 2602, vol. 1, f. 546 (1614).

[32] "[N]on posso mancare di raccomandare l'inclusa supplica di un salvacondotto al padrone del Marino di Marsiglia, che come domanda, Sua Altezza Serenissima lo concede a ciascuno che gliene domanda; e perché ha paura, non gli venga il trabocco addosso, mi ha pregato di mandare la presente cavalcata aperta a sua spese." ASF, MP, 2139, f. 353, 09/10/1604, Matteo di Terentio to Marcello Accolti.

[33] The passports granted to Ottoman Muslims (which also promised safe-conduct in Livorno itself) should also be understood as a response to systemic insecurity. Cf. Calafat, "Une mere jalousée," 400–1.

intended not only to assuage security concerns, but also to mitigate the risks of setting up enterprises in a foreign land. At least 117 foreign patentees settled in Livorno or Pisa; applying a company multiplier of four to their sixty patents produces an estimate of 240 "industrial migrants" to Livorno, mostly concentrated in the early seventeenth century.[34] These individuals came from all parts of the Mediterranean world (Fig. 2.2). Regardless of their own religious affiliation, presumably they felt more secure in the new commercial-industrial zone of Livorno and Pisa, which offered an unusual measure of toleration and had fewer guild restrictions than Florence. As with other immigration pathways, agents abroad or local officials were the first to make contact with prospective entrepreneurs. They transmitted proposals back to Florence, negotiated terms, and evaluated the trustworthiness of individuals. The risk of opening a new enterprise was formidable when immigration was involved, and at least some merchants were unwilling to change places without first getting a patent. For instance, in 1602 Cosimo Baroncelli wrote from Antwerp to discuss the possibility of establishing a sugar refinery in Livorno. A group of Zeeland merchants interested in the scheme only wanted to come if they were granted a privilege (which however seems never to have happened).[35]

The grand duke also granted patents establishing foreign consulates: the Genoese (1597), English (1597), Dutch/Germans (1597), French (1597), and Armenians (1626). These institutions differed in important ways from their medieval predecessors. In the Middle Ages, consuls protected their communities against arbitrary local government and provided jurisdiction for internal legal disputes. These prerogatives were secured by trading agreements between a local ruler and a merchant community, or between two rulers via diplomatic agreement. Many of these customs had fallen into desuetude by the late Renaissance, and nowhere more so than in Livorno itself. As previously, the consuls of Livorno organized the ritual life of their communities, or acted as translators and witnesses. They did not retain the right to judge cases, however, even when both parties were co-nationals. Instead, consuls served more as channels of immigration and trade for a newly founded city than as commercial protectors in the traditional sense. Initially, consuls were Catholics bound to the Medici regime. But from the 1620s on, consuls increasingly served as spokesmen of their titular merchant communities and (less reliably) of their sovereigns back home. This transition was complete by the last third of the seventeenth century.[36]

[34] Most patents were written in the name of only one or two people "and company." Four per patent is a conservative estimate. Agnolo Maria Carbucci's damask concern in Florence employed five people. Luca Colombini and Antonio d'Austria represented a company of eight people when they requested an import prohibition on their patented cages. Abram Isdrael promised to employ fifty people in his proposal for a fustian workshop. Two fishermen with a crew of twenty-four obtained a fishing patent. ASF, Riformagioni, 19, ins. 19l; ASF, Riformagioni, 20, ins. 8; ASF, Riformagioni, 20, ins. 127, ff. 733–735; ASF, PS, 189, f. 198.

[35] ASF, MP, 5155, f. 376, 03/07/1602 [AD], Cosimo Baroncelli to Belisario Vinta.

[36] ASF, MP, 1829, f. 126; Baruchello, *Livorno e il suo porto*, 350–7; Castignoli, "Le prime patenti consolari," 56–61; Engels, *Merchants*, 125–6; Filippini, *Il porto di Livorno*, vol. 2, 399–414; Villani, "'Una piccola epitome di Inghilterra'"; Villani, "I consoli della nazione inglese a Livorno"; Zamora

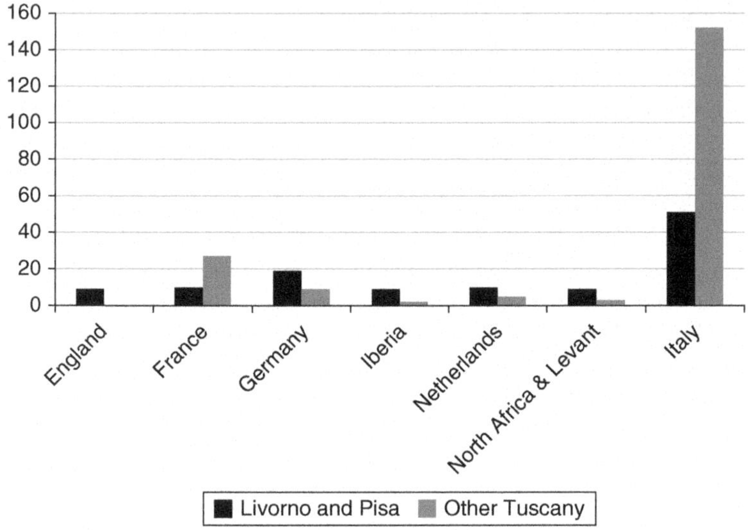

Fig. 2.2. Geographic origin of industrial and commercial patentees, 1574–1720.
Source: ASF, PS, 188–196.

NEGOTIATING TRADE AND SETTLEMENT

Patents, safe-conducts for individuals, and consular privileges were the most concrete supplements to the body of legislation that directed settlement in Livorno. They were the documentary aspect of a strategy of assuring immigrants that they would find genuine opportunities in the new port. There was a social aspect as well. In the earliest decades of Livorno's growth, the grand duke relied upon his network of agents to steer merchants, ships, and other settlers to Tuscany. These men served as valuable go-betweens because they were embedded in foreign societies but nonetheless enjoyed the grand duke's favor (and pay). Representatives stationed in France, Iberia, England, and the Netherlands promoted Livorno as a matter of course. The grand duke also employed informal "emissaries"—loose affiliates of the regime who advertised Livorno to their friends whether in letter or in person.[37]

Jan Van der Neesen's experience in the Netherlands between 1605 and 1612 sheds light on how agents shepherded people to Tuscany. A Flemish Catholic who

Rodríguez, "Privato versus pubblico"; and Calafat, "Une mer jalousée," 410–38. The English consul Thomas Hunt testified that English mariners remained in Livorno on their own volition (1608) and translated a letter into Italian written by one of his conationals (1617). Andrea Signorini, the consul of the Armenians, also served as a translator and legal aid for those under his charge. ASF, MP, 1802, 11/02/1608, Opinion of Pietro Cavallo; ASL, CGA, 2602, vol. 2, 04/29/1617; ASL, CGA, 2602, vol. 2, 09/17/1628; see also "Making Policy by Supplication" in chapter 3.

[37] Cools et al., eds, *Your Humble Servant*. On Tuscan agents, see Crinò, *Fatti e figure del Seicento anglo-Toscano*; Brege, "The Empire That Wasn't," *passim*, esp. 26–31; and "Institutions and Economic Thought" in chapter 3.

had served the grand duke since the early days of Ferdinando's reign, over the years Van der Neesen acted in a variety of confidential capacities throughout western Europe. In 1611 the Inquisition spirited away a crypto-Jew named Diego Lopez to a hidden location near Antwerp. The event terrified the Portuguese New Christians trading in the city. Arguing that Antwerp was no longer safe and that "the Inquisition reigns more than ever in Lisbon," Van der Neesen assured the Portuguese that they could travel to Pisa "with all their belongings under the protection of His Highness [Cosimo II], so peaceable and good, where their nation receives excellent treatment and privileges."[38] In offering these assurances, Van der Neesen proceeded with the utmost secrecy, working through a third party. His efforts bore fruit when Lanzelotto da Sorra immigrated along with his wife and six children. Da Sorra, reputed to be worth 200,000 scudi, was just the sort of well-connected mercantile "Portuguese" the regime wanted. Van der Neesen thought that his happy reception in Tuscany would encourage other families in Antwerp to make the move as well, and he was right: Da Sorra's "very rich brother" came the following year, after seeing how well his relative had been treated.[39]

Before changing places, immigrants had to be confident that their persons and property would be secure, and that they would find good prospects in their new home. Personal contact with individuals known to be close to a ruler helped resolve these questions. Men like Van der Neesen moved freely in worlds where regime officials did not have ready access. In addition, they could make drafts on Florentine banks abroad or furnish documents such as passports that pledged a ruler's word. Insecurity in the Mediterranean did not affect all groups alike, however. The position of Jews differed from that of armed pirates or Dutch merchants. As a result, the content of the assurances the Medici and their agents provided differed, as did the terms of negotiation.

The confiscation of goods was a common threat to trade in the early seventeenth century. Grain for instance was the kind of commodity that tempted princes during times of famine. Merchants needed to be certain that the Medici would not requisition their grain or force them to sell it at below-market rates. It was a lesson that Ferdinando learned the hard way. In the spring of 1591 he imposed an export-prohibition on the huge amounts of grain that were arriving in Livorno. The outcry must have been intense. "To alleviate all doubt," Ferdinando issued a decree a couple of months later denouncing as "vain suspicion" the notion that his regime would again detain grain in Livorno. Ferdinando's successors made the mistake of

[38] "Et a Lisbona regna più che mai l'Inquisitione"; and "...con tutto il loro havere sotto la salvaguardia di Sua Altezza Serenissima nostro signore così pacifico et buono, dove intendono che la lor natione riceve buonissimo trattamento et meglio privilegi." The quotes are from ASF, MP, 4259, ins. 1, f. 16, 03/31/1611, Jan Van der Neesen to Belisario Vinta; and Ibid., f. 14, 01/28/1611, Jan Van der Neesen to Belisario Vinta. On Van der Neesen, see ASF, MP, 322, f. 88; and Guarnieri, *Il principato mediceo*, 91ff.

[39] ASF, MP, 4259, ins. 1, f. 38, 04/13/1612, Jan Van der Neesen to Belisario Vinta. Over the following year Van der Neesen settled several other Portuguese to Tuscany, whether in Livorno or Pisa is unclear. Ibid., f. 18, 04/01/1611; f. 21, 04/17/1611; f. 24, 06/17/1611; f. 25, undated; f. 30, 11/18/1611; f. 38, 04/13/1612.

blocking grain exportation only twice, in 1621 and 1636; fear of alienating foreign merchants made these measures unpopular, and they were quickly abandoned.[40]

The grand duke's direct purchases helped channel ships toward Livorno, but it was the regime's behavior as a scrupulous rather than coercive buyer that made the port a permanent market for grain. During normal years, grain arrived from south-central Italy and was distributed throughout northern Italy. In times of crisis, grain came from all over the Mediterranean world.[41] In those bad years, the Office of Plenty (Abbondanza) purchased huge quantities in Livorno—enough to feed ten percent of Tuscany. The regime needed to act quickly. One official wondered whether he should have standing orders to buy, "because often ships stay only for three or four days, and that is not enough time to arrange the deal, send word [to Florence], and wait for a resolution. This is especially true given that the flow of information is observed by many people, apparently by tipping the postal boys or guards of the city gates."[42] The Medici bureaucracy purchased grain in Livorno without coercion. That made them just one (albeit large) buyer on the market, and it reassured merchants that Livorno was safe for business.

Before the free port became an established institution, trade rested on the grand duke's personal reputation for fair dealing. To celebrate the election in 1605 of the short-lived Medici Pope, Leo XI, an agent threw a "superb banquet" in Amsterdam for the city's leading merchants. Jan Van der Neesen (who was present) reported that Dutch captains and mariners gave glowing reports of their reception in Livorno: "They said that if His Highness should ever need two or three hundred warships, they would fall over themselves to serve him."[43] By 1605 Livorno had already earned something of an international reputation for toleration, commerce, and crusading—or rather, Ferdinando I had a reputation for treating foreigners well in Livorno. It was one that his regime constantly sought to uphold for the good of trade. Moments of crisis could nonetheless expose the fragility of Livorno's free port, as a conflict between Ferdinando and the Dutch East India Company (VOC) reveals.

In 1606 the grand duke authorized Van der Neesen to purchase a ship in Amsterdam christened the *Livorna*.[44] After Van der Neesen bought the ship, prepared

[40] Pult Quaglia, *"Per provvedere ai popoli,"* 114–39: quotes are on 123. In a very different context, Ferdinando III attempted (and failed) to place controls on the international grain trade in 1792. Addobbati, *Commercio, rischio, guerra*, 255.

[41] The regime accordingly allowed merchants to stockpile grain in Livorno even during tough times: ASG, AS, LCL, 2675, 10/08/1653, report by Giovanni Domenico Gavi. See "Mediterranean Commerce in a Global Age" in chapter 6.

[42] "[P]erché molte volte vengono navi o altri vasselli che anno stallia di tre o quattro giorni, et non ci è tempo a praticare la compera, darne conto, et aspettare resolutione; oltre che è osservato da molti li andamenti degli avvisi, e con mezzo di mancie da garzoni delle poste da uffitiali della porte si sente." ASF, MP, 2586, ff. 29–30, 8/29/1601, Jacopo Ricciardi to the Archbishop of Pisa. Ricciardi worried about grain speculators driving up prices.

[43] ASF, MP, 4750, ff. 652 and 657, 04/27/1605, Van der Neesen to Vinta. The agent was a member of the Lus family, probably Abraham, in whose home Van der Neesen lodged: ASF, MP, 938, ff. 665–67, 12/01/1606, Abraham Lus to Belisario Vinta. On the Lus family, see Engels, *Merchants*, 136–7.

[44] Guarnieri, *Il principato mediceo*, 91ff. Buying and selling ships was a regular but never routine business. That is one reason why cultivating relationships with captains and mariners occupied much

its crew, and contracted with mariners to escort it to Livorno, the States General sequestered the *Livorna* on the grounds that the ship was needed in their upcoming war against Spain.[45] In reality, some Dutch merchants feared that the grand duke was planning a commercial voyage to the East Indies that would compete with their own trade.[46] Van der Neesen urged Ferdinando to retaliate by seizing the goods of three VOC members trading in Livorno, whom he listed by name. The regime decided that such a drastic course would imperil the free port and instructed their agent not to make threats touching on the liberties of Livorno.[47] Unfortunately, Van der Neesen had not waited to hear from Florence before intimidating the VOC. The slowness of information occasionally obliged agents to act on their own (fallible) judgment.

Grain merchants were hesitant to do business with Livorno in this unsettled environment. According to the Florentine patrician Bartolomeo Corsini, an investor in the grain trade, Van der Neesen told the merchants of Holland that Dutch ships and goods in Livorno would be seized if the *Livorna* were not liberated. Given this suspicion, many of the shippers destined for Livorno with grain were uncertain about the safety of coming; there was talk of bringing their cargo to the Genoese scale of Portofino instead. Corsini suggested that the grand duke write to Amsterdam "to give word, that the ships can come freely to Livorno and will be freely accepted as in the past, without being harassed in goods or in person . . . and to send them whatever assurances are necessary."[48] Corsini feared that the Genoese would use this opportunity to strike a blow at the commerce of Livorno and urged sending passports to an agent in Portofino, secretly, so that if the Dutch ships alighted there they could head immediately to Livorno. These fears never materialized.

of Van der Neesen's time. See ASF, MP, 4750, ff. 743, 746, 08/25/1606, Van der Neesen to Belisario Vinta; f. 756; f. 760, 10/09/1606; f. 777, 05/22/1607; and f. 778, 05/25/1607. On ship purchasing in Livorno, see ASF, MP, 2140, f. 7, 11/26/1606, Ugolino Barisoni to Marcello Accolti; and f. 9, 12/05/1606.

45 Sequestering ships was a common enough occurrence. In 1596–7 Elizabeth I detained a grain ship coming from the Baltic and bound for Tuscany, despite having promised to provide passports. In 1595 and again in 1601 Ferdinando urged Elizabeth (at war with Spain) not to attack the ships of the "Portuguese" who had settled in Tuscany. Diaz, *Il Granducato di Toscana*, 333–4; Baruchello, *Livorno e il suo porto*, 246; Fischer, *Vivere fuori dal ghetto*, 82; and in general, Steensgaard, "Consuls and Nations."

46 The VOC's fears about the purpose of the *Livorna* were justified. Although the Medici did not have a fully developed plan, a prospective voyage to the Indies was under debate. ASF, MP, 938, f. 765, 10/14/1606, Isaac Lus to the Grand Duke, and f. 799, 10/17/1606, Abraham Lus to Belisario Vinta; ASF, MM, 97, ins. 88, ff. 2–3; ASF, MP, 938, f. 765, 10/14/1606, Isaac Lus to the grand duke, and f. 799, 10/17/1606, Abraham Lus to Belisario Vinta; ASF, MP, 4750, f. 701, 03/21/1606 [AD], Van der Neesen to Belisario Vinta; ASF, MP, 67, f. 279, 09/01/1601, draft of a letter by Belisario Vinta to Jan Van der Neesen.

47 ASF, MP, 4750, f. 760, 10/09/1606, Jan Van der Neesen to Belisario Vinta; ASF, MP, 67, f. 283, 11/03/1606, Belisario Vinta to Jan Van der Neesen.

48 "[E]t di molte nave che erano destinate per Livorno con grani, stavano in dubbia, se dovevano venire o no, mediante detto sospetto. . . . Crederei che fussi bene . . . scrivere al Pungetti che dia parola, che le nave venghino a Livorno liberamente perché saranno accettate liberamente, senza essere molestati, [né] in beni, né in persona, si come è seguito per il passato; se però parrà così a Vostra Altezza Serenissima, e quando Vostra Altezza habbia questo animo, si potrebbe mandare loro quelle fidanze che paressino più necessarie. . . ." MP, ASF, 938, f. 154, 11/09/1606, Bartolomeo Corsini to the Grand Duke.

Thanks to the intervention of the French queen (a niece of the grand duke), the States General released the ship in December and it arrived safely in Livorno the following spring.[49] But the episode highlights the instability of trade at a time when princes routinely preyed on merchants. In this case, Corsini wanted to send merchants and captains passports to ease their minds. Passports were a convenient way of facilitating international commerce because they constituted a written declaration of the prince's *word*. The Medici distributed them freely in the early period of Livorno's growth.[50]

Sephardic merchants had more diffuse security concerns than their Christian counterparts. Jewish historical memory was replete with incidents in which princes curtailed their privileges or expelled them from the realm. No wonder that when Jews renegotiated the Livornina in 1593, they requested the explicit provision, "We order that each of the capitulations contained in these privileges be understood in their clear and pure meaning without any prevarication, and that they be interpreted by our officials and ministers in every way favorable to, and for the benefit of, these merchants."[51] To provide credible assurances, Ferdinando relied on the good offices of Jews close to his regime, who acted as emissaries to cities such as Milan, Ferrara, Venice, and Constantinople.[52] Alone among the "foreigners" of Livorno, Jews were considered Tuscan subjects. The governor used his judicial and policing powers to ensure that they were treated fairly. Most importantly, the grand dukes shielded them from the Inquisition and protected *conversos* who returned to Judaism. By the late-seventeenth century, Jews numbered about three thousand individuals and constituted a tenth of the city's population. The picture was not all rosy, as the grand duke backtracked on a few minor privileges, and the community was rent by intra-Jewish divisions.[53] But by the standards of the day, Livorno deserved its reputation as "the paradise of the Jews."[54]

In courting Jews and merchants, the regime emphasized the scrupulous adherence to its promises. The grand duke provided positive rewards as well. Debt-forgiveness was probably the most important, but Ferdinando I was prodigal in distributing patents, subsidized housing, and loans. Access to credit was a *sine qua non* for immigrants, who ordinarily relied on social networks for supplying cash to meet

[49] ASF, MP, 4750, f. 778, 05/25/1607, Jan Van der Neesen to Belisario Vinta. In addition, Van der Neesen and other agents spent money liberally and called in favors from friends for the liberation of the *Livorna*.

[50] E.g. ASF, MP, 67, f. 10, 07/21/1591; and ibid., f. 191, 06/12/1602. ASF, MP, 67, f. 67 contains a blank passport that officials used as a template.

[51] Quoted by Frattarelli Fischer, *Vivere fuori dal ghetto*, 47; see "The Privileges of Livorno" in chapter 1.

[52] Ibid., 41, 59–61, 90.

[53] Jews were prohibited from taking doctorates at the University of Pisa, and the grand duke placed restrictions on the ability of Jewish doctors to care for Christians, or for Christian servants to work for Jews. In addition, a great deal of tension between Sephardim and other Jews plagued the community. The nation was dominated by rich Sephardic Jews whose ancestors had been expelled from the Iberian Peninsula. Italians were not able to participate in the Jewish government until 1715. Frattarelli Fischer, "Ebrei a Pisa e Livorno."

[54] Guyot de Merville, *Voyage historique d'Italie*, 555–6, quoted by Mangio, "Testimonianze di viaggiatori francesi su Livorno," 315–16.

business necessities.[55] The most famous loan recipient was Thomas Mun, who received forty thousand crowns at zero interest for a year, "although [the grand duke] knew that I would presently send it away in specie for the parts of Turkey to be employed in wares for his countries, he being well assured that in this course of trade it would return again (according to the old saying) with a duck in the mouth."[56] Mun worked as an English factor and also hazarded his own credit by importing lead, tin, alum, and cloth. Ferdinando issued at least sixteen other interest-free loans to entrepreneurs for setting up industries in Livorno and Pisa, to the tune of seventy thousand scudi. Most loans went to textile entrepreneurs, but the grand duke also funded ventures in glass, canvas, ceramics, and cutlery.[57]

Mariners—who had their labor to sell rather than their property to lose—were in a different position than Jews and merchants. Their valuable maritime skills gave them options. A fully equipped ship was always bound to find work—and if not, it could cruise the seas for prey. By 1607 there were nine English vessels (and crews) in the grand duke's service.[58] English merchants in London viewed these as "sequestered" ships, forced into service by the grand duke.[59] From the Tuscan perspective, they were the fruit of negotiated settlement rather than coercion. In 1606, for example, the English ship *Royal Exchange* attacked and captured a rich Turkish prize. The ship's captains brought their booty to Livorno, and many of her mariners enrolled in the grand duke's service. In the meantime, London merchants sent howls of protest to the court of King James. They worried that the sultan would hold them responsible for the depredations of the *Royal Exchange* and thereby endanger their own trading privileges with the Ottoman Empire.[60]

Matters came to a head in 1608 when James sent Sir Stephen Lesieur (d. 1638) as ambassador to negotiate the repatriation of the English mariners and captains, hoping to retain the services of skilled seamen and prevent them from damaging English interests. Lesieur was particularly concerned with inducing the Catholic captains Robert and Giles Thornton to return. He offered Robert a "blank check" for whatever he wanted and pestered his wife while the captain was out of town.[61] According to the Commissary of Livorno, Lesieur "was trying to seduce away servants and subjects in prejudice to His Highness. . . . If Captain Giles and the others want to go to England, they know how to go there without being led by him. His Highness keeps nobody here against his will."[62] In the end, the grand duke released

[55] Arru, "Reti locali, reti globali." In general, see Muldrew, *The Economy of Obligation*; and *Quaderni storici* 136.2 (2011).

[56] Mun, *England's Treasure*, 24. On Mun's time in Tuscany (1598–1607), see de Roover, "Thomas Mun in Italy."

[57] Parigino, *Il tesoro del Principe*, 169 (my calculations); Frattarelli Fischer, *Vivere fuori dal ghetto*, 92.

[58] NA, SP 98/2, 259, 1608.

[59] Pagano de Divitiis, *English Merchants*, 26–8, 45–51.

[60] ASF, MP, 4187, f. 988, 02/03/1606 [AD], Ottaviano Lotti to the grand duke.

[61] 07/28/1609, Ugolino Barisoni to Lorenzo Usimbardi, published in G. Vivoli, *Annali*, vol. 4, 91–2 n. 49. Robert Thornton dwelt in a house that the grand duke gave him "as a free gift"; his brother probably lived there, too.

[62] "[M]a che intendendo ora che non solo va parlando contro il Conte di Warwick, ma in pregiudizio di Sua Altezza procurando di sviarli i servitori e di sollevarli dei sudditi . . . e gli soggiunsi, se il Capitano Giles e quegli altri vorranno andare in Inghilterra, che vi sapranno andare senza esservi

the seamen from his service—though only the Englishmen listed in Lesieur's credentials (not the Brothers Thornton). They were free to go where they would, but most probably chose to remain in Livorno.[63] "The grand duke is a great prince who must be esteemed and considered by everybody," the Commissary explained to Lesieur: "words which the Ambassador took to heart."[64]

The story of the *Royal Exchange* was by no means exceptional in the early seventeenth century. "Sequestered" ships such as the *William & Thomas*, *Triumph*, and *Mayflower* were manned largely by Englishmen.[65] English mariners maintained allegiances to both King James and the grand duke, who competed for their loyalty (and services). Dutch mariners were just as eagerly courted as English ones.[66] Efforts to keep skilled immigrants in Livorno required constant attention on the part of the regime. If Ferdinando "held nobody here against his will," the grand duke nonetheless offered them work, subsidized housing, and diplomatic support in squabbles with their native monarchs.[67]

For men from Protestant countries, the grand duke's war against the Turks was a crucial factor in legitimating their presence in Livorno. The small English community—which at mid-century numbered no more than a hundred people, excluding transient sailors—was initially composed of Catholics and corsairs. These men wrote of their settlement in Tuscany as a function of their personal relationships with the grand duke. Mention of Livorno's privileges are hard to find in their letters. After the 1620s, however, English merchants began using Livorno as their base for commercial expansion in the Mediterranean, and eventually the port served as a way station for English warships as well. These later arrivals were usually Protestants. For the entire seventeenth century, the Medici regime tolerated the presence of such "heretics," but not the open exercise of their ceremonies. Despite these religious difficulties, the strength of the local merchant community and the sheer volume of trade they brought to the port gave the English a predominant voice among foreigners in matters of economic policy.[68] Edward Wright's caution to his countrymen in 1720 nicely evokes English ascendancy in Livorno: "There

condotti da lui, e che Sua Altezza non teneva nessuno contro sua voglia." ASF, MP, 2140, f. 136, 10/31/1609, Ugolino Barisoni to Marcello Accolti [pres.].

63 ASF, MP, 1802, 11/02/1608, Opinion of Pietro Cavallo.

64 ASF, MP, 2140, f. 136, 10/31/1609, Ugolino Barisoni to Marcello Accolti [pres.].

65 Pagano de Divitiis, *English Merchants*, 47–8. She notes that the grand duke and Queen Elizabeth I were engaged in a "fierce contest of international law, to decide whether a merchant's place of origin or his place of residence was to be regarded as legally more important in determining his status. The grand duke eventually won this argument" (p. 28). In fact, the issue was not resolved quickly or completely. The grand duke continued to try to protect his merchants abroad even as he also protected those merchants and seamen who settled in Livorno.

66 E.g. ASF, MP, 2140, ff. 13–14, 12/20/1606, Ugolino Barisoni to Marcello Accolti [pres.].

67 Conversely, the Medici regime kept a close watch on Tuscans abroad, particularly workers who had fled without government permission, and periodically sought to repatriate them; e.g. ASF, Arte della Seta, 176, 28–9.

68 Scrosoppi, "Il porto di Livorno"; Castignoli, "Aspetti istituzionali"; Ciano, "Corsari inglesi"; D'Angelo, *Mercanti inglesi a Livorno*; Hayward, "Gli inglesi a Livorno"; Hayward, "The British Factory in Livorno"; Villani, "'Cum scandalo catholicorum....'"; Villani, "'Una piccola epitome di Inghilterra'"; Villani, "I consoli della nazione inglese a Livorno"; Villani, "Between Anatomy and Politics"; Fischer and Villani, "'People of every mixture.'"

are so many English always residing there, and so many of our merchant-ships use that port, that our language is understood by many natives of that place; so that even in walking along the streets, one should not speak that in English, which he would not care to have a Livornine hear."[69]

Our stories of immigration have two things in common: insecurity and agents. Whether for settlement or trade, whether merchant or mariner, people worried about the reception they would meet with in Livorno. Prospective migrants had to understand the intentions of the Medici, who in turn had to anticipate the security concerns of visitors and settlers. Although the logistical difficulties implied by such negotiations could be formidable—it took time for letters to travel between Florence and the Netherlands—the solutions were relatively simple. Insecurity was a basic fact of commercial life in the early seventeenth century. The Medici were well aware of the typical quandaries in which (for instance) merchants found themselves. The regime could therefore exploit a small number of techniques to assuage their fears: passports, loans, and privileges.

The task of managing negotiations often fell to an informal agent. Agents helped princes make credible commitments by serving as two-way channels of information. They increased not only the density and frequency with which information circulated, but above all, its specificity. They could articulate regime goals, dispel unfavorable rumors, or offer documents *ad personam*. Such tokens of the prince's intentions helped persuade people that their lives and property would be respected in Livorno. In time, the commitment problem that vexed Medici policy faded into insignificance. As its population expanded, relatives or colleagues in Livorno could provide details about the regime's practices in the free port. After all, the grand dukes never seriously infringed on the liberties of Livorno. Their scruples generated the confidence in *consuetudo* (custom) that was dear to the early modern understanding of right order. Contemporaries meanwhile became increasingly aware that it was not in the grand duke's interest to endanger the freedom of a port so central to Tuscan finances. But until these mechanisms were in operation, agents were essential for translating the port's paper privileges into real policy.

THE AGE OF EXPERIMENTATION

The counterpoint to insecurity in the Mediterranean was opportunity. The ease of recruiting foreigners in an era of weak state authority and volatile identity, and the apparent fragility of Spanish control over the sea routes to its overseas empire, made it appear possible for a wealthy state such as Tuscany to dream of mercantile glory on a global stage. Projects for breaking into the Iberian spice monopoly, establishing export industries in Tuscany, and sponsoring exploratory voyages to the Indies hinged upon the construction of a seaport. In retrospect, many of these adventures seemed doomed to fail. But at the time, they were an important reason why the Medici labored to fill their new port with merchants, mariners, and

[69] Wright, *Some Observations*, 374.

artisans. The promises and passports that agents distributed were ultimately backed by the regime's commitment to Livorno itself. Fiscal considerations were not a major motivation behind investment in the port until the mid-seventeenth century. The early grand dukes were bent upon economic expansion in the Mediterranean and beyond.

Few proposals to promote Tuscan commerce were too audacious for Ferdinando I. The grand duke was a voracious consumer of news about the Spanish, Portuguese, and Dutch empires, furnished by agents abroad or garnered from regime friends in Livorno.[70] He too entertained hopes of trading and conquering in the Indies. The problem was that information about opportunities remained uncertain in the first decades of the seventeenth century. Not only was it difficult to predict the profits and costs of a venture, but it was not even clear what business forms were best suited to exploiting the (sometimes imaginary) possibilities in the Indies.[71] Since most information was too general and too varied to be useful in planning specific voyages, experienced seamen were as important as information in getting projects off the drawing board. Fortunately, the Medici found it easy in the early seventeenth century to enroll "defectors" from among Dutch and English seamen who had spent time overseas.

An exploratory voyage to South America illustrates how the Medici regime sought to participate in the Atlantic economy. The ship *Santa Lucia Buonaventura* and a small tartan departed from Livorno in September 1608, bound for the West Indies. Captain Robert Thornton led the voyage while his brother Giles piloted the smaller vessel. At some point the two ships got separated. Robert explored the Guiana, the Orinoco, and the Amazon, and brought six Caribs ("the ones who eat human flesh") back to Florence—five of them died of smallpox, but one survived long enough to learn Italian and serve as a court page (Fig. 2.3).[72] Despite picking up a cargo of natives, Robert failed to sell the ship's merchandise and returned empty-handed. He was lucky to be alive: a couple of mutinous bombardiers had plotted to kill him, steal the ship, and sell its wares. When he discovered their villainy, Robert abandoned the two ringleaders at the mouth of the Amazon and imprisoned the other conspirators in the ship's hold. The *Santa Lucia* returned in July 1609, ten months after its departure and five months after the death of its

[70] While Orazio Della Rena was stationed in Madrid he collected information from Spaniards, Indians, and the Royal Cosmographer which he transmitted back to Florence in 1604. Baccio da Filicaia served for many years as the chief engineer to the governor general of Brazil. When he returned to Portugal, Filicaia sent a letter to the grand duke presenting information about Brazil. The Netherlandish agents Jan Van der Neesen and the Lus family sent weekly reports to Florence. Della Rena's report is in the BNF, Magliabechiano, xxiv, cod. 53, *Descrizione della America*; Filicaia's is in ASF, MP, 949, ff. 1346–49, 08/30/1608; see "Institutions and Economic Thought" in chapter 3.

[71] Contemporaries were uncertain whether state-sponsored monopolies were better than various forms of private enterprise. See Chaudhuri, *The English East India Company*, 38–55; Israel, *Dutch Primacy in World Trade*, 67–73.

[72] Dudley, *Dell'arcano del mare*, vol. 4, 33–4. See Guarnieri, *L'ultima impresa*; and ASF, MP, 1302, f. 20; ASF, MP, 2140, f. 130; and ASF, MP, 2140, f. 715. Robert Dudley (the illegitimate son of the Earl of Leicester) was instrumental in making this expedition possible. For his role in mobilizing the mariners who sailed on the grand duke's venture, see ASF, MP, 2140, f. 131, 10/29/1609, Ugolino Barisoni to Belisario Vinta. On Dudley himself, see Temple Leader, *Life of Sir Robert Dudley*.

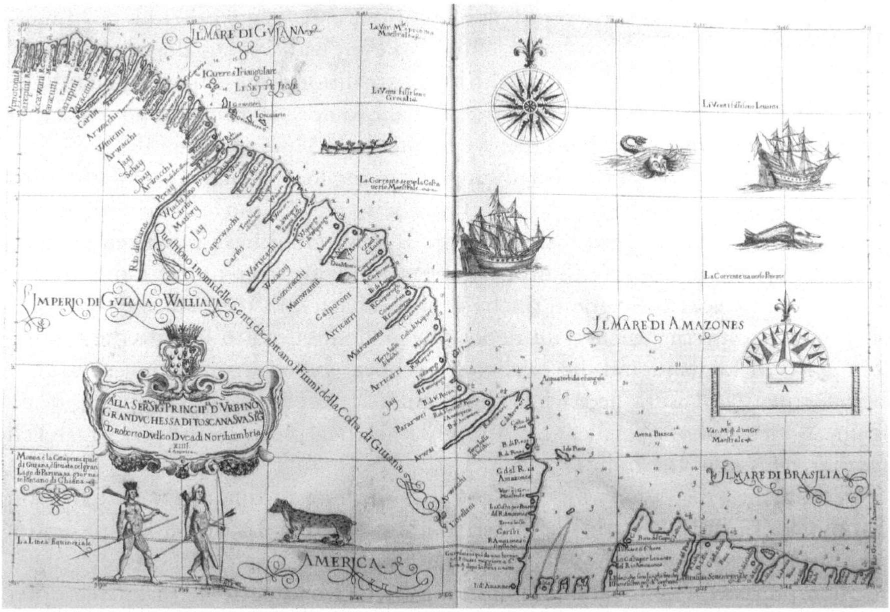

Fig. 2.3. Giuliano Periccioli, "The Amazon and the Coast of Guiana." This is the map that accompanies Robert Dudley's description of Thornton's voyage to Guiana. It is one of the few artifacts of the Tuscan age of exploration.
Credit: Getty Research Institute, Los Angeles (890027).

sponsor, Ferdinando I. Meanwhile, Giles had more success selling their merchandise in "Brazil" but chose not to make any purchases after the authorities there received word of the latest navigation restrictions from Spain. Giles returned in late October 1609.

The Guiana voyage brought together a panoply of interests into one venture: exploring unknown lands, gathering curiosities, discovering precious metals, and celebrating the magnificence of the Medici court.[73] At the most basic level, however, the expedition was an effort to showcase the possibility of direct commerce with America to the merchants of Livorno. Orazio Erbucci had loaded merchandise aboard the *Santa Lucia*, and the ship's priest was supposed to sell it on Erbucci's behalf according to instructions provided by an onsite Dutch expert in American trade.[74] Robert was tasked with discovering gold and drugs, particularly "those minerals beneficial to the memory." He related that the capital of Cayenne, the fabulous Manoa, was a city "rich with gold." The natural resources of the area were a veritable roll-call of colonial desire: there were silver mines, brazilwood, sugar

[73] Findlen and Smith, *Merchants and Marvels*; and Fiorani, *The Marvel of Maps*, chs 3–4.

[74] The priest was Padre Orazione Bennoini and the Dutchman was Jan van Haarlem. On Erbucci's ties with the regime, see ASF, MP, 2140, f. 205, 10/11/1609, Ugolino Barisoni to Belisario Vinta [pres.]; ASF, MP, 1303, f. 250, 08/04/1610, Lodovico Niccolini to Lorenzo Usimbardi [pres.]; and in general, Galluzzi, *Storia del granducato*, vol. 3, bk 5, 285; Guarnieri, *L'ultima impresa*, 16.

cane, white pepper, leopardwood, balsam, cotton, and "many other kinds of merchandise abundant enough to trade." The area even had "spiders that make silk."

Not everybody was impressed with the expedition. The surgeon aboard the *Santa Lucia* remarked that "the countries did afford no such thing" as gold or other resources that would make the territory habitable.[75] More importantly, the grand duke's colonial venture lacked broad support among local merchants or a sustained consideration of whether direct connections between Livorno and the Indies were likely to be profitable. Tuscan ships in the Indies would have provoked staunch military opposition from rival European fleets, implying steep protection costs that would have exceeded the grand duchy's fiscal capacity. In the end, the success of Livorno as an international grain depot obviated any need to imitate the trading companies of England and the Netherlands. Local merchants need not risk funding an expensive Tuscan fleet when they could rely on third-party shipping to do business with Lisbon, Seville, and Amsterdam. The Tuscan state never organized another venture to the Indies.[76]

Despite the frustrations of their colonial dreams, Ferdinando I and his son Cosimo II continued to pursue closer trading relations with the Muslim world. Since peace with the Sublime Porte was impossible as long as the Order of St. Stephen preyed on Ottoman shipping, the Medici had perforce to pursue other opportunities. Ferdinando secured a reciprocal commercial treaty with one of the warring sultans of Morocco in 1604—a worthless document as the country erupted into civil war after the death of Ahmad I al-Mansur in 1603. The grand duke established more fruitful ties with the rebellious Emir Fakhr-al-Din of Saida (1572–1635), who ruled Lebanon as a subject-prince and felt increasingly restless under the Ottoman yoke. These relationships bolstered Livorno's ties to North Africa and the Levant.[77]

The Medici were pragmatic about supporting the commercial and industrial projects of immigrants. Although manufacturing in Florence remained central to the territorial vision of elites, for instance, the regime issued numerous privileges for enterprises in Livorno and Pisa (Fig. 2.4). Partly, this spate of patents reflected an effort to remedy the state's (perceived) industrial malaise at a time when commerce in Livorno was beginning to flourish; partly it helped alleviate the security dilemma that plagued migration, as we saw above. The occupational status of patentees underscores the extent to which merchants were involved in industrial

[75] Davies, *True Relation*, 11 pdf right side (C3r). On Davis, see Neri, *Un schiavo inglese*; and Brege, "The Empire That Wasn't," 299–301, 351–8.

[76] The expedition's failure did not prevent various schemes from falling into the regime's consideration. For instance, in 1629 Giovanni Francesco Buonamici proposed a Dutch-style merchant company: Guasti, "Scrittura in materia di navigazione"; Bonifacio, "Disegno di una compagnia livornese." Genoese colonial projects failed for similar reasons: Giacchero, *Il Seicento*, 372–81; Kirk, *Genoa and the Sea*, ch. 5. See "Old Ambitions and New Methods" in chapter 5 and "Livorno and its Hinterlands" in chapter 6.

[77] See Galluzzi, *Storia del granducato*, vol. 6, bk 6, 191–205; G. Vivoli, *Annali*, vol. 4, 124–6, 163–4; Carali, *Fakhr ad-din II*; and Salibi, "Fakhr-al-Din"; and in general, Tamborra, *Gli Stati italiani*, ch. 4; Salvadorini, "Traffici con i paesi islamici," 208; Engels, *Merchants*, 37. Ferdinando II also pursued a failed project for trade with the Levant after the Ottoman-Austrian peace of 1664: Baruchello, *Livorno e il suo porto*, 359, 414; Guarnieri, *Livorno medicea*, 184–5.

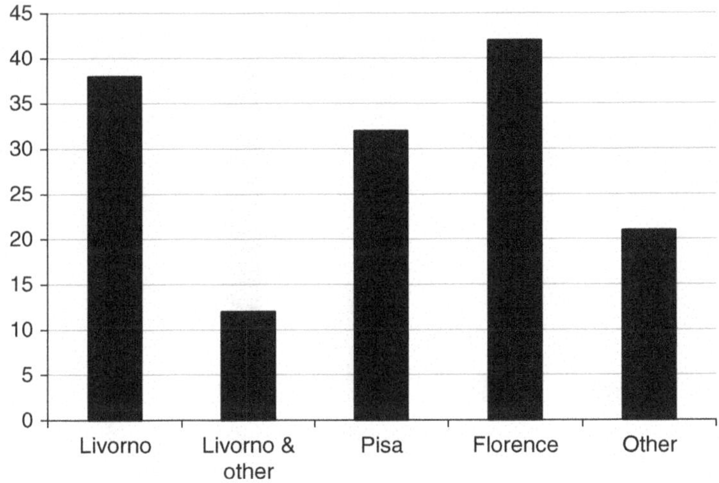

Fig. 2.4. Location of industrial and commercial patents, 1574–1720.
Note: Many patents with unspecified locations (n=172) were probably based in the capital city.
Source: ASF, PS, 188–196.

relations with the Medici regime: eighty percent of patents in Livorno and Pisa went to merchants, in stark contrast to the rest of Tuscany, where artisans and gentlemen predominated (Fig. 2.5). Livorno was well-poised to attract entrepreneurial migration. There were liberal tax exemptions for goods and men. It had easy access to raw materials, and it was an excellent place for observing market trends or staying in contact with distribution networks.[78] Most importantly, there were no guilds. Livorno was as much a free port for commerce as for industry.

Ferdinando issued several patents to Jews for the production of export-oriented textiles in Pisa. For instance, Giuseppe di Salamone received a patent for practicing "three arts that he learned in Constantinople and in other places of the Levant," one of which involved embroidering linen and bombazine in the "Moorish" style.[79] The grand duke also devoted attention to soap. Soap was essential for cleansing wool and, along with fabric dye, was one of the heavy chemicals of early modern industry. As in the case of textiles, Ferdinando encouraged soap manufacturers to settle in his coastal cities. In 1590 a privy secretary began negotiating with Marcantoine Leblanc, a Marseillais soap artisan who claimed Tuscan descent. Leblanc arrived in 1591 with his family in tow, receiving customs exemptions for his belongings, housing, and workspace in Livorno at subsidized rates, and a

[78] Belfanti, "Guilds, Patents, and the Circulation of Technical Knowledge."

[79] ASF, PS, 189, f. 183; ASF, Riformagioni, 18, ins. 116, ff. 715–716. Salamone had already been venting Levantine fabrics at the Pisan fairs before deciding to settle there. Others received similar patents: e.g. ASF, PS, 189, f. 224; ASF, Riformagioni, 20, ins. 36, ff. 228–231; ASF, PS, 190, ff. 8–9; ibid., ff. 27–28; ASF, Riformagioni, 20, ins. 127, ff. 733–735. Frattarelli Fischer, *Vivere fuori dal ghetto*, 89–91; Mazzei, *Pisa medicea*, 8–39.

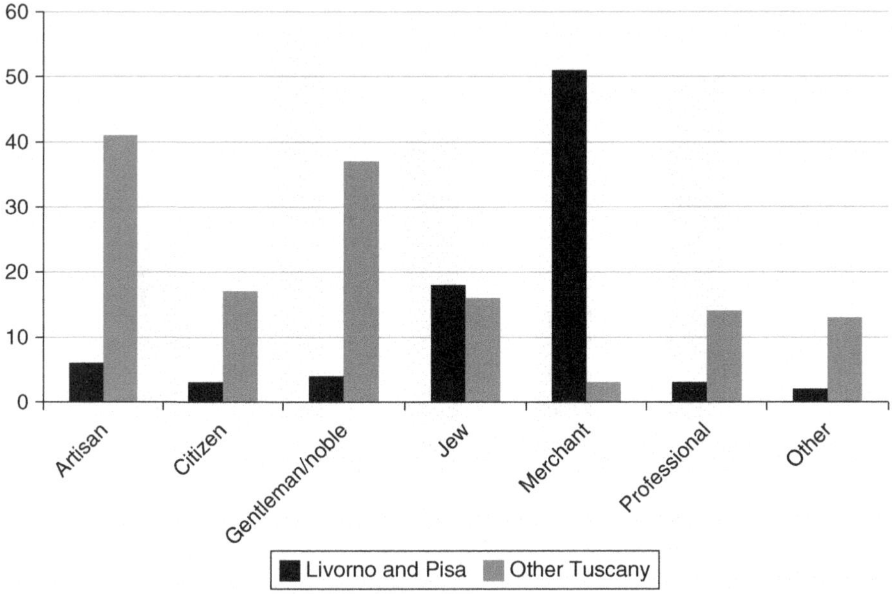

Fig. 2.5. Occupational status of patentees, 1574–1720.

Note: In estimating in-text the percentage of merchant patentees in Livorno and Pisa at eighty percent, I assumed that all Jews ought to be categorized as merchants.

Source: ASF, PS, 188–196.

ten-year monopoly.[80] As his soap was intended for export to western Europe, he was instructed to begin production immediately so that "he could give his manufactured soap to the English ships that will arrive this winter."[81]

The new enterprises, if they did not turn out to be abject failures, often failed to meet expectations. It is possible that the high profits of international commerce crowded out investment in manufacturing. The high labor costs associating with living in the city by the mid-seventeenth century probably compromised industrial development as well.[82] Livorno's only major export industry turned out to be coral manufacturing, which developed without the aid of patents.[83] Pisa saw measured success in silk production but little in other privileged industries, such as glass or

[80] ASF, MP, 280, f. 75. Leblanc was initially uncertained whether he would settle in Livorno or Pisa.

[81] "Inteso che, quando quest'inverno prossimo venivanno le navi Inglesi, egli possa darli della mercanzia del sapone fabbricato." Though the ultimate fate of this soap works is uncertain, Leblanc succeeded in being made French consul in Livorno, and his son fulfilled this role after his death. ASF, Riformagioni, 18, ins. 108, ff. 617–619; ASF, MP, 282, f. 127, 03/04/1591, Ferdinando I to Giulio Brunacci. For a later effort to establish a soap works in Livorno, see ASF, Riformagioni, 43, f. 173.

[82] Sonnino, *Saggio sulle industrie, marina e commercio*, 52; Baruchello, *Livorno e il suo porto*, 173 n., 221–3, 254; Guarnieri, *Livorno medicea*, 73–5, 113, 174, 216–17; Frattarelli Fischer, *Vivere fuori dal ghetto*, 89–92.

[83] A coral patent did go to Giovanni Negrotto for a factory in Pisa in 1603. Trade in raw coral was so intense in Livorno that Negrotto's patent was circumscribed in 1605 and eventually went unenforced, perhaps after the initial monopoly expired in 1608. ASF, PS, 190, ff. 75–76; ASF, MP, 2586, ff. 625–626, 08/20/1605, Cosimo Ricciardi to Marcello Accolti. On coral, see Trivellato, *Familiarity of Strangers*, ch. 9; Grendi, *Il cervo e la repubblica*, 131–62, esp. 151–2.

soap.[84] In spite of their disappointing outcomes, however, these schemes bear witness to the sense of possibility that informed Medici policy in Livorno into the early seventeenth century. Only when the free port came to be understood in terms of the transit and deposit trade did industrial considerations fall by the wayside.

THE WAREHOUSE OF THE MEDITERRANEAN

The first four grand dukes were enamored of the sea. They spent a lot of money on their fleet of galleys and lionized the Order of St. Stephen, whose expeditions cost much more than they earned: in 1626, for example, the six Tuscan galleys cost 154,855 scudi but only garnered some fourteen thousand from its corsair activities.[85] The galleys nonetheless played an important role in coastal defense and in maintaining the Medici family's prestige. The frescoes commissioned to celebrate their naval exploits testify to the sea's role in Medici ideology.[86] Despite the glory, by the 1630s the galleys were exacting a heavy toll on Tuscan finances and could no longer compete with the fleets of the major seafaring nations. Furthermore, the regime had obligations to aid the Catholic war effort in Germany by supplying troops and cash. Ferdinando II began to float the idea of selling his galleys in 1632. This scheme aroused a great deal of controversy among the Order of St. Stephen as well as Tuscan statesmen who prized the independence the galleys afforded: one influential advisor called selling the ships "a base act."[87] In the end, however, Ferdinando sold four of his galleys to agents of Cardinal Mazarin in 1647 for 100,000 scudi. The two that remained were enough for defense and the now-modest needs of the Order. Ferdinando effectuated a shift in military strategy that focused on land defense and symbolic military action abroad. Much new investment went into strengthening the protection of Livorno itself.[88]

As Tuscany settled into humbler ambitions, it increasingly adopted a posture of neutrality in European conflicts. For almost a century, the Medici had maintained a measure of autonomy from Spain by supporting a relatively weak French monarchy whenever possible. But by the 1630s, Iberian might was on the wane and France in the ascendant. In these circumstances, the best that the Medici could hope for was the preservation of the status quo in Italy itself—a quest that prompted its participation in one of the last conflicts in the peninsula, the War of the Castro (1643–5). On this occasion, Tuscany and its allies vanquished the armies of the Barberini papacy. Thereafter Tuscany aspired to maintain the balance of power in Italy and neutrality abroad.[89]

[84] See n. 96 in chapter 1. [85] Capponi, "Le Palle di Marte," 1123.

[86] For example, see Ottavio Vannini's frescoes in the Medici Villa di Poggio Imperiale; and in general, Fiorani, *The Marvel of Maps*, ch. 3.

[87] ASF, MP, 5080, f. 650, 06/01/1632, Orso d'Elci to Francesco de' Medici.

[88] Capponi, "Il sistema difensivo di Livorno," 26. On the debt situation, see Waquet, *Le Grand-Duché de Toscane*, 93–5, 120, 397.

[89] Capponi, "Le palle di Marte," 1127. Giovan Battista Gondi's election as first secretary following the death of Andrea Cioli (1640) signaled the new orientation. The Francophile Gondi had long resided

These geopolitical changes had decisive consequences for Livorno. Strategically, Livorno's neutrality secured the Tuscan coast against wartime depredations and guaranteed access to grain and raw materials. Financially, as a neutral place it could attract (and tax) the commerce of belligerents. The principle of Livorno's neutrality dates back to 1626, when the Spanish king ordered the grand duke as his vassal to close Livorno to English shipping.[90] Refusing such a drastic measure, Ferdinando II agreed only to compel English privateers to return captured goods to their rightful owners. He took similar actions against French privateers around 1640. In 1646 the grand duke announced the neutrality of the port and negotiated terms with the local foreign communities. In 1691 the consuls of the foreign nations signed a neutrality pact under the watchful eye of the governor. An international agreement in 1718 formalized the situation at a European level: even during wartime, the shipping of every nation was welcome in Livorno.[91]

The regime was willing to defend Livorno's neutrality, too. During the First Anglo-Dutch War (1652–4) the belligerents threatened to make war in the coastal waters off Tuscany. A privy secretary wrote to the governor, "You will do everything you can to avoid, *if possible*, any sort of fight. But if you should not succeed, make it known that we will defend the attacked party."[92] The grand duke ordered his military units to the coast. He allowed the English war fleet into the harbor to enjoy the coverage of the fortress's canons. Following a Dutch victory in a naval combat known as the Battle of Livorno (1653), the grand duke temporarily imposed restrictions on the Netherlandish mercantile community as a reprisal against Dutch behavior. Tuscany could stand up for its neutrality even without its galleys.

Ferdinando II reoriented infrastructural investment in Livorno towards the deposit and transit trade. He authorized the construction of new grain silos and another quarantine facility, the lazaretto of San Jacopo. Finished in 1648, San Jacopo was linked by canal to the lazaretto of San Rocco; both were in turn connected to the city's main canals. The most remarkable achievement of his reign was Venezia Nuova ("New Venice"). Venezia Nuova was designed around 1630 as a residential and commercial quarter in the northwestern part of the city. It was built on islands with the assistance of Venetian experts and bisected with canals that serviced a welter of new warehouses. Although building proceeded slowly at first, a renewed interest in financing the venture by the Ceppi di Prato and other investors ensured that the new quarter was complete by the death of Ferdinando II in 1670.[93]

in Paris, and a branch of his family had even been ennobled in France. See Pansini, "Le segreterie del principato mediceo," xlii and n. 145; and Boutier, "Le 'Notizie diverse' de Niccolò Gondi," 1135–6.

[90] While the grand duke was prepared to acknowledge vassalage in the Duchy of Siena, he asserted that he was a free prince in the Duchy of Florence and could dispose of affairs in Livorno as he wished.

[91] Baruchello, *Livorno e il suo porto*, 320–42; Filippini, *Il porto di Livorno*, vol. 2, 207–14; Filippini, "La graduelle affirmation"; Addobbati, *Commercio, rischio, guerra*, 78–81; Aglietti, *I governatori di Livorno*, 80–3, 116, 122; Calafat, "Une mer jalousée," 472–89.

[92] ASF, MP, 1491, 07/11/1652, memorandum by Giovan Battista Gondi. Emphasis in the original. Quoted by Capponi, "Il sistema difensivo," 19. See also Cipolla, *Il burocrate e il marinaio*, 21; Aglietti, *I governatori di Livorno*, 69–70; and in general, Morviducci, "Lo scontro anglo-olandese."

[93] Baruchello, *Livorno e il suo porto*, 302–3, 380–1, 395; Matteoni, *Livorno*, 58–70, 76–82, 89–98. The regime further enlarged the new district between 1690 and 1720.

For Livorno, the fiscal reckoning began even sooner than the sale of the galleys. The outbreak of the War of the Castro in 1641 forced the regime to raise funds and cut costs.[94] In 1643 the grand duke increased transit duties on most goods. In 1646 he imposed the Tenth on rental property, eliminating a long-cherished exemption for inhabitants of the port.[95] More than a simple need for money motivated these decisions, however. The regime was beginning to realize that Livorno had not quite lived up to expectations. While the Customs Office had begun to collect substantial sums for the ducal coffers, the collateral benefits that the Medici had hoped for—the native merchant marine, the increased sale of Florentine textiles, and the development of new industries—had failed to materialize. If the port could not serve as an instrument for commercial expansion, the regime reasoned, it could at least provide a stream of income.

The plan to remake customs in Livorno began in early 1642. In April, a court accountant was sent to examine the records of the Customs Office. Customs Director Pandolfo Attavanti promised to do his best to "bridle these merchants little by little" without alienating them.[96] Following months of rumors, in April 1643 the grand duke commissioned a panel of officials, senators, and Florentine merchants to assist Attavanti and the governor.[97] By June 4 they had redacted their proposals into new legislation. "After seeing what there was to see, and considering what there was to consider," the grand duke raised taxes in the free port across the board. According to the panelists, the grand dukes had lavished money on Livorno for over half a century "without yet having reaped the harvest." Henceforth, virtually all goods transacted in Livorno would pay one-third more in taxes. Wares from beyond one hundred miles would pay two-thirds of the full tax and those within that radius would pay full taxes. The new law doubled stallage and lazaretto fees and increased anchorage prices by a third. It also imposed a tax on the registration of dowries and wills (the *gabella di contratto*) from which the Livornesi had long been exempt. Finally, the perpetual benefit, which allowed duty-free storage of goods so long as they did not change hands, was limited to two years.[98]

Livorno's character as a general emporium justified these measures in the eyes of the panelists. They saw no reason to worry about competition from Genoa, since the increase in taxes would still not equal impositions there. The basic principle of trade in Livorno remained unchanged, they argued: it was easy to store and sell goods in Livorno. If commerce sagged following the reform, it would owe less to

[94] Galluzzi, *Storia del granducato*, bk 7, ch. 9, esp. p. 87.

[95] See "Paperwork and Checkpoints" in chapter 4.

[96] ASF, DG, 77, f. 423, 04/09/1642, Pandolfo Attavanti to Cosimo del Sera. The accountant in question was named Cosimo Gorini, an official of the Guardaroba.

[97] The panelists were Luca degli Albizzi, Alessandro Caccini, Senator Marco Martelli, Cosimo del Sera (the Depositary General), Raffaello Staccoli (the Auditore delle Riformagioni), and Senator Alessandro Vettori (the future Auditore delle Riformagioni). On the rumors, see ASF, MP, 2155, 02/18/1643 [AD], Jacopo Peruzzi to Alessandro Nomi; ibid., 02/20/1643 [AD], Piero del Rosso to Alessandro Nomi; ibid., 04/09/1643, Filippo Jansen[?] to Alessandro Nomi. The Genoese consul Giovanni Stefano Boccalandro also reported on the grand duke's plans to modify the taxation scheme. See e.g. ASG, AS, LCL, 2675, 05/26/1643, 05/17/1644, 06/08/1643, and 07/28/1643.

[98] See ASF, PS, 29, f. 149; Baruchello, *Livorno e il suo porto*, 136, 284–91; Guarnieri, *Livorno medicea*, 174–6.

the tax increases than to the restoration of peace in Europe. The panelists were well aware that merchants would not be thrilled. The governor fretted that "so many things all at once might occasion complaints and laments and produce evil effects"—in short, might aggravate the merchants. He advocated spreading the tax increases out over time. The other panelists, however, believed it was best to publish the entire law at once. That way, merchants would not live in anxiety about the future of taxes in Livorno. "Plus, there may not be another opportunity for a tax increase as now with the wartime expenditures. It would cause a lot more fear to see such lightning bolts in a clear sky."[99]

The regime's calculations proved correct: merchants accepted the new taxes without much protest, given the stability and freedom of commerce in Livorno.[100] In August, for instance, the English consul explained how the East India Company wanted to store goods in Livorno for safety, judging England itself too insecure amidst the tumults of the Civil War.[101] The celebrated advocate of religious toleration, the merchant Henry Robinson (1605–73), had already theorized the possibility of using the Tuscan port as an entrepôt a year earlier, in 1642. Robinson imagined a possible conflict with the Ottoman sultan over the activities of the Algerine corsairs. Such a dispute would assuredly threaten English commerce in the Levant—unless the English could carry on trade via a neutral port. A staple in Livorno could fulfill this function: "which out of some experience had in those parts, I know is practised at present, and make no scruple, but may be perfected hereafter in such ample manner, as we shall stand in need of."[102] Such considerations made it possible for Livorno to serve as an entrepôt for all the commodities of the wider world even without direct ties with the Indies.

The reform of 1643 has sometimes been seen as an unhappy detour in the otherwise smooth unfolding of the free port.[103] While Ferdinando II did raise overall rates, however, he did not impose structural changes on the customs regime. The significance of the legislation lay rather in its recognition of the advantages Livorno could bring to the grand duchy as an international port of deposit, enabling Tuscany to participate in global commerce without altering the institutions of Medici rule. The fiscal benefits were also conspicuous. During the reign of Cosimo I, before the building projects and legislation of the 1590s, Livorno accounted for a tiny percent of the grand duchy's revenue. By the late seventeenth century, it

[99] "[E]t in ultimo perché non si harebbe forse altra volta tanta occasione d'agumento come di presente delle spese delle guerre, et darebbe più spaventi il vedere simili lampi a cielo sereno." ASF, PS, 29, f. 705.

[100] There was some idle talk about returning to the pre-1643 regime when initial customs receipts in the new system were disappointing. There were also a few administrative hitches in implementing the reforms. ASG, AS, LCL, 2675, 08/04/1643, 09/01/1643, 10/13/1643, 12/01/1643, reports by Giovanni Stefano Boccalandro; ASF, MP, 2155, 06/16/1643, Pandolfo Attavanti to Vittorio Nelli; ASF, PS, 29, f. 756; ASF, PS, 29, 09/20/1643, Vittorio Nelli and Andrea de' Medici (the Sea Consuls) to Alessandro Nomi.

[101] ASF, MP, 2155, 08/21/1643, Lelio Talentoni to Alessandro Nomi; and ibid., Morgan Read to Alessandro Nomi.

[102] Robinson, *Libertas*, 11. See Calafat, "Une mer jalousée," 504–8. For the perfection of the entrepôt, see "The Reorganization of Long-Distance Trade" in chapter 6.

[103] Baruchello, *Livorno e il suo porto*, 136, 284–91; Guarnieri, *Livorno medicea*, 174–6.

contributed some ten percent of revenues: a high-profile as well as a high-yield position in the fiscal landscape.[104] In addition, the reform drew attention for the first time to taxes on goods. After 1643, merchants began to demand a permanent and substantial reduction in duties. In 1660, Ferdinando II promised Livorno's foreign merchants that he would consider reducing tariff rates.[105] Instead, in 1676 the grand duke restructured the customs regime in a way that simplified procedures for the deposit and exchange of wares. Medici hospitality toward merchants early in the century prepared the way for a revolution in the handling of goods late in the century.

CONCLUSION

From the accession of Francesco I in 1574 to the death of Cosimo II in 1621, the Medici regime predicated investment in Livorno upon channeling Florentine capital into long-distance commerce. In the early years of the seventeenth century the Medici pursued a kaleidoscope of such projects, including a colonial voyage. But the next couple of decades brought a winnowing of possibility. After 1620, the Medici played a diminishing role in European political life. Ferdinando II (r. 1621–70) was only ten years old when his father died, and the regency that guided policy until his majority—in fact until the death of his grandmother Christina of Lorraine in 1637—was incapable of executing the kinds of projects that Ferdinando I had embarked upon with such brio. By 1640 or so, the port served primarily as a center of redistribution for merchandise plying Mediterranean waters. Florentines had a certain weight in the city's commerce, but it was foreign merchants and local Jews who dominated. Ferdinando II's fiscal reforms endorsed this new status quo.

Livorno exploited the general insecurity of commerce more than any other Christian city in the Mediterranean. The free port evolved amid the weakness of state power over the sea, a maritime economy undergoing rapid change, and the appeal of the Medici crusading program to Protestants and Catholics alike. Livorno's real triumph, however, lay in the courtship of foreign merchants during a turbulent era. Recent literature on historical immigration has been more concerned with how states control visitors than with how visitors "control" states.[106] This perspective elides the power dynamics that prevailed between princes and

[104] There are no exact data on Livorno's contribution to state finance because the Medici regime never produced a unified budget. According to the report published by D'Addario, in 1550 the "customs and other revenues of Pisa" amounted to ten percent of the revenues of the Florentine State (i.e. before the conquest of Siena). The share of Livorno in that figure was probably small: the city did not even have its own customs office yet. Contini shows that customs dues in Livorno contributed about eleven percent of the Depositary General's revenues between 1675–9. Waquet estimates that Livorno contributed nearly ten percent to debt financing in the last decades of the seventeenth and first decades of the eighteenth centuries. D'Addario, "Burocrazia, economia e finanze dello Stato," 436–7; Contini, "La riforma della tassa delle farine," 243; Waquet, *Le Grand-Duché de Toscane*, 379–92.

[105] Giacchero, *Storia economica*, 30.

[106] E.g. Cavaciocchi, ed. *Le migrazioni in Europa*; Moch, *Moving Europeans*; Arru and Ramella, eds, *L'Italia delle migrazioni interne*; Isaacs, ed. *Immigration and Emigration in Historical Perspective*; Moatti and Kaiser, eds, *Gens de passage*; Moatti, Kaiser, and Pébarthe, eds, *Le monde de l'itinérance*, pt 3.

high-status migrants like merchants. The Medici had to bargain extensively to persuade people to settle or trade in Livorno, and this process of negotiation contributed to a permanent shift in the way the regime conceived of the port. One thinks of the migrant-led effort to develop industries in Livorno or Pisa; the decision, under merchant pressure, to liberalize the grain trade; or the work put into settling rich merchants in Livorno, regardless of the commercial needs of Florence. Filippo Sassetti had imagined Livorno as a vehicle for Florentine capitalism in 1577; and while Grand Duke Ferdinando I was nothing if not flexible, he continued to treat the port as a means for expanding the grand duchy's commerce. And yet by the 1640s, the Medici regime began to see Livorno as a neutral center for the deposit and transit of merchandise. This was a logical choice as the new realities of international trade sharpened into focus by the middle of the seventeenth century. But what made it an option at all were the social networks that Livorno had inherited from an earlier period, when the Medici actively courted foreign personnel. These negotiations endowed Livorno with a web of ties that stretched from the Levant to the North Sea.

Livorno went rather further in promoting foreign settlement than any of its Italian rivals, but it was hardly the only port to deemphasize state and religious affiliation in the late sixteenth century. New mercantile tribunals in the major cities assisted merchants' recourse to justice, and their sojourns were facilitated by the easing of customs regulations as well.[107] Foreign hospitality is usually ascribed to the geopolitical condition of Italy after the Renaissance. By this reasoning, Italy provided the interstitial space where the major mercantilist economies could do business on neutral territory. The process of trading and settling in Livorno points to a different interpretation, however. Hospitality developed not so much in dialogue with exclusionary economies, as out of disputes about the relationship between identity and the right to trade. In the late Middle Ages, commercial rights depended on membership in a political community. The instability of religious and political boundaries, and the uncertainty as to which was primary for apportioning commercial rights, created a more complex situation during the late Renaissance. There was indeed a "politicization" of commercial life in this period, but not the one suggested by the term mercantilism. A regime of privileges made trade at once intrinsically personal and also transnational. Commerce flowed along social and religious as well as national lines.

States eventually did develop the power to structure trade according to norms of citizenship and reciprocal trade agreements. But thanks to the examples of Livorno in the south and Amsterdam in the north, they did so in a context that celebrated the virtues of foreign hospitality. In England, the movement toward an

[107] In Genoa, for example, the Magistrato del Mare (Sea Office) was reformed in 1576 and again in 1602; it increasingly handled cases between foreigners. In Naples, local authorities delegated a judge to the various nations, whose merchants nonetheless came to prefer the local courts; and in 1739 the Supremo Consiglio del Commercio (Supreme Council of Commerce) took over the duties of the judge-delegates. Grendi, "Gli inglesi a Genova," 242, 265–7; Brancaccio, *Nazione genovese*; and Zaugg, "Judging Foreigners"; Gelder, *Trading Places*, esp. 58–9; and in general, Fusaro, "Gli uomini d'affari stranieri in Italia," 378–9; and "The Spread of Free Ports" in chapter 8.

immigrant-friendly environment was influenced by examples of free trade and commercial considerations more broadly; it culminated in the Naturalization Bill of 1753. In France, the *droit de aubaine* had long authorized the king to seize the assets of foreigners after their death. Even as Louis IV sought to reaffirm the *droit* throughout his kingdom, maritime cities were exempted from this inhospitable tax for commercial reasons. The abolition of the *droit* in a series of treaties between 1765 and 1787 was likewise motivated by commercial considerations in which the Dutch example was often cited.[108] Political and religious conflict in the decades around 1600 had an enduring legacy for the practice of commercial toleration.

108 See Statt, *Foreigners and Englishmen*, 55–65, 77–92; Sahlins, *Unnaturally French*, 50–2.

3

Institutions, Information, and the Invention of Free Trade

In November 1644, Captain Sebastiano Ferro arrived in Livorno with a cargo of wine. Even before requesting the *pratica* of the port—entry for the purpose of trade—he asked to receive the exemptions of Livorno, "to be sure that in coming onto land he not be molested either in his person or in his goods for civil debts contracted in foreign states."[1] Technically, these exemptions were only applicable to inhabitants of the city. Nonetheless, the Customs Office routinely granted them even to temporary visitors, and in this case Customs Director Pandolfo Attavanti was happy to oblige Ferro. What happened next was therefore quite unexpected. While the regular governor was out roving the Mediterranean with the grand duke's ships, several creditors of Ferro persuaded the acting governor to clap the captain into prison, disable his vessel, and seize his cargo.[2] Attavanti was furious. He declared that this violation of the port's liberties gave merchants a lot to worry about regarding their safety in the port. Captains ought to be protected from such outrages in Livorno by the "public faith and the freedom of the port." Even in more restrictive places such as Genoa and Civitavecchia ship captains were given a "golden bridge" in the interest of commerce. The customs director feared that the attack on Ferro was symptomatic of a new approach by the *auditore* of Livorno, the governor's chief legal counselor. In the preceding months an Armenian and a Venetian who also ought to have been protected by the port's freedoms fell victim to the *auditore*'s zeal. "I don't know whether I have said too much," Attavanti apologized at the end of a rambling letter to the secretary of war in Florence. "I am not angry with anyone but am only obeying Your Excellency's orders."[3]

The detention of Ferro's ship spawned a good deal of paperwork and bureaucratic infighting, which officials first attributed to the disorganization of the relevant legislation, but ultimately to the informal customs of the port. Creditors asserted that Ferro's brother, a corsair, had absconded with prizes on a venture they had invested in, but the details of the case did not interest officials.[4] At stake was the

[1] ASF, MP, 2160, f. 102, 01/31/1645 [AD], Pandolfo Attavanti [pres.] to Domenico Pandolfini.

[2] Livorno's governors were often active in the Order of St. Stephen: Aglietti, *I governatori di Livorno*, 54–8.

[3] "Io non so se mi ho detto troppo, perché non ho collora con nessuno, ma ho obbedito a quanto Vostra Signoria Illustrissima mi ha comandato, e con tale fine Le fo' reverenza." ASF, MP, 2160, f. 102, 01/31/1645 [AD], letter to Domenico Pandolfini.

[4] See the merchants' memorandum by Pellegrino Tidi in ASL, CGA, 2603, vol. 1, ff. 801, 818.

fundamental nature of the port. When the regular governor returned to his office, he disavowed his substitute's actions. The governor did not prosecute captains for debt even when they did not explicitly enjoy the exemptions of Livorno.[5] In any case, he preferred to address the underlying problem: the haphazard organization of the laws and decrees on the subject. Over the next few weeks, legal officials, the governor, and the customs director scoured their archives for documents to shed light on the issue.[6] Customs Director Attavanti asserted on the basis of decrees that the grand dukes had always permitted free comings and goings: "all ships can put in here and pay the anchorage fee and ask for whatever exemptions and safe-conducts they need before stepping onto the land. This is a very usual practice."[7] He granted the exemptions to whoever showed up: "regarding their examination, the whole affair is settled thus: when they are foreigners I ask them whether they have debts with Tuscan subjects or inhabitants; they respond that they have debts with aliens and foreigners; and I cannot deny them [the privileges]."[8] Attavanti explained that this had always been the behavior of his predecessors at the Customs Office, even though no law authorized his office to grant the city's exemptions.[9]

When the secretary of war pressed him further on the issue, Attavanti made a blanket appeal to the traditions of the free port. Although the customs director admitted that his own chancellery did not contain "all of the old documents," Attavanti emphasized that the most important charter, the Livornina, "does not embrace the full extent of the free port." He suggested that the panoply of decrees was stored with the Privy Council in Florence. It hardly mattered in any case. Practice mattered more than documentary precedent in creating a hospitable trade regime. Everybody knew that the custom was that "even our enemies the Turks have enjoyed and continue to enjoy the freedom of this port."[10] Foreigners of any ethno-religious affiliation could trade in Livorno by virtue of its character as a free port. Attavanti won his point and his office continued to manage exemptions as in the past. But the significance of the episode lay in his readiness to ground specific

5 ASF, MP, 2160, ff. 124–25, 02/06/1645 [AD], Ludovico da Verrazzano to Domenico Pandolfini.

6 Ibid., ff. 163, 194, 206, 223, 564, 565, and an unfoliated letter from Alessandro Vettori dated 02/23/1645 [AD]. These letters were all written in February 1645.

7 "[P]uò dare fondo ogni vassello con il pagamento del ancoraggio e domandare esentioni e salvicondotti, che li bisognano prima di venire in terra. E questa è materia così pratichata et antichata di lungo mano." Ibid., f. 157, 02/13/1645 [AD], Pandolfo Attavanti to Domenico Pandolfini.

8 "Quanto poi all'esaminare, strettamente, tutto il negozio havanti fare la concessione del salvo condotto, quando sono forestieri io li domando, se hanno debiti con i sudditi o habitanti [de] li stati di Sua Altezza Serenissima, rispondono, che hanno contratto il debito in stati alieni e con i forestieri, e così io non gliene posso denegare." ASF, MP, 2160, f. 132, 02/16/1645 [AD], Pandolfo Attavanti to Domenico Pandolfini.

9 Attavanti did produce a record that showed the customs director was responsible for enrolling people into the port's privileges as early as 1603. Ibid.; cf. ASL, CGA, 2602, vol. 2, f. 317 (1627).

10 "Si vede bene che sono conservate nella Praticha Segreta e che la consuetudine è stata sempre che fino i turchi, nostri nemici, hanno goduto e tuttavia godono la franchigia del porto, essendo che ci sono venuti e venghano con le loro merchanzie a negotiare liberamente; il che non si costuma in altre scale dove non è porto franco, né in altri luoghi dello stato di Sua Altezza senza il passaporto, e qui possono venire e negoziare sicuramente solo in virtù della franchigia del porto." ASF, MP, 2160, f. 187, 02/19/1645 [AD], Pandolfo Attavanti to Domenico Pandolfini. For judicial rulings that confirm Attavanti's point about the extension of the privileges to Muslims, see Calafat, "Une mer jalousée," 395–7.

policy problems on a general conception of the free port. On its surface, the Sebastiano Ferro episode was a conflict between Attavanti and Livorno's chief legal official over the limits of exemptions in the city. But the debate was responsible for elevating various ducal decrees into canons of local policy. In turn, this helped transform a fluid notion of Livorno's liberties into a practical sense of the free port.

The first jurists who discussed the free port in historical terms saw it as a readily datable creation of the Medici regime. They identified the reform of 1566 by Cosimo I, the Livornina of 1591/93 by Ferdinando I, and the reform of 1676 by Cosimo III as the key moments in its history. Some jurists were aware that the story was more complicated than it seemed. One remarked on the "infinite amplifications and declarations" that composed the free port and noted the distinction between "written law" on the one hand, and "particular orders, practice, and custom" on the other.[11] But like the historians who have followed them, jurists preferred to base their narratives on the grand legislation. There are serious problems with this approach. While it is easy to see purposive state action in the decision to construct port infrastructure and invite foreigners to settle in Livorno, the term "free port" was not even mentioned, let alone defined, in the chief legislation. It remained vague in its sphere—did it pertain primarily to merchants or to their goods?—and in its detailed provisions.

Uncertainties about Livorno's fundamental laws caused periodic confusion, and bureaucratic procedures both formal and informal proved as decisive as legislation in shaping the free port. The Medici had no regular institutional channels with which to craft strategic economic policy or analyze the workings of their customs regimes. Instead, they delegated control over policy development to poorly supervised local officials. This "choice" was made without careful consideration but fully partook of the larger bureaucratic logic of the grand duchy. In this respect, Livorno's distinctive formal institutions functioned in practice much like the rest of Medici Tuscany.[12] Policymaking by the periphery nonetheless provided an excellent mechanism for managing Livorno's unpredictable expansion in the seventeenth century. Local officials collaborated with the merchant community in ways that increased port traffic, promoted foreign settlement, and furthered freedom in the marketplace.

Historians, again following eighteenth-century jurists, have tended to privilege the definition of the free port provided by the Brothers Savary in their 1723 *Dictionary of Commerce*. For them and their readers, free ports were places where merchants of any citizenship or religious status were free to trade on equal terms, and where there were provisions for the duty-free storage and transit of wares.[13]

[11] ASL, GCM, 1025, ins. 13. Modern historians have likewise noted the gradual development of the free port by means of decrees or lenient interpretations of the law, but they have nonetheless emphasized ducal initiative throughout the period from 1566 to 1676. The goal in this chapter and the next is to explain why, as Baruchello put it, a "spirit of unlimited favor towards commerce" animated officials in Livorno despite changing economic and political conditions. See Baruchello, *Livorno e il suo porto*, 125, 267, 292, 367–71; Frattarelli Fischer, "Livorno città nuova"; Frattarelli Fischer, "Livorno 1676"; Addobbati, *Commercio, rischio, guerra*, 71.

[12] On the formal institutions that distinguished Livorno from the rest of Tuscany, see Aglietti, *I governatori di Livorno*, 68, 83–5, 100–2.

[13] See the introduction.

This definition was in fact the outcome of a historical process: the invention of the free port as a set of practices and a discursive tool. Neither the grand dukes who issued Livorno's legislation nor the people who traded there possessed a formal definition of the free port. That notion developed through practical negotiations between merchants and local officials. This historical construction helps account for the free port's double meaning, referring to general hospitality towards goods as well as people, and the consequent tension between its emporium and its entrepôt functions. For the free port emerged not from theoretical reflection, but from the actual experience of commerce (and its management) in Livorno during the first half of the seventeenth century.[14]

THE FREE PORT AS A WORK IN PROGRESS

Livorno was supposed to fulfill the Tuscan elite's longstanding industrial and maritime ambitions. Cosimo's customs reform and Ferdinando's Livornina were the chief elements of a legislative program backed by infrastructure investments, diplomatic initiatives, and a range of efforts to attract commerce to the port. Ferdinando I in particular took a vigorous interest in supervising the minutiae of affairs in Livorno. But after Ferdinando's death in 1609, the regime scaled back its ambitions and finally sold off most of the Tuscan galleys in 1647. In the meantime, privy secretaries enjoyed a freer rein in managing administrative matters in Livorno, especially after Cosimo II's premature demise in 1621 ushered in fifteen years of government by regency. These developments strengthened the role of bureaucratic decision making—not because privy secretaries were unable to exert central authority in any particular instance, but because ordinary administrative procedures made it costly for the central government to maintain constant vigilance. To move beyond a perspective focused on effective state action, it is necessary to pursue another trajectory to explain the elaboration of the free port: bottom-up bureaucratic processes.

When the city's first chronicler wrote about the free port in 1647, he celebrated the "free port" that the grand duke offered to Jews and Greeks.[15] Although the Livornina did not address questions about the presence of Muslims and Protestants, officials adopted a pragmatic policy that quickly grew to encompass a measure of toleration for all foreigners in the city. Muslims did not come in large numbers, as we have seen, but Protestants posed a more sustained challenge to the program of foreign hospitality. Dissimulation among the Dutch and English was high in the early seventeenth century as officials (with the grand duke's approval) turned a blind eye to the spiritual affiliations of the city's inhabitants. This situation evolved

[14] The word *portofranco* is ubiquitous in the Genoese legislation from the 1590s onward; it initially referred to a safe-conduct for grain and later came to mean a duty-free bonded warehouse. There was no notion in Genoa of the *portofranco* as a kind of marketplace. The Genoese model proved much less influential than that of Livorno—at least until the nineteenth century. See Giacchero, *Origini e sviluppo*, 106–7; and "A Complex Institution" in chapter 8.

[15] Magri, *Discorso cronologico*, 98, 106.

into the de facto acceptance of heterodox practices within certain limits. The regime closely monitored religious affairs in the free port, and if a matter threatened public order or relations with Rome, the grand duke was prepared to intervene to restore proper boundaries.[16]

Regulating the marketplace itself was a more complicated process. The customs reform of 1566 and the Livornina granted individuals general safe-conduct from debts contracted outside the state (and before they settled in Livorno). Merchants could also store their wares in the port and re-export them duty-free, so long as such goods did not change owners; and if goods *were* exchanged in Livorno, merchants paid reduced taxes depending on the commodity in question and its origin. Business disputes arising from these arrangements were adjudicated on the basis of a combination of Roman law, local statutes and regulations, and customary norms. The Governor's Court heard most cases initially, an expeditious form of justice that facilitated the flow of commerce. Cases involving more than two hundred lire were easily appealed to two other mercantile courts, the Sea Consuls in Pisa (Consoli del Mare) and the Merchant's Tribunal in Florence (Mercanzia); these cases might end up at still another appeals court in Florence, the Ruota Civile. Livorno was much like other commercial centers in the diversity of venues involved in dispute resolution. The most distinctive aspect of the free port was the extension of judicial protection to all merchants, whatever their ethno-religious affiliation. This protection was the essential legal correlate of foreign hospitality.[17]

Economic life in Livorno also rested on a body of decrees, precedents, and practices that were bureaucratic in nature. Especially in the early decades of Livorno's growth, the local bureaucracy had yet to settle into its standard procedures, and the extent of the city's liberties remained unknown. The requests of merchants generated piecemeal innovations that contributed to defining the free port. Crucial steps towards consolidating a free trade regime in Livorno included the decision to extend privileges to all comers, not merely those who intended to settle in the port; protect from seizure pirated goods purchased elsewhere and sold on the market in Livorno; permit the free trade of both wholesale and retail goods despite the interests of local industry; and extend warehousing rights indefinitely.

After unearthing a number of supplication decrees that were not precisely to the point, Customs Director Attavanti ultimately grounded his defense of Sebastiano Ferro on the traditions of the free port. If officials with archives of laws and rescripts at their disposal made broad appeals to the free port, it is no surprise that individual merchants did the same in their supplications. A good example occurred when two Ragusan ship captains contracted to carry raw wool from Spain to Livorno despite owing money to Tuscan subjects. They undertook to transport it "seeing that the liberties of the port of Livorno have been observed for other people notwithstanding

[16] See "An Expanding Port in a Time of Crisis" in chapter 2.

[17] Baruchello, *Livorno e il suo porto*, 364–5; Addobbati, "La giurisdizione marittima e commerciale"; Trivellato, *Familiarity of Strangers*, ch. 10; Calafat, "Expertises et tribunaux de commerce"; Calafat, "Être étranger"; Calafat, "Une mer jalousée," *passim*. For the gradual development of the judicial authority of the governor and his *auditore*, see Aglietti, *I governatori di Livorno*, 41–2, 45–8, 73–4, 78, 152, 157.

the interest of Tuscan subjects."[18] As the ship drew close to Livorno, however, the Ragusans learned that their creditors intended to detain the ship to satisfy their debts. They requested a safe-conduct for trade "to protect the privileges of the port from corrosion" (as they put it)—and to unload their cargo of wool. Even though the Ragusans' request went against the letter of the city's privileges, which only protected people from debts with alien subjects, the two were granted the exemptions of Livorno. The dictates of law did not prompt the regime to grant such favors; on the contrary, they overrode the letter of the law. They were approved in order to increase the city's commerce and were known as *agevolazioni* or *facilitazioni*—concessions that promoted commerce.[19]

Merchants or captains cited the free port precisely because it was difficult to track down every privilege, exemption, or license, much less the spirit behind the letter of these texts. Their concerns were usually grounded in concrete business problems. For example, a basic question concerned the relationship between predation and legitimate commerce. Two Corsicans, both citizens of Livorno, were involved in buying pirated merchandise in Algiers and selling it in Livorno.[20] In October 1610 they supplicated to recover goods that had been sequestered at the request of the original owner, who claimed that his property had been seized by enemy corsairs at sea and brought to Algiers for sale. The Corsicans were granted the assurance that "vessels and merchants from that part of Barbary may not be harassed" on the grounds that "Livorno is free and open for all businessmen."[21] Though framed as a supplication for safe-conducts *ad personam*, this decision set a precedent incorporated into the customs of the free port. By this act the regime indicated that it would not discriminate against goods purchased in corsair-markets like Tunis or Algiers. The grand duke might have remanded this case to the lower courts, which would have disputed the matter according to the norms of postliminy.[22] He did this when (usually Greek) Christians claimed that Medici galleys had illegally seized their goods, as the direct sale of booty in Livorno was regulated according to strict judicial principles.[23] Instead, the liberties of the free port would protect merchants and the goods they purchased elsewhere,

[18] "[V]edendo massime, che si come ad altri è stato osservato la franchigia del porto di Livorno nonostante l'interesse dei sudditi di Vostra Altezza." ASL, CGA, 2602, vol. 2, f. 12, 10/06/1616.

[19] See "Revenue Collection as Collaboration" and "Fraud, Collusion, and Market Norms" in chapter 4.

[20] The two were Carlo Lorenzi and Rocco Manfredini. See Lami, "I Corsi a Livorno."

[21] "[R]icorsono all'Altezza Vostra Serenissima supplicandola che la restassi servita di farli un libero sicuro salvacondotto, acciò le robbe, che facessero condurre di Barberia in detto porto di Livorno, non fossino per l'avvenire molestate." ASF, Riformagioni, 28, f. 349, 06/19/1611, memorandum by Belisario Vinta; the other part of the quotation is from an earlier supplication by the same supplicants, who believed that "Livorno sia francho libero per tutti negozianti." Ibid., f. 208, 10/19/1610, memorandum by Lorenzo Usimbardi.

[22] Postliminy was under debate in the late sixteenth and early seventeenth centuries, particularly over goods captured by Barbary corsairs, traded legally in Barbary territory, and sold to a European merchant. The tendency was for thinkers to legitimize such trade for pragmatic reasons; in Livorno it was legitimated on grounds of the free port. Rubin, *The Law of Piracy*, 19–32; and Greene, *Catholic Pirates and Greek Merchants*.

[23] ASL, CGA, 2602, vol. 1, ff. 456; ff. 691–696; vol. 2, ff. 383–384; 483; 515–517.

even in North Africa.[24] As late as 1645 the Corsicans' case was still cited along with thirty-four other memoranda important enough for the Customs Office to register in a specific book—a book which officials seem not to have consulted very often, however.[25]

The reform of 1566 had granted merchants the right to store wares duty-free in Livorno for up to a year: the "liberal gift." As the city's commerce expanded, so too did the appetite for warehousing exemptions. In 1605, merchants won the right to keep their *merci sottili* (low-volume, high-value goods) in their own warehouses rather than under lock-and-key in the customs house, as stipulated by law.[26] Rather quickly merchants began to store and access their goods without any monitoring from the Customs Office; observers believed this constituted an important difference between the free port of Livorno and that of Genoa.[27] In 1627, several Livorno merchants supplicated to extend the liberal gift to two years, subject to an annual customs inspection. Just a couple of years later the merchants supplicated again to make the gift perpetual in exchange for an increase in stallage fees. Merchants could now store their goods in Livorno indefinitely without paying duties on their import or export, so long as they did not change ownership. The movement from the "liberal" to the "perpetual" gift is an important marker of the city's role in the deposit and transit trade. It made warehousing exemptions central to the city's identity as a free port. The perpetual gift lasted only until the reform of 1643 reduced the warehousing exemption to two years, although merchants soon won the right to supplicate for its biennial extension. In the end, they enjoyed the same privilege, albeit with more paperwork and bureaucratic oversight.[28]

The supplications of merchant coalitions also shaped the relationship between industry and commerce in Livorno. In 1648, Carlo Antonio Pezzini supplicated for a privilege to produce and distribute silk stockings. Forty-five merchants and shopkeepers sent a collective supplication begging the grand duke to deny Pezzini's privilege. Aside from the fact that the stocking industry would never amount to anything given the competition of established centers in Naples and Messina, they thought it would threaten the wholesale market for stockings in Livorno itself. The customs director concurred with the merchants, remarking: "given that this is a free port for all merchandise alike, [conceding this privilege] would accomplish nothing but obscuring that title for something that could not result in any profit for the customs here."[29] This declaration is one of the earliest to identify the

[24] A similar case occurred two years earlier, when merchants who bought a ship in Algiers successfully defended their purchase against the original Christian owner. The regime even defended the liberties of the port for sugar that had belonged to the Spanish king, was taken by corsairs, and ultimately brought to market in Livorno. See ibid., vol. 1, 03/12/1608; ASF, MM, 30, ins. 7, ff. 1–15.

[25] Filippo Zannetti adduced the Manfredini case from the "libro dove si registrono i memoriali existenti nella Dogana di Livorno." ASL, CGA, 2603, 02/19/1645.

[26] Baruchello, *Livorno e il suo porto*, 280–3.

[27] ASG, CSG, Sala 35, 544, 05/23/1655 [or 1659], anonymous memorandum comparing the two ports.

[28] Ibid., ff. 277–284; 291; ASF, PS, 29, ff. 700–705. A number of these supplications survive: e.g. ASL, Dogana, 3, ff. 20, 24, 77, 78, 91 (all requests from 1648–9). See ASF, MP, 2155, 08/21/1643, Morgan Read to Alessandro Nomi; and in general, Calafat, "Une mer jalousée," 452–7.

[29] "[E]ssendo questo porto francho per tutte le mercantie indifferentemente, non sarà se non un oscurarlo questo nome per una cosa che non può tornare a meo credere in utile alcuno a questa

principle of unrestricted exchange with the free port policy. In the end, Pezzini received only a privilege for the production of silk stockings. There were no prohibitions on sale or distribution.

Officials were well aware that the liberties of the free port were ill-defined. In 1645, the *auditore* of Livorno complained that there was no single repository of texts that defined procedures in the port. "But I have nothing else to say about the exemptions," he commented, "than to observe, that limitations have always been a seminary of disgust."[30] This particular legal official was unhappy with generous interpretations of legislation. The governor and customs director were generally committed to a more pragmatic notion of a free port, however. Attavanti had based his arguments in defense of Sebastiano Ferro on decrees lifted directly from supplications.[31] These were identical in form to the requests of the Corsican traders, the Ragusan ship captains, and Carlo Antonio Pezzini. In the last analysis, Attavanti's case rested less on decrees and more on what his predecessors in office had done: the customs of the port. Many of these practices had originated in supplications, even if the decrees themselves seem to have been forgotten after the immediate decision.

Supplications—and the ducal decrees that answered them—were crucial for defining, even creating, the free port. Precedents were confusing and not readily available. As a result, the early free port was a flexible concept that officials and merchants deployed strategically in their writings. Over time the system of supplications engendered a way of doing things in Livorno that constituted what contemporaries meant by a free port, namely the right of merchants or captains to dispose of their wares with minimal bureaucracy and maximal legal protection; and the right of traders of any national or religious status to do business on equal terms. The Ferro episode helped invent a tradition based on these practices. Supplications created a body of authoritative texts about the free port whose centerpiece was the Livornina, flanked by a thicket of decrees and memoranda.

MAKING POLICY BY SUPPLICATION

Like monarchical power elsewhere in Europe, Medici rule rested on a process of bargaining between center and periphery. The grand duke respected the traditional privileges of his territory's governing bodies while overlaying them with supervisors that enabled him to intervene in the judicial process, balance local interests, and control state finances. Many of these policies hailed from the days of the republic, but the creation of the Medici court and a large bureaucracy transformed the

dogana." ASF, MP, 2324, f. 649, 09/10/1648, memorandum by Alessandro Alammani. See also ibid., ff. 201–202.

30 "Non ho altro senso nell'esentione, che il vedere, che le limitationi, sono sempre un seminario di disgusti." ASF, MP, 2160, f. 564, 02/11/1645, Lelio Talentoni to Domenico Pandolfini.

31 ASF, MP, 2160, f. 141, 02/10/1645, Pandolfo Attavanti to Domenico Pandolfini. He forwarded f. 142, a supplication from 1610; f. 143, a supplication from 1614; and f. 144, an undated safe-conduct.

practice of governance.[32] Supplications are a case in point. In the fifteenth century, rural communities presented their petitions to the Florentine government in person via *oratores*. In the mid-sixteenth century, Cosimo I began personally handling written supplications to provide equity to his subjects. After a few decades of princely intervention, the growing Tuscan bureaucracy replaced the direct attention of the monarch with a system of more or less formalized practices.[33] Local officials often controlled the pace and, in effect, the outcome of the supplication process. And while many of the graces the regime granted lay squarely in the judicial sphere, others had commercial, fiscal, or industrial implications. The supplication was an important conduit for introducing novel procedures or clarifying older regulations. In Livorno, this form of intervention tended to extend rather than limit freedom of trade.

The supplication process was a key dynamic that ordered political and social relations in Tuscany. Historians have focused on the mediation of local officials who stood between the localities, which were intent on preserving their autonomies, and the grand duke, who was concerned with securing obedience and fiscal contributions. By contrast, scholars inspired by neo-institutional economics have concentrated on political bargaining at the center when they investigate early modern politics. They have largely ignored administration in their examination of relations between monarchs and elites.[34] And yet the methodological insights of neo-institutionalist economics offer important tools for historians. Studying the working conditions of local institutions helps us incorporate information flows, and bottlenecks, into our understanding of territorial power in the Ancien Régime. Although officials in Livorno did indeed "mediate," their capacity to do so was determined not by their position relative to the center or periphery, but by their ability to manage the informational difficulties inherent in administering the free port. Even when documentary precedents existed, neither ducal secretaries nor local officials found it easy to retrieve information from their archives. When making decisions about supplications, for instance, officials often had no other choice but to rely on individuals who had a stake in the outcome. The passive nature of the system, in which supplicants took the initiative in framing requests, further diminished the government's role in directing ordinary business. These factors stacked the cards in favor of Livorno's merchants, artisans, and captains.

Princely regimes in sixteenth-century Italy found supplications a potent vehicle for affirming their status as absolute rulers and exercising munificence. An integral element of European political theology, the supplication originated in a judicial

[32] See "The Quickening of Medici Political Economy" in chapter 1.

[33] Cohn, *Creating the Florentine State*; Aglietti, *I governatori di Livorno*, 63–4; Shaw, "Writing to the Prince."

[34] E.g. North and Weingast, "Constitutions and Commitment"; Rosenthal, "The Political Economy of Absolutism Reconsidered"; Grafe and Gelderblom, "The Rise and Fall of Merchant Guilds." Exceptions are Kiser, "Markets and Hierarchies" (though see the criticism by Vester, "The Political Autonomy of a Tax Farm"); and Grafe, *Distant Tyranny*.

context and was used to overturn court decisions.[35] Whereas ordinary appeals were founded on procedural justice and *ius commune*, supplications were founded on princely grace. In the sixteenth century the supplication evolved to allow intervention in other realms, such as requesting patronage, proposing commercial or industrial monopolies, and raising complaints. A burgeoning contemporary literature urged princes to be generous in bestowing their favors on subordinates. Baldassare Castiglione, for example, praised princes who were "liberal" in dispensing graces.[36] For once, the virtuous counsel of humanists served the interests of princes. Supplications enabled rulers to extend their power over courts and communal governments while satisfying the demands of their subjects, especially the poor and weak (or in Livorno, the rich and powerful).

Supplications were sometimes heard in person, but the practice as a whole was a written substitution for holding an audience. Shortly after the death of Ferdinando I, Camillo Puntomi and his partners requested a privilege for the exclusive right to repair ship keels. They claimed that while alive Ferdinando had promised them the privilege, but the secretary dismissed their claim: "privileges are granted in writing, not *in voce*."[37] Officials were more flexible with licenses, however. A dealer in kitchenware who had twice been imprisoned for illegally selling his wares claimed that he had received a license by verbal agreement; his supplication for written confirmation was approved.[38] If a supplicant's request *was* granted, it was his responsibility to preserve the document and show it to officials when necessary. This archival situation, which thrust responsibility for documentary control onto the supplicant rather than the regime, was one reason why the system of supplications proved a rather passive exercise of central authority.

Virtually every bureaucracy in Tuscany had a collection of supplications, which run into the thousands of volumes. Other regimes also established regular channels to cope with the amount of requests. For instance, the Archivio Segreto Vaticano lists 7,365 volumes in its *Registra supplicationum*. The French collection known as the Trésor des Chartes in the Archives Nationales contains some 9,500 letters of remission for the years 1523–68. Not all supplications were routed through the bureaucracies, however, as many found their way into the letters of prominent officials and courtiers. However they reached the ears of the prince, the sheer number of these documents confirms that the supplication was a central channel of power in the Ancien Régime. Philip II, the paper king, answered no fewer than thirty to forty per day.[39]

35 Although the supplication has roots in antiquity, the practice only (re)assumed bureaucratic dimensions in the papal chancery of the fourteenth century. Bartolini, "Suppliche pontificie"; Repetti, "Scrivere ai potenti"; Nubola and Würgler, eds, *Suppliche e "gravamina"*; Nubola and Würgler, eds, *Forme della comunicazione politica*; and Nubola and Würgler, eds, *Operare la resistenza*; Vallerani, "La supplica al signore e il potere della misericordia."

36 Castiglione, *The Courtier*, 296, 308, 310.

37 ASL, CGA, 2602, vol. 1, 04/20/1609.

38 ASL, CGA, 2602, vol. 2, f. 21, 06/03/1597. See Varanini, "'Al magnifico e possente segnoro,'" 87.

39 Nubola, "La 'via supplicationis,'" 35; N. Davis, *Fiction in the Archives*, 145; Parker, *The Grand Strategy of Philip II*, 28; and in general, Fosi, "Rituali della parola"; Teuscher, "Chains of Favor"; Pischedda, "Supplicare, intercedere, raccomandare."

The supplications exploited here were composed in the third-person and generally did not bear a signature, date, or place of composition. Most were probably drafted by a notary or scrivener copying from a formulary. From there, the supplicant found an official or ally who transmitted his request to the ducal chancellery. The documents usually contain the name of the supplicant, his town of origin or residence, the nature of his request, and a brief summary of the facts.[40] Thanks to their abundance and formal characteristics, supplications are ripe for quantitative analysis. Unfortunately, these same generic conventions make it difficult to get at the realities they purport to relate. Formulaic language is used both in the relation of facts and in the request for grace. In addition, even detailed supplications contain the fictive elements common to legal cases. Accordingly, scholars have shied away from a quantitative study and focused instead on supplications as a rhetorical form of communication between subjects and sovereigns, a vehicle for conveying grievances and demanding redress.[41] In Livorno, however, an official investigation (*informazione*) exists alongside supplications and offers a further means for contextualizing requests. When read in light of other evidence, a quantitative study provides insight into decision making in Livorno as well as a window upon social and political realities.

This chapter draws upon 772 supplications from the two chief bureaucracies in Livorno: the Customs Office (n=173) and the Governor's Office (n=599). The Governor's Office evolved in an ad hoc manner throughout the long seventeenth century. Institutionalization began with Livorno's elevation to the status of "city" in 1606, when the Governor's Office's incorporated ill-defined powers in the military and civil spheres. Its sphere of competence expanded alongside the formulation of clearer rules; the governor answered directly to the grand duke via the secretary of war and enjoyed a good measure of discretion in disposing of local affairs.[42] The Customs Office, examined in detail in the next chapter, likewise experienced a process of gradual institutionalization. Officials from both offices reported almost daily to a privy secretary on a variety of requests pertaining to economic life. My source selections were conditioned by the surviving material and, where material was abundant, by the beginning and end of reigns; the figure for the Customs Office is so low because many of the documents in its archive were destroyed in the late nineteenth century. While we have no reason to believe that the run of documents is complete, particularly for the earliest periods, supplications were conserved because of their importance in establishing precedents. If we

[40] Quondam, "Dal 'formulario' al 'formulario,'" 130; Orlandi, "Suppliche al Comune di Ancona"; Repetti, "Scrivere ai potenti," 301–13; Belloni, *Suppliche al pontefice.*

[41] Repetti does perform a quantitative analysis, although she lacks the rescripts and *informazioni* on which I draw. Interestingly, she found that economic concerns occupied most of the business of the magistracies she studied in the Duchy of Parma. Such requests stemmed from the circumstances of the supplicants as poor, underemployed, or indebted persons. The mercantile class played a minuscule role in her supplications (2.62 percent): quite contrary to the situation in Livorno. Repetti, "Scrivere ai potenti," 295–6, 312.

[42] A single governor exercised authority in both civil and military matters except for the periods 1649–78 and 1746–57, when there were separate governors for each domain. See Aglietti, *I governatori di Livorno*, 9–12, 17, 25–7, 39–40, 52, 58–64, 70–2, 77–8, 318–19.

cannot be sure of having access to all of the supplications of a given period, at least we can be confident about the importance of those that do survive.[43]

I coded every supplication into one of twelve exclusive categories: privilege, exemption, license, safe-conduct against specific debtors, general safe-conduct to trade in the port, contract enforcement, fine or assessment revision, grant (requests for jobs, pay raises, etc.), abuse report, judicial, administrative, and miscellaneous. I use the term "economic graces" to describe the first seven categories because they shaped commercial and industrial policy in Livorno: discussions citing the *porto franco* occurred almost entirely amidst economic graces. Other supplications certainly had commercial consequences—consider the court cases of merchants—but they did not involve the structure of the free port, or the openness toward goods and foreigners that was peculiar to Livorno. This scheme of categorization is my own, of course: for contemporaries, the distinction between administration, justice, and economic policy was just being born. In practice, however, the boundaries between the twelve categories are relatively clear.[44]

Supplications in Livorno largely served the commercial classes. Requests came primarily from merchants (forty-seven percent) and artisans (seventeen percent) (Fig. 3.1). Only ten percent came from occupations associated with maritime life—ship captains or owners, small boat operators, mariners, and the like. Few of the city's teeming poor supplicated. The presence of laborers and petty mariners is modest compared to the richer, much less numerous mercantile sector. Perhaps the supplications of the poor were less likely to survive or less likely to record their occupations than those of higher status; many of their requests moreover probably pertained to judicial matters and were routed to the Sea Consuls in Pisa. A word of caution is in order. The monikers *mercante* or *negotiante* found in the supplications were not direct expressions of social reality. No doubt many who did business in Livorno arrogated the title of *mercante* without recognition by their peers. Nor do the words distinguish between the big wholesale merchants and smaller-scale operators. But thanks to the process of investigation described below, supplicants had to make their designations plausible or risk being exposed as frauds.

At any rate, it is clear that the commercial classes found it possible to utilize the system of supplications to promote their interests. About forty-five percent of the cases handled by the Governor's Office, and nearly eighty percent of the cases handled by the Customs Office, dealt with the economy (Fig. 3.2). Remaining documents mainly pertained to judicial or housing matters. Although both offices dealt with requests for privileges, exemptions, licenses, and safe-conducts, the policing of economic life lay in the hands of the governor. It was his office that enforced contracts, handled requests for safe-conducts, and managed court cases. Only in cases of penalty revisions did the two offices share the burdens of policing, since both bodies could levy fines under certain conditions. A practice originally instituted

[43] The documents come from: ASL, CGA, 2602: 1592–1629 (n=408); ASL, CGA, 2603: 1640–8 (n=148); ASL, CGA, 2608; 1680–2 (n=43); ASL, Dogana, 3: 1648–53 (n=173). I read only three years of the 1680s records because it was evident that supplications dealt almost entirely with housing and judicial matters.

[44] See Mannori and Sordi, *Storia del diritto amministrativo*.

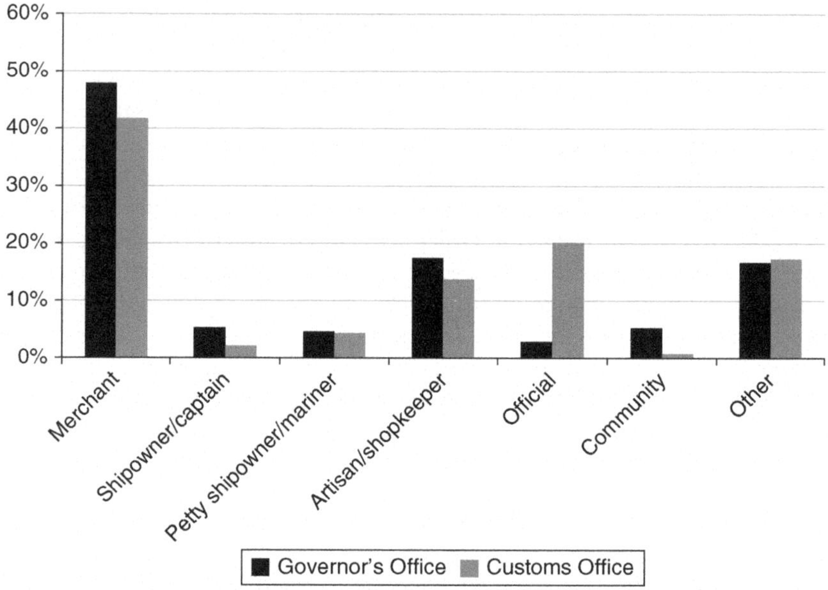

Fig. 3.1. Supplicants by occupational status, 1592–1682.

Note: "Merchant" includes *mercanti*, *negotianti*, and *sensali/mezzani*. Ship-owners or captains include those who described their vessels as *navi*. Those who used terms for small craft such as *leuti* were classified as petty ship-owners or mariners. Artisans or shopkeepers were those who described themselves as practicing a craft, maintaining a shop, or engaged in the retail trade.

Source: ASL, CGA, 2602; ASL, CGA, 2603; ASL, CGA, 2608; ASL, Dogana, 3. See n. 43.

for facilitating justice and empowering the poor became, in Livorno, a tool for manipulating economic policy.

Supplications pertaining to the free port dealt with regulating contracts, ownership, exchange, and the customs regime. They rarely dealt with the religious aspects of foreign hospitality. There are a few examples. When the priests of Livorno objected to the practice of Christian women nursing Jewish babies in 1625, they protested with a supplication.[45] But urgent religious matters could scarcely be decided by petition. For instance, in 1643 an English Protestant preacher arrived in Livorno and dwelt in the house of the merchant Robert Sainthill. The governor initially took no action, worried about "disgusting the [English] nation, which thanks to its stay here has brought so much traffic and commerce to this city."[46] Under pressure from the archbishop of Pisa, the governor finally instructed Sainthill to expel the preacher. The merchant then drafted the inevitable supplication, claiming that as a foreign agent he was entitled to hold religious services in his house. But in the end, he decided to go directly to Florence, perhaps because he knew that supplications were inappropriate for resolving such an affair. Religious issues required direct, high-level interventions because of their delicate political implications.[47]

[45] ASL, CGA, 2602, vol. 2, f. 249.

[46] Villani, "Cum scandalo catholicorum…," 9–13.

[47] Sainthill's audience went well, and he returned with assurances that the grand duke violated only after Rome ratcheted up pressure against tolerating a Protestant preacher in Livorno, who was duly sent home.

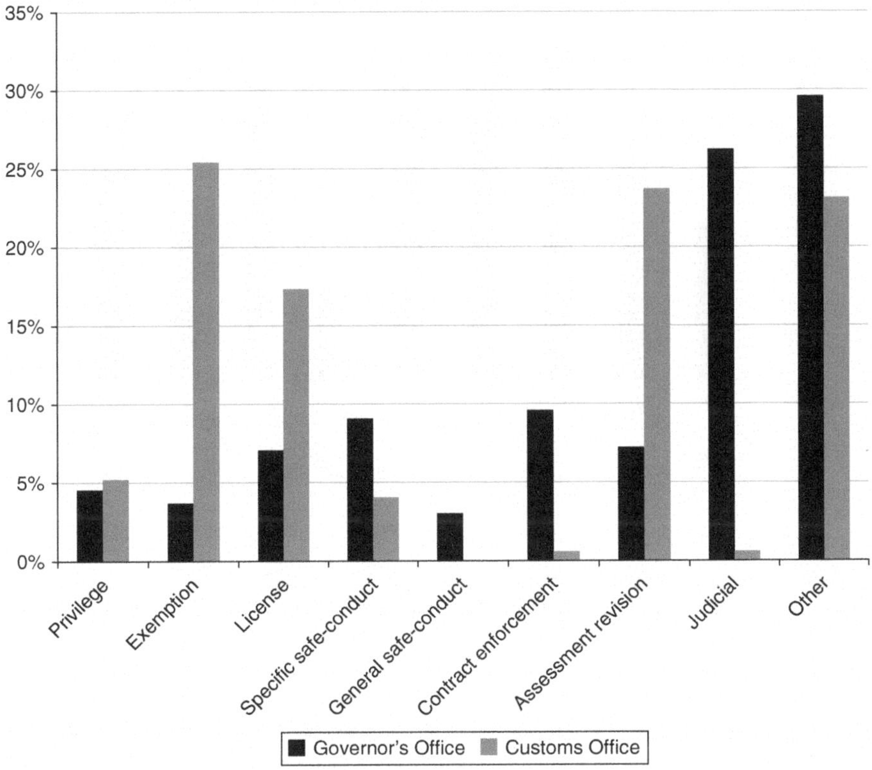

Fig. 3.2. Supplications by type, 1592–1682.

Note: Privileges were requests to be the exclusive producer, distributor, or tax farmer of a good. Exemptions were requests to avoid paying a tax, to receive a lower tax rate, or to get permission to engage in some form of economic activity without paying a tax. Licenses were permission to engage in economic activity while nonetheless paying the usual taxes (e.g. privateering patents). Specific safe-conducts protected individuals from prosecution by a list of creditors. Bankrupt merchants requested such safe-conducts to ensure orderly repayments to creditors or to protect themselves from malicious creditors. The general safe-conduct protected individuals from any civil debts contracted outside Tuscany, or with non-Tuscan subjects. It was equivalent to "taking the exemptions" of Livorno and was sometimes redundantly requested by potential immigrants. Contract enforcement supplications were requests for the government to enforce a contract, compel payment, or settle a debt. These were efforts to intervene in the ordinary course of justice, as normally the governor or the Sea Consuls in Pisa would have heard such cases (I placed requests for enforcement of judicial decisions in the judicial category). Assessment revisions were requests to have an assessment or fine reduced or an extension on payment. The majority of these were supplications to the Customs Office asking for an extension on tax dues or (for smugglers) a penalty reduction.

Source: ASL, CGA, 2602; ASL, CGA, 2603; ASL, CGA, 2608; ASL, Dogana, 3. See n. 43.

The regime had a marked preference for granting supplications. Out of 639 supplications with known resolutions, the grand duke granted sixty-seven percent (Fig. 3.3).[48] At a basic level, the desire among European rulers to exercise their

[48] The figures break down to an acceptance rate of eighty-five percent for the Customs Office, and sixty-one percent for the Governor's Office. The lower proportion for the Governor's Office is accounted for by instances in which the grand duke remanded a supplication to the governor's own court. At that point they become ordinary judicial cases.

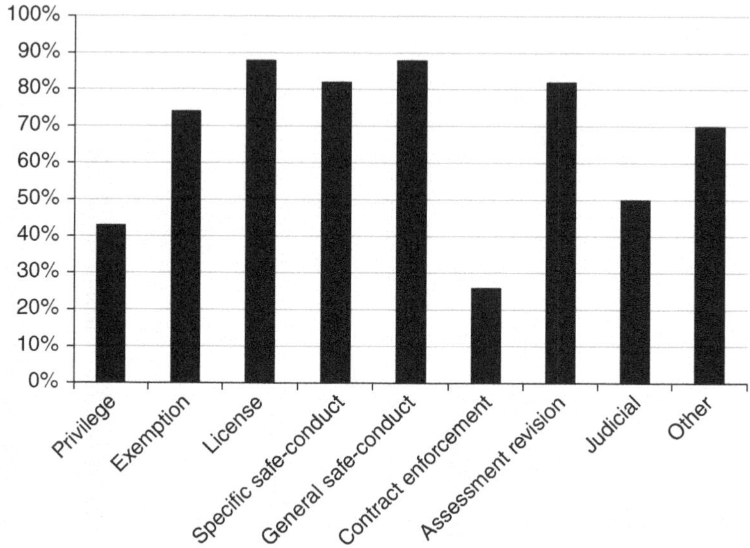

Fig. 3.3. Acceptance rates of supplications by type, 1592–1682.
Source: ASL, CGA, 2602; ASL, CGA, 2603; ASL, CGA, 2608; ASL, Dogana, 3. See n. 43.

generosity explains this finding: Natalie Zemon Davis found that over ninety-three percent of pardon-seekers at the Paris Conciergerie between 1564 and 1580 won the king's grace for homicide.[49] But other processes also account for the high acceptance rate. Supplications were drafted in a stereotypical manner that reflected the conventions of the genre and the known preferences of the regime. The merchants of Livorno were aware of the grand duke's standards for granting safe-conducts from debt, for instance. In addition, there is evidence for "pre-selection" whereby individuals lobbied with local officials before submitting their supplications. The high approval rate marks the success of officials in mediating affairs in the port by vetting requests, supporting measures they liked, and blocking proposals they disliked. It does *not* represent the efforts of merchants in Livorno to overstep the authority of local officials by appealing to the central government. In most cases the grand duke and his secretaries had no knowledge of a matter until a supplication brought it to their attention. It was then delegated back to Livorno for investigation. Although supplications were a princely institution, they reinforced rather than undermined the power of the local bureaucracies.

The documents afford some tantalizing glimpses into negotiations between supplicants and local officials. When the English refugee Sir Robert Dudley wanted a privilege for his new method of dyeing silk, he wrote to the governor of Livorno

[49] N. Davis, *Fiction in the Archives*, 52. Davis focused on supplications for capital crimes, which had distinct procedures that differed substantially from practices in Livorno. The French courts conducted their ratification process according to judicial norms, whereas the investigations I studied in Livorno were conducted by officials according to bureaucratic norms (ibid., 8–11).

to settle his supplication ahead of time.[50] Another official discussed the safe-conduct of a gentleman from Padua with a privy secretary before drafting the supplication.[51] The pre-selection process was part and parcel with the traffic in personal recommendations, and it was indeed common for officials to use a form of the word *recommend* when forwarding along a supplication.[52] As a result, they were reluctant even to accept supplications of which they disapproved, or which they did not find convenient for the grand duke. The assistant director of customs wrote to one secretary, "I've done my best not to trouble Your Lordship about the Netherlander who is owed money by those old butchers, but he has been so insistent that I could not escape forwarding his supplication."[53] Failed requests did not generate a large body of rejections because many were probably blocked even before reaching the grand duke.

Supplications in Livorno often became public knowledge. There was no pretense to secrecy, partly because supplicants handed their requests directly to the governor, the customs director, or one of their underlings to transmit back to Florence.[54] These men read and discussed supplications before sending them along. But the practice of information gathering was public in a more direct sense. If the grand duke asked the governor to evaluate a supplication, the governor sent one of his lackeys through the marketplace looking for the interested parties. For instance, when the commissary of Livorno needed to compile a report on the alabaster industry, he sent a man to talk with the privilege-holder Innocentio Nerucci. Nerucci's shop was always closed, and eventually the commissary himself decided to pay the artisan a visit: "Passing by I asked a mason who was working there where the master of the workshop was, and he told me that he had gone to the fairs. Apparently Innocentio is the type of man who works only when he has to."[55] Livorno was small. Most business took place in the Piazza Grande, in the government offices that flanked the piazza, or in the nearby dockyards. Nor were officials the only people flitting to and fro asking questions. The city's scores of brokers who negotiated sales between wholesale merchants were also conduits of news. In Livorno, there were few barriers to the rapid circulation of information about supplications or commerce more generally.

[50] ASF, MP, 1305, f. 51, 07/03/1610 and 07/10/1610, Robert Dudley to Fra Antonio Martelli. Evidently the letters were forwarded to the ducal secretary Lorenzo Usimbardi.

[51] ASF, MP, 2140, f. 27, 01/26/1607 [AD], Ugolino Barisoni to Marcello Accolti. For other examples see ibid., f. 286; f. 830; f. 853.

[52] ASF, MP, 2140, ff. 133, 142; f. 847 (in which Ludovico Niccolinì denies his "recommendation"); ASF, MP, 2139, f. 346; f. 353; f. 463.

[53] "Io sono stato alla dura più che io ho potuto per non dar fastidio a Vostra Signoria per conto del fiammingo che ha d'avere da quelli bechai vecchi, ma lui importuna tanto me che non ho potuto fuggirlo intorno a rimandare il suo memoriale." ASF, MP, 2139, f. 470, 12/17/1605, Matteo di Terenzio to Marcello Accolti.

[54] ASF, MP, 2140, f. 147; ff. 152–153; f. 211; f. 407; f. 647.

[55] "Ho mandato più volte a bottega di detto Innocentio per intendere da lui quanto gli occorra dire, et sempre è stato trovata la bottega serrata, et passando io di là, domandai a un muratore che vi travagliava dove era il maestro della bottega, et esso mi rispose, che era andato alle fiere. Innocentio per quanto vi sente è persona che sta a bottega quando non può fare altro, et che è sviato la sua parte." ASL, CGA, 2602, vol. 1, f. 328f, memorandum by Ugolino Barisoni.

The information-gathering process and the publicity it generated minimized the tendency for supplicants to make patently false claims. A few did not resist the temptation to lie, however. The debtor Michele Tilche asserted that most of his creditors supported his supplication for safe-conduct, but his request was denied after officials discovered that Tilche had larded his petition with the names of non-creditors.[56] This example is significant because safe-conducts were routine business in Livorno, and it shows that even simple supplications received a measure of direct examination. Requests for privileges, licenses, and exemptions triggered more thorough investigations. Of course, the regime could make mistakes in evaluating a supplicant. When a former butcher for the galleys requested a three-year safe-conduct from his creditors to pay back his contract fees, the commissary of Livorno observed that the impecunious man was thought to be quite wealthy when he had been granted the contract.[57] Nevertheless, I have found few instances in which officials reported outright lying in supplications. Successful liars would be impossible to detect, of course, but the practices of information gathering made lying difficult.

It appears that pre-screening in Livorno was less effective in conflict-prone situations. Requests for privileges, contract enforcement, and judicial interventions were denied more often than other kinds of supplications—acceptance rates were only forty-three percent, twenty-six percent, and fifty percent, respectively.[58] These cases involved third parties and hence possible conflicts of interest. Exemptions and licenses could be granted to one individual without directly affecting others. By contrast, exclusive privileges antagonized people who were already producing or dealing in a good. For instance, Giulio Romano's proposal to create a privilege for weighing the grains used by the Cathedral Workshop (Opera del Duomo) was denied because the Customs Office's corporate stevedores already enjoyed that right by custom. In cases of contract enforcement, the regime strongly preferred the judicial process over direct intervention. Even when a baker asked for a mutual friend to adjudicate over payment from a merchant who was supposed to invest in his shop, the grand duke preferred to follow the ordinary course of justice.[59] These norms of equity were a function of the judicial legacy of the supplicatory process. According to one French jurist, established interests were ipso facto legitimate and could not be infringed upon in adjudicating supplications. This principle lay behind the process of investigation and consultation conducted by public officials.[60]

Taken as a whole, the supplications suggest that a creative period in Livorno's political economy came to an end by the 1640s. Sufficient sources for comparison

[56] ASL, CGA, 2603, vol. 2, 950–1.

[57] ASL, GCM, 2602, vol. 1, f. 324, 07/15/1608. The butcher received a one-year safe-conduct.

[58] See Fig. 3.3. Abuse reports also had a low acceptance rate (thirty-six percent), but the small number of cases (only fourteen) makes it difficult to draw conclusions. The low acceptance rate of judicial supplications in the Governor's Office (forty-nine percent) is compensated by the twenty-four percent of cases remanded to the governor's own court by the grand duke.

[59] ASL, CGA, 2602, vol. 1, f. 345.

[60] Rebuffus, "*Tractatus de supplicationibus*," 301; see Zendri, "Il 'Tractatus de supplicationibus.'"

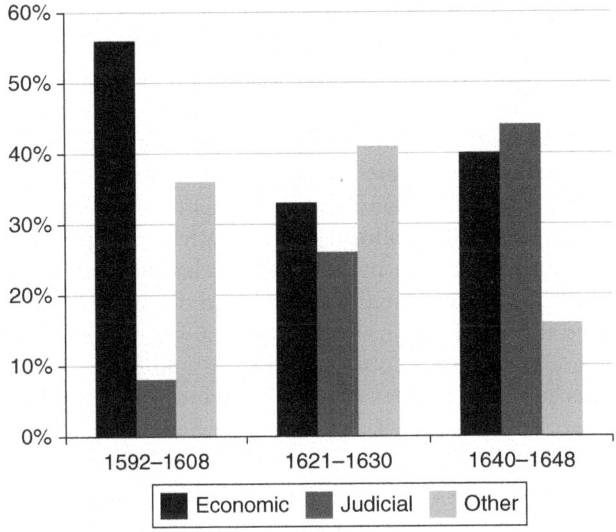

Fig. 3.4. Supplications to the Governor's Office by type, 1592–1648.

Note: Economic supplications comprise privileges, exemptions, licenses, safe-conduct against specific debtors, general safe-conduct to trade in the port, contract enforcement, and fine or assessment revision.

Source: ASL, CGA, 2602; ASL, CGA, 2603; ASL, CGA, 2608. See n. 43.

exist only for the Governor's Office (Fig. 3.4). In earlier decades, the governor dealt with a great variety of supplications. The uncertainties posed by immigration, new commerce and industries, and maritime insecurity all required his attention. Over time, however, the practices associated with the free port became increasingly regular thanks to the institution of supplications. Informal traditions based on older decisions obviated the need for innovative economic supplications. More of the governor's business was occupied with judicial matters or safe-conducts against creditors. Supplications were more often remanded to his court than decided by the grand duke. The arc of legislation confirms this chronology as well. Ferdinando I and Cosimo II issued a welter of decrees for regulating the minutiae of economic life in Livorno, but new legislation likewise diminished towards the middle of the century.[61]

The simpler profile of requests by the 1640s reflects a change in the status of Livorno as the free port became an institutional reality. In its early days, the system of supplications revolved as much around economic policy as around judicial affairs. But by the 1640s—by the period of the ruckus over Sebastiano Ferro—supplications were a scene for routine rather than innovation. Yet perhaps "routine" does not do the phenomenon justice. Some supplications served as a form of political ritual by which the merchant community conveyed its requests to the grand duke. For example, in 1651 the Victual Office (Grascia) demanded a payment of one lira for

[61] Cantini, *Legislazione Toscana*, vols 12–15; and G. Vivoli, *Annali*, vols 2 and 3.

every 150 pounds of biscuit that two merchants imported from Naples. "Not having ever heard of any tax on such merchandise in this free port besides the customary stallage and gabelle paid to the customs house," the merchants supplicated for liberation from the Victual Office's imposition—"especially since they unloaded under the good faith of the customs officer whom they asked before unloading what such merchandise was supposed to pay."[62] The customs director agreed with the merchants and urged the grand duke's clemency. Although the details are murky, this episode reads like political conflict rather than genuine uncertainty about the liberties of the port. For by then, officials had long since amassed a body of practical knowledge, documented precedents, and assumptions about the free port that rendered the supplication superfluous as a tool of policy invention.

The supplication system in theory allowed the grand duke to intervene at will in the lives of his subjects. In virtually every instance, however, he followed the recommendation of local officials. This was true for both complicated business and mundane matters, for which the grand duke or his secretary simply wrote *non altro* ("not otherwise") or *così si fa* ("do it this way") at the end of the official commentary. Sometimes a dissatisfied privy secretary asked for further information, but such cases were infrequent.[63] It goes without saying that local officials were not disinterested analysts of commerce, committed ideologically to norms of free trade. Except for the *auditore* of Livorno, virtually all of the port's top officials hailed from the Tuscan and especially Florentine patriciate.[64] In their memoranda they sought to affirm their loyalty to their superiors and safeguard their own careers. Their decisions nonetheless created a freer marketplace. Partly that outcome depended on supplication procedures and poor monitoring from Florence. Partly it depended on a larger culture of collaboration in which local officials routinely privileged the interests of foreign commerce.

In the early days of Livorno, merchants negotiated directly with local officials over a host of matters via supplications. This practice changed as the number of merchants in the city grew and, in the eyes of officialdom, the complexity of the city's affairs. In 1601, there were perhaps twenty-three merchants in Livorno, including brokers. That figure grew to almost three hundred by 1642.[65] Increasingly,

62 "[E]t per non havere questa sorte di mercantia mai sentito in questo porto francho altro aggravio che del solito stallaggio e gabella dovuta alla Dogana, supplicano Vostra Altezza Serenissima a comandare che, pagando questi a suo tempo, siano liberati dall'altra pretensione della lira per ogni 150 libbre, massime havendolo fatto scaricare sotto buona fede di questo doganiere, al quale avanti di scaricarlo in terra domandorno che spesa pativa simile sorte di mercantia, et esso li disse, che non pagava altro alla dogana." ASL, Dogana, 3, ins. 174, 10/06/1651.

63 E.g. ASL, CGA, 2602, vol. 2, 06/14/1619.

64 Among governors, the outliers were Giovanni Canaviglia (from Naples) and Giovanni Manoli Volterra (a Greek Uniate). Among customs directors, Paolo Poltri and Francesco Terriesi were of relatively modest origins. Many subordinate customs officials were also from important families, however. For the names and status of officeholders, I have consulted Niccolò Arrighi's *Teatro di Grazia e di Giustizia*, ASF, MM, 414, ff. 99–102; Aglietti, *I governatori di Livorno*, app.; and Litchfield; *Emergence of a Bureaucracy*, 364–82.

65 Fasano Guarini, "La popolazione," 203, 212; see too Baruchello, *Livorno e il suo porto*, 382. For the size of the merchant community in the late eighteenth century, see n. 87 and attendant text in chapter 7.

officials found it easier to negotiate with consuls or other representatives than with the entire ensemble of merchants in the city.

It is possible to trace this transition to a scarcity of Spanish reales in the winter of 1644–5, when the grand duke saw an opportunity to establish Florentine coin as the only tender in Livorno. Commodities would be exchanged in Tuscan coinage pegged to a specific exchange rate. The governor convoked the merchant community to discuss the proposed monetary reform, but the chaotic meeting broke up without resolution. The governor's account portrays the challenge of managing consensus in Livorno when every merchant had a voice. The English and Dutch wanted to be able to negotiate in every kind of currency, including local pieces of eight or doubloons; the Florentines and French were of divided minds. "Faced with this great confusion—for there were many of us present—and without hope of a genuine resolution, I begged these gentlemen to be satisfied if each nation selected two people to gather the opinion of their merchants and convey to me in writing their view of the matter."[66] The governor's professed inability to grasp currency issues did not do him any favors as a mediator. "Every little courtier among them is much more of a merchant than I am and therefore understands this business better."[67]

The Customs Office was more attuned to the perspective of foreign merchants. "No doubt it may seem strange at first glance that the money of our prince must be renounced, against the custom of every other country," wrote Customs Director Attavanti. "But considering that this place is different from others, and that affairs here are in the hands of foreigners that do business in the aforesaid regions, they necessarily need pieces of eight."[68] The merchants came out unanimously against the proposed currency rules two days after Attavanti wrote his memorandum. The deputies signed their document "as a bunch," since (as the governor put it) they were all in agreement; in fact, their arguments were similar to that of the customs director, suggesting that the latter had guided their deliberations.[69] The Customs

66 "[S]i che havendo visto una gran confusione (perché eramo molti) senza poter sperare veruna conclusione, risolvei di pregar quei signori di contentarsi che ciascuna natione facesse elettione di due persone le quali, sentito che havessero il parere dei loro mercanti, referissero in scritto a me qual fusse il lor senso in questa materia." ASF, MP, 2160, f. 34, 01/13/1645 [AD], Ludovico da Verrazzano to Domenico Pandolfini.

67 "Hanno sentito, doveranno pensare ancora loro a qualche mezzo termine potendo essere che ogni signore cortigiano de loro siano [sic] molto più mercante di me, et per conseguenza intenda meglio questo mestiero." ASF, MP, 2160, f. 36, 01/10/1645 [AD], Ludovico da Verrazzano to Domenico Pandolfini.

68 "Non è dubbio che a prima vista, che la moneta del nostro principe, habbia da esser recusata, pare cosa strana, fuori di quello si costuma in tutti li altri paesi, ma considerato che questo paese è differente dalli altri, e che il negotio oggi, è in mano de forestieri, che hanno il traffico nelle sopranominate provincie, necessariamente hanno bisogno delle pezze da otto." ASF, MP, 2160, f. 39, 01/16/1645 [AD], Pandolfo Attavanti to Domenico Pandolfini. According to Attavanti, the price of reales in Florentine scudi had increased six percent over recent months, primarily because the Spanish had not sent its usual shipment of coins to Italy, but also because speculators in Genoa and Livorno had engrossed the coins to sell them at higher prices. Volatility in the exchange markets moreover had upset the profits of the foreign-based bankers who supplied credit to traders in Livorno. The customs director believed that the scarcity of reales would cease when the English Civil War came to an end and the Spanish treasure fleets began to sale again.

69 ASF, MP, 2160, f. 61, 01/18/1645 [AD], Ludovico da Verrazzano to Domenico Pandolfini; ibid., f. 37, 01/21/1645 [AD], Niccolò degli Albizzi to Domenico Pandolfini; ibid., f. 38, 01/21/1645 [AD], Vincenzo Salviati to Domenico Pandolfini.

Office prevailed, and the free circulation of all currencies according to market prices remained the established policy. Later attempts to impose Florentine money on Livorno likewise met with frustration.[70]

When historians speak of negotiations in the port, one should imagine local officials spending hours in the governor's palace or the customs house trying to get the city's leading merchants to agree with one another on matters ranging from technocratic best practices to fiscal policy. Officials must have listened carefully to merchants while trying to steer discussions in directions that would be amenable to their superiors in Florence. Perhaps they practiced linkage as well, bargaining extraneous favors for reaching consensus on the matter at hand. The regime did not gather all information possible and base its decision on the best analysis; people such as the governor or the secretary of war were unable to evaluate the intricacies of commercial policy (the customs director was different). The regime cared primarily about three issues: ensuring that merchants remained in Livorno, that the port's commerce continued to grow, and that the Customs Office collected more revenue for the grand duke. It was more important for merchants to be cooperative than it was to alight on the most efficient policies. This process privileged consensus and ensured, as best as possible, that merchants would abide by regulations given the enormous potential for fraud. It also enabled the officials and merchants of Livorno to present a unified front in discussions with the central government. Negotiations were ultimately backed by the threat, rarely voiced, that merchants could take their business elsewhere. This possibility was much more real in the mid-eighteenth than the mid-seventeenth century, as we shall see. In daily practice, consensus was fostered more by the bonds of collaboration than by reason of state.

INSTITUTIONS AND ECONOMIC THOUGHT

Livorno provides an example of how organizational dynamics shaped an important concept of early modern political economy. When the Medici decided to transform Livorno's infrastructure and legislative framework, the term "free port" signified merely a "port with privileges."[71] It referred to the ability of foreigners to settle in Livorno regardless of ethno-religious affiliation. The phrase acquired a precise rubric of policies as well as a "general notion of unrestrained liberty" through memoranda produced in the context of local institutions.[72] While the state was implicated in

[70] ASF, MP, 2168, ins. 7, 10/14/1648, Morgan Read to Domenico Pandolfini; see too the discussion about bills of exchange in "The Abolition of Tariffs" in chapter 5. A debate later in the year over weights and measures followed a similar trajectory. See ASF, MP, 2161, f. 159, undated but likely September 1645; ASF, MP, 2161, f. 160, memorandum by Antonio Maria Pitti and Dionisio Zeffi; ASF, MP, 2161, f. 158, Ottavio Bartoli to Domenico Pandolfini; ASF, MP, 2161, f. 541, 10/02/1645, Lelio Talentoni to Domenico Pandolfini. The weights and measures remained an issue for some time: debate raged from the 1750s to 1783–4, when a new system of weighing was implemented. Baruchello, *Livorno e il suo porto*, 496–9.

[71] Ibid., 267. [72] See n. 47 in the introduction.

the creation of these institutions, it was not necessarily capable of directing their subsequent development. Historians of political economy, focused on concerns about imperial rivalry or changes in moral philosophy, should direct their attention to institutions as well. While those loftier themes were crucial for introducing cultural elites to the problem of economic development, most writing on commercial matters during the seventeenth century took place with more practical aims in view. The evolution of the free port was part of the haphazard development of institutions for regulating economic life: in the case of Livorno, the Customs Office and the Governor's Office.

The system of supplications was embedded in the larger structure of how the Medici organized and used commercial information. Contrary to some historiography that has glorified early modern information management, neither the central government nor the local bureaucracies in Livorno had the capacity to utilize their archives effectively for most commercial matters.[73] Supplications were an important vehicle for discussion about political economy precisely because the state lacked a body for handling similar material. Yet the state machinery for processing supplications was not adept at calibrating Tuscan commercial strategy; the system was erected to make judicial decisions rather than revise ongoing projects. The central government rarely issued follow-ups or excavated information from its archives. There was no routine inquiry into commerce or forum for debating industrial goals. When merchants or artisans crafted a supplication over a particular question, bureaucrats were responsible for discovering precedents in the records of their chancelleries and grilling supplicants on the details of their requests. To facilitate these tasks, offices kept books of rescripts which preserved the grand dukes' decisions in previous matters as well as indexed important business by subject. The meticulousness of their record keeping should not be exaggerated, however, and information gathering relied more on face-to-face discussion than on archival research.

Consider the story of the Neapolitan merchant Salvatore Bernardi. Bernardi had bought a silk-stocking workshop (and its privilege) shortly after 1616. To make good on his investment, he supplicated for further "assistance" from the grand duke, requesting a second patent for making wax-dyeing pigments.[74] The privy

[73] Preto, *I servizi segreti di Venezia*; Dooley and Baron, eds, *The Politics of Information*; Fasano Guarini and Rosa, eds, *L'informazione politica in Italia*; Head, "Knowing Like a State"; de Vivo, *Information and Communication*; Friedrich, "Government and Information-Management," 539–63; Soll, *The Information Master*. These writers generally emphasize informational success rather than failure (though see 238–48 in de Vivo on the Venetian government's handling of the Interdiction Crisis). For a more balanced account, see the Spanish bureaucracy's inability to adjust imperial strategy in light of experience. Parker, *The Grand Strategy of Philip II*, ch. 1.

[74] ASF, PS, 190, ff. 192–193; ASL, GCM, 2602, vol. 2, ff. 100 and 124. The patent had originally been granted to Scipione Schiavo (also a Neapolitan) as a "school" or workshop in Livorno to train impoverished young women to make stockings. The enterprise was supposed to provide jobs for poor girls in danger of falling into less savory occupations; to underscore the connection between good training and good morals, every year the grand duke gave five dowries to the young women of the stocking school. The venture operated at a loss, however, because Schiavo could not find enough skilled silk spinners in the city, and it was soon sold to Bernardi. On such charity workshops, see Terpstra, "Apprenticeship in Social Welfare" and Terpstra, "Making a Living."

secretary Lorenzo Usimbardi forwarded Bernardi's supplication to the governor of Livorno for comment, as was standard. The governor found in his chancellery records that a Piedmontese artisan had sent a similar supplication a year earlier for the production of lead oxides to Usimbardi, who had forwarded it to the customs director for further investigation. The customs director's report was not favorable to the Piedmontese artisan, judging by Usimbardi's exacting comments at the foot of the memorandum: "Explain what profit this will bring, how many people it will employ, how certain he is of using the 2,000 scudi he's asking for assistance, and in what time [he will repay the loan]."[75] Whereupon the artisan "never said anything more" and probably left Livorno altogether, although officials were not sure about his fate: they had neglected to pursue the matter.

The pigment affair remained closed until Bernardi's request a year later. When Usimbardi received this supplication, he did not look through his own archives to compare it to similar requests or to verify Bernardi's credentials. He merely wanted to hear from the governor and the customs director "how he's done with the stocking workshop and whether the supplicant is up to the task of working in the new industry he proposes."[76] Only now did officials leave their archives to conduct an on-the-ground investigation. Evidently, Bernardi had been so incompetent that the school had to be entrusted to somebody else; rumors were circulating that he had also abused the "modesty" of the women under his charge. The travails of the Neapolitan merchant need not detain us further, although it goes without saying that Bernardi failed to receive the pigment privilege under these circumstances. The point is that inquiry into the stocking factory began only when Bernardi requested a second privilege. Neither the privy secretary nor local officials in Livorno made deft use of their archives or proactively investigated enterprises in the free port; even a patent-holding silk workshop was nearly unknown to them. They gathered much of their information in person, and they did so only when prompted by the ordinary procedures for evaluating a supplication.

The supplication process generated thousands of memoranda, which are the early documentary record of the free port. It is important to distinguish this genre from other forms of writing about political economy, such as published pamphlets or legal treatises. Memoranda investigated questions of fact and only rarely offered theoretical discussions. Their writers usually progressed from the particular to the general, from the merits of the case at hand to a general approach to the issue. Moreover, before offering his own opinion, the writer usually presented a list of precedents that bore on the decision; of course, due to the disorganization of the archives, this list was often incomplete and sometimes done by memory. Most importantly, memoranda were set in a policy process. They were composed in

[75] ASL, GCM, 2602, vol. 2, 06/14/1619. The Piedmontese artisan was named Giovanni Antonio Arnolfini; the customs director was Cosimo Castiglioni. Lorenzo Usimbardi was the principal privy secretary involved with Livorno affairs in the early seventeenth century; on his family and career, see Fantoni, "Dalla provincia alla capitale."

[76] ASL, GCM, 2602, vol. 2, f. 111, 04/18/1620. The new manager was the more competent Pierfrancesco Tamagni.

response to a privy secretary's request for more information and were supposed to form the grounds for a decision. Because the genre was so coherent, an ambitious writer could also use his brief strategically, as a platform for showcasing his ideas or urging a change in policy.

The signal importance of the memorandum for political economy may be established by comparing it to the larger universe of economic writing associated with Livorno. Ducal secretaries regularly received information in the form of news, digests, and the letters of agents who had standing orders to report on commercial developments. For example, Jan van der Neesen sent dozens of letters from the Netherlands back to Florence detailing the possibility of establishing commercial ties between Livorno and the Indies, the organization of Dutch trade, and other economic information.[77] The Medici information network has been celebrated for its high quality during the late sixteenth and early seventeenth century. The extent and suppleness of the network was undoubtedly impressive, especially for such a small state, but it is important to observe that translating information into policy outcomes was efficient only for "hot" political or commercial affairs—those that commanded the regime's focused attention.[78]

Officials in Livorno also collected economic information. The captain of the port sent almost daily briefs to Florence detailing the provenance and cargos of ships that arrived in Livorno. His reports served an essentially political purpose of monitoring the armaments passing through the port. The Health Board transmitted similar information for ships arriving with suspect health patents to prevent the spread of plague to the port.[79] In addition, every year the Customs Office prepared a general balance sheet to track fiscal revenues. All of these records have been exploited by modern historians to trace the development of Livorno's trade, although they served other purposes in the seventeenth century. Only the customs balance was occasionally used in contemporary discussions of the free port.[80]

Ducal secretaries had difficulty exploiting the torrent of information that came their way. Often it was put out to pasture in the personal archives of the recipient. Busy secretaries rarely dug through their records to build a picture of trading opportunities in Holland (for example) or to compile trends for the price of grain in Livorno. They did not use their archives to assess ties between Livorno and its Tuscan hinterland; to analyze the relationship between policies that favored the port of deposit versus those that favored maritime expansion; or to track the behavior

[77] ASF, MP, 4750, f. 665, 05/06/1605; f. 675, 08/09/1605; f. 676, 08/16/1605; ff. 722–724, 05/31/1606; f. 756, undated but from late 1606; f. 781, 06/19/1607; and ASF, MP, 4259, ins. 1, 12/06/1605. All letters are from Jan Van der Neesen to Belisario Vinta. See "Negotiating Trade and Settlement" in chapter 2.

[78] Cf. Dooley, "Art and Information Brokerage," 81–95; Dooley, "Making It Present," 95–114; Rodríguez, "War, Trade, Products and Consumption Patterns."

[79] Apparently, though *portate* had been collected for some time, the customs director only began forwarding them to Florence in 1609. ASF, MP, 2140, f. 648, 05/04/1609, Ludovico Niccolini to Lorenzo Usimbardi. For more on these sources, see "Mediterranean Commerce in a Global Age" in chapter 6 and the appendix.

[80] By the mid-eighteenth century, in a quite different context for economic knowledge, summary tables on ship arrivals were also used to examine the state of commerce. Addobbati, *Commercio, rischio, guerra*, 53.

of rival ports, apart from taking note of major legislation issued by competitors. Secretaries almost always asked their usual correspondents to pen responses to specific questions even when they could have excavated such information from their own troves of letters, memos, and news reports. Most everyday business consisted of just such question-and-answers, since it would have been impossible to index all proper names mentioned in letters, let alone subject matters. This procedure meant that many memoranda merely rehashed data or perspectives presented piecemeal over previous correspondence. Like the most advanced of their contemporaries in Venice or Spain, Tuscan secretaries organized their files according to strategic objectives and drew upon them when producing statements of policy.[81] Most commercial information escaped their principles of organization, however. Matters pertaining to the free port were delegated to local officials working through memoranda.

Another reason the memorandum reigned supreme was the absence of published treatises on political economy in seventeenth-century Tuscany. The Renaissance florescence of commercial writing came to a halt in the early seventeenth century, when the Medici grand dukes squelched public discussion of the *arcana imperii* and suppressed virtually all publication touching upon political life in Tuscany.[82] Commercial discussion, perhaps because Botero had succeeded so well in marrying it to reason of state, could scarcely be framed in a politically neutral way. In addition, the fecklessness of representative institutions meant that there was little incentive to court popular opinion by publishing on political economy. The major representative bodies in Tuscany were the forty-eight-person Senate and the Council of 200. The members of both were hand-picked by the grand duke as honors that carried no real power. The supremacy of the Medici and the narrow political class discouraged the publication of commercial reflection. Memoranda (including those linked to supplications) provided the context for many discussions until Tuscans began to print economic texts again in the twilight of the Medici dynasty.

Different institutional arrangements may well have changed the nature of economic discourse in the grand duchy. Other countries had more regular feedback mechanisms for linking policy and commercial strategy. For example, in Venice the Trade Board (Cinque Savi alla Mercanzia) played an active role in vetting petitions on economic matters and occasionally proposed new measures. Under the system of *intendants* supervised by Colbert, France had a cadre of agents trained in gathering information and in superintending state-backed projects. The presence of representative bodies mattered, too. The *Collegi* in Genoa were the major venues in which the navalist faction sought to implement its policy of commercial expansion. Navalists unleashed a flurry of publications in the mid-seventeenth century glorifying the mercantile identity of their city to win public support. The English ruling class was larger than Genoa's, and in a state of rapid evolution owing to

[81] Pansini, "Le segreterie del principato mediceo"; Fusai, *Belisario Vinta ministro e consigliere*; Waquet, *Le Grand-Duché de Toscane*, 501–4; Fantoni, "Dalla provincia alla capitale."

[82] The ban on publication was a means of silencing Florence's republican heritage. Callard, *Le prince et la république*; Jurdjevic, *Guardians of Republicanism*.

economic expansion and political controversy. Commercial writers employed extensive pamphleteering to influence Parliament (not to mention back-room dealing).[83]

Throughout Europe, however, much discussion about the economy occurred in political or mercantile bodies erected for other purposes: the guilds, mints, customs houses, and monopoly companies that had their own mechanisms for supervising or manipulating the economy. The early history of political economy has a bureaucratic flavor because these institutions were often the primary ones charged with evaluating economic ideas.[84] Historians of seventeenth-century political economy have focused on printed sources and powerful states. They have dwelt on Holland, France, and England and marginalized Italy, perhaps because inhabitants of the peninsula did not publish widely on the subject until the Enlightenment.[85] The example of the free port indicates that print was not the only vital medium in the development of early modern commercial thought, and historians' focus on printed sources obscures debates that occurred largely in manuscript.[86] Manuscript discussions unfolded in the context of the messy institutions described here, with their poorly supervised officials, disorganized archives, peculiar procedures, and entitled interest groups.

CONCLUSION

The free port developed along two trajectories, a legislative and a bureaucratic one. The legislative process produced the constitutive (or fundamental) policies that defined the free port. It may be characterized by a model of punctuated equilibrium in which new legislation radically altered the city's prospects for commerce—the reform of 1566, the Livornina of 1591/93, the reform of 1643, and the reform of 1676. New policy orientations typically germinated in regime circles. The grand duke would commission a panel of courtiers and secretaries to consider the issues,

[83] Borgherini-Scarabellin, *Il magistrato dei Cinque Savi*; Gelder, "How to Influence Venetian Economic Policy"; Soll, *The Information Master*, ch. 5; Kirk, *Genoa and the Sea*, ch. 5; Brewer, *The Sinews of Power*, ch. 8. The Genoese *Collegi* comprised the senate, privy council, and doge in joint session. It is worth contrasting the navalist debates in the *Collegi* (which occurred in print as well as manuscript) with that concerning economic change in Spanish Milan, which occurred predominantly in manuscript: Vigo, *Nel cuore della crisi*, apps.

[84] See Minard, *La fortune du colbertisme*, 151–253; D. Smith, "Structuring Politics," 490–537; Ashworth, "Quality and the Roots of Manufacturing 'Expertise,'" 231–54. See "Merchant Expertise and State Institutions" in chapter 5.

[85] An indication of print production may be gauged by a search on *The Making of the Modern World*, an online collection of texts pertaining to political economy (accessed 04/28/2012). Between 1600 and 1699, the collection contains items sorted by language as follows: Spanish (104), Italian (142), German (189), Dutch (286), French (680), and English (4,086). These results are impressionistic, of course. The collection is biased towards English and features, in addition to works on political economy, legislation, political or legal treatises, and the like. Nevertheless, in ranking and order of magnitude, they confirm the figures for Spanish, English, and French economic publications presented by Bonney, "Early Modern Theories of State Finance," 171, 223, 223 n. 391.

[86] Bonney's survey for instance focuses exclusively on print sources: "Early Modern Theories of State Finance," 164, 224–5. The chief exception to the neglect of manuscript sources are the memoranda of Colbert, which even in their own day received a great deal of attention due to the position of their author.

draft new legislation, and set forth provisions for execution. Only the task of publicizing and implementation fell to local authorities. The legislative process was a top-down procedure, controlled by high ministers and with only consultative participation from local officials. Their policy innovations were related to the geo-political considerations that preoccupied such ministers, thereby wedding the grand legislation of the free port to the dictates of reason of state and the evolving fortunes of the grand duchy.[87] By contrast, the bureaucratic process was a bottom-up phenomenon. It produced regulatory policies but also sometimes revised the fundamental laws. It operated discursively by generating knowledge about the free port as well as practically, through the resolution of supplications and informal negotiations. The bureaucratic process obeyed an institutional rather than geo-political logic.

Scholars have generally attributed the diversity of free ports to geopolitical situation, in which a state's commercial power and trading system accounted for the character of a port. This perspective often emphasizes purposive princely action: rulers guided by reason of state pursued the true interests of their realm, given its situation in the play of economic and political forces. This style of explanation certainly carries weight in accounting for differences between cities like Livorno and Marseilles, which discriminated against non-native shipping; or between European and Caribbean ports, where exemptions were linked to the colonial system of their mother countries. It has less traction when considering the free ports in north-central Italy. The Italian ports shared a general geopolitical outlook—they belonged to rich but small states at the crossroads of Mediterranean trade—but none experienced the economic dynamism of Livorno or matched the extent of its freedom of commerce. The relative neutrality of Tuscany did distinguish Livorno from other Italian ports, but institutional factors were even more decisive.

Contemporaries (sometimes of a more institutionalist cast than historians) widely attributed the Tuscan port's success to the Livornina. This is a gross oversimplification. The Livornina only became the cornerstone of the free port in the 1640s, and despite its significance in regulating Jewish communal life, the text was not a central mechanism for attracting trade and settlement. Rather, Livorno's free port was a complex of formal and informal practices embedded in the fundamental institutions of the grand duchy. It was nourished not only by Ferdinando's legislation, but also by the lack of effective central oversight over local officials or their relations with merchants. The ensemble of practices that constituted the free port could not therefore be copied simply by lowering duties or welcoming foreign merchants. Rivals implemented their policies in very different contexts. Although Livorno was well known as a model in Italy and throughout Europe, its peculiarities were difficult to emulate.

[87] See, for example, the role of the Customs Office in the reforms of 1643 and 1676. Other important legislation followed a similar logic, not only for Livorno but for Tuscany as a whole: e.g. ASF, Riformagioni, 31, ff. 382, 484; ASF, MM, 328, ins. 48.

4

Governance and Tax Collection in a Free Port

One of the tales of the *Decameron* describes the travails of a young Florentine merchant in Palermo. Boccaccio begins the story by reminding readers of customs procedures in seaports. Upon arrival a merchant brings his merchandise to the customs house. After presenting officials with a written description of his wares and their value, his merchandise is placed under lock-and-key in one of the storerooms. "The officers then record all the details in their register under the merchant's name, and whenever the merchant removes his goods from bond, either wholly or in part, they make him pay the appropriate dues."[1] Brokers use their access to these registers to negotiate business deals among merchants. In the story, Madonna Jancofiore—one of those Palermitan women who were "lovely of body but strangers to virtue"—exploits her friendship with a broker to defraud the young Florentine of his wealth. The merchant was too proud, and too bankrupted by her duplicity, to let her get away with it. The plucky Florentine in fact makes a handsome profit off Jancofiore while exacting his revenge. "On perceiving that she had been outwitted, Jancofiore lamented long and bitterly... frequently repeating to herself the old saw: *Honesty's the better line, when dealing with a Florentine.*"

A few features of Boccaccio's customs house are worth noting. It was a bonded (i.e. sealed) warehouse, best adapted to the low-volume, high-value goods that plied Mediterranean waters. These articles were kept under physical control by officials, who also tracked their quantity and value in a series of registers. Merchants only had access to their wares under state supervision. Brokers consulted customs records to arrange deals and were thus essential mediators of commerce. The system was anything but airtight—Boccaccio recounts several deceptions of a fiscal rather than amatory nature—but it worked well in the restricted universe of late medieval trade.

The deepening of the marketplace and the expansion of the state made Boccaccio's customs house into something of a literary artifact by the seventeenth century. It is nonetheless a useful benchmark for evaluating control over international trade. All customs houses had to meet the same basic tasks. Levying taxes was a problem of collecting and exploiting information about the flow of goods;

[1] The quotes are from Boccaccio, *The Decameron*, 632–3, 644 (Day 8, Story 10). Boccaccio's account is quite accurate: see Dollinger, *The German Hansa*, 98–106, 182–3; Ogilvie, *Institutions and European Trade*, 46, 140, 288–9; and Purcell, "The Ancient Mediterranean."

that in turn meant coercion in the form of guards and supervision in the form of accounting and inspection.[2] Customs houses in early modern Europe underwent key structural changes with respect to their medieval predecessors. They multiplied personnel and checkpoints to accommodate the crush of new merchandise. More importantly, they experimented with various ways of adjusting the spatial or temporal aspects of oversight. The "customs house" was no longer a single facility, but a congeries of warehouse and administrative buildings linked together by a single institutional body. In that sense, the customs house itself became as intangible as the market forces it was supposed to regulate.

The customs house is one of the unsung heroes of the seventeenth century. It was where merchants met the state during the heyday of commercial capitalism. And the state, hungry for revenue as never before, found customs duties to be a critical source of income—often supplying between ten and thirty percent of the fiscal yield.[3] At the same time, princes also cultivated programs of economic growth that entailed the manipulation of customs levels and rules. Giovanni Botero was not alone in praising the customs—"there is no revenue more legitimate or just"—while insisting that tariffs must be tailored to the needs of the state.[4] The new political economy complicated collection procedures and increased the scope of activities under the aegis of the customs house. Strategies of control were always a compromise between fiscal, industrial, and commercial goals (not to mention the realities of the marketplace).[5]

Because customs duties—tariffs on external trade—constituted a conspicuous dimension of state finance, the rise of the fiscal-military state appears to be at odds with the rise of free trade. How could governments lower tariffs while locked in a desperate search for short-term revenue? The tension was real, but some states found means of displacing customs duties to accommodate freer trade. The port of Amsterdam is the most famous example. Goods were free to move through the city upon payment of low import and export duties, about five percent each. Low duties were supplemented by excise taxes on beer, food, fuel, and other consumer commodities.[6] It is easy to see intimations of modernity in these policies, and there

[2] Waquet, *Le Grand-Duché de Toscane*, 245–315.

[3] Customs accounted for between fifteen and twenty percent of government revenue in seventeenth-century Venice. They made up between thirty and forty percent of revenue in seventeenth-century England, and about twenty-five percent during the eighteenth century. They constituted a smaller but salient percentage of revenue in the Netherlands: twelve percent in the early 1640s, devoted to the maintenance of the Dutch navy. The customs (*traités*) were more marginal to French finance. Rapp, *Industry and Economic Decline*, 141; Pezzolo, *Il fisco dei veneziani*, 76; Braddick, *The Nerves of State*, 49–50; Brewer, *The Sinews of Power*, 98; 't Hart, *The Making of a Bourgeois State*, 86, 100–8; Wolfe, *The Fiscal System of Renaissance France*, 343–54; Matthews, *The Royal General Farms*, 130–4.

[4] Botero, *Della ragion di stato*, VII, 186. Broggia, who cited Botero, made this a principal of his system. Besold, though ambivalent, recognized the practical centrality of duties to state revenue and industrial policy. So entrenched was the notion of raising revenue through the customs that Petty expended much effort in trying to shift taxation away from the customs to the excise. Broggia, *Trattato*, ii–iii, 46–7, 97–8; Besold, *De aerario publico discursus*, 77–82; Petty, *A Treatise of Taxes & Contributions*, 37–8, 75.

[5] A point also made by Braddick, *The Nerves of State*, 58–9.

[6] See Israel, *Dutch Primacy in World Trade*, 280; 't Hart, *The Making of a Bourgeois State*, 103, 112–13, 117 n. 64, 123–9; de Vries and van der Woude, *The First Modern Economy*, 98–103, 122,

is no question that they fascinated contemporaries. But a genealogy of free trade that begins in Amsterdam distorts important elements of the story. Free trade policies were not reducible to tariff levels in the early modern period: storage and transit incentives were its more common attributes. Focusing on tariff levels rather than rules makes early modern commerce look a lot less free than it truly was in many localities. This optic can also distort our object of inquiry, by misdirecting attention to state-level policies rather than the local institutions that attempted to implement them. At the level of individual ports, we can detect how a new infrastructure of power was deployed that made the marketplace a more capacious place regardless of tariff rates.

This view of early modern trade helps us situate Livorno, that other epicenter of cosmopolitan commerce. Much of its customs regime before 1676 resembled systems elsewhere in Europe: invasive but dishonest customs officials; a tremendous amount of paperwork necessitated by complex procedures of control; and high formal tariffs, modified depending on the provenance, destination, or exchange of a good. Yet these features were consistent with the openness to foreigners, provisions of debt forgiveness, non-discriminatory market, and transit incentives for which Livorno was famous. In comparison with Boccaccio's customs house, the free port implied a relaxation of physical and temporal control over goods while attempting to maintain fiscal control. Commodities were free to move about the city without supervision, and taxes were determined and levied only after a transaction. The customs house had ballooned to encompass the entire city (Fig. 4.1).

The mechanics of the early free port reached their full development during the tenure of Pandolfo Attavanti (1640–8). We shall therefore focus on his administration in our examination of the Customs Office between 1566 and 1676. As we saw in the previous chapter, Attavanti was involved in the formation of a canon of texts delimiting the free port. He also helped draft the reform of 1643, the most significant effort to raise commercial taxes in Livorno during the entire Medici period. Although this act earned him the odium of the merchants, their relations with him nonetheless grew, if not cordial, at least complicit over time.[7] A series of corruption abuses finally brought an end to Attavanti's eventful career and precipitated legislation geared toward establishing greater independence between the Customs Office and the Health Board, which regulated quarantine facilities. His tenure illustrates not only how the Medici regime sought to structure trade in the free port, but also the disorders that made it the most open marketplace in southern Europe.

280, 494–5; Fritschy, "The Efficiency of Taxation in Holland"; Gelderblom, "The Organization of Long-Distance Trade."

[7] ASG, AS, LCL, 2675, 07/28/1643, report by Giovanni Stefano Boccalandro; quoted by Giacchero, *Storia economica*, 24; Baruchello, *Livorno e il suo porto*, 285–6. Attavanti's support for the reform of 1643 may be surprising given the intimate relations between merchants and the Customs Office. Attavanti probably doubted his ability to oppose a group of six high-status ministers charged with the task of increasing exactions in Livorno. Nor might Attavanti have wanted to object, even though his office would bear the brunt of merchants' discontent. It was an opportunity to deliver more of what the grand duke wanted most: revenue. See "The Warehouse of the Mediterranean" in chapter 2.

Fig. 4.1. Giuseppe Maria Terreni, "View of the Piazza Grande." The arcaded building to the right is the Customs Office, built towards the end of Attavanti's tenure because its old location at the New Gate (Porta Nuova) permitted too much fraud. The Governor's Palace is on the left.
Credit: Bibliothèque nationale de France, Paris.

SMALL BUREAUCRACY, BIG PORTFOLIO

Commercial competition and the pressures of warfare—or of defense, for neutral states like Tuscany—led to a lumpy but unprecedented increase in the scale of early modern government. There was a dramatic growth in the fiscal bureaucracy, whether privatized in tax farms, delegated to local authorities, or managed by the central government.[8] The manner in which states deployed their burgeoning bureaucracies could make it easier or harder for merchants to deal in certain goods, do business with certain people, or meet their obligations toward the government.[9] Occasionally, effective control took the form of a new corps of officials whose status depended on their office (rather than nobility or wealth) and who implemented a relatively impersonal, rational set of rules. The English excise administration is a

[8] Tilly, *Coercion, Capital, and European States*, 79; Waquet, *Le Grand-Duché de Toscane*, 93–5, 120; Brewer, *The Sinews of Power*, 65–8; 't Hart, *The Making of a Bourgeois State*, 187–91, 205–8; and in general, Parker, *The Military Revolution*; Bonney, ed., *Economic Systems and State Finance*; Bonney, ed., *The Rise of the Fiscal State*.

[9] Weber, *Economy and Society*, 956–1044; Mann, *The Sources of Social Power*, 444–78; North and Thomas, *The Rise of the Western World*; North and Weingast, "Constitutions and Commitment"; Root, *The Fountain of Privilege*; Acemoglu et al., "The Rise of Europe."

good example of this.[10] More often, bureaucracies were embedded in the patrimonial structures of the Ancien Régime. Departments had conflicting jurisdictions, unprofessional officeholders, and an idiosyncratic mélange of rules and customs. Such imperfect bureaucracies did not spell inevitable doom for commerce, however. The broader institutional and market contexts were more important than the professionalism of departments in promoting trade.[11]

Tuscany was an early bureaucratizer. The grand duchy had already inherited the administration of the Florentine Republic and the substantial reforms enacted in the 1540s by Cosimo I, who doubled the permanent bureaucracy in the early part of his reign while eviscerating the power of the old elective magistracies. Even so, between 1551 and 1695, the size of the Tuscan bureaucracy doubled again, and the number of fiscal officials grew by about 123 percent.[12] This administration took shape around the grand duke's effort to transform the Florentine patriciate into reliable servitors of the state. It was not especially impersonal or rule-oriented, however, and nowhere less so than in Livorno itself. Recordkeeping was poor. Revenue collection was personal. Rules were abundantly present but often ignored, disputed, or confusing. These "defects" did not owe to the patrimonial status of office holding, in which officials treated their offices as property, but to the complexity of procedures, the inability of the Customs Office to routinize tasks, and the constant collaboration between officials and merchants.[13]

The Customs Office was a tiny outfit when it got its own director in 1566. At the time, it counted only seven officials and twelve porters, and it was still an appendage of Pisa's customs house. About forty years later, in 1604, the office had increased to ten officials and some thirty porters. There was another new guard, a treasurer, and an assistant director. By the end of the century, it had twenty-two officials and fifty porters. Among the new officials were more guards and inspectors, more assistant administrators, and ministers with entirely new duties. This growth in personnel was accompanied by an expanding sphere of competence and increasingly complicated formal procedures. By the mid-seventeenth century, the Customs Office was practically if not legally independent from Pisa (Fig. 4.2).[14]

[10] Ashworth, *Customs and Excise*, esp. 90–3, 118, 120.

[11] For the impact of ground-level institutional arrangements and the internal size of the market, see Epstein, *Freedom and Growth*; Grafe, *Distant Tyranny*.

[12] I have excluded rotating magistracies from these calculations. Litchfield, *Emergence of a Bureaucracy*, app. A and p. 81; cf. Waquet, *Le Grand-Duché de Toscane*, 244, 432–51, 491–506.

[13] Cf. Litchfield, *Emergence of a Bureaucracy*, esp. 5–67; and the criticism in Waquet, *Le Grand-Duché de Toscane*, ch. 11; and Fasano Guarini, "Potere centrale e comunità soggette"; Fasano Guarini, "Camerlenghi ed esazione locale."

[14] The Customs Office's lack of independence in the early period is illustrated in the fact that the Sea Consuls of Pisa issued regulations concerning it on at least two occasions, in November 1578 and July 1582. The Sea Consuls also had a hand in crafting a law from December 1591. G. Vivoli, *Annali*, vol. 3, 152, 156–7, 186. On personnel, see Mannini, "La riforma," 73; Cantini, *Legislazione Toscana*, vol. 14, 287–90, 05/29/1604, Regolamento per la dogana di Livorno; ASF, MM, 414, Arrighi, *Teatro di Grazia e Giustizia*, vol. 2, f. 98; Waquet, *Le Grand-Duché de Toscane*, 554; and Addobbati, "Livorno: fronte del porto," 252–6. There were still only twenty or so officials when the General Tax Farm took over in 1741 (it eliminated the customs director and inflicted pay cuts on remaining officials).

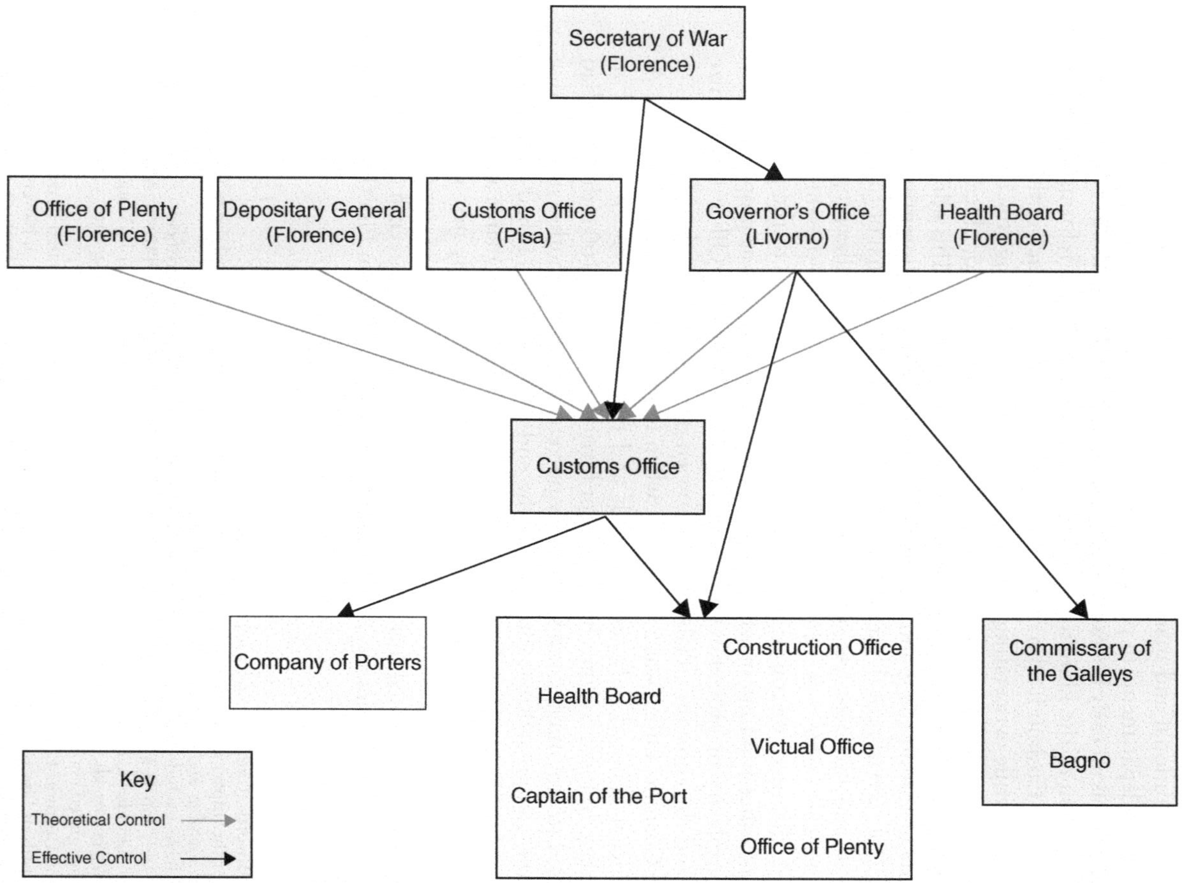

Fig. 4.2. The Customs Office and the organizational hierarchy. Theoretically, several organizations exerted oversight over the Customs Office—not least, the Governor's Office in Livorno and the Customs Office in Pisa. In practice, the Customs Office of Livorno was dependent primarily upon the secretary of war in Florence. Both the Customs Office and the Governor's Office jointly supervised many of the other institutions in Livorno.

The recruitment process in the Customs Office was typical of Ancien Régime bureaucracies. Access to a position was conditioned by family connections, and offices themselves were treated essentially as ecclesiastical benefices. Attavanti for instance owed his position to military service with Prince Matthias de' Medici and his connection by marriage with Ludovico da Verrazzano, admiral of the Order of St. Stephen and future governor of Livorno.[15] Out of ninety-seven men listed in an early eighteenth-century catalog of officeholders, the same family name appears twenty times (i.e. ten patronyms appear twice); no family monopolized the Customs Office, but having a relative in the office gave job aspirants an advantage. The tendency toward nepotism certainly exceeded the impulse to promote from within the institution. Longitudinal information, though incomplete, suggests that only eight individuals held more than one position in the Customs Office. Ottavio Cappelli's career was therefore unusual: he served as assistant director until 1614, customs officer (*doganiere*) until 1621, and finally director proper until his death in 1640. It was more common for officials to remain in their offices: though many died or were promoted elsewhere within their first three years (thirty-five percent), almost as many held their positions for ten years or more (twenty-nine percent). While the Customs Office should not be viewed as patrimonial in the sense of heritability, internal promotion was rather unusual.[16]

Customs officials remained enmeshed in patronage networks based in Florence. The extent to which these networks pervaded the Customs Office is clearest in the contest among job seekers whenever an official died or relocated. When Cappelli died, for example, at least three people sought his post—which ended up going to still a fourth individual, the short-lived Giulio Bracciolini (Attavanti's immediate predecessor).[17] But patronage conditioned bureaucratic life in more structural ways. Attavanti's underling, Customs Chancellor Filippo Zannetti, was a fierce rival of the customs director. Eager to please their common superior in Florence, the Secretary of War Alessandro Nomi, Zannetti generally wrote more informative letters than Attavanti. Shortly after Attavanti's appointment, the chancellor sent Nomi a few cartons of produce from Genoa—including "ripe artichokes and peas"—to demonstrate his devotion. A few months later,

[15] ASF, MP, 2153, 01/24/1642 [1641 ab inc. pres.], Pandolfo Attavanti to Alessandro Nomi.

[16] Niccolò Arrighi's *Teatro di Grazia e di Giustizia*, ASF, MM, 414, ff. 98–112. These figures are very rough. They exclude relatives who do not share patronyms, and they do not include minor officials until the late seventeenth century. The full "data set" includes ninety-seven names, but Arrighi provides longitudinal data only for five offices totaling forty-eight office holders. These figures moreover offer only one slice at the official class of Livorno. Ideally, we would have a list of office holders both ducal and municipal for the entire city. How typical were individuals like Jacopo Peruzzi, who was made director of the Construction Office after serving as *doganiere*, but who eventually achieved the position of customs director? Or of Alamanno Venerosi, who also started as *doganiere*, but eventually became director of the Victual Office?

[17] The failed aspirants were Giovanni Battista Talducci, Bastiano Buonaccorsi, and Jacopo Peruzzi. Other examples: Filippo Zannetti tried to get a job for his brother in the vacant post of the Cancelleria del Fisco. And when the director of the Construction Office, the indefatigable Jacopo Peruzzi, heard a rumor that Attavanti was to be promoted, he did not hesitate to put himself forward as a replacement. ASF, MP, 2150, 05/10/1640, 05/13/1640, and 05/20/1640; ASF, MP, 2151, ins. 5, 07/13/1641, and ins. 6, 08/15/1641, 08/21/1641; ASF, MP, 2155, 02/18/1643, Jacopo Peruzzi to Alessandro Nomi.

Nomi showed his appreciation for the presents by giving Zannetti four prosciuttos. The chancellor was astounded that he had been vouchsafed such an honor, which "took his breath away."[18]

Though competition for patronage made for some disharmonious relations among officials, it did not compromise the integrity of the Customs Office. To be sure, deflecting responsibility was an art that bureaucrats quickly mastered. The chancellor Zannetti accused Attavanti of "using the mantel of another" to cover himself during a bout of mutual recriminations that arose when nobody alerted the secretary of war of a death in Livorno.[19] Such emulous behavior among customs officials rarely interfered with their duties or the cohesion of their institution, however. In most cases, they defended their jurisdiction against outside attacks, whether by officials in Livorno or in Florence. Internal dissension had little effect on tax collection.

A Genoese observer of the late seventeenth century remarked that Livorno's Customs Office had "very few ministers" relative to the commerce it regulated: for him, this was a principal secret of the free port's success.[20] And in fact, its twenty-two officials were a pathetically small cadre in comparison to establishments elsewhere. The Genoese and Venetian customs houses had substantially more accountants, inspectors, and guards despite handling a similar amount of traffic as Livorno.[21] Bigger ports had more than a commensurate number of officials: Amsterdam had about ninety, for instance, and a veritable army of officials monitored movement through the port of London. Control throughout French tax farms was likewise intense (if ineffective).[22]

Personnel was one problem; oversight was another. Customs houses in other ports were subject to far more scrutiny than in Livorno. The Casa di San Giorgio in Genoa produced an endless stream of inquiry into the efficiency of its customs collectors, as the interminable reports to its chancellors testify. In late-eighteenth century England, the Customs Board heard ten thousand petitions annually from the Port of London alone, and another nine thousand from the outports.[23] Such supervision helps explain why officials elsewhere in Europe had a reputation for rigor wholly absent from the free port. It is true that the autonomy merchants enjoyed in storing and transporting their wares in Livorno necessitated a smaller corps of guards than in other ports. But there was a real deficiency of manpower for inspections and bookkeeping. Shortfalls in oversight contributed to the rank growth of customs fraud in the free port.

Even by Tuscan standards, the Customs Office of Livorno was a relatively modest establishment. The Customs Office of Pisa was a substantially larger organization, for instance, even though it did much less business. It had some forty-four

[18] ASF, MP, 2151, ins. 2, 02/18/1641 [AD], Filippo Zannetti to Alessandro Nomi; ASF, MP, 2151, ins. 3, 05/15/1641, Filippo Zannetti to Alessandro Nomi.

[19] ASF, MP, 2154, 08/08/1642, Pandolfo Attavanti to Alessandro Nomi.

[20] ASG, AS, 1011, anonymous memorandum; quoted by Giacchero, *Storia economica*, 63.

[21] See "A Complex Institution" in chapter 8.

[22] 't Hart, *The Making of a Bourgeois State*, 205; Hoon, *The Organization of the English Customs*, 132–67; Matthews, *The Royal General Farms*, 88, 110, 118, 131, 207.

[23] ASG, CSG, Sala 35; Hoon, *The Organization of the English Customs*, 65.

officials, excluding porters and guards: twice the number in Livorno. Customs officials in the free port made substantially more money than their colleagues in Pisa, however, who between emoluments and salary earned only between forty and fifty percent of what officials in Livorno made. This pay differential suggests that the grand duke's ad hoc policies resulted in overloading tasks onto current staff (with recompense) rather than creating new personnel as needed.[24] Accounting control was likewise lax in Livorno. In Florence, three accountants in a department known as the Inferno reviewed accounts to ensure that merchants actually paid what they owed on the books. A pity that every customs house didn't have its own Inferno![25]

PAPERWORK AND CHECKPOINTS

Customs officials in every port sought to monitor the movement of goods while exercising control over the sedentary population (inhabitants) and the roving people who entered for business purposes (merchants, sailors, captains). But while contemporary theorists waxed enthusiastic about the prospects of state control over the movement of goods and people, in practice customs houses were troublesome executors of the sovereign will.[26] Tax regimes rarely constituted calculated responses to the difficulties of enforcing regulations. The Customs Office in Livorno is a case in point. It coped with the vast increase in commerce with haphazard and ineffective measures. Its accumulation of new duties, personnel, and procedures obeyed a bureaucratic rather than a fiscal logic. In the end, the Tuscan state got its money the same way it got commercial growth in Livorno: the unplanned, ill-monitored delegation of affairs to local institutions.

The Customs Office's primacy in commercial affairs was by no means assured in the early seventeenth century. Until 1609, a single chancellor served both the office and the commissary of the galleys. What was worse, the commissary—who had been Ferdinando I's trusted agent in Livorno but was less close to his successor Cosimo II—was accustomed to intervening in the port's economic life, "which causes a lot of confusion and bad service for a number of reasons, not least because he does not have experience in such affairs."[27] A 1609 rescript granted the Customs Office its own chancellor and archives, independent of the commissary of the galleys.

[24] This comparison examines pay among the key administrators in both customs houses: *provveditore, cancelliere, camarlingo, doganiere, sotto-provveditore, sotto-cancelliere*, and *sotto-doganiere* (or *primo veditore* in Pisa). When the *provveditore* is included in the basket, the average pay difference was thirty-six percent; when he is removed, the average pay differential was fifty-two percent. Arrighi, *Teatro di Grazia e Giustizia*, ASF, MM, 414, ff. 1–24, 98–112.

[25] Like the Inferno, the Ufficio de' Soprassindaci was also charged with reviewing accounts. The success of these institutions should not be exaggerated: many debtors were in permanent arrears. Local officials, for their part, found it easy to deceive their overseers by doctoring the books. Waquet, *Corruption*, 50–7; Waquet, *Le Grand-Duché de Toscane*, 298–9, 422–5.

[26] On fantasies of state control, see Wakefield, *The Disordered Police State*; cf. Raeff, *The Well-Ordered Police State*; Gorski, *The Disciplinary Revolution*; and Foucault, *Security, Territory, Population*.

[27] In 1613 the commissary also lost criminal jurisdiction to the governor. G. Vivoli, *Annali*, vol. 3, 173 (for the quote); idem, vol. 4, 186–7; Aglietti, *I governatori*, 18, 40.

Meanwhile, the governor played a role in managing commercial and industrial life in the city throughout the first decades of the seventeenth century. He attended to supplications from merchants and artisans, enjoyed the right to regulate aspects of the retail trade, and defended the privileges of the free port—especially the provisions surrounding foreign hospitality. Thereafter, the governor continued to manage delicate commercial affairs in collaboration with the customs director. But as the governor's military and political duties multiplied, he ceded much of his powers in the economic sphere to the Customs Office.[28]

The Customs Office ultimately owed its growth to the supervisory problems associated with the expansion of traffic. Virtually every law or regulation began with a nod to the disorders that new commerce occasioned; it was a cliché of policy discourse in Livorno. As Attavanti put it, speaking of why it was impossible to settle all outstanding accounts in December:

> that order was issued when the port of Livorno was still at a tender age, when commerce was just getting started, and it was easy for the customs officer to punctually fulfill the regulation. But since business has always increased, to the profit of His Highness, it has become difficult even for previous customs officers to observe the full rigor of this law.[29]

In addition to the growth of commerce, it is possible to distinguish three drivers of the Customs Office's institutional evolution. The construction of new infrastructure meant a greater need for staff on the ground, to monitor access points and enforce regulations. In addition, new initiatives such as privileges, tax farms, or novel imposts obliged the office to undertake expanded duties or enact special rules. As its sphere of competence grew in scope, then, it also got more involved. Lastly, customs fraud was endemic, and measures to fight fraud complicated rather than simplified procedures.

Warehouses, port entrances, and lazarettos all needed guards and other personnel. In 1582, for instance, the customs director complained that the office was in dire need of a new guard to open warehouses and another to look after anchorage taxes, since the current one was inept. Evidently it remained difficult to find competent people for this position: less than a decade later, there were still only two guards, one of whom was illiterate. The proliferation of new warehouses throughout the seventeenth century only aggravated the need for guards.[30] The expansion of Livorno's defensive system likewise created checkpoints that required monitoring.

[28] My account differs from those of other historians, who have seen the governor as the chief protector of Livorno's trade. Aglietti furthermore emphasizes the Customs Office's strict subordination to the Governor's Office. Although the governor did have the formal right of control over the Customs Office, he was often a neglectful supervisor. His reputation as protector of commerce hails from the mid-eighteenth century. See Baruchello, *Livorno e il suo porto*, 362–3; Aglietti, *I governatori di Livorno*, 28–9, 42–3, 51, 115, 177–9; "Making Policy by Supplication" in chapter 3; and "The Council of Commerce and the Crisis of Representation" in chapter 7.

[29] "[E] perché fu disposto detto ordine in quel tempo che il porto di Livorno era di tenera età, che appunto principiava il negotio, non si rendeva difficile al doganiere di eseguire detto ordine con puntualità, ma da poi che il negotio è andato sempre augumentando in benefitio di Vostra Altezza, si è reso anche più difficile etiam a tutti li doganieri antecessori a questo il potere osservare il rigore di questa legge." ASF, MP, 2163, f. 644, 03/08/1646, Pandolfo Attavanti to the grand duke. See too n. 47 in this chapter.

[30] G. Vivoli, *Annali*, vol. 3, 148–9, 03/23/1581, rescript by Concino; ibid., 179–80, 02/12/1590.

During the 1630s, for example, a decision to enlarge the outer walls created two entrances and a new linkage to the canal.[31] The staffing problem was especially acute in the quarantine buildings. The first lazaretto was built in 1582–3 by the lighthouse. In 1597, a more substantial one named San Rocco was constructed, and a third called San Jacopo was erected in 1643. The custodians of the three lazarettos held sensitive positions. The quarantine was unpopular among merchants and mariners, the former wanting their goods in hand, the latter to load new cargo and be on their way. Custodians did not always resist the temptations of malfeasance and were therefore instructed to record the quantity and owner of every good undergoing "the purge" (Fig. 4.3).[32]

The Customs Office also assumed duties distinct from its "natural" role as tax collector. By virtue of presiding over a guild-free city, from the beginning the office regulated the activities of artisans or shopkeepers. This included licensing their activities, balancing free competition against the norms of a living wage, and mediating between wholesale commerce, industry, and petty trade. Other rulings intended to clarify the institutional landscape in Livorno further affirmed the Customs Office's preeminence in economic affairs. In 1578, for instance, the grand duke gave it a treasurer and simultaneously created the Construction Office.[33] These decisions set up the Customs Office to be the major landlord in Livorno. Not only did it license local shopkeepers and artisans, in other words, but it often owned their shops as well.

The establishment of the Jewish Loan was another instance of expanding powers. By 1644 the grand duke was in dire need of cash to support the wars in Germany and Italy. In April he turned to the Jewish community of Livorno for a loan of 100,000 scudi, promising lenders an annual interest of six percent. The offer was attractive to merchants anxious to find a secure investment during war-troubled times. Inevitably, it was the customs director who led negotiations over the loan and his office that administered it. The first installment was for 7,000 scudi, which Attavanti sent to Florence in two carriages accompanied by a convoy of soldiers. Over the next eight years Jews invested more than sixty thousand scudi in the fund. It all meant more paperwork, from keeping the books, disbursing interest payments, and tracking the inheritance claims of deceased investors. When Attavanti's successor joined the Customs Office in 1648, the Jewish Loan was in disarray. Not only had interest not been paid for some time, but the account books themselves were not being kept according to proper standards. Most of the books were simply blank: no official had been named as bookkeeper when the fund was first set up. It took six months to designate an accountant and assign a wine tax as a revenue stream to fund interest on the loan.[34]

[31] Matteoni, *Livorno*, 73–4.

[32] Ibid., 38, 76; G. Vivoli, *Annali*, vol. 4, 469–70; Cantini, *Legislazione Toscana*, vol. 14, 287–90, 05/29/1604, *Regolamento per la Dogana di Livorno*.

[33] G. Vivoli, *Annali*, vol. 3, 147.

[34] ASF, MP, 2159, ins. 6, 04/21/1644; ibid., ins. 5, 05/30/1644; ASL, Dogana, 3, 03/06/1647; ibid., ins. 28, 08/19/1648; ASG, AS, LCL, 2675, 04/20/1644, report by Giovanni Stefano Boccalandro; Frattarelli Fischer, *Vivere fuori dal ghetto*, 149–50. On the fiscal crisis of the 1640s, see "The Warehouse of the Mediterranean" in chapter 2.

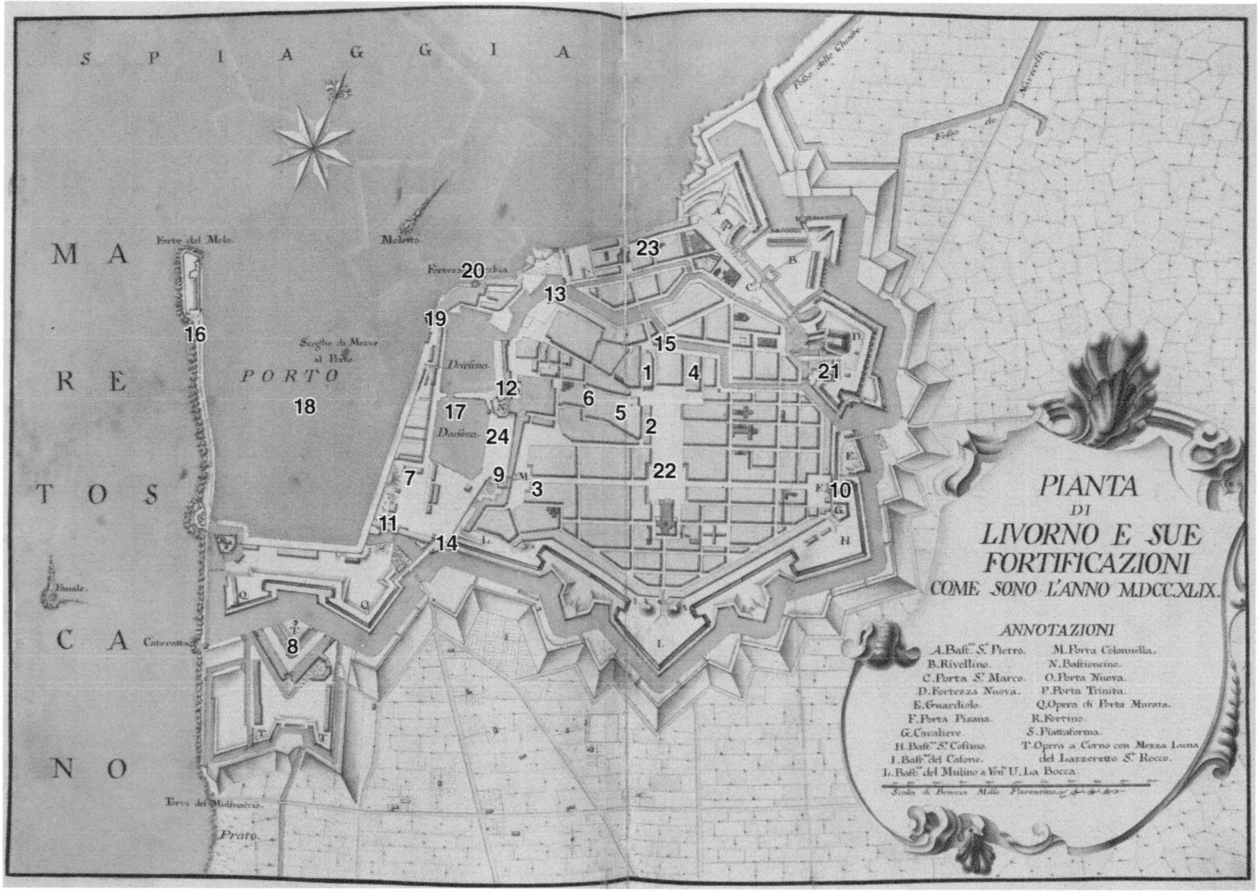
PIANTA
DI
LIVORNO E SUE
FORTIFICAZIONI
COME SONO L'ANNO M.DCC.XLIX.
ANNOTAZIONI
A. Bast.ne S.t Pietro.
B. Rivellino.
C. Porta S.t Marco.
D. Fortezza Nuova.
E. Guardiolo.
F. Porta Pisana.
G. Cavaliere.
H. Bast.ne S.t Cosimo.
I. Bast.ne del Cafone.
L. Bast.ne del Mulino a Vent.o
M. Porta Colonnella.
N. Bastioncino.
O. Porta Nuova.
P. Porta Trinita.
Q. Opera di Porta Murata.
R. Fortino.
S. Piattaforma.
T. Opera a Corno con Mezza Luna del Lazzeretto S.t Rocco.
U. La Bocca.
SPIAGGIA
MARE TOSCANO
PORTO
Forte del Molo
Moletto
Fortezza Vecchia
Scoglio di Mezzo al Porto
Darsena
Fanale
Cateratta
Torre del Mulinaccio
Prato
Fosso delle Chiatte
Fosso de Navicelli
1
2
3
4
5
6
7
8
9
10
11
12
13
14
15
16
17
18
19
20
21
22
23
24

Fig. 4.3. Map of Livorno.

Credit: Ministero dei Beni e delle Attività Culturali e del Turismo.

This map was produced in 1749, a century after the period examined in this chapter. I have added numerals to designate the principal checkpoints and institutions involved in the city's economic life. Note the network of canals that facilitated the movement of goods within Livorno and that connected the free port to the Arno River. For a map indicating the city's religious topography, see Trivellato, *The Familiarity of Strangers*, 75. For the placement of the following features, see Matteoni, *Livorno*, 43, 69, 85, 107, 134.

Features:
1. Customs Office
2. Governor's Palace
3. Construction Office
4. City Hall (Palazzo della Comunità)
5. Bagno
6. Military Bakery (Biscotteria)
7. Arsenal
8. Lazaretto of San Rocco
9. Colonnella Gate
10. Pisan Gate
11. Walled Gate (Porta Murata)
12. New Gate
13. Porticciola dei Navicelli
14. Porta ai Capuccini
15. Porticciolo
16. The Mole
17. The Harbor
18. The Port
19. The Bocca (Mouth of the Port)
20. Old Fortress
21. New Fortress
22. Piazza d'Armi (Piazza Grande)
23. New Venice
24. Monument of the Four Moors

The imposition of the Tenth in 1646 constituted the single biggest expansion of the Customs Office's powers in the entire period. Every landlord or renter in Livorno had to report their homes, warehouses, and shops at the rate of eighteen soldi per one hundred on annual rent; only the personal dwellings of real estate owners were exempt. Attavanti, convinced that revenue from the Tenth would amount to little in comparison to customs receipts, urged the grand duke (in vain) to postpone or moderate the unpopular imposition. In fact, although the customs director was correct in terms of gross revenue, the Tenth did provide a significant stream for funding the public debt.[35] But from the point of view of the Customs Office, the Tenth necessitated another series of registers, provisions for preventing fraud, rules for punishing violations, and guidelines for forgiving delinquents. The office hired an assessor to handle the new duties, and its chancellor received a pay raise in recognition of the more demanding workload.[36]

New policies meant more complicated procedures. This was as true for the Tenth as for the few goods that required licenses. In 1645 the grand duke authorized a Tuscany-wide tax farm for tobacco. Henceforth, everybody possessing more than four ounces of tobacco had to sell it to the contractors or deposit it under lock-and-key in the customs house as it awaited export. Merchants who wanted to transit tobacco overland needed to obtain a special bull from the Customs Office, which collaborated (half-heartedly) with the tax farm to ensure compliance.[37] Wine and grain were also subject to a constellation of regulations that varied from year to year, depending on the harvest and a merchant's political connections. Licensed goods at once created a new layer of bureaucracy and opened up a new field of contraband.[38]

Further complications ensued from the port's distinctive liberties. The customs cordon between Livorno and Tuscany created confusion and occasioned special regulations for the Livornesi. Residents' exemption from import taxes on goods for their own consumption led to abuses almost immediately, for instance, as the crafty Livornesi used their privileges to buy goods for resale. A resolution in 1581 specified that only small quantities were appropriate for the use of inhabitants, such as two loaves of pepper or sugar, and must be bought with the license of a customs official. The exemption of the Livornesi did not mean an exemption from paperwork for the Customs Office.[39] Debt-forgiveness constituted another problem. Tuscan subjects availed themselves of Livorno's exemptions to protect themselves

[35] ASF, MP, 2162, f. 682, 04/11/1646, Pandolfo Attavanti to Domenico Pandolfini; ASF, MP, 2163, f. 29, 05/14/1646, Ludovico da Verrazzano to Domenico Pandolfini; and Waquet, *Le Grand-Duché de Toscane* 376, 405–6.

[36] Cantini, *Legislazione Toscana*, vol. 17, 235–8, 01/12/1646, *Ordinazione e Legge sopra le Decime*; ASL, CGA, 2603, vol. 1, f. 836, Pandolfo Attavanti to Domenico Pandolfini; ibid., f. 848, 03/17/1645, a rescript by Domenico Pandolfini; ASL, Dogana, 3, ins. 11, 03/28/1648, Lelio Talentoni to Domenico Pandolfini.

[37] Cantini, *Legislazione Toscana*, vol. 17, 203–5, 05/11/1645.

[38] ASF, PS, 13, ins. 58.

[39] The situation remained confused until the exemption's elimination in 1643. G. Vivoli, *Annali*, vol. 3, 149, 164–5.

against creditors without actually residing in the port. According to a law from 1602, reissued the following year, anybody who adduced the privileges of Livorno in court had to secure proof of residence in Livorno from the customs director. Merchants who participated in the fairs of Pisa moreover needed to obtain special licenses for their unsold goods to enjoy the benefits of storage in Livorno.[40]

The prevention of fraud could get quite involved. As a politicized commodity, for example, grain was associated with a complex regime of monitoring. Among proposals for thwarting tax fraud that were vetted by one committee in 1646: bakers could no longer receive flour at the harbor without a license; ship owners could only hand over flour after furnishing lading bills to the Victual Office; lending flour under the name of third parties was to be prohibited; flour coming from overland routes must enter through the Pisan Gate, where a minister would track its movement in a register; bakers could not buy flour directly from importers but must procure it from authorized brokers with documents approved by the Victual Office; the official in charge of weights and measures must keep track of all the flour he weighed. These provisions were all intended to limit abuses.[41]

Above all, paperwork. The expansion of paperwork in Livorno is one record of the weakness (relative to its ambitions) of the early modern state. Local officials faced many difficulties in attempting to police the movement of goods and people. They had poor techniques for verifying the ownership of goods. They suffered from a chronic lack of manpower among guards and accountants. And as we will see, they labored under a system of incentives that tolerated a welter of fiscal abuses. The regime did have some choices. It could simplify the tax regime, modify the object of a tax (it was easier to count beasts than weigh cuts of meat), or intensify efforts to control.[42] In Livorno the third option was often the favorite until the reform of 1676, and more control meant more paperwork. We have encountered several occasions when the Customs Office had to keep another register, authorize another permit, or sign another lading bill: when a ship arrived, when goods entered or left the lazaretto, when a resident claimed exemptions for personal consumption, when the regime implemented the Tenth, when the grand duke farmed the tobacco tax, when punters loaded flour aboard their barks. Paperwork was one way of securing compliance with the basic goals of economic policy—but it did so only *post festum* and with middling success. The means of state coercion were too weak to deter many violators, and the complexity of regulations and rudimentary methods of tracking movement created ample space for evasion. So all this state production of documentation did not have a disciplining effect on the population of captains, merchants, and petty dealers who were its object. But it does constitute an archive of their unruliness.

[40] Cantini, *Legislazione Toscana*, vol. 22, 10–13, 09/10/1602; G. Vivoli, *Annali*, vol. 3, 268, 12/11/1603. The treasurer of the commissary (later of the Customs Office) or of the town had to authenticate the proof.

[41] ASF, MP, 2162, ff. 5–6, 01/01/1646, Ludovico da Verrazzano to Domenico Pandolfini.

[42] Waquet, *Le Grand-Duché de Toscane*, 256–8.

REVENUE COLLECTION AS COLLABORATION

Customs collection in the Ancien Régime could be a vexatious process. As Lewes Roberts noted in his *Marchants Mappe of Commerce* (1638), the customs differed from place to place and from season to season, as well as in the manner of assessment. Tariffs were often unpublished or difficult to consult, moreover, so merchants needed to be vigilant against officials who levied according to caprice rather than law:

> All these things and many others, as necessary to this commerce, must be truely learned; for ignorance herein is not pardonable, and is ever a prejudice to him that is found to exercise trade; for the rigor and strictnesse practised in sundry countries herein against merchants is extreame, whereas these customes are not duely and truely to the utmost satisfied and paid.[43]

No doubt Roberts was sincere in his anxiety about duties. But in comparison with other forms of taxation, the customs gave rise to especially intricate forms of collaboration between merchants and officials: rigor was by no means the norm everywhere. Customs houses were permanent establishments that attempted to control the goods of a relatively stable group of traders. There were few one-off transactions between officials and merchants, who often kept a running account with a particular customs house. In all but the largest markets such as Amsterdam or London, customs officials were bound to merchants through frequent, multiplex interactions. The same factors that made the customs a useful source of revenue to the early modern state—their exaction at concentrated checkpoints that monitored a restricted, easily-identified clientele—also thickened collaborative ties.

In few places did merchants find a more complaisant environment than Livorno. After all, wasn't it a free port? From the point of view of the Customs Office, however, key arrangements of the pre-1676 regime aggravated tax collection. The city's freedoms did not envision the indiscriminate right to low-duty trade in Livorno, but rather a panoply of exemptions, each of which created its own paperwork and opportunities for confusion. Customs officials needed to keep track of the provenance and destination of wares; their length of stay in Livorno; and whether they changed ownership. Given that merchants stored their goods in their own warehouses, it was difficult to exact the appropriate taxes without securing their compliance. The procedures for revenue collection created powerful incentives for collaboration between merchants and their regulators.

Merchants furnished the lion's share of the revenue collected by the Customs Office, although not solely in the form of duties. In January of every year, the customs director sent an annual report to a supervisory board. Most receipts were categorized as "ordinary revenues" and "extraordinary revenues" (Fig. 4.4). Ordinary revenues were those from import and export taxes. The more diverse extraordinary revenues included fees for licenses, monopoly contracts, and the sale of property. Rental income constituted a significant heading as well. By contrast, stallage taxes,

[43] Roberts, *The Marchants Mappe of Commerce*, 25–6; and in general, 23–8. The travails of the mercer Cornelis Jansen in Venice well illustrate Roberts's point: Gelder, *Trading Places*, 67–71.

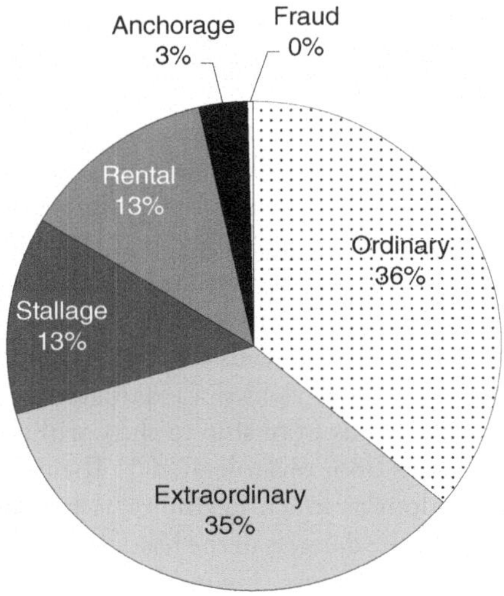

Fig. 4.4. Customs revenue by category, 1640–8.
Source: ASF, Soprassindaci e Sindaci, 469–470. For the complete revenue figures, see app. 9.

paid for goods stored in Livorno, amounted to only eleven percent of customs receipts, and anchorage fees on ships totaled only three percent. The fines collected for various customs violations were negligible—not because fraud was unimportant, but because officials turned a blind eye to its practice or colluded with scofflaws. Overall, at least half of all income owed directly to wholesale merchants or captains; indirectly, even more.[44]

Free port procedures complicated the collection of ordinary revenue, that is, taxes on imports and exports. According to the liberal gift, goods could be stored duty-free in Livorno for up to two years as long as they did not change hands, and the gift was routinely extended indefinitely via supplication.[45] One did not pay duties at the moment of importation, as taxes varied according to the duration of their storage in Livorno, whether they changed ownership, and their final destination. Instead, merchants registered every good that arrived for them with a book known as the survey (*campione*). The survey organized accounts by trading house and kept track of the taxes due on merchandise that entered the port. Every December merchants were supposed to settle accounts with the

[44] This estimate assumes that merchants or captains paid all of the anchorage, stallage, warehouse, and lazaretto fees, half of the remaining rental fees, and two-thirds of the ordinary revenue. The key question is how much ordinary revenue from import/export taxes came from merchants who traded their wares in Livorno's marketplace (transshipped goods did not pay ordinary taxes if they did not change ownership). Since the buyer rather than the seller paid ordinary taxes after a sale, the issue is what proportion of transactions concerned the international wholesale market, and what proportion the local retail market. While data are scarce, we have no reason to believe that retail absorbed anything like the wholesale market. For that reason, I have assumed that wholesale merchants furnished two-thirds of the ordinary revenue.

[45] See chapter 1, "The Quickening of Medici Political Economy," and chapter 3, "The Free Port as a Work in Progress."

Customs Office, with taxes due on some goods while others were transferred to the next year's survey.[46] The survey was then sent to the Customs Office of Pisa, which exacted fines for unpaid accounts.[47]

Monitoring the goods that entered and exited Livorno was an intricate process. Uncooperative merchants simply concealed taxable goods under cover of the liberal gift, or they deceived the office by not reporting transactions. After a seller made a deal, he declared to officials that he had been unable to sell his goods and removed them from Livorno duty-free by virtue of the liberal gift. He then shipped them to another destination on the buyer's account. Under these conditions, it was impossible to exact export duties—officials stopped even trying to do so by the 1580s or 1590s—and import duties yielded a negotiated sum at best. Some merchants also used to exchange goods from ship to ship, without ever bringing them onto dry land to be taxed; this, too, was tolerated.[48] The ease of violating customs rules induced officials to adopt as much flexibility as possible. When a group of merchants complained about the dangers of the hasty settling of accounts, Attavanti readily took up his pen in their defense (Fig. 4.5).[49]

Extraordinary income sheds further light on relations between merchants and customs officials. A balance sheet from 1645–6 reveals that property sales were the biggest source of extraordinary revenue—not surprisingly, given the decision to sell off ducal lands in the 1640s (Fig. 4.6). Most buyers were the Italian merchants or professionals who became the nucleus of the local elite.[50] Among the income from licenses granted to local shopkeepers (tavern owners, butchers, wine dealers, etc.) were broker fees. Brokers, who negotiated sales between wholesale merchants, were the most important licensed professionals in the city. In June 1651, there were 170 brokers in the city paying 100 scudi apiece to practice. The Customs Office relied upon the merchant community to verify whether an individual was

[46] ASF, MP, 2151, 02/27/1641 [AD], Pandolfo Attavanti to Alessandro Nomi. This is probably the "libro dei debitori e creditori" mentioned by Waquet; the information from this book was then compiled into the *ristretto* which is the source of our revenue data. See ASF, DG, 76, f. 734, 01/22/1641, Pandolfo Attavanti to Cosimo del Sera; Waquet, *Le Grand-Duché de Toscane*, 420, 428. On the *fido di dogana* in the nineteenth century, see Fettah, *Livourne et les grandes places marchandes*, 210.

[47] The accountant, Lorenzo Scarlatti, did not complete the 1645 survey until July 1646. Pisan officials complained that their colleagues in Livorno were using the extra time to collect penalties and share the proceeds among themselves, thus depriving the Customs Office of Pisa of an emolument—which may well have been true. But the Customs Office of Livorno successfully argued that the expansion of commerce and the imposition of the Tenth made it impossible to settle all accounts in December. The regime's "solution" to the problem of keeping records up to date was not more accountants or simpler rules, but merely the toleration of dilatory accounting. ASF, MP, 2160, f. 303, 04/12/1645, Lorenzo Scarlatti to Domenico Pandolfini; ASF, MP, 2161, f. 680, 07/04/1645, Domenico Pandolfini to Lorenzo Scarlatti; ASF, MP, 2163, f. 135, 06/06/1646, Li ragionieri straordinari della Dogana di Pisa to Domenico Pandolfini. Ibid., f. 639, 12/17/1646, Lorenzo Scarlatti to the grand duke; ibid., f. 644, 03/08/1647 [AD], Pandolfo Attavanti to the grand duke; ASF, MP, 2163, f. 648, 06/24/1647, Lorenzo Scarlatti to Domenico Pandolfini; ASL, Dogana, 3, inss. 53, 83, and 184. See the quote by Attavanti associated with n. 29.

[48] Baruchello, *Livorno e il suo porto*, 155; Filippini, *Il porto di Livorno*, vol. 1, 80; Addobbati, *Commercio, rischio, guerra*, 68.

[49] His successor did likewise, though perhaps more reluctantly. ASF, MP, 2163, f. 337; ASL, Dogana, ins. 83; and ibid., Alemmani's letters from 08/25/1649 and 09/23/1649.

[50] Frattarelli Fischer, "Case e proprietari," 369–72.

Arriving	Exempting	Taxing & Tracking
1. The Captain of the Port records the cargo of every arriving ship. He sends a copy of this information to the Customs Office, which registers it in a book called "di portata." Large ships must furnish the Customs Office with a more detailed report called a "portata distinta."	1. Merchants who receive merchandise from ships or the lazaretto do not pay anything except stallage and quarantine fees. Goods not disembarked pay no taxes, except for stallage fees.	1. Merchandise unloaded without having been registered in a *portata* or gotten license from the *doganiere* is forfeit. Likewise, merchandise transferred from one ship to another must be registered in a *portata*. The efficacy of these measures depended on the vigilance of the guards.
2. Merchandise listed in either *portata* book are transferred to the survey, organized alphabetically by merchant house. The margins of these *portate* are marked with the corresponding page number in the survey.	2. Merchandise imported on account of a particular merchant enjoys the "liberal gift": wares shipped by sea for more than 100 miles do not pay taxes, so long as they are shipped by their owner or his factor; but they pay the full tax if reexported to a location within 100 miles of Livorno.	2. When merchandise enjoying the liberal gift is shipped by sea, the exporting merchant makes a declaration that the merchandise did not change ownership. If he is caught lying, his merchandise is forfeit on account of the fraud.
3. Goods from the Levant or places suspected of plague, as well as some items from Holland and England, are placed in quarantine.	3. Merchandise that changes ownership in Livorno pays 2/3 of the import taxes if transshipped beyond the 100 miles, and the full tax if sent to a locality within 100 miles of Livorno.	3. The buyer (not the seller) pays duties to the Customs Office when merchandise changes hands.
4. The release of merchandise from quarantine is authorized by an order from the customs officer to the chief of the lazaretto, after said merchandise has undergone the due period of purgation.	4. Merchandise shipped over land from Livorno does not enjoy the liberal gift. However, the factor in Pisa who ships it onwards pays only a third of the export tax.	4. Export taxes must be paid within two months of exportation; otherwise exported goods owe a fourth more as penalty. By contrast, anchorage, stallage, and quarantine fees must be paid within a few days to a few weeks after arrival.
5. Merchants bring wares from ship or quarantine directly to their own warehouses. All transport of merchandise should be performed by the Company of Porters; in practice there were other porters and stevedores who carried out this work as well.	5. Goods that arrive by land via Pisa are entered into the survey and must be exported within a year to enjoy the liberal gift; otherwise they are subject to the ordinary taxes.	5. If merchandise enjoys the liberal gift and is not exported with two years, it must be transferred to a new survey. Since goods lose their exemptions after two years, merchant nations must also supplicate for the extension of the liberal gift.

Fig. 4.5. Routine customs procedures *c.*1650.

Source: ASG, AF, 1201, 02/05/1653, report by Giovanni Domenico Gavi.

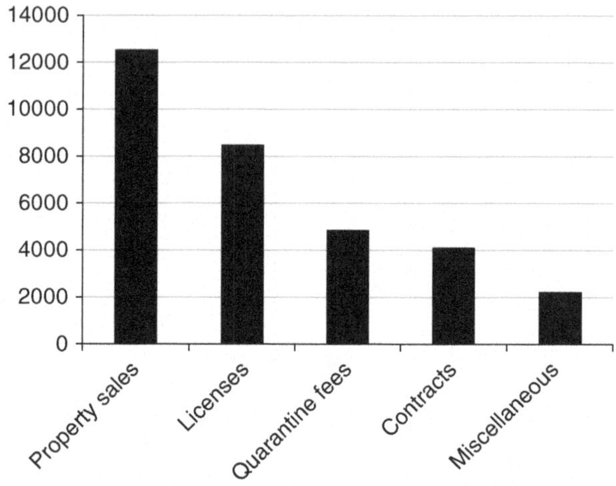

Fig. 4.6. Extraordinary revenue by category, 1645–6 (in scudi, two-year average).

Note: When expressed in lire, the total differs slightly from that reported in the general revenue data: the 1645 figure is 1.6 percent higher in Fig. 4.4.

Source: ASF, MP, 2163, end of filza.

an active broker and hence liable for the brokerage tax.[51] The quarantine fees for goods undergoing the purge likewise constituted a significant source of revenue and were paid entirely by merchants or captains. In addition, the contracts category included income from various monopoly contracts, such as the Company of Porters, the weights and measures, and the moat fisheries. Although these contracts did not involve extensive negotiations with merchants, officials consulted them when mercantile interests were at stake.[52]

Landlord activities also implicated the Customs Office in relations with merchants. Rent on warehouses constituted the single biggest heading in this category (Fig. 4.7). Each guard monitored access to several warehouses and, in theory, merchants moved controlled goods in and out of their storage facilities only in their presence. Such commodities included wine, grains, iron, tobacco, and some spices. Much daily activity in the city must have involved a merchant shuffling to his warehouse, accompanied by an official or a guard peppering him with questions about his business deals.[53] That was the law, anyway. In practice, trusted merchants had a lot of liberty to dispose of their goods without supervision. On balance, the Customs Office probably had an easier time with its merchant-renters than with other groups of renters. Collecting from the city's poor tenants was a

[51] E.g. ASF, MP, 2324, f. 430; ASL, Dogana, 3, ins. 129. See Addobbati, *Commercio, rischio, guerra*, 139–40.

[52] E.g. ASF, MP, 2150, ins. 2, 04/20/1640, Ottavio Cappelli to Antonio Simoni; ibid., ins. 3, 07/04/1640, Giulio Bracciolini to the secretary of war; ASF, MP, 2324, ff. 201–202. On the Company of Porters, see Addobbati, "Livorno: fronte del porto."

[53] G. Vivoli, *Annali*, vol. 3, 242–5, 03/16/1603; ibid., 73, 05/20/1609; ASL, Dogana, 3, ins. 26, 07/03/1648; ASL, Dogana, 3, ins. 105, 01/28/1650.

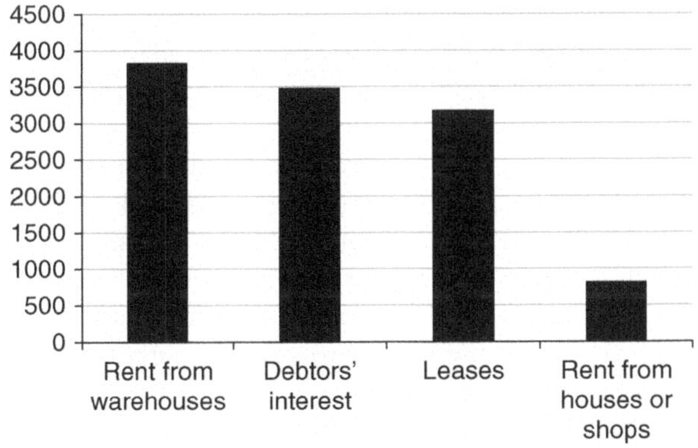

Fig. 4.7. Rental income by category, 1645 (in scudi).

Note: The rental income of 11,308 scudi totals 79,156 when expressed in lire. That is eighteen percent higher than the figure reported in Fig. 4.4. The discrepancy would be even higher if the housing managed by the Customs Office on behalf of the Ceppi di Prato or the Order of St. Stephen were taken into account (according to the same document, that amounted to another six thousand scudi, for a grand total of 17,348 scudi: forty-eight percent higher than the total reported in Fig. 4.4 when expressed in lire). What accounts for this huge difference? Perhaps the table of rental income was calculated before actual returns entered the till. The rental income *ristretto* was compiled in mid-December 1645, while the Customs Office's efforts to settle accounts went into June of the following year. Rental or housing debts were especially difficult to recover.

Source: ASF, MM, 313, ins. 37.

perennial challenge. When Attavanti arrived in Livorno in late 1640, he found that some open accounts were as old as twenty-five years.[54]

Anchorage and stallage fees represented infrastructure taxes, intended to recoup the grand duke's expenses in administering the port of Livorno. In the 1640s, stallage fees provided only a modest income for the Customs Office (a little over ten percent of revenue). Exaction presented challenges comparable to the collection of ordinary duties—keeping track of the goods that entered the port and the duration of their sojourn—and had its own opportunities for error.[55] By contrast, the anchorage was the easiest tax to collect in the Customs Office's portfolio, if also one of the least lucrative. Ship captains had to pay a tariff according to the size of their vessels for the right to harbor in Livorno. In comparison with merchandise, ships were big, visible, and easy to count. The office did not enforce payment of anchorage fees upon arrival but exacted them some time while a ship remained in

[54] ASF, DG, 71, f. 247, 07/04/1640, Giulio Bracciolini to Cosimo del Sera; ASF, DG, 72, ff. 380–82, Pandolfo Attavanti to Cosimo del Sera. Rental deals were made formally at an auction, but terms and rates were often arranged ahead of time. ASF, MP, 2151, ins. 2, 04/14/1641, 04/14/1641, Filippo Zannetti to Alessandro Nomi.

[55] For example, the English merchants Jacob Man and Thomas Forster claimed to have been rushed into paying the stallage in December 1647 by the treasurer Tiberio Brandi, who a few months later was ejected from office for embezzlement (see n. 82). The following December they found themselves under pressure to shell out again for the fee they already paid. When officials looked at the books, they observed that the deposit to Tiberio Brandi had only been made in the name of Jacob Man. A result of the hasty settlement of which the merchants complained? In any case, the Office treated it as a personal payment to Brandi and not the Fisc, since they were worried that merchants might step forward with similar complaints against the disgraced Brandi. ASL, Dogana, 3, ins. 52, 01/11/1649 [AD].

port. Nevertheless, administrative laxity could frustrate the collection of even this simplest of taxes. The guardian of the Porticciolo was charged with keeping track of anchorage duties. For unknown reasons, at least one guardian had allowed his debtor-book to languish at his post for almost a year.[56]

Our tour of the customs regime is accurate for the period before 1676. The office collected much of its taxes directly from merchants. It had good reasons for winning their goodwill and cooperation in doing so, since procedures were involved and readily cheated. And as we have seen, the office often relied upon merchants for information, whether in evaluating a supplication, contemplating a policy change, or establishing the list of brokers. The early free port made it possible for merchants to store and redistribute their wares from Livorno, in short, but at the expense of great administrative complexity.

Customs houses almost everywhere faced similar difficulties in collecting their duties, and they made similar compromises. Regimes had a limited palette of techniques at their disposal for controlling the flow of goods and people. Whether their policies discriminated against certain wares or merchants, whether there were incentives for transit or storage, whether the customs formed an integral part of commercial strategy or simply a source of revenue divorced from larger goals: the motives do not matter. Once a state decided to enforce controls, it had little choice but to deploy more paperwork, checkpoints, guards, and inspectors. These measures made it possible to collect more revenue than ever before. They also entangled the customs house in the objects of its regulation: the merchants.

FRAUD, COLLUSION, AND MARKET NORMS

When the long-serving Customs Director Ottavio Cappelli died in May 1640, it transpired that Cappelli "*did many things without informing the governor, especially in releasing merchandise that was being purged in the lazaretto*. In that matter he acted according to his whim."[57] At the helm of the Customs Office for almost twenty years, Cappelli had ample opportunity to make decisions without informing his superiors. The governor wanted his successors to be less independent. But though Attavanti as customs director was supposed to keep his betters apprised of his actions, he proved just as difficult to monitor as his predecessors. The office's sphere of competence was so varied and its affairs so vast that many decisions were never reported. The lack of supervision made it safe for officials to skim from the fisc or collude with merchants. Whether as agent or abettor, the Customs Office was implicated in much of the fraud that took place in the city. Nowhere was abuse more rampant than in the Health Board, which imposed quarantines on goods and

[56] Cantini, *Legislazione Toscana*, vol. 14, 289, 05/29/1604.

[57] "*Devo bene rappresentare a Vostra Signoria Illustrissima che il Provveditore Cappelli faceva molte cose senza darne parte al governatore, particolarmente in materia di dare pratica a mercantie che facevano la purga al lazzaretto*, nel che si governava a suo capriccio." ASF, MP, 2150, ins. 3, 05/26/1640, Giulio Montauto to Antonio Simoni (italics underscored in the original). Cappelli's immediate successor was Giulio Bracciolini, who died in October after a few months in office. Bracciolini was replaced by Attavanti.

mariners as part of its fight against plague. Attavanti's tenure came to an end in June 1648 when he was arrested for accepting bribes to shorten quarantine times.

Attavanti was hardly the only official in Europe implicated in fraud. The customs everywhere were hotbeds of abuse.[58] Unfortunately, it is notoriously difficult to quantify fraud. It is much easier to trace its modalities, analyze the institutions that permitted it to flourish, and assess its importance in the evolution of a commercial system.[59] For Livorno it is possible to document an atmosphere of complicity in which officials embezzled money, took bribes from merchants, neglected to punish wrongdoers, and turned a blind eye to the misdeeds of their associates. Unlike elsewhere in Italy, where relational fraud predominated, much of this malfeasance was transactional in nature: merchants and captains paid bribes in exchange for favors from the Customs Office. Nor should we assume that officials had a dirty conscience about their behavior. They argued against the strict application of the law in Livorno, whose commerce benefited from lax rules and careless scrutiny. Corruption in the free port was an extension of the marketplace beyond the bounds set by law. It benefited both officials and merchants—for a fee.[60]

A handful of heavily taxed commodities were especially likely to lead lives of crime: salt, victuals, tobacco, wine, and textiles. Most of this fraudulent merchandise began its career in Livorno, as goods arriving in the port benefited from tariff reductions for overland transit to adjacent states. Along the way many never left Tuscany. The black market for such goods could be quite large. In 1748, the General Tax Farm collected 64,640 lire from the salt tax in Pisa. The following year, after a concerted attack on abuses, the tax yielded 97,100 lire—the illegal salt market was almost half as big as the legitimate one. The regime of privileges and exemptions created a space for fraud to thrive. The numerous customs offices rarely shared information or coordinated anti-fraud measures, while bureaucratic collusion compounded the situation.[61]

The inability of the Customs Office to control the porous borders of Livorno was a structural feature of life in the port. In 1648 the customs house moved from the Porta Nuova in old Livorno to the more central Porticciolo, where punters and porters transported wares into and out of the city (Fig. 4.8).[62] Although the purpose of the move was to better monitor the flow of goods, people continued to use the port's other entrances to escape the vigilance of customs officials. The customs director therefore asked the grand duke to issue a decree making the Porticciolo the

[58] 't Hart, *The Making of a Bourgeois State*, 108–12; Ashworth, *Customs and Excise*, chs 9 and 10, esp. 150–9; Braddick, *The Nerves of State*, 160–3; Matthews, *The Royal General Farms*, 138–44.

[59] In his earlier work, Waquet emphasized the illegitimacy of the Medici regime as an important motive for corruption among "republican" patricians; but his later work focuses more on the informational difficulties inherent in control. Waquet, *Corruption*, 44–50, 73–4; 77, 82–3, 129–5; Waquet, *Le Grand-Duché de Toscane*, 451–79.

[60] On the market function of corruption, see Root, "The Redistributive Role of Government." For relational customs fraud in Liguria, see Tazzara, "Against the Fisc and Justice," 364–5.

[61] Waquet, "Aux marges de l'impôt," 80; cf. for the black market in England, Ashworth, *Customs and Excise*, 201, 324.

[62] G. Vivoli, *Annali*, vol. 4, 488–9; ASG, AS, LCL, 2675, 07/31/1647, report by Giovanni Maria Boccalandro. Before 1633 the customs house was located in the Piazza d'Armi.

Fig. 4.8. Giuseppe Maria Terreni, "View of the Porticciolo." Wares were unloaded at the Porticciolo to be carried to the nearby Customs Office. This was one of the major hotbeds of customs fraud in the city.

exclusive checkpoint for goods entering Livorno. Feckless to prevent fraud, the regime resorted to decrees and prohibitions that signaled the grand duke's displeasure more than they established new norms. When lawbreakers did get caught, some secured a penalty reduction via supplication or had the governor provide summary justice. But the small amount of fines exacted suggests that few violators were apprehended.[63]

Emoluments represented an official's cut of the office's activities and were supposed to foster professionalism in the discharge of duties, including the scrupulous detection of fraud. For example, the customs chancellor received a third of the revenue that butcher licenses yielded. The customs director got ten and a half lire whenever a ship registered its manifesto to the captain of the port, and he got four soldi and two denari for every pound of salt that went into a warehouse. These perquisites could dwarf an official's regular pay. In 1648 the customs director received 240 scudi in salary but could expect some thirteen hundred in emoluments. No wonder officials protected their fees with spirited defenses and careful archival research.[64] Nevertheless, the emolument system was not designed to minimize

[63] ASF, MP, 2153, 06/18/1642, Filippo Zannetti to Alessandro Nomi; ASF, MP, 2154, 10/10/1642, Pandolfo Attavanti to Alessandro Nomi; ASF, MP, 2161, f. 489, Lelio Talentoni to Domenico Pandolfini; ASL, CGA, 2602, vol. 1, 12/23/1602; ibid., vol. 2, 03/14/1626; ASL, CGA 2603, vol. 2, 03/05/1646.

[64] ASF, MP, 2168, ins. 6, 09/09/1648, Filippo Zannetti to Domenico Pandolfini; ASF, MP, 2151, ins. 4, 06/12/1641, Pandolfo Attavanti to Alessandro Nomi; ASF, MP, 2153, 01/24/1642 [AD], Pandolfo Attavanti to Alessandro Nomi.

fraud. Officials split between a third and a fourth of the fees associated with fraud penalties. This cut, divided among so many officials, was less than any one individual could have earned by permitting a transgression in exchange for a gift. Sometimes an emolument outright encouraged fraud. The Customs Office collected fees for other bodies, including the Florentine Secretariat and the Customs Office of Pisa. It appears that officials in Livorno sometimes negotiated with merchants for a smaller but illicit fee for themselves rather than turning over the full payment to an outside organization.[65]

There were other reasons not to pursue delinquents too aggressively. The Customs Office had to work closely with merchants during revenue collection. The thicket of paperwork that legitimate trade had to navigate put a premium on good relations between officials and their "clients." Pursuing the letter of the law was a way to antagonize merchants and threaten the prosperity of the port; indulgence earned officials gratitude, whereas exactitude earned enmity. Customs officials favored accommodation whenever possible. This approach provided a bountiful enough harvest for the grand duke's exchequer. It also ensured that merchants had a dominant voice in policy discussions and led officials to relax the law whenever they could get away with it.

Officials referred to the strict application of customs regulations as the *rigore della legge*. They disapproved of this "severity of the law" and urged a more lenient approach toward administering the port's customs. For example, when a privilege-holder who had the exclusive right to manufacture and sell coral asked customs officials to do a better job enforcing his privilege, Attavanti demurred. He did not deny that abuses were rife: merchants were importing coral and keeping it in their houses, packaging it with other goods, or even storing it in churches. Nevertheless, the Customs Office wanted no part in punishing violators. According to Attavanti, insisting on the letter of the coral privilege would contravene the norms of the free port. At most, the coral producer should maintain his own spies to catch smugglers in action. "Otherwise I see no remedy. And in this place such rigor would not be acceptable and in fact would damage the port. It is necessary to differentiate this town from the other cities of the state, where things are handled more severely."[66] Many of Attavanti's colleagues agreed that Livorno was a place where allowances needed to be made.[67] Typically, officials only approved of rigor when it was a question of subjecting mariners and merchandise to the regulations of the Health Board—and often not even then.[68]

[65] See ASF, MP, 2153, 02/01/1641 [AD], Filippo Zannetti to Alessandro Nomi; ASF, MP, 2152, ins. 3, 11/06/1641, Filippo Zannetti to Alessandro Nomi; see n. 47. In Bordeaux, too, the emolument system exacerbated official complicity in fraud: Marzagalli, *Bordeaux et les États-Unis*, 98–101.

[66] "[E] se cotesto corallaco è tanto bene informato, et ha tanta cognitione dove si facciano questi contrabandi, bisogna che tenga delle spie che vadano querelando questo e quello, come è detto alla giustitia, altrimenti non ci veggo rimedio, et in questo paese questo rigore non piacerebbe, e per conseguenza sarebbe di danno del porto, essendo necessario differentiare questo paese dalle altre città dello stato, dove le cose passano più strette, ma qui son tutte natione forestiere avvezzi in questa larghezza, che non è possibile ridurla al termine che vorrebbe il corallaco." ASF, MP, 2160, 02/10/1645 [AD], f. 145, Pandolfo Attavanti to Domenico Pandolfini.

[67] E.g. ASF, DG, 71, f. 247, Giulio Bracciolini to Cosimo del Sera; ASF, MP, 2150, ins. 6, 09/08/1640, Morgan Read to Antonio Simoni.

[68] E.g. ASF, MP, 2150, ins. 4, 11/24/1640, Giulio Montauto to the secretary of war; ASF, MP, 2163, f. 446, Lelio Talentoni to Domenico Pandolfini.

The Health Board was the site of open and perpetual scandal. The personnel of every ship that arrived from Western Europe and had spent at least forty days at sea enjoyed immediate access to Livorno; its goods were put into quarantine for only fifteen days. Provisions were even more generous for the fish ships that carried salted herring and cod from the Atlantic Ocean. However, quarantine could be substantially longer if a ship had called in other ports, come from the Ottoman Empire, or sailed during times of plague. Theoretically, judgment about a ship's health patent lay with a secretary in Florence, but as so often, local officials made decisions with little supervision and much generosity. As the customs director explained in 1612, "regarding the complaints that merchants are making of me for the goods that come from the Occident and are subject to the purge, they know that in this matter I am lenient rather than rigorous.... Merchants have no reason to criticize me, especially since I favor them in their expenditures whenever possible."[69] Despite such courtesies, merchants saw the Health Board as a form of commercial espionage, allowing Tuscan officials access to their cargo lists and shipping schedules. Quarantine also occasioned substantial delays. Merchants often pressured the customs director to license their wares as quickly as possible.[70]

In January 1648, Attavanti authorized the release of the *Gallina Bianca* from quarantine before it underwent the necessary purge.[71] This choice precipitated an avalanche of criticism about Attavanti's behavior at the Health Board that eventually encompassed his management of the customs as well. The atmosphere was no longer propitious for bending the rules. His protector, the governor Ludovico da Verrazzano, had recently died. The patrician Cosimo Riccardi took Verrazzano's place in April. Riccardi was preoccupied with the fear of plague that was sweeping over the city, prompting calls for stricter quarantine regulations.[72] In other words, a few contextual changes transformed Attavanti's routine act of leniency into a serious abuse. What happened during his disgrace reveals a lot about the limits of Florentine authority in Livorno and the complicit relations between merchants and officials in the free port.

Always jealous of its quasi-independent stepchild in Livorno, the Health Board of Florence championed tougher policies and won an ally in the port's new governor. In early May 1648, the grand duke supported legislation that eliminated the customs director's ability to make unilateral decisions. It clarified the chancellor's secretarial duties and mandated the creation of a new register (yet another!) that logged the board's every decision. This reform entailed the only significant institutional loss to the customs directorship in the seventeenth century—and

[69] Quoted by Cipolla, *Il burocrate e il marinaio*, 52.

[70] The register of *portate* kept by the Customs Office was by no means secret. In 1655, for example, the Genoese consul sent a copy to his superiors, who were curious about the extent of trade between Finale Ligure and Livorno. ASG, AS, LCL, 2675, 03/31/1655, report by Giovanni Domenico Gavi.

[71] Cf. ASF, MP, 2167, f. 74, 01/25/1648 [AD], Giovanni de' Medici to Domenico Pandolfini.

[72] ASF, MP, 2167, 02/24/1648 [AD], Giovanni de' Medici to Domenico Pandolfini; ibid., f. 609, 05/12/1648, Cosimo Riccardi to Domenico Pandolfini. And in fact, a minor plague did strike the city the following year: Aglietti, *I governatori di Livorno*, 66.

not coincidentally, Attavanti was the only director in Livorno to lose his job over an abuse.[73] Henceforth, the director no longer received quarantine emoluments and had less incentive to take a role in the body's deliberations. Nevertheless, the customs chancellor remained a key figure on the restructured Health Board and had his own salary increased. The reform left the Customs Office's prerogatives intact even as it imposed limits on the director himself.[74]

The new governor Cosimo Riccardi summoned Attavanti and the other Health Board members to his palace to read aloud the new orders. Then he bade his chancellor to go to the lazaretto to record all the goods undergoing quarantine in the novel register. As Riccardi implemented the reforms, however, he found that the extent of abuses far exceeded what he had imagined. By the end of May, the governor was in Florence discussing the affairs of Livorno with the grand duke. The customs chancellor was anxious to demonstrate his good behavior; and in early June, the guardian of the lazaretto and the doctor of the Health Board of Livorno testified that Attavanti continued to abuse his power. These officials had probably been complicit in the wrongdoing that predated Riccardi's reform and wished to clear their names. The Health Board of Florence commissioned a special investigator named Domenico Puccini to look into corruption. At this stage, the merchants and officials of the city closed ranks around Attavanti—or, to be more precise, they did little to aid the investigation of an outsider such as Puccini.[75]

As was common among officials whose gig was up, Attavanti gathered some of the account books and fled Livorno shortly before Puccini's arrival (though he was soon arrested).[76] The investigator published a notice that everybody who knew of wrongdoing by Attavanti should step forward. He quickly discovered that the facts surrounding the *Gallina Bianca* were "very serious" and that the abuses of Attavanti's administration were "infinite," but Puccini had difficulty gathering the evidence he needed to convict the customs director. The merchants of Livorno were reluctant to attack Attavanti, and the Jewish community actually passed an ordinance prohibiting their members from doing so. After hearing the notice, a broker publicly stated that "anybody who complained [about Attavanti] would be considered an informer."[77] Meanwhile, the *auditore* Talentoni was growing

[73] Though Assistant Director Alessandro degli Alessandri lost his job for embezzling quarantine money in 1716. Waquet, *Corruption*, 38.

[74] In the Florentine Health Board's judgment, the customs director had arrogated but never legitimately possessed this oversight. ASF, Sanità, 64, 9–10, 05/09/1648, Magistrato di Sanità di Firenze to Cosimo Riccardi; ASF, MP, 2167, f. 774, 06/10/1648, Lelio Talentoni to Domenico Pandolfini.

[75] The guardian was Niccolò Allegroni (who later came under examination) and the doctor was Cesare Monti. ASF, MP, 2167, f. 609, 05/12/1648, Cosimo Riccardi to Domenico Pandolfini; ASF, MP, 2167, f. 722, 05/30/1648, Filippo Zannetti to Domenico Pandolfini; ASF, Sanità, 183, ff. 214 and 247, 06/06/1648, Ulivo Dei to the grand duke; ASF, MP, 2168, ins. 9, 11/15/1648 and 11/19/1648, Domenico Puccini to Domenico Pandolfini. Further rationalization of the Health Board occurred in the 1660s: Cipolla, *Il burocrate e il marinaio*, 105–9.

[76] Flight made it easier to request ducal clemency and mobilize one's social network. Waquet, *Corruption*, 37; cf. ASF, MP, 2167, f. 295, 03/13/1648 [AD], Lelio Talentoni to Domenico Pandolfini.

[77] "Un tal Bichiera sensale nel sentire il bando disse pubblicamente, che chi si lamentasse sarebbe stato stimato una spia.... E perché sebbene il Signore Auditore non dice nulla, pare nondimeno, che

uncomfortable with the investigation and encouraged Puccini to use less rigor. The investigator encountered similar difficulties while trying to reform the Health Board of Livorno. "Although this magistracy holds many meetings and grand discussions, it makes few resolutions; few understand, some are party to the merchandise, the governor is suspicious, and the *auditore* is timorous. Your Excellency can imagine how things are."[78] Even the governor Riccardi, who had instigated the investigation, turned against Puccini's activities.

The *omertà* of the Livornesi indicates yet another ground for solidarity between merchants and the Customs Office: intricate, habitual collusion. Everyone knew about fraud, legislation complained about it incessantly, but it took an outside investigator to name it explicitly. The culture of complicity made an interloper like Puccini extremely unpopular. But despite the closed lips of the Livornesi, Puccini managed to collect enough damning evidence against Attavanti to convict him before the Health Board in Florence. The erstwhile customs director, stripped of his office in June, spent almost all the following year in prison. In June 1649, he was transferred to house arrest in Florence and won his liberty, on bail, in July.[79]

Recall that Attavanti's predecessor, Ottavio Cappelli, had acted "according to his whim" in regards to the quarantine. An identical abuse brought down Attavanti's career: doling out health licenses without authorization from his superiors. Captains and merchants paid bribes to Attavanti in exchange for special treatment; perhaps the reluctance of merchants to denounce him stemmed from their complicity. Certainly the health patent had a reputation for being a saleable commodity. A couple of decades later, as casual an observer as Samuel Pepys remarked in his diary that one could be purchased in Livorno for a piece of eight, and that quarantine regulations were a mere "cheat." According to Pepys, rumor had it that one could not only purchase an inexpensive health bill, but, for a rather steeper fee (ten pieces of eight), one could even deny a patent to one's enemy.[80]

The local institutional landscape aggravated abuses at the Health Board. The board was only peripherally related to the Customs Office's core activity of collecting revenue, since shortening the period in quarantine did not diminish fees.[81] Nor did distributing health patents threaten the Customs Office as an institution. If anything, relaxing the quarantine was yet another way to promote trade. In addition, oversight was weak and the risk of getting caught was low. Officials must have asked themselves before accepting a bribe: how likely was any particular good or mariner to be a carrier of plague? Merchants, for their part, viewed quarantine

non approvi, che si passi a più rigore, ma si lassi la libertà alla gente di fare le doglienze volendo." ASF, MP, 2167, f. 793, 06/14/1648, Domenico Puccini to Domenico Pandolfini; and on the merchants and Jews, ASF, MP, 2167, 06/13/1648, Domenico Puccini to Domenico Pandolfini; ASF, MP, 2167, f. 820, 06/22/1648, Domenico Puccini to Domenico Pandolfini.

78 "È ben vero che questo magistrato fa molte radunate, gran discorsi, e poche resoluzioni; pochi l'intendono, alcuni sono interessati per le mercanzie, il governatore sospettoso, l'auditore timoroso, a tal che Vostra Signoria Illustrissima può immaginarsi come passino le cose." ASF, MP, 2167, f. 863, 06/30/1648, Domenico Puccini to Domenico Pandolfini.

79 ASF, Sanità, 184, ff. 50, 79, 82, 166, 182.

80 *The Diary of Samuel Pepys*, ed. Wheatley, vol. 3, 352.

81 ASF, MP, 2166, ins. 6, 09/04/1648, Filippo Zannetti to Domenico Pandolfini.

as an expensive and pointless hassle. The push for rigor came entirely from the center. The Health Board of Florence sought—usually in vain, in this instance with some success—to exercise authority over its daughter institution in Livorno.

Other officials tolerated notorious abuses in the customs and the quarantine because they themselves were in on the act. Shortly before Attavanti's fall, in March 1648, the customs treasurer Tiberio Brandi fled to the Chiesa della Madonna when he learned that Puccini was on his way to investigate the finances of the Customs Office. Brandi owed seven thousand scudi to the grand duke: his large family and low pay had compelled him to dip into the till. The *auditore* Talentoni rightly predicted that the grand duke would show Brandi clemency, especially considering the high cost of living in Livorno.[82] Meanwhile, Puccini's hunt for testimony impressed the grand duke, who extended the investigator's remit that July to encompass abuses in the *bagno*. Puccini issued a notice for "every slave, whether Christian, Turk, or Moor, as well as every other minister or official of the galleys and *bagno*" to step forward to detail transgressions.[83] He unearthed plenty of evidence that tips, extortions, and other gifts were as common there as in the Customs Office.

Since so many officials were involved in fraud, they hesitated to inform on one another lest their own peccadilloes come to light. They did not so much accuse their colleagues as couch their criticism in rumor. For instance, *auditore* Lelio Talentoni heard the licensed tavern keepers complaining that some punters had illegally sold wine from their boats. One of these punters hailed from Attavanti's estate and was thought to be a client of the customs director. "But because they have not yet reappeared, I fear that the customs director has caught wind of the lament of the tavern keepers and sent word for them not to come back."[84] Talentoni was not assertive about getting to the heart of the matter and had no desire to antagonize Attavanti. Insinuation was the bureaucratic language of fraud par excellence because it was vague and not likely to be acted upon. It protected

[82] Brandi lost his job, but he avoided debtor's prison, found bondsmen to guarantee his debt, and obtained a reimbursement schedule of 500 scudi per year. Brandi (who had served for twenty-five years as treasurer) was hardly alone in his defalcations: Tuscan treasurers had free access to the till and were accountable for the money under their charge only when it was needed. The grand duke finally began to crack down on wayward treasurers with two laws in 1677 and 1681. See ASF, MP, 2167, f. 277, 03/11/1648 [AD], Pandolfo Tidi to Domenico Pandolfini; ibid., f. 281, Lelio Talentoni to Domenico Pandolfini; ibid., f. 288, 03/12/1648 [AD], Lelio Talentoni to Domenico Pandolfini; ibid., Alessandro Vettori to Domenico Pandolfini; ibid., 03/18/1648 [AD], Lelio Talentoni to Domenico Pandolfini; f. 295, 03/13/1648 [AD], Lelio Talentoni to Domenico Pandolfini; ASF, DG, 101, f. 467, 04/15/1648; f. 471, 04/22/1648, both Pandolfo Attavanti to Cosimo del Sera. Among Brandi's many supplications in ASL, Dogana, 3, see ins. 59, 03/08/1649 [AD]; for other examples, Waquet, *Corruption*, 38–42; Waquet, *Le Grand-Duché de Toscane*, 454–8, 462, 476–7; and Filippini, *Il porto di Livorno*, vol. 2, 320–1 and n. 11.

[83] "[S]i fa pubblicamente sapere a ciascuno huomo di ciurma tanto cristiano, che turco o moro, quanto a qualsivoglia altro ministro et ufficiale delle galere e bagno, che dopo la pubblicazione del presente bando, deva venire avanti detto delegato [Puccini] e palesare tutti gli aggravi, che ciascuno haverà ricevuto da detti Francesco Pepi e Marco Fabbroni." ASF, MP, 2168, ins. 1, 07/02/1648.

[84] "E trovai che dieci giorni avanti erano partiti con li fiaschi vuoti, per riempirli e ritornare prima della settimana santa; ma perché sino ad hora non sono comparsi, ho paura che il Signore Provveditore che ha penetrato la doglienza degli hosti, non gli habbia mandato ad avvisare e che non tornino." ASF, MP, 2167, f. 442, 04/08/1648, Lelio Talentoni to Domenico Pandolfini.

the complainer while not provoking a thorough inquiry.[85] Family ties among officials and the profits of intramural complicity further consolidated the "law of silence" that reigned in Livorno.[86]

Customs fraud was a price regimes everywhere paid in their effort to tax commerce. It was part of the structure of control that appeared alongside efforts to collect revenue and police customs boundaries. Corruption was especially intractable in Livorno. In part, fraud owed to the nature of the free port as a zone in which local duties and rules differed from those in Tuscany as a whole. Price differences made it profitable for merchants to smuggle into the hinterland goods purchased in Livorno. In addition, the free port's storage and transit incentives created a space for customs abuse by separating the moment of importation from the assessment of fees and the payment of dues. Lots of paperwork and inadequate manpower made it easy for goods to slip outside of regulations. The bureaucratic structure further compounded opportunities for fraud and complicity. Officials served long tenures and were poorly monitored by their supervisors in Florence. Nor were they encouraged to discharge their duties in an impersonal, regular, disinterested manner. A culture of laxity prevailed in Livorno to which merchants and officials alike subscribed. Rigor was bad for business and it was bad for the free port. This attitude did not create fraud per se, but it probably soothed guilty consciences by assuring officials that their illicit dealings did, in the end, also serve the grand duke.

The expansion of Livorno entailed the haphazard growth of the Customs Office and, with it, the capacity of officials to dispose of matters in the free port as they saw fit. But if weak central oversight made it possible for officials to create their private bailiwicks, they were hardly the only beneficiaries of the system. The merchants with whom they dealt also had many opportunities to cheat regulations, ranging from bribery in the quarantine to the illicit exchange of goods under pretext of the exemptions. These abuses earned Livorno a reputation as the most libertine of free ports. We should not exaggerate the fiscal ravages of corruption, however. Embezzlement probably amounted to around one percent of total revenues in the grand duchy.[87] Other kinds of fraud—bribery and smuggling—clearly promoted the port's commerce. By how much? It is impossible to say, but there is no doubt that lax administration gave Livorno an edge over its rivals in Italy.

CONCLUSION

The Customs Office deployed traditional means for administering the early free port. Its apparatus of control, inherited from the Middle Ages and codified in 1566, resembled that used elsewhere in the Ancien Régime. It attempted to corral

[85] Other examples of oblique accusations: ASF, DG, 71, f. 233, 06/13/1640, Giulio Bracciolini to Cosimo del Sera; ASF, MP, 2152, ins. 4, 10/19/1641, Pandolfo Attavanti to Alessandro Nomi.

[86] Waquet, *Corruption*, 108–13; Waquet, *Le Grand-Duché de Toscane*, 442–3, 465–6.

[87] Ibid., 476–7.

goods and merchants within a restricted space; appraise the value of wares; track dues owed over an extended period of time; and inspect goods periodically to ensure compliance. Derogations from ordinary customs procedures entailed a multiplication of paperwork: almost everywhere, licenses for certain goods like grain, and in Livorno, provisions for storage and transit. Just as free port policies evolved piecemeal during the early seventeenth century and with little central oversight, so too did the means of implementing policies evolve gradually and even opportunistically. New procedures, personnel, and policies hived onto current institutions rather than prompting the regime to survey the bureaucratic landscape anew. Contemporary economic thought did not invite such scrutiny, as we have seen, and the Medici bureaucracy delegated most decision making to local institutions.

The customs were traditional in style, but not in scope. The fiscal-military states of Europe had voracious appetites for customs revenue (for all kinds of revenue). Whether by using more manpower or more checkpoints, regimes intensified control whenever possible. Most states pursued programs of commercial and industrial expansion as well. The customs played a role of the utmost importance in these schemes, so much so that mercantilism is sometimes glossed as a system of import and export controls. Free port policies likewise manipulated the customs for commercial growth: in that sense, too, Livorno was of a piece with its epoch. The centrality of the customs to projects of economic expansion gave officials an important voice in the formulation of economic policy. Officials continued to collect taxes, as always, but they also curated trade statistics, negotiated with merchants, kept regimes informed about fluxes in trade and industry, and advised on changes in policy. The state's interventions in economic life transformed the customs house into a kind of regulatory body.

Despite its similarity to other customs administrations, the free port was distinguished by its provisions for the warehousing and transshipment of goods. For there were two approaches to free trade in early modern Europe: one based on the lowering of tariff levels, as in Amsterdam, and another based on the manipulation of tariff rules, as in Livorno. Lowering tariffs made simpler demands on customs officials, who needed to monitor only the entry and exit of merchandise. Incentives for the deposit and transit of goods entailed steeper transaction costs, since officials needed to supervise exchange as well; rules about provenance and destination further burdened oversight. The complexity of the early free port was not an impediment to its economic development, however. The customs almost everywhere were plagued by similar costs, but without corresponding benefits for the treatment of goods. At any rate, given systemic instability, foreign hospitality was more important than customs incentives for attracting commerce until the second half of the seventeenth century. The grand duke only sought to simplify procedures (and hence reduce transaction costs) when competition among neighboring ports threatened Livorno's commercial position.

The two paths to free trade throw into relief the fiscal choices that confronted early modern states. The Dutch excise was critical for raising revenue given the low level of customs duties: free trade came with high consumption taxes. By contrast, free ports such as Livorno created a cordon between the free zone and its hinterland, where import and export duties remained in place. So, free trade of either kind entailed a displacement of maritime duties—onto inland boundaries in the case of Livorno, or onto municipal bureaucracies in the case of Amsterdam. The imposition of an excise was politically costly in comparison to customs houses, even if its fiscal potential was higher. Contemporaries were amazed that Dutchmen were willing to pay such high consumption taxes. The profound legitimacy of the Dutch political regime probably made the excise palatable, but it also rendered Amsterdam's example difficult to imitate. Livorno offered a more appropriate paradigm for monarchs who were conscious of the political friction that an excise administration would cause.

Merchants were more concerned with the commercial than the political implications of free trade policies. From their perspective, the Amsterdam and Livorno models were functionally equivalent for most of the early modern period. This situation began to change with the unification of internal customs during the eighteenth century, and the growing exposure of inland areas to international commerce via better road networks and ultimately the railroad.[88] We associate Amsterdam with modern free trade because long-distance trade increasingly affected life in the hinterland by the late eighteenth century. Only when this "territorialization" of international commerce occurred did the economic differences between the two systems become fully apparent: the Amsterdam model became free trade pure and simple, with its market methods for allocating resources; while the free port became a kind of mercantilist device meant to control the impact of the international market on the hinterland economy. But both cities provided comparable templates of free trade during the long seventeenth century.

Locating free trade in a matrix of privileges and exemptions has important consequences for understanding the development of the marketplace. In emphasizing the rise of mercantilist policies such as navigation requirements and tariff barriers, historians have posited a radical break with the medieval past as the polities of Europe turned commerce into an "affair of state."[89] This procedure ends by ratifying Adam Smith's conception of the mercantilist system regardless of how many criticisms one directs at the coherence of mercantilist theory. It also implies that commodity markets emerged out of inter-state competition rather than economic fundamentals. In my view, the expansion of the marketplace was more important than mercantilist policy in shaping the course of European commerce. Increasingly complex customs rules emerged piecemeal out of medieval practices to accommodate the growth of trade: a less radical break with the past than histories of commerce typically envision. The process whereby Boccaccio's customs house transformed itself into the commodity market owed essentially to commercial realities—and to negotiations between merchants and the local officials who were called upon to tax their activities.

[88] See Braudel, *Civilization and Capitalism*, vol. 3, 289–92.
[89] Hont, *Jealousy of Trade*, 23.

5

Disembedding the Marketplace

In 1676, the grand duke eliminated taxes on imports and exports while imposing an elevated stallage tax, the fee paid to house goods in Livorno. Merchants paid the stallage only once and thereafter could store, trade, or re-export their wares without further bureaucratic oversight. Contemporaries were impressed. As the French traveler Jean-Baptiste Labat put it in the early eighteenth century: "Each parcel pays two piasters to enter, whether it contains silk or paper, whether it weighs one hundred pounds or fifteen hundred: it always pays the same duty." Livorno was therefore a place of "enormous parcels," where merchants carefully incorporated several packages into a single oversized bundle. Taxing by parcel moreover spared merchants "those annoying visits" that were so usual elsewhere in Europe. "You know exactly what you have to pay, you pay it, and you're done."[1] Labat was not quite correct. While goods were taxed according to a public tariff and by parcel rather than value, they did pay different rates. Luxury articles owed more than ordinary goods: following his example, silk paid six lire per bale, whereas paper paid only 1.5 lire. Nevertheless, the reader who remembers the mountains of paperwork that the old customs procedures generated will appreciate Labat's enthusiasm for the new system.[2]

The reform of 1676 marked a critical juncture in Tuscan political economy. Grand Duke Cosimo III (r. 1670–1723) ruled during an epoch of unprecedented commercial competition. Livorno, though well-positioned in Mediterranean trade, was not immune from this pressure. Stallage receipts from the free port declined by about eight percent during the period 1666–75 in comparison with the previous decade, signaling an infirmity in Livorno's role as international entrepôt; the crisis in commerce became undeniable after neighboring Marseille was itself made a free port in 1669.[3] Cosimo III sought to reinforce the entrepôt of Livorno while improving the economic condition of the grand duchy. He entrusted this task to his depositary general, Francesco Feroni. For the first time in Tuscan history, the state had something like a minister for the economy. Cosimo's reliance

[1] Labat, *Voyages*, vol. 2, 131–2. The Venetian consul in Livorno spoke of the new procedures in substantially similar terms: see G. Mori, "Linee e momenti," 14. The impression must have stuck with Labat, who remarked that Civitavecchia could replace Livorno's role in long-distance trade by emulating the free port's policies: see Toti, *Storia di Civitavecchia*, 196–7. Labat's account had an important role in transmitting the Livorno model of the free port to northern Europe: see Hovy, *Het voorstel van 1751*, 181.

[2] The complete tariff is reproduced in Filippini, *Il porto di Livorno*, vol. 1, 185–98.

[3] See "The Abolition of Tariffs" in this chapter.

on advisors such as Feroni signaled a new (and in some respects successful) effort for the regime to gain a firmer grip on the regulatory apparatus of the state.

Sandwiched between the Peace of Westphalia in 1648 and the onset of the First Anglo-Dutch War in 1652, 1650 is a good starting date for the age of commercial rivalry as an organizing perspective on European politics. Two corollaries of this new environment bore directly on the experience of Livorno. First was a heightened anxiety about the economic activities of foreigners or, more exactly, about the flow of wealth over which they presided: one legacy of the rise of national accounting. The regime's approach to the expansion of trade and industry involved a self-conscious reliance on Tuscan resources; Livorno was supposed to host a native merchant marine and an active commerce. A second and more subterranean process was the search for economic expertise. It was common during the sixteenth and early seventeenth centuries to rely on the advice of institutions such as customs houses, but by the second half of the seventeenth century European states began to experiment with more deliberate forms of securing counsel. Cosimo III's use of ministerial panels is one token of this change, as is the authority he granted to Francesco Feroni. Such novel forms of policymaking made it possible to restructure the free port despite the opposition of customs officials in Livorno.

Commercial rivalry often involved tariff barriers, navigation requirements, and the use of armed force. The story of the Atlantic world is told largely around the construction of closed and militarized colonial spheres, as well as the means by which merchant networks circumvented the pretensions of state control. In the central Mediterranean, however, the pursuit of commercial rivalry had the paradoxical effect of liberalizing long-distance trade. Numerous port cities, Livorno first of all, lowered tariff and non-tariff barriers to international commerce. It is therefore fruitful to locate European political economy as much in institutions for formulating policy as in the policies themselves, which varied widely—in the installation of more vigorous consular establishments, the proliferation of advisory boards, and the recruitment of economic ministers such as Feroni. These developments amounted to the institutionalization of political economy understood as a field of social action rather than a set of policies.

Even the free port of 1676, that quintessential act of Livorno exceptionalism, partook of common patterns of state development. European states were eager not only to increase their revenue and promote their commerce, but also to make their institutions more effective servants of the royal will. To gain administrative control over their territories, rulers set up new bodies to outflank older institutions (e.g. the *intendants* of France) or founded new loci of power (e.g. the excise office of England). These were intensive efforts at state control. The reform of 1676 exemplifies a different strategy: simplification. This option was well suited to states such as Tuscany, whose ruler lacked the means to pursue more intensive paths of state development. It was also a route that contemporaries hailed as especially conducive to commerce. The worship of simplicity was as common among the capitalists of yesteryear as it remains today. Ironically, when Chateaubriand denounced the "vulgar modernity" of customs checkpoints in 1850—one of the earliest contemporary usages of that term—he might just as accurately have taken the absence of inspections as a sign of modernity.[4]

The tariff of 1676 took its place alongside the Livornina as one of the sacred scriptures of the free port. But whereas the older legislation articulated the principle of foreign hospitality, the reform proclaimed new norms for the treatment of goods. The suppression of ordinary taxes spelled the end of particular incentives for the deposit and transit of merchandise; with their disappearance, the apparatus for regulating exchange within the city vanished. For individual merchants, the new dispensation eliminated many of the vexations characteristic of the pre-1676 customs regime (and which were common throughout Europe, as Labat reminds us). Yet at a broader level, the new tariff marked a bureaucratic withdrawal to the margins of the marketplace. Taxes were now levied at the moment in which goods arrived in port: the state disclaimed oversight of their transactional destiny unless goods passed into the Tuscan hinterland. This act might appear at first blush to be an indecent concession to foreign merchants, the defeat of the State at the hands of Capital. In fact, in both intent and outcome, the new customs regime protected the entrepôt of Livorno without compromising the economic integrity of the grand duchy.

OLD AMBITIONS AND NEW METHODS

Everywhere, projects and projectors. Neither was new to the European scene in the latter half of the seventeenth century—they were swarming around Italy a century earlier—but they now commanded an unprecedented amount of esteem and institutional power. Jean-Baptiste Colbert, French minister of finances from 1665 to his death in 1683, is emblematic of the new stature of economic projecting. He superintended port projects, industrial enterprises, trading companies, tax reforms, and a network for gathering statistics.[5] Contemporaries were impressed (and perturbed) by his activities, which they imitated whenever possible. It was a common belief that a state's viability amidst the rivalries of the international order depended on its commercial power. To paraphrase Clausewitz, trade was politics by other means. The first golden age of political economy was an era of unrelenting and increasingly global warfare.

Tuscany was not a major contender in these conflicts. Still, Cosimo III's projects for renewing the grand duchy's economy were at one with the age. His measures bear a superficial resemblance to those of Ferdinando I. Like his illustrious ancestor, Cosimo III promoted the sale of Florentine textiles via Livorno and sought to use the port to gain direct access to the Indies. His regime took steps to bind the city more tightly to its hinterland while fostering a native Tuscan elite there. But if

[4] Chateaubriand, *Mémoires d'outre-tombe*, 331.

[5] Soll, *The Information Master*, esp. 67–83; Wakefield, *The Disordered Police State*, *passim*. See "The Quickening of Medici Political Economy" in chapter 1, esp. n. 32.

Cosimo III tapped into long-standing goals of Medici political economy, he faced a different commercial environment than previous grand dukes and adopted a new approach to decision making. His style of leadership represented an effort to manage the nexus of interests that bedeviled policy in Livorno as elsewhere in the grand duchy.[6]

Generations of scholars have located the nadir of Tuscan history in Cosimo's reign. In their view, Cosimo was a religious bigot who surrounded himself with close relatives and presided over an economy that reached new lows of desperation. Recent research has begun to overturn this assessment. The economic outlook of his reign no longer appears as gloomy as it once did. The population of Tuscany, especially in rural areas, grew about twenty-five percent despite brief famines in 1678–9 and 1709–10. Low grain prices throughout the period underlay this growth. High wine prices meanwhile stimulated the planting of vineyards and inaugurated the wine exports for which Tuscany is famous today. In addition, just as the commerce of Livorno began to stagnate, the reform of 1676 launched a bout of expansion that lasted for forty years. The grand duke worked hard to ensure that Tuscany rode the tide of renewed prosperity—a prosperity of which, in fact, his government seems to have been unaware.[7]

The regime pursued a series of plans for reforming state institutions. These included reworking the flour tax (1671 and 1678) and remodeling both the Office of Plenty (1671) and the Victual Office (1681).[8] Livorno's reform of 1676 was a similarly far-reaching measure, and it was followed in 1678 by a reassessment of the Wool Guild of Florence, which had long exerted an outsized influence on Tuscan policy.[9] A privy secretary captured the conservative spirit of these reforms when he called for "a general visit to all magistracies with the object of investigating and discovering exactly if any defect or abuse has appeared that compromises justice and hurts the poor."[10] The regime modified the old laws of Tuscany to create a more efficient and just state, but it did not desire to recast society on new foundations.

Cosimo III entrusted these initiatives to a team of ministers working in concert. He did not operate through the individual secretaries, bureaucratic pathways, and traditional magistracies that had dominated the policy process after the death of his grandfather, Cosimo II (1621). The grand dukes had occasionally relied on policymaking-by-panel, but Cosimo III's general reliance on such *congregazioni*

[6] My interpretation differs from that of Baruchello, who (like most scholars until recently) sees Cosimo III's reign as one of stasis and traces efforts to promote commerce with the hinterland to the reign of Francis Stephen. Baruchello, *Livorno e il suo porto*, 448–51; and "Livorno and its Hinterlands" in chapter 6.

[7] Malanima, "L'economia Toscana nell'età di Cosimo III"; Pult Quaglia, "Politica annonaria e congiuntura economica"; and Pult Quaglia, *"Per provvedere ai popoli,"* 226–35. On efforts to promote Tuscan wine abroad, see ASF, MM, 368, ff. 1–185 and ibid., 369, ins. 1.

[8] Contini, "La riforma della tassa delle farine." Many of the Office of Plenty reformers were involved in other panels: Ascanio Sanminiati, Carlo Torrigiani, Alamanno Arrighi, Orazio Marucelli, Niccolò Martelli, and Francesco Tempi.

[9] Martelli, "'Nec spes nec metus,'" 151–2.

[10] ASF, Regio Diritto, 6036, 09/23/1675, Francesco Panciatichi to Ferrante Capponi, quoted by Verga, "Appunti per una storia politica," 340.

(advisory committees) marks a novel departure in Tuscan history. Two figures stand out from Cosimo's inner circle for their attention to commerce in Livorno: Ferrante Capponi and Francesco Feroni. Their aims, habits of thought, and ability (sometimes inability) to collaborate conditioned policymaking for the next two decades.[11]

Francesco Feroni (1614–92) was the son of a modest dyer of Empoli. He died as the Marquis of Bellavista and depositary general of Tuscany, the grand duchy's highest financial officer, having made his fortune through "sweat, hard work, and great effort . . . without the support or help of anybody."[12] He built his fortune investing in grain and slaves over the course of nearly three decades in Amsterdam. He was an attentive observer of the French, Dutch, and English scenes and played a role in defending the neutrality of Livorno during the First Anglo-Dutch War (1652–4). When prince Cosimo passed through Amsterdam on his grand tour in 1667 and again in 1669, he stayed in Feroni's home and was impressed by the merchant's energy and vision. Upon becoming grand duke the following year, Cosimo entreated Feroni to return to Tuscany to assume the position of depositary general; after much wrangling over issues of social status, the businessman finally agreed. This man, who had a reputation for being a "terrible" and "most subtle and quibbling" person, was Tuscany's most acute analyst of international trade.

Feroni returned to Tuscany with infinite admiration for English and Dutch political economy, measured respect for Jean-Baptiste Colbert, and withering disdain for Florence. At least three overarching goals informed his thinking. Feroni wanted to market more competitive textiles by lowering manufacturing costs while maintaining quality. He believed higher grain prices and lower wages could make "lazy" Florentine artisans more industrious. Secondly, manufactures (and money if necessary) would serve to buy raw materials such as wool. Finally, Florentines would sell textile products abroad by establishing commercial houses in such nerve centers of trade as Cadiz and Izmir. To this end he proposed a Florentine Indies Company to be based jointly in Lisbon and Livorno. Feroni was the first Tuscan policymaker of importance to ground his plans for commercial expansion on agricultural prices and wages: an unusually coherent vision of the economic process. Since he never wrote a treatise expounding his ideas, which he always deployed discursively to support his policy positions, I will examine them as occasion requires.[13]

[11] C. Vivoli, "I lavori pubblici sotto Cosimo III"; Martelli, "'Nec Spes Nec Metus,'" 143–4. There was also a "Congregazione di Livorno" that included Feroni, Capponi, and the *auditore della Camera granducale*, although this congregation does not appear to have corresponded to an institutional reality. See Baruchello, *Livorno e il suo porto*, 421 and Aglietti, *I governatori di Livorno*, 85–6. The loftiest affairs of state, such as diplomacy and nominations to office, continued to be directed by the council established by Ferdinando II. The council declined in the 1670s as a result of the death of important members between 1675 and 1680, such as Cardinal Leopoldo, Gabriello Riccardi, and Ferdinando Bardi.

[12] ASF, MP, 4260, ff. 382–385, 05/24/1668, Francesco Feroni to Apollonio Bassetti, quoted by Cools, "Francesco Feroni," 355. See Benigni, "Francesco Feroni"; and Morviducci, "Lo scontro anglo-olandese." Feroni's arrival in Amsterdam coincided with the second wave of Italian immigration there. Lesger, "Clusters of Achievement"; Bicci, "Immigration and Acculturation."

[13] Benigni, "Francesco Feroni," 176.

Ferrante Capponi (1611–89) also helped direct Cosimo III's political economy. He belonged to a prestigious if not especially wealthy branch of the Capponi clan. A jurist by profession, he served as *auditore di Livorno* early in his career and thereafter took a supervisory interest in that tribunal. He accumulated several high-profile offices under Ferdinando II, including *auditore* of the Order of St. Stephen, and became Cosimo III's chief legal expert. Although he did not write as loquaciously about his commercial ideas as Feroni, he was conversant with contemporary business law and, judging by the personal fortune he built, more than a little familiar with the practical side of business. If Feroni's letters are alive with his boisterous personality, Capponi is almost invisible behind the poise of an impeccable courtier. It is no wonder that the nobleman-lawyer often clashed with the commoner-merchant over matters both substantive and incidental. In intra-regime conflicts, Capponi served as the representative of the traditional elite against the upstart Feroni.[14]

A new silk shop marked Feroni's first efforts to revitalize Florentine industry. The depositary general developed a plan in collaboration with Capponi to open a silk manufactory with a capital of 21,000 scudi and the promise of further financing down the road. Under Capponi's tutelage, the Order of St. Stephen contributed 14,000 scudi in order to invest something of the vast patrimony it had accumulated over the previous century. Feroni furnished the rest. They intended for the shop to serve as a model for Florentine industry, and according to their calculations, it was supposed to provide work for some seven hundred Florentine laborers. The depositary general imported cloth samples from Spain and Florence for exemplars: superfine ribbons, taffeta, rashes, and other light silks.[15]

The shop ran into immediate difficulties that reveal the limits of regime consensus. It turned out that the shop supervisor, Balestri, was impoverished and had exaggerated his experience in the silk business. Capponi and Feroni agreed that it was best to find a companion for Balestri who had some capital of his own to assure his honesty and hard work. The search for a second manager exposed friction between the two ministers that Feroni turned into an attack against Florentine merchants. "I cannot agree with the suspicious and timid dealings of these men," Feroni complained. "I have entrusted tens of thousands of scudi to people much inferior to Balestri, such as ship captains or supercargoes, who own nothing but what they travel with. I have always been treated well by them, although it's true that I always

[14] Capponi was steeped in commercial jurisprudence. Through his ties to the Roman jurist Cardinal Giovanni Battista de Luca (1614–83), he encountered contemporary utilitarian and contractarian ideas. In addition, the cardinal's secretary, Ansaldo Ansaldi (1651–1719), was a former apprentice of Capponi's and the future author of an important handbook of commercial law. Ansaldi, *De commercio et mercatura*; Lauro, *Il cardinale Giovan Battista de Luca*.

[15] ASF, MP, 1744, ins. 1, 11/17/1673, Ferrante Capponi to Francesco Panciatichi. Before his return to Tuscany, Feroni helped the ducal envoy Cosimo Ciferi spy on the methods of wool production practiced in Holland, England, and northwest France. He also tried to found commercial houses before his return and railed against the Tuscan bureaucracy. ASF, MP, 4261, n. 347, 01/08/1672, Francesco Feroni to Apollonio Bassetti; Benigni, "Francesco Feroni," 175. Ciferi's expedition foreshadowed the industrial espionage of Pietro Guerrini in the 1680s. See Martelli, ed. *Viaggio in Europa di Pietro Guerrini*; and Cipolla, *Before the Industrial Revolution*, 156.

paid them well. But here people are suspicious of everything and want to pay little."[16] Feroni exploited a small dispute over business to attack the "suspicious" and "timid" habits of Florentine capitalism. It was one of his favorite critiques.

The silk venture's second problem concerned its profitability as an enterprise. The shop was running higher than expected costs, which Feroni attributed to high wages. According to his diagnosis, the root of the problem was low agricultural prices and lazy workers, who could earn their living by a modicum of work. Feroni proposed lowering real wages by increasing the price of food. That would induce the labor force to work harder and enable manufacturers to produce more cheaply. Feroni appealed to the example of Dutch workers: "I myself saw in Leiden that it costs much less to press wool and turn it into cloth than it does here, and the cost of living is higher than here. But that nation works incessantly all day long, eating while they work, and only returns home at night. From their assiduity they do more work and earn more than these [Florentines], who only want to work half the day."[17] In this letter to a privy secretary, Feroni asked the regime to abandon its long-standing commitment to providing the Florentine poor with cheap provisions. A few months later he advocated putting a "fat tariff" on foreign victuals. His views were politically incorrect to the extreme. "One should not attribute this argument to me," he told the secretary, "because it would serve as a pretext for the spiteful to incite the plebes against me."[18] He was incensed when the shop failed to produce the one hundred taffetas he had scheduled for Cadiz and again fulminated against Florentine labor. This time he advocated hiring "castigators" to literally beat the artisans into working harder.

The fate of Balestri's shop is not known for certain, but it probably did not leave him a ruined man. In 1688 he received a twelve-year patent for a new type of cloth press. In addition, the Order of St. Stephen continued to invest substantial sums in textile companies alongside private investors throughout the 1670s and early 1680s.[19] While wool production in Florence continued its terminal decline, silk

[16] "Del rimanente io non posso accordare la mia natura con questi sospettosi e timorosi trattati di questi signori, avendo io fidato le decime di migliaia di scudi a persone molto più inferiore del Balestri, come sono stati i capitani e sopraccarichi delle navi, che non havevano altro, solo quello che seco conducevano per mare, e posso dire havere da tutti ricevuto buon conto, vero è che anco ho la loro provvisione bene pagata, ma qui sospettiamo di tutti, e si vuole dare poco." ASF, MP, 1523, ff. 251–255, 11/24/1673, Francesco Feroni to Apollonio Bassetti. Interestingly, Capponi initially attributed suspicion of Balestri to Feroni himself: ASF, MP, 1744, ins. 1, 11/17/1673.

[17] "Ho reconosciuto che in Leida si spende molto meno nel mangolare la lana e ridurla in panno, di quello si fa qua, e pur il vivere è più caro di qui; ma come travaglia quella nazione incessantemente tutte il giorno facendo il suo denaro sopra il lavoro, e solo la sera tornando a casa. Da questa loro assiduità ne succede col far più lavoro, guadagnano da vantaggio di questi, che solo la metà del giorno vogliono travagliare." ASF, MP, 1523, ff. 282–84, 12/13/1673, Francesco Feroni to Apollonio Bassetti. Concern about the relationship between wages and industriousness was typical of the age, in Italy and elsewhere. Sella, "The Rise and Fall of the Venetian Woollen Industry," 120–1; Hont, *Jealousy of Trade*, 59–62, 246–58.

[18] "Che questa sia mia speculazione non deve dirsi, poiché servirebbe di pretesto a maligni per incitare la plebe contro di me, come con difficultà non reconosce il suo bene, prende in mala parte quello che in suo benefizio si opera." ASF, MP, 1523, ff. 282–284, 12/13/1673, Francesco Feroni to Apollonio Bassetti.

[19] ASF, PS, 194, f. 59; ASF, *Tribunale di Mercanzia*, 10846, f. 161; ibid., 10847, ff. 136–137, 164–165; ibid., 10848, ff. 93, 111. See Martelli, "'Nec Spes Nec Metus,'" 149.

production leapt from an annual output of around ten thousand cloths at the middle of the seventeenth century to about eighteen thousand by the time of Cosimo III's death in 1723.[20] The regime's efforts to revitalize industry in Florence therefore met with some success. One anonymous Englishman remarked around 1678 that the Florentines "are in reality a very honest and fair dealing sorte of people," and he praised their reliability in comparison to Bolognese manufacturers.[21] Feroni's verdict on Florentine merchants and artisans was certainly too harsh.

Feroni also sought to increase the presence of Florentine capital in the Mediterranean. As he put it, "without taking risks we're not going to earn any profits; we're always going to remain little fish unless we leave the Arno."[22] The outbreak of the Third Anglo-Dutch War (1672–4) was an opportune time to expand the commercial services offered by the neutral Florentines. In the early 1670s, he himself opened operations in Livorno, Cadiz, and Messina; for these ventures he partnered with other members of the Florentine merchant elite.[23] The partnerships did not go off without a snag. It was difficult to find a qualified Florentine for the post in Messina. The only one reputed capable of the task did not want to leave Tuscany, prompting Feroni to lament the sorry state to which the former mercantile powerhouse had been reduced. To supply the deficiency, the depositary general parted with one of his own apprentices, "a young man of excellent accounting ability, who has facility with four languages, and who is most apt for managing correspondence."[24] Although Feroni continued to mock the abilities of Florentine merchants, the regime's efforts bore fruit in the launching of new ventures abroad. Tuscans maintained operations in Amsterdam, Marseilles, Lyons, Madrid, Lisbon, London, Cadiz, Seville, and Smyrna.

With commercial and industrial ambitions reignited, the old dream of using Livorno as the base for a trading company resurfaced in regime circles. The latest incarnation of this project was a Portuguese-Tuscan corporation modeled after the English East India Company. The Florentines proposed that the company raise a capital of 1,800,000 ducats through publicly tradable shares. Company ships would have a monopoly over the trade in coral, based in Livorno, as well as the colonial products of the Indies, including spices, saltpeter, tobacco, brazilwood, and sugar. Any merchant wishing to participate in the trades that bound Livorno

20 Malanima, *Decadenza*, 295, 314–16.

21 Quoted by Poni, *La seta in Italia*, 105.

22 "Mio Signore, senza risicare non si può guadagnare; si resterà sempre pesciolini se non ci partiamo dal'Arno." ASF, MP, 4261, n. 400, 07/15/1672, Francesco Feroni to Apollonio Bassetti.

23 Including members of the Guadagni, Rinuccini, Riccardi, and Del Rosso families. These last two were contacts Feroni had first secured while in Amsterdam. For Cadiz, see ibid., n. 374, 04/15/1672; ASF, MP, 1523, ff. 230–232, 11/13/1673; ibid., ff. 251–255, 11/24/1673; ibid., ff. 309–310, 02/08/1674; ibid., ff. 322–323, 03/03/1674. For Messina see ibid., ff. 230–232, 11/13/1673; ibid., ff. 246–247, 11/20/1673; ibid., ff. 251–255, 11/24/1673.

24 "[A] tale segno è ridotta la città di Firenze di non havere una persona capace di governare il negozio. Io sono per preporgli un giovane buonissimo scritturale, chi ha quattro lingue franche, e puole tenere tutta la corrispondenza delle lettere essendone capacissimo." ASF, MP, 1523, ff. 246–247, 11/20/1673, Francesco Feroni to Apollonio Bassetti. For ventures abroad, see ASF, Carte Strozziane, I serie, 106, ff. 150–153, 1672; Malanima, "I commerci del mondo."

and Lisbon to the Indies would have to rent space aboard company ships. In effect, the company would function as a para-governmental organization connected to the Portuguese and Tuscan crowns. The Genoese were expected to be financial backers of this project and may have been angling for their own monopoly. The specter of competition with Genoa pervaded Tuscan discussions of the project.[25]

When the counter-proposals of the Portuguese king reached Tuscany in July 1674, the Tuscan response was guarded. Feroni sounded out the opinions of the commercial elite. Francesco Tempi, one of Livorno's richest traders, came out clear against the proposal. After confessing himself "stunned" by the amount of money needed for the company, he wanted to know what contribution was expected from the merchants of Livorno. Few people wanted to invest in such risky and distant ventures, tying up money for years while their Genoese creditors merely collected interest. Investing money in such an enterprise was like "sowing seeds in barren ground." The Tuscans would end up subsidizing the commerce of the Portuguese without any benefit to the state, since Tuscan products had little market in the Indies—as was the general predicament of European traders in the East. Without the prospect of selling Tuscan goods, the proposal was "not even worth thinking about." In any case, Tempi doubted that anybody in Lisbon or Florence had the experience to succeed in the venture. Instead, he suggested that the Tuscans ask the Portuguese king for permission to send only one ship to the Indies, with the normal convoy, along with a few trusted people who would learn how to manage such grand affairs. This approach would spare investors from pouring their money into such an elaborate venture all at once, and would allow the business to develop in stages.[26]

Tempi's peers shared his concerns about markets for Tuscan goods and the viability of native business skills. In early October, several Florentines gathered in a private home to discuss the proposal and draft a response to send to Lisbon. The roster was chosen with care. As the chief legal and financial experts of the grand duchy, Ferrante Capponi and Francesco Feroni were responsible for coordinating discussions. Francesco Tempi attended because of his stature in Livorno. Other members were invited because of their longstanding business ties to Portugal.[27] With the exception of Feroni, all participants in the meeting belonged to illustrious Florentine lineages. Their deliberations led to a broader reflection on the Tuscan dependence on foreign shipping. The men agreed that demand for Tuscan products was weak in the Indies, and that they would have to avail themselves of the money and goods of foreigners to bring off the venture. In order to be profitable the Tuscans needed permission for ships to sail directly from Livorno to Goa, without having to pass through Lisbon. Unfortunately, "the want of national mariners and reliable agents" made it difficult to establish native shipping in

[25] ASF, Auditore dei Benefici, 5686, proposed contract for trade with the Indies. See Baruchello, *Livorno*, 436–7; Zamora Rodríguez, "Privato versus pubblico," 51.

[26] ASF, Auditore dei Benefici, 5686, 07/29/1676, Francesco Tempi to the grand duke.

[27] The meeting included Francesco Feroni, Ferrante Capponi, Senator Buonaccorsi, and members from the Bracci, Scarlatti, Torrigiani, Marucelli, and Manetti clans. See ASF, Auditore dei Benefici, 5686, undated memorandum, presumably by Ferrante Capponi.

Livorno. Tuscan merchants had no choice but to employ foreigners if they wanted to send ships to the East. Relying on the Baltic nations was risky because of problems of trust and physical security. The stronger nations—the Dutch, English, and French—were impossible options because of their monopolistic policies. When it came to navigation, Livorno was no Venice or Genoa, and neither of those places could compete autonomously in the Indies.[28]

By the early 1670s, the Tuscan merchant elite had reached an accurate understanding of the relationship between maritime power and colonial commerce. There was no way for Tuscany to participate in the Indies trade on competitive terms. The grand duke did not confront this problem haphazardly, through a system of patronage that linked ducal secretaries to particular agents or officials, as in the early seventeenth century. Instead, he called upon a panel of experts to coordinate opinions based on their experience and social status (with all that such status implied for mobilizing capital and personnel). This procedure had long been used to develop monetary policy during moments of crisis or to reform guild regulations, city privileges, and magistracies. But under the superintendence of Feroni and Capponi it was used to develop commercial and industrial plans for Tuscany as a whole. Alongside the secretaries who made decisions, the officials who lobbied for them, and the individuals who developed proposals, now stood supervisors with some claim to expertise.

Feroni, like some of his contemporaries, was attentive to who could legitimately participate in policy discussions. He complained that courtiers did not know the first thing about commerce. While waiting in an antechamber before an audience with the grand duke, he declared that "a courtier cannot be a good merchant, nor the latter a courtier, since the two men are of a different profession."[29] What sparked Feroni's observation was a dispute earlier that day in the Mercato Nuovo, in which a "man of substance" dismissed worries that bills of exchange were being filled in Livorno rather than Florence. The courtier believed that as long as Livorno belonged to the grand duke, it did not matter where the banking was taking place. As a merchant, Feroni could not refrain from explaining that currency was hemorrhaging out of Livorno because "seven-eighths" of the port's merchants were foreigners who brought their profits home to their native countries. Feroni often vented his frustration against the hordes of courtiers he found in Florence and lauded courts that prized merchants over the "useless nobility."[30]

Nevertheless, Feroni did not believe merchants alone ought to make policy. His views on good government and his ambivalence about merchant expertise are best captured by his analysis of Jean-Baptiste Colbert. He criticized Colbert for forcing

[28] ASF, Auditore di Benefici, 5686, 10/08/1674, meeting minutes. See ASF, *Carte Strozziane*, I serie, 106, ff. 165–168; ASF, MP, 4260, ff. 382–385, 05/24/1668, Francesco Feroni to Apollonio Bassetti; Benigni, "Francesco Feroni," 502–3.

[29] "[G]li dissi che un cortigiano non poteva farsi buon mercante, né questo cortigiano, perché ambi sono di professione contraria, né potrebbono bene operare se facessero l'uno, la professione del'altro." ASF, MP, 1523, ff. 309–310, 02/08/1674 [1673 ab inc.], Francesco Feroni to Apollonio Bassetti.

[30] ASF, MP, 4261, n. 216, 10/03/1670, Francesco Feroni to Apollonio Bassetti, quoted by Benigni, "Francesco Feroni, Empolese," 509. "Seven-eighths" was an exaggeration; the real figure was about a third.

nobles and citizens to invest in his India companies, which "out of his pure fantasy" he expected would win France the better part of global trade. Instead, Colbert had plunged his nation into commercial wars that had bankrupted the treasury.[31] The highly partial advice of merchants had led Colbert to embark on such a disastrous course. For Feroni, Colbert's folly served as a warning to princes accustomed to taking counsel from merchants. Blinded by their own self-interest, merchants unwittingly led rulers into catastrophe. Nor did Feroni trust the bureaucracies to fulfill their own duties honestly, let alone supervise commerce and industry.[32] The best policies were those advocated by divine wisdom: "May god plant in the mind of the Most Serene Grand Duke new rules of government to save this city and his state from the incredible misery that comes from regarding the interest of individuals and not that of the public."[33] God may or may not have instilled wise policies in the brain of the devout Cosimo III: what is certain is that the grand duke entrusted decisions to ministerial panels that sought to minimize the impact of individual interests on policy. They analyzed the Tuscan economy more systematically than was normal in bureaucratic or secretarial networks.

Two features distinguish Feroni's approach to economic life from that of his predecessors. The structuring of incentives was central to Feroni's manipulation of economic life. He eschewed cultural explanations of the nature of workmen in Florence in favor of economic rationales: low wages made for industrious laborers. Likewise, he applied managerial principles to the treatment of the silk workshop, as indeed merchants had done since the Middle Ages. In analyzing the Lisbon project, he recognized not only the need for proper training of maritime personnel, but above all, that state-supported enterprises must satisfy the profit and risk requirements of merchants. These moves were a hallmark of economic thought in the period, which began to treat economic life as a gigantic system of incentives and disincentives.[34]

In addition, Feroni visualized the economic space as bounded by states competing with one another over wages, shipping, industry, and so forth. Individuals, whether worker or merchant, belonged to a single state, upon whose ledger their activities redounded. Gone was a belief, central to the experience of Livorno in an earlier epoch, that individuals might at once be a servant of the grand duke while remaining English or Dutch. "Foreign" had become a category that did not admit of overlap with one's own economic or political spheres. When an English merchant settled in Livorno, he and his commerce remained English. Such at least was

[31] ASF, MP, 1523, ff. 266–69, 12/05/1673, Francesco Feroni to Apollonio Bassetti.

[32] Ibid., ff. 345–46, 03/25/1674, Francesco Feroni to Apollonio Bassetti.

[33] "Iddio faccia concepire nella mente del Serenissima Gran Duca nuove regole di governo per sollevare questa città e suo stato dalle miserie miserabili che si vanno preparando, tutto quello viene fatto riguarda al interesse particolare e non al pubblico." ASF, MP, 1523, ff. 327–330, 03/06/1673, Francesco Feroni to Apollonio Bassetti.

[34] The calculations performed by the regime resembled those long practiced by individual merchants (Dahl, *Trade, Trust, and Networks*, esp. 211). Of course, Sassetti himself had seen incentives as central to attracting trade in his 1577 *Treatise*, but the microanalytic approach became quite common by the late seventeenth century.

the theory: in practice, foreign merchants in Livorno developed ties to the local community that analysts such as Feroni ignored.[35]

For Tuscany, the most significant departure did not lie in the realm of commercial theory, however, but in Cosimo III's attempt to find new channels for managing his projects. His experiment in policymaking did not quite revolutionize the policy process in Tuscany. It was too closely linked to the personalities of Capponi and Feroni to survive their deaths in 1689 and 1692, respectively. Nevertheless, the embodiment of political economy in a couple of top ministers was typical of the era. Their activities were part of a European-wide effort to institutionalize the making of economic policy. In the early seventeenth century, the interventionist program articulated by Giovanni Botero ran up against the pathetic limitations of state power. New institutions (or roles, in the case of Feroni) represented an effort to utilize state resources more effectively, to make projects more successful by better matching means to ends.

THE ABOLITION OF TARIFFS

From the moment the regime redoubled its efforts to promote Florentine industry and trade, it immediately encountered the weakness of Tuscany vis-à-vis foreign mercantile interests. We have already seen Feroni lamenting that most of Livorno's trade was in the hands of aliens and fretting about the competitiveness of Florentine textiles. He also despaired of establishing a native merchant marine in the face of Dutch, English, and French competition. And yet, Feroni and his allies authorized the reform of 1676, which eliminated tariffs and confirmed Livorno's status as a port open to foreign nations. The paradox is why a regime conscious of its weakness would extend privileges that appeared to benefit outsiders at its own expense. Why would an arch-mercantilist like Feroni confirm the ascendancy of foreigners in a Tuscan port?

Three explanations shed light on Feroni's actions. The most important factor was the 1669 declaration establishing a free port in Marseille. It was not so much the bargaining power of foreign communities in Livorno as the threat posed by the loss of French commerce that explains the timing of the new legislation. But it is also worth observing that the reform of 1676 entailed simplified rules rather than a mere lowering of customs duties. The new tariff owed to Feroni's commitment to streamlining revenue collection on grounds of good governance, not just the remorseless pressures of commercial competition. And lastly, while the stature of foreign merchants in Livorno was increasingly seen as a problem, Feroni did not believe that the extension of the free port would necessarily compromise the grand duchy's commercial power. The reform was accompanied by measures to create a native mercantile elite and thicken linkages between Livorno and its hinterland.

[35] This is evident for example from the funerary monuments that Englishmen constructed in Livorno: see Lille, "Under all the eyes of the Christian world"; see too "An Expanding Port in a Time of Crisis" in chapter 2.

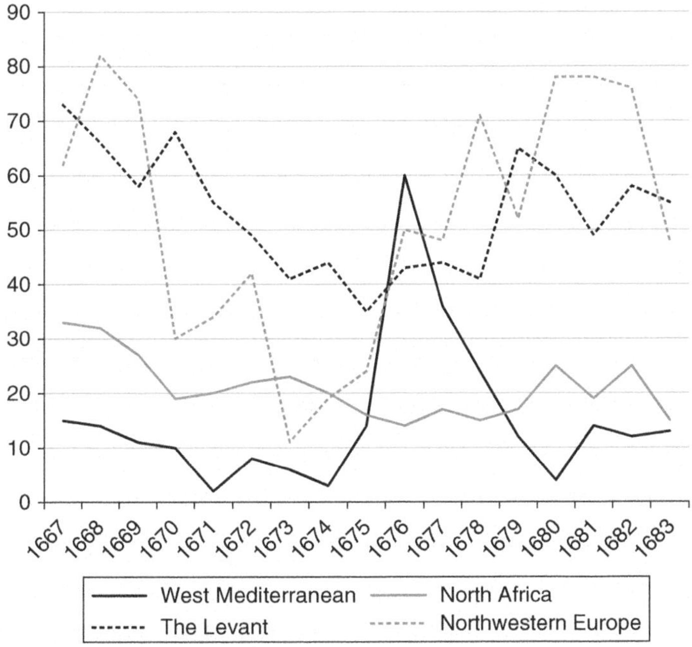

Fig. 5.1. Long-distance ship arrivals in Livorno, 1667–83.
Note: For my methods for reconstructing the shipping curve, see app. 12.
Source: ASL, Sanità, 67, 68, 69, and 71.

The 1669 declaration making Marseilles into a free port had swift repercussions for Livorno. The French consul remarked, "as to French commerce in this city, it is very thin, since after Marseilles became a free port, we stopped sending our Levantine merchandise there; one doesn't conduct half the business that one used to before, and we do not send half the French ships we used to."[36] The statistics bear out the consul's analysis. Long-distance shipping declined by thirty-one percent in the five years after 1669 (Fig. 5.1 and Table 5.1); losses were especially catastrophic in regards to shipping from Spain and northwestern Europe, which declined by seventy-seven percent. Revenue indicators also show a decline during these years: for instance, the stallage, the most important index of long-distance shipping, declined by twelve percent in the seven years following 1669. The free port of Marseilles struck directly at Livorno's role in the deposit-and-transit trade between East and West, probably by sapping French use of the port.[37]

[36] Letter by Pierre Cotolendy to the French Secretary of Maritime Affairs, 08/21/1671, as quoted by Filippini, *Il porto di Livorno*, v. 2, 157. On the free port of Marseilles, see n. 82 in chapter 6; and "The Spread of Free Ports" and "A Complex Institution" in chapter 8.

[37] Despite a crisis in long-distance trade, regional commerce in the port was unaffected. The anchorage tax, which reflected local as well as long-distance shipping, actually increased slightly in this period, by three percent. In addition, taxes on victuals such as wine, grain, and oil—the preeminent goods of local trade—showed no signs of crisis (some were even growing). Such commerce was more

Table 5.1. Commercial indicators, 1665–74

	Long-distance ship arrivals	Ordinary rev. (lire)	Anchorage rev. (lire)	Stallage rev. (lire)	Extraordinary rev. (lire)	Victual rev. (lire)
1665–9	802	748,545	85,735	362,237	815,579	353,255
1670–4	551	800,748	88,511	318,915	775,053	352,559
% Change	-31%	7%	3%	-12%	-5%	0%

Source: apps 9 and 12.

The French effort to divert trade away from Livorno points to the intensification of commercial competition throughout the Mediterranean. Another token of this rivalry was the development of a stronger consular regime. Because the size of the merchant community had expanded so much, Tuscan ministers were finding it increasingly difficult to negotiate individually with merchants as they had done at the beginning of the seventeenth century. Consuls or their deputies now served as officials' points of contact, and these consuls were bound more closely to their metropoles than in earlier decades. Without exaggerating the unity of aims among merchants—after all, Englishmen in Livorno were in competition with one another—the new consular situation enabled foreign communities to present a more unified front in their negotiations with the regime. Merchants no longer phrased requests solely in terms of a particular merchant's interests. Consuls involved themselves in the supplications of their co-nationals even when requests did not touch upon community affairs.[38]

An index of the transformation of merchant-regime relations in Livorno is the diminished vitality of supplications to the Governor's Office. In the early part of the century, the governor had spent much of his time negotiating with merchants and handled a variety of cases; only sixteen percent of his cases were categorized as judicial. This figure climbed to about forty-five percent during the 1640s. By 1680–2, most of the supplications he heard (sixty percent) were judicial in nature (Fig. 5.2). They were also less likely to involve commerce than in the early period. A typical example was a Jewish widow named Benvenuta Sacerdote who had carnal relations with another Jew and was imprisoned for some time. She claimed that she was seduced; the Jewish community, in a long memorandum, contended that she had lived a scandalous life and wanted both her and her lover exiled. In the end, the grand duke let her languish in prison while her court case proceeded in the ordinary tribunals.[39] The system of supplications had returned to its original function of overturning or appealing court cases. The rate of supplication approval also declined to only thirty percent, suggesting that pre-selection was less important than at the beginning of the century.[40] There is no doubt that the

closely related to the underlying economic realities of the region than with the commerce of deposit and transit. See "Regional Exchange between Land and Sea" in chapter 6.

[38] Calafat, "Être étranger dans un port franc," 119–22; see n. 36 in chapter 2, and "Making Policy by Supplication" in chapter 3.

[39] ASL, GCM, 2608, ff. 416–417.

[40] Out of thirty cases with known resolutions, only nine were approved.

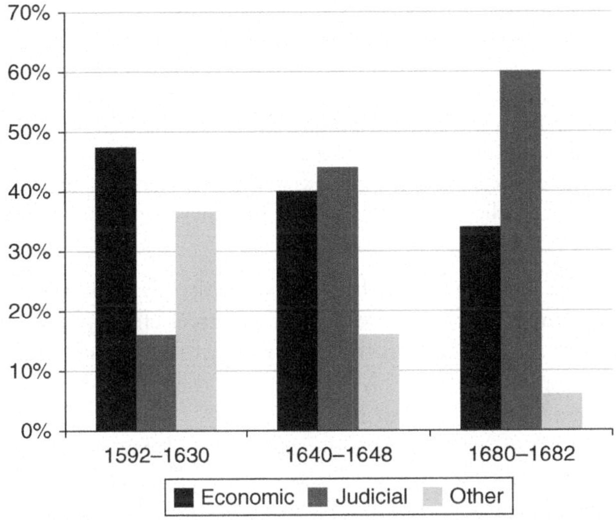

Fig. 5.2. Supplications to the Governor's Office by type, 1592–1682.
Source: ASL, CGA, 2602; ASL, CGA, 2603; ASL, CGA, 2608; see chapter 3, n. 43.

Governor's Office continued to grow more powerful during this period. Rather, this trend indicates that the locus of negotiations had shifted away from supplications and toward more structured interactions with the consuls of foreign communities.

The stronger consular regime, linked to the tightening of national boundaries in Livorno, contributed to a new fear of foreign domination. Anger at aliens had even penetrated the Customs Office, long the most stalwart ally of foreign merchants in the city. Although customs officials continued to furnish the quarantine favors that had ended Attavanti's career, it had grown pricklier in other respects.[41] For instance, the merchant Robert Balle complained, on behalf of the English nation, of the unwonted "fervor" the customs accountant had used in exacting fines for unpaid herring accounts from the annual survey. The English found support against this "extravagance" in the ducal secretary Ferdinando Bardi, who ordered the accountant to treat merchants with the customary indulgence.[42]

As customs director, Camillo Capponi undoubtedly condoned the greater rigor. A relative of Ferrante Capponi and later his adopted son, Camillo served as director from 1670 to 1680. He was one of the sharpest critics of the status of foreigners in Livorno. In a petition a few months before the reform, several consuls and leading merchants held Capponi responsible for harsher inspections of their goods. By their lights, the Customs Office's severity did not stem from justified fears that merchants were eluding duties, but from the "self-interested passion" of officials eager to collect penalty fees. What a change from the 1640s! These methods struck

[41] ASF, MP, 2198, ins. 3, 05/17/1675.
[42] ASF, MP, 2198, ins. 2, 04/13/1675, Robert Balle to Ferdinando Bardi. See Fisher, "Robert Balle."

"terror" into the heart of the business community. Capponi's response was derisive:

> The complaints of those merchants tend toward their usual object, namely to remove their merchandise from the eyes of the guards and to enjoy a more-than-generous liberty; to be able to import and export despotically and without bridle any kind of merchandise…And where at present, thanks to the privileges they enjoy, they practically pay taxes only on the goods they want, when they want, they would rather be assured of not having to pay anything at all.[43]

Capponi argued that merchants in Livorno were already endowed with a "more-than-generous," almost despotic, liberty of commerce. He implied that they often broke the few laws that existed, to the detriment of the grand duke's coffers, and hardly merited ampler privileges. Merchants for their part accused Capponi of beginning to "tiranize more then ordinary."[44]

Camillo Capponi's attitudes reflected a concern with fortifying Tuscany against foreigners. For example, when foreigners sought to fish in a newly discovered coral zone in September of 1675, Capponi took immediate action to ensure that Tuscans enjoyed the exclusive right to fish there. He sent a minister to investigate and found that some twenty-seven barks, mostly belonging to foreigners, were fishing in the spot. Without waiting for orders from Florence, Capponi conferred with several officials in Livorno, including the governor and the general of the garrison. His colleagues agreed that the situation was urgent and ordered an armed felucca to guard the fishery until approval arrived from Florence.[45] One customs official calculated that God had sent this "blessing" to provide work for two hundred and fifty fishermen supporting many impoverished Tuscan families.[46] It did not seem fair to him that any of this boon go to foreigners, and the grand duke agreed. But as so often in the annals of efforts to succor the poor, the epilogue to this episode is less optimistic. Camillo Capponi reluctantly concluded in June of the following year that there were not enough native coral fishermen to take advantage of the windfall. He asked that the industry be open to at least some foreigners.[47]

Despite a rising animus against foreigners, the free port of 1676 was the fruit of their initiatives. Ferdinando II's reforms in 1643 had raised tariffs on some goods while eliminating the perpetual gift that allowed merchants to store wares in Livorno indefinitely without paying duties. Tuscan fiscal obligations in the Thirty Years' War justified these measures. After the Peace of Westphalia in 1648 and the acceleration of commercial rivalry in the second half of the century, the English

[43] ASF, MP, 2198, 12/09/1675, Camillo Capponi to Ferdinando Bardi, quoted by Mangiarotti, "Il porto franco," 54. The merchants' petition, dated 12/02/1675, is inserted into Capponi's letter. On customs rigor in these years, see Baruchello, *Livorno e il suo porto*, 303–4.

[44] NA, SP 98/16, 03/04/1676, Robert Balle to Joseph Williamson, quoted by Calafat, "Une mer jalousée," 460.

[45] ASF, MP, 2198, ins. 3, 09/15/1675, Camillo Capponi to Ferdinando Bardi; and ibid., 09/18/1675. The foreign coral fishermen were probably Genoese.

[46] ASF, MP, 2198, ins. 3, 10/02/1675, Pier Lorenzo Poggiali to Ferdinando Bardi; see ibid., ins. 2, 01/21/1676, Curzio Poli to Ferdinando Bardi.

[47] Ibid., ins. 5, 06/12/1676, Camillo Capponi to Ferdinando Bardi.

began to request lower tariffs. The need to draft a supplication every year for an extension of the liberal gift (a two-year exemption on storage duties) also rankled the foreign communities. In 1660 Ferdinando II finally agreed to lower tariffs, and though he took no action, neither merchants nor officials forgot about his promise.[48] Nevertheless, the regime did not feel foreign pressure so keenly as simply to cave into their demands, even after Colbert declared Marseille a free port in 1669. The son of the French consul in Livorno believed that customs officials refused to write the appropriate memoranda on the subject, "since immediately upon this affair's conclusion many of them would be dismissed."[49]

Merchants sent a deputation directly to the grand duke in early December 1675, circumventing Camillo Capponi and the regular channels of communication between Florence and the free port. By February 1676 serious discussions about the free port were underway. Feroni held meetings at his house in Florence to study the tax regime, and the Venetian resident wrote that the "duke is totally immersed in the business of the customs of Livorno."[50] Feroni again butted heads with the patrician elite, led by Ferrante and Camillo Capponi. They disapproved of any modification on the grounds that foreigners already enjoyed excessive privileges in Livorno. In the end, Feroni prevailed. Cosimo had tremendous faith in the financial acumen of his depositary general, who argued that his proposals would increase revenue while simplifying administrative processes. On March 9, the merchant community submitted a single fictitious supplication with some fifteen headings outlining the new proposal. Their memorandum was incorporated wholesale into the legislation, which Cosimo III (holding court in Livorno) approved the following day.[51]

The key innovation was the elimination of ordinary taxes. Henceforth, merchandise imported into Livorno paid only a one-time stallage tax assessed on the number of parcels rather than by weight or value. The new stallage fee was far higher than the old one, but on the whole, it is likely that overall rates declined slightly for most commodities. Goods could be stored indefinitely, traded, or exported without paying further taxes. Previously, during the regime of the liberal gift, duties on goods depended on provenance, length of storage, and changes in ownership. Now, "once they declare [their wares] to the Customs Office and pay the stallage, merchants are free from all verifications and formalities."[52]

[48] Giacchero, *Storia economica*, 30; Calafat, "Une mer jalousée," 460.

[49] Pierre Cotolendy to the French maritime secretary, 02/29/1676, as quoted by Filippini, *Il porto di Livorno*, vol. 1, 80. Cotolendy was wrong, however: the size of the Customs Office did not shrink until the coming of the General Tax Farm, and then only barely. See n. 14 in chapter 4.

[50] ASV, Dispacci degli Ambasciatori di Senato, Firenze, 81, f. 40, quoted in Frattarelli Fischer, "Livorno 1676," 51. Interestingly, most letters from the Genoese consul Domenico Gavi from early 1676 are missing from their regular repository; perhaps they were taken to be examined in detail by elite Genoese politicians or officials.

[51] ASF, MP, 2272, 03/10/1676 [1675 ab inc.]. On Capponi's opposition, see Baruchello, *Livorno*, 293–4, 300 n. 1. The process of negotiating taxes was common in Tuscany: Waquet, *Le Grand-Duché de Toscane*, 234–5.

[52] From article VII of the new tariff, published in Filippini, *Il porto di Livorno*, vol. 1, 185–98.

The law made all of Livorno a free trade zone, though the text did not specifically mention the term free port.[53] From the point of view of foreign trade, the sole taxes were for commercial services—the maintenance of warehouse and port facilities. At least, the tariff appeared to nod toward this principle while in fact differentiating goods by value. Bulky or inexpensive goods owed smaller stallage fees than valuable goods such as silks or spices, even though the former required more extensive facilities than the latter. The ideal of administrative simplicity underlay the reform, rather than any theory of international trade. The desire to simplify grew out of the dystopian reality of collecting taxes in Livorno, that is, out of practice. In addition, contemporary thinkers also hailed the virtues of simplicity in matters of tax collection. Partly, they distrusted the honesty of officials, who supposedly thrived amidst labyrinthine rules. But complicated regulations were an evil in themselves by multiplying the occasion for evasions, arbitrary appraisals, bookkeeping errors, and vexatious delays for merchants. Efficiency was a major concern among fiscal writers of the latter half of the seventeenth century (and ever since).[54]

Although one often measures centralization in early modern Europe by the numerical growth of bureaucracy, simplification was also a tool of statecraft for exerting greater control over one's territories. It was effective precisely because so many of the officials and institutions that regimes had to work through were unreliable servitors of the central will. One thinks of the incompetent officeholders, overlapping jurisdictions, and tangle of immunities for which the Ancien Régime is famous. On the other hand, this same nexus of interests made simplifying reforms a politically costly enterprise, rarely enacted though often lauded.[55] Reform was possible in Livorno because local elites stood to benefit from it, apart from a small number of customs officials; had the Customs Office been larger, reform would have been even more controversial. The grand duke had plenty of room for maneuver in the rather under-institutionalized free port. Elsewhere in Tuscany the path to simplification was more tortuous and less effective.[56]

The new tariff was a resounding success. Customs receipts increased by almost a third in the following decade, and long-distance shipping increased by almost two-thirds (Table 5.2).[57] Two great periods during the Medici era may thus be distinguished: one, a steady growth in revenue that began in 1590 and plateaued in the 1640s; and a second spurt of growth in the wake of the reform of 1676, which plateaued in the 1710s (Fig. 5.3). Each of these epochs had distinct customs regimes. The early phase was free trade entwined with dogged efforts of bureaucratic

[53] If the concerns of eighteenth-century jurists are an indication, the regime avoided enshrining the term "free port" into legislation for fear of setting a legal precedent. See Aglietti, *I governatori di Livorno*, 13; and "The System of Livorno" in chapter 7.

[54] Bonney, "Early Modern Theories of State Finance," esp. 165, 173, 178, 186, 215.

[55] See the faltering efforts of Genoa and Marseilles to simplify their customs administrations described in "A Complex Institution" in chapter 8.

[56] Waquet, *Le Grand-Duché de Toscane*, 98, 257, 261–3, 307–8.

[57] Cf. Frattarelli Fischer, "Livorno 1676," 53, who provides a comparison of stallage revenue but does not take ordinary revenues into consideration. Note that the Customs Office of Pisa suffered as some of the goods that used to go over land (such as merchandise from Lucca) now went by ship to Livorno. In 1679, for instance, it saw two thousand fewer parcels than before the reform.

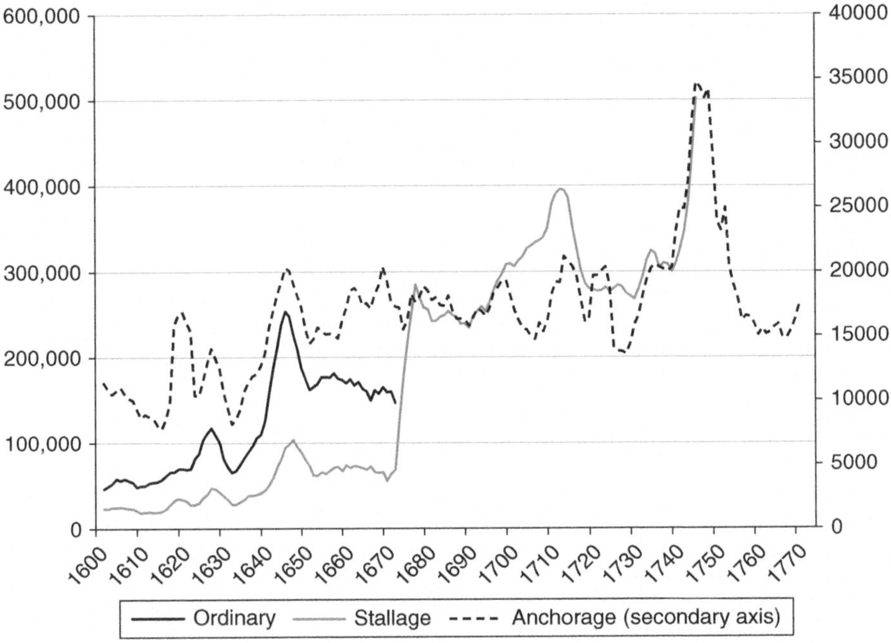

Fig. 5.3. Customs revenues in Livorno, 1600–1775 (in lire, five-year moving average).
Source: ASF, Soprassinadaci e sindaci, 469–74. See app. 9.

supervision. The movement, sale, and warehousing of goods required a welter of documentation. There was ample opportunity for merchants and officials to cheat amidst the complexity of these arrangements. The new dispensation of 1676 reduced transaction costs as well as fraud. This simpler system encouraged merchants to ship their goods through Livorno rather than its competitors. The Customs Office had an easier time collecting taxes and merchants had fewer incentives to bilk the system. The new law thus created a mutually beneficial situation: it was cheaper for merchants and more lucrative for the grand duke.

Tax collection continued to depend to some extent on good relations between merchants and officials. For instance, within a few months of the reform several English merchants complained about the irregular levying of anchorage taxes. Camillo Capponi believed that the consul had no grounds for asserting that English ships were being assessed beyond their due. According to the customs director, ministers at the harbor received no cut of anchorage fees and had no motivation to collect more than the appropriate amount. When a returning ship arrived, officials saw what it had paid in the past; and when a new ship appeared, one determined from its cargo bill the anchorage tax by estimating the ship's tonnage. If there was a discrepancy, the customs director brought in experts such as merchants and captains to determine the tonnage.[58] Whether English complaints

[58] ASF, MP, 2198, ins. 5, 06/27/1676, Camillo Capponi to Ferdinando Bardi.

Table 5.2. Commercial indicators, 1670–84

	Long-distance ship arrivals	Stallage/ ordinary rev.	Anchorage rev.	Extraordinary rev.
1670–4	551	1,119,663	88,511	775,053
1675–9	749	1,476,971	91,307	930,537
1680–4	911	1,424,851	88,123	1,008,227
% change (through 1679)	36%	32%	3%	20%
% change (through 1684)	65%	27%	0%	30%

Note: Stallage taxes have been combined with ordinary taxes for the years 1670–6 to provide a more reliable indicator (the elevated stallage fee was intended to compensate for the elimination of ordinary taxes in early 1676). Most of the taxes on victuals were eliminated in 1676; for that reason they have not been included in the table.

Source: apps 9 and 12.

were warranted is unclear; it is possible that Capponi sought to exact vengeance by implementing the new tariff with the utmost rigor. The more interesting point is that assessment of the anchorage relied only partially on technical criteria (the cargo bill). Social collaboration remained important in establishing dues.

For the stallage fee, officials needed to verify that individual parcels were of reasonable size and contained only one taxable parcel. Apparently, it was common for merchants to package several bales into a single oversized bundle. Officials eventually came to turn a blind eye to this form of fraud. For instance, when Peter Langlois failed to denounce a parcel of "extraordinary size" (composed of five packages of textiles), he was guilty of a double fraud, both creating a compound parcel and then not reporting it to the Customs Office. He should have suffered a fine of fifty scudi per parcel as well as the seizure of the goods; instead, the customs director proposed a fine of only fifty scudi, "treating the said parcel as a single one."[59] Likewise with the transfer of parcels from ship to ship: in theory, there was to be a fifty scudi penalty per parcel if it was moved in the harbor without being reported to the Customs Office; in practice this too was tolerated, both because the Medici regime did not want to alienate traffic, and because it did not want to provoke disputes with foreign powers (which extended national protection to vessels bearing their flags). The habitual bending of the rules gave officials some latitude in exerting power over individuals merely by insisting on the letter of the law.[60]

Although no tax system can ever be completely automatic or impersonal, the tariff of 1676 substantially reduced the involvement of the Customs Office in the ordinary affairs of merchants. Collusion and bribery became less frequent. Instead, the reform transferred the locus of fraud from Livorno itself to the borders the city shared with the grand duchy. From the regime's perspective, the problem now lay in combatting smuggling between the free zone and its hinterland. But the new tariff was less successful in displacing customs officials as mediators between the

[59] ASF, MP, 2277, 12/10/1732, Pitti to Rinuccini; quoted by Filippini, *Il porto di Livorno*, vol. 2, 121. Labat provided the same testimony about large compound-parcels in the passage quoted in n. 1.

[60] Addobbati, *Commercio, rischio, guerra*, 68.

merchant communities and the central government. Amidst heightened competition in the Mediterranean and the dizzying expansion of Livorno's own trade, the customs director remained the "chief of commerce in this port."[61]

The regime enacted several measures for promoting the grand duchy's commerce following the extension of the free port in 1676. These included efforts to foster a native elite, reroute finance to Florence, and empanel a deputation of merchants. Although variants of these initiatives run through our entire period, during Cosimo III's reign they were marked by a concern for securing Tuscan independence from foreign domination. Foreigners were so deeply implicated in the economic functions of Livorno that these proposals generally failed to achieve their aims. Nevertheless, in this period contemporaries rarely linked the problem of foreigners to the free port as a policy device. Instead they attributed it to specific disorders in Livorno that could be modified or amended without impugning the port's fundamental institutions.

One way to bind the port to the grand duchy was to create a larger local elite, more rooted in Tuscan than foreign interests. Ferdinando I had capped citizenship at one hundred in order to guarantee his control over a small ruling class. These men swapped municipal honors among themselves and represented the interests of the town in such matters as church affairs or service contracts. In 1681 Cosimo III decreed that the citizen roster was open for additional candidates. Soon Livorno had some fifty-six new citizens. They included Catholic merchants and captains as well as ducal functionaries. The capstone of this move was the nomination of Livorno as a *città nobile* (noble city) in 1720. Henceforth, Livorno's leading citizens could apply for patents of nobility and participate in the Order of St. Stephen.[62] The grand duke also sanctioned a variety of measures to expand participation for Jews in the affairs of the semi-autonomous Jewish community. Jews remained neither full-fledged Tuscan subjects nor foreigners, but had their special status confirmed. As in the early seventeenth century, norms of citizenship continued to be renegotiated in Livorno late into the Medici period. But now, the aim was to integrate the city into Tuscan society rather than populate it with merchants.[63]

In 1683 Cosimo attempted to restore Florence as the financial center of Tuscany. Over the course of the seventeenth century, international merchants increasingly routed their bills of exchange through Livorno rather than the capital city—there was, indeed, a relative shortage of money in Florence, where only a

[61] ASG, AF, 1217, 08/19/1722, report by Bartolomeo Domenico Gavi.

[62] The institution of a Casa Pia in 1682 (a second was established by Carlo Ginori in 1756) is a token of the city's civic development as well. See Frattarelli Fischer, "Livorno 1676," 63–5; Aglietti, *I governatori di Livorno*, 86–8; the 1681 law is in ASL, Comunità, 4, f. 195, 03/12/1681 [1680 ab inc.]. On Frenchmen enrolled as citizens, see Filippini, *Il porto di Livorno*, vol. 2, 399–414. For the nobility of Livorno, Marrara, "Livorno città 'nobile'"; and Verga, *Da "cittadini" a "nobili,"* 524–6. For an example of the social ascent of a mercantile family, see Ruiu, "La famiglia Sproni fra Comunità"; and for the grand duchy in general, Benadusi, *A Provincial Elite*.

[63] In the Jewish community, the number of governors increased from eighteen to thirty in 1690, and from thirty to sixty in 1693. These measures excluded Jews of non-Iberian origin from government. Toaff, *La nazione ebrea*, 170–8; Frattarelli Fischer, *Vivere fuori dal ghetto*, 178–84.

few big banking houses continued to do business.[64] Merchants preferred to take or give bills in Livorno, where money served the needs of commerce, rather than be forced to keep agents in Florence. Feroni expressed anger about this situation as early as 1673–4. In his view, which was shared by many of his colleagues, "Livorno was supposed to serve for buying and selling merchandise, but it should rely on [Florence] for money with bills of exchange, as the custom has always been."[65] It took another decade for the regime to craft a response. In late June 1683, several Florentine merchants promised to open commercial houses in Florence with big capital endowments in return for exchange bills being handled in Florence rather than Livorno.[66] They wanted to control on behalf of the port's merchants all bills involving Venice, Rome, Naples, and the Fiera di Novi (i.e. the Genoese exchange fairs). In short, the city's patricians intended for Florence to serve as a financial center in regards to its dealings with other Italian markets.

The grand duke approved their proposals, but the new restrictions agitated merchants of Livorno into writing long memoranda against the measure. Each nation had its own reasons for alarm. The Dutch, for example, argued that the free use of letters of exchange was necessary for expeditious shipping. Florentines could not be trusted to consign money to foreigners "with the generosity and promptness that business requires."[67] The proposal would divert navigation away from Livorno, as the Genoese, the chief financiers in the port, put their money in places that imposed fewer restrictions. The grand duke's advisors found most of the merchants' arguments "imaginary" and were derisive of the notion that the free port protected the use of bills of exchange in Livorno. But in the end, "to demonstrate how much [the grand duke] esteems the supplications brought to him," the regime restored the exchange market to Livorno; only the Fiera di Novi remained in Florence. Henceforth, Livorno's role as a center of finance eclipsed that of the capital city.[68] The free port remained a target of legislation late into Cosimo III's reign, but there were no more attempts to control its traffic by fiat.[69]

Trouble with foreign merchants was common in port cities. Often, anti-foreigner sentiment was aimed at protecting local monopoly rents against competitors. Native merchants in Venice, Genoa, and Marseille (for instance) inveighed against

[64] Waquet, *Le Grand-Duché de Toscane*, 97, 101, 118–19.

[65] "[L]a piazza di Livorno doveva servire alle compre e vendite di mercanzie e qui ricorre per il denaro coi cambi come sempre è costumato." ASF, MP, 1523, ff. 309–310, 02/08/1674 [1673 ab inc.], Francesco Feroni to Apollonio Bassetti. A few months earlier, the grand duke reissued a law that mandated bills of exchange must only be paid or received in Florence, if the payee or receiver (or his procurator) was in Florence. Bills were often due in Florence for people whose business and residence were in Livorno. Cantini, *Legislazione toscana*, vol. 18, 349–51; Baruchello, *Livorno*, 426, 430–2.

[66] ASF, MM, 324, ins. 3, f. 2, 06/28/1683.

[67] ASF, MM, 324, ins. 3, ff. 30–32.

[68] "[H]a voluto con la solita sua generosità far conoscere a tutte le nationi che negoziano in Livorno quanta stima facia delle supplicazioni portateli." ASF, MM, 324, ins. 3, f. 26. For the development of the financial market, see "The Reorganization of Long-Distance Trade" in chapter 6, esp. nn. 40–2.

[69] There were decrees targeting fictitious contracts (1687), refining anchorage procedures (1693), authorizing freedom of commerce in the liqueur trade (1694), prohibiting vagabondage in the city (1697), regulating damages (*avarie*) (1701), and imposing penalties on those who sold or produced fake coral (1707). Baruchello, *Livorno e il suo porto*, 435–6.

foreigners who undercut their sales abroad or brought their wares directly to the metropole. Conflict over the rights of foreign traders was just one front in the endless tug-of-war between local urban elites and the territorial states.[70] The situation of the free port was different. Livorno was discovering new problems in light of the principles of national accounting. The free mobility of their wares and their wealth made foreign merchants a difficult constituency to control, not only because they could turn elsewhere—this was a bigger risk in the eighteenth than in the seventeenth century—but because their allegiance could not be counted on. When they retired, they brought their earnings back home rather than investing them locally. Most importantly, their activities could have unforeseen and unpalatable effects on the hinterland economy. These were the perils of free trade.

MERCHANT EXPERTISE AND STATE INSTITUTIONS

When was economic expertise first embodied in institutional form? A handy answer might be the mid-eighteenth century, with its explosion of publications, translations, academies, and university chairs devoted to political economy. If true, the science of commerce would appear as a strict concomitant of the burgeoning public sphere. But the first institutions expressly created to proffer economic advice appeared about a century earlier in the form of trade boards and chambers of commerce. These organizations were creatures of the state, peopled by officials and merchants. The presence of the latter should hardly be surprising. Merchants had long been the recognized experts of commerce. They trumpeted their particular expertise whenever possible, stressing their virtuous commitment to the public good.[71] If political philosophers in the eighteenth century decided that the merchant class constituted an invisible but ferocious check on the arbitrary power of princes, during the seventeenth century it was princes—and republics, too—who harnessed mercantile expertise to serve their interests.[72]

Merchants and other "businessmen" regularly served as informal consultants long before they received their own organs. The Customs Office of Livorno was by no means the only institution that delivered expert economic advice to a prince in collaboration with local merchants. In Italy, for example, the guilds inherited from the Middle Ages gradually morphed from cartels of producers into regulatory or advisory bodies. They served the interests of governments who required information about market conditions, tax procedures, and the status of workers.[73] Beyond Italy, the most conspicuous of the new commercial institutions were the various

[70] See Braudel, *The Mediterranean*, vol. 1, 338–44.

[71] E.g. Peri, *Il negotiante*, vol. 1, 1–6; and in general Poettinger, "Etica mercantile e sviluppo economico." Such assertions should be read in light of anxieties about the merchant-citizen discussed by Pocock, *The Machiavellian Moment*, 389–93, 446–51, *et passim*; and Hont, *The Jealousy of Trade*, 201–22. Northern Italians had long recognized the civic dignity of merchants: Jurdjevic, "Virtue, Commerce, and the Enduring Republican Moment."

[72] Cf. Hirschman, *The Passions and the Interests*, 69–75, 82, 132.

[73] M. Costantini, *L'albero della libertà economica*; Mackenney, *Tradesmen and Traders*; Guenzi, *La "fabbrica" delle tele*; Poni, "Norms and Disputes"; Cerutti, *Mestieri e privilegi*; Migliorini, *Il sistema*

India companies that proliferated throughout northwest Europe. Owing to the social eminence of many of their merchants, as well as to the political and fiscal implications of their activities, companies became important participants in the policy process wherever they appeared. As such, they were often purveyors of commercial memoranda and pamphlets.[74]

Seventeenth-century rulers received a vast amount of counsel from the bodies they erected or co-opted to manage their economic ambitions. This "institutionalization" of economic thought via customs houses or guilds was quite ad hoc. The foundation of expertise organizations therefore represented a stark departure in intent. Precocious Venice appears to have been the first to institute a Board of Trade, as its Cinque Savii alla Mercanzia is often translated. This body was staffed by Venetian patricians and served as the government's clearinghouse for economic information and projects.[75] But the movement to institutionalize commercial advice did not really get underway until the mid-seventeenth century. A Chamber of Commerce was established in Marseilles in 1650; and the monarchy installed many such chambers throughout France in 1701.[76] England, too, was experimenting with new ways of formulating commercial policy. Lewes Roberts complained in 1641 that "ordinary states-men doe neither seriously consider, nor truly weigh the reall benefits that arise to a kingdom and people by the hand of traffike."[77] Commonwealth merchants established the Council of Trade in 1650 to tailor fiscal policies toward commercial development. Other European states throughout the first half of the eighteenth century were keen on these institutions, too: the Papacy, Naples, and the German states set up similar operations.[78] It would be anachronistic to see chambers of commerce as pressure groups while treating trade boards as disinterested organs of governance. These institutions varied greatly in their structures, the backgrounds of their staff, and their specific powers. But all had one thing in common: they were meant to furnish actionable advice in matters of commerce.

Late in his reign Cosimo III established a Deputation of Commerce on the advice of the customs director. The deputation's origin lies in a credit crisis that struck Livorno along with other Mediterranean ports in 1715 in the aftermath of the War of Spanish Succession.[79] Customs Director Giacinto Del Vigna (in office

delle arti; Merlo, *Le corporazioni, conflitti e soppressioni*; and the articles in Guenzi et al., *Guilds, Markets, and Work Regulations*.

[74] Adams, *The Familial State*, 49–58, 113–22, 127–36; Stern, *The Company-State*, 14 and ch. 4.

[75] See "Institutions and Economic Thought" in chapter 3, esp. n. 83.

[76] Gras, "Les chambres de commerce," 550–89, 680–740; Lafon, *Les Députés du Commerce et l'Ordonnance*; Schaeper, *The French Council of Commerce*, 73–98.

[77] Roberts, *The Treasure of Traffike*, 67. On the council, see Brenner, *Merchants and Revolution*, 602–8.

[78] Inner Austria established a Council of Commerce in 1717–18, followed later by a school for the maritime arts (1754). A Giunta di Commercio was formed in Messina in 1724. Naples erected a Giunta di Commercio in 1735 and, to replace it, a Supremo Magistrato di Commercio (1739). Dubin, *The Port Jews of Habsburg Trieste*, 11–13; Martini, "Le condizioni economiche di Messina," 13; Brancaccio, *Nazione genovese*, 168; Robertson, *The Case for the Enlightenment*, 332–3.

[79] This deputation was not the first of its name. In April 1642 a *deputazione* was established composed of the governor, the consuls, and four businessmen. Another in May 1692 was created comprising the customs director and three businessmen to regulate the city's brokers. These were short-lived committees rather than permanent institutions. See Guarnieri, *Livorno medicea*, 176.

between 1716 and 1726) had a good grasp of economic affairs thanks to his years as a merchant in Amsterdam. In mid-1717, Del Vigna developed a plan for the deputation as a means for merchants to propose collectively "what would best conserve and increase commerce."[80] This was a consolidation of the decision system that had developed from the 1640s on. The deputation consisted of men chosen by the consuls with Del Vigna's input: four foreigners (one English, French, Dutch, and Flemish) and four Italians, of whom two were Tuscans. Two Jews deputized by their community were separately involved. Their objective was to maintain consensus while developing new measures to promote the port's trade. A few years later a modest judicial role was given to the deputation's members.

The Deputation of Commerce had a checkered career and met only sporadically over the next couple of decades. Its most interesting proposals were geared toward developing ties between the hinterland and the free port by building new storage facilities for oil or constructing a road to bypass Liguria on the overland route to northern Italy. These projects remained on the drawing board. The deputation succeeded best when performing that old trick of the city's merchants: protecting the liberties of Livorno. They rallied against the Monte di Pietà (a public pawn and lending body) when its officials sought to search ships for contraband paper. They united against a rumored Jewish proposal for a soap monopoly. Most importantly, the deputation whipped Livorno's merchants into a frenzy against the Jewish tobacco monopoly that would remain a shrill complaint for decades to come. The deputation represented an attempt to institutionalize the status quo, but almost imperceptibly it dissolved back into the old system of ad hoc consultations with consuls and deputies.[81]

The deputation is notable less for what it achieved than what it failed to do. Institutionally, it favored the interests of private merchants and offered them few incentives to consider the broader Tuscan good. Henceforth Livorno merchants looked longingly at the deputation as a model for the ideal representation of their interests. By contrast, those in the central government doubted whether the deputation could ever be trusted to look after broader public concerns such as revitalizing the hinterland economy. It is sufficient to note the deputation's docket in 1730: regulating trade with a new law on bills of exchange, creating mechanisms for the quick obtainment of payments, and ending certain jurisdictional confusions. These were all sensible measures, but they focused narrowly on the interests of merchants and scarcely touched the industrial or commercial prospects of the grand duchy.

As the case of the Deputation of Commerce indicates, economic thought participated in a broader field of institutional emulation. States set up boards of trade and chambers of commerce in imitation of one another and in response to a

[80] Quoted by Baggiani, "Tra crisi commerciale," 691.

[81] Baggiani sees the protest against the tobacco contract as the first explicit appeal to promoting a free marketplace in Livorno, particularly with reference to access to the national market (ibid., 705.) He overstates the case. Appeals to liberty as a general stimulus to trade were common in mercantile memoranda for at least a century, as were objections to rigorous contraband inspections. The deputation's attack on the tobacco monopoly was about the dangers of rigor to Livorno's commerce. The potential for developing a Tuscan market was muted.

commonly felt need for a more institutionalized approach to economic intervention. Commercial rivalry, then, was not the only new arrival on the scene in the latter half of the seventeenth century. One concomitant was a new forum for airing economic ideas and making policy. This dual function turned out to be a liability for the deputation, tainting both its expertise and its policy recommendations. Feroni believed that "a courtier cannot be a good merchant, nor the latter a courtier." The problem with the deputation was that it put the merchant into the position of being a courtier: an advisor to the ruler. Could one trust his advice?

Chambers of commerce were the first organizations erected for the purpose of furnishing expert advice on commercial matters. It is true that institutions such as customs houses or guilds had inadvertently fulfilled this role in the past and continued to do so in the future. The new chambers of commerce adopted many of the practices of these older institutions. They conducted business through bureaucratic memoranda. They often had ancillary duties, such as managing projects or hosting tribunals. They were staffed by merchants as well as government officials. Only by abusing the term could they be said to be institutions of the public sphere: they were creatures of the state. These bodies, purveyors of unabashedly "interested" analysis, stood at the border between pre-scientific and scientific political economy. Over time it became evident that councils offered problematic advice for precisely that reason: one Englishman observed in 1695 that merchants were acting as "judges of their own complaints... no man in the actual part and converse of trade can be equal and different in the determination of controverted matters in traffick."[82] The mechanism that such bodies employed for securing consensus was typical of the Ancien Régime: the composition of discordant interests, negotiation. But their claims to expertise were central to their authority—claims contested by later proponents of scientific economics who sought to appropriate for themselves the mantle of disinterested expertise.

CONCLUSION

The latter half of the seventeenth century inaugurated an age of conscious experimentation in economic policy. The reform of 1676 was one aspect of this creative moment. With this decree, the Medici regime eliminated import and export duties in Livorno and imposed a public tariff based (nominally) on the commercial services rendered by the port: docking and storage facilities. Its principle was simplification, in accordance with the dictates of contemporary fiscal theorists. Simplicity offered three virtues: efficiency, equity, and—from the point of view of central authorities—control. The pursuit of bureaucratic simplicity exemplified by the tariff of 1676 was relatively common under the Ancien Régime, despite its reputation for byzantine institutional solutions. Few efforts were as successful as in Livorno, however, where the grand duke enjoyed an exceptional degree of freedom of action.

[82] Brewster, *Essays on Trade and Navigation*, 38–9. For Brewster's discussion of free ports, see n. 6 in chapter 8.

Waquet argued that Tuscan institutions by the mid-seventeenth century functioned in a kind of "dynamic stasis" similar to an ecological system: everything was in motion, but little changed. While this position has come under attack by specialists, who have pointed to undeniable transformations under Cosimo III, in my view his critics have not addressed the tacit considerations that shaped Waquet's interpretation. Behind the controversy about Tuscan institutions is a deeper question posed by Franco Venturi: whether fundamental reform was possible under the Ancien Régime; or whether revolution was necessary to untangle the knot of privilege and particularism that bedeviled European institutions.[83] Did the state have the capacity to enact rationalizing, universalizing interventions against the claims of entitled stakeholders? The tariff of 1676 was certainly one such reform: a far-reaching simplification of procedures in the face of opposition by the Customs Office and Florentine patricians. Nevertheless, although rivals imitated the free port as best they could, few Italian regimes could enact such thoroughgoing interventions. Elsewhere in Tuscany, too, the grand duke was constrained by traditional fiscal structures, not to mention the power of the nobility and the church. Livorno was the exception that proves the rule.

Administrative simplicity had significant consequences for the commercial development of Livorno. The reform of 1676 lowered the transaction costs associated with the deposit, transit, and exchange of merchandise in the free port. Transaction costs are one of the costs of trade, along with taxes and transport expenses; lower transaction costs are associated with larger and more efficient markets. The new tariff gave the free port a differential advantage in attracting long-distance commerce over its rivals, where transaction costs as well as customs duties remained higher. The new tariff did leave in place taxes for the storage of wares and the anchorage of ships. Trade in commodities can never be entirely free in the sense of frictionless: material goods require transport infrastructure and warehouse facilities. That is why most economists believe that it is legitimate to defray such expenses via taxation for commercial services, not unlike charging to use a toll road. The invention of commercial services was an unexpected legacy of Livorno's incentives for the deposit and transit of merchandise.

Recall that Labat had mistakenly declared that *all* parcels paid the same rate. Whether this remark reflected a slip of the pen, a faulty memory, or actual confusion about procedures, Labat's error is a telling one. It offers further confirmation that customs rules were at least as important as the level of duties. What was significant for merchants was not the rates themselves, but the simplicity of procedures and lack of interference in their affairs. Labat's comment is revealing in another way, too. The tariff of 1676 was not a pure instantiation of the principle that free trade required taxing only for commercial services: duties continued to depend on the value of goods. Nevertheless, their designation as anchorage and

[83] See Waquet, *Le Grand-Duché de Toscane*, *passim*, but esp. 514–27 on Cosimo III's court and character; Waquet's position came under assault throughout Angiolini et al., *La Toscana nell'età di Cosimo III*. On the dialectic between reform and revolution, see Venturi, *The End of the Old Regime in Europe, 1768–1776*, 130–1, 198; and Venturi, *The End of the Old Regime in Europe, 1776–1789*, vol. 1, 299.

stallage fees gestured in the direction of taxing solely to defray infrastructural costs. In addition, the toleration of "enormous parcels" further divorced the link between the value of goods and the duties they owed. If a small bale of silk paid the same dues as a huge bale of silk, it was apparent that merchants were paying taxes primarily by parcel rather than by the quality of a good. The grand duke finally acknowledged this principle in 1779 when he reduced the stallage fee to a simple tax of one lira per 1,000 pounds of deposited goods.[84]

The tariff of 1676 represents a milestone in the disembedding of the marketplace, that is, in rendering the market as autonomous as possible from social oversight. Price formation in the early free port was conditioned by procedures for regulating the exchange, transit, and taxation of goods. By minimizing bureaucratic supervision over exchange, the new tariff constructed the marketplace as a kind of black box of redistribution: the state undertook to establish and police the infrastructure of trade, but it withdrew from monitoring transactions themselves. Henceforth, market forces determined the price of commodities for sale in Livorno. This brave new world of capitalism was limited to real commodities and to long-distance exchange. Labor and land were unaffected. Commodity markets in the Tuscan hinterland were also unchanged; they remained subject to traditional fiscal structures. Administrative simplification and the consequent reduction in transaction costs constituted a controlled withdrawal of the state from the marketplace.[85]

In a sense, the free port was a weapon of the weak, a gambit for marginal countries to participate in global trade while reaping collateral benefits such as revenue from commercial services or neutrality in international disputes.[86] Nevertheless, although foreign merchants advocated changing the customs regime, no outside power foisted the reform of 1676 on the grand duchy. Simplifying customs procedures was part of a well-articulated strategy for connecting the free port to the Tuscan hinterland and to more distant markets. Yet the new tariff did have important consequences for the position of foreign communities in Livorno. The reduction in transaction costs that boosted the port's commerce also affected the organization of foreign commercial networks, particularly among the English. As far-flung mercantile interests converged more intensively on Livorno, the status of the free port became an issue of general diplomatic significance.

The renewal of conflict in Europe with the Nine Years' War (1688–97) and the War of Spanish Succession (1701–14) weighed heavily on Tuscan finances. To meet his military aid obligations, the grand duke imposed several new taxes and instituted a new public debt fund in 1692.[87] But most damaging of all was the inability of Cosimo's sons to produce heirs. European intriguers began to toy with

[84] Baruchello, *Livorno e il suo porto*, 312–15.

[85] See "People and Commodities in Early Modern Trade" in the introduction.

[86] See Hovy, *Het voorstel van 1751*, 165; Kirk, *Genoa and the Sea*, 184.

[87] These were the *colletta universale*, a tax on stump-footed animals (mules, asses, and horses), and a tax on wigs. The fund (*monte*) was redeemable, but due to persistent financial shortfalls as well as difficulties in collecting the new taxes, another, non-redeemable fund was instituted in 1706. See Pansini, "Per una storia del debito pubblico e della fiscalità"; and Waquet, *Le Grand-Duché de Toscane*, 96–8.

the idea of a post-Medici Tuscany in 1708, once it became clear that neither Ferdinando de' Medici (d. 1713) nor Gian Gastone (r. 1723–37) would have issue. With a succession crisis looming over Florence for almost thirty years, the regime consumed most of its energy in trying to secure the grand duchy's independence. Their efforts were in vain, however. The Treaty of the Quadruple Alliance (1718, confirmed in 1721) conferred the Tuscan succession on the Spanish Infante Carlos over Cosimo III's objections that the neutrality of Livorno was best served by Tuscan independence. In 1731 Spanish troops occupied the city to prepare the way for Don Carlos. The dangers of a politicized Livorno became evident to the English when, during the War of Polish Succession (1733–8), the Habsburgs threatened to besiege the port. Vigorous action by the English fleet prevented this crisis. During the peace negotiations that began in 1735, three years before the conflict's end, the entire grand duchy was given to Duke Francis Stephen of Habsburg-Lorraine, and the signatories officially recognized the neutrality of Livorno.

The last of the Medici was the cynical, indolent, and obese Gian Gastone. When he finally expired in 1737, Tuscany passed to the Lorraines and was ruled from Vienna for two and a half decades. Before the handoff, in early July, the governor of Livorno received word via Francis Stephen's representative that "all the privileges, freedoms, liberties, and exemptions were to be most punctiliously maintained."[88] Merchants in particular were to be treated in the "usual manner" in accordance with prevailing norms: *a forma delle leggi veglianti*. But it was not long before the new regime subjected the customary practices of the port to a sustained assault.

[88] Aglietti, *I governatori di Livorno*, 90–103 (quote on p. 90); see too Guarnieri, *Livorno medicea*, 197–8, 237–48; G. Mori, "Linee e momenti," 15; Diaz, *Il Granducato di Toscana*, 516–45; Verga, "Appunti per una storia politica"; Verga, "Dai Medici ai Lorena"; and Verga, "Lotta politica e riforma delle istituzioni."

6

Brokering Trade in the Central Mediterranean

The Venetian consul in Livorno looked upon the elimination of customs duties in 1676 with a measure of alarm. He complained that the remaining stallage fee was "already pathetically small" and that the customs regime offered "an infinite number of other facilitations."[1] There was little doubt in his mind that foreign merchants would continue to prefer trading in Livorno rather than Venice. Whereas more distant observers were preoccupied with the long-distance connections of the free port, the consul was equally concerned about Livorno's relationship to the Italian hinterland. Manufactured goods sent overland to the free port paid "a pittance" to transit through the Tuscan territory. Not only would Venice lose out on long-distance transit, but it also stood to lose the battle for control over the Italian hinterland as well.

It makes sense that the consul of Venice would take care to piece together the relationship between the port, its hinterland, and the Mediterranean Sea. Yet the Italian hinterland has long been minimized in accounts of Livorno's economic development. "To tell the truth (it might seem a paradox), Livorno contributes little or no profit to Tuscany. It's like that mouth full of apples that Samson once found: it was the mouth of a dead lion."[2] So wrote the political economist Gian Rinaldo Carli (1720–95) in his *Political and Economic Essay on Tuscany*. The lion in his simile refers to the emblem of Florence—once one of the foremost economies of Europe, but extinct by the early seventeenth century. The implication was that Livorno's commerce had little to do with its hinterland. When Carli published this essay in 1757, his interpretation was already making headway on the Italian scene, and it has since come to govern accounts of the free port. It is assumed that Livorno developed as an exclave whose economic relations with Tuscany could be safely ignored; and likewise that Tuscany was little affected by Livorno for good or ill.[3] This chapter reassesses the relationship between port and hinterland, arguing that Livorno's commercial life, while bound to change throughout the Mediterranean world, was also tied to economic life in north-central Italy. If part of the history of Livorno faces outward, into the sunny light of the Mediterranean, the other faces toward Florence in "the forgotten centuries."[4]

[1] G. Mori, "Linee e momenti," 14.
[2] Carli, "Saggio economico e politico." See Baruchello, *Livorno e il suo porto*, 309.
[3] See n. 8 in the introduction.
[4] The phrase is from Cochrane's eponymous book.

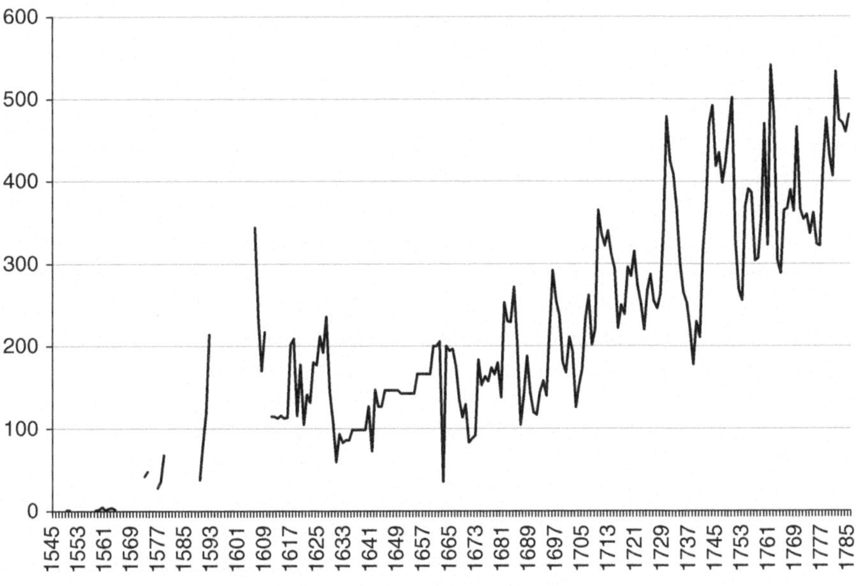

Fig. 6.1. Long-distance ship arrivals in Livorno, 1545–1790.

Note: The key "seams" in these data are 1610/11, 1666/7, 1683/4, and 1700/1, representing different sources or the work of a different scholar. The data are "inflated" for the period 1590–1610 and 1684–1790, with respect to the period 1612–83; for that reason, the curve must be read in light of fiscal data as well as regional shipping figures, when they are known. For my methods for constructing a single curve out of such disparate data, see app. 13.

Source: Braudel and Romano, *Navires et marchandises*, 79–87, 109; Filippini, *Il porto di Livorno*, vol. 1, 44; vol. 2, 149–50; Ghezzi, *Livorno e il mondo islamico*, 20, 69; Ghezzi, *Livorno e l'Atlantico*, 32; Engels, *Merchants, Interlopers, Seamen and Corsairs*, 225–6; ASL, Sanità, 67, 68, 69, and 71.

At first blush, chronology supports Carli's view about the separation between port and hinterland. Livorno's economic take-off began in 1590, just as Dutch and English ships appeared on the Mediterranean scene. By then, the Florentine wool industry was in decline and its merchants were in retreat as international bankers; many of its commercial houses abroad closed up shop a few decades later. The story of Livorno thus seems connected to the rise of the Atlantic world and the origins of modernity, whereas that of Florence points to the decline of the Italian Mediterranean (Fig. 6.1).[5] But there are good reasons for rejecting this narrative. From an empirical perspective, substantial economic ties bound Livorno to its hinterland; the economy of north-central Italy was implicated in the ongoing transformation of long-distance trade. In addition, recent revisions in our picture of economic change after the Renaissance have cast doubt on the world systems perspective that proclaims the peripheralization of Italy. A less global, more regional approach is essential for understanding the early modern Mediterranean.

During the late Middle Ages, merchants from north-central Italy acted as commercial and financial middlemen. Their profits came in part from geographic

[5] E.g. Braudel, "L'Italia fuori d'Italia," 227; Pagano de Divitiis, "Il porto di Livorno," 64–77.

brokerage, in part from industries that enjoyed privileged access to raw materials and export markets. The establishment of direct ties between Western Europe and the Indies was once thought to have inaugurated Italian decline. Giovanni Botero, for one, complained that "we Italians are too fond of ourselves and are too much the uncritical admirers of our own ways, when we prefer Italy and its cities over all the rest of the world."[6] He emphasized Italy's marginal position vis-à-vis the Atlantic, the peninsula's political fragmentation and subjection to Spain, and its rulers' focus on corsairing rather than commerce. More specialized research has modified Botero's view, revealing an "Indian summer" for Italy that lasted until 1620 or 1630. Even after the crisis of the mid-seventeenth century, Italy conserved though it did not grow its wealth—a feat made possible by the resilience of Italian manufacturing in silk and other luxuries, ongoing agricultural development in the north, and the formation of more diversified urban economies. We should speak of the loss of Italian hegemony to northwestern Europe rather than of decline.[7]

World systems theorists have built their interpretation of Mediterranean history on an obsolete portrait of Italian decline. By their lights, the Mediterranean became a de-industrialized appendage of first Dutch and later English capitalism. On its own, the new view of Italian economic resilience would suggest a more nuanced picture of change in the central Mediterranean, in which a core economy in north-central Italy remained capable of resisting the incursions of northern capitalism. Yet historians have leveled searching critiques against world systems theory itself, emphasizing the modest incidence of oceanic trade in even the most globalized of European economies until the mid- to late eighteenth century. Economic development occurred through the exploitation of near rather than distant peripheries—the hinterlands of the Baltic, for example, instead of the Americas. Discarding world systems theory opens up the possibility of explaining change in the Mediterranean without invoking the notion of northern European domination. It also carries forward the search for a less-deterministic and more conjunctural account of economic life in the early modern period.[8]

MEDITERRANEAN COMMERCE IN A GLOBAL AGE

The revolution that began in 1492 had profound effects on long-distance commerce in the Mediterranean. During the late Middle Ages, Genoa and Venice had exerted monopolistic control over certain routes and used violence to exact trading privileges. They specialized in luxury commodities, the so-called rich trades. While the new discoveries threatened the super-profits that flowed into Genoa and Venice from these arrangements, they did not lead to a general restructuring of capillary exchange. Most wholesale commerce remained in the hands of a large number of

[6] Botero, *On the Causes of the Greatness of Cities*, 63.

[7] See "Free Ports in the Central Mediterranean" in the introduction, esp. nn. 15 and 16.

[8] Pomeranz, *The Great Divergence*; Ormrod, *The Rise of Commercial Empires*; Acemoglu et al., "The Rise of Europe"; de Vries, "The Economic Crisis of the Seventeenth Century"; Zahedieh, *The Capital and the Colonies*.

merchants of all the sea's ethno-religious communities. But the rise of the Atlantic World did affect long-haul routes in the Mediterranean, especially by the late sixteenth century. First, given the impossibility of direct relations between distant producers and consumers, hub markets spread throughout the region as a means of managing distribution networks; there was a growing need for geographic mediation that Italian ports were well-placed to fulfill. At the same time, maritime insecurity after the Battle of Lepanto (1571) promoted a preference for definite routes and traveling in convoys. These tendencies favored the use of ports as long-distance entrepôts.[9]

Trade may proceed directly from port to port, or indirectly via an entrepôt such as Livorno. The more commerce resembles a spoke-and-wheel system geared around a central port, the more hierarchical the system; it becomes more dispersed as direct ties prevail. A horizontal structure of trade indicates the existence of a common marketplace, in which each area exchanges its surplus with another on terms of relative parity. By contrast, a more hierarchical system indicates the dependency of peripheral markets on a core one. Such central places collect and redistribute produce, while reaping profits from commercial mediation.[10] These principles are helpful for examining trade relations *within* as well as *between* regions. Regions connected at only a few nodal entrepôts suggest a hierarchical control over trade flows; regions connected at many points suggest a more integrated market.[11]

The extent to which commerce concentrates in a particular port depends on various considerations about market accessibility. There is a trade-off between the costs of operating direct connections and the longer distances of indirect connections. Given the economies of scale inherent in shipping, a hub may be preferred if costs associated with the hub are low enough. In the present day, technological improvement tends to be the most important factor in lowering trade costs: one need only think of the impact of the railway, steamship, or telegraph. The late-medieval invention of the oceanic sailing vessel likewise had a profound effect on trading patterns. In the early modern period, however, organizational changes were more important, such as the reduction in transaction costs associated with free port policies, or a decline in transport costs through maritime insurance. Infrastructural investments were relevant, too, although for our purposes it is best to assume that infrastructure was roughly comparable among major port cities.

[9] G. Mori, "Linee e momenti," 9. See too the introduction to chapter 2.

[10] C. Smith, "Regional Economic Systems"; Paynter, *Models of Spatial Inequality*; de Vries, *European Urbanization*, chs 2 and 6. For historical applications, see S. R. Epstein, "Cities, Regions and the Late Medieval Crisis"; J. Goldberg, *Trade and Institutions*, ch. 8; and Cronon, *Nature's Metropolis*.

[11] Economic regions have fuzzy boundaries. Here, I shall treat Livorno's hinterland as comprising Tuscany and parts of north-central Italy, which relied upon the free port for access to maritime markets. I shall define its region as the set of port cities stretching from the southern coast of France to Sicily (i.e. the Tyrrhenian): an arc of dense ties made possible by small-scale shipping. In theory, North Africa might have been included within the regional boundaries of Livorno. It was easily reached by many Tyrrhenian vessels and exported some of the same products as southern Italy. But for cultural and political reasons, the Health Board subjected shipping from North Africa to quarantine regulations, and I have followed suit to facilitate the quantitative analysis of Livorno's trade. On defining regions, see de Vries, *European Urbanization*, 83–4.

In the seventeenth century, for instance, Livorno had about two thousand meters of dock space, versus three thousand in Genoa and seventeen hundred in Marseille; all three ports faced the same difficulties in keeping their harbor floors clear of silt.[12] The principal factors shaping port agglomeration were network externalities and a differential lowering of trade costs: some ports were cheaper to utilize than others, and they were also better connected to other destinations.[13]

In the late sixteenth century, connections between Italian and northern ports were still fairly haphazard. From the vantage of Livorno we can discern the rise of shipping services from northwestern Europe and the establishment of diasporic trading networks linking Italy to the Levant and North Africa (*c.*1590–1630); the emergence of a multilateral trading regime oriented around the use of entrepôts and the further extension of diasporic networks (*c.*1640–80); and the consolidation of a multilateral trading regime (*c.*1680–1720). Rather than reducing port hierarchy, the rise of northern shipping initially exploited it by intensifying the entrepôt trade in Livorno. But by the third decade of the eighteenth century, northern cities began to extend their reach directly to secondary ports such as Naples and Ancona, thereby suppressing vertical ties between Italian havens. Underlying the moment of commercial concentration and later dispersion were organizational changes that lowered trade costs, first in Livorno and ultimately throughout much of the central Mediterranean.

Livorno was a second-tier port in the period 1573–85. It imported raw wool for Florentine industry and goods from the "floating bazaars" that alighted in its small port: cotton, cochineal, alum, sugar, and so forth. Trading ties were least hierarchical in the regions nearest to the port: Spain and North Africa. Seville mediated much of Livorno's trade with northwestern Europe, transshipping products such as salted fish, lead, and tin.[14] Trade with North Africa was relatively diffuse, although the overall number of ship arrivals was rather small. By contrast, Livorno's ties with the Levant were mediated primarily through Alexandria (seventy percent). Its connections with northwestern Europe were just as weak: London alone accounted for nearly seventy percent of all ships from northern Europe (Fig. 6.2). The main goods traded were the same ones Livorno got from Seville, further indication of fragile links to the north: lead, tin, copper, bronze, and salted fish. Fragmentary as the data are, it is clear that Livorno was a regional port of the west Mediterranean. Ties with the Levant and northern Europe were mediated by Alexandria and London—in part reflecting limited trade between the Atlantic and the Mediterranean, in part the marginality of Livorno in such far-flung exchange networks.

Famine in the early 1590s launched Livorno on its career as a major port. As grain imports nearly quadrupled, the number of ships alighting in the port more

[12] Doria, "Gestione del porto," 152, 163.

[13] Combes, Mayer, and Thisse, *Economic Geography*; Ducruet, Notteboom, and Langen, "Revisiting Inter-Port Relationships"; Redding, Sturm, and Wolf, "History and Industry Location." For historical applications, see Menard, "Transport Costs and Long-Range Trade," 269–75; and Grafe, *Distant Tyranny*, 91–3, 198–9.

[14] Cadiz includes San Lucar and Seville: Braudel and Romano, *Navires et marchandises*, 48.

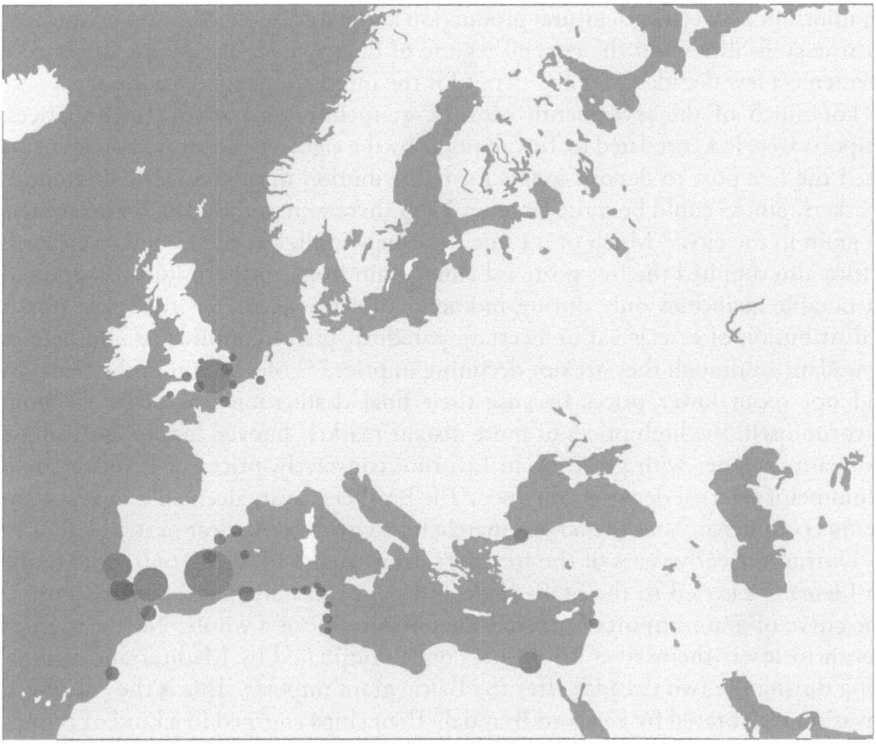

Fig. 6.2. Long-distance connections, 1573–85 (ship arrivals).
Source: Braudel and Romano, *Navires et marchandises*, 39–53. See app. 14.

than doubled. Henceforth, Livorno was an important center of the grain trade, especially during times of crisis.[15] In the early seventeenth century, the amount of grain imported by Livorno was dependent on demand in Tuscany and environs. Imports were modest in good years and very high in bad years. The source of the grain was quite variable—a point worth insisting on, since some scholars maintain that the arrival of Baltic grain in the 1590s signaled a major turning point in history. Mediterranean grain remained important throughout the seventeenth century, contributing on average seventy-three percent of Livorno's imports; only in times of famine did Baltic grain arrive in impressive quantities. The winter of 1590–1 represents the moment when northern Italy began to summon distant calories *when necessary*—and helped facilitate the participation of northern shipping, first Dutch and later English, in the carrying trade in Mediterranean grain.[16] Livorno's role as a cereal port contracted after the famines of 1645–9, as political instability limited exports from the Baltic and population decline in Italy restored

[15] Ibid., 117; and Ghezzi, *Livorno e l'Atlantico*, 107–18. See nn. 8 and 40–2 in chapter 2.

[16] Cf. Tabak, *The Waning of the Mediterranean*, 85, 213. Dutch commerce in the Mediterranean declined after 1645 because demand for Baltic grains declined, not because of the end of the Twelve Years' Truce. See Ghezzi, *Livorno e l'Atlantico*, 113, disputing Israel, *Dutch Primacy in World Trade*, 91–101.

equilibrium between agricultural production and mouths to feed.[17] Yet investment in storage facilities and the general regime of liberty made it easy for Livorno to reemerge a few decades later as a depot for the international grain trade.[18]

For much of the seventeenth century, grain imports tracked Tuscan prices. Imports were less correlated to Tuscan prices by the eighteenth century as merchants used the free port to deposit grains for redistribution throughout Mediterranean markets. Stocks could be quite large: in 1745 there were some 219,264 hectoliters of grain in the city.[19] Much of it came from Italy itself, but the Levant and North Africa also supplied the free port; as before, grain from northern Europe appeared in notable quantities only during moments of acute need. Livorno's role in the redistribution of cereals led to a certain paradox: "grains continue to rain here in abundance although they are not declining in price."[20] More grain in the free port did not mean lower prices because their final destination was often far from Livorno itself: the high prices of more distant markets buoyed local ones. Famine in Spain was met with great joy in Livorno; conversely, prices in Livorno could plummet if external demand collapsed. The Brothers Savary deemed it "a very dangerous commerce," and the largest merchant houses steered clear of it.[21]

During the early years of the free port, from about 1590 to 1650, port traffic in Livorno was tied to the grain trade and hence to Italian agricultural output; the curve of grain imports mirrored the port's traffic as a whole. Northern ships began to insert themselves into routes once dominated by Mediterranean shipping during the two decades after the Baltic grain imports. This is the "northern invasion" celebrated by Fernand Braudel. Their ships engaged in a kind of tramping between the Iberian Peninsula, North Africa, and Italy itself. During the second and third decades of the seventeenth century, northern shippers extended their range to ports in the Levant. Yet northern shipping never dominated everywhere or at any one place for long: even on routes from Izmir and Alexandretta, Mediterranean carriers still accounted for an average of twenty-nine and thirty-four percent of arrivals, respectively. Elsewhere, ties with Livorno were controlled by southern French shipping, and on a few routes, Italian shipping still mattered

[17] Ghezzi, *Livorno e l'Atlantico*, 115; Malanima, *La fine del primato*, 157. The Italian population declined by twenty percent (2,600,000 people) between 1600 and 1660; most of the decline occurred after 1630.

[18] During the Medici period, Livorno could store at least 161,454 hectoliters of grain; by the mid-eighteenth century, it could store somewhat less (102,889 hectoliters) because many facilities were out of use. They could be repaired or used in a pinch, though, as could facilities in Pisa. These figures do not evidently include private grain storage. Filippini, *Il porto di Livorno*, vol. 2, 318–19; Pult Quaglia, "Mercato dei prodotti agricoli," 117–19.

[19] Filippini speculates that Livorno's days as a grain emporium were numbered by the early eighteenth century, and that local demand became increasingly important to Livorno's trade. Yet his own numbers belie this view. Assuming that Livorno imported all of its grain—its consumption was about eighty thousand hectoliters a year during the middle of the century—it appears that total imports (exports plus consumption) in the late eighteenth century, the period from 1779–83, was rather high compared to annual imports earlier in the century: 168,322 hectoliters (1701–15), 242,581 hectoliters (1723–37), and 422,020 hectoliters (1747–51). These numbers suggest a rise in grain imports until the middle years of the century, followed by a decline to levels nonetheless comparable to earlier decades.

[20] Riencourt, 4/29/1710, as quoted by Filippini, *Il porto di Livorno*, vol. 2, 345.

[21] Filippini, *Il porto di Livorno*, vol. 2, 340, 345–8; Savary quotation on 348.

(such as the North African ports). The evidence from Livorno confirms the fundamentally competitive nature of the shipping sector during the seventeenth century. Merchants in the major ports had options when deciding whose ships to use for transporting their wares.[22]

Without the profits from shipping services, the English and the Dutch would not have been able to do much business in Italy. The balance of trade between Italy and northwestern Europe stood in the former's favor throughout the seventeenth century. Silk was an especially high-value Italian export. In the 1660s, English consumption of Italian silk accounted for fifty-five percent of their peninsular imports by value (and fifteen percent of all their Mediterranean imports). Overall, the English exported to the Mediterranean only about seventy-five percent of what it imported from the region, and the trade deficit with Italy was even more marked.[23] The English relied on the carrying trade and currency exchange to make up the shortfall. To state the same situation from the Florentine point of view: the ongoing success of the silk industry depended on foreign demand that would have been wholly ineffectual were it not for the rise of the northern carrying trade.[24] Thomas Mun understood this point perfectly, having himself worked in Livorno as a factor: "The value of our exportations likewise may be much advanced when we perform it our selves in our own ships, for then we get not only the price of our wares as they are worth here, but also the merchants gains, the charges of ensurance and fraight to carry them beyond the seas."[25]

The seventeenth century brought intensified ties with northern Europe, extensive use of northern shipping, and connections (via Atlantic entrepôts) to overseas commodities. In the very long run these relationships reconfigured the commercial order throughout the Mediterranean. Yet northern shipping did not at first affect underlying commercial and productive patterns. Products such as salted fish, lead, tin, and woolens were the basis of English relations with Livorno until the end of the seventeenth century; for the Dutch, grain and shipping services were the foundation. With the exception of shipping, the principal trades were in low-value bulk commodities and industrial raw materials: substantially similar to commerce a century earlier. Yet continuity is only part of the story. Three indicator commodities provide insight into the multifaceted process of economic change in the central Mediterranean: sugar, pepper, and cotton.

Pepper reveals the relationship between the overland route from Asia versus the sea routes via the Atlantic maritime empires. Portuguese pepper appeared in Livorno only around 1575, and it did not predominate over overland pepper until about 1600. During the first decades of the seventeenth century, Portuguese spices arrived in Livorno in impressive quantities—yet by 1625, three-quarters of pepper

[22] Greene, "Beyond the Northern Invasion," 43; see app. 15 for data on connections with the Levant.

[23] Pagano de Divitiis, *English Merchants*, 127, 126, 144. Her estimates are based on trade through London, which accounted for the overwhelming majority by value of all traffic between the two macro-regions.

[24] Ibid., 25–6, 123–7; Ghezzi, *Livorno e l'Atlantico*, 51–3, 134; Israel, "The Phases of the Dutch Straatvaart"; and de Vries and van der Woude, *The First Modern Economy*, 379–82, 412–23, 488.

[25] Quoted by Pagano de Divitiis, *English Merchants*, 131. On Mun, see n. 56 in chapter 2.

arriving in Livorno came via the northern countries, and that figure soon increased to over ninety percent. Meanwhile, quantities almost trebled: from an annual average of 577 quintals during the period 1612–26, there arrived in Livorno some 1,622 annually during the period 1626–66. Not only was the brief Portuguese monopoly on pepper over by 1620, but the English and the Dutch furnished Livorno with a much larger quantity of the spice than other suppliers ever had.[26] Yet we should not assume that the sea routes always delivered monopoly profits to the seafaring nations of the Atlantic. Pepper prices fell with respect to their sixteenth-century levels—suggesting a competitive environment in the Far East of which Mediterranean consumers were one beneficiary.[27]

Sugar is an indicator of the plantation economy in the New World and refineries in the Old. Brazilian sugar was the predominant source for Livorno's sugar in the period prior to 1642; thereafter Dutch and English sugar predominated. Overall sugar imports nearly doubled in the late 1650s. There are two things to note about these developments. First, Egyptian sugar accounted for a substantial proportion of Livorno's imports during the period 1627–56, suggesting that Mediterranean producers were responding to the same price signals as planters in the New World as late as the mid-seventeenth century—even if the latter ultimately overwhelmed them. This point is worth emphasizing, since scholars often stress the divergent destinies of the Mediterranean and the Atlantic rather than the threads that unite them. Second, the strict correlation between Atlantic sugar production and imports in Livorno suggest that Mediterranean markets were key to the expansion of sugar. The free port alone absorbed twenty-two percent of Dutch sugar exports. The growing demand for such a costly substance indicates the affluence of the Mediterranean, not its backwardness. The tragic apparatus of Atlantic slavery was initially oriented toward satisfying sweet tooths in Italy and the Ottoman Empire.[28]

Commodity production in the Mediterranean itself also evolved in the seventeenth century. Cargos of wax from North Africa, linen from Egypt, and cotton from the Levant increased over the period. The rise of cotton was especially striking. Livorno was a principal center of collection and redistribution of this fiber (Fig. 6.3). Unlike the slave plantations that made sugar the period's most notorious success story, cotton was grown by a vast number of small-scale producers throughout the eastern Mediterranean. For that reason it did not generate the super-profits that Atlantic plantations produced for their owners. While some scholars see this organizational structure as a sign of Mediterranean backwardness, we should remember that the benefits of cotton cultivation accrued to a broad swathe of farmers rather than a narrow band of planters. Exchange was governed by market forces and production was competitive.[29] Moreover, throughout the seventeenth

[26] Braudel and Romano, *Navires et merchandises*, 49, 84, 119; Ghezzi, *Livorno e l'Atlantico*, 139–47.

[27] De Vries and van der Woude, *The First Modern Economy*, 430–1, 437; Chaudhuri, *The English East India Company*, 327–8.

[28] Ghezzi, *Livorno e l'Atlantico*, 156, 157, 163.

[29] The extent to which landlords, tax farmers, and members of the political class appropriated peasant surpluses remains uncertain, although exploitation probably grew during the seventeenth and

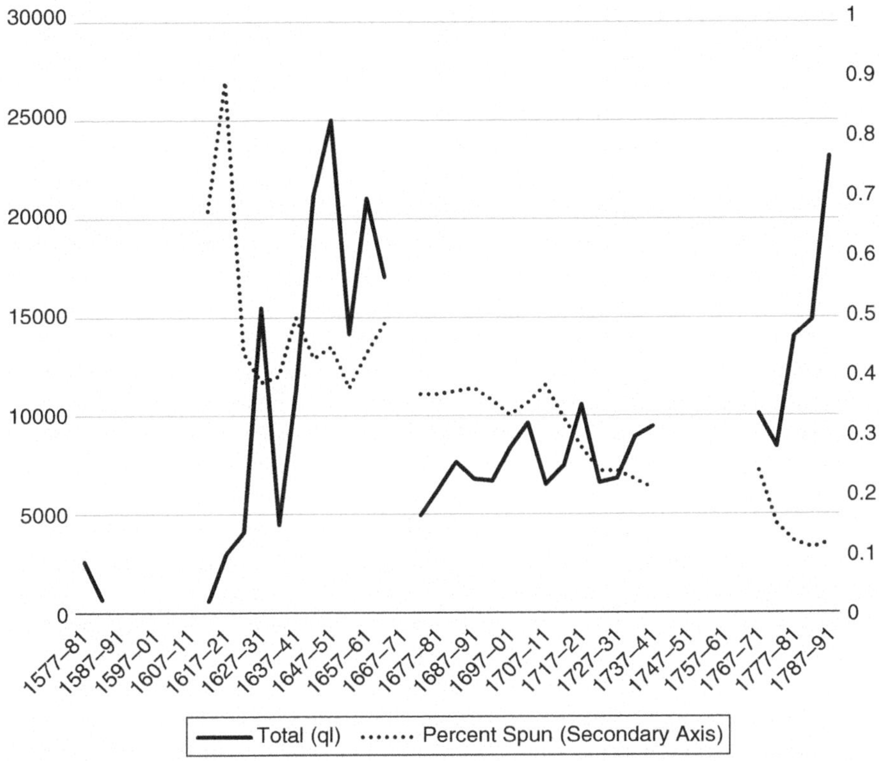

Fig. 6.3. Cotton imports, 1573–1797.

Note: I have placed all data on a quinquennial cycle beginning in 1577. This has necessitated some interpolation, since the Braudel and Romano data were quite fragmentary, and since Filippini presented his data at a range of intervals. See app. 16.

Source: Braudel and Romano, *Navires et merchandises*, 115; Ghezzi, *Livorno e il mondo islamico*, apps; Filippini, *Il porto di Livorno*, vol. 2, 128–9.

century, an average of forty-five percent of cotton arrived in Livorno already spun (yarn was worth between 1.5 to three times the price of raw cotton); the spread of cotton culture was thus compatible with some industrial preparation of the fiber. It was not until 1715 that the proportion of yarn out of total cotton imports collapsed, first to twenty percent until about 1737, and thereafter to only ten percent. The decline in yarn did not owe to de-industrialization, however, since the Ottoman Empire continued to produce yarn until the last decades of the eighteenth century. It owed to a preference for raw cotton among European producers, including Italian ones, who wanted to control the spinning process.[30]

eighteenth centuries. Inalcik and Quataert, eds, *An Economic and Social History*, vol. 1, 161–2; vol. 2, 448, 673, 681, 687; Riello, *Cotton*, 42–4.

30 The partial decline of the cotton trade around 1670 is to be attributed to the rise of Marseille and the florescence of a calico industry there during the 1670s and the 1680s. After the expansion of cotton cultivation in the West Indies after 1760, most cotton imports were intended for production in Italy. Ghezzi, *Livorno e l'Atlantico*, 163; Raveux, "The Birth of a New European Industry,"

THE REORGANIZATION OF LONG-DISTANCE TRADE

In the initial phase of its career as entrepôt, merchants from northwestern Europe used Livorno as a base for purchasing goods from Italy, North Africa, and the Levant; Italian merchants and Sephardic Jews mediated the exchange of northern wares for Mediterranean goods. This system of overlapping trading networks was made possible by Livorno's regime of foreign hospitality and persisted throughout the Ancien Régime. Yet maritime insecurity and the market rigidities involved in managing commerce among far-flung markets imposed limitations on commercial growth, felt especially by the principal carriers. English, Dutch, and French captains sought to maximize their cargos while minimizing time spent in port. Merchants also sought inexpensive and more secure shipping. Two transformations helped consolidate Livorno's role in commercial brokerage. The first were the warehousing incentives that culminated in the tariff of 1676. The second was the development of the convoy system that reduced maritime insecurity after 1650.[31] The convoys entailed inelastic routes that privileged Livorno as a center for the collection and redistribution of merchandise.[32] Taken together, these changes amounted to a substantial decline in the cost of using Livorno as a hub for indirect trade—not only for long-distance commerce, but also for local and regional exchange.

Livorno now stood at the center of a multilateral system of exchange in which wares were stockpiled in the free port before transshipment to further destinations. The logic of this commerce was simple: "after unloading merchandise destined for here, they load goods for Izmir and the Levant. Upon their return they stop here, leaving many wares from the Levant (silk, cotton, leather wares, wax, mohair, cloth, taffeta, Persian goods) and picking up alum, rice, gall nuts, tartar, irises, and the same Levantine wares in their warehouses."[33] Multilateral trade was practiced by English, Dutch, and French merchants, who used it to accumulate the currency reserves necessary for commerce with Italy, the Levant, and East Asia. It entailed the transshipment of non-national goods from more distant locales; and the maintenance of collection points such as Livorno for the maximal exploitation of shipping networks and the minimization of costs. This system promoted new levels of exchange with the world beyond the Mediterranean. The consolidation of sea routes eliminated some intermediaries and reduced

291–306: esp. 298, 302; Riello, *Cotton*, 200; Mazzaoui, "The First European Cotton Industry"; Inalcik and Quataert, *An Economic and Social History*, vol. 2, 703.

[31] The Dutch convoy system took shape in the early seventeenth century, but became more regular after 1650. The first English convoy arrived in Livorno in 1651. The French system followed—albeit more sporadically and with greater resistance among Marseillais merchants—in 1662. Rambert, *Histoire du commerce de Marseille*, 599–600; Pagano de Divitiis, *English Merchants*, 56–63; Israel, "The Phases of the Dutch Straatvaart," 9, 13, 23; Addobbati, *Commercio, rischio, guerra*, 115–16; Ghezzi, *Livorno e l'Atlantico*, 99–105.

[32] English or Dutch convoys typically stopped in Cadiz, Alicante, and sometimes Genoa on their way to Livorno; and thence they stopped in Naples or Messina before continuing on to Izmir. They almost always alighted again in Livorno before sailing for the Straits of Gibraltar. In addition to the details in Ghezzi and Pagano De Divitiis, see the amusing if misleading account in R. Davis, *The Rise of the English Shipping*, 246–7.

[33] Quoted by Frattarelli Fischer, "Livorno 1676," 46.

transaction costs, which could then be recapitalized for trade. When the English resident in Florence crooned about Livorno having become "the scale or magazin of an universall English trade," he was eulogizing a wider transformation in economic organization.[34]

The tariff of 1676 intensified commercial patterns that had been in the making for decades. The Levant now accounted for about forty percent of Livorno's long-distance trade, which became ever more concentrated on the port of Izmir with the consolidation of the multilateral trade regime. The Ottoman Empire exported a vast array of raw materials and agricultural produce to Livorno; it sent few manufactures westward with the exception of rugs.[35] All of this commerce was entangled with connections in northern Europe, principally England and the United Provinces. The English and the Dutch accounted for about forty percent and ten percent respectively of Livorno's long-distance imports in the early eighteenth century. Among the most important imports were salted fish, colonial goods, raw materials, and textiles.[36] As with the Levantine trade, intermediation was central: the free port was "the emporium, or magazine general for English manufacturies, and goods of all kinds, and it was from hence, that not only the cities in Italy, but other countries were supplyd, sending the produce of their several countries to barter or exchange, for such English goods as they had occasion for."[37]

Given that northwestern Europe and the Levant held pride of place in the deposit and transit trade, it is not surprising that relations with the western Mediterranean were proportionally modest. North Africa accounted for only ten percent of Livorno's long-distance trade in the period 1676–1790. On the other hand, commerce with the Iberian Peninsula witnessed a substantial transformation during the mid-eighteenth century with respect to the products exchanged and the volume of merchandise. In addition to wool and diminishing shipments of currency, Spain furnished new products such as wine, aquavit, sugar, and silk handkerchiefs. Lisbon also connected Livorno to Brazil and India. For instance, Livorno imported pepper and sugar from Brazil, and Livorno merchants exported coral to Goa in exchange for diamonds.[38] Long-distance trade with the Iberian Peninsula accounted for three percent of Livorno's imports in 1735 and twenty percent in 1792: the higher figure marks the intensification of ties with Spain after 1750.[39]

The development of financial services was one adjunct of Livorno's new role in international commerce. Europe's trade imbalance with the Ottoman Empire was

[34] Quoted by Pagano de Divitis, "Il porto di Livorno," 54; see also ibid., 44–7, 51–2; and Pagano de Divitis, *English Merchants*, 92–7. On the difficulties of distance, see Braudel, *Civilization and Capitalism*, vol. 2, 170–1.

[35] Filippini, *Il porto di Livorno*, vol. 2, 61.

[36] Ibid., vol. 1, 45, 56, 63. Relations with other countries in northern Europe were modest: three percent of long-distance imports in 1735. Apart from the fish ships of Newfoundland, relations with the colonial sphere were inconsequential.

[37] NA, CO, 388/95, 07/11/1765, report by John Dick.

[38] Trivellato, *The Familiarity of Strangers*, ch. 9. Nevertheless, Portugal accounted for a slender proportion of Livorno's trade—only 0.8 percent of imports in 1735 and 0.6 percent of exports in 1792.

[39] Filippini, *Il porto di Livorno*, vol. 1, 45, 56; see also Bardiot, "Marseille dans la compétition industrielle," 59–85, 63–5, 81–4.

ultimately funded by silver extracted from Spanish mines in the Americas. And yet money appeared infrequently in Livorno during the first half of the seventeenth century, indicating that the port did not yet form part of a regular system of exchange between East and West, even if it was well-connected to both through bilateral channels. This situation changed in the mid-1650s, when impressive amounts of silver began to appear in Livorno aboard Dutch and English ships. Both nations were now purchasing more in the Levant than they could pay for in kind; and silver rather than credit was the solution, since "Christian documents do not hold credence in Turkish courts."[40] As with other commodities, currency could be imported and exported freely in Livorno; the grand duke favored these arrangements by minting coins for trade in the East.

Other financial services were not far behind the development of these currency flows. By the early 1690s, a clearing house enabled merchants to adjust their credits and debits.[41] Meanwhile, the insurance industry flourished to the extent that merchants throughout the Mediterranean relied on it to insure their shipping, whether or not their wares passed through Livorno itself. By the mid-eighteenth century, Livorno's insurance market was nearly as developed as those of London or Amsterdam (and charged similar rates). By the latter years of the century, even shippers engaged only in local trade often took out policies in Livorno. By then, the financial sector was independent of commerce in the free port, although officials continued to treat it as ancillary. When insurers proposed a reform to give themselves additional protections in 1769, the authorities deferred to current practices, lest "merchants lose heart and abstain from insuring [their wares] in Livorno."[42]

Livorno was the first city that Uzbek visited on his fanciful tour of Christendom. The hero of Montesquieu's *Persian Letters*, Uzbek sailed from Izmir directly to the free port, "the most prosperous town in Italy."[43] Both his provenance and his destination were typical of the era, and they remind us that the free port's role in long-distance exchange had consequences for the movement of people as well as information. The same factors that made Livorno such an attractive destination for goods also made it a transit hub for individuals and their letters. For instance, the Armenian epistolary network relied upon Livorno for disseminating its news, so that although Venice was closer to the Levant than the Tuscan port, it had to wait a week longer for its letters. Such informational dependency was characteristic of most places in the central Mediterranean during the seventeenth and eighteenth centuries. Superior access to information was yet another aspect of Livorno's market domination.[44]

[40] Pagano de Divitiis, *Il porto di Livorno*, 62–9: quote on 65.

[41] Baruchello, *Livorno e il suo porto*, 423–8; Stumpo, "La circolazione monetaria"; Ghezzi, *Livorno e l'Atlantico*, 133–8.

[42] Baruchello, *Livorno e il suo porto*, 491–3; Addobbati, *Commercio, rischio, guerra*, 126–9, 152–3, 176–87, 222–3: quote on 186. The size of the insurance market increased substantially in the decades after 1740, when Livorno's long-distance traffic was in the midst of crisis.

[43] Montesquieu, *Persian Letters*, 71.

[44] Aslanian, *From the Indian Ocean to the Mediterranean*, 111; Braudel, *The Mediterranean*, vol. 1, 366–7; and in general Calafat, "Une mer jalousée," 493–5.

Despite Livorno's role in connecting the Mediterranean to northwestern Europe, it never became an "Italian Marseilles."[45] It did not develop direct connections with the Americas or Asia until the last decade of the eighteenth century; its commerce with these places continued to be mediated by Iberian, French, English, and Dutch ports. So while Livorno was the Italian city most closely associated with the expansion of global trade in the early modern period, it remained dependent on other entrepôts for access to colonial markets. This status was not imposed by geographic or market limitations, but by the success of the great powers in protecting their overseas monopolies. No Italian state could compete in the armed commerce of the colonial sphere. Conversely, the free trade regime consolidated around Italian ports like Livorno constituted a breach in mercantilist efforts to control overseas trade. For instance, English merchants purchased Persian silk in Livorno rather than directly in the Levant, as the Navigation Acts envisioned. Navigation rules could not be enforced in the Mediterranean because the openness of Italian ports made it easy for merchants to evade national regulations.[46]

REGIONAL EXCHANGE BETWEEN LAND AND SEA

Livorno's role in brokering trade between the Levant and northwestern Europe was linked to the city's position in regional distribution. As the English consul pointed out, "the commerce carried on in this city, is closely and strictly connected with most cities and towns in Italy, and not confined to Tuscany alone."[47] With the expansion of its long-distance commerce, Livorno increasingly pooled regional commodities for shipment overseas, while also distributing goods from the Levant and northern Europe to neighboring ports in the Tyrrhenian. It also imported goods for distribution throughout north-central Italy, from Milan to Rome. The proliferation of ties between northern Europe and various Italian ports after 1720 struck directly at these trades.[48]

Livorno developed as a major regional port soon after its exordium in the international grain trade. In 1593, regional shipping accounted for only a third of Livorno's traffic, dominated by massive shipments of Baltic grain; but by 1607, regional shipping accounted for two-thirds of Livorno's commerce. The early development of Livorno "corresponded to a kind of drainage of all nearby commerce in the Tyrrhenian Sea."[49] The free port reordered commerce everywhere

[45] Filippini, *Il porto di Livorno*, vol. 1, 63; see Addobbati, "Oltre gli intermediari," 146 n. 6, 149, 170, 173, 180–1.

[46] Pagano de Divitiis, "Il porto di Livorno," 54–62.

[47] NA, CO, 388/95, 07/11/1765, report by John Dick.

[48] The debate engendered by the crisis focused on relations between Livorno and its hinterland, rather than the evolving dynamics of regional trade. See "The Council of Commerce and the Crisis of Representation" in chapter 7.

[49] In 1593, there were 214 *navi* and 103 other ships; and in 1607, 344 *navi* and 1,093 other ships. The overwhelming majority of those other ships hailed from ports in the Tyrrhenian. These figures likely overstate the transformation in commerce, though, since data for the earlier years (1573–93) were based on Health Board *portate*, while the later years (1607–10) were based on summary bureaucratic records. Braudel and Romano, *Navires et merchandises*, 80, 109–13: quote on 90.

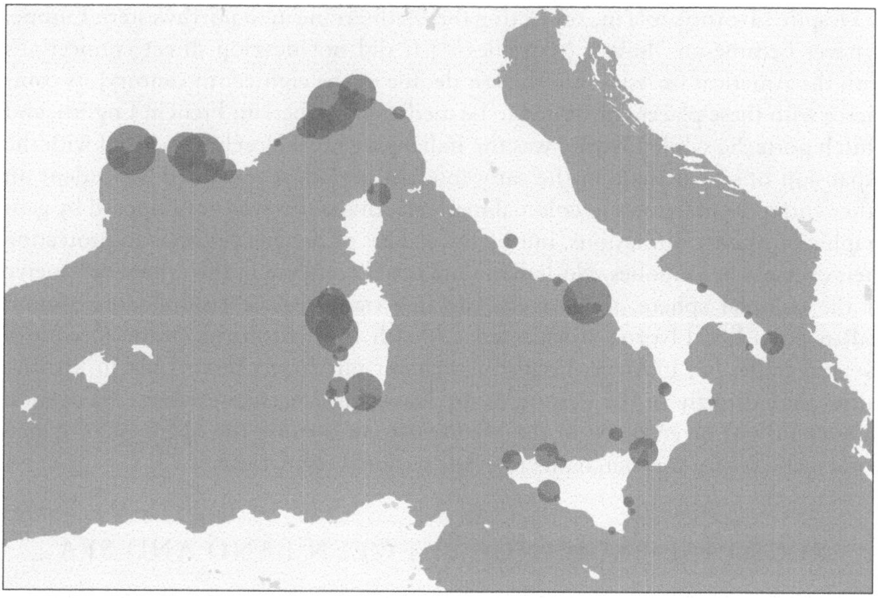

Fig. 6.4. Regional connections, 1657–8 (ship arrivals).
Source: Ghezzi, *Livorno e il mondo islamico*, 89–106. See app. 17.

along the coast from southwestern France to Naples. In the year from June 1616, ninety-four percent of Livorno's traffic consisted of small lateen-style ships, the vast majority of which represented regional trade. During that same period, two thousand small vessels passed through Livorno without disembarking goods: evidence of its centrality among ports-of-call and of the number of ships that swarmed like flies about the Tyrrhenian Sea.[50]

Data from 1657–8 provide further evidence of Livorno's exalted position in the regional hierarchy of ports. Health Board authorities monitored local trade during those years because of pestilence in nearby areas. During that biennium, the Health Board registered 553 small vessels from the Kingdom of Sicily, Sardinia, Corsica, the Pontifical States, and southern France (Fig. 6.4). In comparison to other figures on regional shipping, this number is unaccountably low—perhaps a third of what might be expected—indicating either that the Health Board did not record every ship that alighted, or that its unwonted severity discouraged casual shipping.[51] In any case, the data suggest generalized connections to adjacent areas rather than solely with metropoles such as Naples or Messina: we find notable ties to all second-tier ports in the region and more tenuous ones with a host of smaller cities. This pattern of generalized connectivity to second- and third-tier ports persisted until at least the mid-eighteenth century.

[50] Frattarelli Fischer, "Livorno 1676," 55.

[51] Ciano, *La sanità marittima nell'età medicea*, 82; Ghezzi, *Livorno e il mondo islamico*, 89; and in general, Cipolla, *Il burocrate e il marinaio*.

Table 6.1. Ship cargos from Sicily and southern Italy in 1675, *c.*1700, and 1734

	1675	*c.*1700	1734
Grain	35%	45%	27%
Wine	6%	10%	29%
Silk	48%	16%	5%
Spice	6%	2%	11%
Other food	8%	16%	22%
Other raw material	4%	2%	15%
Coral	25%	1%	4%
Fish	2%	3%	12%
Fruit	1%	5%	8%
Oil	0%	5%	7%
Manufactured good	7%	2%	6%
Ships with identified cargo	121	192	274
Total cargo ships	133	217	276
Total unknown ships	18	3	2

Note: Figures are calculated from the "ships with identified cargo" category. The other totals are presented for reference; vessels known to be empty are excluded from the table entirely. Percentages total more than one hundred because ships often carried more than one good. Offering such percentages was more feasible than calculating actual import levels given the condition of the sources, which only reliably indicate the quantity of grain and silk imports. "Fruit" is only fresh fruit, principally lemons and oranges; dried fruits were placed with "Other food," along with nuts and miscellaneous nutrients. "Spices" included sugar, tobacco, cacao, as well as more local products such as coriander or salt. Manufactured goods were mainly *seterie* and *stracci* (scraps of silk).

Source: ASF, MP, 1612 (1675); ASF, MP, 1542 (May 1699–April 1700); ASF, MP, 2308 (1734).

The *avvisi da mare* (sea reports) that survive for the late Medici period offer especially detailed information about the nature of regional shipping, including their cargos. Regional trade was generally complementary rather than competitive with respect to long-distance commerce, with some notable exceptions. Vessels from Sicily and southern Italy for instance brought grain and silk, two goods imported from the Ottoman Empire as well; but they also carried olive oil, wine, fruit, fish, and coral to the free port (Table 6.1). Much of this traffic was exclusively regional: the sale of produce for local consumption. But Livorno also connected regional exchange networks to those of long-distance commerce: silk from Naples, olive oil from southern Italy, coral from the coastal shoals, and alum from the papal mines at Tolfa were all destined for sale further afield. Conversely, vessels that arrived with empty holds intended on picking up cargo in the free port for distribution elsewhere in the region.[52]

Raw silk, one of the few commodities that competed with Ottoman imports, offers especially eloquent testimony to the importance of regional trade. In 1675, silk imports from the Tyrrhenian sphere were over *twice* those from the Levant; and in 1734, they were over *three* times such imports. Even at their lowest in 1700, regional imports still constituted about half of Levantine imports (Table 6.2). These goods were all intended to feed the silk industry, the principal export of

[52] Ghezzi, *Livorno e il mondo islamico*, 91–105.

Table 6.2. Silk imports in Livorno in 1675, *c.*1700, and 1734 (Tuscan pounds)

	1675	*c.*1700	1734
Italian Sphere	354,230	48,750	106,110
Long-Distance	175,050	112,725	31,320
Total	529,280	161,475	137,430

Note: The Italian sphere, as elsewhere in this chapter, encompasses the trading arc from southern France through Sicily. It is possible that a large amount of silk from Marseille was of Levantine origin, since Marseille imported plenty of silk from the Ottoman Empire (though its ties to the Kingdom of Naples were important, too). There are other elements of uncertainty, too: the figure for the Italian Sphere is calculated at 500 Tuscan pounds per bale, versus 450 Tuscan pounds per bale for Levantine silk, in accordance with a contemporary table of weights and measures. This procedure might exaggerate the difference between imports from the two spheres. On the other hand, this exaggerating effect was probably dampened by the low multiplier I used for regional silk imports when the documents reported a vessel as carrying silk without specifying an actual figure: two bales per vessel, while the average was closer to six bales per vessel. In any case, it is clear that Ghezzi's figures on imports from the Muslim Mediterranean offer a very partial portrait of raw silk imports in the free port. To his annual average of 163,161 pounds during the period 1612–66, we must imagine the equivalent or more in regional raw silk. See Ghezzi, *Livorno e il mondo islamico*, 130.

Source: ASF, MP, 1612 (1675); ASF, MP, 1542 (May 1699–April 1700); ASF, MP, 2308 (1734).

Tuscan as well as Bolognese manufacturing. The decline of silk imports by the early eighteenth century had two causes: the success of sericulture in north-central Italy and the proliferation of direct ties between Marseille and southern Italy, which cut out Livorno's role in commercial mediation. Industry in Florence and Bologna was still buoyant.

Livorno remained central to Italian markets throughout the eighteenth century, though not without important changes. At its height around 1720, twenty-five percent of the total tonnage of ships that entered its harbor hailed from Italian ports. Italian imports into Livorno amounted to a third of total imports (33.4 percent) in 1715 and just a little less in 1735. The stability of this percentage figure conceals an important change. While Livorno's commerce with the Levant and the western Mediterranean held steady between 1715 and 1735, commerce with northern Europe fell by three million *livre tournois* and commerce with Italy fell by two million *livre tournois.* The other decline was with North Africa: another one million *livre tournois.* Since North Africa was just a hopscotch from Sicily, we can see that the decline in trade with northern Europe occurred alongside a fall in regional trade. Initially, this was a crisis in Livorno's brokerage between Atlantic and Italian markets.[53]

The consolidation of the free port facilitated commerce between the Atlantic and the Mediterranean, but it also fostered a dynamic that undermined its own success. The concentration of long-distance trade in Livorno provoked aggressive policy imitation among Livorno's neighbors, who sought to attract commerce via

[53] Filippini, *Il porto di Livorno*, vol. 2, 149–50. The timing of the 1720 change was brought on by a crisis in European trade, finance, and politics, but its long-term impact depended on the proliferation of free ports in the region. See Baggiani, "Tra crisi commerciale"; and "The Spread of Free Ports" in chapter 8.

controlled liberalization; the free port's advantages were under perpetual threat from its rivals during the eighteenth century. In addition, while warehousing commodities in a node like Livorno enabled merchants to respond flexibly to price signals throughout the Mediterranean, the arrival en masse of perishable goods such as fish created sudden gluts in the market. Merchants sought to remedy predictable episodes of oversupply by seeking direct ties to consumers. To a greater extent than ever before, Atlantic goods could be exchanged for local produce in ports such as Naples or Messina, bypassing Livorno as a nexus of exchange.[54] For example, during the long seventeenth century, alum from the papal mines tended to be pooled in entrepôts like Livorno or Genoa. This practice was most marked between 1676 and 1720: but thereafter the entrepôt commerce among Italian ports declined very rapidly (Fig. 6.5).[55] What was true of papal alum was true for

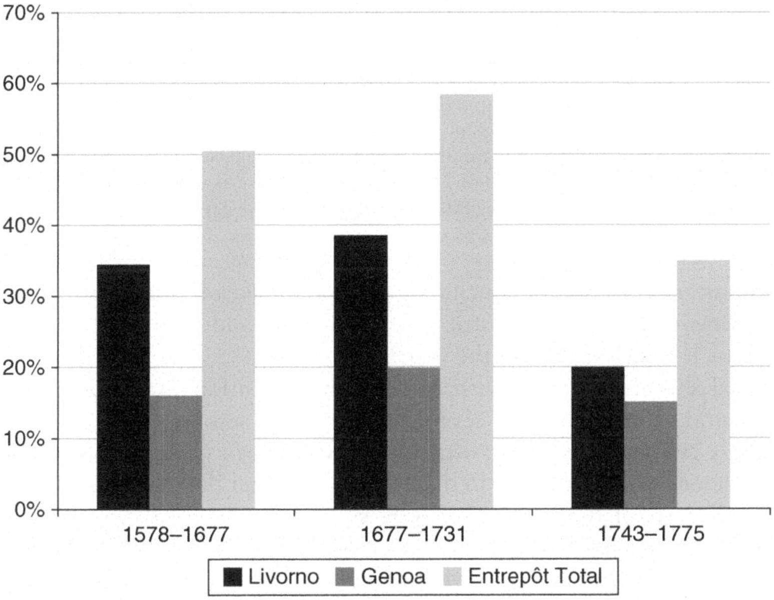

Fig. 6.5. Tolfa alum sent to Livorno and Genoa as a percentage of all shipments to Italy, 1578–1775.

Note: The totals slightly exaggerate the role of Genoa and Livorno, since Delumeau's figures actually pertain to Liguria and Tuscany. The overwhelming majority of alum shipments to those regions passed through the two entrepôts.

Source: Delumeau, *L'Alun de Rome*, 287.

[54] There were always some direct ties between northwestern Europe and the secondary ports of Italy during the seventeenth century. A few northern vessels alighted in Civitavecchia to load alum for shipment beyond the Strait of Gibraltar. In addition, the English undertook some direct trade in fish, olive oil, wine, and wheat as early as the 1670s, although it does not seem that their efforts bore fruit until *c.*1730. Delumeau, *L'alun de Rome*, 197–8; Pagano de Divitiis, *English Merchants*, 62–3, 69–75, 124–5; Chorley, *Oil, Silk, and Enlightenment*, 24–5, 30–2; Visceglia, "Commercio e mercato," 166–70; Di Vittorio, *Il commercio tra Levante*, 121.

[55] If the figures from southern France are included in the Italian trading sphere, port hierarchy declines less, because Marseille was able to control the alum trade along the entire southern coast of

Table 6.3. Two indices of maritime concentration in 1675, *c.*1700, and 1734

Sub-region (primate city)	1675	*c.*1700	1734
Adriatic (Venice)	69 (60%)	41 (21%)	114 (41%)
Liguria (Genoa)	228 (71%)	253 (45%)	357 (58%)
Sicily (Palermo)	163 (42%)	112 (16%)	137 (25%)
Southern Italy (Naples)	199 (57%)	190 (51%)	198 (37%)
Southern France (Marseille)	173 (56%)	202 (59%)	150 (40%)

Note: This table presents two different ways of conceptualizing trade concentration. It was constructed from a database of ship arrivals organized by city and sub-region. Ships that had alighted in another port en route to Livorno were eliminated from the set, thus leaving only direct connections. The figures in parentheses represent the percentage of ship arrivals from the metropole of each sub-region: e.g., in 1675, seventy-one percent of all direct ties between Liguria and Livorno were mediated by Genoa. The other figure represents the coefficient of variation: the standard deviation of ship arrivals from within each region divided by the mean, multiplied by 100. Thus, to continue with the example: in 1675, fifty-six ships came from Genoa, eight from Finale, six from Portovenere, two from La Spezia, and another seven from seven different ports. The average number of arrivals per port was thus 7.18, the standard deviation was 16.37, and the coefficient of variation was 227.93. The coefficient of variation unites in a single measure both the number of ports in a sub-region with which Livorno had connections as well as the intensity of these relations. The two indices do not necessarily yield identical results. For example, the notable increase in Liguria's coefficient of variation across the three time periods conceals an important fact: that the dominance of Genoa itself declined in 1700 with respect to the two other periods, as secondary ports such as San Remo and Portovenere challenged metropolitan commerce. These second-tier ports multiplied their own ties to Livorno at the expense of both third-tier ports as well as Genoa. More often the two indices move in tandem, however.

Source: ASF, MP, 1612 (1675); ASF, MP, 1542 (May 1699–April 1700); ASF, MP, 2308 (1734).

other important commodities, including grain and olive oil from southern Italy. If Livorno remained a center of distribution for foreign and local goods, its supremacy was much less clear than in the past.[56]

Regional shipping patterns also confirm the transition to a more horizontal trading world. Throughout the seventeenth century, second- or third-rank ports increasingly circumvented their own metropoles in favor of direct ties to Livorno. This movement reached its apex in the half-century after the reform of 1676, when virtually all parts of the Tyrrhenian were subject to Livorno's centripetal power (Table 6.3). In the table, a lower coefficient of variation indicates more generalized connections to Livorno and hence the free port's dominance; a higher coefficient of variation suggests less generalized connections, as metropoles mediated local commerce. By 1734, Livorno's golden age had come to an end, with rival ports having reasserted their economic power over their maritime domains.

Rival ports imitated Livorno's own virtues by building better port infrastructure, cultivating foreign merchant communities, and improving their customs regimes. These policies shifted the cost-benefit analysis away from indirect shipping through the Tuscan port and toward direct ties with its neighbors. As the English consul wrote in 1765, other Italian states "actually now import some part of the products

France. See Delumeau, *L'alun de Rome*, 270–7; and more generally, ibid., 193, 217, 250, 285–302. For the florescence of Civitavecchia's commerce during the mid-eighteenth century, see Toti, *Storia di Civitavecchia*, 492–3.

56 Blando, "Da un 'monopolio naturale,'" 15, 18.

of Great Britain directly to their own ports, without having entire recourse to Leghorn; the advantage arising from hence to their own subjects and to their revenues is too obvious to need any other motive."[57] The establishment of direct ties between northern Europe and the ports of Italy is a sign of crisis from the point of view of Livorno. For the region as a whole, though, it is an indication of market development. The multiplication of linkages between Italy and northern Europe facilitated the exchange of Italian produce for Atlantic commodities at the greatest possible advantage given prevailing conditions.

Soon after the crisis in mediating commerce with northern Europe, Livorno faced a challenge in its Levantine commerce. The French ambassador in Istanbul estimated that trade between Livorno and Istanbul diminished by twenty-eight percent between 1686 and 1782; there were probably similar declines with respect to other Levantine ports. Evidence from Marseille indicates a notable growth in the French port's imports from the Levant between 1735 and 1755. These imports, paid for by an immense expansion of French cloth exports, undoubtedly affected Livorno's trading position in the Levant.[58] The resurgence of Ancona and Venice was probably even more important in siphoning off Livorno's commerce with the East. Long-distance ship arrivals about doubled in Ancona after it became a free port in 1732, from fifty annually in the period 1722–31, to over one hundred in the following decade. A report to the Venetian Trade Board observed, "not only is Ancona in a position to distribute and exchange merchandise between East and West, much like Livorno, but also to introduce and disseminate goods at the mouth of the Po all throughout upper and lower Lombardy."[59] Venetian commerce with the Levant was itself expanding after 1740. By 1776, Livorno accounted for an average of only fifteen percent of the imports and thirteen percent of the exports of the principal Levantine ports; its competitors saw a corresponding rise in their trade. At stake in this commerce was not long-distance brokerage, but the trade between the Levant and the hinterlands of north-central Italy.[60]

Italian ports competed with one another not by extending state power as in the Middle Ages, but by attracting commerce through more liberal customs regimes and hospitality to foreign merchants. By contrast, Marseille relied on the backing of the French state, which was moderately successful in enforcing navigation laws and erecting a consular system throughout the Ottoman Empire.[61] When the Tuscan authorities signed peace treaties with the Barbary states in 1748–9, Italian

[57] NA, CO, 388/95, 07/11/1765, report by John Dick.

[58] Carrière, *Négociants Marseillais*, vol. 1, 44–50, 404–6. Carrière expresses reservations about the reliability of the import values, however, given how widely they fluctuate.

[59] Report from 6/21/1735, reproduced in Caracciolo, *Le port franc d'Ancône*, 126–30: 128; the shipping figures are from 113. Although Caracciolo does not provide provenance data, it is clear that Ancona's commercial growth owed to ties with the Levant, mediated by French ships, as well as to direct ties with northwestern Europe. See ibid., 149, 157, 242.

[60] The calculation is an unweighted average of the figures provided by Filippini for Alexandria, Aleppo, Izmir, Istanbul, and Salonica. Filippini *Il porto di Livorno*, vol. 1, 68–9; vol. 2, 135–9; Georgelin, *Venise*, 80, 114–18, 132–44.

[61] But it remained possible for ethnic minorities such as Sephardic Jews to exploit these arrangements for their own benefit—and for the benefit of the intermediary ports out of which they operated, such as Livorno. Trivellato, *The Familiarity of Strangers*, ch. 4.

ports saw a pretext for tightening quarantine restrictions against Livorno (on the supposition that plague controls were weak in North Africa). Such a maneuver was possible only because of the fragility of Livorno's regional commerce, which suffered a permanent loss of twenty-five percent of its regional trade with respect to the first half of the eighteenth century.[62]

An age of polycentricism and instability that began before 1590 with the dissolution of medieval trading patterns gave way after 1650 to the consolidation of Livorno as a central hub. Its rise was part of a larger phase of agglomeration throughout the Mediterranean, best typified by Livorno's sister port of Izmir. These centers of deposit made possible new levels of exchange between the region and the larger world. But as trade costs in the central Mediterranean fell and as export volumes increased, the terms of the trade-off shifted in favor of direct connections. There arose in the central Mediterranean a second polycentric age characterized less by instability than by competitive commercial institutions. Livorno inhabited a less hierarchical commercial space; its rivals established more direct ties with northwestern Europe and came to manage the redistribution of goods in their own hinterlands.

All was not lost, however. Southern Italy continued to send produce or raw materials (grain, wool, raw silk) to northern Italy via Livorno, in exchange for manufactures like velvet and silk. The north also continued to export the luxury wares for which the Italian peninsula was famous, such as jewelry, pearls, perfumes, and paintings. Livorno itself exported coral and, increasingly, straw hats: one of the few triumphs of Tuscan rural industry. The port also continued to redistribute overseas products such as sugar, coffee, or salted fish. Even some of the old long-distance mediating trade remained intact. The English continued to rely on Livorno for purchasing Italian silk, for instance, and the Dutch even intensified their dependence on the Tuscan port throughout the eighteenth century. The free port's sustained prosperity until the end of the Ancien Régime owed to network externalities via its merchant communities, exceptional warehouse capacity, and persistent (though diminished) advantages in its tariff regime.[63]

LIVORNO AND ITS HINTERLANDS

The evolution of Livorno's trade cannot be told solely from the seaward perspective. The small ships buzzing around the Tyrrhenian were ferrying goods to and from its Italian hinterland—or rather hinterlands, since the catchment zone of the free port varied over time. A memorandum by the merchant Giuliano Ricci in

[62] The annual average of small ship arrivals for the period 1701–50 was 5,174; it was only 3,895 during the period 1751–90. Baruchello, *Livorno e il suo porto*, 491–3; and Filippini, *Il porto di Livorno*, vol. 2, 131–3; Di Vittorio, *Il commercio tra Levante*, 101–5, 113–17.

[63] Livorno accounted for fourteen percent of Dutch trade in 1734, sixteen percent in *c.*1742, seventeen percent in *c.*1753, fourteen percent in 1778, and twenty-eight percent in *c.*1785. Figures calculated from Snapper, "De generale listen"; and Oldewelt, "De scheepvaartstatistiek van Amsterdam." For the other information in this paragraph, see Filippini, *Il porto di Livorno*, vol. 1, 50; Dal Pane, *Lo Stato Pontificio*, 249.

1757 suggests that contemporaries were worried about a competitive spiral, by which Italian regimes offered ever more generous terms for attracting commerce to their ports. Such competition affected Livorno directly (through port traffic) and indirectly (through ties with the hinterland). The next stage of Ricci's analysis indicated that a more fundamental problem lay in the Tuscan economy, however: "it is an object of pity to see within the Grand Duchy... the desolate cities and countryside, whose inhabitants barely have enough to live on, unable to devote themselves to industry or to agriculture for not being able to hope to profit."[64] Ricci attributed this desolation to import and export barriers. He would have been more accurate had he denounced the sharecropping system that retarded rural involvement in the marketplace. But it is hard to disagree with Ricci's broader point: as rival ports developed closer ties with their hinterlands, Livorno had to rely on the economic prospects of Tuscany alone.

In the mid-seventeenth century, Tuscany was still thought to be in essence a manufacturing nation. As one anonymous writer opined, "Florence conquers through its industry and its parsimony," not through the "fertility of its soil or its spacious meadows."[65] Many Florentines held the opposite view a little over a century later. "Nature has made us an agricultural nation. She has given us a moderate climate as well as land appropriate for vegetation, blessed with the greatest articles of agriculture, such as grain, wine, olive oil, legumes, and dry fruits of all species; and all in the greatest abundance." The difference between these quotations encapsulates the fate of Tuscany in discourse more than reality. As late as 1757, the region remained an exporter of manufactured goods, principally high-value silk garments (fifty-five percent of all exports). The myth of the decline of Tuscany has some basis in fact, of course. In the early seventeenth century, the international network of Florentine merchants contracted, reducing the profits from commercial mediation. The rise of silk moreover compensated only in part for the decline of wool; in the mid-eighteenth century, textiles accounted for eighty-five percent of the aggregate product of the industry's heyday. But if Tuscany collected fewer profits from abroad than it had during the Renaissance, it remained a rich and developed land.

Livorno provided Tuscany with access to international markets and mitigated the forces of decline. It altered the economic geography of the grand duchy without fundamentally reshaping institutional or social arrangements within the hinterland. And yet a venerable tradition emphasizes the free port's independence from its hinterland economy. The most reliable estimate is from 1762: that year, about twenty-three percent of all Tuscan exports passed through Livorno. This figure is often cited to highlight the poverty of relations between Tuscany and the free port.[66] That estimate represents a secular low, however, given the eighteenth-century

[64] Quoted by G. Mori, "Linee e momenti," 16.

[65] This and the following quote in Malanima, *Decadenza*, 177, 197.

[66] The figure is from Sonnino, *Saggio sulle industrie, marina e commercio*, 82–6; it is repeated by G. Mori, "Linee e momenti," 17; and Malanima, *Il lusso dei contadini*, 112. Sonnino also says that eighty-one percent of all Tuscan imports came via Livorno, a figure less often quoted but just as significant as export totals.

shift in textile exports to the land routes of eastern Europe. In addition, Livorno was critical for importing raw materials and nutrients, as one would expect for a developed economy of the epoch. It is simply inaccurate to assert that trade with Tuscany "constituted the least part of the commerce of this port."[67] Livorno fulfilled multiple and overlapping roles during its glory days as an international entrepôt, to which relations with its hinterland were key.

Grain was the most important bulk commodity that passed between Livorno and Tuscany. The market in the free port was well-integrated with the principal grain markets of the western Mediterranean, but its relationship to the hinterland was complex. Exports from Tuscany were forbidden, with exceptions for coastal lands and those belonging to the grand duke or public institutions; export rights were also granted via special license whenever domestic supplies were assured.[68] As for imports, waterways were a key variable: wherever water reduced transport costs, along the Maremma or the Arno River, the grain trade conditioned agricultural prices.[69] The customs barrier between Livorno and the Tuscan hinterland was modest: grain faced a tax of 0.5 lire per *sacco*, amounting to about five percent during times of low prices or 2.5 percent during times of high prices. Tuscan grains commanded a premium with respect to those in Livorno because of their higher quality. The governor of Livorno estimated in 1767 that it was only profitable to bring grain into Tuscany when prices in the hinterland were three lire higher than in Livorno—a substantial differential for a commodity whose price varied between ten and twenty lire per *sacco*. The international market kept prices in Livorno high enough that merchants rarely found it worthwhile to ship grain into Tuscany.[70]

For a populous country like Tuscany, however, the fundamental problem was securing access to grain in bad years, when prices were high. The Office of Plenty organized immense purchases of grain in Livorno for consumption in the hinterland—supplying the needs of ten to fifteen percent of the population during famines; more often it made purchases toward the end of the agricultural year to bridge supply and demand until the harvest. We have already mentioned the grain purchases of the early 1590s, so important for launching Livorno onto its international career. In March 1631, the Del Beccuto firm purchased 7,367 hectoliters for the Office of Plenty—nearly all the grain purchased that month by the regime and enough to feed half the population of Florence. In harvest year 1772–3, 182,821 hectoliters of foreign grain were imported into the grand duchy, some sixty percent of all foreign grain that entered the port that year; a decade later, eighty-six percent

[67] Official remark in 1789 quoted by Baruchello, *Livorno e il suo porto*, 510.

[68] Such exports could be high—landowners in the Pisan countryside exported 17,108 hectoliters of grain during the quinquennium of 1681–6, for instance, and 65,923 hectoliters during the subsequent five years. These exceptional years bear comparison to maritime imports: the quinquennial average during the period 1612–66 was 232,610 hectoliters of grain; Tuscany could thus export between seven percent and twenty-eight percent of what the free port imported by sea. See Pult Quaglia, "Mercato dei prodotti agricoli," 109–10; and Ghezzi, *Livorno e l'Atlantico*, 112.

[69] Parenti, *Prezzi e mercato del grano*, 238–56, 262–3; see also McArdle, *Altopascio*, 29, 38.

[70] Pult Quaglia, *"Per provvedere ai popoli,"* 116–17 and 126–7.

of foreign grains passed from Livorno into Tuscany.[71] Livorno imported other alimentary goods on behalf of Tuscany, too. For instance, fish was an essential source of protein for urban residents, and not only during Lent, since Tuscany remained short of pastureland until the late seventeenth century.[72]

Livorno also received provisions from the Tuscan interior—wine, olive oil, and meat. The quantities involved are clearest for wine. In 1730 the customs director calculated that Livorno imported 125,000 barrels of Tuscan wine and 25,000 barrels of foreign wine; a third of the foreign wine would be re-exported, but the vast majority of Tuscan wine was consumed by inhabitants in the free port.[73] In addition, the Office of Plenty sold subsidized bread directly to consumers in Livorno—crowding out private bakers, who by 1730 provided only about a fifth of what the public body distributed.[74] In terms of provisioning, Livorno was well-connected to its hinterland. When needed the free port funneled huge amounts of grain to the interior; it consumed local produce such as wine; and it was regulated according to the same administrative principles as other towns in Tuscany.

It is doubtful whether more developed agricultural connections between Livorno and Tuscany would have been feasible during the early modern period. High grain prices in Tuscany were usually accompanied by high prices on the international market, not because of interdependence but because of common harvest behavior. Livorno's stature in the grain trade did, however, make it cheaper to provision Tuscany than it might otherwise have been. Had Tuscany been forced to make recourse to some other grain entrepôt—for instance Genoa or Marseille—it would have paid additional charges for transit and insurance; and had it instead sent agents directly to grain-producing regions, as in the 1590s, it would have incurred search and information costs. Alternative policies might have promoted grain markets, such as the elimination of export barriers (to provide incentives to improve yield) or the liberalization of land tenure rules (to make Tuscan agriculture more responsive to price signals). European states rarely considered such policies until the mid-eighteenth century, and their effects when implemented were ambivalent. In the meantime, it was better to have a grain entrepôt at one's doorstep than to rely on a rival for access to grain.

For Florentines of the sixteenth century, the silk and wool industries were the "two beautiful eyes... set in the front of the head."[75] They accounted for almost all industrial exports. The wool industry's raw materials arrived by sea, since Tuscan

[71] Ibid., 132–3; Filippini, *Il porto di Livorno*, vol. 2, 337; Bertelli, "Un'azienda commerciale," 44–6.

[72] Annual imports via Livorno, Ancona, and the Romagna totaled about 366,087 pounds of sea fish and 329,232 freshwater fish in the early 1670s. Imports of fish to Livorno in those years were around ten thousand to fifteen thousand barrels per year. Some of this was exported to other ports for redistribution to Naples, Ancona, or Venice. Pult Quaglia, *"Per provvedere ai popoli,"* 221; Ghezzi in *Livorno e il mondo islamico*, 53; Ghezzi, *Livorno e l'Atlantico*, 51–6; see also Sonnino, *Saggio sulle industrie, marina e commercio*, 63–5, 85.

[73] Pult Quaglia, *"Per provvedere ai popoli,"* 195, 215, 230; Pult Quaglia, "Mercato dei prodotti agricoli," 135–6; cf. Pagano de Divitiis, "Il porto di Livorno," 46.

[74] Pult Quaglia, *"Per provvedere ai popoli,"* 165–6.

[75] Quoted by Malanima, *Decadenza*, 172.

wool was only used for low-quality local products. The most reliable estimates, those for 1590, indicate that Tuscan wool consumption was an important component of Livorno's overall trade in that commodity: wool destined for Tuscan production accounted for thirty percent of all wool that passed through the port that year (Table 6.4). Although later estimates are more conjectural, they confirm the ongoing importance of Livorno to Tuscan wool manufacturing. In 1670, perhaps fifty percent of all wool consumed in the state passed through the free port; at the same time, Tuscan consumption itself accounted for about a third of Livorno's traffic in raw wool. At an industry low around 1720, Tuscany still imported a third of the levels of the 1590s, both to satisfy what remained of the export industry as well as to supply the internal market for woolens.

Silk, the major growth industry of early modern Tuscany, was a different matter. North-central Italy satisfied much of its demand for raw silk through domestic sericulture. Livorno furnished the remainder: in the early eighteenth century, for instance, Tuscany still met a quarter of its demand for raw silk through imports from Sicily and southern Italy. How much did this commerce matter to Livorno? In 1675, the free port imported 529,280 pounds of raw silk; that figure should be paired with the 52,244 pounds imported by Florentine industry not too long before, in 1660: Florentine industry alone consumed about a tenth of Livorno's imports of raw silk. That figure as a proportion of Livorno's commerce apparently grew in later decades. In 1734, Florentine industry imported some 23,944 pounds of raw silk, almost twenty percent of maritime imports that year (137,430 pounds). Even with the spread of sericulture, the industry's needs constituted a sizable fraction of Livorno's commerce in raw silk.[76]

Wool and silk were by no means the only industrial raw materials to pass through Livorno. In the 1760s, Tuscans imported thirty percent of their linen in the form of Alexandrian raw flax via the free port (2,176,962 pounds annually). In 1734, Livorno imported 2,249,700 pounds of raw flax: just about enough to supply Tuscan demand as estimated a few decades later. Although we do not possess comparable consumption figures for the seventeenth century, we know that Livorno imported per year some 3,054,624 pounds (from 1636–48) and 1,403,369 pounds (from 1649–66) of Alexandrian flax; Livorno in the mid-seventeenth century thus imported about as much flax as its Tuscan hinterland would consume a century later. Virtually all cotton that entered Tuscany likewise passed through Livorno, principally from the Ottoman Empire. Such imports reflect the diffusion of cotton textiles from the late seventeenth century on, although Tuscan peasants themselves still consumed only modest amounts of cotton. In addition, an enormous quantity of leather hides was imported every year from North Africa, in part to supply the industry for leather wall-hangings (*corami*)—one of the quintessential luxuries of Baroque Italy.[77]

[76] See Table 6.2; and on Florentine imports, Malanima, *Decadenza*, 108, 113, 350.

[77] On flax, see Malanima, *Il lusso dei contadini*, 69; and Ghezzi, *Livorno e il mondo islamico*, 244; the 1734 calculation is from ASF, MP, 2308. On cotton, see Malanima, *Il lusso dei contadini*, 70; and "Mediterranean Commerce in a Global Age," esp. nn. 29–30. On *corami*, see Ago, *Gusto for Things*, xxvi, 79–80.

Table 6.4. Wool imports and consumption in Tuscany, estimated, 1590–1762 (Tuscan pounds)

	*c.*1590	*c.*1620	*c.*1670	*c.*1730	1762
Imports via Livorno					
Islamic World		428,085	348,950	2,027,900	
Spain		508,247	460,600	30,800	
Italy		548,155	362,340	407,750	
Total	5,602,345	1,484,487	1,171,890	2,466,450	
Florentine consumption					
Spanish wool	1,188,000	681,269	12,384		60,187
Roman wool	612,000	681,269	279,211		184,941
Barbary wool	0	0	35,837		
Total	1,800,000	1,362,538	327,432	281,561	
Other domestic consumption	415,040	415,040	445,470	506,328	538,437
Total Tuscan wool consumption	2,215,040	1,777,578	772,902	787,889	
Estimated sea consumption	1,701,520	1,229,424	410,561		
Livorno imports as % of Tuscan consumption	77%	69%	53%	54%	
Tuscan consumption as % of Livorno's traffic	30%	83%	35%	17%	

Note: During the last decade of the sixteenth century, about two-thirds of the industry's wool came from Spain and the rest from the Papal States; by 1620, about half came from Spain and half from the Papal States; and around 1670, about eighty-five percent came from the Papal States, eleven percent from the Barbary States, and four percent from Spain. For 1762, the Florentine industry sourced three-quarters of its wool from the Papal States and the rest from Spain. The other import totals for the Florentine industry are unfortunately not specified by origin. Other domestic industries also exploited foreign sources of wool: perhaps twenty-five percent of internal demand was met through importation in 1762, likewise primarily from the Papal States. Unfortunately, we do not possess estimates for the sourcing of local wool for earlier periods. Population increases would have increased wool imports, whereas pasturage expanded during this same period, auguring for a reduction in imports. Given these contradictory movements, it is best simply to index the 1762 figure to the Tuscan population for our comparison years. In addition, we also do not know how much Roman wool arrived by sea. We will assume that half of the wool from the Papal States arrived by sea in Livorno, as did all Spanish or Barbary wool. We also possess information on wool imports into Livorno drawn from Health Board records. The most reliable figure concerns wool imports in the early 1590s. The figures for 1620 involve a certain amount of estimation: Ghezzi provides annual data only on wool imports from the Islamicate world; in addition, his data exclude any wool coming from southern Italy. I have estimated Spanish wool imports by subtracting Spanish wool known to have arrived in Livorno from the Islamicate world from the total amount of Spanish wool used by the Florentine industry in that year; such a procedure assumes that all Spanish wool entering Livorno was destined for Florence. The real figures must have been higher, since Livorno also supplied Spanish wool to other Italian markets. In addition, I have estimated wool imports from the Papal States for 1620 by assuming that half of all Roman wool arrived in Livorno by sea (this procedure likewise assumes that all Roman wool arriving in Livorno was destined for the Tuscan market). My procedures for estimating imports in 1620 assumes minimum import levels and probably exaggerates somewhat the role of Tuscany in Livorno's wool trade. We are on firmer ground for the 1670 and 1730 import figures, because the *portate* records for those years include regional imports.

Sources: Braudel and Romano, *Navires et merchandises*, 114; Ghezzi, *Livorno e il mondo islamico*, 233, 242, 264, 269, 275, 281; Malanima, *Decadenza*, 95–5; Malanima, *Il lusso dei contadini*, 72–3; ASF, MP, 1542; and ibid., 2308.

Tuscan industrial exports were often launched to market via the free port. Livorno was important to the Riccardi family's strategy in the seventeenth century: in 1629, for instance, their investments in Livorno and Pisa amounted to four thousand scudi in each place, earning exceptionally lucrative profits of 18.2 percent and twenty percent. The sale of Florentine textiles was a critical aspect of their business there, alongside the purchase of raw materials and grains. Livorno's role as a channel for exports endured despite a shift in Tuscan textile markets from western Europe to east-central Europe by the early eighteenth century. Livorno remained one of the principal markets for the Baldi firm even in 1725, for instance, and Antonio Casini sold a fourth of his medium-quality Prato textiles to merchants in Livorno. Woolens and felt hats produced in regional centers such as Pontedera and Pescia also found vent in Livorno.[78]

Despite inevitable computational imprecision, it is worth comparing the value of Tuscan industrial exports through Livorno with that of manufactures imported by sea. About fifty thousand wool garments (principally Dutch and English) were imported annually into Livorno around 1670, most destined to be transshipped to southern Italy or the Ottoman Empire. At the same time, merchants exported a little over three thousand Florentine silk garments through the free port. Since silk garments were substantially more expensive than wool ones, about five times as expensive, Florentine exports alone were worth a third of total textile imports from northwestern Europe. A similar calculation from the early eighteenth century suggests that Tuscan silk exports accounted for seventy percent by value of all woolens imported into the free port. Florentine silk passing through Livorno clearly represented an important tranche of the free port's trade in manufactured goods.[79]

The wider Italian market for raw materials and industrial exports sheds further light on relations between port and hinterland. Industries in Milan, Bologna, and other cities relied on the free port for their imports of wool, cotton, flax, and hides, not to mention ancillary materials like mordants or dyes. In exchange, products such as glass, waxworks, and textiles plied Italian roads for export by sea. Bologna for instance consumed seven percent of all alum that Livorno imported during the period 1677–95; and that city alone accounted for about fifty percent of all goods in transit with Livorno.[80] Overall, by the mid-eighteenth century, imports accounted

[78] Malanima, *Decadenza*, 269; Malanima, *Il luso dei contadini*, 80–1, 88; Malanima, "Le attività industriali"; and in general, Mazzei, *Itinera Mercatorum*, *passim*.

[79] During the period 1663–9, England and the Netherlands exported 51,271 garments per year to Livorno; meanwhile, the Florentine silk industry produced 10,177 garments per year, a third of which were exported via the sea route through Livorno: 3,392 garments. The ratio of silk to wool, assuming one silk garment equals five wool ones: thirty-three percent. Between 1705–50, thirty-two percent of Tuscan silks were exported via the free port, or 5,085 garments per year out of an annual production of 15,462. That amounted to 372 quintals of silk goods per year. During those same years, Livorno imported annually about 2,694 quintals of woolens. The ratio: sixty-nine percent. Silk garments ranged in value between 2.5 to ten times the value of wool garments; I have opted for a multiplier of five. Calculations based on Malanima, *Decadenza*, 353; Pagano de Divitiis, *English Merchants*, 91, 133–56; and Filippini, *Il porto di Livorno*, vol. 2, 125–7, 310. See in general Sonnino, *Saggio sulle industrie, marina e commercio*, 84–6.

[80] Delumeau, *L'Alun de Rome*, 286–7, 298; on the goods exchanged between Bologna and Livorno, see Dal Pane, *Economia e società a Bologna*, 333ff.

for about two thirds and exports a third of goods in transit between Livorno and the states of north-central Italy. This "imbalance" reflects the development of industries serving local rather than export markets; that is, it points to the rise of rural industry and peasant consumption, both of which proceeded more intensely in Tuscany's neighbors than in the grand duchy. Despite the lacunae in our sources, the picture is clear: Livorno's hinterland included Lombardy, Emilia-Romagna, Le Marche, and the Papal States. Their export industries relied on the free port almost as much as Florence itself.[81] Treating those states as part of Livorno's hinterland would reveal substantially higher figures than those calculated for commerce with Tuscany alone. When the spread of free port institutions led to a contraction of Livorno's hinterland in the mid-eighteenth century, the effect on its commerce was profound because the hinterland was indeed "closely and strictly connected" to maritime trade.[82]

The changing profile of elite investment strategies highlights how Livorno plugged Tuscany into international markets. Until the early seventeenth century, Florentines invested in business activities abroad as much as in Florence itself. This network of merchants was responsible for creating the famous fortunes of the Renaissance. Then, under pressure from commercial and industrial competition, Florentine foreign investments declined markedly. Braudel deemed this "defection of the bourgeoisie" among the most blameworthy in western Europe.[83] Yet the recall of Florentine capital from abroad did not mark a wholesale retreat from international commerce. Florentines invested heavily in silk production and in commercial enterprises via limited-liability partnership contracts that enabled elites to minimize risk and day-to-day involvement in business affairs. The new commercial firms were based in Florence or Livorno, where they imported grain or raw materials and exported manufactures. Such operations were possible because Livorno merchants had agency relations throughout Europe and the Mediterranean.[84]

The records of the del Beccuto firm illustrate the use Florentine capitalism made of the free port in the seventeenth century. The firm was active in Livorno from 1630 to 1639. Del Beccuto traded on its own account as well as on commission. Its densest ties were with Tuscany and northern Italy, the west Mediterranean stretching from southern France through the Iberian Peninsula, and with southern Italy from Sicily through Latium (Table 6.5). The firm imported far more from the western Mediterranean and northern Europe than it exported; most of its export activity was oriented toward Italian markets (seventy-seven percent). These figures

[81] Sonnino, *Saggio sulle industrie, marina e commercio*, 87–90; Pagano de Divitiis, "Il porto di Livorno," 51–2; Sella, "Industrial Raw Materials"; cf. Malanima, *La fine del primato*, 112–21.

[82] Marseille was fortunate by comparison, serving three provinces throughout the eighteenth century: Languedoc, Provence, and the Lyonnais. In 1789 imports via the hinterland amounted to seventy-four million *livres tournois*, about thirty-two percent of the total of all imports and exports through the French port (230 million). Had Marseille faced competition from rival ports in southern France, that figure would have been rather lower. Carrière, *Négociants Marseillais*, 583–4.

[83] Braudel, *The Mediterranean*, vol. 2, 725–6.

[84] Carmona, "Aspects du capitalisme toscan"; Malanima, *Decadenza*, 138–41; Litchfield, "Les investissements en commerce des patriciens florentins"; Litchfield, *Emergence of a Bureaucracy*, 205–12.

Table 6.5. Geography of the activities of the del Beccuto firm based in Livorno, 1634–5

	Import Rank	Export Rank	Import (%)	Export (%)	Total Rank	Total %
Tuscany	11	27	10%	22%	38	17%
N. Italy	9	39	9%	31%	48	21%
S. Italy	17	30	16%	24%	47	21%
West Med.	51	19	49%	15%	70	31%
N. Europe	17	5	16%	4%	22	10%
Levant	0	4	0%	3%	4	2%
Total	105	124	100%	100%	229	100%

Note: Although Bertelli shows the relative magnitude of various exchanges, she was unable to reduce various measures to a single value, and it is not always clear how she arrived at her graphical representations. I have reformulated her work using simple rank orderings for her basket of goods: worked silk, hides and leather, wool textiles, spices, raw silk, and raw wool. Then I combined the rank orderings to provide a kind of balance sheet for imports and exports. To illustrate my procedure: since Florence's rank in Livorno's imports of worked silk was three, its rank on wool textiles was four, its rank on raw silk was one, and its rank on raw wool was three, its overall rank in Livorno's imports was eleven. Its rank in the firm's Livorno exports was seventeen (three for worked silk, four for leather, three for textiles, two for spices, one for raw silk, and four for raw wool). Florence's total rank score in the firm's activities is therefore twenty-eight (eleven for imports, seventeen for exports)—accounting for over two-thirds of the firm's business in Tuscany, which had a total rank of thirty-eight.

Source: Bertelli, "Un'azienda commerciale," unpaginated maps.

confirm Livorno's role in exchange with the hinterland of north-central Italy: goods moved inland along the Arno to Florence, then to Bologna, and onward for sale through the Po River Valley. Ties to other cities in the Mediterranean and southern Italy were mediated by large cities—Marseilles, Lyons, Barcelona, and Madrid in the west, and Rome, Naples, Palermo, and Messina in the south.[85] The del Beccuto records offer little evidence concerning Livorno's role in the deposit and transit of wares between northwestern Europe and the Levant. Florentine capitalists kept themselves distant from such commerce, participating indirectly via Sephardic, English, Dutch, and French traders in Livorno.[86]

By way of contrast, consider Ergas & Silvera, a Sephardic firm active in Livorno from about 1705 to 1745. Unlike Tuscan firms such as the del Beccuto, Ergas & Silvera did not concentrate their business activities in the western Mediterranean or the Italian hinterland. They were instead focused on long-distance trade in which a handful of cities played roles of the first importance: Genoa and Marseilles in the Tyrrhenian; Aleppo, Cyprus, Izmir, and Venice in the Eastern Mediterranean; and Amsterdam and London in northern Europe. To the Levant they exported Italian silks, French and English woolens, dyestuffs, glasswork from Venice and the Netherlands, and sugar and spices from the Indies. Their principal Ottoman import was raw cotton, but they also did business in raw silk, Asian spices, and

[85] Bertelli, "Un'azienda commerciale," 13–20, 27, 30–1. Although legally independent, the del Beccuto firm was part of a network supervised by the Salviati family firm in Florence that included subsidiaries in Pisa, Bologna, and Piacenza.

[86] Two decades later, the Saminiati firm had a similar trading network, though its connections with the Levant and North Africa were more developed. Braudel, *Civilization and Capitalism*, vol. 2, 184–5.

Table 6.6. Geography of Florentine investments, early seventeenth century

	Florentine investment, 1602–4	Del Beccuto firm in Livorno, 1634–5
Tuscany and Northern Italy	29%	38%
Southern Italy	51%	21%
Iberia	8%	31%
Northern Europe	2%	10%
Levant	3%	20%

Sources: Litchfield, *Emergence of a Bureaucracy*, 207–10; Table 6.5.

other produce. Ergas & Silvera concentrated their activities in emporia that collected and redistributed regional produce.[87]

The development of the free port made it possible for Florentines to conduct business without leaving Tuscany—though this convenience came at the cost of intermediation profits, which now went to other parties. The commercial geography of the firms based in Livorno or Florence resembled that of the old foreign ventures, weighted toward interests in the Iberian and Italian peninsulas, with a smattering of investments further afield (Table 6.6). From the Florentine perspective, Livorno represented a degree of continuity with sixteenth-century commerce. Recall that Filippo Sassetti had lamented the tendency of Florentines to trade with the Levant via Ancona or Venice rather than travel there directly. Tuscan merchants in the early modern period generally spurned Sassetti's advice to travel to the East: but unlike those whom he criticized, they could conduct their long-distance trade through Livorno itself, without relying on foreign ports.[88]

THE LIMITS OF MARKET DEVELOPMENT

Despite enduring connections between the free port and its hinterland, industrial trends in Tuscany bore little direct relation to the development of Livorno. The wool industry suffered from an increasingly inhospitable market environment, in which import-substitution policies narrowed vent in Western Europe, while sales in the Ottoman Empire faced competition from cheap imitations.[89] Under these circumstances, Florentine manufacturers might have lowered the quality and hence the price of their wares, but lowering quality was not a genuine option, since rural labor was not widely available for exploitation: sharecropping arrangements minimized peasant involvement in market-oriented activities. Instead, Florence specialized in high-quality, urban-based wool production despite increasingly restricted markets for their products. On the positive side of the ledger, the

[87] Trivellato, *The Familiarity of Strangers*, 121–7, 201–5.

[88] See n. 50 in chapter 1 and associated text.

[89] See Rapp, "The Unmaking"; moreover, procuring high-quality wool became more difficult given the rise in Spanish wool prices. Malanima, *Decadenza*, 303.

silk industry was undergoing an expansion that lasted deep into the eighteenth century. Unlike wool, the silk industry thrived in an urban environment in spite of higher labor costs. At the same time, thanks to state-supported policies of mulberry planting (which had a low opportunity cost for sharecroppers), sericulture expanded throughout north-central Italy. Meanwhile, appetites for expensive silks seemed insatiable with the spread of fashionability throughout Europe. For silk, in short, Florence enjoyed a growing market, easy access to raw materials, and a favorable labor situation—including the opportunity to exploit female workers in Florence and other cities.

Contemporaries were incorrect to attribute the wool industry's decline to the "ease in procuring foreign cloth imported so readily from Livorno."[90] While at least twenty-five percent of such foreign woolens came through the free port—the real figure was higher owing to contraband—the dynamics of industrial transformation owed little to Livorno. In line with their cohort throughout Europe, Florentine patricians embraced lives of fashion in the latter half of the seventeenth century. Even the clergy had a passion for foreign cloth, "made mostly by heretics," to such an extent that "the churches and convents have been transformed into warehouses of foreign textiles."[91] And yet this consumption did not destroy the Florentine wool industry, which had experienced severe decline much earlier in the century. Nor was the peasantry to blame. Despite moralist anguish about rural extravagance, few peasants were wealthy enough to buy even modest luxuries. Livorno only became an avenue for cheap textiles after late eighteenth-century reforms lowered costs on the movement of goods within Tuscany and, to a lesser extent, between Livorno and its hinterland. Only then did the Tuscan countryside fully enter into the market system.[92]

The same factors that conditioned industrial transformation affected market development more generally. The sharecropping system limited the spread of specialized production for market, keeping mixed crop profiles oriented toward subsistence and deterring peasants from selling their labor to industry or cultivating their own plots of land. Agricultural output grew through extensive rather than intensive means: through extending the sharecropping system to woodlands and land reclamation, rather than innovation and specialization. The Tuscan economy grew through the increased exploitation of natural resources.[93]

[90] Quoted by Malanima, *Il lusso dei contadini*, 141. The figure is from ibid., 112; and in general, see ibid., 145–58; Malanima, *Decadenza*, esp. 80, 295, 314; Brown and Goodman, "Women and Industry in Florence"; Pagano de Divitiis, *English Merchants*, 133–41; Battistini, *Gelsi, bozzoli e caldaie*; Goldthwaite, *The Economy of Renaissance Florence*, 255–62 and 336–40; Tazzara, "Capricious Demands."

[91] Quoted by Malanima, *Il lusso dei contadini*, 108.

[92] Only a small class of prosperous sharecroppers with large holdings benefited from a rise in agricultural prices; for the new class of elite sharecroppers, buying *local* textiles became feasible. These transformations benefited Tuscan proto-industry rather than foreign manufacturers. Malanima, *Il lusso dei contadini*, 109–10, 150–8; McArdle, *Altopascio*, 176–81; and Benadusi, *A Provincial Elite*, ch. 7.

[93] Historians have been unanimous in attributing the limits of the rural marketplace in Tuscany to sharecropping, and I have followed them pending newer research. Elsewhere in Europe, however, sharecropping was not incompatible with market development. It is possible therefore that mixed cultivation itself must bear some responsibility for orienting producers toward auto-consumption. In addition, larger forms of social and political domination probably aggravated the effects of sharecropping. See

As late as the mid-eighteenth century, families only sold about one-sixth of their produce, using the proceeds to purchase textiles and iron goods. Auto-consumption was the norm, and peasant purchasing power remained low, on the order of ten lire per person; the peasant had "just enough income for a miserly living."[94] Given this set of institutional arrangements, constraints on Tuscany's market development were powerful no matter the extent of Livorno's integration into international maritime flows.

Agricultural contracts were the most important constraint on market development, though not the only one. Livorno was a free trade zone separated from its hinterland by a customs cordon. Merchants paid ordinary rates whenever their goods entered Tuscany proper (except for transit). Commerce within the grand duchy also suffered from a warren of internal tolls—about a hundred, clustered along geographic or political frontiers.[95] Contrasting the cordon separating free trade in Livorno from controlled trade in "Tuscany" minimizes the problem, then: that cordon was just one of many that stretched from the coast to Florence and beyond. These tolls were a legacy of the piecemeal construction of the territorial state in the late Middle Ages. And yet their overall effect on export industry was modest. Duties for raw materials were hardly exorbitant. Gian Rinaldo Carli estimated that four internal tolls added twelve percent to the price of a bale of wool on its journey from Livorno to Cortona, the entire length of Tuscany from the sea to the Apennines: each toll added about three percent to the price of the bale.[96] These were maximal estimates. Tax collection during those years was especially rigorous owing to the General Tax Farm, a foreign outfit that administered Tuscan taxation after the demise of the Medici dynasty. More typically, producers and merchants benefited from a regime of fiscal laxity.[97] In any case, duties on raw materials constituted only a small portion of costs. More important in determining the fate of export industry was the structure of the labor market and demand for finished products.

The channels between Livorno and its hinterland were as open as Tuscan institutions allowed them to be. For food commodities, for which transport could amount to a high proportion of costs, ready access to the international market probably minimized price volatility and lowered overall prices during famine years. Livorno also probably attenuated the dislocations associated with industrial transformation by facilitating access to raw materials and promoting industrial exports

Sereni, *History of the Italian Agricultural Landscape*, 119–21, 157–62, 194–5, 234–5; Giorgetti, *Contadini e proprietari*, 278–314; McArdle, *Altopascio*, esp. 31–2, 101–5, 126–7; Ambrosoli, *The Wild and the Sown*, 60–8, 141; Battistini, *Gelsi, bozzoli e caldaie*, 109, 116–23, 127–8, 136, 156, 187; and on Renaissance sharecropping, Balestracci, *The Renaissance in the Fields*; and Emigh, *The Undevelopment of Capitalism*. For sharecropping elsewhere, see Musgrave, *Land and Economy in Baroque Italy*, 51, 86–96, 119–26; and Hoffman, *Growth in a Traditional Society*, 65–9.

[94] Malanima, *Il lusso dei contadini*, 43–5: quote on 45. When rural export industry began to develop after 1730, it quickly developed ties with Livorno: ibid., 123, 133 n. 270; Malanima, *Decadenza*, 327; and in general de Vries, *The Industrious Revolution*, 73–121.

[95] S. R. Epstein, "Market Structures"; Pult Quaglia, "Confini doganali, politica, economia."

[96] Carli, "Saggio economico e politico," 356–61; see also Sonnino, *Saggio sulle industrie, commercio, e marina*, 31–2; and Waquet, *Le Grand-Duché de Toscane*, 276.

[97] See the complaint of the linen dealers of Arezzo about rigor in 1767: Malanima, *Il lusso dei contadini*, 116.

on the best possible terms. Florentine producers and merchants certainly made good use of the commercial networks that radiated out of the free port. Yet given the modest incidence of transport expenses in the final price of luxury textiles—on the order of one percent—the free port brought only small benefits to Florentine producers, who could easily have used land routes to procure raw materials and ship their wares.[98] On the other hand, given the retreat of Florentine patricians from the active management of business concerns, access to an international merchant community within the borders of Tuscany probably fostered industrial investment that might have gone to land instead. Minimizing business risk was a primary goal of the Florentine elite in the seventeenth century.

The free port's most conspicuous economic benefit was the city itself. Livorno experienced high population growth, fueled in the early days by infrastructural expenses and sustained by the proceeds from the city's commercial services. The rise of Livorno changed the demographic profile of the grand duchy. The population of Tuscany increased by thirty-four percent between 1552 and 1784, but the population of Livorno, Pisa, and their immediate hinterlands increased by 270 percent (Table 6.7). Most of this growth occurred in the two cities, closely linked to the service and port industries. The rest occurred in rural parts of the diocese, where the spread of sharecropping and the clearing of new lands were underwritten by opportunities for marketing produce to the two cities. The growth of Livorno and Pisa channeled immigration from regions with dismal prospects to an area with an expanding economy.[99]

Table 6.7. Livorno, Pisa, and demographic change in Tuscany, *c.*1550–1800

Year	Pisan diocese	Livorno & suburbs	Pisa & suburbs	City pop. (w/suburbs)	Rural pop.	Total Tuscan pop.	Notes
1552/1557	27,991	480	9,940	10,420	17,571	710,712	
1612/1622	52,780	11,954	15,461	27,415	25,365	772,746	a.
1640/1642	43,683	11,954	12,902	24,856	18,827	621,441	
1737/1738	69,823	30,897	14,015	44,912	24,911	838,252	b.
1765	99,744	34,538		34,538	65,206	944,225	c.
1784	103,775	37,286	17,747	55,033	48,742	980,894	d.
1794	123,664	41,278	19,960	61,238	62,426	1,037,488	e.

Note: The Pisan diocese includes Pisa, Livorno, and their countryside. The rural population is denoted as anybody living in the diocese but not in Pisa or Livorno (hence, various small towns are counted here as "rural"). The total Tuscan population comes from Del Panta's diocesan figures.

a. The Pisa/Livorno data this year were calculated using the *podesterie* and *vicariati* data rather than diocesan data.
b. City of Pisa figure is for 1745.
c. Livorno's population taken for 1761.
d. Livorno's population is an average of the figures for 1778 and 1787.
e. Livorno's figure is for 1793.

Sources: Del Panta, *Una traccia*, 32, 44–5, 49, 54–6; Trivellato, *The Familiarity of Strangers*, 54–6.

[98] Pagano de Divitiis, *English Merchants*, 91.

[99] It is possible that demographic growth in the cities slowed the formation of a class of landless laborers in Tuscany who might have facilitated the spread of rural industry; but as we have seen, institutional structures bear the brunt of the blame for the lassitude of rural textile production. Della Pina, "La formazione di un nuovo polo demografico," 51–2; Malanima, *Il lusso dei contadini*, 145–58.

If Livorno did not foster further market development in the Tuscan hinterland, it did facilitate its access to international markets. Herein lies the paradox of the free port. It became a central participant in the organization of early modern commercial life. It pioneered novel free trade institutions and served as a node in a set of exchange networks that stretched across the globe. By contrast, market structures in the Tuscan hinterland hailed from the late Middle Ages and resisted further integration with the international marketplace at its doorstep. The substantial flow of commodities between hinterland and port did not exert a catalytic effect on Tuscan political economy. There are several ways of reading this predicament. We might view Livorno's limited impact on regional transformation in Polanyian terms as successful social control over the market. In this vein, the regime and the landowning elite insulated themselves from the dislocations of economic change. We might also view the situation as a failed transition to capitalism, confirming (as a negative example) the importance of rural arrangements to the creation of modern market relations. Livorno would thus offer a lesson on the limits of trade to transform backward societies in the hinterland.

Polanyian and Marxian optics both assume that the main problem is the relative stability of Tuscan institutions in the face of changing patterns of European trade. But perhaps the true explanandum lay not in failure to change, but in the economic fundamentals of international trade. The expense of shipping grain into Tuscany offers some indication of why commerce did not have the impact one might have expected. The organizational and institutional improvements associated with maritime commerce had little effect over land routes. Transit costs in landlocked areas remained high for most trade. Unless good roads and navigable rivers facilitated the capillary distribution of produce, Tuscany had a limited capacity to exploit the ghost acres of the Americas or the feudal acres of the Baltic.[100] The overwhelming majority of economic activity was thus oriented toward agricultural production for local consumption. There, in the hinterland, commerce rapidly lost its revolutionary potential. Under these circumstances, the industrial development of Tuscany was unlikely to proceed much farther even with fewer tolls, better agrarian contracts, and more peasant involvement in the marketplace.

CONCLUSION

Few ports in the Mediterranean experienced sustained growth during the seventeenth century—and those that did were linked to the expansion of the Atlantic economies, apparent proof that they "owed their prosperity to the decadence of the world that produced it."[101] The elegiac tone that suffuses writing about the waning of Renaissance commerce is misplaced, however. During the golden ages of Venice or Genoa, long-distance trade stood in the hands of aspiring monopolists whose commercial networks rested on exclusionary privileges and the use or threat of

[100] The idea of ghost acres is from Pomeranz, *The Great Divergence*, 275–6.
[101] Pagano de Divitiis, "Il porto di Livorno," 76; see also Pagano de Divitiis, "Porti italiani," 357–85.

violence. A handful of urban patriciates captured commercial riches, which they used to lord it over their fellow citizens and dominate the countryside. By contrast, organized violence played a minimal role in structuring the maritime regime centered on Livorno. Institutional change promoted new levels of exchange between northwestern Europe and the central Mediterranean. Such far-flung commerce lay behind the prosperity of ports like Izmir and Livorno—but only in part. The free port also brokered trade with regional ports in Italy, which remained well-connected to the currents of international trade. The Mediterranean did witness the decline of individual port cities and the world they had created: but there appeared something new and creative in its wake.

A regional perspective illuminates the ongoing distinction within the Mediterranean between cores like north-central Italy and peripheries like the Kingdom of Naples. Although the world of Renaissance trade evaporated, the seventeenth century confirmed a longstanding division within the peninsula. North-central Italy resembled the advanced economies of the day. It imported raw materials and nutrients, sustained an impressive degree of domestic industry, and exported luxury manufactures. Meanwhile, the south continued to export agricultural goods such as grain, olive oils, and raw silk. Much work remains to be done in delineating the regional economy and in piercing the urban veil that makes it hard to detect rural industries or peasant participation in the marketplace. But as the evolution of Livorno's hinterland indicates, commerce did not map neatly onto the political boundaries of north-central Italy.[102]

The enduring stature of north-central Italy as a core economy also has implications for our picture of economic change in the Mediterranean. The capacity of long-distance commerce to restructure local economies was limited until late into the Ancien Régime. The dominance of northern shipping did not translate into economic dominance more generally; the carrying trade was essential for providing the purchasing power with which northerners bought Italian commodities. The new forms of commercial organization did bring some sectors of the Mediterranean and the Atlantic worlds closer together. It made the fortunes of cities like Livorno or Izmir, while challenging former hegemons like Genoa or Venice. Yet the ramifications of long-distance commerce were muted for Mediterranean economies as a whole. Even the case of Livorno, where one might have expected to see profound transformations in the countryside, illustrates this point. The development of the free port altered the demographic profile of Tuscany. Yet this shift was a consequence of the growth of commercial services in the city, not a function of the international marketplace. New patterns of long-distance trade had a modest effect in reshaping economic life in the rest of Tuscany.

What was true for Tuscany was also true elsewhere. The regionalization of Venetian trade involved more intense ties between Venice and its hinterland, matching the trade profile for north-central Italy as a whole: the export of manufactured goods, the import of victuals and raw materials. Although commercial statistics for

[102] Braudel's notion of "the quadrilateral" deserves more attention: see *The Mediterranean*, vol. 1, 387–94.

the Kingdom of Naples are spotty, there is little doubt that growth in trade ties was strongest with Marseille: this new connection should be viewed as an extension and intensification of the north/south divide in Italy to encompass the adjacent coast of France. The highly fragmented coast of Genoa, maximally exposed to maritime trade, might appear to have been an exception to the rule: but here, too, the economy felt the "tug" of nearby places much more strongly than distant ones, of Marseille to the west and Livorno to the south. Even the sub-regions of the Ottoman Empire, where scholars used to delight in detecting the early signs of European dominance, maintained substantial economic autonomy deep into the eighteenth century.[103] The vast majority of production and trade had at best a regional identity, despite the effects of long-distance exchange. There are no grounds for positing economic dependence on the distant economies of northwestern Europe.

The core-periphery model is important for understanding global economic disparities today, but it is less helpful for interpreting the premodern world. The contemporary situation is produced by industry operating under increasing returns to scale and very low transport costs. But between the invention of the sailing ship and the industrial revolution, changes in trade costs were determined by policy and organization rather than technology. Any lowering of costs was highly localized; it affected particular cities more than entire regions, let alone the globe. The policies associated with the free port promoted the agglomeration of commerce around Livorno at the expense of nearby ports; as rivals enacted their own free ports, the advantages of routing commerce through Livorno diminished and a phase of dispersion set in. In both cases the underlying productive and commercial economies of the Italian hinterland remained stable. The marketplace had to wait until the coming of the steam engine before it could set about remaking hinterlands on a massive scale.

There is no doubt that the economies of northwestern Europe grew faster than those of the middle sea. North-central Italy was one of the richest cores of the Old World, but its aggregate output scarcely grew during the seventeenth and eighteenth centuries. Yet it is beside the point to ask whether the Mediterranean as a whole declined vis-à-vis the Atlantic world. Internal heterogeneity remained more important than the aggregate of relations between macro-regions. Livorno's role was to perpetuate the dominance of north-central Italy over surrounding areas, wherever cheap maritime transport made such dominance feasible—southern Italy above all. Despite the loss of its export markets in the Levant to the English and Dutch, despite the decline of its fleets and monopolies, the region remained a diversified core economy. Livorno's position in long-distance brokerage, its role in connecting northwestern Europe to the Levant, rested on the shoulders of a rich Italian hinterland.

[103] On Venice, see Rapp, *Industry and Economic Decline*, 144–9, 159–64; and especially the essays in Lanaro, *At the Centre of the Old World*. On Liguria, Tazzara, "Against the Fisc and Justice," 367–9. On Naples, Carrino and Salvemini, "Porti di campagna, porti di città," *passim*. On the Ottoman Empire, Inalcik and Quataert, *An Economic and Social History*, 214, 474, 505–7, 520, 525–6, and 725. See too "Economic Change in the Italian Mediterranean" in chapter 8.

7

Livorno and the Science of Commerce in Enlightenment Tuscany

Institutional practice in Livorno underwent a significant shift when the crown passed to Francis Stephen of Habsburg-Lorraine. The new grand duke, and Holy Roman Emperor from 1745, ruled Tuscany from Vienna via a regency council. To simplify his administration, Francis Stephen farmed out the grand duchy to a French-led company called the General Tax Farm in 1741. The General Tax Farm collected almost all taxes in the state for twenty-seven years. Not only did the farm transform local administrative norms in Livorno, substantially reducing official interventions in economic life, but it also helped redefine the free port's relationship with the grand duchy. The customs director's role in mediating Livorno's commerce depended on a tacit bargain between the prince and the local administration. As long as tax receipts remained high, the customs director had great latitude to manage the port as he saw fit. The introduction of a new tax-collection regime broke this compact and spelled the end of the particularism that animated the city's commerce. The governor stepped up to fill some of the roles of the customs director, but doing so set him up for prolonged opposition with the Lorraine government.[1]

The regency and the leading classes of Livorno agreed that the port's commerce was suffering a deep malaise. They erected a Council of Commerce in 1747 to promote Tuscan economic interests however possible. Unlike the earlier Deputation of Commerce, the new council excluded merchants from its roster and had few administrative powers. It was intended to provide a more objective view of economic matters than the General Tax Farm, which opposed any measure that would compromise its receipts. The council and the farm often clashed over who was entitled to set economic policy. An older historiography attributed the rise of scientific political economy in Tuscany largely to outside stimuli: to the appearance of French Physiocracy and the accession of an enlightened monarch. More recently, historians have shown that native traditions such as the social thought of Antonio Ludovico Muratori and the agricultural economics of Sallustio Bandini paved the

[1] On the Tax Farm, see Waquet, "Les fermes générales"; Waquet, "La ferme de Lombart"; Waquet, *Le Grand-Duché de Toscane*, 548–71; Waquet, *Corruption*, 186–9. On the regency, see Verga, *Da "cittadini" a "nobili"*; Diaz, Migliorini, and Mangio, *Il Granducato di Toscana*; Contini, ed., *La reggenza lorenese*. For Livorno, see Baruchello, *Livorno e il suo porto*, esp. 301; Mangio, "Commercio marittimo"; Baggiani, "Tra crisi commerciale."

way for the reception of foreign economic ideas.[2] More important than the question of sources, however, are questions of process. The conflict between the Council of Commerce and the General Tax Farm was of the first importance in mediating the birth of Tuscan political economy. Contemporaries saw a close relationship between decision making procedures, economic ideas, and policy outcomes.

Soon after acceding to the throne and relocating to Florence, Peter Leopold (r. 1765–90) eliminated the General Tax Farm and abolished the Council of Commerce. Instead, he relied upon Florentine institutions to canvass policy ideas and surrounded himself with advisors well versed in current economic thinking. Under their guidance, the regime turned its attention to agriculture and eradicating internal barriers to trade. Livorno's hospitality to foreigners and its liberty of commerce won the admiration of many observers, but its exceptionalism was a problem for reformers who sought to place the state under a uniform system of administration and taxation. In this context, the free port seemed at best irrelevant and at worst pernicious. Although its privileges remained intact until Italian unification, Livorno was no longer central to Tuscan economic strategy.

The two moments of reform in Tuscany—the first with the regency and the second with Peter Leopold—are often identified with two successive phases of Habsburg reform more broadly: a centralizing thrust motivated by cameralism; and a program of social improvement inspired by the principles of the Enlightenment. For Tuscany as for other states, one typically identifies the overarching goals of reform, the individuals who originated and implemented policies, and the primary obstacles to change. In this model, reform radiated from regime elites while sometimes being stymied by constituencies such as the nobility, the municipalities, or the Church.[3] By contrast, this chapter describes an interactive logic in which opposition to reform in Livorno transformed the opponent itself. In its institutional structure and its relationship to Tuscany, Livorno appeared not to have followed Peter Leopold on the path of reform. But the free port's mode of governance was in fact completely transformed by the new political practices of the mid-eighteenth century. In defending itself against reform as defined by the center, the free port adopted the rhetorical and political values of the center itself.

THE COUNCIL OF COMMERCE AND THE CRISIS OF REPRESENTATION

The commercial crisis in Livorno that began in the 1720s was related to market development and the spread of free ports throughout the central Mediterranean.

[2] Mori, *Le riforme leopoldine*; Venturi, *Settecento riformatore*, vol. 1; Mirri, "La fisiocrazia"; Mirri, "Fisiocrazia e riforme"; Wahnbaeck, *Luxury and Public Happiness*.

[3] In general, see Scott, ed. *Enlightened Absolutism*, esp. his introduction, 1–35; Asch, "Absolutism and Royal Government." On the Italian states, see Valsecchi, *L'assolutismo illuminato*; Venturi, *Settecento riformatore*, vols 1 and 5:I; Capra, "Riforme finanziarie"; Capra, "Habsburg Italy"; Rao, *Il Regno di Napoli*; Grab, "The Politics of Subsistence"; Grab, "Enlightened Absolutism"; Mirri, "Dalla storia dei 'lumi'"; and Imbruglia, ed., *Naples*.

These external problems did not forestall a debate about whether the port's policies were to blame, however. As early as 1726, in a broadsheet entitled *Reasons shewing that Leghorn cannot be deemed a free port*, the English argued that the grand duke had abrogated the regime of liberty and toleration. The piece began with a rather imaginary history of the customs in which the "artful" grand duke began "incroaching upon the freedom of the port" by making merchants pay duties (i.e. stallage fees) immediately upon the arrival of goods in Livorno.[4] More to the point were complaints about tax farms on luxury articles such as tobacco, writing paper, and a few unspecified goods that would have included coffee, chocolate, tea, and brandy. "These instances are sufficient to prove, that if Leghorn was once a free port, it is not so at present." Such farms were authorized to make rigorous inspections and indeed constituted conspicuous breaches in Livorno's free trade regime. Complaints grew shrill with the advent of the General Tax Farm in 1741.

Vienna deputized Emmanuel Richecourt (1697–1768) as its secretary of finance in Tuscany. Gradually, Richecourt became the most important minister in the regency. Upon his arrival in Florence he immediately decried the institutional confusion that bedeviled Tuscany: "The government of this place is a chaos almost impossible to disentangle.... It seems like one had purposefully knotted up affairs so that it is impossible to perceive them clearly."[5] A group of French businessmen approached the new regime with an offer to contract for the tax collections in late 1737. It took three years to conclude a deal. Richecourt saw an opportunity to extinguish what remained of the ancient republican establishment while rendering state administration more efficient. The General Tax Farm afforded an occasion to remove Florentine patricians from offices and fill the bureaucracy with provincial notables and middle-class lawyers. The company improved tax collection by eliminating special favors and clamping down on contraband: revenue increased by twenty-two percent between 1738 and 1758.[6] These measures made the farm immensely unpopular, and nowhere more so than in Livorno. But they transformed the old style of free trade, with its exemptions, undocumented graces, and complicities, into a modern administration of laissez-faire. The regency, as the inexorable executor of laws, meant to create a uniform juridical field for trade.

The transition to Lorraine rule posed stark challenges to leadership in Livorno. The General Tax Farm eliminated the position of customs director and thereby displaced the functions he had performed. Meanwhile, the governor proved unable to maintain his full independence vis-à-vis the central government. Previously, the customs director and the governor reported primarily to the secretary of war. This made for uncluttered decision making that often favored interests in Livorno over broader concerns. But the Lorraine had the governor report to four bodies: the regency for business having to do with politics and public health; the Consulta for

[4] BL Lansdowne MS 1037. On the commercial context, see "Regional Exchange between Land and Sea" in chapter 6 and "The Spread of Free Ports" in chapter 8.

[5] Quoted by Venturi, *Settecento riformatore*, vol. 1, 47.

[6] From about nine million to eleven million lire. The salt and the tobacco monopolies saw similar increases: Dal Pane, *La finanza toscana*, 64–5. See also Litchfield, *Emergence of a Bureaucracy*, 265–335; Verga, *Da "cittadini" a "nobili,"* 104–6 *et passim*.

judicial matters; and the war and finance councils for their respective affairs. Often, the governor had to negotiate with the tax farm as well. These developments created a crisis of representation whereby merchants found it difficult to bend regime policy to their interests.[7]

Soon after arriving, Richecourt surveyed several opinions about how to revive commerce in Livorno. One merchant, Giovanni Pietro Ricci, urged the creation of a general director of commerce in Tuscany. He compared the Tuscan economy to a garden overgrown with weeds and subject to an erratic environment:

> The garden of Tuscany is continually assailed by the perpetual fickleness of its climate, and by its lack of order and the separation of its flowers, which are all of different species and contrary to one another. Poisonous weeds easily sprout there, so that it is difficult to disturb them because the roots of the weeds are entwined with those of the flowers.[8]

In this analogy, the "weeds" were slothful workers, an excess of lawyers, Florentine guild regulations, and a host of monopolies that choked off economic growth. The proposed director, as gardener of commerce, would transmit merchant requests to the monarch and oversee a chamber of commerce: mediation, in a word.

Although Ricci's views did not carry the day, the regency remained interested in institutional change. In the end, Livorno's old Deputation of Commerce served as the point of departure for new ideas. Captain of the Port Pierre d'Hiarce presented the first detailed plan for an organization in January 1745. His memorandum proposed a body that was essentially similar to the deputation—which he preferred to call a Council of Commerce, since people "are more prejudiced against names than against the things themselves."[9] D'Hiarce noted the defunct role of the customs director as "conservator and protector of commerce and of merchants, indeed of the privileges of the port of Livorno." In the era of the General Tax Farm, the city's merchants needed a patron: the proposed council. For d'Hiarce as well as for Ricci, the issue of representation had come to govern policy discourse in Livorno.

[7] Aglietti, *I governatori di Livorno*, 13 n. 10, 117, 120–3; Aglietti, "Giuliano Capponi governatore di Livorno," 41–2. In 1746, the separation of the governor's civil from his military powers further weakened his authority, although this power was restored under Governor Bourbon del Monte.

[8] "Questo giardino della Toscana è incessantemente combattuto da incostanza perpetua del suo clima, e per mancanza d'ordinamento o separazione dei suoi fiori, che sono tutti di specie differenti, e contrarie l'una dalle altre, con altrettanta facilità vi germogliano erbe velenose, quant'è la difficoltà di sturbarle a motivo dell'intrecciamento delle radici dell'erbe assieme con quelle dei fiori." ASF, Finanze, 800, 09/28/1738, Giovanni Pietro Ricci's *Proposizioni di Commercio*. See ASF, Reggenza, 12, ff. 299–305, 12/30/1737, Richecourt to Francis Stephen; ASF, Reggenza, 218, n. 26, 06/28/1738, n. 26, 06/28/1738, Baron Pfütschner and the Marquis Bartholomei; Thompson, "Progetti in vantaggio"; and Mangio, "Richecourt e il miraggio dell'Oriente."

[9] "[B]ien des gens se laissent plus prévenir contre les noms que contre les choses mêmes." ASF, Finanze, 800, memorandum for the establishment of a council of commerce in Livorno, 01/08/1745. The other quote, also from this memo, is: "Le provéditeur de la Douane a des tous temps été regardé comme le conservateur et protecteur du commerce es des négotiants ainsi que de la franchise du port di Livourne." The regime had also solicited information about foreign chambers of commerce as models: see ASF, Finanze, 800, ins. 2; ibid., ins. 3; ibid., ins. 6, 01/05/1745, Nicola Columbo to a "Don Pietro." See in general Mangio, "Commercio marittimo," 904.

The enterprising minister Pompeo Neri (1706–76) wrote a memorandum on the council several weeks later. From an important family near Volterra, Neri trained as a lawyer and served in minor offices between 1729 and 1735. He became secretary to the regency in 1737 because, as its president remarked, "he is a very wise and diligent young man." Neri put this diligence to use in several groundbreaking treatises on Tuscan law as well as by reforming the land tax in Lombardy. After he returned from Milan in 1758, he served as one of the regime's most trusted and influential ministers. On the matter of the proposed council, he fleshed out a position that minimized the role of Livorno in the policy process. He did not get his way on this point, but his interpretation of the free port gained traction in the coming decades.[10]

According to Neri, the old Deputation of Commerce had been deficient in both composition (by including merchants) and competence (by handling judicial matters). Merchants loathed exposing their "commerce, books, and sensitive information" to men with whom they might do business or with whom they were in competition. In any case, there was no need for the proposed council to discharge judicial functions. After all, Livorno had grown from a "little uninhabited castle" into a substantial port without the assistance of a merchant's court. Neri examined other potential roles for the council. He dismissed the idea that it could administer a trading venture like the famous companies of the Dutch, English, and French. Nor could it serve as a forum for experts to recommend ways to increase commerce and industry. Without the money to effectuate its proposals, it would be in danger of becoming a "sterile academy of projects," a locus for grandiose plans that would never materialize.[11]

Neri argued that geography and neutrality made Livorno an ideal port of deposit for foreign nations. The free port had so little to do with its hinterland that Livorno began to flourish only when Florentine commerce had fallen into decadence. The problems of the Tuscan economy were internal to the state and had nothing to do with the free port. Since Livorno's commerce had always been divorced from its hinterland, the maritime knowledge merchants and officials commanded was useless. They certainly could not "formulate projects worthy of attention."[12] Ministers based in Florence had a better grasp of the "interior commerce of the country" and the "faculties of its inhabitants." For Livorno, all that the government could do was "not ruin the favorable arrangements" by which the port flourished. This was the first time an official sidelined Livorno as a locus for Tuscan economic strategy. Significantly, Neri did not cite the free port policies in accounting for Livorno's success: geopolitics constituted a sufficient explanation. Like some of his contemporaries, Neri was convinced that "fostering agriculture and industry" ought to be the sole end of economic policy. These goals were linked to the "internal regulation

[10] Verga, *Da "cittadini" a "nobili,"* 169–206; Fratoianni and Verga, eds, *Pompeo Neri*; the quote is from Litchfield, *Emergence of a Bureaucracy*, 269.

[11] ASF, Finanze, 800, ins. 5, 01/30/1745, published by Misul, *Le arti fiorentine*, vol. 2, 13–26. On this memorandum, see Verga, *Da "cittadini" a "nobili,"* 199–202; for Neri's prior experience in Livorno reforming the *bagno*, see ibid., 181 n. 27.

[12] These quotes are from the memorandum reproduced in Misul, *Le arti fiorentine*, vol. 2, 20–1.

of a country" rather than its port city. He doubted that Livorno had much to contribute to the development of the Tuscan economy. There was no reason why the merchants of Livorno, experts only in the maritime trade of other nations, should be involved in formulating policy.

With most of the reasons one might have supported the Council in tatters, Neri proposed his solution: the creation of a body that fulfilled the duties of the old customs director. He was more precise than d'Hiarce in specifying the services this official provided before the advent of the General Tax Farm. The customs directors "were always individuals of mercantile mind and spirit, but who because of their office could not engage in business in Livorno and were therefore a channel through which the prince could obtain impartial information about the current state of commerce in Livorno."[13] Neri's comments signal a new tendency for the central government to conceptualize the erstwhile customs director as a channel of information rather than local decision maker, mediator, or dispenser of favors. Needless to say, merchants and officials never fully accepted Neri's arguments. Although the Livornesi conceded the need for internal reform in Tuscany, they continually defended the free port's liberties and asserted their city's relevance to policymaking. But they agreed with Neri on the critical need for mediation. In the coming decades, the Livornesi developed an analysis that linked the disappearance of the customs director to the crisis in commerce and the rigors of the General Tax Farm.

The Council of Commerce emerged a year and a half later as a compromise between d'Hiarce's and Neri's proposals. Attentive to securing disinterested advice, the council excluded merchants from its deliberations. It had only five members: the governor as president, the captain of the port, two counselors, and a secretary. Its remit excluded civil and criminal justice, apart from the merchant marine. Contrary to Neri's recommendation, however, it was charged with the maintenance of commerce and with proposing projects conducive to that end. Indeed, far from sharing Neri's assessment of Tuscan political economy, the regency embarked on a series of measures that recall old Medici ambitions. They included the construction of a native marine, the marketing of Tuscan textiles, and the establishment of new industries. As Neri predicted, the council did become a "sterile academy of projects"—but it also enabled the governor to assume mediating duties that were once fulfilled by the customs director.[14]

The council's chief competence became the Tuscan merchant fleet. This was established by edict in 1746 after a debate involving the Council of Commerce and the principle merchants of Tuscany. Foreigners were excluded from consultations because, as the council put it, "foreign nations must necessarily resent the promotion of Tuscan navigation." The edict envisioned the use of native ships and seamen to carry on Tuscan trade with the Levant and North Africa following the

[13] Ibid., 25.

[14] Francis Stephen authorized the council on 10/01/1746. See ASF, Reggenza, 105; and ASL, GCM, 1, ff. 500–528, Relazione del Governo Civile, del Commercio, e della Marina Mercantile di Livorno.

peace treaties of 1747.[15] Tuscan shipping indeed grew over the following decade and a half, primarily because the Seven Years' War opened a space for neutral shipping (many Tuscan ships were owned by Frenchmen). But the coming of general peace in 1763 and a rupture with Algeria in 1764 destroyed this fragile fleet.[16]

It is impossible to separate the history of the Council of Commerce from the personality of Marquis Carlo Ginori, governor of Livorno from 1747 to 1757 and president *ex officio* of the council. Ginori (1702–57) belonged to an old Florentine family that had taken an entrepreneurial turn in recent generations. After successful careers as merchants, his father and uncle had served successively as customs director in Livorno. They had bestowed on Ginori a commercial network beyond Tuscany as well as an array of fiefs within the grand duchy. Ginori was on the losing side of the pro-Bourbon, anti-Lorraine party in 1737 and later lost in a factional struggle against Richecourt, whom he considered a personal enemy. Ginori was convinced that Richecourt failed to transmit his reports to Vienna or, worse, twisted his proposals beyond recognition. He viewed the regency as a malignant force and often went above its head, sending missives directly to Francis Stephen or his imperial counselors. He brought a prickly pride to what he called his "miserable governorship" in Livorno.[17]

Ironically, given Pompeo Neri's disdain for useless schemes, Ginori turned out to be the most tireless promoter of projects in Livorno's history, even after an edict removed this authority from the council in 1748. To name just a few: he developed plans for the merchant marine and a native shipbuilding industry, for producing and marketing textiles, and for founding companies to deal in insurance and bills of exchange. The council was so dependent on the energies of Ginori that his successor, the old soldier Filippo Bourbon del Monte (1708–80), complained it was impossible to study his many projects because Ginori had kept them in his private files. Instead, "hoping to get no little help from the opinion of such an enlightened minister," Bourbon del Monte had to compile a list of schemes mentioned in Ginori's correspondence. Between the records in Livorno and those in Florence, they found twenty-three projects. The regent remarked: "I am astounded that since these are matters dealt with by the Council of Commerce that there is not a copy and a register in the archives of the council."[18] Poor recordkeeping in the free port was not only a seventeenth-century phenomenon.

[15] Cantini, *Legislazione toscana*, vol. 26, 89 (10/10/1746); ASF, Reggenza, 646, ins. 11, 01/23/1747; ibid., 01/29/1747, the Council of Commerce to the regency. The quote is from Mangio, "Commercio marittimo," 911.

[16] Baruchello, *Livorno e il suo porto*, 454–69; Mangio, "Commercio marittimo," 911–23, 933–7; Filippini, *Il Porto di Livorno*, vol. 2, 146. The merchant marine embroiled the council in a broad defense of the grand duke's jurisdiction over Livorno. This meant tightening the definition of Tuscan subjecthood, controlling the activities of Tuscan consuls abroad, affirming the port's neutrality, and asserting full sovereignty over Livorno in legal or diplomatic matters. See ASF, Finanze, 799, ins. 1748; Filippini, "La graduelle affirmation"; Aglietti, *I governatori di Livorno*, 171–80.

[17] Verga, *Da "cittadini" a "nobili,"* 187–8; Alimento, "Tra 'gelosie' personali"; Addobbati, *Commercio, rischio, guerra*, 163–4, 175.

[18] "...sperando di ricavare non poco aiuto da sentimenti d'un ministro così illuminato"; and "Resto bensì maravigliato che essendo affari trattati dal Consiglio del Commercio ^non sia copia e registro^ nella Segreteria del Consiglio suddetto." The quotes are from ASF, Finanze, 799, f. 69,

Ginori's projects shared a number of elements. He treated Livorno as an intimate part of Tuscan political economy and was willing to modify the policies of both port and hinterland to achieve his aims: expansion of trade and the merchant marine in Livorno, growth of agriculture and industry in the grand duchy. He favored the elimination of corporatist restrictions on industry, advocating free trade in raw materials throughout Tuscany and the right to establish ventures in the countryside. He supported measures to revive agriculture, such as a company to reclaim coastal swamps with Tuscan capital (Richecourt opposed this last project for the same reason he supported the General Tax Farm: the suppression of the old Florentine patriciate). In Livorno, Ginori even wanted to favor Tuscan nationals and their commerce over those of other nations. Quoting Montesquieu, he urged a general reduction of duties on goods imported and exported on Tuscan bottoms. This proposal, modeled after the navigation laws of England and France, struck directly at the principles of equality that lay at the heart of political practice in Livorno, as d'Hiarce observed. Ginori took a national view and was even willing to compromise the sacrosanct laws of the free port—when it suited his purposes. He could also be a staunch defender of the city's privileges.[19]

Ginori blamed the regency and the General Tax Farm for their purblind resistance to his ideas and rigorous adherence to the letter of the law. When asked towards the end of his life why the commerce of Livorno continued to decline, Ginori responded with a long memorandum in which he seemed to have lost all patience with his superiors. He was tired of "those subtleties and contradictions that often produce too many letters and an unbelievable mess of papers."[20] Ginori argued that his projects would have restored Livorno and Tuscany alike to a flourishing state. But all had been rejected. He named a few other causes of Livorno's troubles, such as the multiplication of free ports and the uncompetitiveness of Tuscan products on the international market. But rigor was the real problem: "The most certain, the most real, and the principal operating cause of the evil, cannot be attributed to anything but to the rigor with which merchants are treated, instead

01/13/1758, Bourbon del Monte to Botta Adorno; and ibid., f. 68, 01/21/1758, Botta Adorno to Bourbon del Monte. See too ASF, Reggenza, 77, 02/11/1757, Botta Adorno to Bourbon del Monte. On Bourbon del Monte, see Aglietti, *I governatori di Livorno*, 118.

[19] A few weeks earlier the Livorno merchant Giuliano Ricci had written a memorandum that echoed Ginori's views. These perspectives were in line with the form of mature mercantilism that swept over Italy in the 1740s and were shared by Vienna, which took some measures (such as tariff reductions) to bind its far-flung possessions more closely together. See ASF, Finanze, 799, ins. 1, E; Baruchello, *Livorno e il suo porto*, 307, 471–6; Mangio, "Commercio marittimo," 921; and Venturi, *Settecento riformatore*, vol. 1, 497–8.

[20] "[T]engo per certo che invece d'andare al bramato fine da me propostomi nell'esporre sotto gli occhi della Maestà Sua Imperiale un fatto costante e palpabile perché egli potesse poi deputare quelle persone che credesse più proprie per l'esame delle cause, e de rimedi, tengo dico per certo che si caderà sempre più nella confusione, e in quelle implicanze e contradizioni che spesso produce un troppo lungo carteggio, e la soverchia farragine de fogli, la molteplicità de quali argomento del seguito altre volte ad altra non serve che ad accrescere la confusione, e a suscitare le difficoltà e gli equivoci." ASF, Reggenza, 77, 02/11/1757, Carlo Ginori to Giovanni Antonio Tornaquinci. See ibid., 01/24/1757, Ginori to Tornaquinci, and ibid., 01/26/1757, Tornaquinci to Ginori.

of protection and favors. And all my projects tending to implement these favors have been rejected."[21]

Ginori attributed the rigor to the General Tax Farm's zealous pursuit of profit. To make good its contract, the company put its short-term interests ahead of the general good, "exactly like a merchant." Such an arrangement did little for Tuscany, and Ginori all but accused the farm of arrogating the state: tax farmers were private subjects who acted like public authorities. He contrasted their "rule" with the good old days of the Customs Office: "Although the Customs Office was an administration on behalf of the sovereign, over its officials there stood a director, a minister who was a consummate businessman, well-intentioned, and who regarded himself as the spirit of the commerce of Livorno. He had the full confidence of the sovereign and the greatest authority." This minister performed special favors for merchants without having to wait for permission from Florence. Affairs were conducted with "ease, expedition, rapidity, and to the satisfaction of merchants." But now, the farm regulated the least thing that occurred in Livorno, and it did so by insisting despotically on the letter of the law rather than on the interests of the state.[22]

Ginori died a couple of months after his long complaint, but his intervention provoked a prolonged debate about the status of Tuscan political economy. In May the General Tax Farm repudiated Ginori's "voluminous" memorandum with a brief response. The farm met the governor's charges with flat denials: "a convincing proof of which is that there have been no formal and verified complaints."[23] Their reply did not settle the matter. In late 1757, the regency asked the new governor of Livorno, Bourbon del Monte, to solicit merchant opinion on the causes of the port's crisis. Some individuals proffered their views, and the English, Dutch, French, and Jewish nations all produced lengthy memoranda detailing Livorno's languishing commerce. The writers consulted one another in drafting their memoranda, which later became prestigious documents and perhaps circulated after their production.[24]

The merchant memoranda assessed the situation of the free port in terms that were broadly similar to those of Ginori. All noted the proliferation of free ports as a cause for decline. They urged improving ties to the hinterland by lowering export

[21] "[L]a più certa, la più reale, e la principal causa operatrice del male, non ad altro deve attribuirsi che al rigore con cui invece di protezione e facilità si sono trattati i mercanti, e si sono rigettati tutti i progetti tendenti a mettere in pratica le predette facilità." Ibid.

[22] "[Q]uest'Appaltatore è tutto paragonabile ad un mercante, il quale cerca di fare i suoi negozi, non avendo in vista che il lucro presentaneo… . [P]oiche sebbene la Dogana fosse in amministrazione per il sovrano, pure sopra i ministri della medesima vi era un provveditore, ministro, che era una persona consumata negli affari del commercio, bene intenzionata, e che riguardandosi come l'anima del commercio di Livorno, era dell'intera, e piena confidenza del sovrano, e ne aveva tutta la maggiore autorità." Ibid.

[23] "^Una prova convincente essendone il non riceversi reclami formali e provati.^ E che invece di erigere nuovi dazi e gabelle, come viene gratuitamente supposta, egli [l'Appalto Generale] è in grado di produrre molti esempi delle moderazioni o riduzioni di gabelle." ASF, Reggenza, 77, 05/06/1767.

[24] For the solicitation, see ASF, Finanze, 799, ins. 1757, 12/27/1757. Giuliano Ricci submitted a memo qualifying some of his analysis from the previous January: ASF, Finanze, 799, f. 107, 01/07/1758. The Jewish, Dutch, and French memoranda are in ibid., ins. 1. The English memorandum is in the archives in Turin: Mangio, "La memoria presentata." For their possible circulation, see ASL, GCM, 964, pp. 75–6, 03/02/1768. In general, see Baruchello, *Livorno e il suo porto*, 476–502.

duties on primary materials and eliminating guild restrictions. And although they did not dare criticize the regency, they excoriated the General Tax Farm. The Dutch likened the farm to a short-term land tenant concerned only with exploiting the land as much as possible during his tenure. By contrast, a "true owner" (*padrone naturale*) made calculations for the long term and was willing to take the time to plant trees or vines. Where leniency was needed, the farmers favored severity; where lower taxes were necessary, they raised them. They were fanatical in pursuit of contraband. By contrast, the customs director had been "the mediator for the prince's graces and favors," solicitous of both the grand duke and the merchants.[25] By the late 1750s, consensus in Livorno was that the General Tax Farm was the cause of the port's ills, and the establishment of a disinterested mediator akin to the old customs director was the best remedy.

In June 1758, the secretary of finances asked Bourbon del Monte to verify the claims of the memoranda by scouring local records for the favors merchants used to enjoy. This was not the first time that the regency had shown itself to be ignorant about customs procedures: a few years earlier, they had ordered a search through old supplications expecting to find suppliants described as "subjects" in their requests, only to discover that merchants referred to themselves as "servants" or "beggars" (*oratori*).[26] Likewise, the new search did not conform to expectations. Bourbon del Monte advised the regency to give up on the investigation. There was no doubt that the former customs directors had frequently departed from the rigors of the law to promote commerce—and that Vincenzo Pitti had done so "capriciously and without leaving a paper trail"—but it was impossible to get at the truth without consulting somebody practiced in the ways of the Customs Office. Why bother stirring up old affairs? The governor proposed that all capacity to perform favors beyond the letter of the law be denied to the farm and be given instead to a customs director *pro tempore*.[27]

The General Tax Farm prepared its response in November with the full support of the regency. Bourbon del Monte was instructed to assemble the "most honest and accredited" merchants of the port to communicate a reply. When the governor asked whether he should give them a copy, he was told that merchants could take notes if they wanted, but that there would be no process of "coming to terms": this was not about securing consensus, as in the days of yore, but compliance.[28] The tax farm conceded little to the merchants. The farmers contended, inaccurately, that their administration had been *more* generous with favors than the old customs directors. More generally, they were content to cite the law rather than dispute questions of fact or prudence. Even when addressing criticisms about its use of

[25] ASF, Finanze, 799, ins. 1, D, f. 18.

[26] ASF, Reggenza, 65, 11/03/1751, the regency council to Donato Redi; and ibid., 11/08/1751 and 12/13/1751, Donato Redi to the regency council.

[27] ASF, Finanze, 799, 06/28/1757, Bourbon del Monte to Botta Adorno. See also ibid., 06/09/1758, the secretary of finances to Bourbon del Monte; 06/14/1758, Bourbon del Monte to Botta Adorno; 06/20/1758, Botta Adorno to Bourbon del Monte; ibid., 07/04/1758, Botta Adorno to Bourbon del Monte.

[28] ASF, Finanze, 799, 11/28/1758, letter to Bourbon del Monte; ibid., f. 65, 12/01/1758, Bourbon del Monte to the regency council; ibid., 12/05/1758, Botta Adorno to Bourbon del Monte.

rigor, the farm adopted a legalistic posture. In the end, the director *pro tempore* would be permitted to concede all certain favors authorized by law, but his scope for independent action was strictly circumscribed.[29]

Pompeo Neri had been correct to fear that foreign merchants would be unreliable allies in the development of the Tuscan economy. They wanted a return to the way things had been before the farm. As though to underscore the fecklessness of the Council of Commerce, several months after the farm delivered its final report, the merchants presented a collective petition begging for a solution to their complaints. This time, rather than talk through the council, they requested the presence of a high official from Florence capable of serving as a negotiator. Bourbon del Monte suggested that Neri himself would be an ideal candidate and offered to house him during his stay in Livorno. The imperial regent in Florence was nonplussed. To his mind, it was not appropriate for merchants to treat with one of the principal ministers of the regency every time they had a new complaint. The government had done more than enough to accommodate their views through the normal pathways. Nor was it necessary for merchants to be apprised of the confidential instructions given to the customs director *pro tempore*: "Either merchants will be content with their treatment by the customs director, in which case they have no reason to know the director's secret instructions, or they will think themselves maltreated and can bring their complaints to court."[30] The regency could not have been more indifferent to the practice of consensus in Livorno.

The Council of Commerce was a paper institution, incapable of accomplishing its projects. It had life only through the strong personalities of its presidents, governors Ginori and Bourbon del Monte, and the energy of its secretary, Francesco Giuseppe Pierallini (1721–93). Its archives were hardly even distinct from that of the Governor's Office.[31] Writing in 1765, Bourbon del Monte could not bring himself to defend the council to the new grand duke, Peter Leopold. The commerce of Livorno "is entirely foreign, having to do with transit, and depends on the will of foreigners."[32] The governor emphasized that the only projects worth pursuing were those that increased the "favors and conveniences" of trading in Livorno, or

[29] ASF, Finanze, 799, 11/28/1758, nn. 1–2, 7.

[30] "O i mercanti saranno contenti del contegno, che userà con essi il Direttore della Dogana, e in questo caso sarà loro inutile di conoscere il tenore delle istruzioni segrete del prefato Direttore, o crederanno di esser aggravati, e ne potranno far ricorso al giudice camerale." ASF, Finanze, 799, ins. 1759, 08/21/1759, Botta Adorno to Bourbon del Monte. The petition may be found in ibid., 05/18/1759, and other letters of interest are ibid., 05/21/1759, Bourbon del Monte to Botta Adorno; 05/26/1759, Botta Adorno to Bourbon del Monte; 05/28/1759, Bourbon del Monte to Botta Adorno; and 07/21/1759, Botta Adorno to Bourbon del Monte.

[31] ASL, GCM, 1025, n. 15, *Progetto per la soppressione del Consiglio di Commercio*. Anonymous, but written by a source close to Bourbon del Monte or Pierallini. On Pierallini, see Aglietti, *I governatori di Livorno*, 105.

[32] "Ma l'indole e la natura del commercio di Livorno non è suscettibile di sistemi e di regolamenti. Egli è tutto straniero e di transito, e dipende dalla volontà dei forestieri... onde non altri progetti e sistemi possono farsi relativamente al commercio di Livorno, che l'augumentare le facilità ed i comodi, e lasciare i negozianti in una piena libertà di dirigere come li piace le loro intraprese. E questa è la ragione, per la quale il Consiglio di Commercio nel decorso di diciannove anni dalla sua creazione, non ad altro è servito, che a soprintendere alla Marina Toscana." ASL, GCM, 1, ff. 500–528, *Relazione del governo civile, del commercio, e della marina mercantile di Livorno*. The quotations are from

which left merchants with "a full liberty to direct their businesses as they see fit." Bourbon del Monte noted that the council was incapable of discharging the crucial task—mediation—and proposed that its powers over the marine be entrusted to an individual minister. The Council of Commerce was dissolved four years later without opposition. With its abolition in 1769, the locus for policy formulation shifted to Florence itself. Even the governor had come to share Pompeo Neri's opinion, first aired two decades earlier.[33]

For Bourbon del Monte, the commerce of Livorno was "not susceptible to systems or rules."[34] The remark was meant to underscore the failure of the council's many projects. In fact, the city and its institutions were more receptive to formal rules than the governor admitted. Bourbon del Monte, in opposition to the General Tax Farm and later to the grand duke, himself drew upon Enlightenment norms to transform the traditions of the free port into a regular system of governance. The Livornesi were correct to cashier the farm for wanton rigor. Under the banner of a more rational administration, it eliminated the old practices of cooperation and collusion over which the customs director had presided. The governor ultimately affirmed a version of the old way of doing things that resembled the system created by the farm.

THE SYSTEM OF LIVORNO

During the Medici period, local officials showered merchants with a host of formal and informal favors without notifying the central government. The advent of a new dynasty, the General Tax Farm, and (after 1750) Enlightenment thinking precipitated substantial changes in administrative arrangements. The General Tax Farm evaluated the requests for special dispensations that used to fall under the customs director's purview. The rigor with which the farm discharged its duties ultimately rationalized relationships between officials and merchants. The General Tax Farm's methods thus served the purpose that Vienna had envisioned for it: to make a more efficient administration without calling into question the fiscal and political institutions of the state. In Livorno, the farm succeeded not by reeducating its personnel in the principles of good government, but because the Governor's Office itself adopted a more rationalistic style of governance to preserve the city's liberties. With the disappearance of the customs director, the governor was now responsible for protecting the commercial freedoms of the port. His defense of the city's privileges entailed a creative reinterpretation of traditional practices broadly in line with Enlightenment norms of governance. Enlightenment arrived in

ff. 509–10. This memorandum was drafted by Bourbon del Monte or Pierallini under the former's supervision.

33 ASL, GCM, 964, pp. 451–2, 11/30/1768; ASF, Finanze, 795, ins. 1769, 02/24/1769. The new grand duke's arrival in 1765 saw a stillborn proposal to set up a secretariat for the port's affairs in Florence. Lauretta, "Il Progetto"; cf. Baruchello, *Livorno e il suo porto*, 500–2.

34 ASL, GCM, 1, ff. 500–528, *Relazione del governo civile, del commercio, e della marina mercantile di Livorno*: quote on f. 509.

Livorno to defend the free port against external threats—first the farm, later the government in Florence. Bureaucratic conflict was the midwife between the old style of free trade and the new.

The profile of supplications illustrates the new style of Lorraine rule. Supplicants asked for far fewer licenses and exemptions than their predecessors—indeed, not one request out of ninety-six in the late Leopoldine period was classified as an exemption (Fig. 7.1). The number of penalty reductions more than doubled. These were almost entirely requests for fine forgiveness in fraud cases, which ballooned thanks to the farm's fight against smuggling. The general safe-conducts (i.e. city privileges) issued late in Leopold's reign were part of an effort to define debt forgiveness more precisely, to limit the port's attractiveness to the rabble who "live at the expense of society like little fish on the vast bodies of whales."[35] Safe-conducts defending merchants against individual debtors were no longer even acts of grace: they were automatic so long as certain conditions were met. These changes formed part of an administrative revolution that saw exemptions as pernicious and licensing as a matter of bureaucratic routine. They signal the transformation of a system of special favors into a framework of legal rationality.[36]

The new regime preferred to treat all merchants alike and dispensed favors less through individual supplications, than by framing general rules. The General Tax Farm conceded few exceptions to the tariff of 1676, "and these only for goods

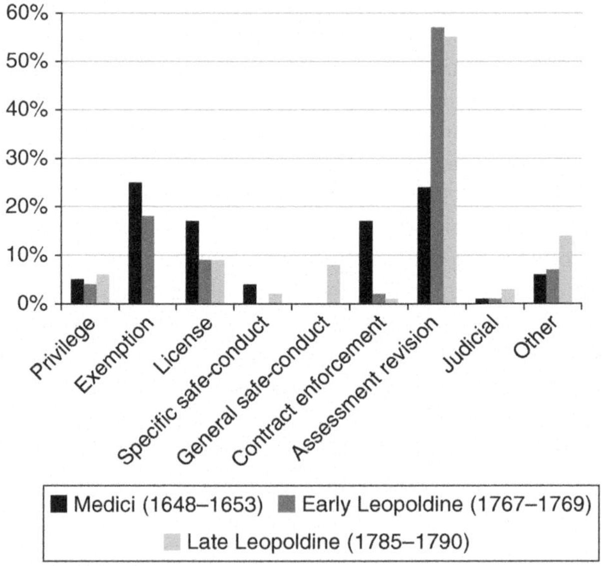

Fig. 7.1. Supplications to the Customs Office by type, 1648–1790.
Sources: ASL, Dogana, 12, 13, 21, 22, and 23; and n. 43 in chapter 3.

[35] The quotation is from a later screed against Ferdinando I's legislation: Ricci, "Livorno," 10.

[36] On general safe-conducts, see ASF, Reggenza, 646, ins. 9, 07/15/1747; ASL, Dogana, 21, ins. 8, 02/20/1786; on specific safe-conducts, see ASL, GCM, 963, ff. 14–15, 02/17/1766.

belonging to crowned heads."[37] Jean Pierre Pugnaire did not receive a formal exemption as part of his ceramics patent, for instance, but an annual tax reimbursement called a bounty. Likewise, officials limited the need for special licensing whenever possible. For example, in 1771 one official devised a plan for eliminating coffee-house licensing; since coffee did not (despite old prejudices) promote idleness, it was not necessary to regulate the number of such establishments. When merchants spoke of "favors," of *facilità* and *agevolazioni*, they now referred less to supplications than to interventions for remedying a general problem or establishing a new rule for everybody.[38]

Nothing had characterized the relationship between the Customs Office and merchants better than widespread complicity in fraud. Medici officials abetted fraud to facilitate tax collection, promote commerce, and increase their own pay. The General Tax Farm, jealous of its short-term profits, took a more stringent approach—not always successfully. For example, ship captains in the 1750s routinely traded in contraband tobacco and liquor off the docks, within plain sight of the city's officials. The farm advocated shipboard visits to arrest scofflaws and adduced the opinion of "all the jurists in the state" to justify their rigor. In this case, the Council of Commerce headed by Ginori convinced the regency that inspections, though technically licit, would be politically inconvenient.[39] More often the farm fought fraud with clear support from Florence and Vienna. It sometimes penalized resident merchants who lied about the size or contents of a parcel. But the farm's most numerous victims were the peasants, punters, and stevedores who did the actual smuggling on behalf of rich clients.

The crusade against fraud that the General Tax Farm prosecuted with such glee was actually a fight against the poorer classes whom merchants employed to carry contraband into Tuscany. Merchants, who once accounted for most requests among surviving supplications, now scarcely enjoyed a plurality. Instead, we find more artisans, more mariners, and more laborers (Fig. 7.2). The story of Maria Maddalena Giovacchini, from the countryside near Pescia, is typical. On August 18, 1767, an informant alerted customs guards to the fact that Giovacchini had purchased a piece of scarlet silk and stitched it under her skirt. When she approached the Pisan Gate, the guards frisked her in the presence of two witnesses and found the silk hastily affixed to her garment. She was imprisoned, assessed a twenty-five lire fine, and required to forfeit the silk. Her brother drafted a supplication asserting her innocence. The farm argued that the deed was "premeditated, and not without a certain malice."[40] It emphasized the utility of import prohibitions in general, citing a law from 1738. Although the Farm

[37] ASL, Dogana, 12, 02/09/1767.

[38] On Pugnaire, see ASL, Dogana, 21, 09/23/1785; on coffee, ASL, GCM, 966, ff. 77–78, 04/22/1771.

[39] ASF, Reggenza, 646, ins. 64, 03/29/1753.

[40] "[I]l detto contrabbando fu premeditato, e non senza un'evidente malizia, dimostrandolo appieno l'essere la detta saija non *cucita alla rustica*, ma semplicemente infilzata, e imbastita con pochi, e lontanissimi punti di colore diverso, senza cintole, senza pieghe, il che non può dirsi l'uso di campagna." ASL, Dogana, 12, ins. 65, 10/21/1767.

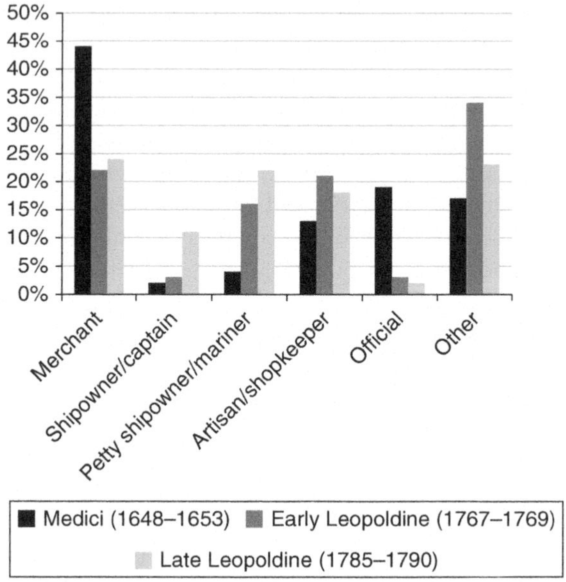

Fig. 7.2. Occupational status of Customs Office supplicants, 1648–1790.
Sources: ASL, Dogana, 12, 13, 21, 22, and 23; and n. 43 in chapter 3.

cautioned against any clemency, Giovacchini did receive a partial grace: her freedom and a fine reduction.[41]

The General Tax Farm was relatively successful in fighting smuggling, though less so in Livorno than elsewhere in Tuscany. The free port remained a place where contraband entered the hinterland as long as it was profitable to subvert import restrictions. The supplications are an index of the rigor that the farm brought to the Customs Office, however: fewer exemptions and licenses, and the aggressive pursuit of fraud. These practices fostered a new attitude among officials in Livorno that outlasted the existence of the farm.[42] This did not occur because the farm trained officials in the secrets of rational administration, or because it cleared away a century and a half of procedural thickets so that Livorno's bureaucrats could implement the law more effectively. The General Tax Farm wrought its transformation inadvertently: local officials adopted the posture of administrative rationalism to fight its policies. Often, as when they made their case against Giovacchini, the farmers found it necessary to interpret Tuscan legislation or discuss general principles of political economy. Their arguments were usually founded on a kind of vulgar Colbertism, when they were not just appeals to the letter of the law. But

[41] E.g. ASL, Dogana, 12, ins. 121, 12/16/1768; ASL, Dogana, 12, ins. 74, 07/08/1769; ASL, Dogana, 13, ins. 93, 10/13/1769. One woman was caught three times smuggling cloth into the mainland: ASL, Dogana, 12, 05/19/1769. Marzagalli calls this form of fraud "filtration," and it seems to have been common between major ports and their hinterlands: *Bordeaux et les États-Unis*, 87–92.

[42] For instance: the governor had no tolerance for complicity and urged the highest standards in selecting customs guards. ASL, GCM, 963, f. 75, 07/07/1766.

they affected the discursive strategies of their opponents, namely the Governor's Office and the Council of Commerce.

The establishment of the General Tax Farm not only created a more implacable style of regulation in Livorno, but it also added a new voice to the policy process. In the past, individuals made requests through the customs director or governor, who forwarded a supplication to a privy secretary. The secretary might consult the textile guilds if a request touched upon their interests; otherwise, he simply endorsed the decisions of local officials. But until its abolition, the farm had an almost imperious voice in determining policy. We have already seen Ginori attribute the failure of his projects to the opposition of the General Tax Farm. In fact, during his tenure as governor, the regency often supported the farm as much out of political as policy reasons: Richecourt hated Ginori and feared the governor's influence over the Florentine patriciate. Bourbon del Monte was more successful than his predecessor in navigating projects through to approval, though even he had to defend his office's role in the process.[43] We shall examine one such case, notable for what it reveals about how the mechanics of decision making were entwined with debates about the character of the free port.

A Swiss merchant named Guillaume Aubert (1722–98), who had been involved in mining and other enterprises in Tuscany, was interested in establishing a factory in Livorno to produce Genoese velvet. Bourbon del Monte developed a plan with Aubert to erect the factory in the suburb of San Jacopo, where construction began around 1751 to provide a place for the mariners and shipwrights of the merchant marine. Since the marine had not met the expectations of its planners, San Jacopo remained underpopulated. It was time (in the governor's view) to expand settlement and industrial privileges in the district.[44] Aubert's project nonetheless met intense opposition. The silk guilds in Pisa and Florence worried about competition over raw material and export markets. The General Tax Farm concurred, emphasizing that a velvet factory in San Jacopo went against the letter of the law as well as its spirit. Worse, the project promised to threaten the silk industry, "the only well-established livelihood of the greatest part of Tuscany."[45] In the farm's view, Aubert's velvet factor would also open a field for potential contraband that would be hard to control. The factory would be bad for the farm, bad for the royal treasury, and bad for the grand duchy.

The Council of Commerce was the last to express its opinion on Aubert's factory. Bourbon del Monte produced a fifty-five-point memorandum to refute the arguments advanced by the project's detractors. He also enlarged on broader issues. It was a recognized truth that industrial development was essential to a state and its economy: "It is sufficient to cast an eye on what people have written concerning commerce, which these days has practically become a science." He disputed the

[43] Cf. ASL, GCM, 964, pp. 160–2, 04/29/1768.

[44] ASF, Finanze, 800, ins. A, 07/18/1760, Bourbon del Monte to Francesco Pecci. For a similar project, see ASF, Reggenza, 646, ins. 13, 12/23/1746, 01/18/1747, 01/21/1747, letters between Carlo Ginori and Giovanni Antonio Tornaquinci. On the construction of the suburb, see Matteoni, *Livorno*, 113–18.

[45] ASF, Finanze, 800, ins. A, 07/28/1760; 09/15/1760; 10/02/1760. The quote is from 11/19/1760.

idea that Livorno should be considered a foreign country, uninvolved in the wellbeing of the Tuscan hinterland. On the contrary, Livorno had a primary role to play in the development of the territorial economy: "This is not the first time this is said, but to render the commerce of this port less passive and foreign, it is necessary to multiply the produce of Tuscany and grow its industries, and this second object (I repeat) can more easily be done where there are businessmen to undertake enterprises, than in other parts of Tuscany."[46]

The General Tax Farm posed a severe challenge to the old bureaucratic circuit, wherein things were arranged in Livorno and agreed upon with little fuss by a privy secretary. The farm ranged widely over legal and practical terrain to argue against any innovation that might affect the fisc.[47] In the Aubert case, they also employed the protectionist arguments of the guilds even though, strictly speaking, such material lay beyond their remit. The special status the farm enjoyed as the chief investor in the grand duchy, as well as the breadth of its argumentation, encouraged the governor to adopt more systematic analysis to advocate his projects. Thus, like his predecessors, Bourbon del Monte discussed the costs and profits of a proposal and the relevant body of legislation. Unlike them, he also embedded his arguments in general principles of the free port or even in the new science of commerce. Sometimes this strategy persuaded the regency, as here: Aubert did receive many of his requests. But often it did not.

Officials did a lot to clarify the "system of Livorno" during the years of rigor brought on by the General Tax Farm. The first complaints about illicit traffic in tobacco and liquor in the harbor go back to 1746, when it was decided that known violators of the law would be apprehended as soon as they touched land, but not on their vessels. Officials literally parleyed with criminals such as ship captains without deigning to lay hands on them.[48] The farm by contrast advocated rigorous shipboard inspections to ferret out contraband. The governor and his jurists argued throughout the 1750s that, despite the ineffectiveness of the current procedures, inspections would have been so obnoxious to the merchant community as to deal a mortal blow to Livorno's commerce. Nevertheless, the spectacle of open disobedience of the law continued to rankle the regency. In 1762 it asked a series of questions about whether the nature of the free port permitted the inspection of

[46] "Io non credo un problema ma una verità dimostrata, che l'introduzione di nuove manifatture sia sempre uno dei maggiori avvantaggi del commercio, e in conseguenza dello stato. Basta dare un'occhiata a tutti quelli che anno scritto nella materia del commercio, che in oggi si è voluta ridurre ad una scienza." And: "Né sarà questa la prima volta, che è stato detto, che per ridurre meno transitorio e straniero il commercio di questa piazza, converrebbe pensare a moltiplicare i prodotti della Toscana ed accrescere le manifatture, e questo secondo oggetto lo torno a ripetere può ottenersi più facilmente qui ove sono dei negozianti che possono tentare delle imprese, che in altre parti della Toscana." Ibid., undated (late 1760), memorandum by Bourbon del Monte, LIV and LIX.

[47] Thus, the farm opposed Pietro Martin's silkworks for the same reasons it opposed Aubert's. But it supported privileges that promised to increase tax yields, as Antonetto Orazio Gaetano's failed request for a privilege for his soap factory in Livorno. ASF, Finanze, 800, ins. M, 01/23/1762; ibid., ins. 8, 08/13/1753.

[48] ASL, Reggenza, 646, ins. 64; 07/16/1746, dispatch from Vienna to the regency; ibid., 08/19/1746, the *auditore* of Livorno to the secretary of state; ibid., 12/27/1749, the rescript; ins. 64, 12/27/1749, unknown to the *auditore* of Livorno.

vessels. The response, crafted by the port's two best legal experts, Giovanni Giacomo Baldasseroni (1710–68) and Francesco Giuseppe Pierallini, reframed the policies of the free port in terms of eighteenth-century Enlightened absolutism.[49]

The lawyers began by paraphrasing Savarys' definition of a free port as a place where ships of every nation can alight and where merchants are free to import, export, and deposit their merchandise without paying duties. They noted that there has never been a free port that fulfilled the definition perfectly, since "in all ports, even free ones, the import and export of merchandise is subject to certain laws that restrict the unbridled liberty that the general idea of a free port contains." But rather than decry that "unbridled liberty," which would have been a normal move for memoranda during the Medici period, the writers formulated a legal argument that put the free port on a new basis:

> Whatever the true definition of the term *free port* may be, it is certain that according to the common understanding it does not mean anything more than a privileged port, to which its sovereign had granted some particular exemptions. So it is impossible to form an idea of the free port in general, but one can certainly assert that its nature depends on that law the sovereign was pleased to endow it with. It carries only those privileges and exemptions that he wanted to give it.[50]

The writers argued that the chief legislation (1566, 1591/93, 1676) contained the entirety of the free port, along with a couple of lesser laws. From these principles, they adduced that the prince was free to change the laws of the port at will. They cited several decrees where he did just that. "So it's evident that the free port does not have a particular and determined nature, but it is what the sovereign who has dominion wants."[51]

Baldasseroni and Pierallini observed that the tariff of 1676 explicitly permitted customs officials to inspect ships. The merchant nations could not object to inspection on legal grounds. The prince was free to order ship inspections with or without new legislation. The only question was prudence, and this hinged on "principles very different and distinct from the nature of the free port."[52] To wit, whether it was worth risking controversies with foreign courts who were sure to defend their flags' honor; and secondly, whether additional rigor would deter foreign merchants from doing business in Livorno. The two lawyers recommended against changes in policy.

In exalting the absolute authority of the prince, the writers of this memorandum did not intend to encourage him to take arbitrary actions. Their purpose was to situate the practices of the free port in a juridical framework that made it easier to

[49] On Baldasseroni, see Addobbati, *Commercio, rischio, guerra*, 118 n. 14.

[50] "Ed è certissimo che qualunque ne sia la vera definizione, la parola porto franco secondo la comune intelligenza altro non vuol dire, che un porto privilegiato, ed al quale sono concesse dai respettivi sovrani alcune particolari esenzioni. Di modo che non è possibile fissare un'idea del porto franco in genere, ma può con sicurezza asserirsi che la loro natura dipende da quelli leggi, che al sovrano è piaciuto di prescrivere, e porta seco soltanto quei privilegi ed esenzioni, che egli ha voluto accordare." ASL, GCM, 1025, ins. 13.

[51] "Adunque egli è evidente, che il porto franco non ha una natura particolare e determinata, ma è tale quale lo vuole il sovrano, che ne ha il dominio." Ibid.

[52] "Il non farsi tali visite, ed il non mandarsi ad effetto le perquisizioni benché ordinate dalle leggi, dipende da due principii affatto diversi e distinti dalla natura del porto franco." Ibid.

speak of political economy in Livorno in systemic and universal terms. The principles of prudent policy, rather than the letter of the law, were to guide the prince. Other memoranda of this period attest to the same attitudes. Officials in Livorno made use of this language to defend the "traditional" practices associated with the free port. It was a new justification for *facilità*, *agevolazioni*, and *commodità*—understood less as grants to individual merchants on a particular basis, as in the Medici era, but as a permanent institution of laissez-faire. More often than ever, officials grounded their decisions or recommendations in terms of the unwritten constitution of the port.[53] Needless to say, defending the port's traditions also helped officials protect their own prerogatives from assault by the General Tax Farm and Peter Leopold.[54]

Approaches to information gathering offer a case in point. In the earlier period, even the most mundane supplications generated thorough investigations. But by the mid-eighteenth century, officials considered it their duty to respect the privacy of merchants. When Andrea Fantozzi supplicated for a license to export 64,000 pounds of tallow, the privy counselor Orsini Rosenberg asked for a host of details: who drafted and presented the supplication, whether Fantozzi already owned the tallow or, if not, from whom he intended to buy; what the cost of the tallow was; and whether anybody else was involved in the business deal.[55] Bourbon del Monte replied with indignation. In the governor's view, such questions amounted to an "interrogation," a "trial against one or more merchants of this marketplace over a commercial enterprise," all the more unnerving since Fantozzi had asked the sovereign's permission beforehand. Such a manner of proceeding violated the "constitution" of the port, which was to allow merchants to pursue their business with minimal intrusions. Bourbon del Monte complied with the bare minimum of Rosenberg's request, describing how Fantozzi had no buyers in mind but had learned from Livorno's brokers that one required a princely dispensation to export Tuscan tallow. The governor reiterated that such questions (de rigueur in the past) were inopportune in Livorno.[56]

[53] Bourbon del Monte employed this argument when opposing the establishment of printing privileges in Livorno and when opposing the activities of the Deputation on Manufactures. ASL, GCM, 963, ff. 356–58, 08/31/1767; ibid., ff. 342–343, 12/30/1767.

[54] Pompeo Neri's strategy of detailed historical analysis served a similar end of affirming traditional practices over Lorraine novelties. See Verga, *Da "cittadini" a "nobili,"* 209, 217, 229; and the discussion of his memorandum on Livorno in "The Council of Commerce and the Crisis of Representation."

[55] ASL, GCM, 5, f. 156, 02/23/1768, Orsini Rosenberg to Bourbon del Monte. Followed by ASL, GCM, 964, pp. 63–4, 02/26/1768, Bourbon del Monte to Orsini Rosenberg; ASL, GCM, 5, f. 197, 03/08/1768, Orsini Rosenberg to Bourbon del Monte; ASL, GCM, 964, p. 95, 03/11/1768, Bourbon del Monte to Orsini Rosenberg.

[56] These were recurring themes for officials in Livorno. There are other examples from the same period: for instance, the reluctance to investigate a Turk's activity in the tobacco trade. Prevailing customs procedures made it impossible to gather detailed commercial statistics. Even for as important a matter as the grain trade, officials only tracked grain stored in public facilities. See ASL, GCM, 966, pp. 38–9, 02/20/1771; ASL, GCM, 963, ff. 154–56, 01/30/1767, Bourbon del Monte to Orsini Rosenberg; Dal Pane, "I lavori preparatori," 278–80; and Filippini, *Il porto di Livorno*, vol. 2, 332. Ironically, a decade earlier the General Tax Farm had also argued that it was against the rules of the port to monitor commerce. They adopted this view to oppose one of the projects of Governor Ginori.

The new terms for speaking about Livorno were its "system," "constitution," "maxims," or "principles." If the governor exploited such language when discussing economic affairs, he did the same when talking about judicial arrangements. When a scrivener—"with black hair, a reddish mustache, white skin, and chestnut-colored eyes"—fled from Civitavecchia to Livorno for having counterfeited currency, the regime in Florence was happy to comply with Rome's request for extradition. But Bourbon del Monte explained that the system of Livorno did not permit extradition. Instead, criminals were the occasion of an elaborate pageant: the government made a show of preparing to arrest offenders while notifying them secretly that they had better leave Livorno of their own volition.[57] If the criminal left Livorno by ship, he was a free man. Moreover, "to make the affair more believable," the secretary of war would issue a public writ for a criminal's arrest, while sending confidential instructions to the governor not to violate the maxims of the port.[58]

The officials of Livorno placed the city's privileges on a new foundation. In the Medici period, customs, precedents, and practices dominated discourse about the free port. Now, writers rested their arguments on the language of political economy: the systems, maxims, and principles devised by famous writers. The development of European legal and commercial writing in the previous century is the broad context of this transformation, but its timing in Livorno was shaped by the decades-long crisis in its trade, the rigors of the General Tax Farm, and finally by the unifying efforts of Peter Leopold. When Governors Carlo Ginori and Filippo Bourbon del Monte defended the privileges of Livorno, effectively assuming the mantle of the vanished customs director, they did so on the same grounds that its critics used to attack the free port. The new way of doing things in Livorno, for all its similarities to the past, bore the imprint of Enlightenment.

THE PRIVILEGES OF LIVORNO IN THE AGE OF ENLIGHTENED REFORM

Livorno's stature in the economic strategy of the grand duchy owed to the centuries-old commitment to selling Florentine textiles abroad. Time and again, the grand dukes had sought to exploit the networks converging on the free port to sell woolens and silks to the Levant. The most cherished dream in this project was the creation of a native merchant marine. But once the domestic economy deposed export industry as the central pole in Tuscan thought, Livorno no longer appeared

ASF, Reggenza, 77, 05/06/1657. For similar opposition to the collection of statistics in a port city, see Rambert, *Histoire du commerce de Marseille*, 256–63.

[57] ASL, GCM, 3, ff. 121–22, 03/07/1767; ASL, GCM, 963, 03/09/1767, Bourbon del Monte to Orsini Rosenberg. The scrivener was named Giuseppe Siciliano. On Bourbon del Monte's principles, see ASL, GCM, 958, "Massime di Governo e altre istruzioni per l'uso," quoted by Aglietti, *I governatori di Livorno*, 105.

[58] ASL, GCM, 966, pp. 19–21, 01/25/1771, Bourbon del Monte to Simonetti; see Aglietti, *I governatori di Livorno*, 178–9.

to be the key channel for economic growth. Gone were fantasies of navigation and the markets of the East. The new goal was to produce low-quality textiles for domestic consumption and to export the agricultural produce of Tuscany, it did not matter aboard whose ships. This vision inspired Peter Leopold to eliminate internal trade barriers and free the grain trade. His reforms were informed in part by French Physiocracy, but also by native strands of thought such as the agricultural turn launched by Sallustio Bandini and the liberal mercantilism of Carlo Ginori. The ultimate victory of the domestic perspective owed less to its persuasiveness—many of the same arguments appeared in both strands—than to disputes about institutions that ended in defeat for Livorno. The question of *how* reform should occur was a critical issue in the middle of the eighteenth century. The crux lay in who was entitled to participate in policy discussions and how it would be possible to organize the immense new library of economic ideas. For reformers, it was impossible to entrust the state's economic development to Livorno, with its entrenched foreign nations and peculiar traditions. Tuscans never definitively solved these problems, but they did transfer the locus of formulating strategy from Livorno to Florence, thereby excluding foreign interests from the policy process.

The turn towards agricultural thinking was taken by Sallustio Bandini (1677–1760). Bandini, from a patrician family in Siena, fixed his gaze on the desolate coastal zone that ran along southwestern Tuscany, known as the Maremma. Bandini argued that restrictive grain policies had been the bane of the Maremma. Lowering and simplifying grain taxes would create strong incentives for development in the region. He argued for consumption-led growth that would provide peasants with the means (produce and money) with which to stimulate supply. Bandini's *Discourse on the Maremma* (1737) had little to say about manufacturing and only mentioned Livorno as a market for grain.[59] He presented a vision of economic growth divorced from industry and navigation. The *Discourse*, though not published until 1775, circulated in manuscript from the time of its composition. Pompeo Neri, a friend of Bandini and a convert to his ideas, probably took the lead in passing it around ministerial circles.[60]

Meanwhile, debates in Livorno over the Council of Commerce and the ongoing crisis in trade turned the trickle of printed texts on political economy into a flood by the early 1750s. Governor Carlo Ginori was an important figure in the transmission of these writings. His memoranda cited liberally from Forbonnais's translation of Jerónimo de Uztáriz (a Spanish political economist) and from Montesquieu's *Spirit of the Laws* (1748). Merchants in Livorno followed his example.[61] Ginori promoted the publication of an edition of Girolamo Belloni's *On Commerce*, prefaced with translations of two English histories of commerce, and an *Introduction to the Practice of Commerce* that fused various French and

[59] Bandini, *Discorso sopra la Maremma di Siena*, 270.

[60] For its manuscript circulation, see Bonelli, "Premessa"; Diaz et al., *Il Granducato di Toscana*, 81 n. 2. In 1767 Neri wrote a *Discourse on the Grain Question* that was heavily indebted to Bandini. See Venturi, *Settecento riformatore*, vol. 1, 334–40.

[61] E.g. ASF, Reggenza, 77, 02/11/1757; ASF, Finanze, 799, ins. 1, D. For the reception of Montesquieu, see Mirri, "Profilo di Stefano Bertolini"; and Verga, *Da "cittadini" a "nobili,"* 82f.

English works on the subject. These texts argued that international commerce created prosperity and ennobled those who participated in it. The prince, sacrificing the short-term interests of his treasury, should eliminate internal duties and export taxes: customs must be used to develop the entire state. Printing such works was part of a maneuver intended to defend the liberties of the free port, nourish the city's commerce, and strengthen the Tuscan economy. Agrophilic thought was not the foe in Ginori's offensive. The General Tax Farm and those officials who were exasperated with Florentine industrial decline were its targets.[62]

Assessing the relationship of this intellectual activity to the policy process is not easy. Sometimes texts directly inspired a project. For instance, Ginori got the idea for an insurance company in Livorno from the entry "Compagnie d'Assurance" in the commercial dictionary of the Brothers Savary.[63] Their writings on the mercantile companies of the Atlantic powers also convinced him that it was impossible to break into the colonial sphere by the creation of a Tuscan rival, leading him to pursue alternative plans. In this respect, printed treatises functioned the way memoranda and legislative documents had since the mid-sixteenth century: as a source for models, analysis, and ideas. Their real novelty concerned authority and institutions. The introduction of such treatises made inescapable the problem of who was entitled to set policy and how foreign models were to be incorporated into a state's policies.

Ginori proposed the establishment of an academy of commerce in Livorno. In his words: "an academic society, to spend a few hours every week in discussion, and to do useful projects to encourage commerce and show the way to extend it.... And because this is a free port, and consequently a general warehouse for merchants of all nations, the members could be chosen from all nations."[64] Inspired by mid-century cosmopolitan ideals, Ginori imagined that academy members would combine practical knowledge about Tuscan and foreign economies alike. One of its proposed tasks would be especially condign to an academic body: editing a florilegium from the "many new and old books concerning this science," that is, a judicious selection of the best writing on commerce, industry, and agriculture. The analogy between academies of natural philosophy and the proposed society was irresistible: "The members of so many different nations united together could contribute a lot by bringing us those ideas and teachings that we do not have here." Merchants and travelers could present information gleaned from their peregrinations but impossible to gather from books.

The formulation of commercial policy had vexed Tuscans long before Ginori confronted the issue. Francesco Feroni, for instance, believed that only merchants had the experience necessary for policy discussions but fretted about the distorting effects of their self-interest. The inability of merchants to offer disinterested advice had also troubled the debate over establishing the Council of Commerce.

[62] Venturi, *Settecento riformatore*, vol. 1, 452–3; Mangio, "Commercio marittimo," 930–2; Addobbati, *Commercio, rischio, guerra*, 63 n. 39; Alimento, "Tra Bristol ed Amsterdam."

[63] Alimento, "Tra 'gelosie' personali," 78 and 93 n. 96.

[64] This and the following quotes in ibid., 78–9. As Alimento notes, Ginori's project was similar to that of Plumard de Dangeul, *Remarques sur les avantages et les désavantages de la France*, 170–2.

But the development of a science of commerce divorced expertise from experience: merchants no longer needed to be the sole purveyors of policy advice. There were authoritative books for that purpose. In addition, the new territorial economics made merchants appear peripheral to the improvement of agriculture and domestic industry. Ginori's arguments for basing an academy in Livorno fell on deaf ears. Why not establish it in Florence, where the landed proprietors of Tuscany lived and where there could be no question of crafty, self-interested merchants?

The Accademia dei Georgofili ("Academy of Nature-Lovers") was founded in 1753 as an agricultural society. It drew its inspiration in part from the work of Bandini, in part from Ubaldo Montelatici's *Treatise on the Means for Making Agriculture Flourish* (1752). Except for its focus on rural economics, the new body functioned much like Ginori's proposed academy for commerce: it gathered information, promoted research, debated best practices, and corresponded with agronomists beyond Tuscany. Its members were patricians with (dubious) claims to disinterested expertise. The Georgofili played a role in preparing legislation, especially in the 1760s and early 1770s. Richecourt, for example, occasionally attended sessions to solicit their advice. During the great inquest on the Tuscan economy, the deputation sought the advice of the Georgofili on agriculture. The academy also helped draft the reform of contracts between landowners and tenants. Important ministers were Georgofili, as was the economist Ferdinando Paoletti, whose *True Means for Making Societies Happy* (1772) inspired reformers to liberalize the grain trade. The older Florentine academies, once devoted to literary games, also came to discuss economic matters. In 1784, at the height of Leopold's reforms, thirty-five percent of ministers participated in the academies.[65]

The rise of public opinion also provided a new venue for discussion about political economy. The roots of public opinion in Tuscany stretch back to the Galilean establishment and legal studies at the University of Pisa, whose professors instructed many of the mid-century ministers responsible for Tuscan reform. The extinction of the Medici and a press law in 1743 that limited the church's involvement in publications made it easier to circulate ideas in Florence than at any time since the days of Machiavelli. Giovanni Lami's *Literary News*, founded in 1740, kept Tuscans abreast of the latest Italian and foreign books in political economy. Lami and his allies provided another channel through which Tuscany absorbed foreign economic writing. Florentines also published translations of French and English works.[66] Public opinion mattered not only for securing consent for the regime's policies, but also for generating elite consensus about the best approach to economic life.[67]

[65] Dal Pane, "I lavori preparatori," 274; Mirri, "Un'inchiesta Toscana"; Cochrane, *Tradition and Enlightenment*, 54; Venturi, "Quattro anni di carestia"; Litchfield, *Emergence of a Bureaucracy*, 280; Pasta, "L'Accademia dei Georgofili."

[66] Carranza, "L'Università di Pisa"; Cochrane, *Florence in the Forgotten Centuries*, 317–96; F. Waquet and J.-C. Waquet, "Presse et société"; and Mirri, "Per una ricerca sui rapporti fra 'economisti' e riformatori toscani."

[67] Landi, *Il governo delle opinioni*, ch. 3, n. 74; and more generally, Habermas, *The Structural Transformation of the Public Sphere*; Melton, *The Rise of the Public in Enlightenment Europe*; and Soll, *Publishing the Prince*.

Institutions such as the Accademia dei Georgofili and public opinion transformed the problems of authoritative policymaking that had plagued Tuscany since the 1670s. The Florentine Chamber of Commerce, established in 1768, was another such organization. Centered around Florence, these bodies offered an alternative to the liberal mercantilism promoted in Livorno.[68] There, the experiment with the Council of Commerce had ended with the governor replacing the defunct customs director as the representative of the mercantile classes. The new Florentine institutions formulated projects that did not depend on the consent of foreign merchants in Livorno. Ministers had a common set of principles with which to make decisions and more authoritative ways of resolving uncertainties. Of course, the existence of an academy such as the Georgofili did not guarantee consensus; on several occasions it empowered an opposition. But the locus of discussion was now in Florence.[69]

The problem of Livorno played a role in this shift. Pompeo Neri's view about the relationship between the free port and its hinterland economy came to be widely shared among contemporary observers.[70] The real debate lay in managing the policy process. Francesco Maria Gianni (1728–1821), the energetic collaborator of Peter Leopold, offered a retrospective analysis that struck directly at this issue. For Gianni, Livorno had usurped its role in the deliberative process to win greater liberties for its merchants at the expense of Tuscan interests. Gianni transposed Livorno's dispute with the General Tax Farm into a conflict with the reforming state of Peter Leopold.[71] He traced the evils of Livorno to the reign of Gian Gastone, the last of the Medici. The city had been corrupted by the vices that stemmed from wealth: a permissive government and a corrupt administration. These imparted to Livorno a "character of depravity that was not afterwards corrected."[72] The court of Francis Stephen was inundated with projects geared towards enriching the city and extending its commerce. "One did not speak of Tuscany in Vienna except in relationship to Livorno, the emperor had ears for nothing else, and Livorno supplied the ideas, projects, and hopes for riches that nourished the fancy of that prince."[73] Livorno's obsessive pursuit of wealth dictated policy in Tuscany without regard to the public good.

Gianni was an apologist for Peter Leopold, of whose reign he was a chief architect. But even Gianni admitted how little they accomplished in Livorno. True, the grand duke hemmed in the "arbitrary authority" of the governors and moderated the bribes officials exacted.[74] But in general, it was hard to achieve the regime's goals in Livorno because officials found a thousand ways to oppose measures and

[68] Ristori, *La Camera di Commercio*; Baggiani, "Progresso tecnico e azione politica." See too the other essays in Barsanti et al., *La politica della scienza*.

[69] See for instance the controversies regarding the conduct of the general survey of 1766–7 in Dal Pane, "I lavori preparatori," 290–2; Pasta, "L'Accademia dei Georgofili," 490–1; Mirri, "Un'inchiesta Toscana."

[70] For instance, according to Gian Rinaldo Carli, the barrier to growth was not so much high taxes as jurisdictional chaos, internal tolls, and guild monopolies. Tuscan poverty stemmed from a lack of a "just and nutritive circulation" of goods and riches. Carli, "Saggio economico e politico," 354–5. See the introduction to chapter 6.

[71] Diaz, *Francesco Maria Gianni*; and Cochrane, *Florence in the Forgotten Centuries*, 399–400.

[72] Gianni, "Discorso," 295. [73] Ibid., 296.

[74] Ibid., 299. The following quote is on p. 298.

exploit their ties to ministers in Florence: they knew how to "make the echo of the mercantile city reverberate" throughout the land. The governor was backed (even controlled) by his nefarious advisor: the *auditore* Francesco Giuseppe Pierallini. Thanks to his mastery of the archives, Pierallini managed access to information about Livorno for almost four decades: "He came to govern the governors, to direct the spirit of all officials, and to provide the bureaus and ministers of Florence with everything they did not know relating to Livorno: and what they knew was truly little, and he always made it a secret of his craft."[75] Pierallini put his talents to use by defending abuses that served the interests of local commerce at the expense of the grand duchy.

Gianni regarded Livorno as a foreign colony in Tuscan territory. Although on balance it was advantageous to stay connected to the international marketplace, in Gianni's view the benefits the free port offered to the fisc amounted to something of a wash, given the high costs of administering the city. He ended his discourse by listing his recommendations for fixing governance in Livorno and binding it more closely to the hinterland. These appear pell-mell for thirteen pages, ranging from the civic to the moral: "everybody knows that our police force is more occupied with whores and whore-ism in Livorno than with anything else."[76] Gianni's advice was also directed toward refashioning the port's role in the policy process. He advocated creating a differential tariff for the benefit of Tuscan products and ensuring that foreign consuls were treated as private individuals, not representatives of foreign nations. "The aggregate of merchants of various nations cannot be legitimately represented, since all their interests are merely individual, sometimes opposed."[77] He wanted more submissive governors, selected by merit and loyalty rather than high birth; and a reform of the judicial system that would break the authority of *auditori* like Pierallini.

Peter Leopold's reforms were oriented toward rationalizing Tuscan institutions. The grand duke believed that ministers should set policies while, thanks to a more simplified administration at the local level, subjects were free to pursue their own interests within a more rational structure of incentives. Accordingly, the number of offices in the bureaucracy fell by thirty percent between 1736 and 1784. Many magistracies were suppressed; those that survived were reorganized, restricted in their spheres of competence, and inserted into a better defined hierarchy of offices.[78] Among the many reforms enacted by Leopold's ministers, the most important included the general economic survey conducted in 1766–7, the dismantling of the guild system (completed in 1780), the progressive liberalization of the grain trade from 1766–78, and the creation of a customs union in 1781.[79] At the broadest level, one might see these measures as an effort to dismantle the paternalistic state of the Medici by clearly separating jurisdiction from administration.

[75] Ibid., 314; see too Lauretta, "Il Progetto," 54. Cf. Baruchello, *Livorno e il suo porto*, 349–50.

[76] Ibid., 318. [77] Ibid., 313.

[78] Litchfield, *Emergence of a Bureaucracy*, 313–29; Mangio, *La polizia toscana*; Sordi, *L'amministrazione illuminata*, chs 1 and 3; Aglietti, *I governatori di Livorno*, 168–70, 185–8.

[79] Baruchello, *Livorno e il suo porto*, 316; Dal Pane, "I lavori preparatori"; Mirri, *La lotta politica*; Venturi, "Quattro anni di carestia"; Becagli, *Un unico territorio gabellabile*. The only remaining internal tolls were at the gates of the major cities: Florence, Siena, Pisa, and Pistoia.

The reforms gave Peter Leopold a reputation as one of Europe's most enlightened rulers. He even drafted a secret constitution that would have given Tuscany a general assembly and transformed the grand duchy into a limited monarchy. This plan foundered on opposition from Vienna and many of his own ministers.

Unless it served the interests of their city, Livorno's officials were not active in Peter Leopold's reforms and sometimes used their authority to thwart them. Consider Governor Bourbon del Monte's response to the Deputation of Manufactures. The deputation intended to gather data about industry throughout Tuscany as part of the grand duke's general survey. When its members approached the governor, he told them that their request was inopportune because "merchants were not inclined to give any account of their affairs."[80] They might be suspicious that the gathering of information would be the first step in making Livorno's industry dependent on magistracies in Florence. "It is useless to mix in Livorno with the rest of Tuscany in whatever is related to commerce, but [necessary] to consider it quite distinct from the rest of the state." Rather than lament the gulf between Livorno and its hinterland, Bourbon del Monte exaggerated the separation to protect the independence of the city's merchants from outside interference. It was a settled principle that the government not inquire into the affairs of merchants in the free port. After providing several citations from his archives, Bourbon del Monte declared that the only legitimate role for the government was to create a welcoming atmosphere for commerce and eliminate barriers to trade. The governor suggested that the deputation consult the memoranda of 1758 or the records of the General Tax Farm. He was not going to offer further assistance.[81]

When Bourbon del Monte died in 1780, Peter Leopold was supposed to have remarked, "now we have reacquired Livorno."[82] At its most ambitious, the grand duke's legislation sought to integrate Livorno politically, juridically, and economically with the rest of the state. But opposition in Livorno hampered the regime's efforts. In late 1780, the office of *auditore* was split between an "*auditore* of the tribunal," with a judicial function, and an "*auditore* consultant," an advisor on political and economic matters. Pierallini became the *auditore* consultant and assumed many of the mediating roles once performed by governors Ginori and Bourbon del Monte. The new governor, less forceful than his predecessors, was unable to prevent Pierallini from simply moving the archives of the governor's office into a room adjoining his own apartments. Gianni was not exaggerating when he accused Pierallini of making his mastery of the archives into a trade secret. Contrary to his expectations, Peter Leopold did not obtain greater control over Livorno after the governor's death. Instead, Livorno acquired in Pierallini a new guardian of its interests.[83]

80 ASL, GCM, 963, ff. 342–343, 12/30/1767, Bourbon del Monte to the Francesco Pecci, quoted by Aglietti, *I governatori di Livorno*, 134. See the previous letter from Francesco Pecci in ASL, GCM, 4, f. 568, 12/26/1767.

81 ASL, GCM, 964, pp. 43–4, 02/10/1768, Bourbon del Monte (or Pierallini) to Francesco Pecci. See Pecci's earlier letter in ASL, GCM, 5, f. 54, 01/21/1768, and two subsequent letters in the exchange in ASL, GCM, 5, ff. 174, 181, 02/27/1768, and ASL, GCM, 964, 75–6, 03/02/1768. On commercial statistics, see n. 56.

82 G. Vivoli, *Annali*, vol. 1, 269.

83 Aglietti, *I governatori di Livorno*, 126–7, 133–9, 149–55. Pierallini had already increased his authority over judicial matters with a legal reform in 1774. The archive escapades are recounted on p. 166. Governor Francesco Seratti's travails with his archives are discussed on pp. 12 n. 8 and 14 n. 12: the poor governor couldn't even find a copy of the Livornina in his records!

The reforms Leopold did succeed in enacting helped perfect the system of Livorno. Far from hurting the interests of foreign merchants, they facilitated them. A few years after coming to office, he issued a law on brokers that satisfied long-standing demands of merchants.[84] He also published tariffs for quarantine fees so that factors could not deceive their correspondents by pocketing the difference between the actual costs and the ones reported to their principals, "to the discredit of the port." His regime eliminated many of the city's local monopolies, such as the tax farms that managed bread, meat, and fishing, and created a freer environment for the retail trade. He reduced many of the export taxes on Tuscan goods such as ceramics, glass, olive oil, leather, and marble. Above all, administrative reform. Several rulings eliminated bureaucratic abuses by supplying more precise instructions, clarifying hierarchies, and providing better salaries to remove temptations for bribery. A 1781 law further simplified the exaction of the stallage duties. These measures made Livorno like itself, only more so.[85]

Toward the end of his reign, Peter Leopold expressed the system of Livorno in almost exactly the same language Bourbon del Monte had used twenty years earlier. The grand duke urged the scrupulous protection of the city's privileges for foreigners and its laws on neutrality. Commerce must be left free and unrestricted, as Livorno was in essence a port of deposit and transit, nothing more. It could profit Tuscany only as an outlet for local goods and for the revenue generated by its commercial services. The chief difference between the governor's language and that of the grand duke lay in new proposals. Peter Leopold closed his account by cautioning the reader never to waste time with industrial enterprises, commercial companies, and financial schemes. These projects were illusions. "The government cannot do anything more than provide the greatest possible ease and convenience."[86]

The merchant community was as vibrant as ever. During the reign of Peter Leopold, there were about two hundred merchants and one hundred and fifty commercial houses in Livorno at any one time: perhaps thirty of the houses were Tuscan, fifty were Jewish, and the rest were foreign, the most numerous of whom were the English, but which also included Dutch, Armenians, Greeks, French, and other Italians. There were another two hundred and fifty brokers, some of whom secretly acted as merchants, and a large community of cashiers, accountants, and business apprentices. Everybody put on airs, and the monarch complained more than once about the luxury, gambling, libertinage, ambition, and vainglory of the city's merchants. The governor did not moralize, however: "Frugality and parsimony are fine things elsewhere," he declared, but not in Livorno.[87] This bustling

[84] See Addobbati, *Commercio, rischio, guerra*, 136–7, 142–4, 178–82, 195–202, 204, 213–14, 227–30.

[85] Pietro Leopoldo d'Asburgo Lorena, *Relazioni*, vol. 3, 60–71; Sonnino, *Saggio sulle industrie, marina e commercio*, 39–43; Baruchello, *Livorno e il suo porto*, 311–15; Addobbati, *Commercio, rischio, guerra*, 212–13. See the conclusion to chapter 5.

[86] Pietro Leopoldo d'Asburgo Lorena, *Relazioni*, 60–1; cf. the quote by Bourbon del Monte in n. 32, and the remarks in "Free Ports in the Central Mediterranean" in the introduction.

[87] ASL, GCM, 1, f. 498, 09/14/1765, quoted by Addobbati, "'La frugalità e l'economia sono ottime altrove'"; Aglietti, *I governatori di Livorno*, 193–4. For Peter Leopold's views, see his *Relazioni*,

Fig. 7.3. Antonio Piemontesi, "The Merchant's Office." From left to right, the maps on the wall are of Spain, Livorno, and Italy.
Credit: Camera di Commercio di Livorno.

community, about a third the size of Marseille's at the end of Leopold's reign in 1790, could look forward to a period of dizzying economic expansion until Napoleon conquered Livorno in 1807 (Fig. 7.3).

The battles between the governor and Peter Leopold had their root cause in the earlier, protracted war between the Council of Commerce and the General Tax Farm. The problems Livorno posed defined some of the terms of his reforms. But despite helping inspire some of the new policies that characterized his reign, little changed in the free port. The real enemy of Peter Leopold's reforms was not the governor as such, but rather, the system of local collaboration and representation that came into being during the first decades of the seventeenth century. Elites in Livorno welcomed some innovations: the abolition of the General Tax Farm in 1768, the freeing of the grain trade, and the dissolution of corporatist restrictions. But they brooked no interference in their affairs and no alteration to the status of foreign merchants. As a result, Livorno's role in formulating policy in the grand duchy of Peter Leopold was minimal, and it was peripheral to his vision for economic growth. Gone were the days when the grand duke might say, "Livorno is the key to my states," as Ferdinando I had in 1603.

vol. 3, 62. For the business community, see Filippini, *Il porto di Livorno*, vol. 1, 75–8. On Livorno in the Napoleonic and post-Napoleonic periods, see Baruchello, *Livorno e il suo porto*, 519–21; Mangio, *Politica toscana e rivoluzione*; LoRomer, *Merchants and Reform*, ch. 1; Filippini, *Il porto di Livorno*, vol. 3; Addobbati, *Commercio, rischio, guerra*, 249–50; Fettah, "Temps et espaces des trafics portuaires"; Fettah, "Livourne: cité du Prince, cité marchande"; and Fettah, "Livourne et les grandes places merchandes."

CONCLUSION

If Peter Leopold's project was "to assimilate as much as possible the system of Livorno to the rest of the grand duchy," one might assert the converse with equal truth: his goal was to assimilate the grand duchy to Livorno.[88] The desire to bind the free port to the hinterland was not new to his regime; similar efforts punctuated the reigns of Ferdinando I, Cosimo III, and Francis Stephen. The locus of reform was the true novelty. Peter Leopold's interventions were aimed at remaking the Tuscan hinterland. His program of liberalization simplified administration throughout the grand duchy, while at the same time reducing barriers to free commerce and production. His reforms were an ideologically robust extension of the same principles that had evolved piecemeal (and without ideological coherence) in Livorno itself over the previous two hundred years. This is not exactly a case of the center mirroring the periphery. While there were connections between Peter Leopold's program and Livorno's experiments with free trade, best exemplified by the figure of Carlo Ginori, the free port was only one of many models that Tuscan reformers had at their disposal. Livorno's significance lay in the debate over the proper method for articulating economic advice and policy.

The rise of scientific political economy was one of the hallmarks of Enlightenment reform. The Tuscan case suggests that the new political economy is notable less for its substantive ideas than for its epistemic and institutional foundations. Livorno had long served as the grand duke's canvas for economic projects. But the interested nature of the city's counsel—its entanglement in private and indeed foreign mercantile concerns—compromised the free port's claims to formulate policy for Tuscany as a whole. Despite broad agreement among Tuscan statesmen regarding the necessary agricultural and industrial policies, controversy raged about the institutional arrangements appropriate for managing economic counsel. "Economists argue less about whether their field is a science than do practitioners of some other fields of social science," noted Thomas Kuhn. "Is that because economists know what science is? Or is it rather economics about which they agree?"[89] The creation of a new community for producing economic knowledge was the critical achievement of Enlightenment political economy.

Economic societies such as the Accademia dei Georgofili defined themselves in opposition to the form of expertise represented by the Council of Commerce. At first glance, the two bodies appear to have had little to do with one another: one was self-interested, bureaucratic, and privileged; the other was disinterested, civil, and voluntary. The reciprocal antagonism was not accidental, however. The commercial advice offered by the council or the earlier Deputation of Commerce was meant to show how the private interest of merchants aligned with the interest of the prince and the commonwealth. As the troubled history of the Council of Commerce suggests, such bodies were at once a culmination of traditional modes

[88] The quote is from Aglietti, *I governatori di Livorno*, 149. Cf. Baruchello, *Livorno e il suo porto*, 504–5.

[89] Kuhn, *The Structure of Scientific Revolutions*, 161.

of economic advising and a turning point in the history of political economy, pointing towards a new kind of epistemic community: the economic society.[90] Samuel Madden, one of the founders of the Dublin Society (a model for the Georgofili), took inspiration from institutions like chambers of commerce, "to say nothing of Holland, whose government is nothing more than a great council of merchants."[91] Yet the academies constituted a different sociological form, more indebted to the norms of the Republic of Letters than to the political institutions of the Ancien Régime: reciprocity, non-hierarchy, and openness. Economic societies might have been modeled on commercial councils, but they were also in competition with them. Their claims to offer disinterested expertise, cull the best from international thought, and harness practical knowledge were intended to undermine the old political venues for proffering economic advice.

The formal independence enjoyed by economic societies was an important element of their authority, but it should not be taken at face value. With the Georgofili as with other societies, membership included regime officials and people with intimate government ties, not to mention merchants. Economic societies represented the delegation of state powers to a group of individuals who, in the guise of private citizens, acted on behalf of the state. It would be naive to take them as an exuberant expression of the public sphere. Their claims to disinterested knowledge must likewise be qualified. The Georgofili facilitated the incorporation of landowning and cultural elites into the formulation of political economy. They aspired to intervene in the lives of the peasantry and the working poor. An aura of class control hovered about the academy's expertise.[92]

It is also important not to exaggerate the success of the new societies in resolving the epistemic problems of the social sciences. Despite much handwringing and efforts to improve the Accademia dei Georgofili, a participant in 1777 observed that "the assembled members are pathetic, and seen from close up the meetings are risible."[93] Many societies had difficulty getting their members to attend sessions, let alone undertake the projects of practical knowledge they envisioned. When they did meet, societies nourished a considerable amount of internal disagreement. Nevertheless, even amidst conflict, the new societies fostered certain discursive norms and practices. Societies created not so much a unitary consensus as a common space that defined who was entitled to make certain kinds of arguments and the manner in which one could make them.

[90] See "Merchant Expertise and State Institutions" in chapter 5.

[91] Samuel Madden, as quoted by Livesy, "The Dublin Society," 63.

[92] Bödeker, "Economic Societies in Germany," 193, 210–11; Bonnyman, "Agrarian Patriotism," 42–3; Engelhardt, "Patriotic Societies," 227–8. For Tuscany, see Mirri, *Proprietari e contadini*, 224–9; and Becagli, "The *Georgofili*," 114.

[93] Giuseppe Bencivenni Pelli, as quoted by ibid., 125; see too Shovlin, "The Society of Brittany," 75.

8

Free Trade before Liberalism

Genoese officials followed the rise of Livorno with a mixture of envy and apprehension. Their Casa di San Giorgio, which supervised revenue collection and administered the public debt, received a stream of reports detailing the workings of Livorno's free port and outlining projects to fix Genoa's own system of tax-exempt warehouses. A memorandum from 1655 is a typical specimen of their concerns. Its author analyzed the effectiveness of Livorno's Customs Office as an institution, the ease of transacting and transshipping wares in the free port, and the commercial connections of its foreign merchants. Typical, too, were his niggling proposals for competing with Livorno. Even as simple a proposition as allowing merchants to store goods in their own warehouses troubled the writer, who fretted about the ensuing opportunities for fraud. At least his recommendation that Genoa treat Jews with greater "courtesy" was taken up by the republic in just those years, albeit halfheartedly. The reform of Livorno's free port in 1676 further aggravated Genoese anxiety about its rival's institutions.[1]

Livorno's influence was felt most strongly on the Italian scene, which was a region of intense maritime competition and a lush profusion of free ports. The spread of free ports has often been lamented as both cause and consequence of northern Italy's economic decline. For Enlightenment thinkers, they promoted foreign domination of Italian commerce, hurt local manufacturing, and threatened a just fiscal and political order. One economic writer admitted that free ports made commerce "flourish marvelously," for instance, but at the cost of "prostituting" it to foreigners.[2] Modern world-systems theory has echoed and formalized this view. According to this interpretation, the opening of Italian ports to foreign merchants facilitated the subordination of Italy to the more dynamic economies of northwestern Europe.[3] Undoubtedly, most free ports were responses not only to opportunities in the commercial landscape, but also to a competitive situation in which ports had little option but to follow suit when a nearby rival lowered duties or welcomed foreigners: "for he who remains alone is deserted."[4] But the network of free ports did not merely

[1] ASG, CSG, Sala 35, 544, 05/23/1655, sommario. See also the memorandum from the late seventeenth century in ASG, AS, 1011, quoted at length in Giacchero, *Storia economica*, 59–64; ASG, AF, 1201, 02/05/1653, report by Giovanni Domenico Gavi; ASG, AS, 1011, memorandum from *c.*1670 on reforming the free port of Genoa; and ASG, AF, 1217, anonymous early eighteenth-century memorandum comparing Livorno and Genoa.

[2] Broggia, *Trattato*, 98 and 101.

[3] See n. 11 in the introduction.

[4] Genovesi, *Lezioni di commercio*, vol. 1, 319. Broggia, *Trattato* 104, 115, 117–18 makes a similar point.

serve the interests of hegemons such as England, France, and the Dutch Republic. It benefited Italy, too, by fostering commercial integration and generating revenue from commercial services. Above all, it kept Italy connected to the currents of international trade during a profound phase of economic restructuring.

Livorno played a privileged role in early modern discussions about free ports. The city was "born of commerce" and was famous for its regime of toleration, flourishing foreign communities, pervasive liberties, and (after 1676) procedural simplicity.[5] Officials of other Italian governments meticulously studied Livorno's free port as they sought to implement their own policies, and contemporary pamphleteers regularly cited Livorno in their arguments as well. The Whig publicist Sir Francis Brewster, who leveled one of the earliest critiques of the free port in his 1695 treatise, found it necessary to begin with Livorno, "because I take that in all its circumstances to be the first complete precedent in Europe."[6] Tuscany was not merely a reactive player in the development of political economy, forced to catch up with developments elsewhere—despite the perception of Italian thinkers during the Enlightenment. Through its port of Livorno, Tuscany was a source of creativity for all of Europe.[7]

There were four phases in the geographic diffusion of free ports. The first was a Tyrrhenian period, from 1590 to 1650. Goaded by Livorno's success, Genoa and other neighboring localities attempted to implement their own free port policies. There followed an expansionary phase, 1650 to 1740, when free ports appeared throughout Western Europe and especially in the Italian peninsula: Trieste, Ancona, Messina, Marseilles, Nice, Tangiers, Dunkirk, Althona, and Hamburg. Thereafter free ports gradually fell out of fashion in Europe, but by the mid-eighteenth century colonial powers were creating a bewildering number of them in the Caribbean Sea, including in Martinique, Guadeloupe, Tobago, Jamaica, and Saint-Domingue (Haiti). Later they spread to East Asia and North America. So, free ports were first an Italian, then a Western European, later an Atlantic, and ultimately a global phenomenon.[8] As though to underscore the institution's Italian origin, writers occasionally used the term *porto franco* instead of its translation. "[Dunkirk] might have been brought to have been a porto franco, a free port," complained the English patriot James Howell after a treaty returned Dunkirk to the French.[9]

Like every process of emulation, the spread of the free port involved experimentation, hesitation, and about-faces. Actual free ports differed widely in legislative intent and institutional structure. In the end, few proved quite as hospitable as Livorno. Regimes usually worked within existing institutional arrangements in the hopes of salvaging traditional fiscal and commercial goals. Their compromises

[5] Peri, *Il negotiante*, vol. 3, 141. See too Guyot de Merville, *Voyage historique d'Italie*, 549–57; Labat, *Voyages*, vol. 2, 79–106; Nugent, *The Grand Tour*, vol. 3, 374–7.

[6] Brewster, *Essays on Trade and Navigation*, 29.

[7] Cf. S. Reinert, *Translating Empire*, 186–232.

[8] McCalla, "The Geographical Spread of Free Zones." Hamburg (1713/1748) and Emden (1751) should be added to the table of free ports declarations in Tazzara, "Managing Free Trade," 495–7. See Hovy, *Het voorstel van 1751*, 169, 172, and 180.

[9] Howell, *A Discours of Dunkirk*, 3. Other examples: Feliu de la Penya, *Fenix de Cataluña*, 111; Montanus, *De nieuwe en onbekende weereld*, 489.

often imposed more supervision of merchants and their goods, when they did not end in outright limitations of liberty. The freest ports were new cities that had not played a starring role in a state's prior fiscal apparatus. In that sense, free trade sprouted its most vigorous roots in the institutional wastelands of the Ancien Régime: Livorno, Ancona, and Trieste in Italy, or the free ports of the Caribbean islands. But the phenomenon was not as marginal as this geography might suggest. The vast amount of maritime traffic that passed through free ports made them a crucial conduit for international commerce. In addition, free ports were conspicuous. Political economists could not help but ponder their virtues and weaknesses. There are three intertwined stories to tell: the institutional reception of the free port, its economic consequences, and its impact on economic thought.

THE SPREAD OF FREE PORTS

In their *Universal Dictionary of Commerce* of 1723, the Brothers Savary observed that all the port cities of Italy modeled their customs regime on either Livorno or Venice. After some further discussion, they concluded that those two ports were ultimately rather similar in their actual level of duties and hospitality toward foreign merchant communities.[10] The notion that all significant Italian ports had a similar customs regime became a commonplace during the Enlightenment. From the Italian perspective, the proliferation of free ports was the most important institutional response to the changes in global trade after 1500, attenuating rather than accelerating economic decline in Italy. Here we will trace the path to convergence along two key axes: openness to foreigners, and the structure and level of tariffs.

The Brothers Savary were correct to emphasize Livorno's influence throughout the region. The port's legislation was a direct inspiration for laws issued in Genoa (1609, 1654, 1670, 1708, 1729, et al.), Nice (1613, 1648, 1667, and 1749), Civitavecchia (1630, 1692, 1742), Naples (1633, 1739), Modena (1652), Messina (1719, 1732), Trieste (1719, 1725), and Ancona (1732). Livorno served as a significant model beyond the Italian peninsula as well, ranging from Marseille (1669) to Marstrand (1775). Italian governments scrutinized the latest policies of their rivals, debated the effects they would have on local trade, and crafted counter-responses. Englishmen also delighted in alerting governments to the virtues of the free port, which they shopped about from ruler to ruler: "which as it is a convenience, so consequently the more free ports wee have the greater is the convenience in itselfe."[11] For that

[10] J. Savary des Bruslons and P.-L. Savary, *Dictionnaire universel*, vol. 2, 1777–8. Broggia makes a similar point in the *Trattato*, 104.

[11] The English resident in Tuscany in 1668, Sir John Finch, as quoted by Pagano de Divitiis, *English Merchants*, 117. On the influence of the Livorno model, see Georgelin, *Venise*, 99–102; Frattarelli Fischer, *Vivere fuori dal ghetto*, 55; Fettah, "Livourne et les grandes places marchandes," 212; Meijling, "La lenta diffusione di un modello"; Calafat, "Une mer jalousée," 497–9, 540–5. For the ports themselves, see Luzzatto, "Il portofranco di Trieste"; Babudieri, *L'espansione mercantile austriaca*; Cova, *Commercio e navigazione*, 9–23; Dubin, *The Port Jews of Habsburg Trieste*, ch. 1; da Silva, "Nice dans l'économie méditerranéenne"; Di Vittorio, *Il commercio tra Levante Ottomano e Napoli*, 12–13; Martini, "Le condizioni economiche di Messina," 1–33; Delumeau, *L'alun de Rome*, 189–90.

matter, English policy in Tangiers, Port Mahon, and Gibraltar was also indebted to the example of Italian free ports.

Livorno's principal competitors were Genoa, Venice, Ancona, and Marseille. The first two were the capital cities of sovereign states and heirs to an illustrious maritime past. Ancona and Marseille were both provincial ports, although the Papacy had more freedom of action in the former than the French king had in the latter. All four ports grew more tolerant of foreign merchants in their midst, and all except Marseille also relaxed customs restrictions. It is likely that Livorno's rivals would have implemented a more liberal customs regime even in the absence of pressure from the Tuscan port. The old city-states of the Middle Ages had flourished amid navigation laws and customs restrictions. The larger commercial environment of the seventeenth and eighteenth centuries made for more intense maritime competition in the Mediterranean, especially in regions dense with coastline and fragmented in political authority.[12]

Genoa tinkered incessantly with the free port policy. Temporary measures for combating bad harvests in the early 1590s were rolled into a limited free port in 1595, which offered safe-conduct for anyone who brought ships laden with grain. In 1609 a regulation opened Genoa up to ships bearing merchandise from beyond Liguria to the west or the Tiber to the south (thus excluding Livorno). Goods could be trans-boarded from one ship to another and only paid one percent of their value on re-export. Over the course of the seventeenth century, several other laws made it easier to move foreign goods through the port, and navigation restrictions against trade with Livorno were eliminated in 1670. The process culminated in 1708 with an effort at full liberalization on the Livorno model: when tax receipts dropped precipitously, Genoa returned to a somewhat more restrictive pattern. Genoese experimentation with the free port was bedeviled by competing policy goals. The aristocratic republic sought to make Genoa a crossroads of Mediterranean commerce, a center of industry, a well-provisioned capital city, and a headquarters for a renewed merchant marine.[13] But the force of competition was relentless. "A few days ago the Republic of Genoa has made its free port," observed one official in Livorno. "Although it hardly approaches the privileges of Livorno . . . the Senate has no other purpose but to damage this port, and is pure emulation."[14]

Genoa was more resistant to foreign merchants in its midst. Some foreign communities did expand. In 1616, for instance, the Netherlandish community got its own consul, and there were perhaps four Dutch commercials houses in Genoa by the 1620s and 1630s. Mostly futile efforts to woo Armenians began in 1624. In 1654, Genoa redoubled its efforts to settle foreign merchants and Jews. But apart from some thirty French and Genevan merchants by the early eighteenth century, Genoa never hosted large and deeply rooted foreign merchant communities. Genoese policy toward Jews remained vacillating, with a tendency now to restrict,

[12] See Pagano de Divitiis, "Porti italiani," 357–85; and "Free Ports in the Central Mediterranean" in the introduction.

[13] Giacchero, *Origini e sviluppi*, 13, 19–20, 47, 94–105, 107, 145–6; Grendi, "Traffico e navi," 351; C. Costantini, *La repubblica di Genova*, 323–34; Kirk, *Genoa and the Sea*, 154–80, esp. 167–70.

[14] Quoted by Giacchero, *Origini e sviluppi*, 96.

now to loosen regulations and a propensity to make ad hominem distinctions between rich and poor Jews. Perhaps the city's abundant local capital accounts for its lack of resolution, at least until the plague of 1656–7 temporarily deranged the Republic's wealth.[15] But even if Genoa remained rich in capital, its stingy hospitality was a missed opportunity in terms of international connections. This did not escape contemporaries. Lewes Roberts thought that Genoa could have competed handily with Livorno if it threw open the doors to foreign traders: "but I referre this point, and publish to the world their owne common proverbe which admits hardly any merchants to live or thrive amongst them, *Genoa fatta per noi*, their citie is onely made for themselves."[16]

Genoa's path toward the free port was marked by frequent, obsessively detailed legislation. By contrast, Venice adopted an ad hoc approach because it was difficult to secure legislative consensus for radical departures in tax policy. Successive regulations entailed the outright lowering of duties, often for specific goods, and a relaxation of the navigation laws that had been a linchpin of the Venetian system since the Middle Ages. For example, during the sixteenth century duties on silk goods were gradually lightened because of concerns about maintaining the city's industrial position. In 1626, the Venetians lowered import duties on goods arriving from the *Ponente*—that is, on the commerce of the Dutch and English. In 1646, the Senate granted equality to all Christians in Venice to participate in the Levant trade. The declaration of a free port in 1662 suppressed entry duties for goods arriving by sea. Another free port declaration, this time extending to exports as well as imports, was issued in 1736 (the first had been abandoned after twenty years). In reality, these were just legislative milestones: customs duties on a whole panel of goods declined throughout the sixteenth and seventeenth centuries.[17] Venice manipulated tariff levels rather than warehousing and transit incentives, as in Livorno or Genoa, but the outcome was similar. Competition to attract commerce to the wealthy, fragmented, harbor-rich Italian peninsula led to lower duties and milder navigation laws.

During the Middle Ages and most of the Renaissance, foreign merchants occupied a marginal or controlled position in the leading mercantile cities of northern Italy. In Venice, this control is best exemplified by the *fondaco*: a building used for housing foreign merchants and their wares, but also for monitoring them. The loss of the carrying trade and Venice's transformation from an international emporium to a regional port created a new scope for foreign merchants to operate within the city itself. Throughout the first half of the seventeenth century, some thirty Dutch

[15] Giacchero, *Storia economica*, 45, 77, 104; Giacchero, *Origini e sviluppi*, 22, 105, 131, 209–10, 232 n. 19; Grendi, "Traffico e navi," 350; Engels, *Merchants*, 120–2; Kirk, *Genoa and the Sea*, 155, 176–9.

[16] Roberts, *The Marchants Mappe of Commerce*, 92–3.

[17] Customs rates varied between four percent and thirteen percent by the late seventeenth century—probably closer to the former, owing to systematic under-appraisals. Beltrami, "La crisi," 317; Sella, *Commerci e industrie*, 89–92; Lane, "The Merchant Marine"; Georgelin, *Venise*, 57–83: esp. 70, 77; M. Costantini, "La regolazione dei dazi marittimi"; M. Costantini, *Porto navi e traffici*, 21–4, 36–41; Molà, *The Silk Industry*, 63–8, 75–85; Fusaro, "Les Anglais et les Grecs," 619–20; Gelder, *Trading Places*, 57, 72, 87, 93–4, 102, 145–8.

merchants were active in Venice at any one time. There were also perhaps twenty English merchants present, although they remained for shorter stays. These northerners did not reside in fondacos; nor did the large population of Greeks, most of whom were Venetian subjects, who flocked to the Serenissima. Controls remained for other groups, however. The community of Jews lived in the city's three ghettos, and Ottoman subjects usually resided in the *Fondaco dei turchi* established in 1621. The hundreds of German merchants who did business in the city often remained in their fondaco as well. In short, foreign merchants found Venice a more hospitable marketplace after 1550 or so, although the legal regime that regulated their presence was ad hoc and at times incoherent.[18] One Genoese writer—no doubt conscious of the inhospitality of his own city—saw Venice as the "fatherland of every nation."[19] For him, commercial toleration brought marvelous benefits to Venice despite the "mutual hatreds" arising from differences in language, religion, and customs.

The papacy's port of Ancona was one of the Serenissima's fiercest enemies during the eighteenth century: Ancona, "such a deadly and dire port for our city."[20] Ancona had already experienced a golden age during the sixteenth century, when Filippo Sassetti had admired its low transit taxes and facilities for foreigners. Growth petered out during the late sixteenth century owing to maritime insecurity, the persecution of Jews, and competition from Venice and Livorno. The city's commerce declined, but the memory of its glory days remained. The awakening of papal political economy in the 1720s out of its "archaicisms and puerility" created an opportunity for local merchants in Ancona to advocate for a free port.[21] Opponents of the measure argued that Ancona could scarcely ever compete with Livorno, which (they contended) owed its success to geopolitics rather than to policy. Proponents drew upon historical analysis and mercantile calculations to demonstrate that Livorno's privileges were in fact the key to its commerce. The latter arguments won the day. The papacy endowed Ancona with the essential attributes of a free port: open entry for captains or merchants of any nation; and the customs-free sale, storage, or re-export of their wares. Stallage duties were eliminated in favor of an anchorage tax that varied by tonnage and provenance.[22]

Ancona had been famous during the sixteenth century for its Ottoman connections. Although its population of Jews had dwindled during the seventeenth century, a number still resided there in 1710 to carry on relations with the ports of the Eastern Mediterranean. The community of foreigners grew more diverse after the edict of 1732 made it a free port. The most important new arrivals were the

18 Kellenbenz, "Le declin de Venise," 164–5; Fedalto, "Stranieri a Venezia e a Padova," 254–5, 265, 268–9; Fusaro, "Les Anglais et les Grecs," 605; Gelder, *Trading Places*, 100–4, 140.

19 Peri, *Il negotiante*, vol. 2, 117; see too Misson, *Nouveau voyage d'Italie*, vol. 1, 227.

20 From a report by the Venetian Trade Board, quoted by Caracciolo, *Le port franc de Ancône*, 38.

21 Caracciolo, "Il dibattito sui 'porti franchi,'" 540. Imperial representatives keen on destroying Venetian trade also lobbied for the free port of Ancona. Caracciolo, *Le port franc de Ancône*, 81–9. On commerce before 1732, see Earle, "The Commercial Development of Ancona," 43–4; Caracciolo, *Le port franc de Ancône*, 14–28; Segre, "Sephardic Settlements," 124–30.

22 Earle, "The Commercial Development of Ancona," 42; Caracciolo, *Le port franc de Ancône*, 23, 42, 90–5, 249–53.

English, who saw Ancona as a good alternative if Livorno became "clogged with difficulties" after the demise of the Medici dynasty.[23] In theory, merchants who settled in the city with their families benefited from a ten-year exemption from property taxes and other incentives. In practice, locals used their access to public officials to dominate the city's traffic: for instance, Anconitans found it easier than foreigners to obtain licenses for exporting agricultural produce. The foreigners who settled there tended themselves to be big operators. Ancona never developed the deep pool of medium-scale foreign merchants that Livorno and Venice had.

The port of Marseille appears at first blush to have been a case apart. Unlike its Italian cousins, it hosted an active trade in which French ships transported merchandise on behalf of French merchants. Its free port, promulgated by Colbert in 1669, was also more restrictive. This "disguised navigation act" discouraged foreign shipping and was aimed to foster growth in Marseille at the expense of neighboring ports, principally Genoa and Livorno.[24] A prohibitive duty of twenty percent was levied on goods coming from the Levant on non-French ships, or even on French ships hailing from ports in Italy or Spain. Despite these restrictions, trade with Livorno remained significant. Accordingly, in 1688 the tax exemptions were extended to ships that embarked goods in the Ottoman Empire and nonetheless stopped in Italy to unload part of their cargo. Thus adjusted, the twenty-percent duty was effective at excluding foreign shipping, judging by the modest amount of revenue generated by that tax—except during periods of war, when the Marseillais relied on neutral shipping.[25]

Still, the 1669 edict affirmed Marseille's status as a free port in a number of senses. Foreign merchants were welcome to settle and do business in the port. In practice, the municipality discriminated against Mediterranean competitors such as Jews, Armenians, and Italians. That did not mean the city lacked its cosmopolitan aspect: "The quay of the port . . . is continually covered with all manner of figures of all nations and both sexes, Europeans, Greeks, Armenians, Blacks, Levantines, etc."[26] These were temporary visitors, found near the docks rather than in the new city where the *gens de condition* resided. Marseille was more welcoming to northern European merchants, who did not compete with its monopoly with the Levant, as well as to other French merchants and Protestants—though not to French Protestants, after the Edict of Nantes was revoked in 1685. Marseille resembled the Venetian emporium of the Middle Ages, trading directly with the East while permitting northerners to settle in its midst.

There was something of the free port in Marseille's treatment of goods after 1669, too. Wares carried aboard French ships coming from the Levant enjoyed

[23] Ibid., 28, 145–60. The quote is from a 1734 letter from the Count of Essex to the Duke of Newcastle reproduced in ibid., 165. See Capuzzo, "Portifranchi e comunità etnico-religiose."

[24] Dermigny, "Escales, échelles et ports francs," 556.

[25] Bergasse and Rambert, *Histoire du commerce*, 39–44; Paris, *Histoire du commerce*, 8 n. 31, 11, 122–3, 160–1; Takeda, *Between Crown and Commerce*, 25–35.

[26] De Brosses, *Lettres familières écrites d'Italie*, 30–1. On the status of foreigners, see Bergasse and Rambert, *Histoire du commerce*, 18–19, 65, 531; Carrière, *Négociants marseillais*, 70, 259–62, 281; Echinard and Temime, *Histoire des migrations*, 34–46, 53–5, 63, 77, 91; and Takeda, *Between Crown and Commerce*, 97–102.

low, simplified customs duties. Colbert abolished many of the old medieval taxes in his edict. And while his dream of eliminating trade taxes was a failure—the central government imposed several new duties during the eighteenth century—their mode of exaction became more equitable throughout the period. In addition, the municipality fought hard to keep the welter of tax farms outside the city walls. Marseille constituted a kind of exclave from France whose status periodically aggravated relations with Versailles when reformers sought to impose more unified policies on the kingdom.[27] To contemporaries concerned about competition, however, local regulations were by no means simple: one official remarked in 1765 that foreign merchants found themselves "lost in a labyrinth from which they could not escape without having to pay some kind of duty."[28] This was a bit of an exaggeration. Despite substantial differences in customs regime, Marseille inhabited the same competitive environment as Livorno and Genoa, and it employed some of the same methods to attract commerce.

In the early seventeenth century, Livorno had a dramatic customs lead over other ports. For example, in 1628 it cost between thirty and forty pieces of eight for the English to ship a bale of silk to Vicenza (in the Veneto) via Venice, but only ten pieces to ship the same bale overland via Livorno.[29] Such a commanding lead in tariff rates did not last, at least not for maritime traffic (overland transit dues were more variable). Total tax assessments in the principal ports of northern Italy were roughly the same by the early eighteenth century—between five and ten percent for most goods. These figures are comparable to those of Amsterdam, where import and export duties were about five percent each. Given the complexity of tariff rules, however, such averages offer limited insight. Remaining differences lay less in tariff rates than in institutional structure, which varied substantially from port to port.[30]

The consolidation of the system of free ports was part of the creation of a new kind of marketplace. Although not every port was equally hospitable, access to the market depended less than ever before on the social qualities of an individual or group. The "convenience in itselfe" that Englishmen celebrated affected every merchant who alighted in a free port. In addition, the reduction in tariff levels and the simplification of tariff rules implied a decline in the social oversight of the marketplace. Livorno was at the epicenter of these changes, but it was part of a broader disembedding of market structures throughout the central Mediterranean, with important consequences for commercial organization. Armed commerce offered few advantages in this world and had little success. Traditional trading networks remained more competitive than bureaucratic companies in the Italian sphere.

[27] Paris, *Histoire du commerce*, 24–9, 70, 75–8, 319; Carrière, *Négociants marseillais*, 212–19, 317–18; and Takeda, *Between Crown and Commerce*, *passim*.

[28] Quoted by Bergasse and Rambert, *Histoire du commerce*, 225. On the tax regime, see ibid., 222, 267; Paris, *Histoire du commerce*, 117–22, 142–5, 165; and Takeda, *Between Crown and Commerce*, 43–8.

[29] Pagano de Divitiis, *English Merchants*, 115.

[30] Savary, *Le parfait négociant*, vol. 2, 55; J. Savary des Bruslons and P.-L. Savary, *Dictionnaire universel*, vol. 2, 1776–8; Giacchero, *Storia economica*, 54, 59, 66–7, 72; Giacchero, *Il Seicento e le compere*, 606–8; and Gelderblom, "The Organization of Long-Distance," 245.

The disembedding of the marketplace should not be confused with the desocialization of trade itself. The spread of free ports did not promote impersonal exchange—that is, agency relations across cultural and social barriers. On the contrary, the relaxation of state control over trade had the effect of strengthening ethno-religious networks, whether in the familial diasporic form represented by the Sephardim, or the more hierarchical form represented by English factor relationships. What the proliferation of free ports made possible was the entanglement of these separate networks: in markets like Livorno, it was easy for Jewish merchants and English merchants to conduct spot transactions with one another. For merchants, the convergence of disparate networks was a major advantage in using a free port, multiplying the number of potential transactions far beyond the limits of one's own ethno-religious group. Hospitality toward goods and people not only lowered trade costs, in short, but it also increased a port's connectedness to the outside world.

A COMPLEX INSTITUTION

Emulation was a tricky business. King Charles II of England declared Tangiers a free port in 1662. The city ultimately proved too expensive to defend relative to its commercial prospects, and Tangiers was abandoned in 1684. Henry Sheeres (1641–1710), the military engineer appointed to construct the colony's fortifications, thought he knew why the entrepôt had failed. Tangiers had lacked a defined "constitution" laying out its privileges like Livorno and Marseille. The free port of Tangiers was "a trap and a snare to people, [rather] than an incouragement and protection."[31] Sheeres had documents such as the Livornina, the tariff of 1676, and Colbert's 1669 edict in mind when he urged Charles II to grant a constitution for Tangiers. In fact, the challenge in copying policies did not lay in enumerating liberties or setting tariffs, contrary to Sheeres's opinion (which was shared by many contemporaries). The true problem was creating ground-level institutions compatible with a state's larger fiscal system.

Livorno's special success owed in part to the international commercial context, in part to local political structures. It was well situated to benefit from the rise of the Atlantic economies thanks to its position in the Tyrrhenian and the relative neutrality of Tuscany. Livorno also benefited from its status as an extraterritorial enclave with a distinct administrative apparatus. Ancona and Marseille were also provincial ports, but their entrenched elites and ancient institutions limited royal intervention. Genoa and Venice were capital cities whose rulers had to manage subject territory, control regional exchange, and tax local consumption. Geopolitics does not tell the whole story, however. We must also isolate the local institutions

[31] Sheeres, *A Discourse Touching Tanger*, 46–7; see also Petyt, *Britannia languens*, 142–3. On the English occupation of Tangiers, see Games, *Web of Empire*, 293–8. On Sheeres himself, see the entry by J. D. Davies in the ODNB. Dermigny sees the free port of Trieste as a tool to project military and economic power over the sea, and one could make a similar argument for English intentions in Tangiers. See "Escales, échelles et ports francs," 571–4, 581–8.

that mediated liberty in the marketplace. At least three arrangements made Livorno an especially effective free port: the nature of its Customs Office as an organization, the method of levying taxes, and the geographical extent of the free port. These factors reduced the transaction costs inherent in navigating the local market (for merchants) or in taxing commerce (for officials). They were, however, difficult for its rivals to imitate.

Livorno's Customs Office was a unified and autonomous body, and apart from the contentious period of the General Tax Farm, it was not farmed out to contractors. Merchants dealt with only one office and twenty officials, who were by no means zealous exactors of the grand duke's duties. The customs director, as the "chief of commerce," answered on a regular basis only to the secretary of war and enjoyed immense discretion in administering trade.[32] Unlike their colleagues in other ports, after 1676 officials in Livorno did not have to trouble themselves with monitoring the wholesale trade, appraising the value of goods, or tracking the destination of wares. The free port of Ancona came closest to replicating the administrative structure of Livorno. After 1732 there were no import/export duties, and the anchorage tax was managed by the papal government rather than farmed. But no climate of laxity prevailed in Ancona. A strong municipality discriminated in favor of local bigwigs, who used their access to public authority to suppress competition from lesser merchants. Even so, the government followed a line of policy more reminiscent of Livorno than any other port in the region.

Customs offices elsewhere were stricter, more fragmented, and more entangled in extra-commercial considerations. The taxes in Genoa, Venice, and Marseille were usually farmed, and farmers had more powerful incentives to insist on the letter of the law than bureaucrats. In Genoa, for instance, the Casa di San Giorgio sold the revenue streams associated with the free port as five-year tax farms to private consortia. Officials belonged to different tax farms that supervised specific dimensions of the local tax regime. The number of officials was much higher, moreover—according to a count from 1670, the Genoese free port had more than four times as many guards as that of Livorno.[33] In Venice, too, four separate taxes were assessed by different bodies managing foreign trade, and additional organizations were responsible for taxing local consumption. The Trade Board played a similar role as San Giorgio in supervising the tax regime, although its measures also required approval by the Senate. The Venetian government was not as beholden to tax farmers as in Genoa, however. For example, in 1632 the Netherlandish merchants won the right to export silk without paying duties, over the objections of a farmer anxious about his receipts. There is also evidence that officials of one

[32] Giacchero, *Storia economica*, 59–64; J. Savary des Bruslons and P.-L. Savary, *Dictionnaire universel*, vol. 2, 1236–7.

[33] ASG, CSG, Sala 35, 563, ins. 106?, lists eighteen guards at the free port and another thirty-five at various stations in the city (there were only four customs guards in Livorno). The chief tax farms implicated with the free port were the *gabella di grano*, the *caratti sul mare*, the *gabella dei panni*, the *pedaggi*, and the *riva grossa*. See Giacchero, *Il Seicento e le compere*, 128–32, 338, 412–17, 431–3, 573–85; Giacchero, *Settecento*, 21; and Sieveking, *Studio sulle finanze genovesi*, 219–20; C. Costantini, *La repubblica di Genova*, 28–9; Grendi, "Traffico e navi," 351. For the "rigor" of tax farms, see "The System of Livorno" in chapter 7; and in general, Kiser, "Markets and Hierarchies."

farm enforced regulations for all farms, indicating that at least some were loyal to the republic as a whole.[34]

A second difference lay in the mode of exaction. Livorno had always taxed primarily by parcel rather than value of goods. As Filippo Sassetti had observed in 1577, this made assessments easy—particularly for officials who were disinclined to make thorough inspections of merchants' goods. In 1676, Grand Duke Cosimo III eliminated import and export duties in Livorno, instead charging solely for stallage and anchorage. This measure substantially simplified the customs regime. Merchants paid the stallage fees shortly after arrival and could then dispose of their wares without additional oversight. Recall Jean-Baptiste Labat's admiration: "You know exactly what you have to pay, you pay it, and you're done."[35] Ancona went even further than Livorno in streamlining dues on traffic, levying only a single anchorage fee on ships and no fees at all on goods (except for use of the public weigher). Venetian officials looked with helplessness on these "most light and tenuous" taxes.[36]

Genoa, Venice, and Marseille relied on *ad valorem* taxation, which involved time-consuming and error-prone appraisals of merchandise.[37] It also made it less profitable for merchants to prepare the largest possible parcels, as happened in Livorno. More importantly, older ports did not adopt the simple stallage/anchorage tax model. They continued to charge import and export duties, albeit at reduced rates depending on the provenance or destination of a good. This decision entailed an ongoing process of inspection and monitoring to ensure compliance with customs regulations. The French merchant-entrepreneur Joseph Fabre lamented in 1693 that merchants preferred to do business in Livorno, "because there they escape the obstacles they encounter in Marseille."[38] There were two failed proposals to create a free port within the free port of Marseille: a truly duty-free zone.

A third consideration is the geographical size of the free port. In Livorno, the free port encompassed the whole city. Goods were free to move, and merchants were free to do business, within the precincts of the town with minimal supervision. Merchants stored their wares in private warehouses, which they could access without having to consult with customs officials. "There are very few ministers in the customs house," observed one anonymous Genoese commentator, "and they don't store any wares there. Every merchant keeps them along with their keys in their own houses or warehouses."[39] Ancona and Marseille likewise extended their

[34] Beltrami, "La crisi," 315; Sella, *Commerci e industrie*, 71; Rapp, *Industry and Economic Decline*, 139–41; Georgelin, *Venise*, 57–9, 70; Molà, *The Silk Industry*, 83–4; and Gelder, *Trading Places*, 95.

[35] See the introduction to chapter 5.

[36] From a 1735 report by the Trade Board published by Caracciolo, *Le port franc de Ancône*, 126–30: 128.

[37] With one exception. In 1708 Genoa decided to value goods "un tanto per collo" instead of according to an *ad valorem* schedule. The measure did not work and was repealed two years later because it led to a substantial decrease in customs revenue. Giacchero, *Origini e sviluppi*, 155–9.

[38] Quoted by Dermigny, "Escales, échelles et ports francs," 562–3; see Masson, *Port francs*, 70–5. On Fabre, see Takeda, *Between Crown and Commerce*, 44.

[39] ASG, AS, 1011, quoted by Giacchero, *Storia economica*, 63; see Giacchero, *Il Seicento e le compere*, 420–1 for an inventory of the free port from 1656.

free ports to the entire city, though Marseille had to fight strenuously to keep the royal tax farms beyond the city walls. While it is possible to see this policy as a defense of traditional urban liberties, especially in the case of Marseille, officials and pamphleteers argued that it made for a freer marketplace as well.

In Genoa the free port described a set of bonded warehouses cordoned off from the rest of the city. This warehouse zone was only open during business hours and remained under the supervision of a local authority, who regulated access and monitored the guards. In Venice, too, the free port pertained to the warehouses associated with the customs office rather than with the city as a whole. Genoa and Venice were not free ports, in other words: they *had* free ports. Their version of the policy device merited a separate entry in the commercial dictionary: "You put the merchandise . . . in deposit within a huge warehouse that is called the *porto-franco* or free port."[40] This procedure entailed high control costs in the form of more guards and more paperwork intended to maintain the separation, within the city, of exempt goods—those benefitting from the free port—and non-exempt goods. With the modern state's sophisticated bureaucracies and means of monitoring corporations, many special economic zones in the contemporary world indeed extend only to specific factories or warehouses. But in the seventeenth and eighteenth centuries, it was more effective to bestow a franchise on an entire city given the state's limited apparatus of control. That is why the influence of Livorno's model far exceeded that of Genoa.[41]

Lewes Roberts believed that a port's commerce depended less on its geographic situation than on the "libertie and freedome of the place and traders thereinto." He criticized Venice and Genoa for failing to imitate Livorno's example, "would their greedy covetousnesse permit them, and suffer merchants to bring their goods thither upon small charges."[42] In fact, officials in other cities were well aware of Livorno's advantages.[43] But despite endless discussion and much legislation, they knew their institutions were difficult to change. Venice and Genoa were large capital cities whose consumption taxes constituted a significant portion of public revenue. State finances depended on the rigorous separation between international commerce and the local retail trade. It was infeasible to extend the free port to the entire city, consequently, or to orient its commerce exclusively toward the deposit and transit trade. More broadly, the institutional framework inherited from the Middle Ages was better adapted to the monopoly rents afforded by the old navigation

[40] J. Savary des Bruslons and P.-L. Savary, *Dictionnaire universel*, vol. 2, 1191. See in general Minoletti, *I porti franchi*, 9–16. For Genoa, see Giacchero, *Origini e sviluppi*, 23, 46, 121–4; Giacchero, *Storia economica*, 23, 41, 46. For Venice, see Georgelin, *Venise*, 80; Calabi, "Canali, rive, approdi," 777; Calabi, "Magazzini, fondaci, dogane," 190–4, 809–10.

[41] Rondinelli, "Export Processing Zones"; Madani, "A Review of the Role and Impact of Export Processing Zones"; Orenstein, "Foreign-Trade Zones"; Tazzara, "Capitalism and the Special Economic Zone."

[42] The quotes are in Roberts, *The Marchants Mappe of Commerce*, 72–3 and 92, respectively.

[43] For instance, the Venetian consul in Aleppo, Antonio Lippomano, urged making Venice a full free port because "an absolute liberty of commerce causes competition among merchants, which will certainly bring an abundance of merchandise, renown to the marketplace, growth in the customs revenue, and more maritime traffic." Quoted by Sella, *Commerci e industrie*, 40 n. 2.

laws than to a passive entrepôt. The merchant republics of Genoa and Venice had been successful because they could organize collective action and indeed collective violence. But their old institutions persisted in new circumstances: the multiplicity of taxes for a multiplicity of goods; a dense body of local institutions for supervising and deliberating over commercial matters; and a long tradition, instantiated in the physical fabric of the city, in legislation, and in historical memory, of their former commercial system.[44] These things were hard to change. Too many elites were invested in the old institutions for an eagled-eye policy entrepreneur simply to sweep them aside. A similar logic applied to Ancona and Marseille. Though provincial ports rather than capital cities, they had also inherited a rich organizational framework from the Middle Ages. Their institutions strengthened local anti-competitive interests against certain categories of foreign merchant.

Maritime competition supplied the pressure to lower tariffs and liberalize trade restrictions in early modern Italy. Whether such policies were effective owed to administrative logics. Efficient free trade policies minimized intrusive inspections of commercial activity and other barriers to the flow of people and goods. Given the limits of state power, regimes had characteristic ways of simplifying the tax structure and the mode of exaction. Whether a state could avail itself of its options—whether it could craft a "proper" free port—depended on the constraints of the existing institutional landscape. Of course, it would be a truism to assert that local institutions were path dependent, that the glories of the Middle Ages cast their shadow over the succeeding epoch: who would deny it? The point is that implementing free trade required more than the desire or need to do so.

Movement toward liberalization proceeded alongside administrative simplification. This project met its limits in the rigidities of the Ancien Régime. Where regimes enjoyed the utmost freedom of action, as in Livorno, they could permit their ports to adjust to changing circumstances. Elsewhere, municipal privileges or existing fiscal regimes curtailed the capacity of central governments to adapt to evolving market conditions. To some extent, this situation was an obstacle to liberalization throughout Europe, littered as it was with internal customs houses and legions of tax farmers. The eighteenth-century struggle to liberalize commerce was largely a battle against these forces. Eliminating internal barriers to the flow of goods required forcing municipalities and other stakeholders to forgo their traditional perquisites—the defense of which was a crucial component of regime legitimacy. It also meant securing alternative revenue streams such as excise taxes. Displacing customs revenues onto alternative tax structures entailed intensive negotiations with existing interest groups. Effective free ports were not always compatible with a state's basic political economy.[45]

[44] See Tazzara, "Against the Fisc and Justice," 367–9; Rapp, *Industry and Economic Decline*, 141–2, 162–4; Georgelin, *Venise*, 67; and the introduction, n. 12.

[45] S. R. Epstein, *Freedom and Growth*, 14–16, 103–5, 148–55; Grafe, *Distant Tyranny*, 9–11, 138–46; and the conclusion to chapter 4.

ECONOMIC CHANGE IN THE ITALIAN MEDITERRANEAN

The prior achievements of Florentine capitalism continued to pay dividends into the eighteenth century, giving the port of Livorno advantages that rivals could not match even by imitating its policies. Barring extraordinary princely activism, for instance, the free ports of Nice and Villefranche were doomed from the start: "the maine obstacle of trade heere being the too neere neighbourhood of Genoa the rich, and of Leghorne the free, which neither the two townes formerly mentioned can equalize."[46] Economic fundamentals mattered. The most important factors shaping the ultimate success of a free port were infrastructural endowments, network externalities, access to capital, and the productivity of the hinterland. That is why Livorno's main rivals in the Tyrrhenian were Marseille and Genoa rather than Nice and Civitavecchia. In a place like north-central Italy, moreover, the hinterland itself was not a stable reality. Competition over maritime traffic also entailed capturing a larger share of hinterland trade, since land and sea were connected. Free ports were not independent expressions of isolated economies, in short, but rather exerted a complex set of effects on one another as well as on traffic in the interior.

The convergence of tariff levels promoted economic integration among port cities and perhaps to some degree in their hinterlands as well. Genoa's harbor continued to receive an impressive amount of ships throughout the seventeenth century, although it handled a smaller volume of goods after the rise of Livorno. In other words, ships often alighted in both ports. A similar trend occurred in the Adriatic Sea.[47] The inference is that ships were carrying cargoes that were more adapted to the regional markets of northern Italy even as the long-distance transit trade concentrated in Livorno. While gauging the full extent to which the free port network promoted regional integration requires detailed price studies, it seems that northern Italy was better served by maritime traffic in the early modern than in the medieval period. One study suggests that the Pisan grain market became more integrated internationally, first in the decades around 1600 with the expansion of Livorno, and again around 1700—perhaps because of increased competition among Italian ports?[48]

Competition did not stop with maritime tariffs. As duties by sea converged, regimes became increasingly solicitous of reducing overland transit duties. By the early eighteenth century, Italian states sought to improve the roads radiating from their ports, especially those that led into Lombardy and the German lands beyond.[49] As the market became more competitive, cities like Milan enjoyed more

[46] Roberts, *The Marchants Mappe of Commerce*, 47.

[47] Grendi, "Traffico e navi," 327–31, 345, 352; Caracciolo *Le port franc de Ancône*, 117–18; Georgelin, *Venise*, 99–101.

[48] Persson, *Grain Markets in Europe*, 98–9, 110–11. For the fitful process of early modern integration, see S. R. Epstein, *Freedom and Growth*, 38–72, 147–68; O'Rourke and Williamson, "When Did Globalisation Begin?"; Rönnbäck, "Integration of Global Commodity Markets"; Grafe, *Distant Tyranny*, 86–102.

[49] Giacchero, *Storia economica*, 90–107; Venturi, *Settecento riformatore*, 417–20; and Simoncini, "I porti del Regno di Napoli," 20–3.

options in procuring raw materials: Genoa and Venice were Milan's principal suppliers during the Middle Ages, to which Livorno was added in the late sixteenth century. By 1765, commodities such as wool or cotton were about the same price in Milan whether they were imported from Livorno, Genoa, Trieste, or Ancona; even Nice was competitive for certain goods. The result of this dynamic was to regionalize ports vis-à-vis Lombardy: for instance, Trieste tended to send exclusively products from its German or Balkan hinterlands. More distant connections were mediated by Genoa or Livorno.[50]

Rank order analysis offers another indication of more competitive markets in north-central Italy. Table 8.1 measures changes in the size of Italian cities with respect to the overall dispersion of the data set. It shows a marked decline in urban hierarchy during the eighteenth century. More hierarchy suggests a more intense concentration of resources (a higher coefficient of variation); less hierarchy suggests that resources were shared more equally between places (a lower coefficient of variation). Behind this transformation lay the relative decline of old urban centers, the development of industries outside the metropoles, and the articulation of regional exchange networks: in short, the commercialization of the countryside in northern Italy. These changes proceeded alongside the spread of free ports in the peninsula. Maritime free trade was only one cause of the decline in urban hierarchy, which also had to do with the transformation of the city-state into the territorial state. But the results are consistent with more equitable flows of resources throughout north-central Italy. What appeared to a Genoese or Venetian observer as the loss of a glorious merchant marine was an opportunity for other places in the region.

More than in Tuscany itself, where economic growth in the countryside was tied to construction and commercial services in Livorno, the transformation of Italian ports was accompanied by the increased marketization of regional goods. These

Table 8.1. Urban hierarchy in Italy, 1600–1800

	1600	1650	1700	1750	1800
Mean city population ('000)	9.0 (26.9)	(23.6)	8.6 (25.6)	(28.3)	11.3 (31.1)
Standard deviation ('000)	18.6 (28.1)	(24.6)	17.7 (28.5)	(29.8)	19.5 (30.6)
Coefficient of variation	205.4 (104.5)	(104.5)	206.2 (111.6)	(105.1)	173.3 (98.2)

Note: De Vries's database is smaller than Malanima's and relies on a less intensive reading of the secondary literature; these factors account for the higher means and standard deviations. For that reason, I have placed figures from the de Vries database in parentheses; data from Malanima are reported without parentheses. On the other hand, de Vries offers population data at half-century points, making his set more useful for tracking change over time, thereby revealing the decline in hierarchy in the first half of the eighteenth century. Where de Vries listed "unknown," I used the figure reported by Malanima if available; otherwise I averaged the surrounding figures (e.g. Bergamo's population in 1600 and 1700 to estimate 1650). De Vries's figures for Brescia, Cuneo, Fossano, Genoa, Mondavi, Monza, Nice, Savigliano, and Vercelli seemed incredible; I relied on Malanima for those cities. North-central Italy includes Le Marche and Umbria but does not include Latium. In producing this table, I followed the same procedures as S. R. Epstein, "Regions and the Late Medieval Crisis," 20–8.

Sources: Malanima, "Italian Urban Population"; de Vries, *European Urbanization*, app. 1.

[50] Caizzi, *Industria, commercio e banca*, 220–65, esp. the table on 225–6; De Luca, *Commercio del denaro e crescità economica*, 89–90, 145–8. See too "Livorno and its Hinterlands" in chapter 6.

included the agricultural produce of central Italy and the manufactured wares of northern Italy. For instance, Ancona served as a catalyst for the integration of Le Marche into the European economy, as indicated by the movement of grain prices.[51] There also developed a stricter relationship between industry and agriculture in the Veneto and the port of Venice. The volume of Venetian port traffic in the late seventeenth century was comparable to that in the late sixteenth century, although its composition had changed, more geared towards regional exchange than long-distance brokerage. In that thin strip of coastline called Liguria, the market power of Marseille and Livorno made it impossible for Genoa to monopolize regional commerce. Nevertheless, the proliferation of free ports in the Tyrrhenian facilitated the export of local produce—including that quintessential product of Liguria, maritime labor: sailors and fishermen.[52]

REFLECTING ON THE FREE PORT

A freer marketplace was the unintentional outcome of trade rivalry in the Tyrrhenian and Adriatic during the long seventeenth century. Although few officials espoused anything like liberalism in crafting their policies, the logic of rivalry in the politically fragmented region promoted freer trade and also—almost willy-nilly—expressions of proto-liberalism. By the 1760s, officials in Livorno began to understand the workings of the free port within a quasi-liberal framework. In Genoa, too, the aristocrats who staffed the Casa di San Giorgio began to appreciate the "truths" of laissez-faire. The preparations for the 1751 free port law capture this spirit: regulations "cannot obligate merchants to direct their wares except to that market where, having performed the most detailed calculations, their interests are best satisfied."[53]

Broadly speaking, three intertwined strands contributed to the development of ideas about international free trade. The oldest was a juridical tradition stemming from scholastic thought, exemplified by the writings of the Salamanca School or natural law theorists such as Hugo Grotius and Samuel Pufendorf. These authors emphasized the rights of foreigners to travel and do business without state interference.[54] Another strand, associated with debates about the grain trade, referred to the auto-regulation of the market and its stabilizing effect on prices. Physiocrats are the best-known representatives of this perspective, but a variety of political economists adopted this view without subscribing to doctrinaire Physiocracy. Other proponents of free trade were pamphleteers such as Nicholas Barbon and Dudley North. They focused on the commercial benefits that free trade brought

[51] Although for Caracciolo this implied the area's subordination to the economies of northwestern Europe, most of his evidence pertains to the mid-eighteenth century, when such domination is difficult to demonstrate. See *Le port franc de Ancône*, 163–4, 183–96, 241–7.

[52] Georgelin, *Venise*, 90–1; Sella, *Commerci e industrie*, 72–3; and Gelder, *Trading Places*, 77–84; Tazzara, "Against Justice and the Fisc."

[53] Quoted by Bulferetti and Costantini, *Industria e commercio*, 143–4; see too, Giacchero, *Origini e sviluppi*, 205–8.

[54] See Grotius, *Mare Liberum*, 97, 193–7, 209; and Grotius, *On the Law of War and Peace*, 101–2; on the Salamanca school, Grice-Hutchinson, *Early Economic Thought*, 81–121.

a nation. Despite their fame among posterity, however, early analysts of free trade constituted a minority voice in print discussions of political economy. The most successful writers celebrated the pursuit of empire and the jealousy of trade, not the virtues of free exchange. And yet it is precisely in this sphere of pamphleteers, merchant writers, and administrators that discussions of free ports occurred—often in manuscript.[55]

Whereas juridical texts focused on the legal rights of merchants vis-à-vis rulers or enemy powers, free ports raised questions of utility: what were the consequences of encouraging foreign merchants to settle in one's ports? what effect did reducing tariffs have on state revenue and local industries? how should one design rational institutions for administering the customs? The free port was rarely the beneficiary of extended treatises. Instead, officials and merchants were the chief analysts of the free port—not only in Livorno, but also in Genoa, Venice, Ancona, and Marseille. Their ad hoc production of memoranda was conditioned by the local institutional context. From generic conventions to argumentation, this most cosmopolitan of institutions was elaborated in preeminently local discursive frameworks.

Usage of the term "free port" varied throughout the long seventeenth century. In addition to the familiar sense, as a place where foreigners could trade freely or where goods were exempt from customs duties, we find related but distinct meanings. The Duke of Osuna offered free port to the Uskoks of Senj who were expelled by the Venetians in 1618: general safe-conduct.[56] The Count-Duke of Olivares enjoyed a free port for the goods his estates produced, which he sold in the New World without paying a dime to the Spanish king.[57] A free port could simply be a good natural harbor, as with Freeport, Maine, so called for being free of ice.[58] The term carried the general sense of refuge for goods, men, or ships. One writer even likened free ports to God's mercy: "That mercy must be like a free port that opens unto the sea, and affords frank passage upon all occasions, or whither soever we are bound, without paying so much for importation, or so much for exportation."[59] The semantic sphere of the term remained broad because the words "free" and "port" were embedded in webs of meaning independent of their commercial signification.

In the first half of the seventeenth century, writers occasionally cited the free port as a term of political economy, but they did not analyze its meaning or relate free ports to a state's general commercial orientation. Contemporaries tended to highlight a port's hospitality to foreigners rather than customs regime. Thus, Hakluyt referred to Alexandria in Egypt as a free port because of its openness to foreign visitors, as did Venetian consuls: a haven for "friend or enemy" alike.[60]

55 S. Reinert, *Translating Empire*, 70–1.

56 Sansovino, *Venetia città nobilissima et singolare*, 644. In this sense, meaning "safe-conduct," see also Heath, *A Chronicle of the late Intestine War*, 293.

57 Pallavicino, *Opere scelte*, 89.

58 See also Leti, *Teatro gallico*, pt 2, 352; Leti, *Vita di Don Pietro Giron Duca d'Ossuna*, pt 2, 215.

59 Fonseca, *Devout Contemplations*, 148.

60 Hakluyt, *The Principal Navigations*, 414; Pedani, "Venetian Consuls in Egypt and Syria," 20; the quote is from Roberts, *The Marchants Mappe of Commerce*, 100.

But references are fleeting. One indication is the paucity of the term in print until the second half of the seventeenth century. In England, between 1550 and 1599, only one text used the term (Hakluyt), and only nine more texts before 1650. But between 1650 and 1699, forty-three printed works mention free ports. Even Italian sources contain few references to the term in print before 1650, but many thereafter.[61] These findings are not surprising considering the nexus between supplications and policy discourse in Livorno. The early elaboration of the free port as a term of political economy occurred in mercantile circles in Livorno itself or among people familiar with the Tuscan port.

Thinkers in the mid-seventeenth century began to transform free ports into objects of analysis, exploiting them as historical *exempla* for larger programs or as problems requiring expert treatment. They appeared alternately as engines of economic growth or instruments of economic decline, as gardens of cosmopolitan delight or dens of foreign domination. The free port was a slippery object, both because of the rhetorical valences of the term—there was scarcely a more seductive term in all political economy—and because of the difficulty in interpreting actual free ports. The experience of Livorno provided ammunition for supporters as well as critics. On the one hand, the city was a flourishing zone of religious tolerance and rational customs regulations; on the other, its trade was managed by foreign merchants and enlivened by complicit ties between officials and businessmen. For that reason, free ports sat uneasily between Enlightenment programs of commercial rivalry and principles of laissez-faire. The liminal position of free ports indicates the extent to which Enlightenment economic thought was the servant of political projects—of empire, independence, or reform.

The free port's print career began in earnest in Commonwealth England. Benjamin Worsely's *Free Ports the Nature and Necessitie of Them Stated* (1652) offered the first substantial treatment of the term. Worsely argued that deposit ports were necessary due to seasonal fluctuations in production and demand. He advocated creating a "general mart" out of England by erecting free ports throughout the realm and sharply reducing export (not import) duties.[62] William Petty a decade later was the first to note that free ports could raise revenue through the provision of commercial services, "by the expence of sea-men and passengers, hire of labourers, and ware-houses," and a small duty on ships that use the harbor.[63] Like other tract writers in this period, Worsely and Petty were obsessed with emulating (and surpassing) the Dutch. Yet the connection between the entrepôt and the free port

[61] The English figures are based on a keyword search in Early English Books Online (EEBO) on 03/23/2011. From 1550–99, only one item out of 2,321 machine-readable texts contained the term "free port." For 1600–49, there were nine items out of 7,625. For 1650–99, there were forty-three items out of 14,195. Coded texts represent only about twenty percent of all items in the EEBO database. The Italian figures are based on a search in Google Books. Google's database is a blunter instrument than EEBO and rife with duplications. Nevertheless, I found only eight items using the term *porto franco* from 1600–49 (out of 31,400), and sixty-five items for the period 1650–99 (out of 41,400). Usage increased dramatically in the eighteenth century for both languages.

[62] Worsley, *Free Ports*. Worsley was involved in the English Council of Trade that drafted the Navigation Acts. See Brenner, *Merchants and Revolution*, 613f.

[63] Petty, *A Treatise of Taxes & Contributions*, paras 20–2.

came not via Amsterdam but via Livorno. The English started to conceive of the Tuscan port as a center for storage and transit in the early 1640s; and they began seeking ad hoc warehousing privileges even earlier, in the 1620s.[64]

An entrepôt and an engine of growth: there remained only an argument on behalf of foreigners. Roger Coke supplied this in 1675. He framed the problem of resident foreigners in religious rather than national terms. According to Coke, trade between members of different religions was a fact of life and ordained by god: "as every man stands in need of being supplied by another, so does every country."[65] To restrain international commerce was "to violate an institution of God in the conservation of humane society." Coke was sounding here the ancient theme of universal economy, which saw in the unequal distribution of goods a divinely ordained motive for commerce. What was under dispute was not the utility of inter-confessional trade, but its feasibility. He adduced the example of the Jews in Livorno as evidence of successful commercial toleration. For Coke, it was possible to invite foreigners to live in England as well without corrupting the religious mores of the people.

The English reception of the free port reveals that observers did not always differentiate between the emporium (open to merchants) and entrepôt (open to goods) functions of the free port. In fact, the discursive halo around the term appears to have dazzled contemporaries. An Anconitan annalist called free ports "the only infallible means used today by princes to bring trade and riches to their states."[66] Not only did the institution have a magical power to summon trade out of thin air, but it was also supposed to stimulate export industries and provision a state with raw materials, to give "vigor to the spent industrial and commercial life of the country."[67] Colbert's 1669 edict making Marseille into a free port sounded the most exalted notes of which the term was capable, turning trade with foreigners into an argument for international harmony: "commerce is the fittest means for conciliating the various nations... bringing and spreading abundance by the most innocent of paths."[68] The free port was discursively effective because it conjured up visions of miraculous wealth while leaving the details vague: it might be free for some or all merchandise, for some or all shipping, for some or all merchants.

The flexibility of the term "free port" was part of its appeal. But the policy's significance to economic thought lay in how thinkers used it to argue about the toleration of foreigners or the organization of customs duties. Once they subjected the free port to rigorous analysis, however, many writers either circumscribed the utility of the policy or transformed it into a general program of reform. As we have seen, Florentine elites during the Enlightenment grew skeptical that Livorno could

[64] See "The Warehouse of the Mediterranean" in chapter 2 and "The Free Port as a Work in Progress" in chapter 3.

[65] Coke, *England's Improvements*, Apology. Coke had earlier argued for the utility of low customs duties, citing the example of Livorno in *A Discourse of Trade*, 61–2. In general, see Statt, *Foreigners and Englishmen*. On the theme of "universal economy," see Irwin, *Against the Tide*, 15–17.

[66] Quoted by Caracciolo, *Le port franc d'Ancône*, 55.

[67] Caracciolo, "Il dibattito sui 'porti franchi,'" 553; see Kirk, *Genoa and the Sea*, 157–67, 175.

[68] Quoted by Dermigny, "Escales, échelles et ports francs," 553–4.

serve a vital role in the Tuscan economy. Genoese officials by the late 1720s also felt that their free port was a dead end.[69] Thinkers elsewhere in Italy likewise came to believe that free ports promoted foreign over domestic interests. Their view was actuated by a perceived experience of economic and political decline: Italian states, once independent, were now "governed as provinces" by foreign powers and could not set policy according to their own interests.[70] And yet, beyond Italy, free ports occupied an important place in conversations about commerce during the formative period of European political economy. The paradox owes to the incorporation of the term into larger political projects: in Italy, programs intent on securing independence from foreigners, and elsewhere, programs celebrating the cosmopolitan dimensions of commerce and the virtues of free trade.

Carlo Antonio Broggia (1698–1767) was the first Italian writer to censure the free port in print. Often sick, Broggia spent his "troubled existence" working as a drug merchant to support his family and devoted his spare time to intellectual life. He wrote many memoranda in the hope of landing a government job in Naples; in fact, he antagonized a finance minister and spent several years in exile in the late 1750s. Broggia's most important work is the *Treatise on Taxes, Money, and the Management of the Health Board* (1743). He was a zealous disciple of Vico and disavowed all principles of skepticism, epicureanism, and stoicism: ideas associated with contemporaries such as Jean-François Melon or Bernard Mandeville. Broggia's views on currency have often come under attack, then and since. Scholars have been kinder to his analysis of taxation, however, as he argued for simplified customs procedures, moderate duties, the right to export local produce, and the dangers of monopoly. These were all common crusades among commercial writers of the age; Broggia gave these issues a wider audience in Naples by printing them. What was new was his explanation for why free ports were an obstacle to his program.[71]

The rationalization of customs was a crucial plank in Broggia's program, developed at length in the *Treatise on Taxes*. Taxes were grievous to a populace not so much because of their actual level, but because they were *mal situati*, poorly designed. "And so [taxes] are established in oblique and unnecessary ways, with superfluous formalities, astounding subtleties, and incredibly intricate rules and norms." Then, in breathless prose: "policy can discover means that are at once simple natural brief clear efficacious intelligible to everybody, and born of a true science of the world and of commerce."[72] Broggia aimed to moderate customs taxes everywhere (hinterland included) and simplify procedures. He devoted much care to explicating the principles of efficient administration, to remedy the "torture of a caviling customs

[69] Giacchero, *Origini e sviluppi*, 204; see "The Privileges of Livorno in the Age of Enlightened Reform" in chapter 7.

[70] Robertson, *The Case for the Enlightenment*, 358–9 *et passim*; S. Reinert, "Lessons on the Rise and Fall of Great Powers."

[71] Luigi de Rosa called Broggia's a "travagliata esistenza" in his article in the DBI. Broggia's hatred of free ports is one of the oldest elements of his economic analysis, hailing from an unpublished work of 1729. See Ajello, "Nota introduttiva," 999–1000; see too Venturi, *Settecento riformatore*, 483–8, 517–22.

[72] Broggia, *Trattato*, 2.

house." The potential ease of collection was one reason customs duties were among "the most natural" of taxes.[73]

Broggia ascribed a bevy of evils to free ports, that supremely *mal situato* policy. It is true that they attracted wares and merchants, but only by "prostituting" commerce to foreigners.[74] Foreigners could unload their goods for next to nothing in Italian ports, undercutting local industry and flooding the market with contraband and superfluous items, "nourishing the unbridled luxury" of the inhabitants. Although some Italian merchants enriched themselves through this trade, the profit generally accrued to the foreign communities who used a free port. If the policy had been such a success, he wondered, why had Livorno not restored Tuscany to its Renaissance grandeur? On the contrary, free ports served other nations by enabling them to appropriate Italy's crafts, discoveries, and philosophies. Broggia even believed that free ports delivered the final coup to the civic culture of Italy, enervating its citizens and dragging the state into decadence: the source of "countless problems, vices, errors, and distress."

Customs duties could be an instrument for promoting native commerce while at the same time raising state revenue. "And truly, what does the cultivation of commerce benefit the state, if it does not give rise to a substantial emolument?"[75] Toward that end, Broggia proposed moderating tariffs on exports of local goods and produce, while being sure to tax imports of foreign goods when desirable. Far from a general liberty of trade, despite the frequency with which the phrase appears in the *Treatise*, Broggia thought that every customs duty must be assessed on its own merits and made high, low, or moderate as circumstances required. Free ports were a disaster on this count: "To pretend to draw blindly by all possible means an abundance of merchandise for the sole purpose of raising customs revenue is the same as damaging the state: it never promotes commerce in its true essence."[76] Trade was not a good in itself, but only insofar as it benefited the state. Parsimony and industriousness were better than abundance and luxury. The private interest must cede to the public good, and "the good citizen must [be willing] to sacrifice not only his property, but even his life if necessary."[77] Free ports vitiated the citizenry, threatened the state's revenue, and strengthened foreign nations at the expense of Italy.

Broggia's condemnation of free ports did not reach a large audience because his works were not widely read outside of Naples. But one luminary of the Italian Enlightenment, Antonio Genovesi (1713–69), read Broggia carefully and transmitted an authoritative verdict on free ports to his Italian audience. From humble beginnings near Salerno, Genovesi had to cut short his first career as a theologian owing to his sympathy with heterodox ideas. He turned to practical philosophy and foreign commercial thought. An influential patron endowed Genovesi with the first Italian chair of political economy (in "mechanics and commerce") at the

[73] Ibid., 138 and 39, respectively; and in general, ii–iii, 6–7, 15–16, 24, 28, 36–7, 43–9, 64, 122–3, 130–5, 170–1.

[74] This and the following quotes in ibid., 101, 106, and 108–9.

[75] Ibid., 97–8.

[76] Ibid., 123–5; cf. 120.

[77] Ibid., 31; cf. 4–5, 26–7, 74, 85–92.

University of Naples in 1754. For the next fifteen years, he published translations or commentaries on key works of political economy, comparing the diverse economic trajectories of England and Spain, analyzing the predicament of the Kingdom of Naples, and developing these themes in a lecture course for students. The fruit of his labors was his *Lectures on Commerce* (1765). It became a foundational text for the next two generations.[78]

Genovesi believed that a state's wealth and power rested not on its tax receipts, but on the affluence of its inhabitants. Increasing the riches and number of the populace was the primary end of political economy. "The greatest *arcanum imperi* is to ensure that common prejudices tend toward the virtue, wisdom, industriousness, and true wellbeing of the state."[79] External trade was fine so long as it did not serve as a vehicle for foreign nations to flood the market with luxuries. Genovesi had no problem with moderate luxury as such, recognizing that exchange of all kinds was an engine of growth: commerce was "the sweet mistress of all forces, the generatrix of wealth and greatness in the body politic."[80] But for him the development of the Neapolitan economy lay in its domestic industry and agriculture. Like his Tuscan contemporaries, he advocated the liberalization of the grain trade, the elimination of internal barriers to production and trade, and the promotion of local consumption.[81]

At first glance, Genovesi appeared to recommend a policy of protectionism identical to that of Broggia. "The free port was and is the idol of many economists," he remarked.[82] "There are some, who understand 'liberty' to indicate the absolute power of merchants to export or import all kinds of merchandise, without restriction, law, or measure. But this liberty, or rather license, is not found in any European nation, and is contrary to the very spirit of commerce."[83] There was no question that a state's internal ports must be free in order to promote the utmost circulation of produce and manufactures. External ports should be used for the export of local goods and surplus produce and the import of raw materials, and in those respects should be made free. But governments should burden with duties, or prohibit, the import of foreign goods that competed with the local economy. Genovesi thus transformed the question of the free port into one of the most traditional arguments for protectionism. But in doing so, he evacuated his analysis of the statist dimensions so dear to Broggia. He said nothing about the corrupting effects of luxury, the surpassing need to raise revenue, and the dangers of free ports to civic life. The chief point in common was a concern for the liberty of Italian states and their capacity to follow independent policies. He concluded his discussion of free ports by noting that if all neighboring nations had them, then Naples would have

[78] See Venturi, *Settecento riformatore*, 523–33, 565–71, and 632–44; Robertson, *The Case for the Enlightenment*, 347–60; Jossa et al., eds, *Genovesi economista.*

[79] Genovesi, *Lezioni di commercio*, vol. 1, 43; see also 1, 23, 36.

[80] Ibid., 247–8; cf. 298. A footnote makes clear that this point is directed against Rousseau.

[81] Ibid., 273–4, 335. Like Broggia, Genovesi also believed in the virtues of administrative simplicity. Beccaria, too, shared their attitude to "formalities": *Elementi di economia pubblica*, vol. 11, 90–2, 286–7.

[82] Ibid., 319.

[83] Ibid., 270. See too ibid., 261–2, 271–5, 308–18.

little choice but to follow suit. This was the predicament of the Italian peninsula with its crowd of free ports.[84]

Part of Italian skepticism toward free ports stemmed from contemporary agrophilic thinking. Even more important, however, was the round of free port declarations throughout the peninsula during the first half of the eighteenth century. It appeared evident that free ports made it easier for foreigners to sell their goods in Italy, whether legally or not, but had an ambivalent effect on local industry and a detrimental effect on national liberties.[85] The actual performance of free ports was more mixed than most critics allowed. While free ports weakened the hegemonic positions of the old capital cities (Genoa, Venice, Florence), they developed alongside rural industries, market-oriented agriculture, and maritime trade. At base, what Italians were really concerned about was economic interdependence vis-à-vis countries such as France or Britain in light of the peninsula's political weakness. That is, they were worried about the decline in Italian commercial power rather than economic performance as such. Their experience with free ports accelerated the shift toward developing the domestic market for industry and agriculture as a means of protection against powerful outsiders. This project was preeminently political.

Writers outside of Italy took up the free port with gusto just as Italians came to temper their enthusiasm. New cosmopolitan sensibilities were in part responsible for this interest. In the early eighteenth century, the French friar Jean-Baptiste Labat could still be horrified at the toleration of religious minorities in Livorno. The Jews "regard Livorno and the entire grand duchy as a new promised land."[86] They benefited from protections so extraordinary that, according to a Tuscan proverb, "it was better to offend the grand duke than a Jew." Labat's views were old fashioned even by his day, and within a few decades, some of the most important writers of Europe celebrated toleration as a social, political, and cultural virtue. Accordingly, mid-century travelers had nothing but praise for Livorno. Charles Boyle on his grand tour was astounded at the flourishing state of the Jewish community. Then he commented, "all religions are exercised peaceably by the Livornians, who appear, as a modern author expresses himself, 'like a hive of bees without one sting of devotion.'"[87] Joseph Jérôme de Lalande marveled that the Inquisition was almost powerless in Livorno. "Moreover, everybody enjoys a perfect liberty of conscience in this city, which is, so to speak, the patria of the universe."[88] Free ports won praise for the farrago of peoples who flocked to them—not only because such an admixture was good for business, but also because toleration was now an end in itself.

[84] Ibid., 266, 293–4, 319; see too n. 4.

[85] Recall that Tuscans were concerned about how the free port of Livorno corrupted the policy process through inappropriate relations between officials and foreign merchants. The obsession with policymaking was far from absent in Naples, but related less to the free port than to the kingdom's centuries of governance as a province of Spain. Other comments on free ports indebted to Broggia or Genovesi include Pini, *Memoria*, 6; and Gibellini, *Elementi d'economia civile*, 123.

[86] Labat, *Voyages*, vol. 2, 134.

[87] Boyle, *Letters from Italy*, 101. The "modern author" was George Farquhar: see *Love and Business*, 26.

[88] Lalande, *Voyage d'un françois en Italie*, vol. 2, 459.

Foreign commercial writers were less interested in the Babylonian nature of free ports than in their economic implications. They deployed the free port in ways that bore little relation to realities in Italy, or rather, they transformed the term in a manner that escaped the kinds of critiques levied by Italians. The most important figures were Montesquieu, Matthew Decker, and Adam Smith. As with the political economists of Italy, their assessment of the free port hinged upon larger visions of the relationship between state, society, and commerce. All cited in passing the free ports of Italy, especially Livorno, as evidence of the efficacy of free commerce. When they got down to brass tacks, however, they found that the implications of the policy device in the contexts of France or England required a framework quite unrelated to the situation in the Italian Mediterranean.

In *The Spirit of the Laws* (1748), Montesquieu praised states that engaged in the carrying trade of high-volume, low-cost goods. For him, this was a form of commerce for parsimonious republics rather than for monarchies with their tendencies toward luxury. "The thriftiness of the state, which always follows the frugality of individuals, gives its carrying trade a soul."[89] Such republics were ripe for the creation of free ports, making up in mercantile wealth what they lost in customs revenue. In restricting the policy to republican entrepôts, Montesquieu's underlying preoccupation was with controlling the destructive consequences of commercialization on French institutions. Commercial policies only had value in relation to the customs (*moeurs*) of a nation. They needed to serve social and political ends. The kind of freedom he advocated was not a form of commercial libertinage whereby merchants could do whatever they wanted: "this would instead be servitude to commerce."[90] He praised the English navigation laws for subordinating economic to political interests and at once reinforcing liberty, religion, and commerce. But monarchies required different policies.[91]

Montesquieu's conception of the free port was deeply misleading. By limiting the policy to an active-trade entrepôt, he contributed to the anachronistic extension of the term to alien contexts such as late medieval Venice or the cities of the Hanseatic League. In addition, his usage concealed the role of violence inherent in the entrepôt systems of the hegemons of his own day, the English and the Dutch. Montesquieu ignored actual free ports such as Livorno or Marseille, presumably because he shared the concerns of writers such as Genovesi about their impact on the hinterland. Ironically, given his concern with checking the ravages of commerce, it was the passive free ports of Italy that functioned as controlled channels of international commerce, as safety valves between society and the market. They were open to goods as well as foreigners, connecting Italian states to the global economy, but they protected hinterland economies better than most Enlightenment thinkers believed.

[89] Montesquieu, *De l'esprit des loix*, bk 20, ch. 10. The standard translation by Cohler, Miller, and Stone misleadingly translates *commerce d'économie* as "economic commerce," rather than the more idiomatic "carrying trade." On Montesquieu and his thought, see Cheney, *Revolutionary Commerce*, 52–86.

[90] Montesquieu, *De l'esprit des loix*, bk 20, ch. 11. [91] Ibid., ch. 6.

English writers also unmoored the free port from its Mediterranean context, but they did so in a manner that treated the policy as a potentially universal institution of free trade. The first to take this step was Matthew Decker (1679–1749), who has been celebrated as a prophet of free trade for the fervency of his advocacy and the radicalism of his proposals. Born to a Dutch mercantile family in Amsterdam, Decker moved to London in 1702 and established himself as a principal city merchant. For several years he was a member of Parliament and served in key positions in the East India Company throughout the 1720s and early 1730s. His fame rests on his *Essay on the Causes of the Decline of the Foreign Trade* (1744). He employed the peculiar term "free-port trade" to argue for a thoroughgoing reduction in customs duties. He proposed a single tax on luxury consumption, not trade, to provide for government revenue.[92]

Decker cited the success of free ports as evidence for the efficacy of free trade. Genoa, when it had low customs duties, was the storehouse of Italy. He argued that the Ligurian city lost its position when it raised duties and especially after the grand duke of Tuscany made Livorno a free port, "which continuing still free, retains its flourishing condition."[93] Livorno also figured in Decker's relentless assault on monopoly privileges, including those of the East India Company. He denounced the "trifling navigation" conducted by such corporations "in their monopolies to 3/4 parts of the world" in comparison with the unregulated trade to Livorno.[94] Monopoly companies reminded Decker of the fable of the manger dog who denied hay to the horses even though he himself did not eat it: the companies were inefficient at promoting commerce, but jealously guarded their privileges against those who would trade. Decker also observed that free ports, by their concourse of foreigners and merchandise, generated revenue from commercial services—through freightage, boat-hiring, portage, cartage, warehouse-rent, merchants' commission fees, and cooperage: "the universal storehouse of a free-port must bring a vast profit to a country."[95]

Despite his readiness to adduce examples from individual free ports, Decker's program involved a wholesale transformation of Britain for which the example of the free port offered limited guidance. He urged the elimination of internal excises, the end of monopoly companies, and the invigoration of English agriculture through the abolition of land taxes and the free export of local produce. Decker argued for a strict relationship between the trading and agricultural interests, believing that a confused system of taxation had made enemies out of allies. In his view, restrictions on trade depressed agricultural prices and hurt England's commerce. "And they may see the fatal error when it is perhaps too late, trade being like a coy dame, difficult to be brought back when slighted."[96]

Decker was not alone in contemplating the extension of the free port to the entire nation. Discussions in Amsterdam in the 1740s and early 1750s and in

[92] On Decker, see the entry by Perry Gauci in the ODNB.

[93] Decker, *The Causes of the Decline of the Foreign Trade*, 91. He cites Sir Walter Raleigh's *Observations on Trade* for this point, which was also made by Roger Coke's *Discourse of Trade*, cited n. 65.

[94] Decker, *The Causes of the Decline of the Foreign Trade*, 30.

[95] Ibid., 65. [96] Ibid., 5.

Copenhagen in the 1760s envisioned similar projects.[97] But it was Adam Smith who completed the conversion of the free port into free trade. In the academic year of 1763–4, Smith delivered a series of lectures which rehearsed many of the arguments that later appeared in *The Wealth of Nations* (1776). In one passage, he told his students at the University of Glasgow that public opulence depended on the division of labor and hence on freedom of commerce. With customary acerbity he attacked the view that wealth consisted of money and that good policy demanded import restrictions. On the contrary, plenty proceeded from the free flow of money and goods. He concluded:

> From the above considerations it appears that Brittain should by all means be made a free port, that there should be no interruptions of any kind made to forreign trade, that if it were possible to defray the expences of government by any other method, all duties, customs, and excise should be abolished, and that free commerce and liberty of exchange should be allowed with all nations and for all things.[98]

For Smith, the only problem with free trade was the raising of revenue. Accordingly, he devoted about a quarter of the *Wealth of Nations* to finding better ways to "defray the expences of government" than customs duties: taxes on luxury consumption and land rent.

Smith was aware that his version of free trade had never been implemented in Europe. "Though there are in Europe, indeed, a few towns which in some respects deserve the name of free ports, there is no country which does so."[99] Like Decker, he argued that every city or country that had adopted liberal policies had been enriched in proportion to its freedom of its trade. But Smith departed in some passages from a vision of national competition to argue that free trade benefited all participants. He imagined a Europe in which individual states, by embracing his "liberal system" of free trade, could become like provinces in a single continental empire.[100] The idea of the free port had come far since the beginning of the century. From being a tool in national competition—and one the Italians had found rather unwieldy—Smith conceptualized free ports as an emblem of a commercially integrated Europe.

The Italian free port was a zone distinct from its hinterland, marked by a special customs regime and the presence of foreigners. It seemed to enable foreign goods to undercut local manufacturing and promote a passive commerce. For those reasons, Italians saw free ports as a symptom of decline rather than an engine of opportunity. Beyond the peninsula, however, writers focused on the economic prospects the free port offered to powers that maintained an active commerce. Decker and Smith, moreover, mapped the free port onto a national stage. They directed many of their arguments toward inland trade and linked the virtues of a

[97] Hovy, *Het voorstel van 1751*, 218–37; Venturi, *The End of the Old Regime in Europe*, vol. 1, 253; Stapelbroek, "Dutch Commercial Decline Revisited."

[98] A. Smith, "Report dated 1766," 514. Despite the name, the lectures were probably delivered in 1763–4. See the editors' introduction, 5. On Smith himself, see Rothschild, *Economic Sentiments*, esp. ch. 2; Hont, *Jealousy of Trade*, *passim*, esp. chs 5 and 6.

[99] A. Smith, *Wealth of Nations*, bk 4.iii.c.14 (p. 497).

[100] Ibid., bk 4.v.b.39 (p. 538).

free local commerce to a free foreign trade, invoking the free port rhetorically while changing the content of the term. Their version of the policy amounted to a photo negative of that of the Italians. In fact, Italian writers participated in many of the broader currents of Enlightenment political economy, including a concern for developing local industry, removing internal tolls, and promoting agricultural production. Whether they were advocates or enemies of the free port, in other words, thinkers throughout Europe exploited the term for the same ultimate purpose: to urge a more unified and rational internal economy. Free ports like Livorno had to be eliminated for the sake of free trade for the entire nation.

When speaking of free ports, writers were often lead as though by a silver thread to the issue of state revenue. Many were convinced that Livorno yielded untold treasure to the grand dukes. In a grand chronological faux-pas, one popular historian even attributed the Florentine Renaissance to the riches of Livorno: it was the "gold mine" of the Medici, which allowed them "to patronize artists, renovate the arts, and enrich their country with most precious masterpieces."[101] But political economists conducted more systematic investigations of free ports. Commercial pamphleteers focused on the revenues generated not to the state, but to individuals in the form of wages, freight charges, and the like. One could tax the wealth of an industrious citizenry while leaving their commerce free. The luminaries of the Enlightenment, especially Adam Smith, developed these ideas into comprehensive theories of taxation that displaced that most ancient of taxes, the customs, "denoting customary payments which had been in use from time immemorial."[102] They sought better means than customs to raise state revenue. This project was born in the effort to grapple with free trade, whether in the guise of free ports or as a national policy.

CONCLUSION

The spread of the free port recalls earlier patterns of institutional emulation in Italy. The proliferation of the office of *podestà*, the organization of chancelleries, and the establishment of reciprocal diplomatic operations are among the best-known examples from the late Middle Ages. The adoption of the free port entailed a similar process of imitation, nourished not only by shared circumstances, but also by incessant communication: structural similarities and connectedness each had its part to play.[103] Italian officials were careful observers of their neighbors' institutions, of which they were kept informed by consuls, merchants, travelers,

[101] Caraccioli, *Voyage de la Raison en Europe*, 114. Francesco Maria Gianni believed that Livorno generated in revenue about as much as the regime had to invest in its upkeep: see Gianni, "Discorso," 305–6.

[102] A. Smith, *Wealth of Nations*, bk 5.2.k.20 (p. 878).

[103] And not only free ports: chambers of commerce, monopoly companies, tax farms, health boards, and insurance companies were also objects of emulation within and beyond the Italian peninsula. See "Merchant Expertise and State Institutions" in chapter 5; Venturi, *Settecento riformatore*, 420–32; Addobbati, *Commercio, rischio, guerra*, 215; Fettah, "Livourne et les grandes places marchandes," 200.

and immigrants. If they did not implement identical free ports, it was because local context conditioned their choices. Existing institutions and traditions, larger fiscal regimes, and other exigencies of governance meant that few Italian ports were capable or desirous of copying Livorno's policies to the letter.

The movement toward free ports continued a process of economic integration that had begun long before. The ravages wrought by the Black Death and the interminable wars among city states during the fourteenth century might have seemed to betoken the Apocalypse, but they also laid the foundation for regional economic integration within the boundaries of the city state. The spread of local, state-sanctioned fairs is one token of integration.[104] The free ports continued this impulse toward a more unified economic space, albeit with respect to maritime trade and global markets. The freezing of Italian political boundaries in the mid-sixteenth century did not put an end to integration, in other words, but diverted it towards the sea. The process bore some resemblance to the earlier phase of integration, too, when political fragmentation and an abundance of alternative routes encouraged cities to create fairs or minimize transit duties. Relentless commercial competition is one of the red threads running through Italy's history before and after the Renaissance, with fairs strung on the peninsula like so many hundreds of beads. Customs Director Pandolfo Attavanti unwittingly alluded to a deeper truth when he designated Livorno a "continuous fair of foreigners."[105]

The status of foreigners also came to epitomize the perils of the free port. A discrepancy developed between the real impact of free ports on Italian economies, which was positive, and a discursive tradition that saw them as symptoms of foreign domination. Part of this gulf may be explained by a tendency for thinkers to exaggerate the role of long-distance commerce in shaping hinterland economies. More important, however, was a political program for reforming institutions in the interior. By 1730 or so, the problem of decline had sharpened into a central issue of Italian intellectual life. Italians had no way to reverse their loss of commercial power against the likes of Great Britain or France. But they could develop their domestic agriculture and industry, thereby securing as much independence from foreign commerce as possible. When Genovesi likened the free port to a false idol, he did not mean to dismiss the policy's utility for importing raw materials or exporting agricultural produce, but to depose it from its exalted status as agent of commercial expansion. Italy would have to look to its own interior for economic development. *Italia farà da se*, Italy will make itself: this mantra of the Risorgimento had its roots in an older program of political independence and self-help.

In any case, the development of tariff-enclosed national spaces and the invention of the steamship soon rendered the free port an otiose institution. Steamships facilitated direct bilateral trade, thus bypassing waystations such as Livorno. The creation of tariff-enclosed national spaces made the state itself the most relevant free trade area, access to which was regulated by citizenship status and diplomatic agreement. The old functions of free ports as long-distance entrepôts and international

[104] S. R. Epstein, "Market Structures"; S. R. Epstein, *Freedom and Growth*, 59–60, 73–88.
[105] See "People and Commodities in Early Modern Trade" in the introduction, esp. n. 39.

emporia were gradually laid aside. By the early twentieth century, remaining free ports in Europe served primarily as duty-free zones for raw materials awaiting buyers in the hinterland: an early version of just-in-time supply, whereby merchants did not have to pay import taxes until sale was assured.[106] And like scaffolding that could be discarded once an edifice was secure, liberal economists quickly forgot the role free ports had played in the genealogy of free trade. Thinkers did continue to enumerate the benefits of access to a duty-free zone, but their discussions were more indebted to theoretical economics than to the experience of the seventeenth and eighteenth centuries. Free ports became peripheral devices of national policy, more like the Genoese system of bonded warehouses than like Livorno, and they have so remained in the rich world to the present day.[107]

Although increasingly irrelevant to economic strategy in Western Europe, the free port proved useful to European colonial powers in the Caribbean—with a difference. In the Americas, privileges did not define the status of foreign commerce, and foreign consuls were not present. Instead, the American free port was a breach in the colonial system of exclusivity according to which only national merchants and ships were entitled to do business. Metropoles were incapable of enforcing the restrictions by which they sought to control colonial trade. American planters were always willing to sell their tobacco, sugar, or cotton to venders who could furnish them with the goods they lacked. From the 1760s on, colonial powers erected free ports in the region to exert their sovereignty, collect more revenue, and maintain the essentials of the colonial system while conceding something to the planters. These free ports had complicated if generous tax regimes and remained hotbeds of fraud, contraband, and disorder. It was free trade of the unbridled kind.[108]

Such chaos could certainly serve imperialist ends. In 1787, the inspector general of the English customs remarked that free ports in the Caribbean were a means of penetrating the Spanish mainland, "whereby we might enjoy to the extent of the trade, all the advantage of the foreign colonies without being exposed to the expense of establishing or protecting them."[109] They allowed England to sell its industrial goods to the Spanish Americas in exchange for raw materials such as cotton. Free ports were later erected in places such as Hong Kong and Singapore to facilitate the economic penetration of East Asia. Today, their descendants are manufacturing exclaves in developing countries, whose relaxed labor and environmental standards enable the cheap provisioning of the developed world. The Medici had conceived their free port of Livorno as a vehicle for colonial expansion in the Mediterranean and beyond. Now free ports were suitable only for the colonies themselves.

[106] Thoman, *Free Ports and Foreign-Trade Zones*, 9, 51–4.

[107] E.g. Palyart, *Sobre commercio e porto-franco*, 12; Gioja, *Nuovo prospetto delle scienze economiche*, 218–22; Foramiti, *I vantaggi del porto franco*, 6–10. I am indebted to Koen Stapelbroek for the point about the ahistoricism of nineteenth-century reflections on the free port.

[108] Dermigny, "Escales, échelles et ports francs," 604f.

[109] Quoted by Armytage, *The Free Port System*, 58.

Conclusion

Expertise, Rent-Seeking, and the Origins of Political Economy

The Renaissance merchant is a familiar figure. He was a banker, a trader, and an industrial entrepreneur. Whether reluctantly or zealously, he participated in the political life of his city, and he secured his family's splendor by patronizing artists, collecting antiquities, and building a palazzo.[1] But historians have ignored one role of capital importance: Renaissance merchants were the supreme economic experts of their day. As the Ragusan commercial writer Benedetto Cotrugli (*c.*1416–69) observed, merchants could be found conversing with all sorts of people, from princes and kings to artisans and prelates. "Everybody crowds about merchants and is always in need of them," he declared. "Nobody understands better than the experienced merchant the monarchy and government of money in this world, on which all earthly things depend."[2] The merchant alone was initiate into the mysterious ways of money.

Three hundred years later, amidst a pervasive if misleading sense of economic decline, Italian rulers sought better advisors than the merchants they had come to rely upon. Between 1754 and 1772, three academic chairs of political economy were set up in Naples, Milan, and Modena. Intellectuals throughout the peninsula experimented with the creation of a public sphere as a corrective to bad policy. They translated foreign works of political economy with an eye to understanding the peculiarities of the Italian situation. The first of Italy's academic economists, Antonio Genovesi, believed that "commerce is an art, which, like all others, has an end, rules, and principles." Elsewhere he called it a science or a philosophy. Whatever its name, he wanted to instruct the entire "human species" in the secrets of commerce, not just the few.[3] Intellectuals like Genovesi sought to reconstitute economic thought on a new foundation. But how did they depose the previous masters of commercial expertise?

[1] E.g. Sapori, *Il mercante italiano*; de Roover, *The Rise and Decline of the Medici Bank*; Goldthwaite, *Private Wealth in Renaissance Florence*; Goldthwaite, *Wealth and the Demand for Art*, 176–211; McClure, *The Culture of Profession*, 12–13, 22–3, 115–17.

[2] Cotrugli, *Il libro dell'arte di mercatura*, 208.

[3] The quotes are from Genovesi, "Discorso sopra il vero fine delle lettere e delle scienze," as quoted by S. Reinert, *Translating Empire*, 203; and Genovesi, *Elementorum artis logico-criticae*, as quoted by Garin, "Antonio Genovesi metafisco e storico," 15.

In the centuries after Cotrugli, merchants were incorporated as advisors into a swelling state apparatus for regulating economic life, from customs houses and mints to consular regimes and trading companies. The expansion of global trade and the state's new fiscal ambitions thus had a profound impact on capillary governance throughout Europe. This process culminated in the creation of chambers of commerce between the mid-seventeenth and mid-eighteenth centuries. The new institutions were by no means independent of one another: they were the products of obsessive emulation, of models transmitted by merchants and embellished by local officials. These institutions had their own pathways that structured decision making, and the outcome of their deliberations was not merely a policy, but also the set of ideas with which the policy was entangled. In all cases, merchants played an important role in tendering memoranda and representing their opinions. They were not the only actors involved: officials were regular participants, and at times they were joined by jurists, privy secretaries, and patricians. But rulers took the merchant community's claims to expertise seriously, partly because they had an important stake in any decision, and partly for lack of an alternative.

The history of the free port suggests that discursive traditions must be situated within particular institutional landscapes. In Livorno, the bureaucratic process produced a general regime of exceptionalism actuated by close relationships between merchants and officials. By the late seventeenth century, merchants no longer required personal favors, and instead began bargaining collectively to secure the liberties they required. When this intimacy came under attack, officials gradually universalized the liberties of the free port. Except in the sphere of industry, merchants rarely sought monopoly privileges. At a certain level, then, Livorno escaped the kind of rent-seeking typical of the epoch. The port's merchants advocated lower duties on goods, the elimination of import and export restrictions, and greater access to the Tuscan hinterland. Although they did not seek rents, however, they did do their utmost to influence policy outcomes. When Florentines in the mid-eighteenth century turned to political economy, the merchants' role in the policy process of the free port was one of their chief targets.

An influential approach indebted to public choice economics treats policy as a function of "political markets." It sees interest groups competing for policy favors (the demand) from a monopolistic "seller," the government. In this view, the early modern state bartered away long-term economic growth in exchange for short-term revenues. My analysis of the policy process indicates that merchants' efforts to influence policy must be framed alongside the problem of securing expert opinion. Public choice scholarship provides ahistorical accounts of "rent-seeking societies" by ignoring the fact that early modern governments had no access to authoritative, disinterested economic knowledge.[4] Until the development of scientific political economy in the mid-eighteenth century, merchants possessed the most credentialed analyses of economic life. Inevitably, their personal interests colored if not determined their policy recommendations. Often enough they

[4] E.g. Ekelund and Tollison, *Politicized Economies*, *passim*; Root, *The Fountain of Privilege*, *passim*; Ogilvie, *Institutions and European Trade*, 326–7.

wanted monopolies, but as the case of the free port indicates, they frequently sought freedom from regulation as well. The search for a disinterested science was a reaction against relying on merchant advice rather than against the content of that advice per se. As a Venetian economist explained: the state should solicit merchant opinion, but it "should not abandon itself to it."[5] Merchants pursued their own profit rather than the public good; and if they advocated for free trade, that revealed more about their own interests than about the welfare of society. The trouble was that merchant expertise was deeply rooted in the administrative structures of the Ancien Régime. The new science of commerce required a renovation of the policy process.

André Morellet (1727–1819) was an indefatigable visitor of salons and commentator on political economy. Despite his reputation as a critic rather than an original thinker, in one work he was careful to formulate his own arguments: the *Reflections on the Advantages of Freely Writing and Printing on Matters of Administration*. Published in 1775 but written a decade earlier in response to a law against the freedom of the press, this text contains an unusually detailed examination of the policy process. Morellet's aim was to argue that public opinion is a necessary institution for sound policymaking. The prevailing system made it impossible for ministers to make informed decisions and retarded the development of a science of political economy. Public opinion offered a solution to both problems, but it depended on a free press.[6]

The current dispensation permitted self-interested parties to take advantage of ministerial ignorance to promote their agendas. Ministers received countless memoranda (one estimated that he received twelve hundred per year) and were unable to evaluate them: "Let one enter the offices of our ministers, one will see thousands of memorials in which all imaginable projects relating to all parts of administration have been proposed."[7] Most of these projects were idiotic and justly neglected, but even sensible ones remained without purchase. Why? "It is because instead of being spread in public, they have been addressed to the minister, and have not been read." The right to petition was an ancient and legitimate practice in the monarchies of Europe, but Morellet recognized that the bureaucratic chaos it engendered served special interests at the expense of the public. Entrepreneurs and guilds exploited overworked ministers to promote their pet projects or maintain the status quo. They feared putting their proposals before the public. Publicity would make them "blush" to oppose necessary reforms.[8]

Even if ministers could attend to all the proposals that came to their desk, they lacked a science of political economy with which to judge them. For Morellet, only a vigorous public opinion was capable of establishing this science. He believed that the discipline lacked precision and was divided into various camps: those enamored of liberty of commerce, those who confused wealth and money, those who railed

[5] Girolamo Costantini, as quoted by Venturi, *Settecento riformatore*, 513.

[6] Gordon, "'Public Opinion'"; Salvat, "'De la science de l'économie publique' de Morellet."

[7] Morellet, *Réflexions*, 28, as quoted by Gordon, "'Public Opinion,'" 314.

[8] Morellet, *Réflexions*, 26, 33–4. On special interests in France, see Tarrade, "Le groupe de pression du commerce à la fin de l'Ancien Régime"; D. Smith, "Structuring Politics."

against luxury, and those obsessed with state power. To transform such a new field into as systematic a science as that of Copernicus or Newton, Morellet proposed subjecting it to the tribunal of public opinion. The public had its own means of generating consensus: "Whenever a question of political economy is submitted to the judgment of the public by means of the printing press, the minister immediately obtains the judgment of informed men; not because all informed men write, but because they judge writers and their principles, and their opinion quickly forms public opinion."[9] The minister could be assured that any policy approved by public opinion rested on the best available analysis.

Morellet identified a problem with the relationship between special interests and information in the policy process. A science of commerce, regulated by public opinion, would solve governments' problems with information and moderate the dangers of particular interests. His proposal cut at the heart of the traditional relationship between sovereign and subject embodied by the right to petition. At first sight, Adam Smith's analysis seems more preoccupied with haranguing special interests than with managing them. But he too was aware of how interest groups exploited informational problems inherent in the policy process. Smith's *Wealth of Nations* is an attempt to supply public opinion with the tools necessary to evaluate policy.

Smith wrote often about the detrimental effects of special interests on policy. Most interpreters have focused on his attack on collective rent-seeking. Merchants and industrialists, concentrated in cities, found it easier to form coalitions than country gentlemen and farmers. Workers were also capable of "the most shocking violence and outrage," but they could not translate their "tumultuous combinations" into favorable outcomes in the eyes of magistrates.[10] For Smith, this system enabled merchants and manufacturers to set policy in isolation from the concerns of the agricultural and laboring classes. More than once, Smith lamented the "wretched spirit of monopoly" that directed public deliberations. At other times, he spoke of extortion and intimidation. Smith even referred to the industrial and mercantile classes as constituting an "overgrown standing army" that had become so formidable as to "intimidate the legislature" into protecting their interests. Woe to the politician who took a principled stand against them on behalf of the public good: "neither the most acknowledged probity, nor the highest rank, nor the greatest public services can protect him from the most infamous abuse and detraction, from personal insults, nor sometimes from real danger, arising from the insolent outrage of furious and disappointed monopolists."[11]

Though Smith was aware that merchants' mastery over economic analysis played a role in the policy process, he left this function largely unexamined. Merchants and masters, not workers and gentlemen farmers, were the ones who offered "advice" to Parliament. Often, they "represented" their views or "persuaded" the legislature to

[9] Morellet, *Réflexions*, 22; see too his remarks on p. 12.

[10] A. Smith, *Wealth of Nations*, bk 1.vii.13 (p. 84); see also bk 4.ii.21 (p. 462).

[11] Ibid., bk 4.ii.43 (p. 471). For Smith's comments against monopolists, see bk 4.ii.21 (p. 461); 4.iii.a.1 (p. 474); 4.iii.c.9 (p. 493); 5.i.e.18 (p. 741); 5.ii.k.21 (p. 879). For their extortionate practices, bk 4.viii.17 (pp. 647–8). Cf. John Millar's view, quoted by Hirschman, *The Passions and the Interests*, 91.

adopt a certain policy. Once, merchants merely "bethought themselves" and voila, the import tax on beaver skins was nearly eliminated. Only in one passage of the *Wealth of Nations* did Smith elucidate why their advisory tactics were effective, and his explanation points less to intimidation, than to the status of merchants as the experts of economic life. Commercial arguments "were addressed by merchants to Parliaments, and to the councils of princes, to nobles and to country gentlemen; by those who were supposed to understand trade, to those who were conscious to themselves that they knew nothing about the matter."[12] Merchants were self-interested and had a partial view of the economic process, but nobody else could offer politicians superior advice.

Purveying information attended all merchants' efforts to influence policy. Smith positioned his work to provide a legislative science that would replace the need for partial or mistaken "expert" opinion. Toward that end, he took delight in pointing out instances where social actors lacked a keen sense of their own interests.[13] Although Smith thought it was impossible to restrain "the capricious ambition of kings and ministers," he hoped that his science would at least make it possible to attenuate the influence of special interests on policies. "The mean rapacity, the monopolizing spirit of merchants and manufacturers, who neither are, nor ought to be, the rulers of mankind, though it cannot perhaps be corrected may very easily be prevented from disturbing the tranquility of anybody but themselves."[14]

Both Morellet and Smith identified the production of economic knowledge as an essential part of the policy process. Their criticism of the status quo focused not only on the principles of prevailing political economy, but also on the institutions that allowed special interests to play a consultative role in government. Of course, Enlightenment thinkers did not have a comprehensive knowledge of the policy process in their own time, and often they had only a schematic understanding of seventeenth-century administrative procedures. Men like Morellet and Smith were typical in that they privileged the ability of princes, parliaments, and ministers to supervise policy. Their confidence was misplaced. Officials charged with administering economic life created policy through their decisions, non-decisions, and difficulty in mastering the mess of laws and precedents that crowded up their archives. For practical reasons they had little choice but to rely on merchants and industrialists.

Theoretical writers in Italy, like reformers in Tuscany, were also vexed by the problem of expertise. Giambattista Vasco's attack on the guilds is a good example. Vasco (1733–96) was a leading figure of the Enlightenment in Piedmont and a chief channel for introducing Adam Smith's ideas into Italy.[15] His *On Craft Guilds* (1793) offered a familiar critique of corporations. They raised prices, lowered quality,

[12] A. Smith, *Wealth of Nations*, bk 4.i.10 (p. 434). For the other examples in this paragraph, see bk 1.x.c.61 (pp. 157–8); bk 4.vii.b.49 (p. 584); and bk 4.viii.41 (p. 658). Cf. Hont, *Jealousy of Trade*, 55, 104.

[13] A. Smith, *Wealth of Nations*, bk 4.v.a.24 (p. 516); bk 4.vi.22 (pp. 552–3); bk 4.viii.24 (p. 651).

[14] Ibid., bk 4.iii.c.9 (p. 493).

[15] Venturi, "Giambattista Vasco in Lombardia"; Venturi, "Giambattista Vasco, Francesco Dalmazzo Vasco"; Marocco, *Giambattista Vasco*, 123–5.

and restricted the market. More interesting from our point of view is that Vasco mocked the pretensions of guilds or ministers to expert knowledge. "How rare are those men who possess a mastery over an infinity of facts, have a good method for judging them, have the elevated genius for putting them together, and who are without prejudices or private inclinations toward some system, some city or province, some class of men!"[16] Not even guild artisans possessed the knowledge, let alone the disinterest necessary for issuing regulations. For similar reasons, Vasco opposed projects that aimed to intervene in the economy by developing (e.g.) the silk industry at the expense of viticulture. Nobody had the information with which to calculate the cost of shifting resources from current production to some proposed production. Only liberty could direct the economy towards an efficient allocation of resources.

Vasco was dimly aware that his was only a partial solution to the problem of expert advice. He admitted that the government must play a regulatory role in any industry that affected public health or tranquility. This included doctors, chemists, bakers, wine-dealers, writers, painters, and the like. In everything else, the consumer was sovereign. "The habitual diligence of buyers is the best, if not the only restraint" to corrupt business practices.[17] Vasco proposed several ways to ensure that producers sold honest goods, but all depended on the prince's ability to punish wrongdoers. He even proposed unannounced inspections of shops to ensure that artisans manufactured goods according to advertised specifications. "An infrequent visit made without notice to catch delinquents *in flagrante*, and a heavy pecuniary penalty against the same should be enough to defeat the negligence and to overcome the most vile private interest" that leads to fraudulent manufacturing.[18]

Disdain for government projecting—for interventions to stimulate industry and commerce—had a certain affinity with principles of laissez-faire (for producers and merchants) and of *caveat emptor* (for consumers). Under the right conditions, a free economy could be a self-regulating one. What Vasco and most of his contemporaries usually failed to observe is that their proposals presumed a high level of technical expertise in some government quarters. Who would inspect shops and merchandise to ensure that sellers were honest? Who would defend the realm against financial shenanigans? Even in the eighteenth century, the intricacies of money markets were only understood by practicing merchants and financiers. The later development of industrial capitalism has revealed time and again that regulators are drawn from the sectors they are called upon to regulate. Reformers in Leopoldine Tuscany confronted but could not resolve this problem. The conflicts of interest associated with the revolving door are still with us today. The issue first appeared when merchants lost their legitimate role as technical consultants. Their heirs in modern big business remain as active as ever as lobbyists and regulators, of course, but a whiff of illegitimacy hangs over their activities.

[16] Vasco, *Delle Università delle arti e mestierii*, 34.
[17] Ibid., 49; see also 14f. Condorcet had a similar view: Rothschild, *Economic Sentiments*, 167.
[18] Vasco, *Delle Università delle arti e mestierii*, 52.

"Limitations have always been a seminary of disgust." So wrote the *auditore* of Livorno in 1645. By the end of the eighteenth century he would have been more precise: regulation is a seminary of disgust. But in Livorno as elsewhere, the principles of liberty and administrative simplicity did not eliminate the need for economic expertise. Instead, the new science of commerce transferred the locus of authoritative analysis from ground-level operators to central institutions. Local merchants had "interests," officials and intellectuals had "expertise." At first blush, one might view this transformation as an assertion of high modernism against local *metis*, enabling central bodies to steamroll over local knowledge.[19] In fact, it merely changed the terms of negotiation between centers and peripheries, and not always at the latter's expense. Elite commitment to free exchange eliminated some possibilities for rent-seeking, but it also legitimized local business strategies of non-interference. Who knew better than locals what freedoms they required? The system of Livorno, as Governor Bourbon del Monte called the city's laissez-faire regime, did not run itself.

[19] Cf. Scott, *Seeing Like a State*, 309–28.

Appendices

A.1. Patents by decade, 1574–1720

Decade	Number	Percent of Total
1564–73	9	3%
1574–83	25	9%
1584–93	52	18%
1594–1603	50	17%
1604–13	28	10%
1614–23	35	12%
1624–33	17	6%
1634–43	8	3%
1644–53	9	3%
1654–63	21	7%
1664–73	13	4%
1674–83	15	5%
1684–93	6	2%
1694–1703	2	1%
1704–13	2	1%
Total	292	101%

Source: ASF, PS, 188–96. Malanima presented a similar table in *Decadenza*, 150. His figures included printing presses and renewals, which I have excluded.

A.2. Origin of patentees, 1574–1720

Country of origin	Destination		
	Livorno and Pisa	Other Tuscany	Total
England	9	0	9
France	10	27	37
Germany	19	9	28
Iberia	9	2	11
Netherlands	10	5	15
North Africa and the Levant	9	3	12
Italy	51	152	203
Total known	117	198	315
Unknown	16	101	117
Total	133	299	432

Source: ASF, PS, 188–96.

A.3. Location of privileges, 1574–1720

Destination	Number
Livorno	38
Livorno and other	12
Pisa	32
Florence	42
Other	21
Total known	145
Unspecified	172
Total	317

Source: ASF, PS, 188–96.

A.4. Occupational status of patentees, 1574–1720

Occupational status	Destination		
	Livorno and Pisa	Other Tuscany	Total
Artisan	6	41	47
Citizen	3	17	20
Cleric	1	4	5
Gentleman/noble	4	37	41
Jew	18	16	34
Merchant	51	3	54
Professional	3	14	17
Soldier/bombardier	1	7	8
Laborer	0	2	2
Total	87	141	228

Source: ASF, PS, 188–96.

A.5. Supplicants by occupational status, 1592–1682

Occupational status	Customs Office (1648–53)	Governor's Office (1592–1682)	Total	Percentage
Noble	2	16	18	2%
Merchant	58	299	357	47%
Professional	4	15	19	2%
Ship owner or captain	3	33	36	5%
Official	28	18	46	6%
Petty owner or mariner	6	29	35	5%
Artisan/shopkeeper	19	109	128	17%
Laborer	1	14	15	2%
Military	7	20	27	4%
Clergy	10	39	49	6%
City of Livorno	0	28	28	4%
Jewish Community	1	3	4	1%
Miscellaneous Community	0	2	2	0%
Total	139	625	764	100%

Note: See the discussion of the sources in chapter 3, "Making Policy by Supplication."
Source: ASL, CGA, 2602; ASL, CGA, 2603; ASL, CGA, 2608; ASL, Dogana, 3.

A.6. Supplications by type

	Governor's Office (1592–1682)	Customs Office (1648–53)	Total	Percentage
Privilege	27	9	36	5%
Exemption	22	44	66	9%
License	42	30	72	9%
Specific safe-conduct	54	7	61	8%
General safe-conduct	18	0	18	2%
Contract enforcement	57	1	58	8%
Assessment revision	43	41	84	11%
Grant	56	30	86	11%
Abuse report	12	3	15	2%
Judicial	156	1	157	20%
Administrative	62	4	66	9%
Miscellaneous	46	3	49	6%
Total	595	173	768	100%

Note: See the discussion of the sources in chapter 3, "Making Policy by Supplication."
Source: ASL, CGA, 2602; ASL, CGA, 2603; ASL, CGA, 2608; ASL, Dogana, 3.

A.7. Supplication acceptance rates, 1592–1682

	Governor's Office		Customs Office		Total Acceptance Rates
	Accepted	Total	Accepted	Total	
Privilege	10	23	3	7	43%
Exemption	12	19	33	42	74%
License	30	37	27	28	88%
Specific safe-conduct	38	48	7	7	82%
General safe-conduct	15	17	0	0	88%
Contract enforcement	11	46	1	1	26%
Assessment revision	28	36	34	40	82%
Grant	24	40	26	29	72%
Abuse report	4	11	1	3	36%
Judicial	53	108	1	1	50%
Administrative	43	52	4	4	84%
Miscellaneous	20	37	3	3	58%
Total	288	474	140	165	67%

Source: ASL, CGA, 2602; ASL, CGA, 2603; ASL, CGA, 2608; ASL, Dogana, 3.

A.8. Supplications to the Governor's Office by type

Category	1592–1608	1609–20	1621–30	1640–8	1680–2
Privilege	4%	8%	5%	3%	2%
Exemption	7%	4%	2%	3%	2%
License	13%	9%	5%	2%	7%
Specific safe-conduct	8%	7%	10%	11%	9%
General safe-conduct	4%	5%	3%	1%	0%
Contract enforcement	6%	12%	6%	13%	14%
Assessment revision	14%	7%	2%	7%	0%
Grant	12%	11%	10%	7%	0%
Abuse report	1%	3%	3%	2%	0%
Judicial	8%	15%	26%	44%	60%
Administrative	11%	16%	13%	4%	5%
Miscellaneous	13%	2%	16%	3%	0%
Total	142	134	127	149	43

Source: ASL, CGA, 2602; ASL, CGA, 2603; ASL, CGA, 2608.

A.9. Customs receipts in Livorno, 1600–1773 (in lire)

Year	Ordinary	Anchorage	Stallage	Extra Ord.	Victuals	Retail	Fraud	Rent	Other	Total	Notes
1600	36,999	12,837	23,560	39,723			103		130	113,352	
1601	42,709	11,266	14,451	60,114			804		15	129,359	
1602	49,316	12,374	34,863	65,377			310		547	162,787	
1603	58,285	10,742	26,598	99,433			530		622	196,210	
1604	45,502	9522	18,473	38,234			283	42,364	575	154,953	
1605	52,739	10,340	22,862	42,047			405	55,150	408	183,951	
1606	56,482	9375	21,103	29,831			714	58,228	75	175,808	
1607	78,785	13,827	34,665	39,665			327	64,466	1601	233,336	
1608	48,568	12,075	29,984	53,012			868	82,057	2299	228,863	
1609	54,612	7030	14,262	49,895			464	81,431	582	208,276	
1610	41,537	8516	17,754	194,344			456	72,234		334,841	
1611	46,036	8533	20,566	70,856			1485	85,268	210	232,954	
1612	52,064	10,238	22,771	64,231			357	105,342	62	255,065	a.
1613	57,476	8787	17,125	80,278			667	89,260	105	253,698	
1614	54,136	8473	18,682	84,147			638	85,104	546	251,726	
1615	56,819	7580	20,114	93,863			577	80,197		259,150	
1616	51,570	7922	17,429	119,105			1551	85,605	187	283,369	
1617	54,815	7511	23,589	94,808			488	79,292		260,503	
1618	70,143	7266	22,003	84,104			644	78,542		262,702	
1619	77,213	12,609	33,077	87,711			211	77,352		288,173	
1620	76,000	13,737	45,658	86,594			1333	78,561		301,883	
1621	53,148	37,980	39,229	65,954			495	76,468		273,274	
1622	72,205	11,603	35,634	87,542			1257	76,480	919	285,640	
1623	71,386	8335	16,714	70,220			1032	76,019		243,706	
1624	73,021	8404	22,987	110,954			1290	76,501		293,157	
1625	78,878	10,631	23,694	141,554			513	78,892	402	334,564	b.
1626	112,399	12,944	40,176	159,760			743	79,948	14,995	420,965	
1627	103,677	11,244	46,259	176,515			2815	80,088	1725	422,323	

(*continued*)

A.9. Continued

Year	Ordinary	Anchorage	Stallage	Extra Ord.	Victuals	Retail	Fraud	Rent	Other	Total	Notes
1628	150,383	14,140	46,106	242,210			3898	76,519		533,256	
1629	113,881	15,202	43,292	204,722			1611	76,770		455,478	
1630	109,154	16,561	60,690	154,328			2674	69,959		413,366	
1631	69,718	9175	34,452	146,766			13,237	80,442		353,790	
1632	62,125	7246	26,820	143,037			1176	58,529		298,933	
1633	52,641	5117	26,642	149,227			1040	70,774	700	306,141	
1634	66,839	8989	21,712	158,577			2149	73,395	399	332,060	
1635	75,634	10,146	32,256	132,920			1187	74,078		326,221	
1636	80,907	11,157	33,585	110,806			353	64,508		301,316	
1637	96,781	10,993	41,359	158,828			1228	83,753		392,942	
1638	92,454	12,328	41,497	129,036			1557	85,764		362,636	
1639	102,276	12,208	43,490	158,476			2502	86,937		405,889	
1640	110,325	12,675	33,316	130,546			756	81,966		369,584	
1641	128,206	12,076	38,992	160,064			188	86,008		425,534	
1642	116,947	13,976	49,176	165,683			1096	89,140		436,018	
1643	173,235	17,158	58,674	165,202			693	80,203		495,165	
1644	257,991	22,124	73,202	258,204			1377	67,681		680,579	
1645	257,375	19,283	77,020	224,934			2373	64,679		645,664	
1646	252,755	18,685	102,187	227,843			2010	56,705		660,185	
1647	248,849	18,493	96,657	193,182			3905	72,094		633,180	
1648	249,548	22,877	123,467	187,512			5587	37,040		626,031	
1649	230,023	21,171	92,743	149,826	27,728		3838	101,863		420,192	c.
1650	150,995	14,258	104,871	230,672	47,431		5904	64,820		618,951	
1651	166,719	13,876	56,129	149,291	33,657		3015	48,986		471,673	
1652	142,730	14,206	66,997	143,521	26,806		2744	41,473		438,477	
1653	184,281	14,494	79,195	320,676	33,554		2054	36,721		670,975	
1654	165,674	15,122	57,007	256,784	34,009		3743	42,185		574,524	
1655	169,121	15,865	51,286	205,365	30,572		5362	35,253		512,824	
1656	183,806	18,596	53,634	177,386	25,112		2125	29,867		490,526	

1657	181,854	12,718	87,506	206,662	22,444	4216	31,482		546,882	
1658	184,463	13,265	68,825	175,263	25,216	6165	29,834		503,031	
1659	163,578	15,383	75,480	105,962	29,191	3435	33,360		426,389	
1660	193,048	15,575	69,255	179,325	16,622	2138	32,632		508,595	
1661	151,813	16,991	58,705	149,440	22,865.6	2663	28,358		430,835.6	
1662	175,264	19,719	63,380	141,459	26,861.6	4720	40,290		471,693.6	
1663	165,161	18,070	101,640	182,338	49,638	3748	31,530		552,125	
1664	186,743	22,341	59,879	154,577	56,481	5235	22,769		508,025	
1665	158,125	16,579	81,776	183,893	63949.8	5952	21,596		5,318,708	
1666	171,007	15,173	54,080	161,846	63,877	2120	23,647		491,750	
1667	136,024	14,717	54,912	161,724	74,393	2298	24,069		468,137	
1668	149,990	18,960	91,814	167,691	80,239	4021	26,957		539,672	
1669	133,399	20,306	79,655	140,425	70,796	1226	31,416		477,223	
1670	217,858	21,927	48,435	138,114	65,154	5990	20,909		518,387	
1671	151,245	18,679	49,964	160,528	69,164	1887	31,173		482,640	
1672	174,238	22,075	58,103	141,607	71,162	7217	21,035		495,437	
1673	120,292	13,873	41,549	140,299	65,693	4010	26,700		412,416	
1674	137,115	11,957	120,864	194,505	81,386	7714	29,357		582,898	
1675	151,294	19,867	71,826	135,934	72,964	6199	32,668		490,752	
1676	73,028	18,322	329,670	150,474	56,621	4232	48,110		680,457	d.
1677		13,355	312,499	235,391	11,687	6486	34,505		613,923	
1678		17,598	249,719	213,498	13,496	4530	32,753		531,594	
1679		22,165	288,935	195,240	12,222	3831	27,932		550,325	
1680		16,683	244,028	213,624	18,579	6790	33,293		532,997	
1681		20,444	254,955	181,170	17,119	2486	31,970		508,144	
1682		17,439	252,752	243,651	15,977	4311	29,715		563,845	
1683		15,804	239,784	213,564	9904	1843	33,976		514,875	
1684		18,592	217,588	209,394	14,072	2692	35,952		498,290	
1685		17,834	246,154	224,615	27,496	3728	36,397		556,224	
1686		17,301	277,219	232,976	3709	2695	35,851		569,751	
1687		17,242	263,616	245,648	1958	3752	35,923	314	568,453	e.
1688		19,670	265,049	227,480	1697	1340	36,705	421	552,362	

(*continued*)

A.9. Continued

Year	Ordinary	Anchorage	Stallage	Extra Ord.	Victuals	Retail	Fraud	Rent	Other	Total	Notes
1689		13,029	193,905	193,791	3838		3997	37,957	237	446,754	
1690		14,324	232,867	221,946	22,305		1438	41,859	2017	536,756	
1691		17,224	239,011	180,830	46,804		935	33,656	1012	519,472	
1692		17,151	263,929	168,060	53,446		2512	32,733	914	538,745	
1693		17,069	239,852	203,196	44,755		2574	32,841	2479	542,766	
1694		16,304	264,617	194,255	44,266		1769	32,658	1940	555,809	
1695		17,821	262,460	194,526	28,039		3526	27,144	1550	535,066	
1696		16,276	265,688	159,977	26,162		2209	26,130	1336	497,778	
1697		15,213	233,723	168,074	26,301		2390	27,099	930	473,730	
1698		20,318	297,577	168,377	30,714		9423	28,694	398	555,501	
1699		22,644	335,610	203,150	35,084		3629	28,211	738	629,066	
1700		19,363	315,739	166,296	42,910		5467	29,343	755	579,873	f.
1701		18,969	303,613	186,646	43,034		3818	27,521	271	583,872	
1702		15,245	289,370	179,649	34,804		1416	26,681	555	547,720	
1703		14,631	301,545	211,241	26,340		1834	31,481	290	587,362	
1704		16,804	318,137	152,840	46,486		2139	34,505	715	571,626	
1705		15,291	352,229	167,214	59,829		2232	33,921	39	630,755	
1706		16,036	324,714	173,716	44,049		4019	32,144	858	595,536	
1707		14,412	336,860	170,915	36,000		3687	32,743		594,617	
1708		12,149	316,463	164,451	31,812		1081	29,553		555,509	
1709		15,746	336,607	147,965	24,022		1181	29,608		555,129	
1710		21,633	366,048	138,299	78,803		2043	30,984		637,810	
1711		12,572	342,720	139,606	29,309		2102	28,992		555,301	
1712		18,875	392,159	168,678	35,702		1416	29,619		646,449	
1713		22,490	454,654	154,650	20,220		3581	30,144		685,739	
1714		20,421	394,740	151,757	23,368		4340	26,308		620,934	
1715		21,458	393,404	192,528	34,813		1456	27,353		671,012	

1716	22,678	340,614	166,555	40,411	49,280	2810	25,413	647,761	
1717	16,944	344,804	133,930	41,952	48,639	2791	27,378	616,438	
1718	20,438	287,170	142,697	23,077	50,169	1512	26,664	551,727	
1719	16,896	270,707	157,119	23,986	57,494	2537	31,203	559,942	
1720	12,268	265,134	135,284	22,073	58,663	1457	27,674	522,553	
1721	13,671	262,481	134,253	13,762	55,793	2877	25,265	508,102	
1722	18,979	316,072	140,987	23,410	54,304	1707	25,531	580,990	
1723	36,540	280,216	156,351	26,306	56,300	796	26,218	582,727	
1724	16,933	262,139	164,974	20,678	69,550	8632	22,789	565,695	
1725	14,163	268,324	145,909	20,572	50,768	1881	25,429	527,046	
1726	15,174	281,855	137,660	22,629	67,186	2925	24,760	552,189	
1727	11,820	289,261	133,494	17,262	59,709	2276	27,050	540,872	
1728	11,803	298,042	143,860	15,115	59,123	2106	24,935	554,984	
1729	16,056	284,608	200,234	14,085	49,619	1738	27,067	593,407	
1730	13,987	255,821	146,966	23,856	55,290	1647	24,506	522,073	
1731	14,191	244,871	130,723	10,030	61,858	2020	24,718	488,411	
1732	15,963	273,528	144,742	14,019	68,150	5623	24,094	546,119	
1733	19,059	280,914	137,473	14,043	73,338	1331	24,302	550,460	
1734	20,231	345,954	149,149	51,921	49,332	3277	20,828	640,692	
1735	21,451	328,301	138,906	29,472	52,813	800	25,365	597,108	
1736	20,642	341,725	146,436	23,347	56,600	1862	26,333	616,945	
1737	19,961	322,889	143,988	15,834	52,163	1560	27,742	584,137	
1738	20,517	262,874	144,722	24,285	53,380	2277	27,521	535,576	
1739	19,020	264,608	132,740	29,279	63,071	1832	26,623	537,173	
1740	20,746	356,515	148,886	32,654	69,274	2785	23,209	654,069	
1741	19,754	335,000							g.
1742	21,507	280,000							h.
1743	34,219	310,000							h.
1744	28,533	349,000							h.
1745	20,351	459,000							h.

(continued)

A.9. Continued

Year	Ordinary	Anchorage	Stallage	Extra Ord.	Victuals	Retail	Fraud	Rent	Other	Total	Notes
1746		30,446	502,000								h.
1747		45,676	581,000								h.
1748		48,655	621,000								h.
1749		26,484									h.
1750		16,209									i.
1751		33,911									j.
1752		21,059									k.
1753		21,773									
1754		23,086									
1755											l.
1756		15,474									
1757		15,400									
1758		17,742									
1759		16,237									
1760		18,012									
1761		14,954									
1762		12,832									
1763		13,082									
1764		18,870									
1765		15,896									
1766		15,677									
1767		14,871									
1768		14,424									
1769		13,311									

1770	15,707
1771	18,553
1772	19,196
1773	19,883

Note: I would like to thank Lucia Frattarelli Fischer and Andrea Addobbati for providing me with the transcription of the stallage and anchorage receipts.

a. My total differs from the total entered into the accounts slightly (the account total is 251,246).

b. My total differs from the total entered into the accounts by 500 lire.

c. The "victual" heading is my term for the taxes on foreign wine, domestic wine, lemons, oil, and the grain anchorage (which for some purposes is also worth combining with the ordinary anchorage fees).

d. The Reform of 1676 eliminated ordinary taxes and substantially raised stallage fees.

e. The "other" between 1687 and 1706 encompasses various efforts to recover debt owed to the Customs Office.

f. Henceforth, "rent" includes a separate category for "warehouse rental." Warehouse rental appears previously to have simply been included in rent totals. Warehouse rental ranged from between 3% and 15% of total rental income, with an average of 7%.

g. This figure is from 1/1/1740 to 10/31/1740. Henceforth, the "Cala Galera" (a tax on lateen-style ships from the Levant) is added to the anchorage. The stallage figure is lifted from Addobbati, *Commercio, rischio, guerra*, 99.

h. This figure is from 11/1/1741 through 10/31/1742. The stallage figure is lifted from Addobbati, *Commercio rischio Guerra*, 99.

i. This figure is from 11/1/1749 through 8/31/1750.

j. This figure is from 9/1/1750 through 12/31/1750.

k. A return to the calendar year.

l. This year is missing.

Source: ASF, Soprassinadaci e sindaci, 469–74.

A.10. Extraordinary revenue by category, 1645–6 (in scudi)

Category	1645	1646	Average
Property sales	13,185	11,892	12,539
Licenses	8543	8426	8485
Quarantine fees	4483	5214	4849
Contracts	4100	4120	4110
Miscellaneous	1562	2893	2228
Total	31,873	32,545	32,209

Source: ASF, MP, 2163, end of filza.

A.11. Rental income by category, 1645 (in scudi)

Category	Revenue
Rent from warehouses	3832
Debtors' interest	3485
Leases	3174
Rent from houses or shops	817
Total	11,308

Source: ASF, MM, 313, ins. 37.

A.12. Long-distance shipping, 1667–1783

Year	Unknown	Iberian Peninsula	Misc. Italy	North Africa	The Levant	The Regno	The West	Tyrrhenian	West Mediterranean	Total
1667	11	8	0	33	73	1	62	6	0	194
1668	2	0	0	32	66	1	82	11	2	197
1669	5	3	0	27	58	1	74	7	0	175
1670	9	1	1	19	68	2	30	3	3	136
1671	4	1	1	20	55	0	34	0	0	114
1672	8	0	1	22	49	6	42	0	1	130
1673	2	0	1	23	41	0	11	4	1	83
1674	2	0	0	20	44	0	19	3	0	88
1675	4	0	1	16	35	10	24	2	1	92
1676	16	9	2	14	43	31	50	17	1	184
1677	7	6	2	17	44	14	48	7	7	153
1678	12	6	1	15	41	12	71	5	0	163
1679	11	5	0	17	65	0	52	5	2	157
1680	8	1	1	25	60	2	78	0	0	174
1681	6	9	0	19	49	0	78	5	0	166
1682	9	11	0	25	58	1	76	0	0	180
1683	8	5	0	15	55	0	48	4	4	138

Note: This table is based on commands from the Health Board in Florence back to the Health Board in Livorno concerning quarantine times for ship arrivals; they are the sister documentation for the *portate* used by Braudel and Romano, Engels, and Ghezzi (the *portate* in Florence do not survive after 1666).

In compiling these data, I have tried to adhere as much as possible to the methods used by Ghezzi. I have removed corsairing, prize, and war vessels from the totals. I have also applied a convoy multiplier for cases in which the number of convoy ships was not specified. When there were plural ships, but the term convoy was not used, I simply added two ships to my database. When the term convoy (as in "Dutch convoy from Izmir") was used, I applied my convoy multipliers: 7 for the West, 4 for the East. When there were plural ships coming from multiple provenances—e.g. "le merce et robe venute d'Inghilterra, e d'Olanda con le nave descritte nella portata dell'ultimo passato"—I divided the two groups in half; in practice this may have slightly affected country provenances but never my regional totals. When archival information enabled me to fill in some of the convoy information (for instance, official testimony that referenced specific vessels), I only added convoy ships up to the number of 7 or 4, depending on provenance. When there were clear cases of convoy ships listed a few days from vague notice of the arrival of a convoy, I have treated those as part of said convoy and therefore not used the multiplier (so as to exclude possible double counting). In the few cases when the provenance of a convoy was not specified, but its arrival was noted in December or January, it was treated as coming from the appropriate place in the West (e.g. the Dutch and English convoys which arrived on January 27, 1672 were treated as coming from the Netherlands and England respectively). Finally, I added a multiplier of 20% to every month for which Florentine documentation does not survive—that is, the bulk of the data—to further facilitate comparison with the *portate* deposited with the Florentine Health Board. This procedure did not change the shape of the curve but makes it easier to integrate it with the earlier and later periods. Since the documentation in the ASF covers only 30 out of 204 months in this period, the multiplier applied to 174 months. The additional "multiplier vessels" were assigned according to the following ratio: 50% to the West, 30% to the Levant, and 20% to North Africa. This proportion comes from the provenance by region of the 77 cases (over 30 months) for which notices only exist in the ASF. It is not surprising that the ASL documentation is vaguest (i.e. has the most missing ships relative to the ASF documentation) for shipping from northwestern Europe and the Levant, whence came the convoys.

Source: ASL, Sanità, 67, 68, 69, and 71.

A.13. Long-distance ship arrivals in Livorno, 1545–1790

Year	Total	Year	Total	Year	Total
1545		1627	212	1709	235
1546		1628	193	1710	262
1547	1	1629	236	1711	202
1548		1630	144	1712	220
1549	1	1631	109	1713	365
1550	1	1632	60	1714	336
1551		1633	94	1715	322
1552		1634	83	1716	340
1553		1635	86	1717	312
1554		1636	86	1718	294
1555		1637	99	1719	222
1556		1638	99	1720	250
1557		1639	99	1721	239
1558	1	1640	99	1722	296
1559	2	1641	99	1723	285
1560	5	1642	127	1724	315
1561	1	1643	72	1725	274
1562	3	1644	147	1726	252
1563	4	1645	127	1727	220
1564	2	1646	127	1728	268
1565		1647	147	1729	287
1566		1648	147	1730	255
1567		1649	147	1731	246
1568	4	1650	147	1732	263
1569		1651	147	1733	344
1570		1652	143	1734	479
1571		1653	143	1735	425
1572		1654	143	1736	409
1573	42	1655	143	1737	368
1574	48	1656	143	1738	302
1575		1657	166	1739	266
1576		1658	166	1740	253
1577	28	1659	166	1741	221
1578	36	1660	166	1742	178
1579	68	1661	166	1743	230
1580		1662	200	1744	211
1581		1663	200	1745	316
1582		1664	206	1746	369
1583		1665	36	1747	470
1584		1666	200	1748	492
1585		1667	194	1749	419
1586		1668	197	1750	435
1587		1669	175	1751	399
1588		1670	136	1752	423
1589		1671	114	1753	464
1590	38	1672	130	1754	502
1591	82	1673	83	1755	327
1592	120	1674	88	1756	269
1593	214	1675	92	1757	256
1594		1676	184	1758	369
1595		1677	153	1759	391

1596		1678	163	1760	386
1597		1679	157	1761	304
1598		1680	174	1762	307
1599		1681	166	1763	357
1600		1682	180	1764	470
1601		1683	138	1765	323
1602		1684	253	1766	541
1603		1685	230	1767	479
1604		1686	229	1768	304
1605		1687	272	1769	289
1606		1688	204	1770	365
1607	344	1689	105	1771	367
1608	233	1690	139	1772	390
1609	170	1691	188	1773	364
1610	217	1692	143	1774	466
1611		1693	120	1775	366
1612	115	1694	117	1776	354
1613	115	1695	144	1777	360
1614	113	1696	158	1778	337
1615	116	1697	140	1779	362
1616	113	1698	221	1780	324
1617	114	1699	292	1781	322
1618	202	1700	255	1782	417
1619	209	1701	237	1783	477
1620	116	1702	180	1784	431
1621	178	1703	168	1785	407
1622	105	1704	211	1786	533
1623	141	1705	194	1787	475
1624	132	1706	126	1788	471
1625	181	1707	152	1789	460
1626	177	1708	172	1790	481

Notes: Compiling a single table for long-distance shipping is not straightforward, although doing so facilitates inter-temporal (Livorno in 1650 versus Livorno in 1700) as well as inter-port comparisons (Livorno and Marseilles). Braudel and Romano provide data from Health Board records (*portate*) and other sources for 26 out of their 64-year period. Nine of those years are actually split years (i.e. July of 1573 to June of 1674). Since they provide monthly data, for consecutive split years it was possible to add the months together (e.g. 1608 was produced by combining January through June of 1607–8 and June through December of 1608–9). For other split-years I annualized the data by assuming that the half-year was half of the actual number of ships. This assumption is reasonable because on average, traffic from January through June was about equal to the traffic from July through December: arrivals were concentrated in the summer and especially winter months, while slacker in spring and autumn (Ghezzi, *Livorno e l'Atlantico*, 31). Another difficulty is harmonizing the Braudel and Romano data with Ghezzi's series. The basic problem is that while Braudel and Romano provide data by month and ship type, they furnish less information on provenance than Ghezzi. Their discussion of the relationship between the *portate* and their other sources is also less clear. Given these difficulties, it seems best to use their figures for *navi* as the closest approximation to the *portate* data used by Ghezzi.[1] We are on firmer ground with the subsequent period, 1612–66, for which Ghezzi has examined the *portate* and other Health Board documentation in the Florentine archives. Since he grouped his results into five-year totals, I first organized his data into annual totals.[2] Next, since Ghezzi did not examine the Health

[1] Ideally, one could use the proportions found by Ghezzi (70% *navi*, 30% other ships) as an inflator to better reflect the ratio between *navi* and other vessels. On the other hand, one would then have to deflate this estimated figure by the disproportionate amount of Tyrrhenian commerce found by Braudel and Romano, largely absent in Ghezzi's materials. Given the uncertainty surrounding both these operations, it is best to leave Braudel and Romano's figures untouched.

[2] Ghezzi grouped his data in five-year intervals because the date of convoy arrivals—sometimes in December, sometimes in January—produced misleading year-to-year fluctuations. Note that Ghezzi provides specific totals for four years (1642, 1643, 1664, and 1665), which have been incorporated into the data set.

A.13. Continued

Board records in Livorno, I applied an inflator of 5% to account for the lacunae in his documentation (see appendix 12). Fortunately, Engels also provides shipping annual data for 1615–35 that closely corresponds to Ghezzi's totals.[3] I applied the percentile ratios of her figures to my adjusted Ghezzi's totals to provide estimates of annual variation. To illustrate: Ghezzi found 717 ship arrivals in the five-year period 1617–21, 143 ships on average. This figure was first multiplied by 5% for a total of 151 ships on average. For that same period, Engels found 728 ships, although unlike Ghezzi she also provides the annual data. This makes it possible to calculate the percentage contributed by a single year to the total of a given period. In 1617, she found 109 ships: 15% of total arrivals in the period 1617–21. That percentage applied to Ghezzi's figures yields a figure of 113 ships in 1617. The construction of the series from 1667–83 is discussed in appendix 12. Finally, Jean-Pierre Filippini presents two series, the first running from 1684–1700, the second from 1701–1800. Unfortunately, Filippini does not explain the principles by which he constructed his series. He drew from an array of sources. The first series was based on the letters of the customs director of Livorno.[4] For the second and longer series, his footnote cites fourteen volumes from seven collections. The data are organized into *navi* and *bastimenti sottili*. Are the larger *barche* that made up a notable minority of long-distance travel included in the former or the latter category? As with the Braudel and Romano material, it is simply best to utilize Filippini's data while being cognizant of their limitations.

Sources: Braudel and Romano, *Navires et marchandises*, 79–87, 109; Filippini, *Il porto di Livorno*, vol. 1, 44; vol. 2, 149–50; Ghezzi, *Livorno e il mondo islamico*, 20, 69; Ghezzi, *Livorno e l'Atlantico*, 32; Engels, *Merchants, Interlopers, Seamen and Corsairs*, 225–6; ASL, Sanità, 67, 68, 69, and 71.

[3] Her figures differ somewhat from Ghezzi's, since she took into account all arrivals, including of those ships just stopping by on their way to another port. The underlying assumption in this calculation is that Engels's figures accurately reflect the annual variation also found by Ghezzi.

[4] Filippini, "L'attività del porto," 158.

A.14. Port connections, 1573–85 (ship arrivals)

Iberia		North Africa		Levant		Northwestern Europe	
Lisbon	38	Djerba	1	Alexandria	21	London	58
Lagos	23	Sfax	3	Constantinople	7	Harwich	5
Faro	8	Monastir	1	Tripoli (Syria)	4	Southhampton	3
Alicante	119	Tunis	3			Bristol	3
Seville (and Cadiz)	54	Bizerte	1			Yarmouth	1
Barcellona	5	Tabarca	3		32	Inester	1
Tortosa	4	Bastion de France	1			Plymouth	1
Valencia	6	Bône	1			Calais	2
Majorca	2	Algiers	8			Dieppe	3
		Larache	9			Archangel	1
		Cap dou Gué	7			Antwerp	2
Other/Unknown	74	Other/Unknown	4			Other/Unknown	3
Total	333	Total	42	Total	32	Total	82

Note: The figure on connections with London (and the other English ports) is an estimate based on the information Braudel and Romano provide for the period from 1573–93. 45 London ships out of 95 total English ships in the period compares to 34 London ships out of 71 English ships in the period 1573–85. In addition, one should assume that the 33 ships from England with unknown provenance departed from London (i.e. 24 ships in the period before 1590): the overall figure rounds to 58 ships from London, which should be treated as an upper-bound estimate. See ibid., 51.

Source: Braudel and Romano, *Navires et marchandises*, 39–53.

A.15. Connections with Levantine and North African ports, 1612–66 (total ship arrivals in five-year intervals)

	Izmir	Istanbul	Alexandria	Alexandretta	Saida	San Giovanni d'Acri	Cyprus	Tunis	Algiers	Tripoli	Other Levant	Other North Africa	Total
1612–6	5	3	91	0	2	0	2	43	7	3	130	21	307
1617–21	10	5	74	2	3	3	0	60	46	1	176	21	401
1622–6	12	10	79	8	2	7	5	52	64	0	133	21	393
1627–31	23	19	108	14	9	77	12	55	30	1	178	21	547
1632–6	16	13	61	4	1	7	9	17	15	3	163	26	335
1637–41	38	13	144	7	7	2	4	16	7	2	122	23	385
1642–6	26	13	105	7	7	8	12	13	15	7	144	23	380
1647–51	46	20	88	13	15	11	13	21	4	19	125	21	396
1652–6	54	14	119	14	5	10	11	31	15	21	139	21	454
1657–61	62	15	37	25	7	30	3	39	17	36	134	31	436
1662–6	86	13	57	19	4	2	15	42	37	32	154	55	516

Note: I have included shipping from Cyprus and other Greek isles as part of the Levant.

Source: Ghezzi, *Livorno e il mondo islamico*, apps.

A.16. Cotton imports, 1570–1797 (total imports in five-year intervals)

Year	Total (ql)	Percent Spun	Notes.
1577–81	2603.69		a.
1582–6	671.19		a.
1587–91			
1592–6	451.31		b.
1597–1601			
1602–6			
1607–11			
1612–6	586.04	68%	
1617–21	2993.36	90%	
1622–6	4097.72	44%	
1627–31	15,476.68	39%	
1632–6	4479.52	40%	
1637–41	11,270.74	50%	
1642–6	21,181.78	43%	
1647–51	25,006.36	45%	
1652–6	14,151.37	38%	
1657–61	21,026.24	44%	
1662–6	17,053.38	49%	
1667–71			
1672–6	4937	37%	c.
1677–81	6272	37%	
1682–6	7655	38%	
1687–91	6774	38%	
1692–6	6687	36%	
1697–1701	8361	34%	
1702–6	9644	36%	
1707–11	6511	39%	
1712–16	7459	33%	
1717–21	10,563	28%	b.
1722–6	6606	24%	
1727–31	6810	24%	
1732–6	8942	23%	
1737–41			
1742–6			
1747–51			
1752–6			
1757–61			
1762–6			
1767–71	10,103	24%	a.
1772–6	8441	15%	
1777–81	14,021	12%	
1782–6	14,876	11%	
1787–91	23,172	12%	

Note: Braudel and Romano's figure was reported at the very high rate of 1000 pounds per bale; in addition, they do not specify whether it arrived raw or spun. I have used Ghezzi's conversion ratios (1 *balla* raw cotton equals 450 Tuscan pounds; 1 *balla* spun equals 500 Tuscan pounds): assuming conservatively that fifty percent was spun, I have averaged the two estimates (thus: 1 *balla*, 475 pounds). On the conversion rate, see A.20.

a. Estimate based on four years of data.

b. Estimate based on three years of data.

c. Estimate based on two years of data.

Source: Braudel and Romano, *Navires et marchandises*, 115; Ghezzi, *Livorno e il mondo islamico*, apps; Filippini, *Il porto di Livorno*, vol. 2, 128–9.

A.17. Regional connections, 1657–8 (ship arrivals)

Provenance	City	Barche	Tartane	Leuti	Fregate	Felucche	Brigantini	Total
Kingdom of Sicily		53	13			37	1	104
	Agrigento	1						1
	Augusta	1	1					2
	Bari	2						2
	Brindisi	1						1
	Castellammare	1						1
	Crotone	1						1
	Gaeta	1	1					2
	Gallipoli	1						1
	Ischia	2	2					4
	Lipari	4						4
	Messina	11	1			4		16
	Naples	16				25		41
	Palermo	5	3			2	1	11
	Paola					1		1
	Pozzallo					1		1
	San Lucido					3		3
	Syracuse	1						1
	Termini Imerese		2					2
	Torre Anunziata		1			1		2
	Trapani	5	2					7
Sardegna		39		20	96		10	165
	Aranci				8		1	9
	Bosa	3			31			34
	Cagliari	24			4			28
	Castello Aragonese				9		1	10
	Iglesias			3	1		4	8
	Larghè (Alghero)				42			42

	Oristano	4						4
	Porto Torres	6		9	1		1	17
	Portoscuso	2						2
	Sassari			8			3	11
Republic of Genoa		32	11	51		8	9	111
	Finale	2	4	44				50
	Genoa	12		2		4	9	27
	Lerici					3		3
	Oneglia	12	6	5				23
	San Pier d'Arena					1		1
	San Remo	6	1					7
Corsica							11	11
	Bastia						11	11
Papal States							5	5
	Rome						5	5
Southern France (Languedoc/Provence)		77	77				2	156
	Agde	7	2					9
	Aigues-Mortes	3						3
	Antibes		1					1
	Cassis		1					1
	Frontignan	24	24					48
	La Ciotat		5					5
	Marseille	33	14				2	49
	Martigues	2	28					30
	Tolone	8	2					10
Total								552

Note: The very low numbers for the Papal States (and the absence of ships from Civitavecchia) are perhaps accounted for by the severity of plague in the area. See ibid., 89.

Source: Ghezzi, *Livorno e il mondo islamico*, 89–106.

A.18. Supplications to the Customs Office by type, 1648–1790

Category	Medici	Early Leopoldine	Late Leopoldine
	1648–53	1767–9	1785–90
Privilege	5%	4%	6%
Exemption	25%	18%	0%
License	17%	9%	9%
Specific safe-conduct	4%	0%	2%
General safe-conduct	0%	0%	8%
Grant	17%	2%	1%
Contract enforcement	1%	3%	1%
Abuse report	2%	2%	1%
Assessment revision	24%	57%	55%
Judicial	1%	1%	3%
Administrative	2%	1%	0%
Miscellaneous	2%	4%	13%
Total	173	139	96

Source: ASL, Dogana, 12, 13, 21, 22, and 23; and n. 43 in chapter 3.

A.19. Occupational status of Customs Office supplicants, 1648–1790

	Medici	Early Leopoldine	Late Leopoldine
	1648–53	1767–9	1785–90
Merchant	44%	22%	24%
Ship owner or captain	2%	3%	11%
Petty owner or mariner	4%	16%	22%
Artisan or shopkeeper	13%	21%	18%
Official	19%	3%	2%
Laborer	1%	15%	16%
Other	16%	19%	7%
Total	149	89	45

Source: ASL, Dogana, 12, 13, 21, 22, and 23; and n. 43 in chapter 3.

A.20. Units of measure in Livorno

Article	Measure	Tuscan pounds	Metric	Note
Cotton (raw)	balla	450	152.79 kg	a.
	sacco	116	39.38 kg	
Cotton (spun)	balla	500	169.77 kg	
	sacco	142	48.21 kg	
Flax (raw)	balla	1500	509.31 kg	
	balletta	600	203.72 kg	
	sacco	600	203.72 kg	
	cantaro	125	42.44 kg	b.
Silk (raw)	balla (Izmir)	450	152.79 kg	
	balla (Italy)	500	169.77 kg	
	cassa	400	135.81 kg	
	ballotto	225	76.39 kg	
	sacco	225	76.39 kg	
	fagotto	190	64.51 kg	
Wool (raw)	balla	700	237.68 kg	c.
	sacco	165	56.02 kg	
	cantaro	125	42.44 kg	
Wool (cloth)	balla	486	165 kg	

Note: I have privileged the weights and measures used by Renato Ghezzi. Thus, I have preferred his measure of the Tuscan pound at 339.53 grams, rather than the figure of 360 reported by Trivellato, *The Familiarity of Strangers*, xii. When necessary, I have also used Braudel and Romano's figures. This table includes information solely for those commodity calculations I performed myself. Consult the listed sources for the equivalencies of other commodities. See too the terminological note to *The Free Port of Livorno*.

a. Elsewhere, Ghezzi (*Livorno e il mondo islamico*, n. 601) says a bale of cotton equaled 600 Tuscan pounds, but he appears to have preferred 450 pounds for a *balla* of raw silk (*Livorno e il mondo islamico*, 130). Braudel and Romano calculated the bale of cotton at 1000 pounds.

b. By analogy with the cantaro of wool.

c. This was listed as only 400 Tuscan pounds in Braudel and Romano.

Source: ASP, Opera del Duomo, 743–6; *Governo civile e militare*, 35; Braudel and Romano, *Navires et marchandises*, apps; Ghezzi, *Livorno e il mondo islamico*, *passim*, esp. 130, 169; Ghezzi, *Livorno e l'Atlantico*, 15.

Bibliography

Acemoglu, Daron, Simon Johnson, and James Robinson. "The Rise of Europe: Atlantic Trade, Institutional Change and Economic Growth." *American Economic Review* 95, no. 3 (2005): 546–79.

Adams, Julia. *The Familial State: Ruling Families and Merchant Capitalism in Early Modern Europe*. Ithaca: Cornell University Press, 2005.

Addobbati, Andrea. "La giurisdizione marittima e commerciale dei Consoli del Mare in età medicea." In *Pisa e il Mediterraneo: uomini, merci, idee dagli Etruschi ai* Medici, edited by Marco Tangheroni, 311–15. Milan: Skira, 2003.

Addobbati, Andrea. "Oltre gli intermediari: La Anton Francesco Salucci & Figlia alla conquista dei mercati americani (1779–1788)." In *Storia e attualità della presenza degli Stati Uniti a Livorno e in Toscana*, 145–83, 2003.

Addobbati, Andrea. *Commercio, rischio, guerra: il mercato delle assicurazioni marittime di Livorno (1694–1795)*. Rome: Edizioni di storia e letteratura, 2007.

Addobbati, Andrea. "'La frugalità e l'economia sono ottime altrove': lusso e incentivazione dei consumi nella Livorno del Settecento." *Nuovi studi livornesi* 15 (2008): 139–52.

Addobbati, Andrea. "Livorno: fronte del porto: Monelli, Carovane e Bergamaschi della Dogana (1602–1847)." In *I sistemi portuali della Toscana mediterranea: infrastrutture, scambi, economie dall'antichità a oggi*, 245–314. Pisa: Pacini, 2011.

Aglietti, Marcella. "Guiliano Capponi governatore di Livorno tra Medici e Lorena." *Nuovi studi livorensi* 16 (2009): 33–62.

Aglietti, Marcella. *I governatori di Livorno dai Medici all'Unità d'Italia: Gli uomini, le istituzioni, la città*. Pisa: ETS, 2009.

Ago, Renata. *Gusto for Things: A History of Objects in Seventeenth-Century Rome*. Chicago: University of Chicago Press, 2013.

Ajello, Raffaele. "Carlo Antonio Broggia: nota introduttiva." In *Dal Muratori al Cesarotti V: politici ed economisti del primo Settecento*, edited by Raffaele Ajello and Emilio Bigi, 971–1034. Milan-Naples: Ricciardi, 1979.

Albèri, Eugenio, ed. *Le relazioni degli ambasciatori veneti al senato*. Series III, vol. 3. Florence: Società Editrice Fiorentina, 1855.

Alimento, Antonella. "Tra Bristol ed Amsterdam: discussioni livornesi su commercio, marina ed impero negli anni cinquanta del Settecento." In *Dall'origine dei lumi alla rivoluzione: scritti in onore di Luciano Guerci e Giuseppe Ricuperati*, edited by Donatella Balani, Dino Carpanetto, e Marina Roggero, 24–45. Rome: Edizioni di Storia e Letteratura, 2008.

Alimento, Antonella. "Tra 'gelosie' personali e 'gelosie' tra gli stati: i progetti del governatore Garlo Ginori e la circolazione della cultura economica e politica a Livorno (1747–1757)." *Nuovi studi livornesi* 16 (2009): 63–95.

Ambrosoli, Mauro. *The Wild and the Sown: Botany and Agriculture in Western Europe, 1350–1850*. Cambridge: Cambridge University Press, 1997.

Angiolini, Franco. *I cavalieri e il principe: l'ordine di Santo Stefano e la società toscana in età moderna*. Florence: Edifir, 1996.

Angiolini, Franco, Vieri Becagli, and Marcello Verga, eds. *La Toscana nell'età di Cosimo III*. Florence: Edifir, 1993.

Ansaldi, Ansaldo. *De commercio et mercatura: discursus legales*. Rome: Ex typographia Domenici Antonii Herculis, 1689.

Appleby, Joyce Oldham. *Economic Thought and Ideology in Seventeenth Century England.* Princeton: Princeton University Press, 1978.
Armytage, Frances. *The Free Port System in the British West Indies: A Study in Commercial Policy, 1766–1822.* London: Longmans, Green, & Co., 1953.
Arrighi, Giovanni. *The Long Twentieth Century: Money, Power, and the Origins of Our Times.* New York: Verso, 1994.
Arrighi, Vanna, and Francesca Klein. "Da mercante avventuriero a confidente dello stato: profilo di Bongianni Gianfigliazzi attraverso le sue ricordanze." *Archivio storico italiano* 161 (2003): 53–79.
Arru, Angiolina. "Reti locali, reti globali: il credito degli immigrati, secoli XVIII–XIX." In *L'Italia delle migrazioni interne: donne, uomini, mobilità in età moderna e contemporanea*, edited by Angiolina Arru and Franco Ramella, 77–110. Rome: Donzelli, 2003.
Arru, Angiolina, and Franco Ramella, eds. *L'Italia delle migrazioni interne: donne, uomini, mobilità in età moderna e contemporanea.* Rome: Donzelli, 2003.
Asburgo Lorena, Pietro Leopoldo d'. *Relazioni sul governo della Toscana*, vol. 3. Edited by Arnaldo Salvestrini. Florence: Olschki, 1974.
Asch, Ronald. "Absolutism and Royal Government." In *A Companion to Eighteenth-Century Europe*, edited by Peter H. Wilson, 451–63. Malden, MA: Blackwell, 2008.
Ash, Eric H. *Power, Knowledge, and Expertise in Elizabethan England.* Baltimore: Johns Hopkins University Press, 2004.
Ash, Eric H. "Introduction: Expertise and the Early Modern State." *Osiris* 25, no. 1 (2010): 1–24.
Ashworth, William J. *Customs and Excise: Trade, Production and Consumption in England 1640–1845.* Oxford: Oxford University Press, 2003.
Ashworth, William J. "Quality and the Roots of Manufacturing 'Expertise' in Eighteenth-Century Britain." *Osiris* 25, no. 1 (2010): 231–54.
Aslanian, Sebouh David. *From the Indian Ocean to the Mediterranean: The Global Trade Networks of Armenian Merchants from New Julfa.* Berkeley: University of California Press, 2011.
Aymard, Maurice. "La fragilità di un'economia avanzata: l'Italia e le trasformazioni dell'economia europea." In *Storia dell'economia italiana*, vol. 2, edited by Ruggiero Romano, 5–137. Turin: Einaudi, 1991.
Azuni, Domenico Alberto. *Dizionario universale ragionato della Giurisprudenza mercantile*, 4 vols. Nice, 1786–8.
Babudieri, Fulvio. *L'espansione mercantile austriaca nei territori d'oltremare nel XVIII secolo e suoi riflessi politici ed economici.* Milan: Giuffrè, 1978.
Baggiani, Daniele. "Tra crisi commerciale e interventi istituzionali: le vicende del porto di Livorno in età tardo medicea (1714–1730)." *Rivista storica italiana* 104, no. 3 (1992): 678–729.
Baggiani, Daniele. "Progresso tecnico e azione politica nella Toscana leopoldina: la Camera di Commercio di Firenze (1768–1782)." In *La politica della scienza*, edited by Barsanti et al., 285–324.
Balbi de Caro, Silvana, ed. *Merci e monete a Livorno in età granducale.* Milan: Silvana, 1997.
Balbi de Caro, Silvana. "La monetazione granducale per Livorno." In *Merci e monete a Livorno in età granducale*, edited by Balbi de Caro, 147–58.
Baldini, Artemio Enzo, ed. *Botero e la "Ragion di Stato."* Florence: Olschki, 1992.
Balestracci, Duccio. *The Renaissance in the Fields: Family Memoirs of a Fifteenth-Century Tuscan Peasant.* University Park, PA: The Pennsylvania State University Press, 1999.

Bandini, Sallustio. "Discorso sopra la Maremma di Siena," edited by Lucia Connena Bonelli. In *Sallustio Bandini*, edited by George R. F. Baker. Florence: Olschki, 1978.

Bardiot, Nicole. "Marseille dans la compétition industrielle aux XVIIIe siècle: l'essor des soudes siciliennes après la guerre de sept ans." In *Lo spazio tirrenico nella "grande trasformazione,"* edited by Salvemini, 59–85.

Barsanti, Giulio, Vieri Becagli, and Renato Pasta, eds. *La politica della scienza: Toscana e stati italiani nel tardo Settecento*, 2 vols. Florence: Olschki, 1996.

Bartolini, Franco. "Suppliche pontificie nei secoli XIII e XIV." *Bullettino dell'Istituto storico italiano per il medio evo* 67 (1955): 1–187.

Baruchello, Mario. *Livorno e il suo porto: origini, caratteristiche e vicende dei traffici livornesi*. Livorno: Società Anonima Editrice Riviste Tecniche, 1932.

Battaglini, Giuseppe M. *Cosmopolis: portoferraio medicea storia urbana 1548–1737*. Rome: Multigrafica Editrice, 1978.

Battistini, Francesco. *Gelsi, bozzoli e caldaie: l'industria della seta in Toscana tra città, borghi e campagne (sec. XVI–XVIII)*. Florence: Olschki, 1998.

Becagli, Vieri. *Un unico territorio gabellabile: la riforma doganale Leopoldina. Il dibattito politico 1767–1781*. Naples: ETS, 1983.

Becagli, Vieri. "The *Georgofili* of Florence, 1753–1783: From 'Perfect Anarchy' to Royal Academy." In *The Rise of Economic Societies*, edited by Stapelbroek and Marjanen, 96–129.

Beccaria, Cesare. *Elementi di economia pubblica*, vols 11 and 12 of *Scrittori classici italiani di economia politica*. Milan: G. G. Destefanis, 1804.

Beik, William. *Absolutism and Society in Seventeenth-Century France: State Power and Provincial Aristocracy in Languedoc*. Cambridge: Cambridge University Press, 1985.

Belfanti, Carlo Marco. "Guilds, Patents, and the Circulation of Technical Knowledge: Northern Italy During the Early Modern Age." *Society for the History of Technology* 45 (2004): 581–3.

Belloni, Cristina. *Suppliche al pontefice: Diocesi di Trento 1566–1605*. Bologna: Il Mulino, 2007.

Beltrami, Daniele. "La crisi della marina mercantile veneziana e i provvedimenti del 1736 per fronteggiarla." *Rivista internazionale di scienze sociali* 13 (1942): 304–18.

Benadusi, Giovanna. *A Provincial Elite in Early Modern Tuscany: Family and Power in the Creation of the State*. Baltimore: The Johns Hopkins University Press, 1996.

Benigni, Paola. "Francesco Feroni, Empolese, negoziante in Amsterdam." *Rassegna degli Archivi di Stato* 47 (1988): 488–517.

Benigni, Paola. "Francesco Feroni: da mercante di schiavi a burocrate nella Toscana di Cosimo III. Alcune anticipazioni." In *La Toscana nell'età di Cosimo III*, edited by Angiolini et al., 165–83.

Benjamin, Walter. *Illuminations*. New York: Schocken, 1969.

Bergasse, Louis and Gaston Rambert. *Histoire du commerce de Marseille*, vol. 4: *De 1599 à 1789*. Paris: Plon, 1954.

Berner, Samuel. "Florentine Society in the Late Sixteenth and Early Seventeenth Centuries." *Studies in the Renaissance* 18 (1971): 203–46.

Bertelli, Elena. "Un'azienda commerciale a Livorno nel XVII secolo: gli affari del banco di Giulio del Beccuto (1629–1639)." Undergraduate thesis, University of Pisa, 1993–4.

Berti, Luciano. *Il principe dello studiolo: Francesco I dei Medici e la fine del Rinascimento fiorentino*. Florence: Edam, 1967.

Berveglieri, Roberto. *Inventori stranieri a Venezia, 1474–1788: importazione di tecnologia e circolazione di tecnici artigiani inventori*. Venice: Istituto veneto di scienze, lettere ed arti, 1995.

Besold, Christoph. *De aerario publico discursus.* Strasbourg: Zetzner, 1639.
Bethel, Slingsby. *An Account of the French Usurpation upon the Trade of England.* London, 1679.
Biagioli, Mario. *Galileo, Courtier: The Practice of Science in the Culture of Absolutism.* Chicago: University of Chicago Press, 1993.
Biagioli, Mario. "From Prints to Patents: Living on Instruments in Early Modern Europe." *History of Science* 44 (2006): 139–86.
Bicci, Antonella. "Immigration and Acculturation: Italians in Amsterdam." In *Rome-Amsterdam: Two Growing Cities in Seventeenth Century Europe*, edited by Peter van Kessel and Elisja Schulte van Kessel, 248–59. Amsterdam: Amsterdam University Press, 1997.
Blando, Antonino. "Da un 'monopolio naturale' all'altro: il grano e lo zolfo siciliano." In *Lo spazio tirrenico nella "grande trasformazione,"* edited by Salvemini, 1–39.
Boccaccio, Giovanni. *The Decameron.* Translated by G. H. McWilliam. New York: Penguin, 1995.
Bödeker, Hans Erich. "Economic Societies in Germany, 1760–1820: Organisation, Social Structures and Fields of Activities." In *The Rise of Economic Societies*, edited by Stapelbroek and Marjanen, 182–211.
Bonelli Connena, Lucia. "Premessa." In *Sallustio Bandini*, edited by George R. F. Baker. Florence: Olschki, 1978.
Boni, Salvatore. *Corsari nel Mediterraneo: cristiani e musulmani fra guerra, schiavitù e commercio.* Milan: Mondadori, 1997.
Bonifacio, Gaetano. "Il primo governatore di Livorno: Giovanni Volterra (1586–95)." *Bollettino storico livornese* 3 (1939): 343–59.
Bonifacio, Gaetano. "Disegno di una compagnia livornese di navigazione." *Bollettino storico livornese* 4, no. 1 (1942): 49–57.
Bonney, Richard, ed. *Economic Systems and State Finance.* Oxford: Oxford University Press, 1995.
Bonney, Richard, ed. *The Rise of the Fiscal State in Europe, c.1200–1815.* Oxford: Oxford University Press, 1999.
Bonney, Richard. "Early Modern Theories of State Finance." In *Economic Systems and State Finance*, edited by Bonney, 163–230.
Bonnyman, Brian. "Agrarian Patriotism and the Landed Interest: The Scottish 'Society of Improvers in the Knowledge of Agriculture,' 1723–1746." In *The Rise of Economic Societies*, edited by Stapelbroek and Marjanen, 26–51.
Borgherini-Scarabellin, Maria. *Il magistrato dei Cinque Savi alla Mercanzia dalla istituzione alla caduta della Repubblica.* Venice: A. Milani, 1925.
Botero, Giovanni. *Della ragion di stato.* Venice: Gioliti, 1589.
Botero, Giovanni. *On the Causes of the Greatness of Cities.* Translated by Geoffrey Symcox. Toronto: University of Toronto Press, 2012.
Boutier, Jean. "Le 'Notizie diverse' de Niccolò Gondi (1652–1720): a propos de la mémoire et des stratégies familiales d'un noble florentin." *Mélanges de l'école française de Rome* 98, no. 2 (1986): 1097–1151.
Boyajian, James C. *Portuguese Trade in Asia under the Habsburgs, 1580–1640.* Baltimore: Johns Hopkins University Press, 1993.
Boyle, John. *Letters from Italy, in the Years 1754 and 1755, by the late Right Honourable John Earl of Corke and Orrery.* London: B. White, 1773.
Braddick, Michael. *The Nerves of State: Taxation and the Financing of the English State, 1558–1714.* New York: Manchester University Press, 1996.

Braddick, Michael. *State Formation in Early Modern England, c.1550–1700*. Cambridge: Cambridge University Press, 2000.

Brancaccio, Giovanni. *Nazione genovese: consoli e colonia nella Napoli moderna*. Naples: Guida, 2001.

Braudel, Fernand. "L'Italia fuori d'Italia." In *Storia d'Italia*, vol. 2: *Dalla caduta dell'Impero romano al secolo XVIII*, edited by Ruggiero Romano, 2089–248. Turin: Einaudi, 1974.

Braudel, Fernand. *Civilization and Capitalism, 15th–18th Century*, 3 vols. Berkeley: University of California Press, 1982–4.

Braudel, Fernand. *The Mediterranean and the Mediterranean World in the Age of Phillip II*, 2 vols. Berkeley: University of California Press, 1995.

Braudel, Fernand, and Ruggiero Romano. *Navires et marchandises à l'entrée du port de Livourne (1547–1611)*. Paris: A. Colin, 1951.

Brege, Brian Anthony. "The Empire That Wasn't: The Grand Duchy of Tuscany and Empire, 1574–1609." PhD Diss., Stanford University, 2014.

Bregoli, Francesca. *Mediterranean Enlightenment: Livornese Jews, Tuscan Culture, and Eighteenth-Century Reform*. Stanford: Stanford University Press, 2014.

Brenner, Robert. *Merchants and Revolution: Commercial Change, Political Conflict and London's Overseas Traders, 1550–1653*. Princeton: Princeton University Press, 1993.

Brewer, John. *The Sinews of Power: War, Money and the English State, 1688–1783*. Cambridge, MA: Harvard University Press, 1990.

Brewster, Francis. *Essays on Trade and Navigation in Five Parts*. London: Thomas Cockerill, 1695.

Broggia, Carlo Antonio. *Trattato de' tributi, delle monete, e del governo politico della sanità*. Naples: Pietro Palombo, 1743.

Brown, Judith C. "Concepts of Political Economy: Cosimo I de' Medici in a Comparative European Context." In *Firenze e la Toscana dei Medici*, 278–93.

Brown, Judith C., and Jordan Goodman. "Women and Industry in Florence." *Journal of Economic History* 40, no. 1 (1980): 73–80.

Bulferetti, Luigi, and Claudio Costantini. *Industria e commercio in Liguria nell'età del Risorgimento, 1700–1861*. Milan: Banca commerciale italiana, 1966.

Burke, Peter. "On Tacitus." In *The Cambridge History of Political Thought*, edited by J. H. Burns and Mark Goldie, 484–90. Cambridge: Cambridge University Press, 1994.

Caizzi, Bruno. *Industria, commercio e banca in Lombardia nel XVIII secolo*. Milan: Banca Commerciale Italiana, 1968.

Calabi, Donatella. *The Market and the City: Square, Street, and Architecture in Early Modern Europe*. Burlington, VT: Ashgate, 2004.

Calabi, Donatella. "Canali, rive, approdi." In *Storia di Venezia*, edited by Alberto Tenenti and Ugo Tucci, vol. 12: *Il Mare*, 761–88.

Calabi, Donatella. "Magazzini, fondaci, dogane." In *Storia di Venezia*, edited by Alberto Tenenti and Ugo Tucci, vol. 12: *Il Mare*, 789–817.

Calafat, Guillaume. "Expertises et tribunaux de commerce: procédures et réputation à Livourne au XVIIe siècle." *Hypothèses* 14, no. 1 (2010): 141–54.

Calafat, Guillaume. "Être étranger dans un port franc: droits, privilèges et accès au travail à Livourne (1590–1715)." *Cahiers de la Méditerranée* 84 (2012): 103–22.

Calafat, Guillaume. "Ramadam Fatet vs. John Jucker: Trials and Forgery in Egypt, Syria, and Tuscany (1739–1740)." *Quaderni Storici* 143 (2013): 419–40.

Calafat, Guillaume. "Une mer jalousée: juridictions maritimes, ports francs et régulation du commerce en Méditerranée (1590–1740)." PhD thesis, Université Paris 1, 2013.

Callard, Caroline. *Le prince et la république: histoire, pouvoir et société dans la Florence des Médicis au XVIIe siècle*. Paris: Presses de l'université Paris-Sorbonne, 2007.

Cantini, Lorenzo. *Legislazione Toscana raccolta ed illustrata*, 32 vols. Florence: Albizziniana, 1800–32.

Capponi, Niccolò. "Il sistema difensivo di Livorno sotto Ferdinando II de' Medici." *Nuovi studi livornesi* 9 (2001): 15–35.

Capponi, Niccolò. "Le Palle di Marte: Military Strategy and Diplomacy in the Grand Duchy of Tuscany under Ferdinand II de' Medici (1621–1670)." *The Journal of Military History* 68, no. 4. (2004): 1105–41.

Capra, Carlo. "Riforme finanziarie e mutamento istituzionale nello Stato di Milano: gli anni sessanta del secolo XVIII." *Rivista storica italiana* 91 (1979): 313–68.

Capra, Carlo. "Habsburg Italy in the Age of Reform." *Journal of Modern Italian Studies* 10, no. 2 (2005): 218–33.

Capuzzo, Ester. "Portifranchi e comunità etnico-religiose: il caso di Trieste, Fiume e Ancona." *Ricerche di storia sociale e religiosa* 61 (2002): 43–53.

Caraccioli, Louis-Antoine. *Voyage de la Raison en Europe*. Paris: Saillant & Nyons, 1772.

Caracciolo, Alberto. "Il dibattito sui 'porti franchi' nel Settecento: genesi della franchigia di Ancona." *Rivista storica italiana* 75, no. 3 (1963): 538–58.

Caracciolo, Alberto. *Le port franc d'Ancône, croissance et impasse d'un milieu marchand au XVIIIe siècle*. Paris: SEVPEN, 1965.

Carafa, Diomede. *Memoriali*. Edited by Franca Petrucci Nardelli. Rome: Bonacci, 1988.

Carali, Paolo. *Fakhr ad-din II, principe del Libano e la corte di Toscana: 1605–1635*. Rome: Reale Accademia d'Italia, 1936.

Carli, Gian Rinaldo. "Saggio economico e politico sulla Toscana nel 1757." In *Opere*, 336–67. Milan: S. Ambrogio Maggiore, 1784.

Carlos, Anne M. "Principal-Agent Problems in Early Trading Companies: A Tale of Two Firms." *The American Economic Review* 82, no. 2 (1992): 140–5.

Carmona, Maurice. "Aspects du capitalisme toscan aux XVIe et XVIIe siècles: les sociétés en commandite à Florence et à Lucques." *Revue d'histoire moderne et contemporaine* 11, no. 2 (1964): 81–108.

Carranza, Niccola. "L'Università di Pisa e la formazione culturale del ceto dirigente toscano del Settecento." *Bollettino storico pisano* 33–35 (1964–6): 469–537.

Carrière, Charles. *Négociants marseillais au XVIIIe siècle: contribution à l'étude des économies maritimes*. Marseille: Institut Historique de Provence, 1973.

Carrino, Annastella, and Biagio Salvemini. "Porti di campagna, porti di città: traffici e insediamenti del Regno di Napoli visti da Marsiglia (1710–1846)." *Quaderni storici* 121 (2006): 209–54.

Castiglione, Baldassare, *The Book of the Courtier*. Translated by George Bull. New York: Penguin, 2003.

Castignoli, Paolo. "Le prime patenti consolari a Livorno." *La Canaviglia* 6 (1981): 56–61.

Castignoli, Paolo. "Aspetti istituzionali della Nazione inglese a Livorno." In *Gli inglesi a Livorno*, 102–15.

Castignoli, Paolo, and Lucia Frattarelli Fischer. *Bandi per il popolamento di Livorno 1590–1603*. Livorno: Coop. "Risorgimento," 1988.

Cavaciocchi, Simonetta. *Le migrazioni in Europa secc. XIII–XVIII*. Florence: Le Monnier, 1994.

Cerutti, Simona. *Mestieri e privilegi: nascita delle corporazioni a Torino, secoli XVII–XVIII*. Turin: Einaudi, 1992.

Chateaubriand, François René de. *Mémoires d'outre-tombe*, vol 10. Paris: Penaud, 1850.

Chaudhuri, K. N. *The English East India Company: The Study of an Early Joint Stock Company, 1600–1640.* London: Frank Cass & Co., 1965.
Chaudhuri, K. N. *The Trading World of Asia and the English East India Company, 1660–1760.* Cambridge: Cambridge University Press, 1978.
Chaudhuri, K. N. *Trade and Civilisation in the Indian Ocean.* Cambridge: Cambridge University Press, 1985.
Cheney, Paul. *Revolutionary Commerce: Globalization and the French Monarchy.* Cambridge, MA: Harvard University Press, 2010.
Chittolini, Giorgio. *La formazione dello stato regionale e le istituzioni del contado.* Turin: Einaudi, 1979.
Chittolini, Giorgio. "The 'Private,' the 'Public,' the State." In *The Origins of the State in Italy*, edited by Kirshner, 34–61.
Chorley, Patrick. *Oil, Silk, and Enlightenment: Economic Problems in XVIIIth-Century Naples.* Naples: Istituto Italiano per gli Studi Storici, 1965.
Ciano, Cesare. *La sanità marittima nell'età medicea.* Pisa: Pacini, 1976.
Ciano, Cesare. "Corsari inglesi a servizio di Ferdinando I." In *Gli inglesi a Livorno*, 77–82.
Cipolla, Carlo M. *Il burocrate e il marinaio: la "Sanità" toscana e le tribolazioni degli inglesi a Livorno nel XVII secolo.* Bologna: Il Mulino, 1992.
Cipolla, Carlo M. *Before the Industrial Revolution: European Society and Economy, 1000–1700.* New York: Norton, 1994.
Cochrane, Eric W. *Tradition and Enlightenment in the Tuscan Academies, 1690–1800.* Rome: Edizioni di storia e letteratura, 1961.
Cochrane, Eric W. *Florence in the Forgotten Centuries, 1527–1800.* Chicago: University of Chicago Press, 1973.
Codini, Ewa Karwacka. *Piazza dei Cavalieri: urbanistica e architettura dal Medioevo al Novecento.* Florence: Cassa di Risparimo di Firenze, 1989.
Cohn, Samuel. *Creating the Florentine State: Peasants and Rebellion, 1348–1434.* Cambridge: Cambridge University Press, 1999.
Coke, Roger. *A Discourse of Trade.* London: Henry Brome, 1670.
Coke, Roger. *England's Improvements in Two Parts.* London: Henry Brome, 1675.
Cole, Charles Woolsey. *French Mercantilist Doctrines Before Colbert.* New York: Richard R. Smith, 1931.
Coleman, D. C., ed. *Revisions in Mercantilism.* London: Methuen & Co., 1969.
Combes, Pierre-Philippe, Thierry Mayer, and Jacque-François Thisse. *Economic Geography: The Integration of Regions and Nations.* Princeton: Princeton University Press, 2008.
Connell, William J., and Andrea Zorzi, eds. *Florentine Tuscany: Structures and Practices of Power.* Cambridge: Cambridge University Press, 2000.
Contini, Alessandra, ed. *La reggenza lorenese tra Firenze e Vienna: logiche dinastiche, uomini e governo (1737–1766).* Florence: Olschki, 2002.
Contini, Alessandra. "L'informazione politica sugli stati italiani non spagnoli nelle relazioni veneziani a metà Cinquecento (1558–1566)." In *L'informazione politica in Italia*, edited by Fasano Guarini and Rosa, 1–58.
Contini, Alessandra. "La riforma della tassa delle farine (1670–1680)." In *La Toscana nell'età di Cosimo III*, edited by Angiolini et al., 241–73.
Cools, Hans. "Francesco Feroni, intermediario in cereali, schiavi e opere d'arte." *Quaderni storici* 41, no. 2 (2006): 353–65.
Cools, Hans, Marika Keblusek, and Badeloch Noldus. *Your Humble Servant: Agents in Early Modern Europe.* Hilversum: Verloren, 2006.
Costantini, Claudio. *La repubblica di Genova.* Turin: UTET, 1978.

Costantini, Massimo. *L'albero della libertà economica: il processo di scioglimento delle corporazioni veneziane*. Venice: Arsenale, 1987.

Costantini, Massimo. "La regolazione dei dazi marittimi e l'esperienza del 'portofranco' a Venezia tra il 1662 e il 1664." In *La finanza pubblica in età di crisi*, edited by Antonio Di Vittorio, 77–88. Bari: Cacucci, 1993.

Costantini, Massimo. *Porto, navi e traffici a Venezia 1700–2000*. Venice: Marsilio, 2004.

Cotrugli, Benedetto. *Il libro dell'arte di mercatura*. Edited by Ugo Tucci. Venice: Arsenale, 1990.

Cova, Ugo. *Commercio e navigazione a Trieste e nella monarchia asburgica da Maria Teresa al 1915*. Udine: Del Bianco, 1992.

Crinò, Anna Maria. *Fatti e figure del Seicento anglo-toscano*. Florence: Olschki, 1957.

Cronon, William. *Nature's Metropolis: Chicago and the Great West*. New York: Norton, 1992.

D'Addario, Arnaldo. "Burocrazia, economia e finanze dello Stato Fiorentino alla metà del Cinquecento." *Archivio storico italiano* 121 (1963): 362–456.

D'Angelo, Michela. *Mercanti inglesi a Livorno 1573–1737: alle origini di una "British Factory."* Messina: Istituto di Studi Storici "G. Salvemini," 2004.

da Silva, José Gentil. "Nice dans l'économie méditerranéenne." In *Histoire de Nice et du pays niçois*, edited by Maurice Bourdes, 97–134. Toulouse: Privat, 1976.

Dahl, Gunnar. *Trade, Trust, and Networks*. Lund, Sweden: Nordic Academic Press, 1998.

Dal Pane, Luigi. *I lavori preparatori per la grande inchiesta del 1766 sull'economia toscana*. Florence: Sansoni, 1958.

Dal Pane, Luigi. *Lo Stato Pontificio e il movimento riformatore del Settecento*. Milan: Giuffrè, 1959.

Dal Pane, Luigi. *La finanza toscana dagli inizi del secolo XVIII alla caduta del Granducato*. Milan: Banca Commerciale Italiana, 1965.

Dal Pane, Luigi. *Economia e società a Bologna nell'età del Risorgimento*. Bologna: Zanichelli, 1969.

Dandelet, Thomas James, and John A. Marino. *Spain in Italy: Politics, Society, and Religion 1500–1700*. Leiden: Brill, 2007.

Davies, William. *True Relation of the Travailes and Most Miserable Captivitie of William Davies*. London: Nicholas Bourne, 1614.

Davis, Natalie Zemon. *Fiction in the Archives: Pardon Tales and Their Tellers in Seventeenth-Century France*. Stanford: Stanford University Press, 1987.

Davis, Ralph. *The Rise of the English Shipping Industry in the Seventeenth and Eighteenth Centuries*. London: Macmillan, 1962.

Davis, Robert C. *Christian Slaves, Muslim Masters: White Slavery in the Mediterranean, the Barbary Coast, and Italy, 1500–1800*. New York: Palgrave Macmillan, 2003.

de Brosses, Charles. *Lettres familières écrites d'Italie en 1739 et 1740*. Brussels: Editions Complexe, 1995.

de la Court, Pieter. *The True Interests and Political Maxims of the Republick of Holland and West-Friesland*. London, 1702.

de Maddalena, Aldo. "Il mercantilismo." In *Storia delle idee politiche, economiche e sociali*, edited by Luigi Firpo, 637–704. Turin: UTET, 1980.

de Roover, Raymond. "Thomas Mun in Italy." *Bulletin of the Institute of Historical Research* 30, no. 81 (1957): 80–5.

de Roover, Raymond. *The Rise and Decline of the Medici Bank, 1397–1494*. Cambridge, MA: Harvard University Press, 1963.

de Vivo, Filippo. *Information and Communication in Venice: Rethinking Early Modern Politics*. Oxford: Oxford University Press, 2007.

de Vries, Jan. *European Urbanization, 1500–1800*. Cambridge, MA: Harvard University Press, 1984.

de Vries, Jan. *The Industrious Revolution: Consumer Behavior and the Household Economy, 1650 to the Present*. Cambridge: Cambridge University Press, 2008.

de Vries, Jan. "The Economic Crisis of the Seventeenth Century after Fifty Years." *Journal of Interdisciplinary History* 11, no. 2 (2009): 151–94.

de Vries, Jan, and Ad Van der Woude. *The First Modern Economy: Success, Failure, and Perseverance of the Dutch Economy, 1500–1815*. Cambridge: Cambridge University Press, 1997.

De Luca, Giuseppe. *Commercio del denaro e crescità economica a Milano tra Cinquecento e Seicento*. Milan: Il Prolifilo, 1996.

Del Panta, Lorenzo. *Una traccia di storia demografica della Toscana nei secoli XVI–XVIII*. Florence: Universitá degli studi di Firenze, 1974.

Dear, Peter. *The Literary Stucture of Scientific Argument*. Philadelphia: University of Pennsylvania Press, 1991.

Dear, Peter. *Discipline and Experience: The Mathematical Way in the Scientific Revolution*. Chicago: University of Chicago Press, 1995.

Decker, Matthew. *An Essay on the Causes of the Decline of the Foreign Trade*. London, 1744.

Della Pina, Marco. "Andamento e distribuzione della popolazione." In *Livorno e Pisa: due città e un territorio nella politica dei Medici; Pisa e "Contado": una città e il suo territorio nella Toscana dei Medici*, 25–9. Pisa: Nistri-Lischi and Pacini, 1980.

Della Pina, Marco. "La formazione di un nuovo polo demografico nella Toscana dei Medici: Pisa e contado." In *La città e il contado di Pisa*, edited by Mirri, 1–58.

Delumeau, Jean. *L'alun de Rome, XVe–XIXe siècle*. Paris: SEVPEN, 1962.

Delumeau, Jean. "Un ponte fra oriente e occidente: Ancona nel Cinquecento." *Quaderni storici* 5 (1970): 26–47.

Dermigny, Louis. "Escales, échelles et ports francs au moyen âge et aux temps modernes." In *Les grandes escales*, 213–644. Brussels: Recueil de la Société Jean Bodin, 1974.

Descendre, Romain. *L'état du monde: Giovanni Botero entre raison d'état et géopolitique*. Geneva: Droz, 2009.

Di Vittorio, Antonio. *Il commercio tra Levante Ottomano e Napoli nel secolo XVIII*. Naples: Giannini, 1979.

Diaz, Furio. *Francesco Maria Gianni: dalla burocrazia alla politica sotto Pietro Leopoldo di Toscana*. Milan: R. Ricciardi, 1966.

Diaz, Furio. *Il Granducato di Toscana: I Medici*. Turin: UTET, 1976.

Diaz, Furio, Luigi Mascilli Migliorini, and Carlo Mangio. *Il Granducato di Toscana: i Lorena dalla Reggenza agli anni rivoluzionari*. Turin: UTET, 1997.

Dollinger, Philippe. *The German Hansa*. Stanford: Stanford University Press, 1970.

Donati, Barbara. *Tra inquisizione e granducato: storie di inglesi nella Livorno del primo seicento*. Rome: Edizioni di storia e letteratura, 2010.

Donatini, Enzo. *La città ideale: fortezza della Romagna Fiorentina*. Ravenna: Girasole, 1979.

Dooley, Brendan. "Making It Present." In *The Dissemination of News and the Emergence of Contemporaneity in Early Modern Europe*, edited by Brendan Dooley, 95–114. Burlington, VT: Ashgate, 2010.

Dooley, Brendan. "Art and Information Brokerage in the Career of Don Giovanni de' Medici." In *Your Humble Servant*, edited by Cools et al., 81–95.

Dooley, Brendan and Sabrina A. Baron, eds. *The Politics of Information in Early Modern Europe*. London: Routledge, 2001.

Doria, Giorgio. "La gestione del porto di Genova dal 1550 al 1797." In *Il sistema portuale della Repubblica di Genova: profili organizzativi e politica gestionale (secc. XII–XVIII)*, edited by Giorgio Doria and Paola Massa Piergiovanni, 135–98. Genoa: Società ligure di storia patria, 1988.

Dubin, Lois C. *The Port Jews of Habsburg Trieste: Absolutist Politics and Enlightenment Culture*. Stanford: Stanford University Press, 1999.

Ducruet, César, Theo E. Notteboom, and Peter W. Langen. "Revisiting Inter-Port Relationships under the New Economic Geography Research Framework." In *Ports in Proximity: Competition and Coordination Among Adjacent Seaports*, 11–28. Brookfield, VT: Ashgate, 2009.

Dudley, Robert. *Dell'arcano del mare*, 6 vols. Florence: Francesco Onofri, 1646.

Earle, Peter. "The Commercial Development of Ancona, 1479–1551." *Economic History Review* 22, no. 1 (1969): 28–44.

Echinard, Pierre, and Emile Temime. *Histoire des migrations à Marseille*. Vol. 1: *La prehistoire de la migration (1482–1830)*. La Calade, Aix-en-Provence: Edisud, 1989.

Ekelund, Robert B., and Robert D. Tollison. *Politicized Economies: Monarchy, Monopoly, and Mercantilism*. College Station, TX: Texas A&M University Press, 1997.

Elliott, J. H. "A Europe of Composite Monarchies." *Past and Present* 137 (1992): 48–71.

Emigh, Rebecca Jean. *The Undevelopment of Capitalism: Sectors and Markets in Fifteenth-Century Tuscany*. Philadelphia: Temple University Press, 2008.

Engelhardt, Juliane. "Patriotic Societies and Royal Imperial Reforms in Denmark, 1761–1814." In *The Rise of Economic Societies*, edited by Stapelbroek and Marjanen, 212–31.

Engels, Marie-Christine. *Merchants, Interlopers, Seamen and Corsairs: The "Flemish" Community in Livorno and Genoa (1615–1635)*. Hilversum: Verloren, 1997.

Epstein, Stephan R. "Cities, Regions and the Late Medieval Crisis: Sicily and Tuscany Compared." *Past and Present* 130 (1991): 3–50.

Epstein, Stephan R. *Freedom and Growth: The Rise of States and Markets in Europe, 1300–1750*. London: Routledge, 2000.

Epstein, Stephan R. "Market Structures." In *Florentine Tuscany*, edited by Connell and Zorzi, 90–121.

Epstein, Steven A. *Genoa and the Genoese, 958–1528*. Chapel Hill: University of North Carolina Press, 1996.

Fantoni, Marcello. "Dalla provincia alla capitale: gli Usimbardi di Colle alla corte medicea." In *Colle di Val d'Elsa: diocesi e città tra '500 e '600*, edited by Pietro Nencini, 117–37. Castelfiorentino: Società Storica della Valdelsa, 1994.

Fantoni, Marcello. *La corte del Granduca: forma e simboli del potere mediceo fra Cinque e Seicento*. Rome: Bulzoni, 1994.

Fantoni, Marcello. "La formazione del sistema curiale mediceo tra Cinque e Seicento." In *Istituzioni e società in Toscana nell'età moderna*, edited by Claudio Lamioni, 165–78. Rome: Ministero per i beni culturali e ambientali, 1994.

Farquhar, George. *Love and Business: In a Collection of Occasionary Verse, and Epistolary Prose*. London: B. Lintott, 1702.

Fasano Guarini, Elena. *Lo stato mediceo di Cosimo I*. Florence: Sansoni, 1973.

Fasano Guarini, Elena. "Potere centrale e comunità soggette nel Granducato di Cosimo I." *Rivista storica italiana* 89 (1977): 490–538.

Fasano Guarini, Elena. "La politica demografica delle città italiane in età moderna." In *La demografia storica delle città italiane*, 149–91. Bologna: CLUEB, 1982.
Fasano Guarini, Elena. "'Roma officina di tutte le pratiche del mondo': dalle lettere del cardinale Ferdinando de' Medici a Cosimo I e a Francesco I." In *La corte di Roma tra Cinque e Seicento: "Teatro" della politica europea*, edited by Gianvittorio Signorotto and Maria Antonietta Visceglia, 265–97. Rome: Bulzoni, 1998.
Fasano Guarini, Elena. *L'Italia moderna e la Toscana dei principi*. Milan: Le Monnier, 2008.
Fasano Guarini, Elena. "Camerlenghi ed esazione locale: delle imposte nel Granducato di Toscana del '500–'600." In *La fiscalité et ses implications sociales*, 29–49.
Fasano Guarini, Elena. "Center and Periphery." In *The Origins of the State in Italy*, edited by Kirshner, 74–96.
Fasano Guarini, Elena. "Esenzioni e immigrazioni in città tra sedicesimo e diciassettesimo secolo." In *Livorno e il Mediterraneo*, 56–76.
Fasano Guarini, Elena. "I giuristi e lo stato nella Toscana medicea cinque-seicentesca." In *Firenze e la Toscana dei Medici*, 229–47.
Fasano Guarini, Elena. "La popolazione." In *Livorno e Pisa*, 199–215.
Fasano Guarini, Elena, and Danilo Matteoni. "L'Ufficio della Fabbrica." In *Livorno e Pisa*, 149–51.
Fasano Guarini, Elena, and Mario Rosa, eds. *L'informazione politica in Italia (secoli XVI–XVIII)*. Pisa: Scuola normale superiore, 2001.
Fedalto, Giorgio. "Stranieri a Venezia e a Padova, 1550–1700." In *Storia della cultura veneta*, 4/2: 251–79. Vicenza: Neri Pozza, 1984.
Feliu de la Penya, Narcís. *Fènix de Cataluña*. Barcellona, 1683.
Fettah, Samuel. "Temps et espaces des trafics portuaires en Méditerranée: le cas du port franc de Livourne (XVIIe–XIXe siècles)." *Ricerche storiche* 28, no. 2 (1998): 243–73.
Fettah, Samuel. "Livourne: cité du prince, cité marchande (XVIe–XIXe siècles)." In *Florence et la Toscane: les dynamiques d'un état italien, XIVe–XIX siècles*, edited by Jean Boutier, Sandro Landi, and Olivier Rouchon, 179–95. Rennes: Presses de l'Université de Rennes, 2004.
Fettah, Samuel. "Livourne et les grandes places marchandes des routes tyrrhéniennes (XVIIe siècle-première moitié du XIXe siècle)." In *Lo spazio tirrenico nella "grande trasformazione,"* edited by Salvemini, 197–213.
Filippini, Jean-Pierre. *Il porto di Livorno e la Toscana (1676–1814)*, 3 vols. Naples: Edizioni scientifiche italiane, 1998.
Filippini, Jean-Pierre. "La graduelle affirmation de la souveraineté du Grand-Duc de Toscane sur le port de Livourne: les edits de neutralité de la période des Habsbourg-Lorraine." *Nuovi studi livornesi* 16 (2009): 23–31.
Findlen, Paula, and Pamela H. Smith. *Merchants and Marvels: Commerce, Science and Art in Early Modern Europe*. New York: Routledge, 2002.
Fiorani, Francesca. *The Marvel of Maps: Art, Cartography and Politics in Renaissance Italy*. New Haven: Yale University Press, 2005.
Firenze e la Toscana dei Medici nell'Europa del '500. Florence: Olschki, 1983.
Fisher, N. R. R. "Robert Balle, Merchant of Leghorn and Fellow of the Royal Society (ca. 1640–ca. 1734)." *Notes and Records of the Royal Society of London* 55, no. 3 (2001): 351–71.
Fonseca, Cristóbal de. *Devout Contemplations Expressed in Two and Fortie Sermons Upon all ye Quadragesimall Gospells*. Translated by James Mabbe. London: Adam Islip, 1629.
Foramiti, Francesco. *I vantaggi del porto franco*. Venice: Alvisopoli, 1829.

Fortunati, Vita. "Progetti utopici ed architettonici: la città ideale nell'Italia del Rinascimento." In *Le corti e la città ideale*, edited by Gabriella Morisco and Alessandra Calanchi, 33–49. Fasano, Brindisi: Schena, 2004.

Fosi, Irene. "Rituali della parola: supplicare, raccomandare e raccomandarsi a Roma nel Seicento." In *Forme della comunicazione politica*, edited by Nubola and Würgler, 329–49.

Foucault, Michel. *Security, Territory, Population: Lectures at the Collège de France, 1977–1978*. New York: Picador, 2004.

Fox-Genovese, Elizabeth. *The Origins of Physiocracy: Economic Revolution and Social Order in Eighteenth-Century France*. Ithaca: Cornell University Press, 1978.

Franceschi, Franco, Richard A. Goldthwaite, and Reinhold C. Mueller, eds. *Il Rinascimento italiano e l'Europa*, vol. 4: *Commercio e cultura mercantile*. Treviso: Angelo Colla, 2007.

Fratoianni, Aldo, and Marcello Verga. *Pompeo Neri*. Castelfiorentino: Società Storica della Valdelsa, 1992.

Frattarelli Fischer, Lucia. "Proprietà e insediamento ebraici a Livorno dalla fine del Cinquecento alla seconda metà del Settecento." *Quaderni storici* 54, no. 19 (1983): 879–96.

Frattarelli Fischer, Lucia. "Tipologia abitativa degli ebrei a Livorno nel Seicento." *La Rassegna Mensile di Israel* 50 (1984): 583–605.

Frattarelli Fischer, Lucia. "Livorno città nuova: 1574–1609." *Società e storia* 11 (1989): 873–93.

Frattarelli Fischer, Lucia. "Case e proprietari a Livorno nel Seicento." *Quaderni storici* XXXVIII, no. 2 (2003): 363–80.

Frattarelli Fischer, Lucia. "Ebrei a Pisa e Livorno nel Sei e Settecento tra Inquisizioni e garanzie granducali." In *Le Inquisizioni cristiane e gli ebrei*, edited by Giuseppe Galasso. Rome: Accademia nazionale dei Lincei, 2003.

Frattarelli Fischer, Lucia. "La costruzione e il popolamento di Livorno dal 1590 al 1603: i bandi popolazionistici di Ferdinando I." In *Le popolazioni del mare: porti franchi, città, isole e villaggi costieri tra età moderna e contemporanea*, edited by Aleksej Kalc and Elisabetta Navarra, 87–98. Udine: Forum, 2003.

Frattarelli Fischer, Lucia. *Vivere fuori dal ghetto: Ebrei a Pisa e Livorno (secoli XVI–XVIII)*. Turin: Silvio Zamorani, 2008.

Frattarelli Fischer, Lucia. "Livorno 1676: la città e il porto franco." In *La Toscana nell'età di Cosimo III*, edited by Angiolini et al., 45–66.

Frattarelli Fischer, Lucia. "Merci e mercanti nella Livorno seicentesca, 'Magazzino d'Italia e del Mediterraneo.'" In *Merci e monete a Livorno in età granducale*, edited by Balbi de Caro, 65–90.

Frattarelli Fischer, Lucia, and Stefano Villani. "'People of Every Mixture': Immigration, Tolerance and Religious Conflicts in Early Modern Livorno." In *Immigration and Emigration in Historical Perspective*, edited by Isaacs, 93–107.

Friedrich, Markus. "Government and Information-Management in Early Modern Europe: The Case of the Society of Jesus." *Journal of Early Modern History* 12 (2008): 539–63.

Fritschy, Wantje. "The Efficiency of Taxation in Holland." In *The Political Economy of the Dutch Republic*, edited by Gelderblom, 55–84.

Fusai, Giuseppe. *Belisario Vinta ministro e consigliere di Stato dei Granduchi Ferdinando I e Cosimo II (1542–1613)*. Florence: Bernardo Seeber, 1975.

Fusaro, Maria. "Les Anglais et les Grecs: un réseau de coopération commerciale en Méditerranée vénitienne." *Annales. Histoire, Sciences Sociales* 58, no. 3 (2003): 605–25.

Fusaro, Maria. *Political Economies of Empire in the Early Modern Mediterranean: The Decline of Venice and the Rise of England 1450–1700*. Cambridge: Cambridge University Press, 2015.

Fusaro, Maria. "Gli uomini d'affari stranieri in Italia." In *Il Rinascimento italiano e l'Europa*, vol. 4, edited by Franceschi et al., 369–96.

Galluzzi, Jacopo. *Storia del granducato di Toscana*, 11 vols. Florence: Marchini, 1822.

Games, Allison. *The Web of Empire: English Cosmopolitans in an Age of Expansion, 1560–1660*. Oxford: Oxford University Press, 2008.

Garin, Eugenio. "The Ideal City." In *Science and Civic Life in the Italian Renaissance*, 21–48. Garden City, NY: Anchor Books, 1969.

Garin, Eugenio. "Antonio Genovesi metafisico e storico." Introduction to Antonio Genovesi, *Dello stato e delle naturali forze del Regno di Napoli per rispetto all'arti e al commercio*, 3–32. Naples: Città del Sole, 1985.

Gelder, Maartje van. "How to Influence Venetian Economic Policy: Collective Petitions of the Netherlandish Merchant Community in the Early Seventeeth Century." *Mediterranean Historical Review* 24, no. 1 (2009): 29–47.

Gelder, Maartje van. *Trading Places: The Netherlandish Merchants in Early Modern Venice*. Leiden: Brill, 2009.

Gelderblom, Oscar, ed. *The Political Economy of the Dutch Republic*. Burlington, VT: Ashgate, 2009.

Gelderblom, Oscar. "The Organization of Long-Distance Trade and the Dutch Republic, 1550–1650." In *The Political Economy of the Dutch Republic*, edited by Gelderblom, 223–54.

Genovesi, Antonio. "Discorso sopra il vero fine delle lettere e delle scienze." In *Autobiografia e lettere*, edited by Gennaro Savarese, 227–76. Milan: Feltrinelli, 1962.

Genovesi, Antonio. *Delle lezioni di commercio o sia d'economia civile*, 2 vols. Naples: Simone, 1765–7.

Georgelin, Jean. *Venise au siècle des lumières*. Paris: École des hautes études en sciences sociales, 1978.

Germano, Maifreda. *From Oikonomia to Political Economy: Constructing Economic Knowledge from the Renaissance to the Scientific Revolution*. Burlington, VT: Ashgate, 2012.

Ghezzi, Renato. *Livorno e il mondo islamico nel XVII secolo: naviglio e commercio di importazione*. Bari: Cacucci, 2007.

Ghezzi, Renato. *Livorno e l'Atlantico: i commerci olandesi nel Mediterraneo del Seicento*. Bari: Cacucci, 2012.

Giacchero, Giulio. *Storia economica del Settecento genovese*. Genoa: Apuania, 1951.

Giacchero, Giulio. *Origini e sviluppi del portofranco genovese*. Genoa: SAGEP, 1972.

Giacchero, Giulio. *Il Seicento e le compere di San Giorgio*. Genoa: SAGEP, 1979.

Gianni, Francesco Maria. "Discorso sopra a Livorno." In *Scritti di pubblica economia e storico-politici del senatore Francesco Maria Gianni*, vol. 2, 291–321. Florence: Luigi Niccolai, 1848.

Gibellini, Tommass. *Elementi d'economia civile*. Turin: S. Soffietti, 1805.

Gilbert, Felix. *Machiavelli and Guicciardini: Politics and History in Sixteenth-Century Florence*. Princeton: Princeton University Press, 1965.

Gioja, Melchiore. *Nuovo prospetto delle scienze economiche*, vol. 5. Giovanni Pirotta, 1816.

Giorgetti, Giorgio. *Contadini e proprietari nell'Italia moderna*. Turin: Einaudi, 1974.

Gli inglesi a Livorno e all'Isola d'Elba. Livorno: Bastogi, 1980.

Goldberg, Edward. *Jews and Magic in Medici Florence: The Secret World of Benedetto Blanis*. Toronto: University of Toronto Press, 2011.

Goldberg, Jessica. *Trade and Institutions in the Medieval Mediterranean: The Geniza Merchants and their Business World.* Cambridge: Cambridge University Press, 2012.
Goldthwaite, Richard A. *Private Wealth in Renaissance Florence.* Princeton: Princeton University Press, 1968.
Goldthwaite, Richard A. *Wealth and the Demand for Art in Italy, 1300–1600.* Baltimore: Johns Hopkins University Press, 1993.
Goldthwaite, Richard A. *The Economy of Renaissance Florence.* Baltimore: Johns Hopkins University Press, 2009.
Gordon, Daniel. "'Public Opinion' and the Civilizing Process in France: The Example of Morellet." *Eighteenth-Century Studies* 22, no. 3 (1989): 302–28.
Gorski, Phillip S. *The Disciplinary Revolution: Calvinism and the Rise of the State in Early Modern Europe.* Chicago: University of Chicago Press, 2003.
Grab, Alexander I. "The Politics of Subsistence: The Liberalization of Grain Commerce in Austrian Lombardy." *Journal of Modern History* 57, no. 2 (1985): 185–210.
Grab, Alexander I. "Enlightened Absolutism and Commonlands Enclosure: The Case of Austrian Lombardy." *Agricultural History* 63, no. 1 (1989): 49–72.
Grafe, Regina. *Distant Tyranny: Markets, Power, and Backwardness in Spain, 1650–1800.* Princeton: Princeton University Press, 2012.
Grafe, Regina, and Oscar Gelderblom. "The Rise and Fall of Merchant Guilds: Re-Thinking the Comparative Study of Commercial Institutions in Premodern Europe." *Journal of Interdisciplinary History* 40, no. 4 (2010): 477–511.
Gras, Louis-Joseph. "Les chambres de commerce." *Annales de l'école libre des science politique* 10 (1895): 550–89, 680–740.
Greene, Molly. "Beyond the Northern Invasion: The Mediterranean in the Seventeenth Century." *Past and Present* 174, no. 1 (2002): 42–71.
Greene, Molly. *Catholic Pirates and Greek Merchants: A Maritime History of the Mediterranean.* Princeton: Princeton University Press, 2010.
Greif, Avner. "On the Political Foundations of the Late Medieval Commercial Revolution: Genoa during the Twelfth and Thirteenth Centuries." *Journal of Economic History* 54, no. 2 (1994): 271–87.
Greif, Avner. *Institutions and the Path to the Modern Economy: Lessons from Medieval Trade.* Cambridge: Cambridge University Press, 2006.
Grell, Ole Peter and Roy Porter, eds. *Toleration in Enlightenment Europe.* Cambridge: Cambridge University Press, 2000.
Grendi, Edoardo. "Traffico e navi nel porto di Genova fra 1500 e 1700." In *La repubblica aristocratica dei genovesi*, 309–64. Bologna: Mulino, 1987.
Grendi, Edoardo. *Il cervo e la repubblica: il modello ligure di antico regime.* Turin: Einaudi, 1993.
Grendi, Edoardo. "Gli inglesi a Genova (secoli XVII–XVIII)." *Quaderni storici* 39, no. 115, 1 (2004): 241–78.
Grice-Hutchinson, Marjorie. *Early Economic Thought in Spain 1177–1740.* London: Allen & Unwin, 1978.
Grotius, Hugo. *Mare Liberum.* Edited by Robert Feenstra. Leiden: Brill, 2009.
Grotius, Hugo. *On the Law of War and Peace.* Edited by Stephen C. Neff. Cambridge: Cambridge University Press, 2012.
Guarnieri, Giuseppe Gino. *L'ultima impresa coloniale di Ferdinando I dei Medici.* Livorno: Meucci, 1910.
Guarnieri, Giuseppe Gino. *I cavalieri di Santo Stefano (1562–1859).* Pisa: Nistri-Lischi, 1960.

Guarnieri, Giuseppe Gino. *Il principato mediceo nella scienza del mare*. Pisa: Giardini, 1963.

Guarnieri, Giuseppe Gino. *Da Porto Pisano a Livorno città, attraverso le tappe della storia e della evoluzione geografica: studio storico-critico*. Pisa: Giardini, 1967.

Guarnieri, Giuseppe Gino. *Livorno medicea nel quadro delle sue attrezzature portuali e della funzione economica-marittima: dalla fondazione civica alla fine della dinastia medicea (1577–1737)*. Livorno: Giardini, 1970.

Guasti, Cesare. "Scrittura in materia di navigazione del cav. Giovan Francesco Buonamici e da esso mandato nel 1629 a Galileo Galilei." *Archivio storico italiano* 16 (1885): 3–24.

Guenzi, Alberto. *La "fabbrica" delle tele fra città e campagna: gruppi professionali e governo dell'economia a Bologna nel secolo XVIII*. Ancona: Lavoro, 1987.

Guenzi, Alberto, Paola Massa, and Piola Fausto Caselli, eds. *Guilds, Markets, and Work Regulations in Italy, 16th–19th Centuries*. Brookfield, VT: Ashgate, 1998.

Guyot de Merville, Michel. *Voyage historique d'Italie*. The Hague: 1729.

Habermas, Jürgen. *The Structural Transformation of the Public Sphere: An Inquiry into a Category of Bourgeois Society*. Cambridge, MA: MIT Press, 1989.

Hanlon, Gregory. *The Twilight of a Military Tradition: Italian Aristocrats and European Conflicts, 1560–1800*. London: UCL Press, 1998.

Hakluyt, Richard. *The Principall Nauigations, Voyages and Discoveries of the English Nation*. London: George Bishop and Ralph Newberie, 1589.

Hayward, Horace Albert. "The British Factory in Livorno." In *Gli inglesi a Livorno*, 261–7.

Hayward, Horace Albert. "Gli inglesi a Livorno al tempo dei Medici." *Livorno e il Mediterraneo*, 268–73.

Head, Randolph. "Knowing Like a State: The Transformation of Political Knowledge in Swiss Archives." *Journal of Modern History* 75, no. 4 (2003): 745–82.

Heath, James. *A Chronicle of the late Intestine War in the Three Kingdoms of England, Scotland and Ireland*. London: Thomas Basset, 1675.

Heckscher, Eli. *Mercantilism*. London: Allen & Unwin, 1955.

Hirschman, Albert O. *The Passions and the Interests: Political Arguments for Capitalism before its Triumph*. Princeton: Princeton University Press, 1977.

Hoffman, Philip T. *Growth in a Traditional Society: The French Countryside, 1450–1815*. Princeton: Princeton University Press, 1996.

Hont, Istvan. *Jealousy of Trade: International Competition and the Nation State in Historical Perspective*. Cambridge, MA: Harvard University Press, 2005.

Hoon, Evelynola. *The Organization of the English Customs System, 1696–1786*. New York: D. Appleton-Century, 1938.

Hovy, Johannes. *Het voorstel van 1751 tot instelling van een beperkt vrijhavenstelsel in de Republiek*. Groningen: J. B. Wolters, 1966.

Howell, James. *A Discours of Dunkirk with some Reflexes upon the late Surrender therof*. London: Samuel Speed, 1664.

Imbruglia, Girolamo, ed. *Naples in the Eighteenth Century: The Birth and Death of a Nation State*. Cambridge: Cambridge University Press, 2000.

Inalcik, Halil, and Donald Quataert, eds. *An Economic and Social History of the Ottoman Empire*, 2 vols. Cambridge: Cambridge University Press, 1997.

Irwin, Douglas A. *Against the Tide: An Intellectual History of Free Trade*. Princeton: Princeton University Press, 1996.

Isaacs, Anne Katherine. *Immigration and Emigration in Historical Perspective*. Pisa: Pisa University Press, 2007.

Israel, Jonathan Irvine. *European Jewry in the Age of Mercantilism*. Oxford: Clarendon, 1985.

Israel, Jonathan Irvine. "The Phases of the Dutch Straatvaart (1590–1713): A Chapter in the Economic History of the Mediterranean." *Tijdschrift Voor Geschiedenis* 99 (1986): 1–30.

Israel, Jonathan Irvine. *Dutch Primacy in World Trade, 1585–1740*. Oxford: Clarendon, 1989.

Jacob, Margaret C. *Strangers Nowhere in the World: The Rise of Cosmopolitanism in Early Modern Europe*. Philadelphia: University of Pennsylvania Press, 2006.

Jones, S. R. H., and Simon P. Ville. "Efficient Transactors or Rent-Seeking Monopolists? The Rationale for Early Chartered Trading Companies." *Journal of Economic History* 56, no. 4 (1996): 898–915.

Jossa, Bruno, Rosario Patalano, and Eugenio Zagari, eds. *Genovesi economista*. Naples: Istituto Italiano per gli studi filosofici, 2007.

Jurdjevic, Mark. "Virtue, Commerce, and the Enduring Republican Moment: Reintegrating Italy into the Atlantic Republican Debate." *Journal of the History of Ideas* 62, no. 4 (2001): 721–43.

Jurdjevic, Mark. *Guardians of Republicanism: The Valori Family in the Florentine Renaissance*. Oxford: Oxford University Press, 2008.

Kafadar, Cemal. "A Death in Venice (1575): Anatolian Muslim Merchants Trading in the Serenissima." *Journal of Turkish Studies* 10 (1986): 191–218.

Kaplan, Benjamin J. *Divided by Faith: Religious Conflict and the Practice of Toleration in Early Modern Europe*. Cambridge, MA: Harvard University Press, 2007.

Karl, Barbara. "'Galanterie di cose rare….': Filippo Sassetti's Indian Shopping List for the Medici Grand Duke Francesco and His Brother Cardinal Ferdinando." *Itinerario* 32 (2010): 23–41.

Kellenbenz, Hermann. "Le déclin de Venise et les relations économiques de Venise avec les marches au nord des Alpes." In *Aspetti e cause della decadenza economica veneziana nel secolo xvii*, 109–83. Venice: Fondazione Giorgio Zini, 1961.

Kirk, Thomas Allison. "Genoa and Livorno: Sixteenth and Seventeenth-Century Commercial Rivalry as a Stimulus to Policy Development." *The Historical Association* 86, no. 281 (2001): 3–17.

Kirk, Thomas Allison. *Genoa and the Sea: Policy and Power in an Early Modern Maritime Republic, 1559–1684*. Baltimore: Johns Hopkins University Press, 2005.

Kirshner, Julius, ed. *The Origins of the State in Italy, 1300–1600*. Chicago University Press, 1996.

Kiser, Edgar. "Markets and Hierarchies in Early Modern Tax Systems: A Principal-Agent Analysis." *Politics and Society* 22, no. 3 (1994): 284–315.

Kuhn, Thomas. *The Structure of Scientific Revolutions*. Chicago: The University of Chicago Press, 1996.

Labat, Jean-Battiste. *Voyages du P. Labat de l'ordre des FF: prêcheurs en Espagne et en Italie*, 8 vols. Paris: Delespine, 1702.

Lafon, Jacqueline-Lucienne. *Les Députés du Commerce et l'Ordonnance de Mars 1673*. Paris: Cujas, 1979.

Lalande, Jerôme Lefrançois de. *Voyage d'un françois en Italie, fait dans les années 1765 et 1766*, 8 vols. Venice: Desaint, 1769.

Lami, Elisabetta Piccioni. "I Corsi a Livorno nel '600: primo contributo." *Studi livornesi* 5 (1990): 71–9.

La fiscalité et ses implications sociales en Italie et en France aux XVIIe et XVIIIe siècles. Rome: École française de Rome, 1980.

Landi, Sandro. *Il governo delle opinioni: censura e formazione del consenso nella Toscana del Settecento*. Bologna: Il Mulino, 2000.

Lane, Frederic C. “Economic Consequences of Organized Violence.” *Journal of Economic History* 18, no. 4 (1958): 401–17.

Lane, Frederic C. “The Merchant Marine of the Venetian Republic.” In *Venice and History: The Collected Papers of Frederic C. Lane*, 143–62. Baltimore: Johns Hopkins University Press, 1966.

Lane, Frederic C. *Venice: A Maritime Republic*. Baltimore: Johns Hopkins University Press, 1973.

Lanaro, Paola, ed. *At the Centre of the Old World: Trade and Manufacturing in Venice and on the Venetian Mainland, 1400–1800*. Toronto: Centre for Reformation and Renaissance Studies, 2006.

Latour, Bruno, and Steve Woolgar. *Laboratory Life: The Construction of Scientific Facts*. Princeton: Princeton University Press, 1986.

Lauretta, Raffaele. “Progetto per stabilire in Firenze una segreteria per gli affari di Livorno.” *Bollettino storico livornese*, 2, no. 1 (1952): 49–55.

Lauro, Agostino. *Il cardinale Giovan Battista de Luca: diritto e riforme nello Stato della Chiesa (1676–1683)*. Naples: Jovene, 1991.

di Leone Leoni, Aron. *The Hebrew Portuguese Nations in Antwerp and London at the Time of Charles V and Henry VIII: New Documents and Interpretations*. Jersey City: KTAV, 2005.

Lesger, Clé. “Clusters of Achievement: The Economy of Amsterdam in its Golden Age.” In *Urban achievement in Early Modern Europe: Golden Ages in Antwerp, Amsterdam and London*, edited by Patrick Karl O’Brien, 63–80. Cambridge: Cambridge University Press, 2001.

Leti, Gregorio. *Teatro gallico, o vero la monarchia della real casa di Borbone in Francia sotto i regni di Henrico IV, Luigi XIII, e Luigi XIV*. Amsterdam: Guglielmo de Jonge, 1691.

Leti, Gregorio. *Vita di Don Pietro Giron, Duca d’Ossuna*. Amsterdam: Georgio Gallet, 1699.

Lille, Lisa. “‘Under all the Eyes of the Christian world’: comunità e identità nell’antico cimitero degli inglesi di Livorno.” In *Un archivio di pietra: l’antico cimitero degli inglesi di Livorno*, edited by Matteo Giunti and Giaccomo Lorenzini, 39–63. Pisa: Pacini, 2013.

Litchfield, R. Burr. “Les investissements en commerce des patriciens florentins au XVIIIe siècle.” *Annales E.S.C.* 24, no. 3 (1969): 685–721.

Litchfield, R. Burr. *Emergence of a Bureaucracy: The Florentine Patricians, 1530–1790*. Princeton: Princeton University Press, 1986.

Livesey, James. “A Kingdom of Cosmopolitan Improvers: The Dublin Society, 1731–1798.” In *The Rise of Economic Societies*, edited by Stapelbroek and Marjanen, 52–72.

Livorno e il Mediterraneo nell’età medicea. Livorno: Bastogi, 1978.

Livorno e Pisa: due città e un territorio nella politica dei Medici; Livorno, progetto e storia di una città tra il 1500 e il 1600. Pisa: Nistri-Lischi and Pacini, 1980.

LoRomer, David G. *Merchants and Reform in Livorno, 1814–1868*. Berkeley: University of California Press, 1987.

Luzzatto, Gino. “Il portofranco di Trieste e la politica mercantilistica austriaca nel ’700.” *Annali triestini* 23, supp. (1953): 7–17.

Mackenney, Richard. *Tradesmen and Traders: The World of the Guilds in Venice and Europe, c.1250–c.1650*. London: Croom Helm, 1987.

Madani, Dorsati. “A Review of the Role and Impact of Export Processing Zones.” World Bank, 1999.

Magnusson, Lars. *Mercantilism: The Shaping of Economic Language*. London: Routledge, 1994.

Magri, Nicola. *Discorso cronologico della origine di Livorno in Toscana, dall’anno della sua fondazione, sino al 1646*. Naples: Francesco Savio Stampatore, 1647.

Malanima, Paolo. *La decadenza di un'economia cittadina: l'industria di Firenze nei secoli XVI–XVIII*. Bologna: Il Mulino, 1982.

Malanima, Paolo. "Le attività industriali." In *Prato: storia di una città*, edited by Elena Fasano Guarini, vol. 2, 219–69. Florence: Le Monnier, 1986.

Malanima, Paolo. *Il lusso dei contadini: consumi e industrie nelle campagne toscane del Sei e Settecento*. Bologna: Il Mulino, 1990.

Malanima, Paolo. "I commerci del mondo nel 1674 visti da Amsterdam e da Livorno." In *Ricerche di Storia Moderna*, edited by Giuliana Biagioli, 153–80. Pisa: Pacini, 1995.

Malanima, Paolo. *La fine del primato: crisi e riconversione nell'Italia del Seicento*. Milan: Bruno Mondadori, 1998.

Malanima, Paolo. "Italian Urban Population 1300–1861 (The Database)." PDF file, 2005. http://www.paolomalanima.it/ (accessed 5/22/2015).

Malanima, Paolo. "Wheat Prices in Tuscany, 1260–1860." PDF file, 2005. http://www.paolomalanima.it/ (accessed 5/22/2015).

Malanima, Paolo. "L'economia Toscana nell'età di Cosimo III." In *La Toscana nell'età di Cosimo III*, edited by Angiolini et al., 5–17.

Mallet, Michael E. *The Florentine Galleys in the Fifteenth Century*. Oxford: Clarendon, 1967.

Mangiarotti, Anna. "Il porto franco (1565–1676)." In *Merci e monete a Livorno in età granducale*, edited by Balbi De Caro, 36–56.

Mangio, Carlo. *Politica toscana e rivoluzione: momenti di storia livornese, 1790–1801*. Pisa: Pacini, 1974.

Mangio, Carlo. "Commercio marittimo e Reggenza lorenese in Toscana (provvedimenti legislativi e dibattiti)." *Rivista storica italiana* 90, no. 4 (1978): 898–938.

Mangio, Carlo. *La polizia toscana: organizzazione e criteri d'intervento, 1765–1808*. Milan: Giuffrè, 1988.

Mangio, Carlo. "Livorno nel Granducato: un'identità inconfondibile e mutevole." *Rassegna storica toscana* 48 (2002): 7–40.

Mangio, Carlo. "Richecourt e il miraggio dell'Oriente." In *Il Mediterraneo delle città*, edited by Franco Salvatori, 363–76. Rome: Viella, 2008.

Mangio, Carlo. "La memoria presentata dalla 'Nazione Inglese' di Livorno in occasione dell'inchiesta del 1758." In *Gli inglesi a Livorno*, 58–65.

Mangio, Carlo. "Testimonianze di viaggiatori francesi su Livorno fra Seicento e Settecento." In *Livorno e il Mediterraneo*, 306–17.

Mann, Michael. *The Sources of Social Power*, vol. 2: *The Rise of Classes and Nation-States, 1760–1914*. Cambridge: Cambridge University Press, 1993.

Mannini, Brunello. "La riforma della Dogana di Livorno del 1566." *Studi livornesi* 7 (1992): 65–107.

Mannori, Luca. *Il sovrano tutore: pluralismo istituzionale e accentramento amministrativo nel principato dei Medici (secc. XVI–XVIII)*. Milan: Giuffrè, 1994.

Mannori, Luca, and Bernardo Sordi. *Storia del diritto amministrativo*. Rome-Bari: Laterza, 2001.

Mariana, Juan de. *Tractatus VII*. Cologne: Antonius Hieratus, 1609.

Marocco, Gianni, *Giambattista Vasco*. Turin: Einaudi, 1978.

Marrara, Danilo. "Livorno città 'nobile.'" In *Livorno e il Mediterraneo*, 77–81.

Martelli, Francesco, ed. *Viaggio in Europa di Pietro Guerrini (1682–1686)*. Florence: Olschki, 2005.

Martelli, Francesco. "'Nec spes nec metus:' Ferrante Capponi, giurista ed alto funzionario nella Toscana di Cosimo III." In *La Toscana nell'età di Cosimo III*, edited by Angiolini et al., 137–63.

Martini, Raffaele. "Le condizioni economiche di Messina durante il governo di Carlo VI d'Austria (1719–1734)." *Archivio storico siciliano* 29 (1904): 1–33.

Marzagalli, Silvia. *Bordeaux et les États-Unis, 1776–1815: politique et stratégies négociantes dans la genèse d'un réseau commercial.* Geneva: Droz, 2015.

Mascilli Migliorini, Luigi. *Il sistema delle arti: corporazioni annonarie e di mestiere a Napoli nel Settecento.* Naples: A. Guidi, 1992.

Masi, Corrado. "Relazioni fra Livorno ed Algeri nei secoli XVII–XIX." *Bollettino storico livornese* 2, no. 2 (1938): 183–93.

Masson, Paul. *Ports Francs d'autrefois et d'aujord'hui.* Paris: Hachette, 1904.

Matteoni, Danilo. *Livorno.* Bari: Laterza, 1985.

Matthews, George T. *The Royal General Farms in Eighteenth-Century France.* New York: Columbia University Press, 1958.

Mauro, Frédéric. "Merchant Communities, 1350–1750." In *The Rise of Merchant Empires: Long-Distance Trade in the Early Modern World, 1350–1750*, edited by James D. Tracy, 255–86. Cambridge: Cambridge University Press, 1990.

Mazzaoui, Maureen Fennell. "The First European Cotton Industry: Italy and Germany 1100–1800." In *The Spinning World*, edited by Riello and Parthasarathi, 63–88.

Mazzei, Rita. *Pisa medicea: l'economia cittadina da Ferdinando I a Cosimo III.* Florence: Olschki, 1991.

Mazzei, Rita. *Itinera mercatorum: circolazione di uomini e beni nell'Europa centro-orientale 1550–1660.* Lucca: Maria Pacini Fazzi, 1999.

McArdle, Frank. *Altopascio: A Study in Tuscan Rural Society, 1587–1784.* Cambridge: Cambridge University Press, 1978.

McCalla, Robert J. "The Geographical Spread of Free Zones Associated with Ports." *Geoforum* 21, no. 1 (1990): 121–34.

McClure, George W. *The Culture of Profession in Late Renaissance Italy.* Toronto: University of Toronto Press, 2004.

Meijling, Jesper. "La lenta diffusione di un modello: il porto franco da Livorno a Marstrand nel Settecento." *Nuovi studi livornesi* 17 (2010): 95–120.

Mellyn, Elizabeth W. *Mad Tuscans and Their Families.* Philadelphia: University of Pennsylvania Press, 2014.

Melton, James Van Horn. *The Rise of the Public in Enlightenment Europe.* Cambridge: Cambridge University Press, 2001.

Menard, Russell R. "Transport Costs and Long-Range Trade, 1300–1800." In *The Political Economy of Merchant Empires*, edited by James D. Tracy, 228–75. Cambridge: Cambridge University Press, 1991.

Menning, Carol Bresnahan. *Charity and State in Late Renaissance Italy: The Monte di Pietà of Florence.* Ithaca: Cornell University Press, 1993.

Merlo, Elisabetta. *Le corporazioni, conflitti e soppressioni: Milano tra Sei e Settecento.* Milan: FrancoAngeli, 1996.

Milanesi, Marica. *Filippo Sassetti.* Florence: La Nuova Italia, 1973.

Millstone, Noah. *Manuscript Circulation and the Invention of Politics in Early Stuart England.* Cambridge: Cambridge University Press, 2016.

Minard, Philippe. *La fortune du colbertisme: état et industrie dans la France des Lumières.* Paris: Fayard, 1998.

Miner, Jeffrey. "'Lest We Break Faith with Our Creditors': Public Debt and Civic Culture in Fourteenth-Century Genoa." PhD Diss., Stanford University, 2011.

Minoletti, Bruno. *I porti franchi.* Turin: Einaudi, 1939.

Mirri, Mario. "Proprietari e contadini toscani nelle riforme leopoldine." *Movimento operaio* 7 (1955): 173–229.

Mirri, Mario. "Per una ricerca sui rapporti fra 'economisti' e riformatori toscani: l'abate Niccoli a Parigi." *Annali dell'Istituto Giangiacomo Feltrinelli* 2 (1959): 55–115.

Mirri, Mario. "Un'inchiesta Toscana sui tributi pagati dai mezzadri e sui patti colonici nella seconda metà del Settecento: le memorie di Pelli-Bencivenni, Pagnini, Tramontani, e Paoletti." *Annali dell'Istituto Giangiacomo Feltrinelli* 2 (1959): 483–559.

Mirri, Mario. "Profilo di Stefano Bertolini: un ideale montesquieuiano a confronto col programma di riforme leopoldino," *Bollettino storico pisano* 33–35 (1964–6): 434–68.

Mirri, Mario. *La lotta politica in Toscana intorno alle riforme annonarie, 1764–75*. Pisa: Pacini, 1972.

Mirri, Mario. "La fisiocrazia in Toscana: un tema da riprendere." In *Studi di storia medievale e moderna per Ernesto Sestan*, 703–60. Florence: Olschki, 1980.

Mirri, Mario. "Formazione di una regione economica: ipotesi sulla Toscana, sul Veneto, sulla Lombardia." *Studi Veneziani* 11 (1986): 47–59.

Mirri, Mario, ed. *La città e il contado di Pisa nello stato dei Medici (XV–XVII sec.)*. Pisa: Pacini, 2000.

Mirri, Mario. "Fisiocrazia e riforme: il caso della Toscana e il ruolo di Ferdinando Paoletti." In *Governare il mondo: l'economia come linguaggio della politica nell'Europa del Settecento*, edited by Manuela Albertone, 323–441. Milan: Feltrinelli, 2009.

Mirri, Mario. "Dalla storia dei 'lumi' e delle 'riforme' alla storia degli 'antichi stati italiani.'" In *Pompeo Neri*, edited by Fratoianni and Verga, 401–540.

Misson, Maximilien. *Nouveau voyage d'Italie, fait en l'année 1688*, 4th ed., 3 vols. The Hague: H. van Bulderen, 1702.

Misson, Maximilien. *Nouveau voyage d'Italie, fait en l'année 1688*, 5th ed., 3 vols. Utrecht: Guillaume van de Water and Jaques van Poolsum, 1722.

Misul, Rodolfo. *Le arti fiorentine, decadenza e soppressione. Le camere di commercio: origini-modificazioni*. Florence: Seeber, 1904.

Moatti, Claudia, and Wolfgang Kaiser, eds. *Gens de passage en Méditerranée de l'Antiquité à l'époque moderne: procédures de contrôle et d'identification*. Paris: Maisonneuve & Larose, 2007.

Moatti, Claudia, Wolfgang Kaiser, and Christophe Pébarthe, eds. *Le monde de l'itinérance en Méditerranée de l'antiquité à l'époque moderne: procédures de contrôle et d'identification*. Paris: De Boccard, 2009.

Moch, Leslie Page. *Moving Europeans: Migration in Western Europe since 1650*. 2nd ed. Bloomington: Indiana University Press, 2003.

Molà, Luca. "Artigiani e brevetti nella Firenze del Cinquecento." In *La grande storia dell'artigianato*, vol. 3, edited by Franco and Gloria Fossi Franceschi, 57–79. Florence: Giunti, 2000.

Molà, Luca. *The Silk Industry of Renaissance Venice*. Baltimore: Johns Hopkins University Press, 2000.

Molà, Luca. "Il mercato delle innovazioni nell'Italia del Rinascimento." In *Le technicien dans la cité en Europe occidentale, 1250–1650*, edited by Mathieu Arnoux and Pierre Monnet, 215–50. Rome: École française de Rome, 2004.

Montanus, Arnoldus. *De nieuwe en obekende weereld*. Amsterdam: Jacob Meurs, 1671.

Montesquieu, Charles-Louis de Secondat, Baron de. *De l'esprit des loix*, 2 vols. Geneva: Barrillot & Fils, 1748.

Montesquieu, Charles-Louis de Secondat, Baron de. *The Spirit of the Laws*. Translated by Anne M. Cohler, Basia C. Miller, and Harold S. Stone. Cambridge: Cambridge University Press, 1989.

Montesquieu, Charles-Louis de Secondat, Baron de. *Persian Letters*. Translated by Christopher J. Betts. New York: Penguin, 2004.

Morellet, André. *Réflexions sur les avantages de la liberté d'écrire et d'imprimer sur les matières de l'administration*. Paris: 1775.

Mori, Giorgio. "Linee e momenti dello sviluppo della città, del porto e dei traffici di Livorno." *La Regione: Rivista dell'unione regionale delle provincie toscane* 3, no. 12 (1956): 3–44.

Mori, Renato. *Le riforme leopoldine nel pensiero degli economisti toscani del '700*. Florence: Sansoni, 1951.

Morviducci, Marcella. "Lo scontro anglo-olandese avvenuto nel porto di Livorno il 14 marzo 1653, nelle relazioni di Francesco Feroni." In *Livorno e il Mediterraneo*, 395–404.

Muldrew, Craig. *The Economy of Obligation: The Culture of Credit and Social Relations in Early Modern England*. New York: St. Martin's Press, 1998.

Mun, Thomas. *England's Treasure by Forraign Trade*. New York: Macmillan, 1895.

Musgrave, Peter. *Land and Economy in Baroque Italy: Valpolicella, 1630–1797*. Leicester: Leicester University Press, 1992.

Musi, Aurelio, ed. *Nel sistema imperiale: l'Italia spagnola*. Naples: Edizioni Scientifiche Italiane, 1994.

Nadalo, Stephanie. "Constructing Pluralism in Seventeenth-Century Livorno: Managing Religious Minorities in a Mediterranean Free Port (1537–1737)." PhD Diss., Northwestern University, 2013.

Najemy, John M. *A History of Florence, 1200–1575*. Malden, MA: Blackwell, 2006.

Neri, Algerina. *Uno schiavo inglese nella Livorno dei Medici*. Pisa: ETS, 2000.

North, Douglass C., and Robert P. Thomas. *The Rise of the Western World: A New Economic History*. Cambridge: Cambridge University Press, 1973.

North, Douglass C., and Barry Weingast. "Constitutions and Commitment: Evolution of Institutions Governing Public Choice in Seventeenth-Century England." *Journal of Economic History* 49 (1989): 803–32.

Nubola, Cecilia. "La 'via supplicationis' negli stati italiani della prima età moderna (secoli XV–XVIII)." In *Suppliche e "gravamina,"* edited by Nubola and Würgler, 21–63.

Nubola, Cecilia, and Andreas Würgler. *Suppliche e "gravamina": politica, amministrazione, giustizia in Europa (secoli XIV–XVIII)*. Bologna: il Mulino, 2002.

Nubola, Cecilia, and Andreas Würgler. *Forme della comunicazione politica in Europa nei secoli XV–XVIII: suppliche, gravamina, lettere*. Bologna: il Mulino, 2004.

Nubola, Cecilia, and Andreas Würgler. *Operare la resistenza: suppliche, gravamina e rivolte in Europa (secoli XV–XVIII)*. Bologna: Mulino, 2006.

Nudi, Giacinto. *Storia urbanistica di Livorno: dalle origini al secolo XVI*. Venice: Neri Pozza, 1959.

Nudi, Giacinto. "Il progetto di Bernardo Buontalenti per la città nuova." In *Livorno e Pisa*, 15–41.

Nugent, Thomas. *The Grand Tour*, 3rd ed., vol. 3. London: J. Rivington and Sons, 1778.

O'Rourke, K. H., and J. G. Williamson. "When Did Globalisation Begin?" *European Review of Economic History* 6 (2002): 23–50.

Ogilvie, Sheilagh C., *Institutions and European Trade: Merchant Guilds, 1000–1800*. Cambridge: Cambridge University Press, 2011.

Oldewelt, W. F. H. "*De scheepvaartstatistiek van Amsterdam in de 17e en 18e eeuw*." *Jaarboek van het Genootschap Amstelodamum* 45 (1953): 114–51.

Orenstein, Dara. "Foreign-Trade Zones and the Cultural Logic of Frictionless Production." *Radical History Review* 109 (2011): 36–61.

Orlandi, Gianni. "Suppliche al Comune di Ancona (sec. XVI): inventario." *Quaderni della rassegna degli archivi di stato* 97 (2001), 16–22.

Ormrod, David. *The Rise of Commercial Empires: England and the Netherlands in the Age of Mercantilism, 1650–1770.* Cambridge: Cambridge University Press, 2003.

Padgett, John F. "Country as Global Market: Netherlands, Calvinism, and the Joint-Stock Company." In *The Emergence of Organizations and Markets*, edited by John F. Padgett and Walter W. Powell, 208–34. Princeton: Princeton University Press, 2012.

Pagano de Divitiis, Gigliola. "Il porto di Livorno fra Inghilterra e Oriente." *Nuovi studi livornesi* 1 (1993): 43–87.

Pagano de Divitiis, Gigliola. *English Merchants in Seventeenth-Century Italy.* Cambridge: Cambridge University Press, 1997.

Pagano de Divitiis, Gigliola. "Porti italiani nel Seicento e traffici mediterranei." In *La popolazione italiana nel Seicento*, 357–85. Bologna: CLUEB, 1999.

Pagden, Anthony, ed. *The Languages of Political Theory in Early Modern Europe.* Cambridge: Cambridge University Press, 1987.

Pallavicino, Ferrante. *Opere scelte.* Villefranche, 1660.

Palmieri, Matteo. *Vita Civile.* Edited by Gino Belloni. Florence: Sansoni, 1982.

Palyart, Henrique. *Sobre commercio e porto-franco.* Lisbon: Liberal, 1822.

Pansini, Giuseppe. "Le segreterie del principato mediceo." In *Carteggio universale di Cosimo I de' Medici, I (1539–41)*, edited by Anna Bellinazzi and Claudio Lamioni, xi–xlix. Florence: Giunta Regionale Toscana, 1982.

Pansini, Giuseppe. "Per una storia del debito pubblico e della fiscalità al tempo di Cosimo III dei Medici." In *La Toscana nell'età di Cosimo III*, edited by Angiolini et al., 295–317.

Paolini, Aldobrando Giovanni Battista. *Della legittima libertà del commercio*, 3 vols. Florence: Anton-Giuseppe Pagani, 1785.

Pardi, Giuseppe. "Disegno della storia demografica di Livorno." *Archivio Storico Italiano* 76, no. 1 (1918): 1–96.

Parenti, Giuseppe. *Prezzi e mercato del grano a Siena (1546–1765).* Florence: C. Cya, 1942.

Parigino, Giuseppe Vittorio. *Il tesoro del Principe: funzione pubblica e privata del patrimonio della famiglia Medici nel Cinquecento.* Florence: Olschki, 1999.

Paris, Robert. *Histoire du commerce de Marseille*, vol. 5: *De 1660 à 1789.* Paris: Plon, 1957.

Parker, Geoffrey. *The Military Revolution: Military Innovation and the Rise of the West, 1500–1800*, 2nd ed. Cambridge: Cambridge University Press, 1996.

Parker, Geoffrey. *The Grand Strategy of Philip II.* New Haven: Yale University Press, 1998.

Parker, Geoffrey, and Lesley M. Smith, eds. *The General Crisis of the Seventeenth Century.* London: Routledge, 1978.

Pasta, Renato. "L'Accademia dei Georgofili e la riforma dell'agricoltura." *Rivista storica italiana* 105 (1993), 484–501.

Paynter, Robert. *Models of Spatial Inequality: Settlement Patterns in Historical Archeology.* New York: Academic Press, 1982.

Pedani, Maria Pia. "Venetian Consuls in Egypt and Syria in the Ottoman Age." *Mediterranean World* 18 (2006): 7–21.

Pepys, Samuel. *The Diary of Samuel Pepys*, 3 vols. Edited by Henry B. Wheatley. London: George Bell and Sons, 1898.

Peri, Giovanni Domenico. *Il negotiante*, 4 vols. Genoa: Pier Giovanni Calenzano, 1638–65.

Persson, Karl Gunnar. *Grain Markets in Europe, 1500–1900.* Cambridge: Cambridge University Press, 1999.

Pesante, Maria Luisa. "Il commercio nella repubblica." *Quaderni storici* 35 (2000): 655–95.

Pesante, Maria Luisa. "Un pensiero economico laico?" In *Il Rinascimento italiano e l'Europa*, vol. 4, edited by Franceschi et al., 71–102.

Petty, William. *A Treatise of Taxes & Contributions*. London: N. Brooke, 1662.

Petyt, William. *Britannia languens, or a Discourse of Trade*. London: Richard Baldwin, 1689.

Pezzolo, Luciano. *Il fisco dei veneziani: finanza pubblica ed economia tra XV e XVII secolo*. Verona: Cierre Edizioni, 2003.

Pincus, Steve. "Neither Machiavellian Moment nor Possessive Individualism: Commercial Society and the Defenders of the English Commonwealth." *American Historical Review* 103, no. 3 (1998): 705–36.

Pini, Giovambatista. *Memoria del signor Giovambatista Pini coronata dalla Società patria delle arti e manifatture*. Genoa: Eredi di A. Scionico, 1791.

Pischedda, Katia. "Supplicare, intercedere, raccomandare: forme e significati del chiedere nella corrispondenza di Cristoforo Madruzzo (1539–1567)." In *Forme della comunicazione politica*, edited by Nubola and Würgler, 351–82.

Plumard de Dangeul, Louis-Joseph. *Remarques sur les avantages et les désavantages de la France et de la Grande Bretagne*. Leiden, 1754.

Pocock, J. G. A. *Politics, Language, and Time: Essays on Political Thought and History*. New York: Atheneum, 1971.

Pocock, J. G. A. *The Machiavellian Moment: Florentine Political Thought and the Atlantic Republican Tradition*. Princeton: Princeton University Press, 1975.

Poettinger, Monika. "Etica mercantile e sviluppo economico." *Società e storia* 32, no. 125 (2009): 465–502.

Polanyi, Karl. *The Great Transformation*. New York: Farar & Rinehart, 1944.

Pomeranz, Kenneth. *The Great Divergence: Europe, China, and the Making of the Modern World Economy*. Princeton: Princeton University Press, 2000.

Poni, Carlo. "Norms and Disputes: The Shoemakers' Guild in Eighteenth-Century Bologna." *Past and Present* 123 (1989): 80–108.

Poni, Carlo. *La seta in Italia: una grande industria prima della rivoluzione industriale*. Bologna: Il Mulino, 2009.

Preto, Paolo. *I servizi segreti di Venezia: spionaggio e controspionaggio ai tempi della Serenissima*. Milan: Il Saggiatore, 2010.

Pult Quaglia, Anna Maria. *"Per provvedere ai popoli": il sistema annonario nella Toscana dei Medici*. Florence: Olschki, 1990.

Pult Quaglia, Anna Maria. "Confini doganali, politica, economia." In *Frontiere di terra frontiere di mare: la Toscana moderna nello spazio mediterraneo*, edited by Elena Fasano Guarini and Paola Volpini, 78–90. Milan: FrancoAngeli, 2005.

Pult Quaglia, Anna Maria. "Mercato dei prodotti agricoli e magistrature annonarie a Pisa nell'età moderna." In *La città e il contado di Pisa*, edited by Mirri, 57–142.

Pult Quaglia, Anna Maria. "Politica annonaria e congiuntura economica nella Toscana di Cosimo III." In *La Toscana nell'età di Cosimo III*, edited by Angiolini et al., 33–43.

Purcell, Nicholas. "The Ancient Mediterranean: The View from the Customs House." In *Rethinking the Mediterranean*, edited by William V. Harris, 200–32. Oxford: Oxford University Press, 2005.

Quondam, Amedeo. "Dal 'formulario' al 'formulario': cento anni di 'libri di lettere.' " In *Le "carte messaggiere." Retorica e modelli di comunicazione epistolare: per un indice dei libri di lettere del Cinquecento*, edited by Amedeo Quondam, 13–156. Rome: Bulzoni, 1981.

Raeff, Marc. *The Well-Ordered Police State: Social and Institutional Change through Law in the Germanies and Russia, 1600–1800*. New Haven: Yale University Press, 1983.

Raleigh, Walter. *Observations Touching Trade and Commerce with the Hollander and Other Nations*. London: T.H., 1653.

Rambert, Louis Gaston. *Histoire du commerce de Marseille*, vol. 4: *De 1660 à 1789*. Paris: Plon, 1954.

Rao, Anna Maria. *Il Regno di Napoli nel Settecento*. Naples: Guida, 1983.

Rapp, R. T. "The Unmaking of the Mediterranean Trade Hegemony: International Trade Rivalry and the Commercial Revolution." *Journal of Economic History* 35 (1975): 499–525.

Rapp, R. T. *Industry and Economic Decline in Seventeenth-Century Venice*. Cambridge, MA: Cambridge University Press, 1976.

Raveux, Olivier. "The Birth of a New European Industry: *L'Indiennage* in Seventeenth-Century Marseilles." In *The Spinning World*, edited by Riello and Parthasarathi, 291–306.

Ravid, Benjamin. *Economics and Toleration in Seventeenth Century Venice*. Jerusalem: American Academy for Jewish Research, 1978.

Ravid, Benjamin. "An Autobiographical Memorandum by Daniel Rodriga, *Inventore* of the *Scala* of Spalato." In *The Mediterranean and the Jews*, vol. 1, edited by Ariel Toaff and Simon Schwarzfuchs, 189–213. Ramat-Gan: Bar-Ilan University Press, 1989.

Ravid, Benjamin. "A Tale of Three Cities and their *Raison d'État*: Ancona, Venice, Livorno, and the Competition for Jewish Merchants in the Sixteenth Century." *Mediterranean Historical Review* 6 (1991): 138–62.

Ravid, Benjamin. "Venice, Rome, and the Reversion of New Christians to Judaism: A Study in *Ragione di Stato*." In *L'identità dissimulata: giudaizzanti iberici nell'Europa cristiana dell'età moderna*, edited by Pier Cesare Ioly Zorattini, 151–93. Florence: Olschki, 2000.

Rebuffus, Petrus. "Tractatus de supplicationibus, seu errorum propositionibus." In *Commentaria in constitutiones*. Lyons: G. Rovilius, 1599.

Redding, Stephan J., Daniel M. Sturm, and Nikolaus Wolf. "History and Industry Location: Evidence from German Airports." *The Review of Economics and Statistics* 93, no. 3 (2011): 814–31.

Reinert, Erik S. "Emulating Success: Contemporary Views of the Dutch Economy." In *The Political Economy of the Dutch Republic*, edited by Gelderblom, 19–40.

Reinert, Sophus A. "Lessons on the Rise and Fall of Great Powers: Conquest, Commerce, and Decline in Enlightenment Italy." *American Historical Review* 115, no. 5 (2010): 1395–425.

Reinert, Sophus A. "Introduction." In *A "Short Treatise" on the Wealth and Poverty of Nations (1613)*, by Antonio Serra, 1–93. New York: Anthem Press, 2011.

Reinert, Sophus A. *Translating Empire: Emulation and the Origins of Political Economy*. Cambridge, MA: Harvard University Press, 2011.

Repetti, Emanuele. *Dizionario geografico fisico storico della Toscana*, 5 vols. Florence: A. Tofani, 1833–46.

Repetti, Paola. "Scrivere ai potenti: suppliche e memoriali a Parma (secoli XVI–XVIII). Lo stato, la giustizia, la supplica." *Scrittura e civiltà* 24 (2000): 295–358.

Ricci, Giuliano. "Livorno." *Giornale agrario toscano* 11 (1837): 101–16.

Riello, Giorgio. *Cotton: The Fabric That Made the Modern World*. Cambridge: Cambridge University Press, 2013.

Riello, Giorgio, and Prasannan Parthasarathi, eds. *The Spinning World: A Global History of Cotton Textiles, 1200–1850*. Oxford: Oxford University Press, 2009.

Ristori, Renzo. *La Camera di Commercio e la Borsa di Firenze*. Florence: Olschki, 1963.

Roberts, Lewes. *The Marchants Mappe of Commerce*. London: Ralph Mabb, 1638.

Roberts, Lewes. *The Treasure of Traffike, or a Discourse of Forraigne Trade*. London: Nicholas Bourne, 1641.

Robertson, John. *The Case for the Enlightenment: Scotland and Naples, 1680–1760*. Cambridge: Cambridge University Press, 2005.

Robinson, Henry. *Libertas, or Reliefe to the English Captives in Algier*. London: John Sweeting, 1642.

Romano, Ruggiero. "Between the Sixteenth and Seventeenth Centuries: The Economic Crisis of 1619–22." In *The General Crisis of the Seventeenth Century*, edited by Parker and Smith, 165–225. London: Routledge, 1978.

Rondinelli, Dennis A. "Export Processing Zones and Economic Development in Asia: A Review and Reassessment of a Means of Promoting Growth and Jobs." *American Journal of Economics and Sociology* 46, no. 1 (1987): 89–105.

Rönnbäck, Klas. "Integration of Global Commodity Markets in the Early Modern Era." *European Review of Economic History* 13 (2009): 95–120.

Root, Hilton L. "The Redistributive Role of Government: Economic Regulation in Old Regime France and England." *Comparative Studies in Society and History* 33, no. 2 (1991): 338–69.

Root, Hilton L. *The Fountain of Privilege: Political Foundations of Economic Markets in Old Regime France and England*. Berkeley: University of California Press, 1994.

Rosenthal, Jean-Laurent. "The Political Economy of Absolutism Reconsidered." In *Analytic Narratives*, edited by Robert H. Bates et al., 64–108. Princeton: Princeton University Press, 1998.

Rothman, Natalie. *Brokering Empire: Trans-Imperial Subjects between Venice and Istanbul*. Ithaca: Cornell University Press, 2012.

Rothschild, Emma. *Economic Sentiments: Adam Smith, Condorcet, and the Enlightenment*. Cambridge, MA: Harvard University Press, 2001.

Rubin, Alfred. *The Law of Piracy*. Newport, RI: Naval War College, 1988.

Ruiu, Antonio. "La famiglia Sproni fra Comunità di Livorno, Ordine di S. Stefano e nobiltà toscana: l'ascesa di una nuova aristocrazia." *Nuovi studi livornesi* 16 (2009): 97–119.

Sahlins, Peter. *Unnaturally French: Foreign Citizens in the Old Regime and After*. Ithaca: Cornell University Press, 2004.

Salibi, Kamal. "Fakhr-al-Din." *Encyclopedia of Islam*, vol. 2, 749–51. Leiden: Brill, 1960.

Salvadorini, Vittorio. "Traffici e schiavi fra Livorno e Algeria nella prima decade del '600." *Bollettino storico pisano* 51 (1982): 67–104.

Salvadorini, Vittorio. "Traffici con i paesi islamici e schiavi a Livorno nel XVII secolo: problemi e suggestioni." In *Livorno e il Mediterraneo*, 206–55.

Salvat, Christophe. "'De la science de l'économie publique' de Morellet." In *André Morellet: Texts and Contexts*, edited by Dorothy Medlin and Jeffrey Merrick, 65–95. Oxford: Voltaire Foundation, 2003.

Salvemini, Biagio, ed. *Lo spazio tirrenico nella "grande trasformazione": merci, uomini e istituzioni nel Settecento e nel primo Ottocento*. Bari: EdiPuglia, 2009.

Salvemini, Biagio, and Maria Antonietta Visceglia. "Pour une histoire des rapports économiques entre Marseille et le Sud de l'Italie au XVIIIe siècle et au début du XIXe siècle: flux marchands, articulations territoriales, choix politiques." *Provence historique* 177 (1994): 321–65.

Samuel, Edgar R. "'Sir Thomas Shirley's Project for Jewes'—the Earliest Known Proposal for the Resettlement." *Jewish Historical Society of England* 24 (1974): 195–7.

Sansovino, Francesco. *Venetia, città nobilissima et singolare.* Venice: Stefano Curti, 1663.

Sapori, Armando. *Il mercante italiano nel medioevo.* Florence: University of Florence, 1945.

Sassetti, Filippo. *Lettere da vari paesi, 1570–1588.* Edited by Vanni Bramanti. Milan: Longanesi, 1570.

Sassetti, Filippo. "Ragionamento sul commercio ordinato dal granduca fra i sudditi suoi e le nazioni del Levante." *Archivio storico italiano* app. IX, 171–84 (1853).

Savary, Jacques. *Le parfait négociant, ou, instruction générale pour ce qui regarde le commerce des marchandises de France et des pays étrangers.* 2 vols. Paris: Jean Guignard fils, 1675.

Savary des Bruslons, Jacques, and Philémon-Louis Savary. *Dictionnaire universel de commerce*, 3 vols. Paris: J. Estienne, 1723.

Schaeper, Thomas. *The French Council of Commerce, 1700–1715: A Study of Mercantilism after Colbert.* Columbus, OH: Ohio State University Press, 1983.

Schlereth, Thomas J. *The Cosmopolitan Ideal in Enlightenment Thought: Its Form and Function in the Ideas of Franklin, Hume, and Voltaire, 1694–1790.* Notre Dame: The University of Notre Dame Press, 1977.

Schumpeter, Joseph. *History of Economic Analysis.* Oxford: Oxford University Press, 1994 [1954].

Scott, H. M., ed. *Enlightened Absolutism: Reform and Reformers in Later Eighteenth-Century Europe.* Basingstoke, Hampshire: Macmillan, 1990.

Scott, James C. *Seeing Like a State: How Certain Schemes to Improve the Human Condition Have Failed.* New Haven: Yale University Press, 1998.

Scrosoppi, Paolo. "Il porto di Livorno e gli inizi dell'attività inglese nel Mediterraneo." *Bollettino storico livornese* 1 (1937): 339–80.

Scrosoppi, Paolo. "Attività commerciale del porto di Livorno nella prima metà del secolo XVIII." *Bollettino storico livornese* 3 (1939): 41–65.

Segre, Renata. "Sephardic Settlements in Sixteenth-Century Italy: A Historical and Geographical Survey." *Mediterranean Historical Review* 6, no. 2 (1991): 112–37.

Segre, Renata. "La Controriforma: espulsioni, conversioni, isolamento." In *Gli ebrei in Italia*, edited by Corrado Vivanti, 707–78. Turin: Einaudi, 1996.

Sella, Domenico. "L'industria della lana in Venezia nei secoli sedicesimo e diciassettesimo." In *Storia dell'economia italiana*, vol. 1, edited by Carlo M. Cipolla, 542–4. Turin: Einaudi, 1959.

Sella, Domenico. *Commerci e industrie a Venezia nel secolo XVII.* Venice: Istituto per la Collaborazione Culturale, 1961.

Sella, Domenico. "The Rise and Fall of the Venetian Woollen Industry." In *Crisis and Change in the Venetian Economy in the Sixteenth and Seventeenth Centuries*, edited by Brian Pullan, 106–26. London: Methuen & Co., 1968.

Sella, Domenico. *Crisis and Continuity: The Economy of Spanish Lombardy in the Seventeenth Century.* Cambridge, MA: Harvard University Press, 1979.

Sella, Domenico. "Industrial Raw Materials in the Import Trade of Northern and Central Italy during the XVIIth Century." *Journal of European Economic History* 33, no. 1 (2004): 59–70.

Sereni, Emilio. *History of the Italian Agricultural Landscape.* Princeton: Princeton University Press, 1997.

Serra, Antonio. *A "Short Treatise" on the Wealth and Poverty of Nations (1613).* Edited by Sophus Reinert. New York: Anthem Press, 2011.

Shapin, Steven. *A Social History of Truth: Civility and Science in Seventeenth-Century England.* Chicago: University of Chicago Press, 1994.

Shapin, Steven, and Simon Schaffer. *Leviathan and the Air-Pump: Hobbes, Boyle, and the Experimental Life*. Princeton: Princeton University Press, 1985.

Shaw, James. "Writing to the Prince: Supplications, Equity, and Absolutism in Sixteenth-Century Tuscany." *Past and Present* 215, no. 1 (2012): 51–83.

Sheeres, Henry. *A Discourse Touching Tanger*. London: 1680.

Shovlin, John. "The Society of Brittany and the Irish Economic Model: International Competition and the Politics of Provincial Development." In *The Rise of Economic Societies*, edited by Stapelbroek and Marjanen, 73–95.

Siegmund, Stefanie B. *The Medici State and the Ghetto of Florence: The Construction of an Early Modern Jewish Community*. Stanford: Stanford University Press, 2006.

Sieveking, Heinrich. *Studio sulle finanze genovesi e in particolare sulla casa di San Giorgio*. Genoa: Gioventù, 1905.

Simoncini, Giorgio. "I porti del Regno di Napoli dal XV al XIX secolo." In *Sopra i porti di mare*, vol. 2: *Il Regno di Napoli*, edited by Giorgio Simoncini, 1–38. Florence: Olschki, 1993.

Skinner, Quentin. *The Foundations of Modern Political Thought*. Cambridge: Cambridge University Press, 1978.

Smith, Adam. "Report dated 1766." In *Lectures on Jurisprudence*, edited by R. L. Meek, D. D. Raphael, and P. G. Stein, 395–558. Oxford: Oxford University Press, 1978.

Smith, Adam. *An Inquiry into the Nature and Causes of the Wealth of Nations*. Indianapolis: Liberty Fund, 1981.

Smith, Carol A. "Regional Economic Systems: Linking Geographical Models and Socioeconomic Problems." In *Regional Analysis*, edited by Carol A. Smith, 3–63. New York: Academic Press, 1976.

Smith, David Kammerling. "Structuring Politics in Early Eighteenth-Century France: The Political Innovations of the French Council of Commerce." *Journal of Modern History* 74, no. 3 (2002): 490–537.

Smith, Pamela H. *The Business of Alchemy: Science and Culture in the Holy Roman Empire*. Princeton: Princeton University Press, 1994.

Snapper, Frits. "De generale listen van de schepen die in de perioden 1758–1761 en 1783–1786." *Economisch- en sociaal-historisch jaarboek* 42 (1979): 26–44.

Soll, Jacob. *Publishing the Prince: History, Reading, and the Birth of Political Criticism*. Ann Arbor: University of Michigan Press, 2005.

Soll, Jacob. *The Information Master: Jean-Baptiste Colbert's Secret State Intelligence System*. Ann Arbor: University of Chicago Press, 2009.

Sonnino, Guido. *Saggio sulle industrie, marina e commercio sotto i primi due Lorenesi (1737–1790)*. Cortona: E. Alari, 1909.

Sordi, Bernardo. *L'amministrazione illuminata: riforma delle comunità e progetti di costituzione nella Toscana leopoldina*. Milan: Giuffrè, 1991.

Spagnoletti, Angelantonio. *Principi italiani e Spagna nell'età barocca*. Milan: Mondadori, 1996.

Spini, Giorgio. "Introduzione." In *Architettura e politica da Cosimo I a Ferdinando I*, edited by Giorgio Spini, 9–77. Florence: Olschki, 1976.

Stapelbroek, Koen. "Dutch Commercial Decline Revisited: The Future of International Trade and the 1750s Debate about a Limited Free Port." *Annali della fondazione Feltrinelli* 43 (2009): 227–55.

Stapelbroek, Koen, and Jani Marjanen, eds. *The Rise of Economic Societies in the Eighteenth Century*. New York: Palgrave Macmillan, 2012.

Statt, Daniel. *Foreigners and Englishmen: The Controversy over Immigration and Population, 1660–1760*. Newark: University of Delaware Press, 1995.

Steensgaard, Niels. "Consuls and Nations in the Levant from 1570 to 1650." *Scandinavian Economic History Review* 15, no. 182 (1967): 13–55.

Stern, Philip J. *The Company-State: Corporate Sovereignty and the Early Modern Foundations of the British Empire in India*. Oxford: Oxford University Press, 2011.

Stow, Kenneth R. *Catholic Thought and Papal Jewry Policy, 1555–1593*. New York: Jewish Theological Seminary of America, 1977.

Stumpo, Enrico. "La circolazione monetaria sulla piazza di Livorno: le monete Toscane e quelle forestiere, il corso dei cambi." In *Merci e monete a Livorno in età granducale*, edited by Balbi de Caro, 138–46.

Stumpo, Enrico. "Livorno in età granducale: la città ideale e la patria di tutti." In *Merci e monete a Livorno in età granducale*, edited by Balbi de Caro, 105–28.

Symcox, Geoffrey. "Turin ca 1560–1750 Ideal City of the Baroque." In *Le corti e la città ideale*, edited by Gabriella Morisco and Alessandra Calanchi, 223–41. Fasano, Brindisi: Schena, 2004.

't Hart, Marjolein. *The Making of a Bourgeois State: War, Politics and Finance during the Dutch Revolt*. Manchester: Manchester University Press, 1993.

Tabak, Faruk. *The Waning of the Mediterranean, 1550–1870*. Baltimore: Johns Hopkins University Press, 2008.

Takeda, Junko Thérèse. *Between Crown and Commerce: Marseille and the Early Modern Mediterranean*. Baltimore: Johns Hopkins University Press, 2011.

Tamborra, Angelo. *Gli stati italiani, l'Europa e il problema turco dopo Lepanto*. Florence: Olschki, 1961.

Tarrade, Jean. "Le groupe de pression du commerce à la fin de l'Ancien Régime." *Bulletin de la société d'histoire moderne et contemporaine* 14, no. 13 (1970).

Tazzara, Corey. "Capricious Demands: Artisanal Goods, Business Strategies, and Consumer Behavior in Seventeenth-Century Florence." In *Early Modern Things: Objects and their Histories, 1500–1800*, edited by Paula Findlen, 204–24. New York: Routledge, 2012.

Tazzara, Corey. "Managing Free Trade in Early Modern Europe: Institutions, Information, and the Free Port of Livorno." *Journal of Modern History* 85, 3 (2014): 493–529.

Tazzara, Corey. "Against the Fisc and Justice: State Formation, Market Development, and Customs Fraud in Seventeenth-Century Liguria." In *New Interpretations of the Italian Renaissance*, edited by William Caferro, 358–72. London: Routledge, 2017.

Tazzara, Corey. "Capitalism and the Special Economic Zone, 1590–2014." Forthcoming in *New Perspectives on Political Economy*, edited by Sophus Reinert and Robert Fredona. New York: Palgrave Macmillan, 2017.

Tazzara, Corey. "Maintaining Religious Boundaries in Italy during the Age of Free Trade, 1550–1750." In *Jews and the Mediterranean World*, edited by Jessica Marglin and Matthias Lehman. Forthcoming.

Teicher, Anna. "Politics and Finance in the Age of Cosimo I: The Public and Private Face of Credit." In *Firenze e la Toscana dei Medici*, 343–62.

Temple, William. *Observations upon the United Provinces of the Netherlands*. Edinburgh: Jacob Tonson, 1673.

Temple Leader, John. *Life of Sir Robert Dudley*. Florence: G. Barbèra, 1895.

Tenenti, Alberto, and Ugo Tucci, ed. *Storia di Venezia*, vol. 12: *Il Mare*. Rome: Istituto della Enciclopedia Italiana, 1991.

Terpstra, Nicholas. "Apprenticeship in Social Welfare: From Confraternal Charity to Municipal Poor Relief in Early Modern Italy." *Sixteenth Century Journal* 25, 1 (1994): 101–20.

Terpstra, Nicholas. "Making a Living, Making a Life: Work in the Orphanages of Florence and Bologna." *Sixteenth Century Journal* 31, 4 (2000): 1063–79.

Teuscher, Simon. "Chains of Favor: Approaching the City Council in Late Medieval Bern." In *Forme della comunicazione politica*, edited by Nubola and Würgler, 311–28.

Thirsk, Joan. *Economic Policy and Projects: The Development of a Consumer Society in Early Modern England*. Oxford: Clarendon, 1978.

Thoman, Richard S. *Free Ports and Foreign-Trade Zones*. Cambridge: Cornell Maritime Press, 1956.

Thompson, Allen D. "'Progetti in vantaggio del principe, del pubblico e del commercio della Toscana': i mercanti di Livorno e l'economia toscana al momento della successione lorenese." *Critica storica* 28 (1991): 427–87.

Tilly, Charles. *Coercion, Capital, and European States, AD 990–1992*. Malden, MA: Blackwell, 1992.

Toaff, Renzo. *La nazione ebrea a Livorno e a Pisa (1591–1700)*. Florence: Olschki, 1990.

Toti, Odoardo. *Storia di Civitavecchia*, vol. 2: *Da Sisto IV a Pio VI*. Civitavecchia: Ronciglione, 1996.

Trivellato, Francesca. *The Familiarity of Strangers: The Sephardic Diaspora, Livorno, and Cross-Cultural Trade in the Early Modern Period*. New Haven: Yale University Press, 2009.

Tully, James, ed. *Meaning and Context: Quentin Skinner and His Critics*. Princeton: Princeton University Press, 1989.

Vallerani, Massimo. "La supplica al signore e il potere della misericordia: Bologna 1337–1347." *Quaderni storici* 44 (2009).

Valsecchi, Franco. *L'assolutismo illuminato in Austria e in Lombardia*. Bologna: Zanichelli, 1931.

Varanini, Gian Maria. "'Al magnifico e possente segnoro.' Suppliche ai signori trecenteschi italiani fra cancelleria e corte: l'esempio scaligero." In *Suppliche e "gravamina,"* edited by Nubola and Würgler, 65–106.

Vasco, Giambattista. *Delle università delle arti e mestieri*. Milan: Luigi Veladini, 1793.

Venturi, Franco. "Giambattista Vasco in Lombardia." *Atti dell'Accademia delle scienze di Torino* 91 (1956–7): 19–98.

Venturi, Franco. "Giambattista Vasco, Francesco Dalmazzo Vasco." In *Illuministi italiani*, vol. 3. Riformatori lombardi piemontesi e toscani, 757–879. Milan-Naples: Ricciardi, 1958.

Venturi, Franco. *Settecento riformatore*, vol. 1: *Da Muratori a Beccaria*. Turin: Einaudi, 1969.

Venturi, Franco. "Quattro anni di carestia in Toscana (1764–1767)." *Rivista storica italiana* 38, no. 4 (1976): 649–707.

Venturi, Franco. *Settecento riformatore*, vol. 5: *La rivoluzione di Corsica, le grandi carestie degli anni sessanta, la Lombardia delle riforme*. Turin: Einaudi, 1987.

Venturi, Franco. *The End of the Old Regime in Europe, 1768–1776: The First Crisis*. Princeton: Princeton University Press, 1989.

Venturi, Franco. *The End of the Old Regime in Europe, 1776–1789*, 2 vols. Princeton: Princeton University Press, 1991.

Venturi, Franco. *Utopia and Reform in the Enlightenment*. Cambridge: Cambridge University Press, 2008.

Verga, Marcello. "Dai Medici ai Lorena: aspetti del dibattito politico nella Toscana del primo Settecento dall'epistolario di Bernardo Tanucci." *Società e storia* 8 (1985): 927–41.

Verga, Marcello. *Da "cittadini" a "nobili": lotta politica e riforma delle istituzioni nella Toscana di Francesco Stefano*. Milan: Giuffrè, 1990.

Verga, Marcello. "Lotta politica e riforma delle istituzioni nel granducato di Toscana fra Sei e Settecento: una risposta a J. C. Waquet." *Società e storia* IV, no. 54 (1991): 927–36.

Verga, Marcello. "Appunti per una storia politica del granducato di Cosimo III (1670–1723)." In *La Toscana nell'età di Cosimo III*, edited by Angiolini et al., 335–54.

Vester, Matthew. "The Political Autonomy of a Tax Farm: The Nice-Piedmont Gabelle of the Dukes of Savoy, 1535–1580." *Journal of Modern History* 76 (2004): 745–92.

Vidal, Annie. *La pensée démographique: doctrines, théories et politiques de population*. Grenoble: Presses universitaires de Grenoble, 1994.

Vigo, Giovanni. *Nel cuore della crisi: politica economica e metamorfosi industriale nella Lombardia del Seicento*. Pavia: University of Pavia, 2000.

Villani, Stefano. "'Cum scandalo catholicorum…': la presenza a Livorno di predicatori protestanti inglesi tra il 1644 e il 1670." *Nuovi studi livornesi* VII (1999): 9–58.

Villani, Stefano. "'Una piccola epitome di Inghilterra.' La comunità inglese di Livorno negli anni di Ferdinando II: questioni religiose e politici." *Cromohs* 8 (2003): 1–23.

Villani, Stefano. "I consoli della nazione inglese a Livorno tra il 1665 e il 1673: Joseph Kent, Thomas Clutterbuck e Ephraim Skinner." *Nuovi studi livornesi* 11 (2004): 11–34.

Villani, Stefano. "Between Anatomy and Politics: John Finch and Italy, 1649–1671." In *The Practice of Reform in Health, Medicine, and Science, 1500–2000*, edited by Charles Webster, Margaret Pelling, and Scott Mandelbrote, 151–66. Burlington, VT: Ashgate, 2005.

Villani, Stefano. "Donne inglesi a Livorno nella prima età moderna." In *Sul filo della scrittura: fonti e temi per la storia delle donne a Livorno*, edited by Lucia Frattarelli Fischer and Olimpia Vaccari, 377–99. Pisa: Pisa University Press, 2005.

Viner, Jacob. "Power versus Plenty as Objectives of Foreign Policy in the Seventeenth and Eighteenth Centuries." *World Politics* 1, no. 1 (1948): 1–29.

Viroli, Maurizio. *From Politics to Reason of State: The Acquisition and Transformation of the Language of Politics 1250–1600*. Cambridge: Cambridge University Press, 1992.

Visceglia, Maria Antonietta. "Commercio e mercato in terra d'Otranto nella seconda metà del XVIII secolo." *Quaderni storici* 10, no. 28 (1975): 151–98.

Vivoli, Carlo. "I lavori pubblici sotto Cosimo III: disposizioni normative e pratica amministrativa degli uffici preposti al controllo del territorio fiorentino nel Seicento." In *La Toscana nell'età di Cosimo III*, edited by Angiolini et al., 225–39.

Vivoli, Giuseppe. *Annali di Livorno: dalla sua origine sino all'anno di Gesù Cristo 1840*, 2nd ed., 5 vols. Livorno: Bastogi, 1974.

Voltaire, François-Marie Arouet de. *Letters Concerning the English Nation*. London: 1733.

Wahnbaeck, Till. *Luxury and Public Happiness: Political Economy in the Italian Enlightenment*. Oxford: Oxford University Press, 2004.

Wakefield, Andre. *The Disordered Police State: German Cameralism as Science and Practice*. Chicago: University of Chicago Press, 2009.

Wallerstein, Immanuel M. *The Modern World-System*, vol. 2: *Mercantilism and the Consolidation of the European World-Economy, 1600–1750*. New York: Academic Press, 1980.

Waquet, Jean-Claude. "Les fermes générales dans l'Europe des Lumières: le cas toscan." *Mélanges de l'École française de Rome (Moyen âge, temps modernes)* 89 (1977): 983–1027.

Waquet, Jean-Claude. “La ferme de Lombart (1741–1749): pertes et profits d’une compagnie française en Toscane.” *Revue d’histoire moderne et contemporaine* 25 (1978): 513–29.

Waquet, Jean-Claude. *Le Grand-Duché de Toscane sous les derniers Médicis: essai sur le système de finances et la stabilité des institutions dans les anciens états italiens*. Rome: École française de Rome, 1990.

Waquet, Jean-Claude. *Corruption: Ethics and Power in Florence, 1600–1770*. Cambridge: Polity, 1991.

Waquet, Jean-Claude. “Aux marges de l’impôt: fraudeurs et contrebandiers dans la Toscane du XVIII siècle.” In *La fiscalité et ses implications sociales*, 75–94.

Waquet, Jean-Claude, and Françoise Waquet. “Presse et société: le public des ‘Novelle letterarie’ de Florence (1749–1769).” *Revue française d’histoire du livre* 22 (1979): 39–60.

Weber, Max. *Economy and Society*, 2 vols. Edited by Guenther Roth and Claus Wittich. Berkeley: University of California Press, 1978.

Wilson, Charles. “Trade, Society, and the State.” In *The Cambridge Economic History of Europe*, vol. 4: *The Economy of Expanding Europe in the Sixteenth and Seventeenth Centuries*, edited by E. E. Rich and Charles Wilson, 487–575. Cambridge: Cambridge University Press, 1967.

Wolfe, Martin. *The Fiscal System of Renaissance France*. New Haven: Yale University Press, 1972.

Worsley, Benjamin. *Free Ports, the Nature and Necessitie of Them Stated*. London: William Du-Gard, 1652.

Wright, Edward. *Some Observations Made in Travelling through France, Italy, &c. in the Years 1720, 1721, and 1722*. London: Ward and Wicksteed, 1730.

Zahedieh, Nuala. *The Capital and the Colonies: London and the Atlantic Economy, 1600–1700*. Cambridge: Cambridge University Press, 2010.

Zamora Rodríguez, Francisco Javier. “Privato versus pubblico: l’attività dei primi consoli spagnoli nella Livorno granducale.” *Nuovi studi livornesi* 17 (2010): 43–64.

Zamora Rodríguez, Francisco Javier. “War, Trade, Products and Consumption Patterns: The Ginori and their Information Networks.” In *War, Trade and Neutrality: Europe and the Mediterranean in the Seventeenth and Eighteenth Centuries*, edited by Antonella Alimento, 55–67. Milan, 2011.

Zaugg, Roberto. “Judging Foreigners: Conflict Strategies, Consular Interventions and Institutional Changes in Eighteenth-Century Naples.” *Journal of Modern Italian Studies* 13, no. 2 (2008): 171–95.

Zendri, Christian. “Il ‘Tractatus de supplicationibus, seu errorum propositionibus’ di Pierre Rebuffi (1487–1557).” In *Forme della comunicazione politica*, edited by Nubola and Würgler, 35–51.

Index

The manufacturer's authorised representative in the EU for product safety is Oxford University Press España S.A. of El Parque Empresarial San Fernando de Henares, Avenida de Castilla, 2 - 28830 Madrid (www.oup.es/en or product.safety@oup.com). OUP España S.A. also acts as importer into Spain of products made by the manufacturer.
Printed and bound by CPI Group (UK) Ltd, Croydon, CR0 4YY

14/09/2026

02216305-0012